PUBLICATIONS OF THE NEW CHAUCER SOCIETY

THE NEW CHAUCER SOCIETY

Studies in the Age of Chaucer, the yearbook of The New Chaucer Society, is published annually. Each issue contains substantial articles on all aspects of Chaucer and his age, book reviews, and an annotated Chaucer bibliography. Manuscripts should follow the *Chicago Manual of Style*, 16th edition. Unsolicited reviews are not accepted. Authors receive twenty free offprints of articles and ten of reviews. All correspondence regarding manuscript submissions should be directed to the Editor, Sarah Salih, Department of English, King's College London, Virginia Woolf Building, 22 Kingsway, London WC2B 6NR, United Kingdom; e-mail ageofchaucer@kcl.ac.uk. Subscriptions to The New Chaucer Society and information about the Society's activities should be directed to Ruth Evans, Department of English, Saint Louis University, Adorjan Hall 231, 3800 Lindell Blvd., St. Louis, MO 63108–3414. Back issues of the journal may be ordered from University of Notre Dame Press, Chicago Distribution Center, 11030 South Langley Avenue, Chicago, IL 60628; phone: 800-621-2736; fax: 800-621-8476; from outside the United States, phone: 773-702-7000; fax: 773-702-7212.

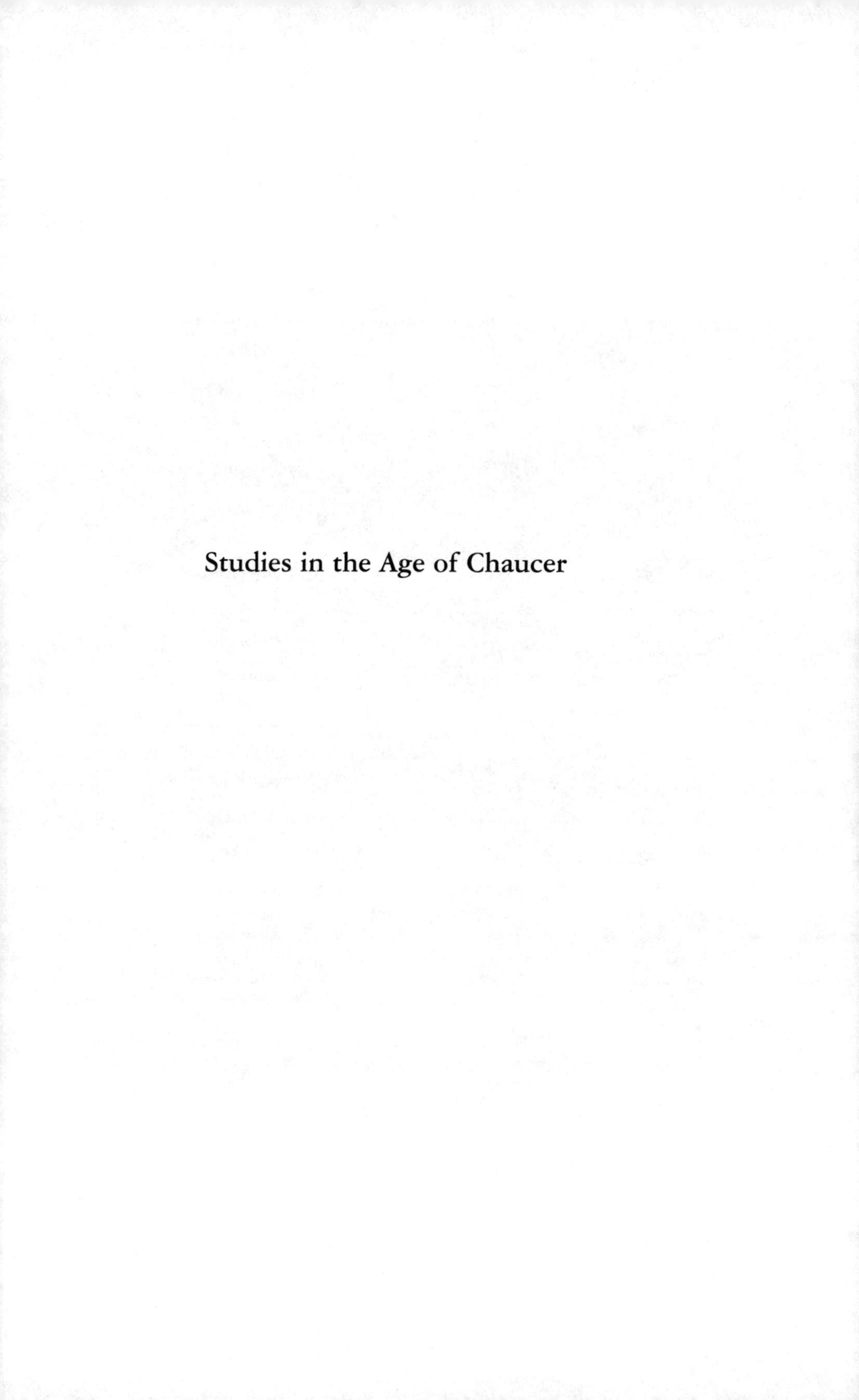

Studies in the Age of Chaucer

Studies in the Age of Chaucer

Volume 36
2014

EDITOR
SARAH SALIH

PUBLISHED ANNUALLY BY THE NEW CHAUCER SOCIETY
SAINT LOUIS UNIVERSITY IN ST. LOUIS

The frontispiece design, showing the Pilgrims at the Tabard Inn, is adapted from the woodcut in Caxton's second edition of the *Canterbury Tales*.

 First edition. Published by University of Notre Dame Press for The New Chaucer Society.

ISBN-10 0-933784-37-6
ISBN-13 978-0-933784-37-6
ISSN 0190-2407

CONTENTS

ARTICLES

REVIEWS

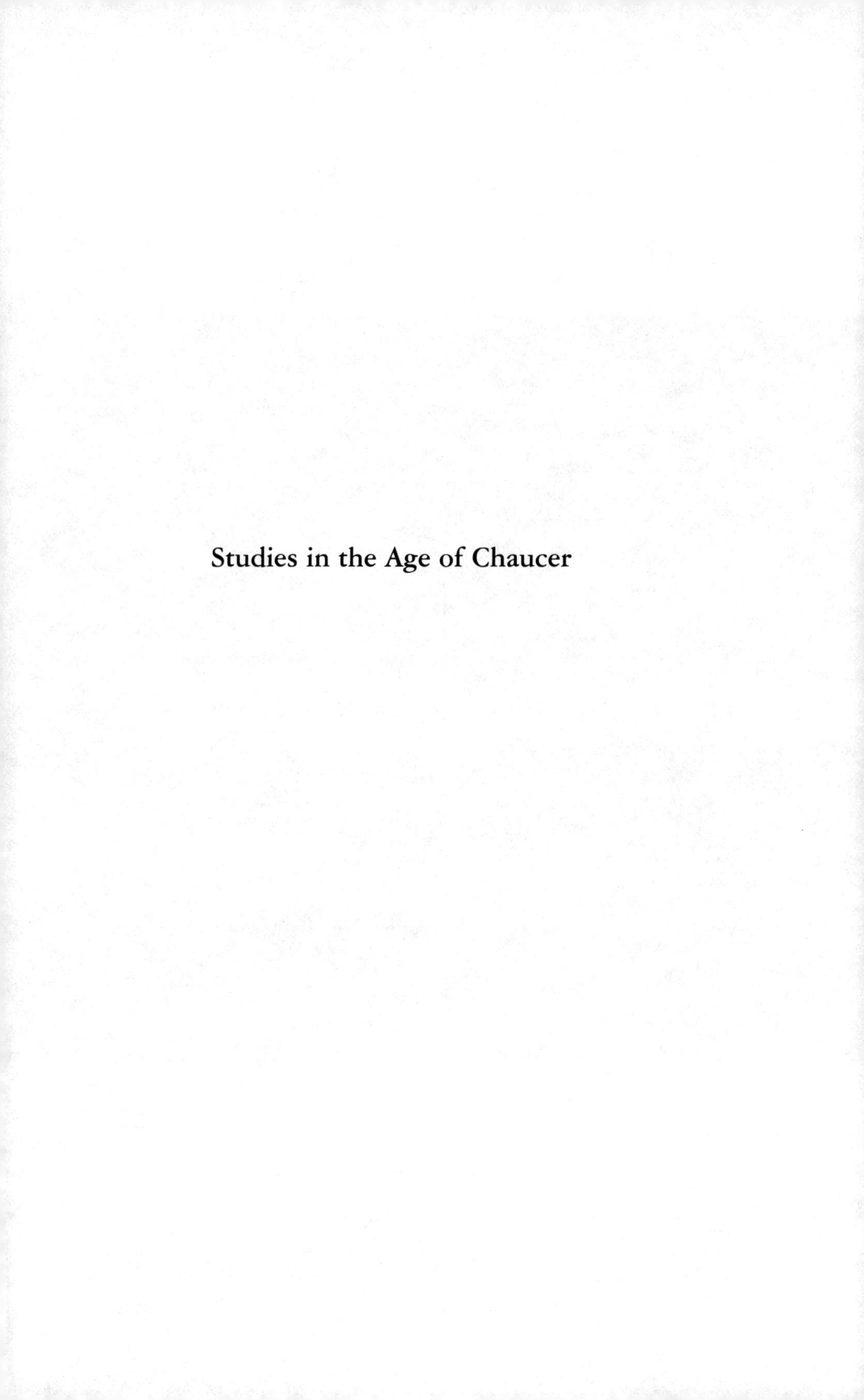

Studies in the Age of Chaucer

The *Pearl*-Poet Manuscript in York

Joel Fredell
Southeastern Louisiana University

ONE OF THE GREATEST MANUSCRIPT TREASURES for medieval literature is the British Library's MS Cotton Nero A.x, which contains four poems we now ascribe to one poet: *Sir Gawain and the Green Knight*, *Pearl*, *Patience*, and *Cleanness*. We have learned surprisingly little about this manuscript over the years, despite the importance of dating and provenance to arguments about *Gawain* and *Pearl*—and to the construction of a *Gawain*-poet or a *Pearl*-poet to supply an authorial identity otherwise missing. For many years the assumed provenance of the manuscript has been "northern" or "northwest Midlands," and latterly associated with Cheshire.[1] However, a substantial body of evidence argues that Cotton Nero A.x as we now have it was produced, at least partially and possibly *in toto*, in York in the early fifteenth century. This evidence offers no new conclusions about the poet, but it does suggest new possibilities, and reveals how little effort has been directed to understanding the object we have, the single witness to some of the most important poems in the canons of literature. Our attempts to recover an underlying poet-genius and that poet's ur-text may not be quixotic goals, but understanding Cotton Nero A.x must come first.

Research for this essay was begun during a National Endowment for the Humanities Summer Institute, "The Cathedral and Culture: Medieval York." Further work was made possible by a Leverhulme Trust Visiting Professorship at the University of York. I would like to thank Paul Szarmach and Linne Mooney, respectively, for their roles in these opportunities, as well as other faculty, staff, and archivists too numerous to mention here.

[1]The contest between "northern" and "northwest Midlands" begins with *Syre Gawayne: A Collection of Ancient Romance-Poems*, ed. Sir Frederic Madden (London: R. and J. Taylor/Bannantyne Club, 1839), 299–307, where Madden identifies a Scottish author for the Cotton Nero poems; and *Early Alliterative Poems in the West-Midland Dialect of the Fourteenth Century*, ed. Richard Morris, EETS o.s. 1 (London: Oxford University Press, 1864), iv–ix, where Morris eponymously locates the dialect of the Cotton Nero poems in the west Midlands. On the northwest Midlands provenances offered for Cotton Nero A.x see below.

Studies in the Age of Chaucer 36 (2014):1–39

At the outset we should recover the manuscript from generations of speculation about the poet's origins and patronage. Much about these poems that has long and confidently been claimed to be Ricardian—that is, a cultural manifestation of the court of Richard II of England—and much about them that has long and confidently been claimed to be Cheshire-based, must be reconsidered in light of the actual object we have. Among the features of Cotton Nero A.x with reasonably secure dating are the illustrations, placed some decades ago by A. I. Doyle in the first two decades of the fifteenth century.[2] However we date the ur-poems themselves, or even the poems we have in Cotton Nero A.x, which were no doubt produced separately from the illustrations, we must consider a Henrician Cotton Nero A.x—that is, from the reign of Henry IV. Audience response to the manuscript cannot, of course, be associated directly with the author's composition of the poems. Nonetheless, the context for the manuscript may well be a factor in the production of the object that we have, undoubtedly part of the only evidence we have at hand for interpretation, and a clue in a long-standing puzzle: why the obscurity that veiled these poetic masterpieces after the cultural moment of Cotton Nero A.x?

I. The Cheshire Hypothesis

A long tradition has argued for the composition in Cheshire of the poems in Cotton Nero A.x, given some dialect features surviving in our sole witness and various internal references in *Sir Gawain and the Green Knight* that could be mapped onto a peninsula in Cheshire. These internal references describe Gawain's journey by means of a series of specific locations through north Wales that end at the Wirral.[3] In that area Gawain asks to be directed to the Green Chapel, but the locals "nikked him with nay" in response (706). Gawain then goes on through a series of wilderness trials that could bring him to the Dales of the north, but more often scholars identify the Green Knight's landscape with the Peak District, which spreads across Staffordshire, Derbyshire, and southern

[2] A. I. Doyle, "The Manuscripts," in *Middle English Alliterative Poetry and Its Literary Background: Seven Essays*, ed. David Lawton (Cambridge: Cambridge University Press, 1982), 88–100.

[3] *Sir Gawain and the Green Knight*, 691–708. All citations are to *The Poems of the "Pearl" Manuscript*, ed. Malcolm Andrew and Ronald Waldron, 3rd ed. (Exeter: University of Exeter Press, 1996).

Yorkshire (713–39).[4] The *Linguistic Atlas of Late Mediaeval English* (*LALME*) seems to support this tradition by locating Cotton Nero A.x's dialect in southeastern Cheshire, near the borders of Derbyshire and Staffordshire.[5] Its location for the manuscript thus suggests a region well away from the Wirral and closer to the Peak District; this rugged region, then, could as easily be of interest to a poet working somewhere in the cluster of population centers and great houses on the other side of the Peak District: that is, on the eastern side of the Pennines.

However, the initial problem with this approach to the origins of all four poems in Cotton Nero A.x is that the apparent harmony between *LALME* and the internal geography of the manuscript's one romance does not speak to the problem of separating out dialects of scribe and poet, nor does it take into account the population movement in late medieval England complicating any assumption that dialect and the location for production will be identical in a given manuscript. Dialect can offer clues to the origins of a poet or scribe, but not so much for later places of residence—and there is no doubt that many poets and scribes were peripatetic. On the first point, the evidence strongly indicates that the scribe of Cotton Nero A.x is some distance from the poet, as Hoyt Duggan has argued.[6] Recently Ad Putter and Myra Stokes have

[4] See, for instance, Ralph Elliot, "Landscape and Geography," in *A Companion to the "Gawain"-Poet*, ed. Derek Brewer and Jonathan Gibson (Woodbridge: Boydell and Brewer, 1997), 108–17; Elliot settles quite specifically on an area east of Leek, Staffordshire, hard by the Peak District.

[5] Angus McIntosh, M. L. Samuels, and Michael Benskin, *A Linguistic Atlas of Late Mediaeval English*, 4 vols. (Aberdeen: Aberdeen University Press, 1986), Linguistic Profile (LP) 26 (1:178 and 3:37–38); for the grid location at the intersection of these three counties (397 364) see the county map at 1:569. On Cheshire gentry who may have been connected to the Cotton Nero poet, see Michael Bennett, *Community, Class and Careerism: Cheshire and Lancashire Society in the Age of "Sir Gawain and the Green Knight"* (Cambridge: Cambridge University Press, 1983); also see further below.

[6] Given the sheer number of scribal errors in the manuscript, J. P. Oakden, *Alliterative Poetry in Middle English*, 2 vols. (Manchester: University of Manchester Press, 1930 and 1935), 2:261–63 argued that Cotton Nero A.x is six or seven removes from the original. Also see the earlier, and relatively full, description of scribal errors in Cotton Nero A.x in *Pearl, Cleanness, Patience and Sir Gawain*, ed. Israel Gollancz, EETS o.s. 162 (London: Oxford University Press, 1923), 7–43. More recently A. S. G. Edwards and Hoyt Duggan have acknowledged a similar distance between Cotton Nero A.x's scribe and poet; Duggan goes on to locate the poet's dialect further south in Staffordshire. See A. S. G. Edwards, "The Manuscript: British Library MS Cotton Nero A.x," in Brewer and Gibson, *A Companion to the "Gawain"-Poet*, 197–220 (198–200); Hoyt N. Duggan, "Meter, Stanza, Vocabulary, Dialect," in the same volume, 221–42. Duggan also offers evidence of metrical corruption in *Sir Gawain and the Green Knight* to argue for that poem's larger number of scribal intermediaries (227).

attacked the *LALME* location for Cotton Nero A.x in some detail, and raise the problem of teasing out separate dialects for poet and scribe. They offer no fewer than 278 points of evidence from the Cotton Nero A.x poems not taken into account in *LALME*, and in the process note that much of the dialect evidence indicates a northern manuscript, including a number of Yorkshire features.[7] Ralph Hanna has also highlighted Yorkshire dialect forms in Cotton Nero A.x that he attributes to the scribe; he further notes that at least one body of linguistic evidence from the Cotton Nero poems argues against Cheshire as the home dialect of the poet.[8] Both of these studies, like Duggan's, demonstrate just how problematic the dialect evidence is when we attempt to separate poet and scribe in a single witness. More important for any discussion of the manuscript, these studies taken together make a compelling case that the *LALME* evidence for Cotton Nero A.x, long assumed as a given, in fact is deeply flawed.[9] A new study must reconsider the larger

[7] Ad Putter and Myra Stokes, "The *Linguistic Atlas* and the Dialect of the *Gawain* Poems," *JEGP* 106 (2007): 468–91; their evidence directly contradicts the long-standing assumption that the *LALME* evidence for Cotton Nero A.x is a settled question, restated a decade before their own study by Duggan, "Meter, Stanza, Vocabulary, Dialect": "The salient features of the phonology and morphology of the scribe who wrote Cotton Nero A.x are well catalogued and need not be repeated here" (240). Evidence for Yorkshire dialect in the scribe includes the broadly northern use of <qu> for /hw/ and the probable use of the verb *gebyrian* in a formulation—"him burde"—testified almost exclusively in central and eastern Yorkshire; and the shortened forms "bos" and "boȝ." Putter and Stokes (471) argue that <qu> is much more common in *Sir Gawain and the Green Knight* and *Pearl*. My own count suggests that occurrences of <qu> are somewhat more common in *Sir Gawain and the Green Knight* (eighty-five) than in the other three poems (thirty-seven in *Pearl*, fifteen in *Cleanness*, four in *Patience*). These disparities are in part a result of text length (*Gawain* 2,530 lines, *Cleanness* 1,810 lines, *Pearl* 1,210 lines, *Patience* 530 lines), though the evidence that *Sir Gawain and the Green Knight* came through more (presumably northern) scribal intermediaries than the other three poems must also be taken into account.

[8] Hanna argues that in "*LALME*'s report of dialects of this region, the coalescence of OE *hw* and OE *cw* is absolutely ubiquitous—as it is also over a large tract of adjacent West Yorkshire. The absence of any evidence for it in the authorial detail of the poem certainly should make one pause over placing the poet in Cheshire (although the possibility remains that he could have been from elsewhere and composed for a Cheshire employer). The logical conclusion would be to place him elsewhere, in an area where *hw* and *cw* had remained separate sounds—either to the south of the region (Shropshire or more southern Staffordshire) or to the east (the eastern half of Yorkshire)." (From a book in progress on Yorkshire writers, kindly supplied to the author.)

[9] One of Angus McIntosh's earliest studies, and apparently the basis for the *LALME* entries on Cotton Nero A.x, declares that the dialect of *Sir Gawain and the Green Knight* "can only *fit* with reasonable propriety in a very small area either in SE Cheshire or just north of the border in NE Staffordshire" given that the evidence is "dialectically homogeneous" (emphasis in original); see Angus McIntosh, "A New Approach to Middle English Dialectology," *ES* 44 (1963): 1–11 (5–6). No account exists in published

body of evidence—indicated most clearly by Putter and Stokes—that now awaits analysis. That analysis cannot be done here, but one conclusion can be drawn in the interim: Cheshire connections for Cotton Nero A.x are still a possibility, but we cannot with certainty privilege Cheshire as a given home base for the poet or for the scribe founded on dialect evidence. Recent analysis points to Staffordshire as a better contender for the poet's home base; I will show in more detail below that Yorkshire is a better contender for the scribe.

To turn to this latter point, while some of the dialect evidence in Cotton Nero A.x points toward Yorkshire for the scribe and/or the poet, negative evidence from surviving late medieval manuscripts argues against Cheshire connections for the scribe, at least. Very few literary manuscripts of any kind from Cheshire in Cotton Nero A.x's period have been identified, and no center of book production seems to have existed there. We have Dublin, Trinity College, MS 155, produced in Lichfield in the 1390s for the Mascy family, but this is an anthology of imported Yorkshire texts.[10] The only manuscripts we have containing texts with a claim to Cheshire origin occur far on either side of our dates for the poems of Cotton Nero A.x. The fairly well-known Harley 2250, which contains the sole witness to *Saint Erkenwald* and one of two for the *Stanzaic Life of Christ*, appears in a paper manuscript from around 1475—long after the period of Cotton Nero A.x and thus of little help in the question of Cheshire material culture around 1400.[11] We also

---

scholarship for any changes in the evidence used between this study and the *LALME* findings, nor any modifications to this specific assertion of homogeneity. A supplemented list of forms in the new online *LALME*, http://www.lel.ed.ac.uk/ihd/elalme/elalme.html, offers much new evidence to consider beyond those raised above, including forms like "saytȝ" and "satȝ" for third-person singular "SAYS" (235–21 in the County Dictionary) only attested in Cotton Nero A.x, but identified in *LALME* as Cheshire by association.

[10] For the connection between the Mascy family and Trinity 155, which the author tries (unconvincingly, in my view) to parlay into more evidence for a Cheshire context for Cotton Nero A.x, see John Scattergood, *Manuscripts and Ghosts: Essays on the Transmission of Medieval and Early Renaissance Literature* (Dublin: Four Courts Press, 2006), 181–97. Major texts in Trinity 155 include Rolle's *Ego dormio* and William of Nassyngton's *Speculum vitae*; on the latter as a Yorkshire production see William of Nassyngton, *Speculum vitae*, ed. Ralph Hanna, 2 vols., EETS o.s. 331–32 (London and New York: Oxford University Press, 2009). *LALME* locates all the scribes writing in English for this manuscript south and west of Cheshire. Scribe 1: Staffordshire (*Linguistic Atlas* grid reference: 418 327, LP 215 [4:237]). Scribe 3: Worcestershire (grid reference: 385 237, LP 7810 [4:250]). Scribe 4: Derbyshire (grid reference: 416 335, LP 184 [1:77]).

[11] On the attempts to ascribe *Saint Erkenwald* to the Cotton Nero poet see most recently Malcolm Andrew, "Theories of Authorship," in Brewer and Gibson, *A Companion to the "Gawain"-Poet*, 28–31 (26–28). The *Manuscripts of the West Midlands* project

have one much earlier manuscript from around 1350, the holograph by Ranulph Higden of his *Polychronicon* (San Marino, Huntington Library, MS HM 132), written while he was at the Benedictine abbey of Saint Werburgh in Chester.[12] But this messy authorial holograph again argues against any organized book production in the area rather than in favor. Assuredly manuscripts—modest ones, in particular—were produced in all sorts of places outside centers of book production.[13] However, Cotton Nero A.x's decorations and its construction as a single-author anthology connect the manuscript to luxury book production whatever we may think of the level of work in the book at hand.[14] As such Cotton Nero A.x raises a particular set of questions about its relationship to book centers that have not yet been broached, let alone answered.[15]

One broad area of misconceptions remains to be addressed: Cotton Nero A.x's relationship to gentry Cheshiremen, as possible patrons but more temptingly as candidates for authorship of the poems, attached to the court of Richard II. Problems in the location of the poet's dialect lead to problems with two other standard parts of the Cheshire narrative about Cotton Nero A.x, such as the various Cheshiremen—John Massey of Cotton, Richard Newton, Sir Richard Craddock—advanced as author of the poems with nothing like proof.[16] Quite simply, we do not have a

notes another literary manuscript that is very likely of Cheshire origins: Oxford, Bodleian Library, MS Bodley 123, also dated to the end of the fifteenth century; see http://www.hrionline.ac.uk/mwm/browse?type = ms&id = 99.

[12] See further N. R. Ker, *Medieval Libraries of Great Britain*, 2nd ed. (London: Royal Historical Society, 1964), 50.

[13] Ralph Hanna, "Some North Yorkshire Scribes and Their Context," in *Medieval Texts in Context*, ed. Graham D. Caie and Denis Renevey (London: Routledge, 2008), 167–91, points to four vernacular manuscripts with devotional texts all connected to Ripon. These associations are not surprising for modest manuscripts; none of these four manifests any signs of deluxe book production beyond a modest pen-and-ink drawing in London, British Library, MS Cotton Galba E.ix, Part 5, fol. 1v.

[14] On the long-standing critical opinion that the decorations in Cotton Nero A.x are crude and unworthy of the name "deluxe," see note 37 below. Important to keep in mind is the fact that the book (after illumination) was hacked down to its present modest size from what were clearly more luxurious margins. Also, judged in relationship to other illuminated manuscripts from the north of England at this time it is far easier to argue that Cotton Nero A.x is the product of skilled professionals.

[15] Kathleen Scott, *Later Gothic Manuscripts, 1390–1490*, 2 vols. (London: Harvey Miller, 1996), 1:34 notes in a survey of provenance for decorated books that Yorkshire is "moderately important" after London and eastern England as a producer; Scott does not mention Cheshire or the *Gawain*-related counties of Derbyshire or Staffordshire in this survey, and no manuscript in her catalogue can be identified with these counties.

[16] See Andrew, "Theories of Authorship." On the sole putative material evidence—William Vantuano's assertion that the name "I Macy" appears in decorative penwork on fol. 62v, and "Macy" on fol. 114r of Cotton Nero A.x—I must agree with Edwards,

Cheshire poet clearly in evidence from dialect or local traditions. Also, one principal area of investigation for the poet has been relations between Richard II and Cheshire, assuming that these relations make likely a Cheshire poet with the courtly experience supposedly necessary to write the courtly *Sir Gawain and the Green Knight* and the elegant *Pearl*. The principal source for this line of argument is Michael Bennett's groundbreaking book on Cheshire gentry.[17] In this early study Bennett focused chiefly on gentry families, and their manor houses in Cheshire, whose associations with Richard might have shaped a local sponsorship for poetry otherwise viewed as far more accomplished than other surviving alliterative romances. Again, this line of argument founders if we do not have a Cheshire poet.

Furthermore, the special relationship between Richard and his major Cheshire supporters in fact occurred in two fairly brief phases separated by a decade. The first was in 1385 to 1387—the earliest date regularly suggested for the Cotton Nero A.x poems these days—a date largely meant to catch this historical moment, actually, for the Cheshire narrative, and largely over after the disastrous defeat of a Cheshire army led by Robert de Vere and Sir Thomas Molyneaux against opponents of King Richard at Radcot Bridge in November 1387, followed by the Merciless Parliament of 1388.[18] Richard did retain some Cheshiremen during the 1390s despite the Cheshire rebellion of 1393 and, of course, famously recruited a band of Cheshire archers for personal protection in a second phase beginning in 1397;[19] he also returned to Cheshire in

"The Manuscript," 98: it is not visible to my eyes even when examining Cotton Nero directly. A new digital facsimile of Cotton Nero A.x is now available in the British Library Manuscript Reading Room without special permission, so high-resolution examination is possible for any interested. See William Vantuano, "A Name in the Cotton MS. Nero A.x. Article 3," *Medieval Studies* 37 (1975): 537–42; and "John de Mascy and the *Pearl* Poems," *Manuscripta* 25 (1981): 77–88.

[17] Bennett, *Community*.

[18] Nigel Saul, *Richard II* (New Haven: Yale University Press, 1997), 172, 187–88, 274 argues that Richard's relationship with Chester was largely based on emotional needs for direct authority and practical positioning for de Vere. Also see R. R. Davies, "Richard II and the Principality of Chester, 1397–99," in *The Reign of Richard II: Essays in Honour of May McKisack*, ed. F. R. H. Du Boulay and Caroline Barron (London: Athlone, 1971), 256–79; and J. L. Gillespie, "Richard II's Cheshire Archers," *Transactions of the Historic Society of Lancashire and Cheshire* 125 (1975): 1–39. The one recent exception to Ricardian dating for *Sir Gawain and the Green Knight* is Francis Ingledew, *"Sir Gawain and the Green Knight" and the Order of the Garter* (Notre Dame: University of Notre Dame Press, 2006); on Ingledew's arguments for an Edwardian context for the composition of the poem see further below.

[19] See Saul's account of these issues in *Richard II*, 219–20, 258, 393–94, and his observation that the Cheshire archers were an idiosyncrasy from the final years of Rich-

these last two years before his abdication. But in this period Richard was also spending serious time and attention on York and Leicester, among other northbound destinations; from 1389 to 1397 evidence of Richard's particular interest in Cheshire is sparse indeed.

In recent years *Pearl* has attracted a growing number of readings that suggest much higher-status contexts for the poet than regional gentry thanks to its array of luxury goods (however Apocalyptic), particularly jewels such as the eponymous pearl.[20] The Cheshire origins of the poet (little attention is paid in these studies to the manuscript outside its putative evidence for Cheshire origins) become far less important to these discussions, though John Bowers would like to use Bennett's approach to map the Cotton Nero poet's work onto the history of Richard's reign from 1387 to 1399.[21] Bowers is careful to note that his arguments "do not assume the author's physical presence at the court and direct patronage from Richard II"; however, that distinction is quickly lost in speculations—such as the presence of the *Saint Erkenwald* poet in London—that point to an underlying assumption of the poet's proximity to Richard's court.[22] Bennett himself has moved toward this view, seeing too much focus on origins for the Cotton Nero poems from regional sources such as Cheshire as "perverse" and arguing instead for an "expatriate" audience resident at a major court such as Richard's; he dates the composition of *Sir Gawain and the Green Knight* to "the late 1390s."[23] Thus the composition of these two most-read works from Cot-

ard's rule, 444–46. On the small handful of Massey family members retained during the 1390s see Bennett, *Community*, 234; and Chris Given-Wilson, *The Royal Household and the King's Affinity: Service, Politics and Finance in England 1360–1413* (New Haven: Yale University Press, 1986), 218. For a few other Cheshire gentry who remained in Richard's service during this period see Bennett, "Historical Background," in Brewer and Gibson, *A Companion to the "Gawain"-Poet*, 83–84.

[20] Notable among these studies are Felicity Riddy, "Jewels in *Pearl*," in Brewer and Gibson, *A Companion to the "Gawain"-Poet*, 143–55; Lynn Staley, "Pearl and the Contingencies of Love and Piety," in *Medieval Literature and Historical Inquiry: Essays in Honour of Derek Pearsall*, ed. David Aers (Woodbridge: Boydell and Brewer, 2000), 83–114; and John Bowers, *The Politics of "Pearl": Court Poetry in the Age of Richard II* (Cambridge: Brewer, 2001).

[21] See Bowers, *The Politics of "Pearl,"* 12–22 and 187–95.

[22] Ibid., 12 and 18; the latter point quotes approvingly Bennett, *Community*, 233. Bowers, *Politics of Pearl*, 191 (citing Gervase Mathew, *The Court of Richard II* [New York: Norton, 1968], 117), eventually asserts that Cotton Nero A.x "was copied from a deluxe manuscript produced during the period of Cheshire privilege at court" for a "backwoods manorial culture"; Bowers, then, follows a long tradition that denigrates Cotton Nero A.x as a crude production.

[23] Bennett, "Historical Background," 77–90; on his dating for *Sir Gawain and the Green Knight* see 88–90. For a book-length discussion of *Sir Gawain*'s connection to the

ton Nero A.x has been positioned recently by a distinguished group of scholars in the last decade of the fourteenth century, and further from Cheshire than Bennett had first encouraged. Although no hard evidence for the poet's presence in London or Westminster emerges, these scholars do make a compelling case for *Gawain* and *Pearl* fitting the cultural environment of the wealthy in the 1390s.

In sum, the whole narrative of Richard and the Cheshire gentry as a creation and performance context for the Cotton Nero poet weakens drastically once we remove some oversimplified Ricardian history, acknowledge the problems of dialect in Cotton Nero A.x, and face the paucity of literary book production in Cheshire. Not only are Cheshire connections largely lost in the recent shift to magnate or royal contexts for the Cotton Nero poet, the readings cited above move the creation of *Gawain* and *Pearl* closer to 1400—and Richard's abdication.[24] If we accept the context for *Pearl* as the 1390s, then the specific texts of Cotton Nero A.x some several versions later (not simply the added illustrations) were likely to have been written even closer to 1400. The implications for Cotton Nero A.x's reception in its own time, which is looking much more like the reign of Henry IV than Richard II, demands some radical reassessment of how we read these great poems. First and foremost, provenance for Cotton Nero A.x itself has been little discussed despite its usefulness as a starting-point. While Cheshire is quite unlikely as the source for a single-author anthology of vernacular romances graced with a substantial program of illuminations, Yorkshire was a center for book production in Cotton Nero A.x's period; some dialect evidence discussed above already points to this region, where York constituted a kind of second city for late medieval England, particularly in the early 1390s when Richard II removed his court there during his struggles with the city of London.[25]

founding of the Order of the Garter in 1349 that eventually argues for the composition of the poem in the 1360s see Ingledew, "*Sir Gawain*," 124 and passim.

[24] Susanna Grier Fein, "Twelve-Line Stanza Forms in Middle English and the Date of *Pearl*," *Speculum* 72 (1997): 367–98 argues for *Pearl*'s dating in the 1380s based on its fairly rare and sophisticated twelve-line stanza. However, other examples of this stanza form include a handful of lyrics in the Vernon and Simeon manuscripts (dated to the last decade of the fourteenth century; Fein notes a topical allusion in onc lyric to 1384 [370]), and the fifteenth-century poem *Pety Job* (for a complete list of what Fein terms twelve-line ballades, including *Pearl*, see 395–97). The 1380s should thus be considered a likely *terminus post quem* for *Pearl* rather than a fixed date.

[25] On these arguments, Richard's subsequent transfer of some royal functions (principally courts of justice) to York, and his support for York demonstrated by the charter of 1396 along with a series of gifts to York Minster, see Caroline M. Barron, "The Quarrel

Furthermore, the evidence we have argues strongly for the creation of Cotton Nero A.x in a period of profound political instability: if the poet did create some or all of his poems in the 1390s, then the scribe of Cotton Nero A.x consequently did his work from the late 1390s to the early 1400s, the decorators did theirs in the early 1400s, and the manuscript as a whole would have been produced across or just after the great rupture of 1399. I will look at the paleographical evidence, and what it can offer for dating, below; nonetheless, however Ricardian we may think the poems, the illuminated manuscript itself is certainly Henrician in its finished state. Cotton Nero A.x, then, was produced somewhere in the umbra of 1399 and the volatile early years of Henry's reign: a point that demands discussion. This point immediately comes into play for the provenance of the manuscript when we consider the state of magnate and gentry cultures in this troubled time. Cheshire in the time of Cotton Nero A.x switched from Ricardian control to the radical instabilities of Henry "Hotspur" Percy after 1399; Hotspur became "king's lieutenant" of Cheshire and north Wales in 1402, then the leader of a rebel army largely raised in Cheshire by the summer of 1403 and subsequently shattered at Shrewsbury.[26] By contrast, during this period in Yorkshire the affinity attached to the major Lancastrian holdings in Yorkshire remained relatively stable, with Ralph Neville's encroachments on Percy interests there only reinforcing this stability, suggesting conditions for literary patronage that are, in fact, reflected in substantial book production in the city of York particularly.[27] Clearly the short-lived Scrope Rebellion in 1405 undermines this picture to a

of Richard II with London 1392–7," in Barron and Du Boulay, *The Reign of Richard II: Essays in Honour of May McKisack*, 173–201; and John H. Harvey, "Richard II and York," in the same volume, 202–15.

[26] Philip. J. Morgan, *War and Society in Medieval Cheshire, 1277–1403* (Manchester: Manchester University Press, 1987), 211–19; R. R. Davies, *The Revolt of Owain Glyn Dwr* (Oxford: Oxford University Press, 1995), 184; Mark Arvanigian, "Managing the North in the Reign of Henry IV, 1402–1408," in *The Reign of Henry IV: Rebellion and Survival, 1403–1406*, ed. Gwilym Dodd and Douglas Biggs (York: York Medieval Press, 2008), 82–104 (90).

[27] Simon Walker, *The Lancastrian Affinity, 1361–1399* (Oxford: Oxford University Press, 1990), passim; Helen Castor, *The King, the Crown, and the Duchy of Lancaster: Public Authority and Private Power, 1399–1461* (Cambridge: Cambridge University Press, 2000), 193–224. For a recent summary of Neville's role in Yorkshire see Arvanigian, "Managing the North," 96–104. On book production and patronage in York during this period note such figures as John Newton and William Gascoigne; Newton in 1414 bequeathed thirty-five manuscripts, several of which are in the York Minster archive and demonstrably of York production.

degree, but not for the Lancastrian affinity itself as loyalists such as William Gascoigne and Thomas Rokeby asserted their dominion in York and Yorkshire more strongly.[28] In short, if we were looking for a stable place during this troubled period for a deluxe book associated with magnate culture—made more deluxe after Henry's accession—the Lancastrian affinity in Yorkshire is a far better bet than anything that might be conjured in Cheshire.

II. A Yorkshire Hypothesis

A possible Yorkshire provenance for Cotton Nero A.x may come as a surprise after decades of complacency about a Cheshire provenance for the poet or the manuscript or some combination of the two. We can add to the dialect evidence the likelihood of a long stretch in Yorkshire early in Cotton Nero A.x's history.[29] The manuscript first shows up in 1614 in the catalogue for the library of Henry Savile, a Yorkshire physician and book collector.[30] It is dangerous to speculate about origins with early modern collectors, but Henry owned works from four religious houses in the city of York—Saint Leonard's, Saint Mary's, Saint Peter's, and the Austin Friars—and the bulk of his collection came from other Yorkshire sources. Another antiquarian and cousin to Henry Savile, William Crashaw, reports in a letter that Henry's medieval manuscripts were acquired by Henry's grandfather "out of the plunder of the monas-

[28] On the Scrope Rebellion see Peter McNiven, "The Betrayal of Archbishop Scrope," *BJRL* 54 (1971): 173–213; Simon Walker, "The Yorkshire Risings of 1405: Texts and Contexts," in *Henry IV: The Establishment of the Regime, 1399–1406*, ed. Gwilym Dodd and Douglas Biggs (York: York Medieval Press, 2003), 161–84; W. Mark Ormrod, "The Rebellion of Archbishop Scrope and the Tradition of Opposition to Royal Taxation," in Dodd and Biggs, *The Reign of Henry IV*, 162–179; W. Mark Ormrod, "An Archbishop in Revolt: Richard Scrope and the Yorkshire Rising of 1405," in *Richard Scrope: Archbishop, Rebel, Martyr*, ed. P. J. P. Goldberg (Donington: Shaun Tyas, 2007), 28–44; and Christian D. Liddy, "William Frost, the City of York and Scrope's Rebellion of 1405," in Goldberg, *Richard Scrope*, 64–85.

[29] Elizabeth Salter, in *Fourteenth-Century English Poetry: Contexts and Readings* (Oxford: Clarendon Press, 1983), 83–85, first noted a possible Yorkshire owner for the Cotton Nero manuscript, suggesting the Nettletons of Hutton Cranswich as mid-sixteenth-century owners of Cotton Nero A.x and the London Thornton manuscript (London, British Library, MS Add. 31042).

[30] Andrew Watson, *The Manuscripts of Henry Savile of Banke* (London: Bibliographical Society, 1969), 68, no. 274. The list was made not long before 1614, and so it is likely that its next appearance with Robert Cotton in 1621 represents a fairly direct transmission; see also Edwards, "The Manuscript," 198.

teries (chiefly northern) and were bequeathed to Savill by his father."[31] In other words, the bulk of Henry's collection was inherited from his Yorkshire ancestors, and Cotton Nero A.x appears in his library catalogue in the midst of these inherited books, not his own additions. Henry's branch of the family back into the fifteenth century seems to have been modest gentry centered around Halifax, southwest of Leeds, but the other branch of Yorkshire Saviles is from nearby Thornhill, around five miles from Halifax and closer to Wakefield within the Lancastrian Honor of Pontefract. This latter branch included MPs and high sheriffs for Yorkshire near to Cotton Nero A.x's time.[32] Thornhill's literal next-door neighbors in the 1390s and early 1400s were the Swillington family, whose patriarch Robert was a long-standing member of John of Gaunt's Privy Council and Steward of Pontefract Castle nearby;[33] so a critical location for the honor of the Duchy of Lancaster—and probably King Richard's bane—was the dominant feature of gentry life here. Leaving aside speculation about magnate associations, though, what we do know about the early history of Cotton Nero A.x suggests that it may have long resided in Yorkshire.

Turning to Cotton Nero A.x itself we must grapple with the fact that we have not found this scribal hand anywhere else.[34] On first glance it

[31] William Crashaw to Isaac Casaubon: "A certain man named Savill, a native of Yorkshire, has in his possession about 500 manuscript volumes . . . [that] were acquired by this gentleman's grandfather [Thomas Savile, d. 1590?] out of the plunder of the monasteries (chiefly northern), and were bequeathed to Savill by his father"; translated in Watson, *The Manuscripts of Henry Savile*, 6.

[32] In the reign of Edward III, Elizabeth Thornhill, the only child of Simon Thornhill, married Sir Henry Savile. The family line of the Thornhills thus ended and Thornhill Manor passed to the Savile family. On the Savile family of Thornhill and Elland in late medieval Yorkshire see J. W. Clay, "The Savile Family," *Yorkshire Archaeological Journal* 25 (1920): 1–6.

[33] For Swillington's membership of Gaunt's Privy Council since at least 1375 see *John of Gaunt's Register*, ed. Sydney Armitage-Smith, 2 vols. (London: Royal Historical Society, 1911), 2:xi. Roger Swillington held the manor of New Hall, Midgley in 1392, the year of Robert's death; another manor in Shelf also held by Roger Swillington passed into the Savile family by the time of Henry VII. See John Crabtree, *A Concise History of the Parish and Vicarage of Halifax, in the County of York* (Halifax: Hartleby and Walker, 1838), 393–94.

[34] Recently two words by an inserted hand in the Ellesmere *Canterbury Tales* (San Marino, Huntington Library, MS El 26 C 9, fol. 74v) have been tentatively attributed by one scholar to the scribe of Cotton Nero A.x; see Jordi Sánchez-Martí, "Adam Pynkhurst's 'Necglygence and Rape' Reassessed," *ES* 92 (2011): 360–74 (368–69). Among the many reasons this identification is highly unlikely are the differences in letter forms *g*, *e*, *t*, and *l*, which cannot be ascribed, *pace* Sánchez-Martí, to an attempt to imitate Pinkhurst.

can seem like an odd, old-fashioned hand for 1400. Some early attempts to date the manuscript paleographically offered the second half of the fourteenth century and the last quarter of the fourteenth century based on similar impressions of this hand.[35] What the Cotton Nero hand reveals, though, is a hybrid of textura and cursive anglicana—specifically a professional scribe practiced in cursive anglicana but not terribly familiar with textura, trying to create a book hand around the turn of the century.[36] Cotton Nero A.x also has a remarkable set of miniatures illustrating the poems; these have been given surprisingly little and often derogatory attention.[37] The most precise dating for Cotton Nero A.x up to now, however, has come from the observation by Ian Doyle that the miniatures in Cotton Nero A.x probably date from the first two decades of the fifteenth century, after the manuscript's text was produced. This assessment rests largely on some costume features, such as the women's *houppelarde* dresses, in the miniatures.[38]

I believe that I can add to this discussion by saying with some certainty that Cotton Nero A.x was decorated, at least, in York in the period Doyle suggests. A cluster of features allows us to assign a York provenance to dozens of manuscripts dating to the last decade of the fourteenth century and the first half of the fifteenth; several decorative features in Cotton Nero A.x occur otherwise exclusively in manuscripts produced in York during this period. Furthermore, the surprisingly large

[35] Attempts to date the hand include *Pearl, Cleanness, Patience and Sir Gawain*, ed. Gollancz, 8 (unnamed experts put the date at the end of the fourteenth century); C. E. Wright, *English Vernacular Hands from the Twelfth to the Fifteenth Centuries* (Oxford: Oxford University Press, 1960), 15 (last quarter of the fourteenth century); A. I. Doyle, "English Books in and out of Court," in *English Court Culture in the Later Middle Ages*, ed. V. J. Scattergood and J. W. Sherborne (London: Duckworth, 1983), 163–81 (166–67) (second half of the fourteenth century); Jane Roberts, *Guide to Scripts Used in English Writings up to 1500* (London: British Library, 2005), 172 (around 1400).

[36] Display hands in York-based notarial documents in the late 1390s, even into 1407, use a mix of letter forms very close to that of the Cotton Nero scribe; see further below.

[37] Most dramatic is the judgment of R. S. and Laura Loomis that the Cotton Nero illustrations represent the "nadir of English illustrative art" in *Arthurian Legends in Medieval Art* (New York: MLA, 1938), 138; this judgment codified the earlier dismissal of the illustrations as "certainly of crude workmanship" in Gollancz's introduction to his EETS facsimile (*Pearl, Cleanness, Patience and Sir Gawain*, 9). Attempts to understand the illustrations on their own terms include Jennifer A. Lee, "The Illuminating Critic: The Illustrator of Cotton Nero A.x," *SIcon* 3 (1977): 17–46; Sarah Horall, "Notes on British Library, MS Cotton Nero A x," *Manuscripta* 30 (1986): 191–98; Edwards, "The Manuscript," 202–19; Scott, *Later Gothic Manuscripts*, 1:10, 2:67; Paul F. Reichart, "'Several Illuminations, Coarsely Executed': The Illustrations of the *Pearl* Manuscript," *SIcon* 18 (1997): 119–42.

[38] Doyle, "The Manuscripts," 92.

number of prestige manuscripts we can locate in this time and place establish a definable book culture in York and Yorkshire that may be directly relevant to Cotton Nero A.x. Much of this supporting evidence comes from devotional books, which may seem like a counterintuitive source for late medieval literary manuscripts. However, liturgical and devotional manuscripts more broadly are valuable repositories for local scripts and local decorations; breviaries and psalters are much easier to locate and date than literary manuscripts in most cases, while providing an encyclopedia of approved graphic elements for book production in a specific time and place. More broadly, we have not adequately examined the dominant forms of book design and production in regional centers such as York, or noted the strong differences with the design of literary manuscripts in London that have become so familiar to scholars in recent years.[39] Establishing a hierarchy of book production and design for regional centers in itself has much to offer these scholars, and in this case to study of Cotton Nero A.x.

A number of devotional manuscripts have a well-established provenance in the city of York during this period, such as the Bolton Hours, a deluxe book produced in York around 1420 for John Bolton, merchant, MP, and mayor of York.[40] In fact, a large body of deluxe liturgical manuscripts firmly given York provenance in this period share many decorative features. A few of those manuscript features, such as the borders and figures, have been discussed by Kathleen Scott and John Friedman.[41]

[39] Given the evidence emerging in the work of Linne Mooney and others that a surprising number of the best-known manuscripts of Langland, Chaucer, and Gower were copied by a small coterie of scribes associated with the London Guildhall, we need to think more about local strategies for presentation of texts in late medieval England; on these London scribes see most recently Linne Mooney and Estelle Stubbs, *Scribes and the City: London Guildhall Clerks and the Dissemination of Middle English Literature 1375–1425* (Woodbridge: York Medieval Press, 2013).

[40] On the Bolton Hours (York, Minster Library, MS Add. 2) see most recently Anneke Mulder-Bakke and Jocelyn Wogan-Browne, eds., *The Bolton Hours of York: Female Domestic Piety and the Public Sphere* (Turnhout: Brepols, 2005); Felicity Riddy and Sarah Rees Jones, "Female Domestic Piety and the Public Sphere: The Bolton Hours of York," in *Women and the Christian Tradition*, ed. Anneke Mulder-Bakke and Jocelyn Wogan-Browne (Turnhout: Brepols, 2006), 215–30; and Sarah Rees Jones, "Richard Scrope, the Bolton Hours and the Church of St. Martin in Micklegate: Reconstructing a Holy Neighbourhood in Later Medieval York," in Goldberg, *Richard Scrope*, 214–36.

[41] Scott, in *Later Gothic Manuscripts*, identifies five major illuminated manuscripts c. 1400 with a definite York provenance and shared decorative features: Boulogne-sur-Mer, Bibliothèque Municipale, MS 93, fols. 1–41v (no. 7) (2:37–39); Brussels, Bibliothèque Royale, MS 4862–4869a (no. 24) (2.97–98); Cambridge, Trinity College, MS O.3.10 (no. 32) (2:117–19); Dublin, Trinity College, MS 83 (2:38); York, Minster Library, MS Add. 2 (Bolton Hours, no. 33) (2:119–21). John Friedman, *Northern English*

Many more that I have examined solidify further a defined York style for the period 1390–1420, and extend these identifications to manuscripts not as deluxe as the Bolton Hours. Specific hands and decorators are shared among these manuscripts for major local families such as the Scropes; clusters of scribes and decorators indicate at least two or three separate production teams co-existing at the time in York. All in all, York had a flourishing book-production trade in a wide range of texts during this period, but for the purposes of this study a sketch of this evidence should provide adequate background for Cotton Nero A.x's production.

The borders in the Bolton Hours are highly typical of the five manuscripts Scott locates in York in the period 1400 to 1420, the same period assigned to the decorations in Cotton Nero A.x.[42] Scott, along with detailed discussions of illustrating hands, notes some consistent features of York borders in this period, including sprigs of white-dotted balls of rose or blue, gold balls between leaves and bar borders, and green wash over pen squiggles.[43] Another deluxe manuscript from this period firmly located in York, however, offers some typical features that clarify and expand Scott's brief lists. York Minster, Additional 383 has the same elaborate borders as the Bolton Hours (figs. 1 and 2).

In the bar border gold balls are visible at the axial angles of leaves sprouting off the borders and virtually every other available line, bar border or not—a feature that is absolutely typical of York borders from several producers in this period.[44] Little pen squiggles, highlighted with

Books, Owners, and Makers in the Late Middle Ages (Syracuse, N.Y.: Syracuse University Press, 1995), 108–47, examines a larger but overlapping group of manuscripts using a much broader regional perspective; also see 237–54 for a useful list of northern manuscripts, though details should be treated with caution.

[42] Friedman, *Northern English Books*, 116 notes a dominating golden element to interlaced borders that can look like pools of gold leaf, along with what he calls "jutting leaves," and in the miniatures a characteristic palette of greens and the famously stiff northern figures. None of these features is more firmly described or located, however.

[43] Scott, *Later Gothic Manuscripts*, 2:118; see further note 44 below.

[44] This feature is well represented in Scott's set of York-produced manuscripts and other well-known deluxe books whose production is equally certain to be placed in York, such as the Pavement Hours (York, Minster Library, MS XVI.K.6); on this manuscript see recently Amelia Grounds, "Evolution of a Manuscript: The Pavement Hours," in *Design and Distribution of Late Medieval Manuscripts in England*, ed. Margaret Connolly and Linne R. Mooney (Woodbridge: York Medieval Press, 2000), 118–38; and brief comments by Friedman, *Northern English Books*, 155 and 162. Although a full discussion of provenance and date is not possible here, other manuscripts with these features and additional elements associating them with York include Oxford, Bodleian Library, MS Laud misc. 84 and MS Gough Liturgies 1; London, British Library, MS Harley 2431; San Marino, Huntington Library, MS HM 1067; and York, Minster Library, MS XVI.P.8.

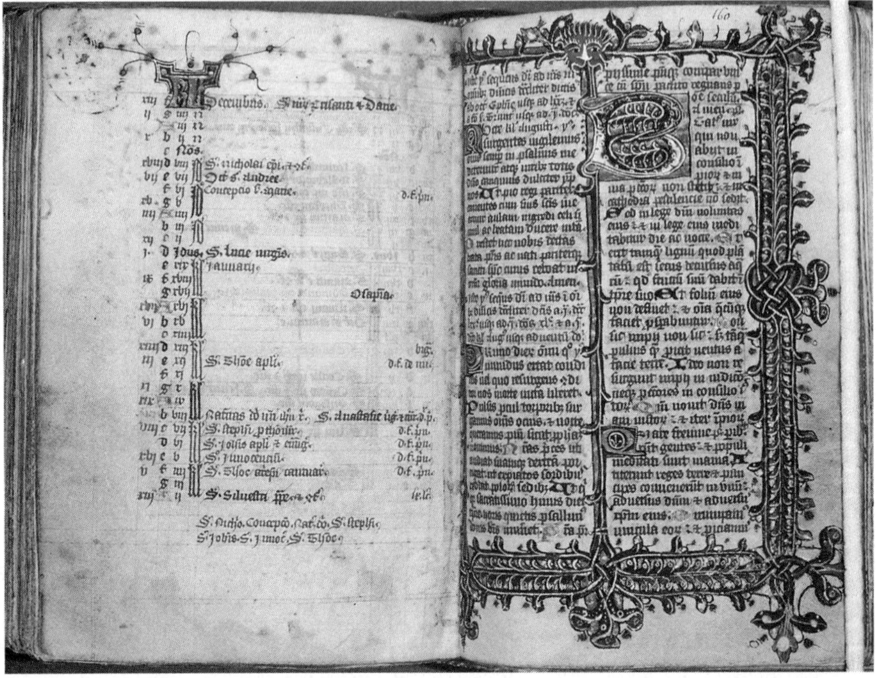

Fig. 1. York, Minster Library, MS Add. 383, fols. 159v–160r; © Chapter of York. Reproduced by kind permission.

Fig. 2. York, Minster Library, MS Add. 383, fol. 160r, detail; © Chapter of York. Reproduced by kind permission.

a green wash, extend from these gold balls, as Scott first noted. Scott dates this decorative device quite precisely to 1410 and thereafter for English manuscripts. [45] However, another striking local feature here is the green wash regularly appearing at the base of sprays, which Scott does not discuss.[46] This little effect is actually far more widespread in the kinds of lesser decoration such as penwork flourishing that Scott does not analyze, and occurs in different forms exclusively in York manuscripts, some of them earlier than 1410.

For lesser initials, as in champes (illuminated small initials) from Add. 383 (Fig. 3), the green wash is applied to the base of penwork sprays in addition to being used on squiggles and balls. Axial balls and green wash over the base of penwork sprays show up in York manuscripts as early as 1390 in one breviary of York use;[47] another York missal, San Marino, Huntington Library, MS HM 1067, combines all these elements in its borders as well (figs. 4 and 5).[48] Although such decorative elements may seem trivial, they are remarkably consistent in manu-

Fig. 3. York, Minster Library, MS Add. 383, fol. 159v, detail; © Chapter of York. Reproduced by kind permission.

[45] Scott uses the effect of green wash on pen squiggles (presumably those squiggles that occur at spray ends and/or off the little balls that cap penwork lines of spray commonly in the early fifteenth century in English manuscripts) to date borders for English manuscripts generally; here she argues that the borders in Trinity O.3.10, because of the "application of green to all pen squiggles in the borders, . . . indicate a later date than Boulogne-Sur-Mer," that is "c. 1410 or slightly later" (2:118). Similarly Kathleen Scott, *Dated and Dateable English Manuscript Borders c. 1395–1499* (London: Bibliographical Society, 2002), 42 argues that this use of green wash is "new" in a manuscript she dates 1410–13.

[46] Friedman, *Northern English Books*, 74 briefly notes the common use of green in northern illuminating generally, but does not note its use in lesser decoration.

[47] Oxford, Bodleian Library, MS Gough Liturgies 1; this border design (though not these features) is also discussed by Friedman, *Northern English Books*, 74 and 133–34.

[48] In C. W. Dutschke, R. H. Rouse, and Richard S. Dunn, eds., *Guide to Medieval and Renaissance Manuscripts in the Huntington Library* (San Marino: Huntington Library, 1989), 246 this manuscript is dated s. XV[1].

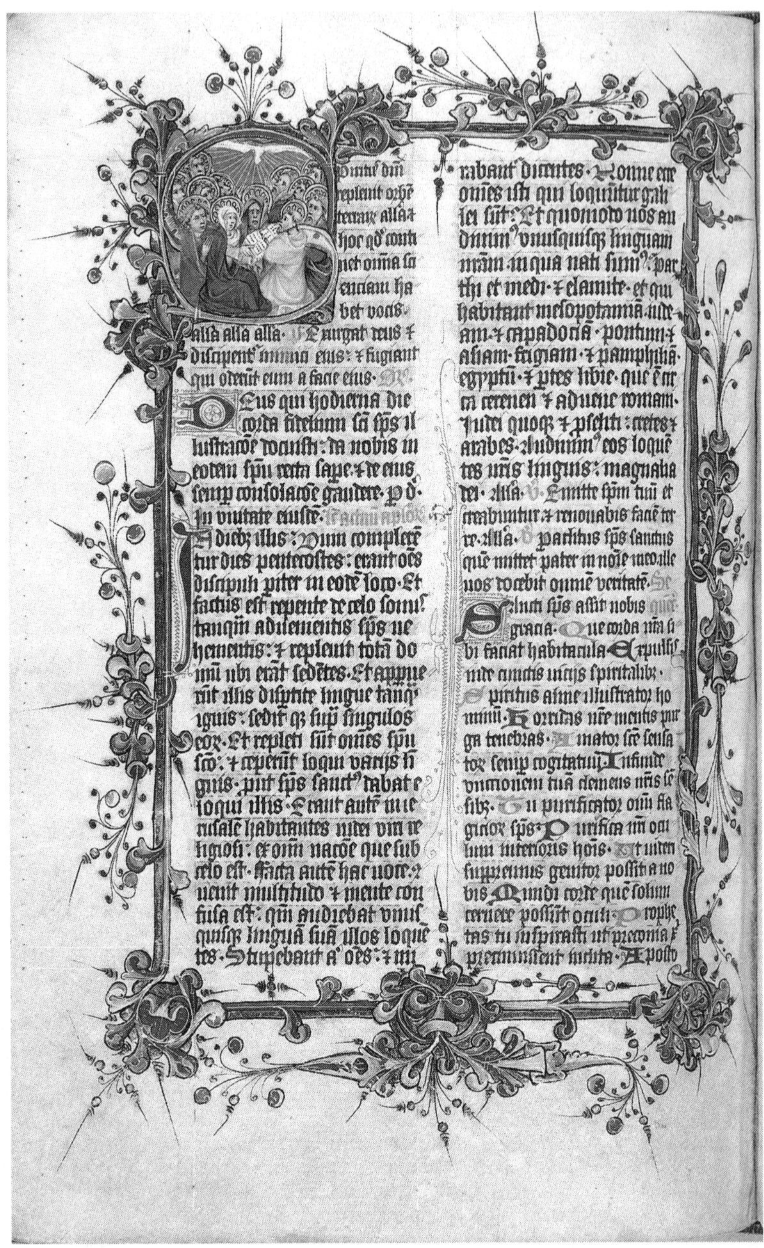

Fig. 4. San Marino, Huntington Library, MS HM 1067, fol. 130v.

Fig. 5. San Marino, Huntington Library, MS HM 1067, fol. 130v, detail.

scripts we can securely attribute to York workshops, and these individual features become a key indicator for York provenance in less elaborate manuscripts. Several other such details could be brought forward here.[49] One detail never before noted, however, proves particularly helpful in identifying manuscripts from York, including Cotton Nero A.x: penwork flourishing for initials in the text. This feature has been beneath the notice of art historians, and rarely engaged with by paleographers. Nonetheless, some distinctive styles and features may identify certain shops and scribes, and flourishing shows up in many manuscripts that are otherwise undecorated; in a surprising number of cases penwork flourishing can be distinctive enough to discern an individual hand within and across manuscripts. This ubiquitous feature has only recently received any sustained attention, with little published documentation yet. Happily, late medieval York has a distinct and exclusive flourishing style. The Bolton Hours, for instance, has typical York bar borders, and green wash at the base of blank-ink sprays radiating from champes, but the previous verso has the much more common penwork initial with contrasting ink flourishing (Fig. 6).

Here we can see the odd flourishing detail that shows up in York manuscripts and nowhere else: sprays of small circles. That detail, in combination with the prominent hash marks (short lines crossing the longer flourished lines) and other features, has a specific use for identifying provenance, since the same decorating hand can be found in other

[49] Another detail that shows up in York manuscripts is a specific sort of lion face given front-on, appearing regularly in the borders of Add. 383. Lions are ubiquitous in medieval decoration, but a particular happy crew-cut lion appears regularly in York historiated initials and in borders from the first decades of the fifteenth century, also being found in the Saint William windows in the Minster: see, for instance, images 4b and 11e from the York Minster collection of the online *Corpus vitrearum medii aevum*, http://www.cvma.ac.uk/index.html. Scott also notes this detail (as a "mask") in her discussion of Cambridge, Trinity College, MS O.3.10, in *Later Gothic Manuscripts*, 2.118.

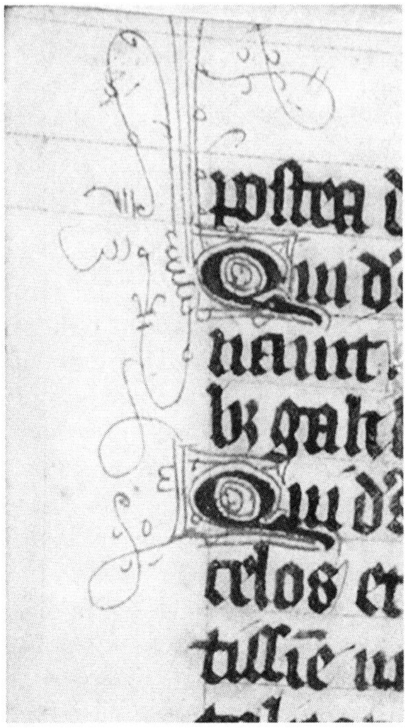

Fig. 6. York, Minster Library, MS Additional 2, fol. 10v, detail.

manuscripts, and solidifies identifications of a common scribal hand in the ever-difficult textura script typical of devotional books in York.[50] More broadly, though, this decorating detail consistently occurs in manuscripts produced in York and can add one more piece of evidence. I will use the term "bubbles" for these circles, given their frequent use in long sprays. A good example of this more exuberant manifestation can be seen in HM 1067 (Fig. 7). As tiny as this detail might seem, after exhaustive search and consultation I can report two findings. First, penwork bubbles of this kind occur in manuscripts that we know from other evidence are from York, in association with all these other York decorative features where they occur, and never yet, at least, in manuscripts that we know are not from York.[51]

[50] The same pen flourishing and the same scribe can be found in Dublin, Trinity College, MS 85; and Cambridge, Clare College, MS G.3.10.

[51] Over the last few years I have examined hundreds of manuscripts, which constitute thousands of penwork initials altogether, to check on manifestations of this flourishing

It is important here to add one cautionary statement: circles are a basic design feature, and occasionally one or two circles show up as a decorative element in pen flourishing outside York. Thus I do not argue that any time a small circle or two show up in penwork decoration we can assume a York provenance for the manuscript. The patterns of bubbles are distinct in York manuscripts in that they float along sprays, inside and outside loops, untethered from other design elements. Nonetheless, using these bubbles to argue a York provenance is much more convincing when they show up in association with other firmly established York decorations and hands, as they do in Huntington 1067, but a full accounting will demand a separate report. Again, the association happens consistently and repeatedly in the period Cotton Nero A.x was produced.

Several questions arise immediately when arguments for provenance depend on relatively modest decoration. One such issue is that small-scale decorators producing modest manuscripts could be influenced by a York model without being in York or another book center where major decoration is most likely to take place; work in pen and ink could be done by the scribe himself wherever he might set up.[52] A *Speculum spiritualium* manuscript from Mount Grace Priory (York, Minster Library, MS XVI.I.9) has sprays of York bubbles in its flourishing much like that illustrated in HM 1067 in Figure 7, suggesting that the manuscript was brought to York for decoration if not the textual production itself, or given to a York-trained decorator in-house. Another devotional collection (San Marino, Huntington Library, MS HM 148) owned by the Ingilbys of Ripley Castle—prominent patrons of Mount Grace—has York green at the base of sprays for an illuminated initial (fol. 23r) and bubbles flanking a pen-and-ink initial (fol. 143r); again, this more modest decorative work could have come from a satellite book center, including Mount Grace itself (Fig. 8).[53]

---

detail and its association with York. Linne Mooney has kept substantial notes over more than a decade for penwork details, including "bubbles" as the keyword for this detail (which I have borrowed here); she graciously searched her notes and database at my request. Neither of us could find a single instance where this feature occurred in manuscripts securely given a provenance other than York.

[52] While it is possible that the scribe does the penwork decoration, we know from many unfinished manuscripts that penwork flourishing in this period often is conducted separately from text production. Furthermore, certain kinds of penwork decoration seem to be consistent work by distinct flourishers operating separately from scribes.

[53] On the latter manuscript see further George Keiser, "The Holy Boke Gratia Dei," *Viator* 12 (1981): 289–317; images for the initial on fol. 143r are available at http://dpg.lib.berkeley.edu/webdb/dsheh/heh_brf?CallNumber = HM + 148.

Fig. 7. San Marino, Huntington Library, MS 1067, fol. 130v, detail.

Fig. 8. San Marino, Huntington Library, MS HM 148. fol. 23r, detail.

This kind of objection could be raised for somewhat later manuscripts such as the Lincoln Thornton manuscript, whose decoration uses several York features including penwork flourishing with bubbles and green wash on the bases of the black-ink sprays in illuminated initials (Fig. 9). Elsewhere I have argued that the more complex decoration in the Lincoln Thornton manuscript was done later by a professional rather than by Thornton himself (who may have done the more simple Lombard initials there and in the London Thornton manuscript), and it is not surprising if Thornton chose a professional connected to a major and nearby bookmaking center like York for the job.[54] This connection may also help explain the remarkable range of romances Thornton managed

[54] Joel Fredell, "Decorated Initials in the Lincoln Thornton Manuscript," *SB* 47 (1994): 78–88; on decoration in the London Thornton manuscript see John Thompson, *Robert Thornton and the London Thornton Manuscript: British Library MS Additional 31042* (Cambridge: D. S. Brewer, 1987), 56–63.

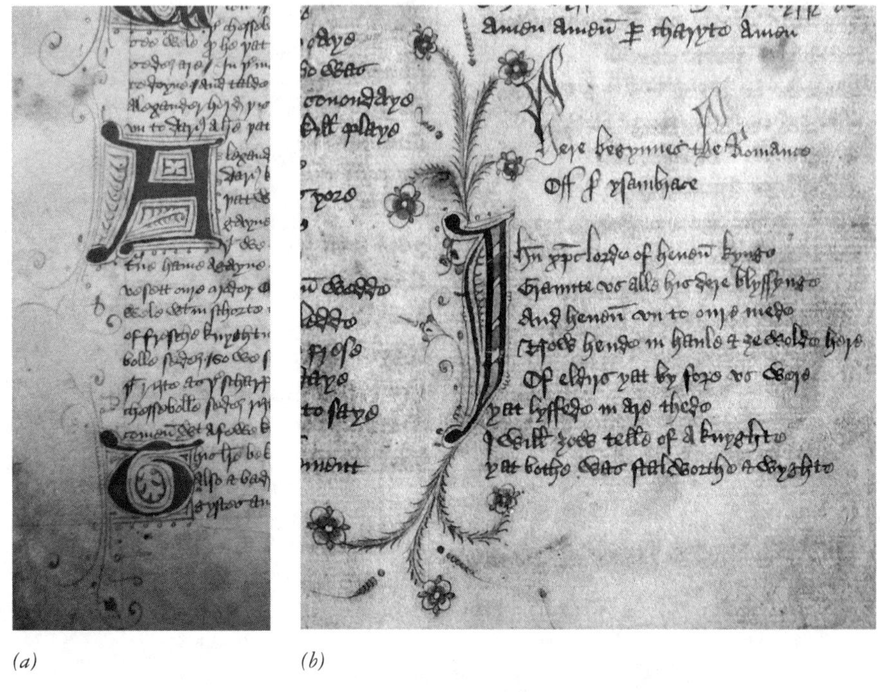

(*a*) (*b*)

Fig. 9. Lincoln, Cathedral Library, MS 91. (*a*) fol. 9v, detail; (*b*) fol. 109r, detail.

to gather. Rather than point to his family associates in the minor gentry nearby as a source of the poems, noting his contact with a major center like York makes far more sense.[55] We cannot say with certainty that these two manuscripts were decorated in York, but the connection to York as a bookmaking center remains crucial: we have to consider the possibility that many more manuscripts and texts than we have previously thought were passing through the literary nexus of York. If, for instance, the Thornton romances were decorated by a York-connected professional, the Thornton texts may well have come from York and/or returned to its book professionals available for copy. York thus may have been a center not just for devotional writing, the focus of so much schol-

[55] York lions show up in the Lincoln Thornton manuscript as a drollery as well on fols. 54r and 66r. For the theory that Thornton's collection of romances came to him from local gentry sources see George Keiser, "Lincoln Cathedral Library MS. 91: The Life and Milieu of the Scribe," *SB* 32 (1979): 159–64.

arly attention recently, but also for the great romance poems moving through the Midlands and north of England then.

To return to Cotton Nero A.x, we can date the penwork decoration to after the text production since it overlaps the scribe's work in several places (Fig. 10). This kind of penwork initial with bubbles and hash marks occurs throughout Cotton Nero A.x.[56] Bubbles are not enough to prove provenance, but the strong association with York decoration argues that they are useful evidence. One more decorative point is relevant here: features of York figure drawing such as hand gestures, and figure drawing generally, where the affinities with the Cotton Nero miniatures are striking.[57]

More broadly, York is the most likely venue for this decoration for a number of reasons. The Cotton Nero A.x illustrations may be crude by the standards of London and the International Style, but they are nonetheless skilled work much like the miniatures in the Bolton Hours, with skillful drapery, use of space, and coloring among their many virtues. These miniatures survive in concert with elaborate and clearly professional penwork initials throughout Cotton Nero A.x. In the north of England no real contenders for this kind of penwork decoration present themselves outside Durham, whose house style in the same period is well documented and quite different from that of Cotton Nero A.x.[58] According to the current state of our knowledge, York is by far the most likely venue for the decoration, at least, of Cotton Nero A.x.

The main hand of Cotton Nero A.x, to come back to that topic, is not so easily located, but we start with the scribe's central and east Yorkshire dialect, and can go on to the hand itself (Fig. 11). The Cotton Nero scribe uses many abbreviations, a remarkable number for a vernacular manuscript written in one column of poetry, but all of them standard for professional scribes writing in English and Latin.[59] The hand is

[56] I am grateful to Michelle Sweeney for pointing out to me, after a talk on York manuscripts, these "bubbles" in Cotton Nero.

[57] Other illuminations probably done in York do exist, and have been given virtually no attention, as in London, British Library, MS Harley 1808, Part 3, a collection of historical texts including one on the building of the city of York, fol. 45v. Here the illuminations share a number of features with Cotton Nero A.x, particularly in figure, gesture, palette, and the peculiar rendering of trees and shrubs. See particularly the *Pearl* miniatures for parallels in palette and natural forms. Scott, *Later Gothic Manuscripts*, 2:67 offers a short list of other miniatures similar in style to those in Cotton Nero A.x.

[58] See Friedman, *Northern English Books*, 208–15 on manuscripts decorated by the Durham master.

[59] Common abbreviations using Latin sigla include *a*m, d*em*, g*er*, g*ra*, m*er*, n*er*, o*ur*, p*er*, p*ro*, p*rop*, q*uod*, t*er*, t*ra*, *us*, v*er*, y*er*, plus the usual m- and n-macrons.

Fig. 10. London, British Library, MS Cotton Nero A.x, fol. 91r, detail; © British Library Board.

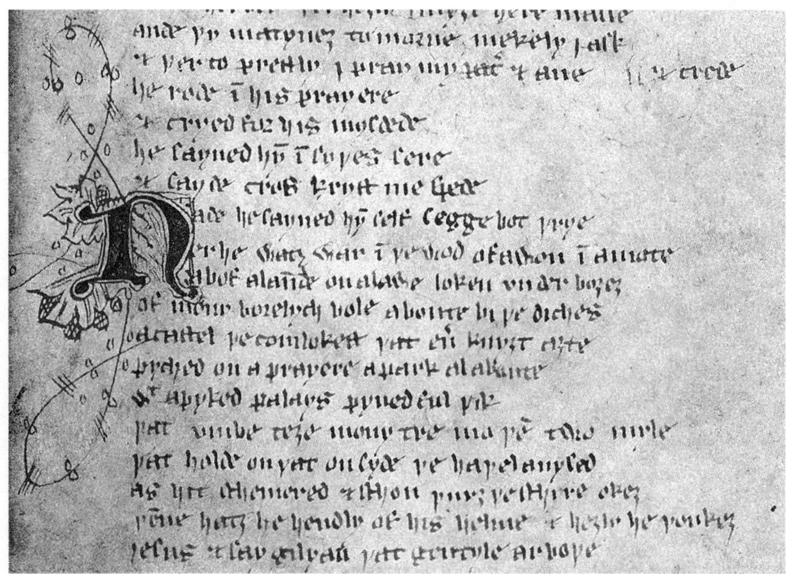

Fig. 11. London, British Library, MS Cotton Nero A.x, fol. 105r, detail; © British Library Board.

also fairly consistent throughout in terms of size, though irregularities in straightness across the manuscript suggest little experience with book hands, formal ruling, or the geometrical rigors of textura. Along with the multitude of abbreviations, one other feature suggests a scribe used to notarial work reshaping his practice for textura: the Cotton Nero scribe uses many bitings and ligatures of the sort professional document producers use to save space, but also seems to improvise his own. Textura script in the period used standard forms of biting such as "da"/"de"/"do," and "ct"/"rt" ligatures (note the "da" biting and "ct" ligature in Fig. 12, from a contemporary York-produced manuscript discussed above). The Cotton Nero scribe includes (and apparently invents) some idiosyncratic forms like the "sp" ligature and the "pe" biting (before the conventional "de" biting) for "spede" (Fig. 13) in a line short

Fig. 12. San Marino, Huntington Library, MS 1067, fol. 130va (line 28), detail.

Fig. 13. London, British Library, MS Cotton Nero A.x, fol. 105r (line 23), detail; © British Library Board.

enough that it hardly needs such economies (see the end of line 6 in Fig. 11). On the other hand, yogh-like zed for final "s" (as in "boȝeȝ," line 3 of Fig. 14) simply is not a glyph used in textura; this common character throughout Cotton Nero A.x reflects Anglo-French writing habits, and suggests a scribe doing specifically notarial work, much of it in French still in this period. Overall the scribal ductus here argues strongly that the scribe produced this work slowly and carefully, trying to reproduce a textura hand with a mixture of elements typical of the last decade of the fourteenth and first decade of the fifteenth century.

Other glyphs point to a textura improvised by a notarial hand, as in the case of the peculiar "o"s that look very much like single-chamber "a"s (Fig. 14: "bot," line 1; "wod," "won," and "mote," line 2; "on," line 3). Textura "o" is formed from deliberate angular strokes that render the letter almost like a hexagon. The Cotton Nero scribe begins the letter "o" with a left-hand half-circle that approximates a textura duct, but an ingrained cursive impulse leads him to pull his second stroke to the right more often than not.

We can see similar habits in contemporary notarial documents from York: textura breaks out occasionally as the higher-order hand in a hierarchy of scripts, but the letter forms are odd and somewhat shaky. In a York probate copy of a will from 1395 (Fig. 15), along with the York bubbles decorating the capital "I" of "In dei nomine Amen" much like

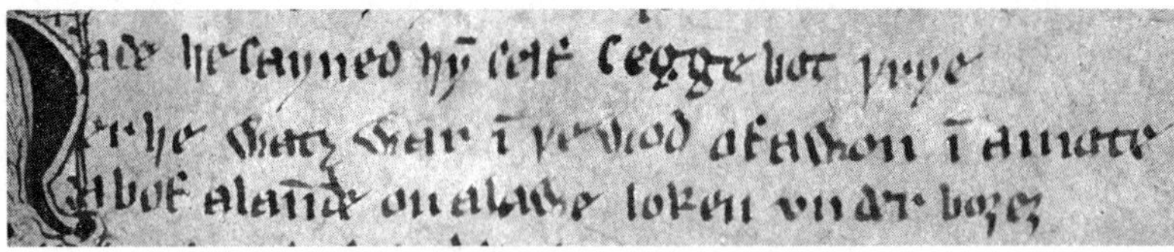

Fig. 14. London, British Library, MS Cotton Nero A.x, fol. 105r (lines 24–26), detail; © British Library Board.

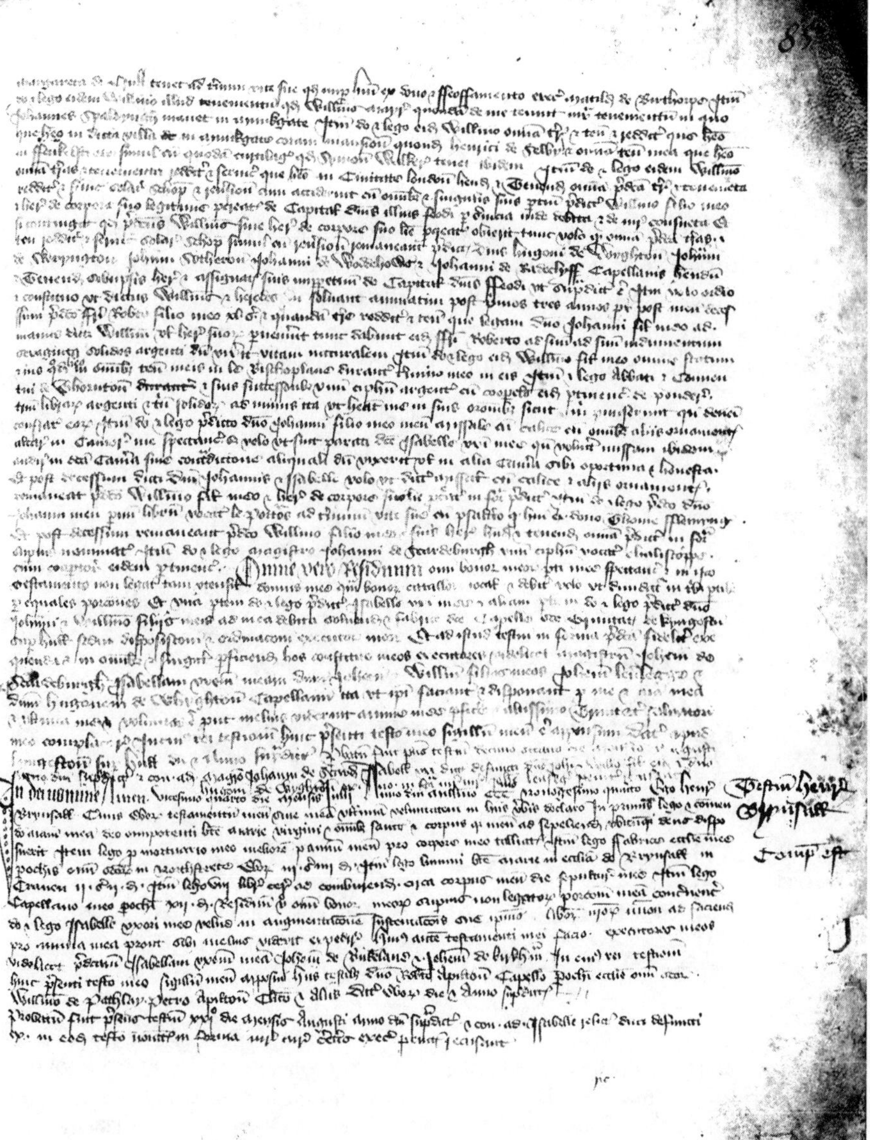

Fig. 15. Henry Brynsall of York, August 21, 1395, Prob. Reg. 1, fol. 85r; reproduced from an original in the Borthwick Institute, University of York.

Fig. 16. Henry Brynsall of York, August 21, 1395, Prob. Reg. 1, fol. 85r (line 28), detail; reproduced from an original in the Borthwick Institute, University of York.

a similar initial "A" in Cotton Nero (Fig. 17), are two breakouts of shaky textura among the cursive. In the two details (figs. 16 and 17a) the textura reveals a secretary (cursive) "d" adding a bastard touch to the first breakout of textura, whereas the traditional uncial form is used in the second breakout.[60] Here again we see a notarial hand improvising a display script; while this script represents another individual hand, its

(*a*) (*b*)

Fig. 17. (*a*) Henry Brynsall of York, August 21, 1395, Prob. Reg. 1, fol. 85r (line 40), detail reproduced from an original in the Borthwick Institute, University of York. (*b*) London, British Library, MS Cotton Nero, fol. 57r (line 25), detail; © British Library Board.

[60] As Parkes and others have pointed out, this substitution is a common feature in what Parkes has called bastard anglicana. In York, though, a city whose most prestigious texts are in a formal textura, this kind of improvisation is more striking.

choice of textura and its odd, semi-skilled expression of that script parallel that of the Cotton Nero scribe.

Throughout these brief textura displays note the inconsistent minims, the frequent cursive start and finish of the penstrokes, and the effects of writing without a ruled line—all much like the unpracticed textura of the Cotton Nero scribe. Textura, in other words, is a well-known script for these York notaries and the Cotton Nero scribe, since it is the dominant book hand in the region at this time. However, scribes who did not normally produce books would combine improvised elements (and York decorations such as the bubbles) with cursive duct to approximate an ideal they knew well, not invent a new book hand like the anglicana emerging for literary texts in the south of England during this period.[61]

These scribal features in Cotton Nero A.x may be more clues than arguments—it remains to compare contemporary notarial and book hands in other regional centers across the north of England. Nonetheless, in notarial documents from York these improvisations and cursive features are also common. York can thank Richard II in part for its status as a notarial center; in 1392 Richard transferred the royal law courts; a large retinue of followers; and, from June to November of that year, himself to York. Guild records from York witness a sudden expansion of several groups of tradesmen—jewelers, not surprisingly, but also scribes.[62] The courts eventually returned south but Richard continued to visit and to shower favors on the city and the Minster through 1396.[63] As England's second city at the time, York's status as an administrative center surely fostered the explosion of book production in this and the following decades in York when Cotton Nero A.x was decorated, if not written.

If Cotton Nero A.x does in some way represent Lancastrian York one

[61] Thanks to recent work by Linne Mooney and Estelle Stubbs, a substantial body of evidence on notarial hands in London during the same period, hands whose work on literary manuscripts we can assess in parallel, is easily available. Briefly, what we see in the work of these London scribes whose individual duct is quite different, such as Adam Pinkhurst and John Marchaunt, is the dominance of a very different set of book hands; they regularly use anglicana script for display in notarial documents, typical in the literary manuscripts they also produced in this period, rather than the textura we see in York notarial documents. One clear reason for this difference is that the anglicana in their entries is already highly developed, with distinct and independent letter forms, not nearly so current as can be found in most notaries of the period. See Mooney and Stubbs, *Scribes and the City*, passim.

[62] *Register of the Freemen of the City of York*, ed. Francis Collins, Vol. 1, *1272–1558*, Publications of the Surtees Society 96 (Durham: Andrews, 1897), entries 1392–98.

[63] Harvey, "Richard II and York," 205–15.

other feature demands attention: the Garter motto that ends *Sir Gawain and the Green Knight* and the textual content of Cotton Nero A.x (Fig. 18). This addition is clearly a display hand, so some variation from the main hand is to be expected.[64] Still, in the "Hony soyt" phrase the "y," the "s," the "a," the "l," and the "p" letter forms are distinctly different in form and duct from the letter forms of the main text (figs. 19 and 20). Here the "l," internal "s," and final "s" are strikingly different in form; distinct differences in duct are clear in the "a" loop and lower chamber, "p" descender, "t" cross-stroke, "o" closure, and "y" descender.[65] Furthermore, the "Hony soyt" phrase is not integrated with the careful layout the Cotton Nero scribe maintains, as is the case at the end of *Pearl*.[66] If we date *Pearl* to the mid-1390s or later, Cotton Nero A.x itself was produced near or after 1400, making the addition

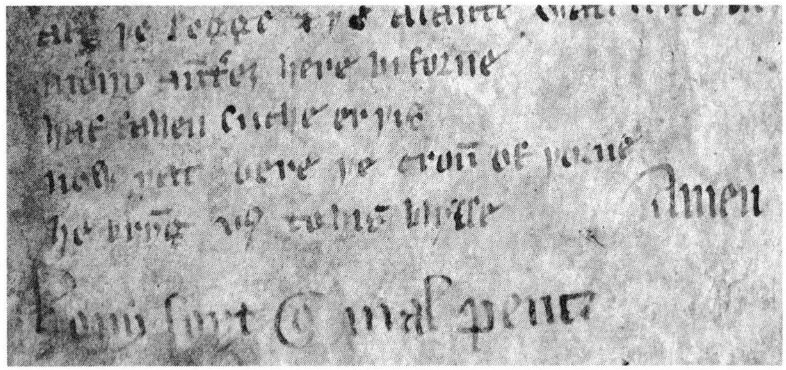

Fig. 18. London, British Library, MS Cotton Nero A.x, fol. 128v, detail; © British Library Board.

[64] Ingledew, *"Sir Gawain,"* 6 and 224 n. argues that the scribe is the same for what he acknowledges is a different script for the Garter motto, following a personal communication from Malcolm Parkes. The declaration in the main text here is far more confident than what is reported from Parkes, who according to Ingledew notes the difference in scripts but is willing to think both scripts are by the same scribe. My own views differ, *pace* Ingledew and the late Malcolm Parkes; see below.

[65] Some variation in duct and letter forms is commonplace in scribes, but the letter forms for "l" and final "s" here are strikingly different, and no parallels for the "Hony Soyt" forms for these two letters occur in Cotton Nero otherwise, including the hand that adds two lines above the illustration on fol. 129r.

[66] "Amen" occurs twice at the end of the final line of *Pearl*, carefully placed on the rule for that line. See London, British Library, MS Cotton Nero A.x, fol. 59v. Reproductions for the entire Part 3 of the manuscript are now available on the *Cotton Nero A.x Project* website, http://www.gawain.ucalgary.ca/.

of the Garter motto by any hand all the more likely to be in Lancastrian times, as the miniatures are quite certain to be.

III. The Witness at Hand

These arguments about Cotton Nero A.x cannot establish dates or certain origins for the poems themselves. Nonetheless, we can look at the context for this precious single witness that gathers together and illustrates various works of a single author at a specific time and place. In other words, while questions such as order and timing for this major poet are critical—the poet may have written these four poems over decades of time in diverse circumstances, or not—Cotton Nero A.x presents a much more definite object of study simply because its producer decided to combine these four poems in a single, unified book. If we accept these dates for Cotton Nero A.x—scribal production near or after 1400 and illumination not long thereafter—this manuscript was born in the remarkable atmosphere of the first years of Henry IV and decorated somewhere along that troubled reign or during the first years of Henry V. These four texts, then, appear in our only witness alongside the outpouring of moralizing poetry from sources as near to the king as John Gower or as distant as the author of *Mum and the Sothsegger*, much of it encouraging penitential stoicism and orthodoxy in unsettled times.[67] Thus a different question arises: why were these poems chosen and combined for a book (and then made luxurious with full-page illuminations), probably in York in the early fifteenth century, at a time when such luxuries were overwhelmingly reserved for sacred texts? As Nicholas Watson has noted, the poems of Cotton Nero A.x are not like the affective texts we often associate with Yorkshire and the north of England in this period; they present a virile, pragmatic spirituality of struggle and penance, of journey and return.[68] Even *Pearl*, a visionary poem suffused with domestic emotions, is nonetheless dedicated to removing affective

[67] On Henry's persona early in his reign as a tolerant figure "who obliged the people by specifically not pressing the nation that he ruled by conquest," see Michael J. Bennett, "Henry of Bolingbroke and the Revolution of 1399," in Dodd and Biggs, *Henry IV: The Establishment of the Regime*, 9–34 (25). On the (tolerated) outpouring of advice to Henry from figures such as Philip Repington (in a letter of complaint Henry apparently solicited) and John Gower, see Frank Grady, "Lancastrian Gower and the Limits of Exemplarity," *Speculum* 70 (1995): 552–55.

[68] Nicholas Watson, "The *Gawain*-Poet as Vernacular Theologian," in Brewer and Gibson, *A Companion to the "Gawain"-Poet*, 293–313.

Fig. 19. London, British Library, MS Cotton Nero A.x, fol. 105r, detail (line 9): "pitosly" in main hand; © British Library Board.

response from its grieving narrator. Also, the "luf-longyng" or "pay" (desire) that drives the jeweler in *Pearl* to his "rasch and ronk" attempt to cross the river (or the desire that drives Gawain to keep the green girdle) is transformed into a call to be obedient to "Pryncez paye"—God's pleasure expressed as royal pleasure; the phrase "prince's pay" is sounded five times in the final fifty lines of *Pearl* at the beginnings and ends of stanzas, culminating in the final line's assertion that we all are servants to "His pay."[69] Here the return of "pay" from the Parable of the Vineyard at the center of *Pearl* (493–744) sees a shift of meaning from "reward" ("þe gentyle Lorde þenne payez Hys hyne" [632]) to "desire." Undoubtedly in the conclusion to *Pearl* "pay" maintains its reminder of God's unquestioned and absolute power to forgive and welcome his "hyne" into his kingdom. Yet the conflict between the Jeweler's "pay" and that of his Lord is a reminder of the limits of human will to assert itself against its sovereign: the Jeweler rebels, loses his vision, pleads with God, and finally resolves that all good Christians must please their prince and achieve reconciliation ("To paye þe Prince oþer sete saȝte" [1201]). This emphasis on limits, obedience, and reconciliation ("saȝte") resonates—whatever the intentions of the poet—in Yorkshire during the time of Henry's pacification of the north and Cotton Nero A.x's production. In the city of York, surviving with surprising dignity the power shift from Percy to Neville and an archbishop's rebellion, the "pragmatics" Watson points out in the *Pearl*-poet take on a political as well as spiritual cast.

All four poems of Cotton Nero A.x are about the loss of perfection

[69] *Pearl*, 1152, 1177, 1167, 1157–1212.

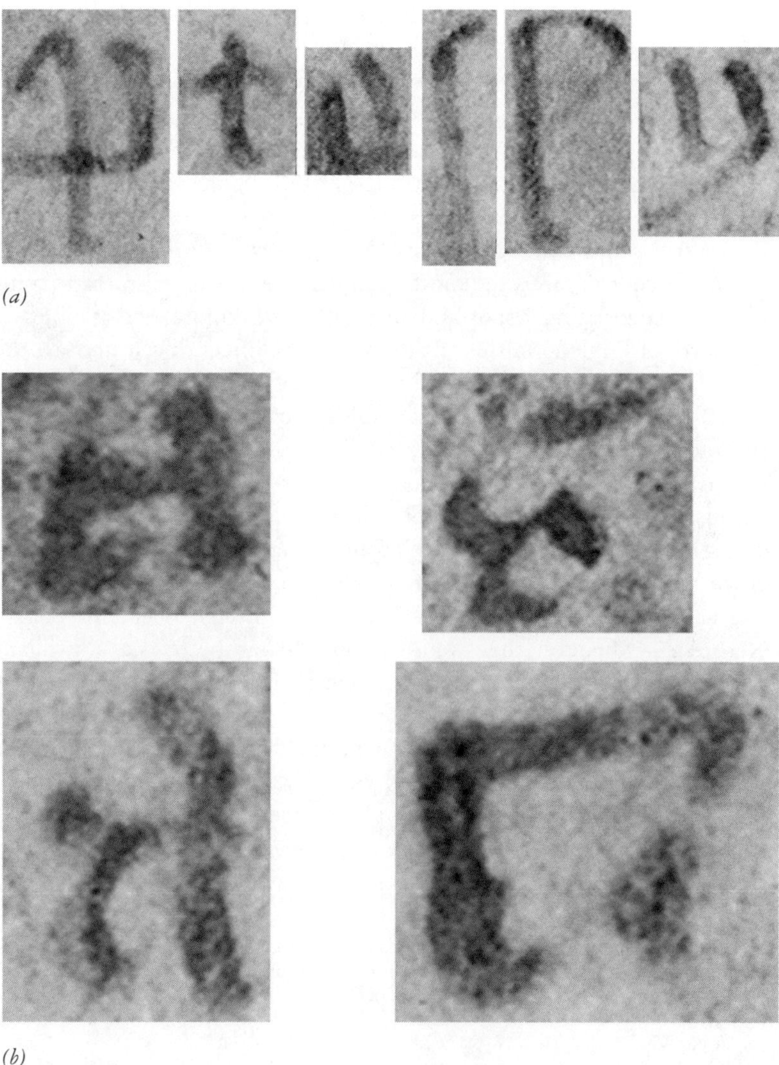

Fig. 20. London, British Library, MS Cotton Nero A.x, fol. 128v, details.
(*a*) comparable letters "p," "t," "o," "s," "l," "y" from "Hony soyt" addition.
(*b*) main scribe (above): "a" (line 28) and final "s" (line 16); "Hony soyt" (below): "a" and final "s."

and the willingness to return to the conditions of the fallen world despite the shame—or "honi"—of individual sin. *Cleanness* echoes the end of *Pearl* with a series of images about the proper approach to and hierarchy in God's court, conceived in terms of "worldly prince" ("wordlych prynce" [*Cleanness*, 49]), and arranged in a kind of sumptuary Calvinism by the richness of clothing (17–50).[70] The framing narrative for Jonah in *Patience* is the narrator's poverty and need to jump when his master sends him on errands (51–52). *Sir Gawain and the Green Knight*, of course, raises the most complex ideas about aristocratic complacency negotiating honor and survival. Furthermore, the troubles in the north of England in the first decade of the fifteenth century saw the death of several prominent local members of the Order of the Garter, and of the relatively unworldly archbishop of York, Richard Scrope, at the pleasure of a worldly Lancastrian prince with his own powerful northern connections.[71] In a period in York where remarkable civic expansion (evidenced by the production of luxury books) co-existed with civil strife literally within the city's walls (where Henry IV had his showdown with Henry Percy, earl of Northumberland in August of 1403) and at its gates in the rising of 1405, the collected poems of Cotton Nero A.x—whenever they were composed—can be read as a brilliant plea for obedience and orthodoxy, a rejection of "mal pens," or wrong thinking.

These very qualities may help explain the fact that this cluster of four poems effectively disappeared from view. Two of the poems are widely regarded as masterpieces of the highest order, yet no other witnesses survive in a region whose appetite for vernacular devotional texts was second to none in England.[72] These poems apparently did not enter

[70] On divine omnipotence in *Cleanness*, also see Watson, "The *Gawain*-Poet as Vernacular Theologian," 306–9, and on 312 his discussion of "aristocratized theology"; and David Wallace, "*Cleanness* and the Terms of Terror," in *Text and Matter: New Critical Perspectives of the "Pearl"-Poet*, ed. Robert J. Blanch, Miriam Youngerman Miller, and Julian N. Wasserman (Troy, N.Y.: Whitston, 1991), 93–104.

[71] On Archbishop Scrope's revolt and execution by beheading see most recently Ormrod, "An Archbishop in Revolt." Prominent aristocrats in this period who were members of the Order of the Garter and beheaded during the transition to Lancastrian rule include William le Scrope, first earl of Wiltshire (beheaded in 1399 at Bristol Castle); three nobles beheaded in 1400 at Bristol after the Epiphany Rising (Thomas le Despencer, earl of Gloucester; Thomas Holland, first duke of Surrey, third earl of Kent; and John de Montecute, earl of Salisbury); and Thomas Percy, earl of Worcester (beheaded in 1403 after Shrewsbury).

[72] For the argument that *The Greene Knight* in the Percy Folio (London, British Library, MS Add. 27879) represents a surviving tradition for *Sir Gawain and the Green*

clerical networks or early print, where a fragment of Margery Kempe's *Book* emerged.[73] Yet even the substantial catalogue of devotional works compiled by Yorkshireman Robert Thornton, here again intermingled with romances, does not include any works even roughly parallel with *Cleanness* or *Patience*, let alone *Pearl* or *Sir Gawain and the Green Knight*.[74] These poems in Cotton Nero A.x, their virile and pragmatic spirituality, may have been enshrined in an illuminated anthology because they served exceptionally well the cultural moment that afforded them reproduction in a luxury book: the early years of Henry IV, whose struggles resonated so powerfully in Yorkshire. It may be that by 1415 the cultural context that prompted the *Pearl*-poet's enshrinement in a decorated single-author anthology had reformed into a northern environment far more receptive to the work of Nicholas Love, Henry Suso, and other explorations of affective devotion within the safer confines of domestic structures.

York is the logical provenance for the Cotton Nero decorations in the period from 1400 to 1420, and the evidence of the decorations supports that provenance. Although the scribal evidence is not yet conclusive, the strong possibility remains that Cotton Nero A.x was produced entirely in York, text and images, along with the fair certainty that the text (if not the poems themselves) was produced in Yorkshire. This connection between Cotton Nero A.x and York offers several new lines of investigation. First, we should look more closely at London aureate poetry—Chaucer, Gower, Hoccleve, Lydgate—manifesting in Yorkshire in the time of Cotton Nero A.x's production, since we have yet to take York's full measure as a center for book production and vernacular

Knight, see *Sir Gawain: Eleven Romances and Tales*, ed. Thomas Hahn (Kalamazoo: Medieval Institute, 1995), ix.

[73] See the eight-page extract, "Here begynneth a shorte treatyse of contemplacyon taught by our lorde Jhesu cryste, or taken out of the boke of Margerie kempe of lyn[n]" (*STC*, 2nd ed., 14924), published by Wynkyn de Worde in 1501. The best overview of late medieval networks for devotional works in the vernacular remains the unpublished dissertation by A. I. Doyle, "A Survey of the Origins and Circulation of Theological Writings in English in the Fourteenth, Fifteenth, and Sixteenth Centuries with Special Consideration of the Part of the Clergy Therein," 2 vols., Ph.D. diss. (Cambridge University, 1953). No such overview for Carthusians exists despite substantial work in the area; for a recent review see Margaret Connolly, "Mapping Manuscripts and Readers of *Contemplation of the Dread and Love of God*," in Connolly and Mooney, *Design and Distribution*, 261–78.

[74] Full accounts of Thornton's manuscripts can be found in *The Thornton Manuscript (Lincoln Cathedral Ms. 91)*, ed. Derek Brewer and A. E. B. Owen (London: Scolar Press, 1975); and Thompson, *Robert Thornton*.

texts. Furthermore, several candidates stand out as potential York patrons of the *Gawain*-poet. Others have pointed to Sir John Stanley and John Macclesfield as possibilities; both are likely to have been in York with Richard II in the 1390s.[75] A duo not regularly associated with the *Gawain*-poet, Thomas Langley (from just across the northern border of Cheshire) and his close working partner Sir James Strangeways (a Cheshireman with a Yorkshire manor), were certainly in York and Yorkshire during the period when Cotton Nero A.x was decorated. Langley was a major figure in book production himself. Though we associate him with a mini-boom in manuscripts at Durham Cathedral after his elevation as bishop there in 1406, he came first to York in 1403 to be installed as a dean just before Archbishop Scrope's death; furthermore, he came to York as a man with the extensive court experience we tend to seek in a patron or transmitter for *Sir Gawain and the Green Knight* and *Pearl*.[76] We also need to investigate book-owning magnate and gentry families connected to Pontefract, to the other honors of Lancaster running north–south through the center of Yorkshire, and to the Nevilles.[77]

Finally, we need to look at the textual community of York with the poems of Cotton Nero A.x in mind, since they represent what may well be the most important intersection of devotional and romance poetry in Middle English, a northern dynamic that looks very different from the aureate poetry developing in the south. We have not fully confronted the frequent associations of devotional and romance texts in the many surviving anthologies and compendia in Middle English despite our attempts at "whole book" analysis, let alone the delicate interplay of genres in individual poems such as *Sir Gawain and the Green Knight*. Similarly, we acknowledge the effects of romance on devotional works such as Nicholas Love's *Mirror of the Blessed Life of Jesus Christ* while not looking closely at the romances in Love's environment in and around

[75] See most recently Bennett, "Historical Background," 75–76.

[76] The fullest account of Langley's career and movements can be found in Ian C. Sharman, *Thomas Langley: The First Spin Doctor (c. 1363–1437)* (Manchester: Dovecote-Renaissance, 1999); on his time in York see especially 60–66. On Langley's role in book production at Durham see Friedman, *Northern English Books*.

[77] One prominent candidate here is William Gascoigne: Yorkshireman; steward of Pontefract Castle by 1391; married to Joan Wyman, daughter of Henry Wyman (goldsmith and Lord Mayor of York 1407–8). Others include Pontefract figures such as Robert Waterton and Thomas Swynford, or Ralph Neville himself, who maintained a base of operations in this period at Sheriff Hutton just outside York.

Mount Grace, in demonstrable contact with the world of York bookmaking just down the road. Cotton Nero A.x's likely presence in York, possibly with the romances of the Thornton manuscript, and certainly with a remarkable body of devotional and dramatic texts, argues for a literary scene in York that should at least complicate any narrative of the "alliterative revival" and the development of northern devotional texts, uncover new readings for the *Gawain*-poet, and demand new ways to assess regional book cultures.

Of Judges and Jewelers: *Pearl* and the Life of Saint John

Susanna Fein
Kent State University

In the Middle English poem *Pearl*, a swooning, grief-stricken Jeweler experiences a gem-studded vision wherein precious stone becomes richly symbolic of heavenly wealth. The Jeweler first apprehends himself to be in a bejeweled landscape, then he perceives a glistening Pearl-Maiden, and ultimately he beholds the Heavenly City walled in diverse precious stones and gated with pearl, wherein gleaming citizens follow Christ "þat gay Juelle" (line 1124) in procession. The twelve gems of the city's foundation and walls conform to the architectural model spelled out in Revelation, which itself stands as the record of a spectacular vision experienced by an earlier, deeply blessed visionary. By medieval tradition, Saint John the Evangelist, the Divine Apostle, was the author of both the Gospel of John and the Book of the Apocalypse. He was also popularly known as Jesus' good friend. Christ had tenderly permitted him to nap on his breast at the Last Supper, a privilege that led John to have extraordinary insight into the ways of God.[1] He was the apostle who had stood with Mary at the Crucifixion and the one to whom the crucified Lord had entrusted his own mother.

Because Saint John, being privy to God's wonders, had witnessed the New Jerusalem, naming its precious stones in his Apocalypse, he also

Early versions of this essay were presented at the 2010 LOMERS Conference on Cotton Nero A.x, University College London, at the University of Connecticut, Storrs, and at the University of Notre Dame. I am grateful to many who offered comments at those forums, as well as to the anonymous reviewers for *Studies in the Age of Chaucer*.

[1] See Jeffrey F. Hamburger, *St. John the Divine: The Deified Evangelist in Medieval Art and Theology* (Berkeley: University of California Press, 2002), who notes that John "provided, together with Paul, the foundations of a theology of vision. . . . John's Gospel made him the first and foremost theologian of the Incarnation and the Trinity. The Book of Revelation, in turn, cast him as the preeminent witness to eternal and eschatological truth" (18).

Studies in the Age of Chaucer 36 (2014):41–76

held honorific status as a gemologist—a reputation much strengthened by lapidarian metaphors, exempla, and moral teachings attached to his hagiography. Traditional episodes in the apocryphal Life of Saint John underscored the apostle's wisdom regarding rocks, gems, and the right valuation of earthly substance as accorded by the Creator. Three of his most famous miracles center on jewels being transformed or exchanged. One of these episodes introduces the apostle into the life of Edward the Confessor, wherein a precious gem comes to symbolize a "Prince's pay." Ultimately, Saint John's narrative becomes entwined with a core national myth of English monarchic privilege—a myth materially invested in the Confessor's shrine at Westminster and the royal crown. Expressed in worldly terms, the contours of Saint John's medieval legend exalt the Divine Apostle as peerless among jewelers.

I offer here a hitherto unexplored perspective by which to understand the trope of the Jeweler in *Pearl*. As the Jeweler's dream unfolds in ineffable splendor, a good deal of its credibility borrows from sanctified authority: Saint John and the vision recorded in Apocalypse. When the narrating "I" exhibits his skill in appraisal and eventually is called a "juelere," this professional identity serves as a crucial marker of similitude to Saint John, the Divine Jeweler of earthly matter and spiritual worth. The narrating "I" performs a role in the poem consistent with his named occupation: he is an expert appraiser of physical substance. A jeweler evaluates things by size, dimension, symmetry, color, and purity. Medieval science and theology held that precious stones and metals possess virtues—magical, God-given properties—that hold potency when in a pure, unalloyed state. By his own introduction, the Jeweler is a creature who by trained discernment deals in quality assessment:

> Oute of oryent, I hardyly saye,
> Ne proued I neuer her precios pere.
> So rounde, so reken in vche araye, . . .
> Queresoeuer *I jugged gemmez gaye*
> *I sette hyr sengeley in synglure.*
> (lines 3–5, 7–8; emphasis added)[2]

[2] All quotations from *Pearl* (London, British Library, MS Cotton Nero A.x, fols. 39r–55v) are drawn from *The Poems of the "Pearl" Manuscript*, ed. Malcolm Andrew and Ronald Waldron, 5th ed. (Exeter: University of Exeter Press, 2007). I have also consulted *Pearl*, ed. E. V. Gordon (Oxford: Clarendon, 1953); and *Pearl*, ed. Sarah Stanbury (Kalamazoo: Medieval Institute Publications, 2001). The poem's 101 stanzas divide into twenty internally linked stanza-groups. In each group, link-words are echoed at the beginning

As a judge of gems, the Jeweler is drawn to objects of refinement, for singular beauty enhances worth, and his now-lost pearl was his most valuable treasure.

Playing a prominent role later in *Pearl*, deep within the vision, is the saint whose own *devysement*—dreaming, narrating, assessing—becomes the spiritualized, extrasensory exemplar for the sensory acumen of the Jeweler. The medieval lapidary tradition, recorded for many centuries in many languages—Latin, French, Old English, Middle English, and so on—promoted John as the authority who reigned supreme among other divine experts in stone, such as Moses and Solomon. The apostle's Revelation held the position of highest honor because it closes the Holy Book. Rather than constructing temples on earth, John saw the truths of heaven itself figured in stone (Fig. 1). As the *North Midland Lapidary* author explains, translating from French, John was God's expert gemologist: "Ye Apocalyps beres wyttnes yt god louyd so well saynt Iohn Euangelist yt he was sent by A aungell to se ye priuytes of paradyse, as it ware by a vysyon; & he saw paradys huge as a cyte, & he saw xi[i] stones, ye whyche saynte Iohn named."[3]

Important work by Tony Spearing, Barbara Nolan, Muriel Whitaker, Rosalind Field, Sarah Stanbury, and others has led us to understand how the *Pearl*-poet borrowed from the tradition of the great illustrated Apocalypses made in France and especially in England, c. 1200–1350.[4] We have grown accustomed to linking the Jeweler's final vision of the

---

and end of stanzas. The numbering of these stanza-groups is supplied in the Andrew–Waldron edition.

[3] *English Mediaeval Lapidaries*, ed. Joan Evans and Mary S. Serjeantson, EETS o.s. 190 (1933; repr. London: Oxford University Press, 1990), 39; see also 17. The text appears in Oxford, Bodleian Library, MS Add. A.106, fol. 45r. I have emended the manuscript reading *xi* to the biblical *xii* (Rv 21:12–21).

[4] A. C. Spearing calls the Apocalypse of Saint John the "main source" for *Pearl* (*The "Gawain"-Poet: A Critical Study* [Cambridge: Cambridge University Press, 1970], 13; see also 108–17); for Spearing's latest views on the *Pearl* narrator, which substantially revise his earlier statements, see *Textual Subjectivity: The Encoding of Subjectivity in Medieval Narratives and Lyrics* (Oxford: Oxford University Press, 2005), 137–73. Key additional studies of the influence are by Barbara Nolan, *The Gothic Visionary Perspective* (Princeton: Princeton University Press, 1977), 157–204, esp. 198–200; Muriel A. Whitaker, "*Pearl* and Some Illustrated Apocalypse Manuscripts," *Viator* 12 (1981): 183–96; Rosalind Field, "The Heavenly Jerusalem in *Pearl*," *MLR* 81 (1986): 7–17; and Sarah Stanbury, *Seeing the "Gawain"-Poet: Description and the Act of Perception* (Philadelphia: University of Pennsylvania Press, 1991), 21–33. See also Theodore Bogdanos, *"Pearl": Image of the Ineffable: A Study in Medieval Poetic Symbolism* (University Park: Pennsylvania State University Press, 1983), 99–142; and Ann R. Meyer, *Medieval Allegory and the Building of the New Jerusalem* (Cambridge: D. S. Brewer, 2003), 137–86, esp. 180.

Fig. 1. Saint John's apocalyptic vision of the twelve gems and twelve gates of pearl of the New Jerusalem. Trinity Apocalypse (Cambridge, Trinity College, MS R.16.2), fol. 25v. Courtesy of Trinity College, Cambridge.

Heavenly City and its procession of virgins led by the Lamb, with Saint John's witnessing of heavenly sights as recorded in Revelation and as fixed in the iconography of the Apocalypse manuscripts. John usually appears in these images, often standing to the side, where he mediates for the reader the exotic, fantastic sights of the Final Judgment.[5] What has been neglected in this assessment, however, is the *full* context for Apocalypse imagery, that is, its traditional setting within Saint John hagiography. What most drew readers to illustrated Apocalypse manuscripts were, of course, the mesmerizing images of Revelation, which extended over many pages. But it was standard practice for scenes from the saint's life to be part of the overall pictorial sequence.[6] The artist of the great English Trinity Apocalypse (Cambridge, Trinity College, MS R.16.2) presents these episodes in colorful panels. Figure 2 shows, for example, John being put on the ship to Rome (top); his coming before the Emperor Domitian (middle); and his torture in a vat of boiling oil (bottom)—events that occurred before John's exile to Patmos, where he received his Revelation. Likewise, the magnificent late fourteenth-century mural painted on the walls of the Westminster Abbey Chapter House preserves similar opening scenes of John's travel by boat.[7] The

[5] A good example can be seen in the Douce Apocalypse (c. 1270), 78, available at http://medieval.library.nd.edu/facsimiles/apocalypse/douce/78.html (accessed July 21, 2013); and see Nigel J. Morgan, *The Douce Apocalypse: Picturing the End of the World* (Oxford: Bodleian Library, 2006). More examples may be seen in Nigel J. Morgan, *Illuminating the End of Time: The Getty Apocalypse Manuscript* (Los Angeles: The J. Paul Getty Museum, 2011); and *The Trinity Apocalypse (Trinity College Cambridge, MS R.16.2)*, ed. David McKitterick (London: British Library, 2005), plates 3(a) and 3(b) (from fol. 4r–v), and Fig. 45 (from the Metz Apocalypse, c. 1250–55, fol. 6r). On the "remarkable outpouring" of illustrated Apocalypses in England, c. 1240–1350, see Whitaker, "*Pearl* and Some Illustrated Apocalypse Manuscripts," 183–84. For a census of English Apocalypses, see Suzanne Lewis, *Reading Images: Narrative Discourse and Reception in the Thirteenth-Century Illuminated Apocalypse* (Cambridge: Cambridge University Press, 1995), 340–44.

[6] The Trinity Apocalypse (c. 1235–50) is the earliest extant English Apocalypse with a pictorial series on the Life of John. See McKitterick, *The Trinity Apocalypse*, Plate 2; and David R. Cartlidge and J. Keith Elliott, *Art and the Christian Apocrypha* (London: Routledge, 2001), 192–93 (Fig. 6.6); Lewis, *Reading Images*, 19–39; and Richard K. Emmerson, "Framing the Apocalypse: The Performance of John's Life in the Trinity Apocalypse," in *Visualizing Medieval Performance: Perspectives, Histories, Contexts*, ed. Elina Gertsman (New York: Ashgate, 2008), 33–56. The Trinity Apocalypse has been made newly accessible by online color facsimile: http://www.trin.cam/ac/uk/james/show /php?index = 1199 (accessed July 21, 2013). Cartlidge and Elliott remark that "[d]uring the twelfth and thirteenth centuries John was arguably the most popular of the apostles; no other apostle has such a volume of stories and images" (182).

[7] Warwick Rodwell and Richard Mortimer, eds., *Westminster Abbey Chapter House: The History, Art and Architecture of "a Chapter House beyond Compare"* (London: Society of Antiquaries of London, 2010); and Tony Trowles, *Treasures of Westminster Abbey* (London:

final panels can no longer be made out, but, to judge by spatial dimensions, the post-Revelation miracles of John were probably included there.

On another front, numerous critics—in particular, Ad Putter, Felicity Riddy, John Bowers, Helen Barr, and Tony Davenport—have advanced richly nuanced readings of the trope of the Jeweler in *Pearl*.[8] Amidst this valuable body of scholarship, which represents many different approaches and potential meanings, materialist to moral, I offer here some new territory for our thinking on the matter. Recovering *Pearl*'s relationship to Saint John's *vita* brings within the poem's immediate ambit a contemporary, clerically sanctioned set of exempla on earthly wealth and heavenly treasure. The *Pearl*-poet develops a series of parallels—some direct, some oblique—between the Jeweler's experiences and Saint John's actions and teachings. For example, when the Jeweler approaches his last vision, he stands like John on a hill near a river—"Tyl on a hyl þat I asspyed / And blusched on þe burghe, as I forth dreued, / Byȝonde þe brok" (lines 979–81)—from which vantage-point he envisions paradise as a well-proportioned city of twelve gems. His account is both verified by his own dream-fortified eyes and dependent on John's master narrative. As he himself states, he is reenacting the saint's sublime experience: "As John þe apostel hit syȝ with syȝt, / I syȝe

Scala, 2008), 150, 152–54. The wall paintings date from around 1395; see Paul Binski, *Westminster Abbey and the Plantagenets: Kingship and the Representation of Power, 1200–1400* (New Haven: Yale University Press, 1995), 187–93. The image of John boarding the ship may be viewed at http://www.english-heritage.org.uk/daysout/properties/chapter-house-and-pyx-chamber/ (accessed July 21, 2013).

[8] Ad Putter, *An Introduction to the "Gawain"-Poet* (London: Longman, 1996), 151–76; Felicity Riddy, "Jewels in *Pearl*," in *A Companion to the "Gawain" Poet*, ed. Derek Brewer and Jonathan Gibson (Cambridge: D. S. Brewer, 1997), 143–55; John M. Bowers, *The Politics of "Pearl": Court Poetry in the Age of Richard II* (Cambridge: D. S. Brewer, 2001), 57, 65, 102–3, 157, and his more recent *An Introduction to the "Gawain" Poet* (Gainesville: University Press of Florida, 2012), 110–12; Helen Barr, "*Pearl*—or 'The Jeweller's Tale,'" *MÆ* 69 (2000): 59–79 (revised and reprinted in her *Socioliterary Practice in Late Medieval England* [Oxford: Oxford University Press, 2001], 40–62); and Tony Davenport, "Jewels and Jewellers in *Pearl*," *RES* n.s. 59 (2008): 508–20. In addition, Mary J. Carruthers examines the poem as "the product of a master jeweler" and stresses the likeness of craftsmanship to thinking and memory ("Invention, Mnemonics, and Stylistic Ornament in *Psychomachia* and *Pearl*," in *The Endless Knot: Essays on Old and Middle English in Honor of Marie Borroff*, ed. M. Teresa Tavormina and R. F. Yeager [Cambridge: D. S. Brewer, 1995], 201–13 [201]). See also Elizabeth Harper, "*Pearl* in the Context of Fourteenth-Century Gift Economies," *ChauR* 44 (2010): 421–39; Lynn Staley, "*Pearl* and the Contingencies of Love and Piety," in *Medieval Literature and Historical Inquiry: Essays in Honor of Derek Pearsall*, ed. David Aers (Cambridge: D. S. Brewer, 2000), 83–114; and Spearing, *Textual Subjectivity*, 137–73, esp. 162–70.

Fig. 2. The Life of Saint John: (*top*) John put on the ship to Rome; (*middle*) John before the Emperor Domitian; (*bottom*) John placed in the vat of boiling oil. Trinity Apocalypse (Cambridge, Trinity College, MS R.16.2), fol. 1v. Courtesy of Trinity College, Cambridge.

þat cyty of gret renoun" (lines 985–86). Later, upon awakening, the Jeweler has absorbed a Johannist comfort as Christ's friend: "For I haf founden Hym, boþe day and naȝte, / A God, a Lorde, a frende ful fyin" (lines 1203–4).[9] By such gradual markers, the poet allows the reader to see the Jeweler as following, however insufficiently, John's profound example. One may compare the method to how Dante fashioned his abashed, alter-ego pilgrim as both a second Paul and a second Aeneas. It may be too much to say that the Jeweler becomes a second John, but despite his mortal frailty and lesser insight, it is Saint John whom he most definitively imitates.

The *Pearl*-poet's device of designating the narrating "I" as Jeweler prepares, therefore, for an unfolding of dreamed revelations that gain spiritual credibility by their modeled likeness to John the Evangelist's visionary experience. Indeed, Saint John eventually becomes the poem's third speaker when the Pearl-Maiden quotes his words for three entire stanzas (73–75; lines 867–900). In the following sections of this article, I will situate the distinctive Jeweler trope of *Pearl* beside the events and lessons of the Life of Saint John, presenting here several strands of evidence. I initially focus on some analogous texts in Middle English that gain moral traction by yoking practitioners of professional appraisal (goldsmiths, jewelers) to themes of judgment. The article's central section then examines the Life of Saint John. I demonstrate how this *vita*—from its most widely known version in *The Golden Legend* to its various glosses by English poets and preachers—is at its core an extensive lesson on the pearl of great price (Mt 13:45–46). My discussion of the Life divides its jewel-related episodes into three types: first, the miracles of gemstones; second, other miracles that expound John's gemlike purity and philosophy on wealth; third, the saint's posthumous miracle with a jeweled ring that ushers Edward the Confessor's soul into bliss. I will conclude this article by examining how the Jeweler/John analogy enlarges meanings embedded in *Pearl*, particularly as regards its treatment of the parable about the pearl of great price. The Life of Saint John depicts an apostle who trades in jewels as he seeks a man willing to sell his most precious gem to gain the Kingdom of Heaven. In this way, its status as a likely influence upon the *Pearl*-poet warrants close attention.

[9] On this passage, compare Spearing, *Textual Subjectivity*, 165–66.

Jewelers in Medieval English Literature

A trained capacity to judge substance and appraise worth defines the Jeweler trope of *Pearl*. In the fourteenth century, situated in the powerful London Goldsmiths' Company, or at least near its periphery, was the trade of jeweler, which had no London guild of its own. Many prominent London goldsmiths identified themselves as both "goldsmith and jeweler."[10] A rule from the Goldsmiths' *Book of Ordinances* illustrates how regulation and measurement—including the quantification of labor and payment—were integral to the goldsmith craft:

> If any workman or labourer asks or receives more than he has worked for: as, for example, if a whole day is allowed for half a day's work, or two or three days for one and a half days' work, or anything else comes to your knowledge that is prejudicial or harmful to the Company, you shall inform the wardens so that they may provide a remedy.[11]

In this ordinance one might hear the Jeweler's practical grounds for resisting the message of the parable of the laborers (Mt 20:1–16) when the Maiden paraphrases it near the center of *Pearl*. In the regulated practices of goldsmiths, this rule of workplace vigilance was part of an oath taken by all laborers belonging to the fellowship.

By eye and instrument, jewelers or goldsmiths measured labor and product, skill and workmanship, chemical purity and perfect beauty in terms of color and light—that is, they judged aesthetic form and execution as a calibrated thing. Literary usages borrowed from real-life practice, wherein goldsmiths reigned as masters in the business of valuation. As authoritative appraisers in the marketplace, goldsmiths were sworn to adhere to rigorous standards. The designated wardens of the Company regulated in London and elsewhere the quality of silver and gold metalwork—including coin, which was assayed on a regular basis for fraudulent levels of alloys. The knowledge of valuation was called a *priv-*

[10] T. F. Reddaway and Lorna E. M. Walker, *The Early History of the Goldsmiths' Company 1327–1509, including "The Book of Ordinances 1478–83"* (London: The Worshipful Company of Goldsmiths [Edward Arnold], 1975), 206–7 n. 131, 300 (John Paddesley), 304 (William Russe), 309 (Richard Stacy). See also John Cherry, *Goldsmiths* (Toronto: University of Toronto Press, 1992), 23–24, 52–64.

[11] "Appendix I: The Book of Ordinances," in Reddaway and Walker, *The Early History of the Goldsmiths' Company*, 209–74 (219).

itee, that is, a secret craft.[12] In medieval literature goldsmiths and jewelers are routinely the offstage, go-to characters who verify values. To recall an instance from Chaucer's *Canon's Yeoman's Tale*: to dupe the priest, the swindler-alchemist canon suggests that the gold he has seemingly produced from a lesser metal be tested, so "unto the goldsmyth" they go, where the rods are put "in assay" and proved to be "as hem oghte be" (VIII.1337–40).[13] As shall be seen, in the Life of Saint John, goldsmiths and jewelers are asked to provide this service.

In countless saints' legends an unjust judge, invariably a pagan worshiper of idols, comes to symbolize the fallibility of the faithless person who lacks spiritual vision, the one who believes only in what can be seen, touched, tasted, or heard. The emperor in the prose Life of Saint Katherine is such a figure who thinks he can tempt the saint into error by promising to erect a statue of her for others to worship. Katherine archly taunts him for his false faith:

> Than þe virgyn began a lytel to smyle and sayde vnto the tiraunt, O how blessed am I þat am worthy so gret priuilege of worschep þat an ymage schold be sette vp for me to be reuerensed and worscheped of men. O hou blessed schall I say I am and I myght deserue to be maad of gold. And ȝeet I schold not be al vnblessed and I myght be of seluer. Bot þan schal þer be *stryf bytwene þe jowelers for þe price weyght & value þat I am of.*[14]

Katherine mocks the tyrant's love of gold and silver by pointing out the strife that would erupt amongst those jewelers who would then evaluate her. The saint deftly equates their materiality with her inquisitor's values. In *Pearl* the Pearl-Maiden's stern corrections of the Jeweler are not, in their way, very far from this tradition of virgin saints boldly facing judges who deem wrongly through sense perception what cannot be rationally known.

Divine justice—and also humans' frail comprehension of it—seems

[12] Ibid., 270 (Ordinance F.90), 278.

[13] *The Riverside Chaucer*, gen. ed. Larry D. Benson, 3rd ed. (Boston: Houghton Mifflin, 1987), 280. An oblique analogy occurs when Griselda is dressed up and then piecemeal-stripped of everything Walter has given her, including jewels (IV.869), while the marquis—as a type of goldsmith or jeweler—relentlessly assays her actual worth. When at last she is proven true, Griselda is adorned in a "clooth of gold that brighte shoon, / With a coroune of many a riche stoon" (IV.1117–18).

[14] *The Life and Martyrdom of Saint Katherine of Alexandria, Virgin and Martyr*, ed. Henry Hucks Gibbs, Roxburghe Club 112 (London: Nichols and Sons, 1884), 1–67 (43; emphasis added).

to preoccupy many alliterative poets. All four Cotton Nero poems share this concern, and in *Pearl* it is insistent, couched in the monitory, even legalistic, speech of the Pearl-Maiden.[15] In the alliterative *Morte Arthure* Arthur's greatness as guardian of justice ultimately resides in his humility before God, not in his pride of earthly conquest.[16] In *Saint Erkenwald* divine justice and heavenly reward come to the virtuous pagan judge who lived before Christ; he judged righteously in unrighteous times, and so is he judged. The alliterative "Four Leaves of the Truelove" is likewise a poem about judgment, contrasting the false judgments of Herod at the Nativity, Pilate at the Crucifixion, and Satan at the Harrowing to the final, eternal judgment of Christ, who appears in a chilling courtroom drama of Doomsday.[17] In its scene of Apocalypse, the poet catalogues a range of powerful men who find themselves before the supreme Judge. The stanza reads:

> He wil schew us His woundes blody and bare,
> As He has sufferd for owre sake, wytter and wyd.
> Kynges and kasors before Hym bus fare;
> Byschoppes and barons and all bus abyd;
> Erles and emperours, nane wyll He spare;
> Prestes ne prelates nor persons of pride;
> *Thar justes and juellarse of lawe or of lare*,
> That now ar full ryall to ryn and to ryd
>   In land.
>   Thar dome sall thai take thare.
>   Ryght as thai demed are,
>   When thay ware of myghtes mare,
>   And domes had in hand.
>
> (lines 443–55; emphasis added)

These powerful men must receive their everlasting dooms, in an ironic reversal of how they apportioned judgments to others in life.

This little-known poem also provides, outside the opening lines of

[15] Bogdanos, *"Pearl": Image of the Ineffable*, 87–98.

[16] See George R. Keiser, "The Theme of Justice in the Alliterative *Morte Arthure*," *Annuale Mediaevale* 16 (1975): 94–109.

[17] "When we ar cald to that courte, behoves us to here; / All sall be thar seyn, bothe bondmen and free; / . . . / We sall seke theder in symple atyre, / Tremland and schakand, as lefe on a tree" (lines 404–5, 417–18). Quotations from "The Four Leaves of the Truelove" are from Susanna Greer Fein, ed., *Moral Love Songs and Laments* (Kalamazoo: Medieval Institute Publications, 1998), 161–254, in which *i/j* orthography is modernized.

Pearl, one of the clearest semantic and alliterative links between judges and jewelers. The pertinent reading occurs in the stanza's seventh line: "justes and juellarse of lawe or of lare." For the reading "iuellarse" found in the London Thornton copy (London, British Library, MS Additional 31042), early editors read instead the word "mellarse," "meddlers."[18] Etymologies were duly sought and found. Magdalene M. Weale derived the word from Old English *maþelian*, *maeþlan*, "to speak, discourse," and translated it "discoursers, disputers."[19] C. L. Wrenn suggested instead that it came from Middle English *medlen*, *mellen* (Old French *mesler*, *meller*), "to meddle," and defined the meaning as "those who meddle with law."[20] The word *mellarse* has thus entered the *MED* as a nonce form of *medlers*, "practitioners" or "meddlers, nuisances."[21] None of this speculation is correct, however, for it is based on misread minims. The phrase reads "justyce & iuellarse" in the manuscript, with the initial *i* of "iuellarse" clearly dotted (Fig. 3). Alliteration with *justyce* verifies the reading, as does the presence of similarly formed initial *iu* for *ju* elsewhere in Robert Thornton's script.[22] The *b*-verse completes the sense of the *a*-verse: "justices of the law" and "jewelers of learning." The line contrasts those who judge things on ground to God who judges them.[23]

[18] "*The Quatrefoil of Love*: An Alliterative Religious Lyric, Now First Edited from Add. MS. British Museum 31042, with Collations from Add. MS. A. 106 Bodleian Library," ed. Israel Gollancz, in *An English Miscellany, Presented to Dr. Furnivall in Honour of His Seventy-Fifth Birthday*, ed. N. R. Ker, A. S. Napier, and W. W. Skeat (1901; repr. New York: Benjamin Blom, 1969), 112–32 (130); and *The Quatrefoil of Love*, ed. Israel Gollancz and Magdalene M. Weale, EETS o.s. 195 (1935; repr. London: Milford, Oxford University Press, 1971), 1–18 (15).

[19] *The Quatrefoil of Love*, ed. Gollancz and Weale, p. 32.

[20] C. L. Wrenn, review of *The Quatrefoil of Love*, ed. Gollancz and Weale, *RES* 13 (1937): 374–77.

[21] *MED*, s.v. *medlere* (n.), def. (a). Compare *Richard the Redeless*, III.335: "And ho-so pleyned to the prince that pees shulde kepe, / Of these mystirmen, medlers of wrongis" (*"Richard the Redeless" and "Mum and the Sothsegger,"* ed. James M. Dean [Kalamazoo: Medieval Institute Publications, 2000], 45).

[22] See, for example, "justices & iugges" (dotted "iu-") in the alliterative *Morte Arthure*, line 246, visible at the base of fol. 55v in the facsimile of the Lincoln Thornton manuscript: *The Thornton Manuscript (Lincoln Cathedral MS. 91)*, intro. D. S. Brewer and A. E. B. Owen (London: Scolar Press, 1975). In the line above, Thornton writes "iolily" ("i-" undotted) for "jolily." (I choose these examples because the Lincoln manuscript is readily accessible in facsimile.) On Thornton's minims, see Mary Hamel, "Scribal Self-Corrections in the Thornton *Morte Arthure*," *SB* 36 (1983): 119–37 (125).

[23] Of interest, too, are the variants found in other copies of *Truelove*. Oxford, Bodleian Library, MS Add. A.106, fols. 6r–14r (c. 1425–50), has the metrically defective "domesmen," meaning "men of judgment, discriminators of worth," a gloss for Thornton's "iuellarse." The third copy, a late printing by Wynkyn de Worde (*STC*, 15345, c. 1510), reads "juges," a synonym that supports the presence of a more difficult alliterating original. A similar misreading of "iuele" as "mele" features in the editorial history of

Fig. 3. Detail from "The Four Leaves of the Truelove." London Thornton manuscript (British Library, MS Add. 31042), fol. 101r. Courtesy of The British Library.

The relevance of this collocation to *Pearl* is worth pursuing.[24] The term *juelere* denotes an activity representative of humanity's reasoning capacity, based on empirical observation, measurement, and practiced experience. Hence, the Jeweler's expert lapidary knowledge, his skill in appraising "gemmez gaye" (line 7), complements the poet's play on ideas of evaluation and value, the key paradox in the parable of the vineyard being how differently man and God assess degree.[25] The link-

Pearl, line 23. See *Pearl*, ed. Gordon, 47; and *Pearl*, ed. Stanbury, 72. Variants of *molere* ("woman") in *Piers Plowman*, A II.83 ("Mede is molere") include "muliere," "medeler," "medlere," "mulyer," and "Iuweler"; Skeat printed "Meede is a Iuweler" ("wealthy person") (William Langland, *The Vision of William Concerning Piers the Plowman*, ed. W. W. Skeat, Vol. 1, EETS o.s. 28 [1867; repr. London: Oxford University Press, 1990], 21 [numbered A II.87]). Compare also the emended line "For oure ioye, oure [iu]ele, Iesu Crist of heuene," in *Piers Plowman*, B XI.184 (William Langland, *Piers Plowman: A Parallel Text Edition of the A, B, C and Z Versions*, ed. A. V. C. Schmidt, 3 vols. [Kalamazoo: Medieval Institute Publications, 2011], 1:462).

[24] The line in *Truelove* might even allude to *Pearl* itself. In Fein, *Moral Love Songs*, 161–67, I demonstrate how the *Truelove*-poet frames the poem with a grieving maiden under a tree because she figuratively resembles Mary at the cross. The *Pearl*-poet's use of the Jeweler/John analogy might possibly have spurred the *Truelove*-poet's creation of a framing conceit based on a holy person's iconography. The transference of the technique to Mary would have been a natural choice given how she is John's counterpart in Passion imagery.

[25] On the Jeweler's problems with "deeming," see Putter, *An Introduction*, 162–77. For some editors' definitions of the Jeweler as a judge of value, see *The Poems*, ed. Andrew and Waldron, 65–66 (note to lines 241–300); and *"The Pearl": A New Translation and Critical Edition*, ed. Sr. Mary Vincent Hillman (Notre Dame: University of Notre Dame Press, 1961), 75–76, 84–85. Cherry discusses the looseness of the term *jeweler* in common parlance: "The exact meaning of the term jeweller in the late Middle Ages is unclear, and it may well have been applied to a variety of activities. It might

words of amount—"more and more," "more," "gret inoghe," "makellez," "neuer þe les" (stanza-groups 3, 10, 11, 13, 15)—expound not just theological doctrines of God's ineffable bounty and perfection; they also reveal the Jeweler's propensity to describe spiritual effects in terms of accessible quantity, of one value measured in reference to another.

A polar opposition in perception marks the mid-point of *Pearl*, where the link-words shift from "more" to "inoghe." The tenth stanza-group ends with the Jeweler asserting, as in the Goldsmiths' oath for laborers, the principle of entitlement to payment according to length of work:

> Now he þat stod þe long day stable
> And þou to payment com hym byfore,
> Þenne þe lasse in werke to take more able,
> And euer the lenger þe lasse þe more.
> (lines 597–600)

At the head of the eleventh stanza-group, the Maiden counters by expounding the boundless grace of God:

> "Of more and lasse in *Godez ryche*,"
> Þat gentyl sayde, "lys no joparde,
> For þer is vch mon payed inlyche,
> Wheþer lyttel oþer much be hys reward."
> (lines 601–4; emphasis added)

Terms of quantity, *more* and *lasse*, transform semantically according to perspective, material or spiritual. As the Maiden instructs in this stanza-group: "the grace of God is gret inoghe" (line 612). The crossover in perspective is brilliantly underscored by a pun in line 601, the poem's central line, the turning-point. Here "Godez ryche" means *both* "God's kingdom" and "God's treasury."[26] In naming the divine realm, the Pearl-Maiden embeds a monetary metaphor. What the wordplay exquisitely denotes is the same unified perspective on wealth persistently

mean a retailer of gemstones or a retailer of goldsmiths' work; it might, however, mean an appraiser of gemstones or simply the craftsmen who cut or set the stones" (*Goldsmiths*, 23).

[26] This pun has been generally passed over by editors. It is partially captured in William Vantuono's translation, "God's realm rich," in *The "Pearl" Poems: An Omnibus Edition*, Vol. 1, *"Pearl" and "Cleanness"* (New York: Garland, 1984), 51. For the primary meaning "kingdom," see *MED*, s.v. *riche* (n.[1]), def. 2. The meaning "wealth, treasury" is easily construed, though: svv. *riche* (adj.), def. 1–3, and *richesse* (n.), def. 1–2.

preached by the Divine Apostle in the stories of his *vita*. According to Saint John's teachings, all created matter—from simple sticks and stones to human souls—constitutes God's treasure, which exists in gradated forms. Souls hold a special value, however, for each one saved will be deposited in and thereby "increase" the treasury of heaven.

The Miracles of the Life of Saint John

Saint John's Miracles of Gemstones

In two major episodes of Saint John's *vita*, the apostle's acts of conversion involve transformed jewels.[27] One miracle provides a lesson on false wealth by means of rocks turned into gems and then back again into rocks. The second involves the smashing of gems and their later restoration to wholeness. When performed by the saint who envisioned the twelve gems of the New Jerusalem, these lapidarian miracles construct a kind of trademark insignia. In the realm of earthly/spiritual valuation, from dross dust to priceless jewels, John is the supreme expert. In *Pearl* the Jeweler acknowledges the quality of the saint's expertise when he addresses the naming of the twelve stones of the New Jerusalem:

> John þise stonez in writ con nemme,
> I knew þe name after his tale. . . .
> I knew hit by his deuysement
> In þe Apocalyppez, þe apostel John.
> (lines 997–98, 1019–20)

Obviously familiar with John's *devysement* in the Apocalypse, the clerical *Pearl*-poet and his audience would also have known the Life of Saint John. The slightly later author of the alliterative *John Evangelist Hymn* calls on his readers' engaged knowledge when he alludes passingly to a well-known miracle of gem transformation. Addressing the saint directly, he declares:

> Thow made golde full gude and gafe þam, I wene.
> Smale stanes of þe see saynede þou þare,

[27] Jacobus de Voragine, "Saint John, Apostle and Evangelist," in *The Golden Legend: Readings on the Saints*, trans. William Granger Ryan, 2 vols. (Princeton: Princeton University Press, 1993), 2:50–55.

And þay warre saphirs, for-sothe, was nane swylke sene.
Sene swylke was þare none
For fine precyouse stone.
The wandes when þou badde
Þay ware gold ylkone.
Þou gafe thaym welthe mare wone
Þan þay euer hadde.[28]

These lines recall John's conversion of sticks and stones to gold and jewels, a miracle frequently recounted in sermons drawing upon the apocryphal events of John's life.

The standard source for the Life of Saint John for English authors, Jacobus de Voragine's *Golden Legend*, strings together stories cobbled from numerous sources (Jacobus names Mellitus, Jerome, Isidore, and Clement, among others), all basically indebted to the ancient, apocryphal Acts of John.[29] Glosses added by preachers and hagiographers helped to illuminate for medieval English worshipers the full arc and import of John's legend. Consistently expounded are John's intimacy with God and his talent for distinguishing false wealth from true.[30] His

[28] The alliterative *Of Sayne Johne þe Euangelist*, lines 174–82, in *Three Alliterative Saints' Hymns: Late Middle English Stanzaic Poems*, ed. Ruth Kennedy, EETS o.s. 321 (Oxford: Oxford University Press, 2003), 10–23, 68–86 (15). In this poem John is introduced with similes to jewels (lines 15–16) before the poet gives this abbreviated account of the miracle of sticks and stones. Ignoring the direct references to jewels in the *vita*, John Scattergood suggests that the allusions derive solely from the gems described in Revelation ("Alliterative Poetry: Religion and Morality," in *A Companion to Medieval Poetry*, ed. Corinne Saunders [Oxford: Wiley-Blackwell, 2010], 329–48 [335]).

[29] Cartlidge and Elliott, *Art and the Christian Apocrypha*, 175–208.

[30] In addition to the alliterative poem cited in note 28 above, the Middle English lives of Saint John consulted for this study are: the verse *De sancto Johanne euangelista* (from the Northern Homily Cycle), in *Altenglische Legenden: Neue Folge*, ed. C. Horstmann (Heilbronn: Von Gebr. Henninger, 1881), 35–42; the verse *Iohan ap.*, in *The Early South-English Legendary; or, Lives of Saints*, ed. Carl Horstmann, EETS o.s. 87 (1887; repr. London: N. Trübner, 1975), 402–17; the verse *De sancto Iohanne ewangelista*, in *The South English Legendary*, ed. Charlotte D'Evelyn and Anna J. Mill, EETS o.s. 236 (1956; repr. London: Oxford University Press, 1967), 3:594–610; the prose sermon *De sancto Iohanne euangelista* (c. late 1380s), in *John Mirk's "Festial," Edited from British Library MS Cotton Claudius A.II*, ed. Susan Powell, Vol. 1, Part 1, EETS o.s. 334 (Oxford: Oxford University Press, 2009), 31–35; *Speculum sacerdotale, Edited from British Museum MS. Additional 36791*, ed. Edward H. Weatherly, EETS o.s. 200 (London: Humphrey Milford, Oxford University Press, 1936), 11–12; the prose *Saint Iohn Euangelist*, in *Virgins and Scholars: A Fifteenth-Century Compilation of the Lives of John the Baptist, John the Evangelist, Jerome, and Katherine of Alexandria*, ed. and trans. Claire Waters (Turnhout: Brepols, 2008), 1–177, 436–49; and the prose *Life of Seynt Iohn Euangelist*, in Cambridge University Library, MS Add. 2604, fols. 11v–21v (transcription kindly supplied by Veronica O'Mara). I have also consulted the late thirteenth-century Anglo-Norman *vita*

is the appraiser's eye whose powers go beyond material surfaces. To his closest apostle, God revealed his own *privetee*, that is, both the divinity of the Word and the apocalyptic vision.[31] In reference to *Pearl*, what become very intriguing are John's two miracles that use jewels as symbolic props. And in one of them miracle-worked treasure is sent to goldsmiths and jewelers—the worldly practitioners—for appraisal.

John's *vita* in the *Golden Legend* opens with a list of his four definitive privileges. These are: (1) Christ held a special love for John; (2) John was a chaste virgin, free from fleshly corruption; (3) God's secrets were revealed to the apostle when he laid his head on Christ's breast at the Last Supper (an English writer explains that he slept softly there; thus the event was a dream-vision);[32] and (4) Jesus entrusted Mary to John's care. After enumerating these special graces, Jacobus tells of John's acts after the descent of the Holy Spirit. He travels to Asia and founds churches, but soon he is summoned to Rome, where Emperor Domitian sentences him to boil in a vat of oil (Fig. 2, bottom). English sermonizer John Mirk calls this experience an "assaye" of John's virtue, as if his exterior mettle is being tested.[33] John's flesh remains untouched, so the angry emperor exiles him to the island of Patmos, where the apostle writes the Apocalypse. When the emperor later dies, John returns to Ephesus and works his next miracle: the raising from death of Drusiana, a virtuous woman.[34]

---

found in British Library, MS Harley 2253, fols. 41v–43v, and the Old French *vita* of similar date in Paris, Bibliothèque nationale de France, fr. 19525, fols. 31r–36r: see Delbert W. Russell, ed., *Légendier apostolique anglo-normand* (Montreal: Presses de l'Université de Montréal, 1989), 50–76; and the translation by Ian Short found on the CD accompanying Morgan, *The Trinity Apocalypse*, CD81-CD94.

[31] The intimacy of the term *privetee*, standard for the John story, held a differently shaded valence among goldsmiths, where it connoted secret skill in assessing monetary worth. In *Pearl* the term evokes the deep mourning of the Jeweler who has lost his "priuy perle" (lines 12, 24), a state that brings him to his vision. In all instances, the word denotes a special kind of access.

[32] "Sein Ion lenede op is brest & and wel softe aslepe lay" (*The South English Legendary*, ed. D'Evelyn and Mill, 3:594 [line 26]). Medieval images of the Last Supper very frequently show John asleep on Christ's breast. For two English examples that predate *Pearl*, see Lewis, *Reading Images*, 28–29 (figs. 13, 15). The Corpus Apocalypse offers a meaningful juxtaposition of this image with John's arrival at Patmos. This illumination may be viewed at parkerweb.stanford.edu/parker/actions/page_turner.do?ms_no = 20 (Cambridge, Corpus Christi College, MS 20, fol. 1r; accessed October 1, 2013).

[33] Mirk, *Festial*, ed. Powell, 32 (line 22). The Anglo-Norman prose life of Saint John (c. 1300) attributes John's survival to his virginity and carnal purity (Russell, *Légendier*, 53 [lines 54–55]).

[34] Whitaker proposes that the Drusiana story contributed to the poet's conception of the Pearl-Maiden ("*Pearl* and Some Illustrated Apocalypse Manuscripts," 186–87). See also *The "Pearl" Poems*, ed. Vantuono, 177.

The succeeding episode introduces the gems concept that runs like a rich vein through Saint John's legend. A philosopher named Craton teaches that people should despise the world. In exuberant response, two youths sell their patrimonies, convert them to jewels, and then smash the jewels to bits before an audience.[35] In both the Trinity Apocalypse (Fig. 4) and the magnificent Saint John Window at Chartres Cathedral (Fig. 5),[36] one can see how an iconography developed for this episode, wherein the youths dramatically raise hammers over the gemstones, a sign of their being smashed to bits. Witnessing this display, John denounces it for three reasons: because it wins men's praise but is condemned by divine judgment; because it cures no vices; and because contempt of riches is meritorious only when wealth is given to the poor. John restores the gems to wholeness, and all three men—youths and philosopher—convert. The proceeds of the sold jewels go to the poor. This miracle causes things of innate value—material gems—to be restored to their natural state for the sake of doing worldly good, and it brings three men to God.

Observing this example, two other rich youths sell all they have, give to the poor, and become followers of John. They would seem to have paid good attention to John's lesson. Later, however, they come to regret their actions when they see their own former servants flaunting costly clothes while they themselves have but one cloak between them. Seeing their sorrow, John asks them to fetch sticks and pebbles, which he converts before their eyes to gold wands and precious jewels (Fig. 6, top). John then sends the youths to goldsmiths and jewelers to have the treasures appraised. In a Middle English version, John "bad þam vnto goldsmithes go / And vnto Jewelers, þat knew / To luke if þai war gude & trew."[37] The two return to report that the experts claim never to have seen gold so pure nor gems so magnificent. John now tells the youths to buy back their former goods, but he warns them that, while

[35] Smashing substandard gems was a prescribed way for jewelers to regulate their craft. See Reddaway and Walker, *The Early History of the Goldsmiths' Company*, 227–28 (Ordinance C.8).

[36] For the early thirteenth-century Saint John Window of Chartres Cathedral in its entirety, see http://www.medievalart.org.uk/chartres/48_pages/Chartres_Bay4 8_key .htm (accessed July 21, 2013). The scene of gems being smashed also appears in a medieval stained-glass window at Lincoln Cathedral: http://www.therosewindow.com /pilot/Lincoln/s29-Frame.htm (accessed July 21, 2013). See also Cartlidge and Elliott, *Art and the Christian Apocrypha*, 185–86.

[37] *Altenglische Legenden*, 37 (lines 224–26).

Fig. 4. The Life of Saint John: (*top*) Craton preaches against riches and orders the jewels destroyed, a command that the youths carry out with raised hammers; (*middle*) John converts and baptizes Craton and his disciples; (*bottom*) Craton and the two youths give money to the poor obtained from the sale of jewels, the two youths become John's disciples, and others are converted. Trinity Apocalypse (Cambridge, Trinity College, MS R.16.2), fol. 28v. Courtesy of Trinity College, Cambridge.

Fig. 5. Listening to the philosopher Craton, the youths raise hammers to smash the jewels. The Saint John Window, Chartres Cathedral. © Dr. Stuart Whatling, Corpus of Medieval Narrative Art.

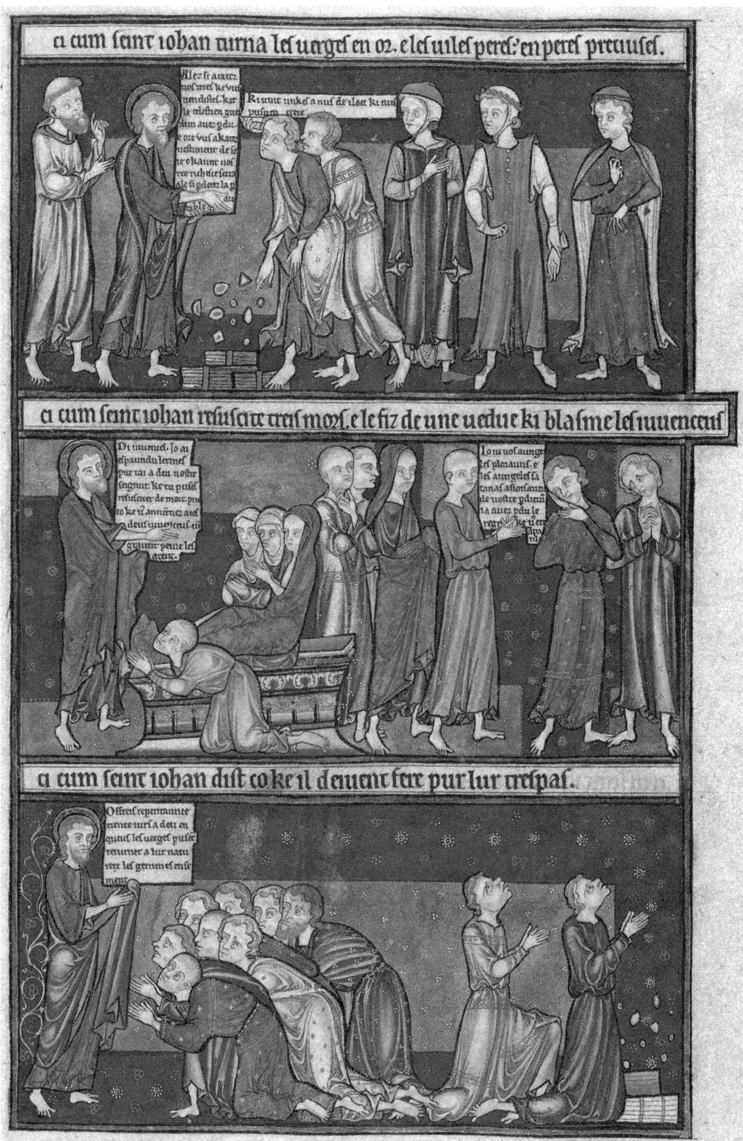

Fig. 6. The Life of Saint John: (*top*) John converts sticks and stones to gold and gems; (*middle*) John raises a dead youth, who tells of the treasures of heaven; (*bottom*) John preaches a sermon, and the youths repent. Trinity Apocalypse (Cambridge, Trinity College, MS R.16.2), fol. 29r. Courtesy of Trinity College, Cambridge.

they can be rich for a time, they shall be beggars for eternity. The Evangelist then pauses to preach a pithy sermon that gives six reasons why one should be deterred from inordinate wealth: (1) because of Scripture (story of Lazarus and Dives); (2) because of Nature (man is born naked and dies without wealth); (3) because of Creation (like the sun, moon, and air, all should be held in common); (4) because of Fortune (a rich man is slave to his money, and he shall be the devil's slave); (5) because of care and worry (one ponders how to get more and how to keep what one has); and (6) because it involves the risk of loss (creating swollen pride, it leads to damnation).

Next comes vivid testimony to show how destructive worldly wealth is, for its price is the loss of paradise. Hearing of a third young man, recently dead, John revives him and asks the youth to tell his two followers what he witnessed in death (Fig. 6, middle). The boy describes the glories of paradise and the pains of hell. He saw the men's angels weeping while their demons gloated, because they had lost, as Jacobus writes, "eternal palaces built of shining gems, filled with banquets, abounding in delights and lasting joys."[38] As in *Pearl* and the Apocalypse, heaven's spiritual wealth is expressed through a witnessing of its jewels. In one version found in the *South English Legendary*, the boy calls the men out for having made a foolish purchase:

> "Allas," he sayd, "wricches vnwise!
> Ʒe haue made *ful euil marchandise*!
> I saw yowre angels wepeand sore
> And deuils laghand ful fast þarfore.
> I saw *a palais of grete cost*
> Þat ʒe haue for ʒowre foly lost."[39]

In most versions the boy then recounts the eight pains of hell, and in the face of this harrowing reality, all three youths implore John for mercy. John tells them to do penance and pray that the newly fashioned gold and gems may revert back to their natural states. This reverse miracle occurs (Fig. 7, top), and "[t]hereupon," according to Jacobus, "the young men received the grace of all the virtues that had been theirs."[40] This miracle exchanges lapidary virtues for the virtues of souls.

[38] Jacobus, "Saint John," 52.
[39] *Altenglische Legenden*, 39 (lines 363–68; emphasis added).
[40] Jacobus, "Saint John," 53.

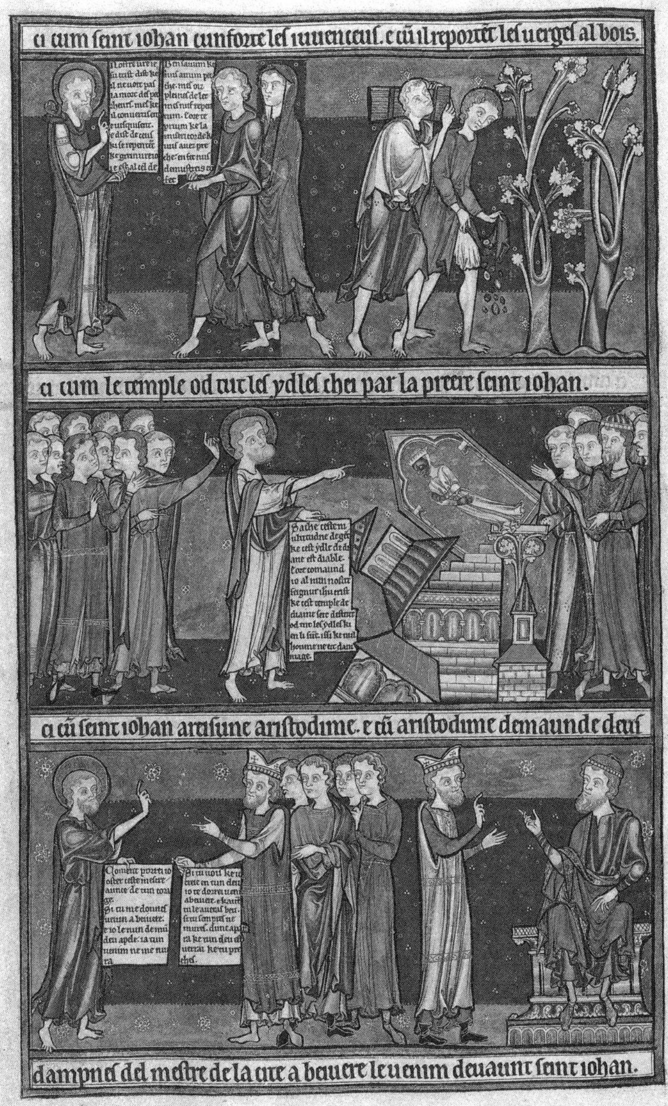

Fig. 7. The Life of Saint John: (*top*) John comforts the youths, and they return the sticks and stones to the woods; (*middle*) John destroys the temple of Diana; (*bottom*) the high priest of the temple challenges John to drink poison, and then he asks the governor of the city for two condemned criminals. Trinity Apocalypse (Cambridge, Trinity College, MS R.16.2), fol. 29v. Courtesy of Trinity College, Cambridge.

Intriguingly, it is by *undoing* a miracle that John delivers his graphic lesson: possession of wealth denotes, in truth, spiritual poverty. Thus do common sticks and stones become a reason to rejoice: forfeited gold and jewels signify that the men's souls are again secure.

The miracles of gems thus progress in meaning. In the first, real gems are smashed and then restored: *natural* riches should be shared with the poor. In the second, seemingly worthless rocks become superior gems, *better* than nature, as assessed by jewelers. The true second miracle happens, however, when the rocks revert to nature and the youths reclaim their own virtues, which will bring them to bejeweled castles of paradise. In accord with John's sermon, men possess an inner gemlike treasure bequeathed by neither Nature nor Fortune but by God, namely, their immortal souls. The levels of vision required to see through to these truths seem to be gradated, first from natural vision to miraculous vision, as when the Jeweler in *Pearl* sees the wondrous pearl upon the Maiden's breast: its quality exceeds anything he has ever before appraised, "So watz hit clene and cler and pure" (line 227). But the next stage takes one to sublime insight, as when John glimpses God's *privetee* and the *Pearl* Jeweler receives sights he cannot describe without recourse to John's language, most particularly, the breast-jewel now become the enthroned Lamb shining pure and gemlike in the midst of the Heavenly City (line 836).

Saint John's Miracles of Dust and Treasure

The Evangelist's next few miracles in his *vita* bring about conversions with variations on the lapidarian motif. By invoking Christ, John causes a heathen temple to collapse, and Diana's statue then shatters to dust (Fig. 7, middle). A false idol is now crushed stone, devoid of any virtue. Soon after, John erects stone churches. And in this section of the legend, John undergoes another physical assay, this one testing his insides, not his flesh, as did the boiling oil. John is made to drink poison, and he survives, according to one English exegete, because he is a virgin and therefore clean inside.[41] The pagan high priest first tests the drug by

[41] A variant line in a sermon by Mirk credits John's survival to his freedom from the venom of lechery: "[For as clene as he was wythout venym of lechery], so clene he was of þat poyson, aftur he hadde dronk hyt" (Mirk, *Festial*, ed. Powell, 32 [lines 35–36]). The bracketed phrase comes from Oxford, Bodleian Library, MS Gough Eccl. Top. 4, fol. 18v (*Mirk's Festial*, ed. Theodor Erbe, EETS e.s. 96 [London: Kegan Paul, Trench, Trübner, 1905], 31 [lines 32–33]). In the Northern Homily Cycle *De sancto Johanne*

poisoning two prisoners (Fig. 7, bottom). Then John has to imbibe the same substance, but it has no effect. Questioning John's power, the priest challenges the apostle to resurrect the two poisoned men. John asks the priest to spread his cloak over them. He does so, and the men revive. Those who witness this miracle convert. John's survival of two bodily assays—his outsides boiled in oil, his insides poisoned—serves to confirm his own gemlike purity.[42]

The legend now introduces one of its most intriguing episodes: the tale of a young man regarded by John as his treasure (Fig. 8). John converts a headstrong youth and places him under a bishop's care. Poorly supervised, however, the youth leaves the bishop and becomes a chief outlaw. John, now a very old man, is distraught because the bishop has lost what John calls his "deposit." Jacobus records here a verbal misunderstanding: the bishop thinks John refers to money, but John means the boy's soul. Despite his age, John mounts a horse and rides full tilt after the boy, who is ashamed and runs away (Fig. 8, middle). But John is determined and overtakes him. The apostle gains the youth's repentance and eventually ordains him as a worthy bishop. English versions gloss this tale in ways that moralize on themes of spiritual wealth. The over-complacent bishop must make account, while John mourns the boy's soul as a lost *tresour*. The lesson is about vigilantly guarding spiritual capital. Without proper guidance, the boy has turned toward material things, becoming a robber. John, however, proves to be a fiercely possessive depositor. Praying to God, John confesses that "A feble tresour ich ches and þoru is [i.e., the bishop's] feble lore / Mi deoworþe tresour ich habbe ilore."[43] John calls the young man his "son" and himself a "feeble father," delineating a parental relationship to the boy. The old man chases the youth in a scene that is well nigh comic; one English hagiographer stresses that John rode as fast as a young man. The tale is figured as a parent's need to restore a dead child, a treasure inadvertently lost. The young man is at once John's child, John's treasure, and the Church as John's legacy. The episode provides an interesting parallel to *Pearl*, especially as it is set within a

euangelista, "assay" is the verb used to describe the taking of the poison (*Altenglische Legenden*, 40 [line 454]).

[42] The poet of the alliterative Middle English hymn addresses the virgin Saint John as a "gem dere and gente" and as "jasper, þe jowell of gentill perry" (*Three Alliterative Saints' Hymns*, 10 [lines 15–16]).

[43] *The South English Legendary*, ed. D'Evelyn and Mill, 3:606–7 (lines 411–12).

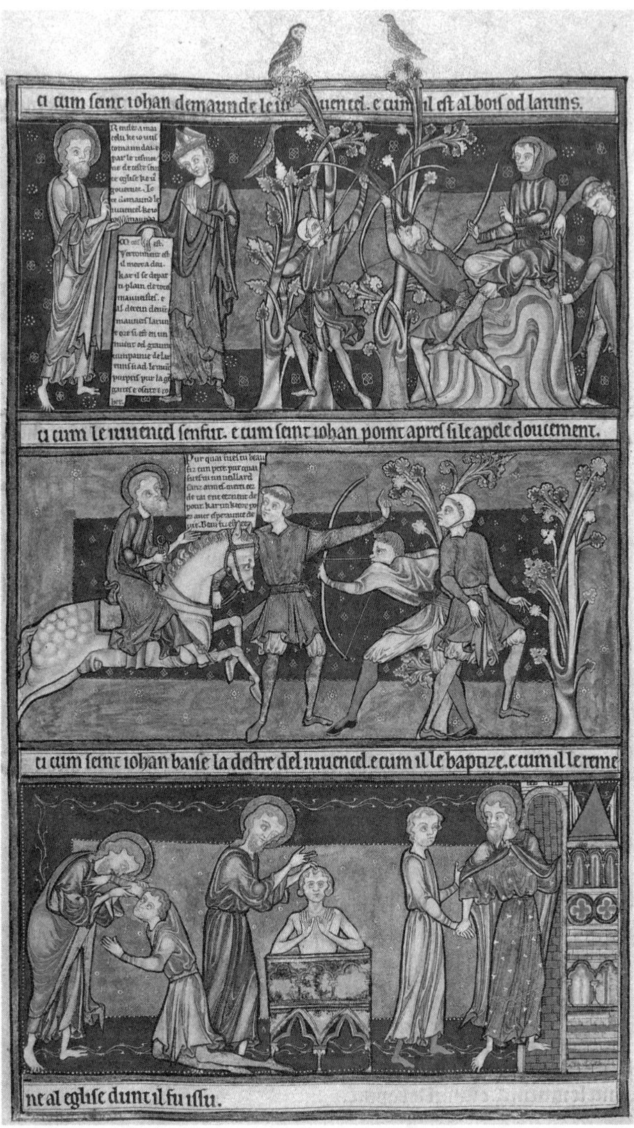

Fig. 8. The Life of Saint John: (*top*) the bishop tells John that the youth has become a robber, and the robbers in the woods; (*middle*) John rides to the woods to find the youth, and the youth runs away from him; (*bottom*) John kisses the arm of the youth, baptizes him, and leads him to church. Trinity Apocalypse (Cambridge, Trinity College, MS R.16.2), fol. 30v. Courtesy of Trinity College, Cambridge.

fertile matrix of gemological tales. The saint who abjures wealth strives desperately here to retrieve his treasure. In Jacobus's version, John declares himself, as *alter Christi*, ready to sacrifice himself to save his son: "I will gladly die for you, as Christ died for all of us. Come back, my son, come back!"[44] John is made God's treasure-seeker, a guardian and banker of souls.

John's other adventures in old age continue to develop the saint's reputation for sublime wisdom. The next one affectionately merges the saint's tolerance for human frailty with his extraordinary power of discernment. Now extremely old, the Evangelist plays with a partridge, and a little boy laughs at his foolishness. John's explanation is that humans must relax and seek solace in order to have the strength for contemplation. The human spirit is like a soaring eagle that rests on the ground after looking straight into the sun.[45] As the author of the *South English Legendary* comments, John's own symbol is the eagle, the bird that soars highest, with vision so acute it can detect the smallest worm on the ground. When John lay his head on Jesus' breast, God's *privetees* were revealed to him, and by such inspiration his Gospel is the most sublime of the four.[46] The Life then records how the aged apostle died on a Sunday as he preached from a grave dug in the church floor. When he departed to heaven, the congregants could find no body, only manna, which was like fine particles of sand, filling his grave. It did not rain down but instead seemed to spring like a well from the ground. This rich manna becomes the closing instance of stone-based particulates in John's legend: crushed gems, gravelly stones, shattered idols, and now fine manna emanating like powdery sand from the ground.

Saint John's Miracle of the Confessor's Ring

To conclude, Jacobus inserts one last miraculous adventure of Saint John: a posthumous sighting of the Divine Apostle in England, in the tale of King Edward's ring, a legend not depicted in the Apocalypses but richly illustrated in the sole manuscript of the Anglo-Norman Life of Saint Edward the Confessor (Cambridge University Library, MS

[44] Jacobus, "Saint John," 54. On John as *alter Christi* and divine, see Hamburger, *St. John the Divine*, esp. 203–4.

[45] Jacobus, "Saint John," 54; *The Early South-English Legendary*, ed. Horstmann, 412–13 (lines 337–52); and *The South English Legendary*, ed. D'Evelyn and Mill, 3:604 (lines 327–54).

[46] *The Early South-English Legendary*, ed. Horstmann, 406–7 (lines 150–66); and *The South English Legendary*, ed. D'Evelyn and Mill, 3:598–99 (lines 151–68).

Ee.III.59). Edward never refuses a favor asked on behalf of Saint John, so when a pilgrim begs alms in the saint's name, the king, lacking his pursebearer, gives the pilgrim a large jewel from his own finger (Fig. 9; fol. 26r). The pilgrim is actually Saint John in disguise, a fact discovered when English soldiers later return the jewel to Edward (fol. 27r), having received it abroad from the same pilgrim (fol. 26v) with the message "He for whose love you gave this ring sends it back to you."[47] By acting as he does, Edward gains the Kingdom of Heaven. Concomitantly, in the context of John's legend, the apostle concludes his search for a man who already knows his treasure on earth. In the illustrations of CUL, MS Ee.III.59, the exchange comes full circle with a scene of Christ receiving Edward in heaven (fol. 29r).[48] The Evangelist finds at last a man—indeed, an English monarch—who knows the lesson of true wealth without having to have it preached to him. The jewel given away in charity returns to Edward as God's grace.

The lives of Saint John and the Confessor are thus fully wedded in hagiography, their union sealed by a symbolism of ring and jewel. After the apostle's two gem-involved miracles, the ring-exchange with Edward expresses the motif for a third time. The bejeweled ring features in the iconography of portraits of King Edward the Confessor (as in the Wilton Diptych, for example). In the Middle Ages the reputed original ring was revered as a relic at Westminster.[49] And the tale of the ring-

[47] Jacobus, "Saint John," 55. The legend of Edward the Confessor's ring first appears in Aelred of Rievaulx's *Life of Saint Edward* (c. 1162–63): *Aelred of Rievaulx: The Historical Works*, ed. Marsha L. Dutton, trans. Jane Patricia Freeland (Kalamazoo: Cistercian Publications, 2005), 20–24, 125–243.

[48] The Anglo-Norman Life of Saint Edward in Cambridge University Library, MS Ee.III.59 is the only extant copy of the life having extensive illustrations. It was composed in England in the late 1230s or early 1240s, perhaps by Matthew Paris, and the manuscript was executed around 1250–60. The full codex may be viewed at the Cambridge University Digital Library: http://cudl.lib.cam.ac.uk/view/MS-EE-00003-00059 (accessed July 21, 2013). This book is stylistically linked with the thirteenth-century Apocalypses that have come to be known as the Westminster Group. See Morgan, *Illuminating the End of Time*, 14–21. It is edited and translated by Henry Richards Luard, *Lives of Edward the Confessor*, Rolls Series 3 (London: Longman, Brown, Green, Longmans, and Roberts, 1858), 1–311. For versions in Middle English, see Grace Edna Moore, *The Middle English Verse Life of Edward the Confessor* (Philadelphia: University of Pennsylvania, 1942).

[49] On Edward's ring and the role of the legend in the history of Westminster Abbey, see Arthur Penrhyn Stanley, *Historical Memorials of Westminster Abbey* (London: John Murray, 1911), 12–29. On the *Pearl*-poet and Westminster Abbey saints, see Ann Astell, *Political Allegory in Late Medieval England* (Ithaca, N.Y.: Cornell University Press, 1999), 132–36; Bowers, *The Politics of "Pearl,"* 29–30, 86–88, and *An Introduction*, 120–21; and also my discussion in note 52 below.

Fig. 9. Edward the Confessor gives his ring to the pilgrim who is Saint John in disguise. The Anglo-Norman Life of Edward the Confessor, Cambridge University Library, MS Ee.III.59, fol. 26r. Courtesy of Cambridge University Library.

exchange still flourishes as a patriotic legend by which to assert the divine authentication of successive English monarchs. Every coronation, down to Elizabeth II's, has featured placement of Saint Edward's Crown (a commemoration of the ring) on the new monarch's head.[50] Edward the Confessor's spiritual goodness and regal identity are perpetually conveyed, therefore, by means of an iconography of the jewel: his magnificent stone is both his salvation and his kingship, given him by God through an exchange with the Divine Jeweler, Saint John.

Given the degree of Saint John's authority in *Pearl*'s visionary makeup, it becomes a real possibility, one worth remarking upon here, that the poem's key framing phrase—"prynces paye" (lines 1, 1201)—is meant as an allusion to the apostle's posthumous English adventure. If Edward the Confessor's ring-exchange is to be recalled in this phrase (set as it is in a poem about jewels, Saint John's apocalyptic vision, and souls purchased for heaven), then fourteenth-century associations with Westminster Abbey, site of Edward's tomb and shrine, would seem to be inescapable. In the *Pearl*-poet's time (whether that was late in Edward's III's reign or during Richard II's),[51] the abbey itself was saturated with a standard image of Edward extending his ring to the pilgrim. The iconography exists, or formerly existed, in (1) the floor tiles of the Chapter House; (2) the paintings on the oak sedilia near the altar; (3) the bas-relief carved above the shrine; and (4) a pair of statues once placed near the shrine.[52]

[50] An ancient crown was used continuously until the crowning of Charles I. It was sold during the Commonwealth and replaced with a copy for the coronation of Charles II. In the fifteenth century, the Palmers Guild of Ludlow commemorated in stained glass the ancillary legend of their own founding by charter of the Confessor. They claimed that those who had conveyed the ring from John to Edward were Ludlow palmers. Edward in these windows bears a prominent jewel at the center of his crown. See Edwin Willliam Ganderon and Jean Lafond, *Ludlow Stained and Painted Glass* (London: Adams Bros. and Shardlow, 1961), 47–52, esp. 50.

[51] See Susanna Greer Fein, "Twelve-Line Stanza Forms in Middle English and the Date of *Pearl*," *Speculum* 72 (1997): 367–98; as well as Bowers, *The Politics of "Pearl."*

[52] For reproductions of these items, see (1) G. B. Gordon, "The Floor Tiles of Westminster Abbey Chapter House," *The Museum Journal* (University of Pennsylvania) 14, no. 4 (December 1923): 288–309 (303); (2) http://www.wmf.org/project/westminster-abbey-sedilia (accessed July 21, 2013); also described by E. W. Tristram, *English Wall Painting of the Fourteenth Century* (London: Routledge and Kegan Paul, 1955), 41, 198; (3) Stanley, *Historical Memorials*, 12; and (4) Cambridge University Library, MS Ee.III.59, fol. 30r (website supplied in note 48 above). The Edward/John iconography was also painted opposite Henry III's bed in the Palace of Westminster (Paul Binski, *The Painted Chamber at Westminster* [London: Society of Antiquities of London, 1986], 40, plates 4, 5). On its appearances elsewhere in England, see Tristram, *English Wall Painting*, 172–73 and Fig. 25.

Aside from its special status in English sacred history and national identity, this last apocryphal story in the Life of Saint John completes the profile of John as a trader in gems material and spiritual, a jeweler with a surpassing eye of discernment for true value. The tale itself, like the other stories of relinquished gems in John's *vita*, is a thinly veiled variant of the parable in Matthew: "The kingdom of heaven is like a merchant in search of fine pearls, who, on finding one pearl of great value, went and sold all that he had and bought it" (13:45–46).

The Jeweler's Pearl of Great Price

The parable is overt in the ancient Acts of John, and, as we have seen, it surfaces in the English version of the *Golden Legend* that has the revived boy testify about the greedy youths' "euil marchandise" in heaven—a term that signifies how John's miracle of sticks and stones had created material wealth but exposed their souls to damnation.[53] Earlier in that same story, John had sent those youths to goldsmiths and jewelers to have their miraculous but poorly conceived treasure appraised. This very scene was chosen for illustration in the Saint John Window of Chartres Cathedral (Fig. 10). In it, Saint John and the jeweler are parallel figures. On the left, God's Divine Jeweler works the miracle of sticks and stones; on the right, a jeweler expertly appraises the new gold and jewels. Saint and jeweler are exactly matched in how they tilt their heads, gesture with their right arms, and occupy the left-hand space of their respective stained-glass compartments. Mimicry of gesture and stance underscores the analogy. In the Chartres window, as well as in the reading I give here of the Life of Saint John, the Divine Apostle is the Divine Jeweler, a discerning knower of real worth. He does not repudiate the world so much as know its exact virtues, which exist along a continuum that extends from earth to heaven. The saint teaches others how to apprehend God's Creation by this true light.

The parable of the pearl of great price appears in *Pearl* with a twist. The biblical merchant is here called a "joueler":

> This makellez perle þat boȝt is dere,
> Þe *joueler* gef fore alle hys god,

[53] Cartlidge and Elliott, *Art and the Christian Apocrypha*, 186; and *Altenglische Legenden*, 39 (line 364).

Fig. 10. Guided by Saint John (left), the youths take the miraculous gold and gems to the jeweler (right) to be appraised. The Saint John Window, Chartres Cathedral. © Dr. Stuart Whatling, Corpus of Medieval Narrative Art.

> Is lyke þe reme of heuenesse clere—
> So sayde þe Fader of folde and flode.
> (lines 733–36; emphasis added)

The poet conflates jeweler and merchant so that the one who sells his matchless pearl will need no outside expert to know its value. He himself is the judge, like the narrating Jeweler. The Jeweler's occupational identity makes for pointed irony when, early in the poem, he finds himself the object of evaluation, the Maiden questioning in the fifth stanza-group (concatenating on "jueler") whether or not he is a "kynde" jeweler, a "gentyl" jeweler, a "joyfol" jeweler, and, finally, in the sixth, judging him to be full of flaws, "lyttel to prayse" and "much to blame." Thus the poem moves steadily toward the narrator's self-evaluation: having superior discernment of surface appearance and inner purity, the Jeweler learns to use that wisdom to see within himself, as the Maiden commands in the sixth stanza-group: "Deme now þyself" (line 313).

In response, in the seventh stanza-group, the Jeweler demurs politely that

> We meten so selden *by stok oþer ston.*
> Þaȝ cortaysly ȝe carpe con,
> I am bot *mol* and manerez mysse;
> Bot Crystes mersy and Mary and *Jon*,
> Þise arn þe *grounde* of alle my blysse.
> (lines 380–84; emphasis added)

Spoken in the first half of the poem, these words carry an air of conventional courtly humility, that is, good social manners, not serious religion. The Jeweler, trying to gain his footing as he speaks to this surprising apparition, evaluates himself by a term—"mol" (dust)—that is the antithesis of a gem dug from the ground. At the same time, he summons the perpetually latent lapidarian pun on "grounde"—both "basis, foundation" and "earthly ground"—that runs throughout *Pearl*. The Jeweler's words here also serve a subtle literary purpose: they introduce the apostle John very quietly into the poem, a good while before he becomes the potent authority for the Jeweler's sublime vision. The Jeweler's mention of Mary, John, and Christ's mercy evokes, furthermore, a brief flash of the Passion scene, where mother and apostle stood together at the foot of the cross, and where Jesus committed Mary to John's care. Just before this brief naming of John, the Jeweler's exclamation "by stok oþer ston" seems a simple, idiomatic way to say "anywhere," but if one allows that its literal sense may be heard—"stock [of wood]" and "stone"—the phrase may latently recall the apostle's well-known miracle of sticks and stones transformed to gold and jewels.[54] And still more, by further metaphorical association, packed tightly in these five lines, stock-and-stone-made-precious might be the cross on Calvary, *grounde* of the Jeweler's bliss.

Later in *Pearl*, when stanza-groups 14 through 17 reverberate with *j*-alliteration (the New Jerusalem and the apostle John), the Jeweler seems to have acquired a more mature knowledge of himself, confessing earnestly and penitentially "I am bot mokke and mul among" (line 905). His capacity to judge himself has deepened, his sharp eye now rightly gauging his own mortal substance. As elsewhere in *Pearl*, the poet's instinct for diptych structuring is exact here. Parallels signal how the poem builds upon a figural analogy between the Jeweler and Saint

[54] *MED*, s.v. *stok* (n.(1)), def. 1a. and 3a.

John.[55] As in the diptych image of the Saint John Window at Chartres, scenes of the Jeweler appraising and being appraised in the first half of the poem, and of the apostle John *devysing* in the second half, are balanced against each other. The stanzas that characterize the Jeweler come at the poem's one-quarter point (stanza-group 5; that is, stanzas 21–25); they are juxtaposed at the poem's three-quarter point by Saint John's vision of the New Jerusalem, in which the Pearl-Maiden relays John's own speech (stanza-group 15; that is, stanzas 71–75). The meaning of the Jeweler most fully unfolds when his visionary experience is revealed to be in shadow likeness to the apostle's crystalline sight. When the Jeweler finds himself incapable of expressing what he envisions, John enters as his holy double, able to *devyse* in the sublime language of Revelation.

Though merely an ordinary man beside the sanctified John, the Jeweler ought not be seen as shallowly materialist in his every response, particularly by the end of the poem. His vision is a gift; he is the privileged seer of secrets. As Beatrice did for Dante, the Maiden made prior request that the Jeweler have this sight of the heavenly Jerusalem (line 965), and, as he witnesses the final procession, the Jeweler exclaims that the experience is greater than any that a waking man could bear:

> Hade bodyly burne abiden þat bone,
> Þaȝ alle clerkez hym hade in cure
> His lyf wer loste anvnder mone.
> (lines 1090–92)

The eyes that see these sights are ghostly, not bodily. Dazzling splendor overpowers his critical faculties, "So watz [he] rauyste wyth glymme pure" (line 1088). The Jeweler, now beholding the Divine Radiance of "Godez Lombe, as trwe as ston" (line 822), experiences the apotheosis of his craft. He envisions a "hundreth þowsandez" pearly souls flocking in legions to sing praise to Christ, "þat gay Juelle" (lines 1107, 1124). He seems wholly, humbly ready to embrace the mystical sense of Jesus' parable, as was expounded by John's *devysement* in his *vita*. Like King Edward with his ring, the Jeweler is ready to relinquish his pearl to

[55] For details of *Pearl*'s symmetrical structure, see Britton J. Harwood, "*Pearl* as Diptych," in *Text and Matter: New Critical Perspectives of the "Pearl"-Poet*, ed. Robert J. Blanch, Miriam Youngerman Miller, and Julian N. Wasserman (Troy, N.Y.: Whitson, 1991), 61–78; and Meyer, *Medieval Allegory*, 167.

enter God's *ryche*. The Jeweler who judged has become the Jewel subject to judgment. In the end, he wishes to pay the Prince his virtuous treasure.

Thus do the apocryphal Life of Saint John and its popular exegesis in England and on the Continent profoundly inform the poetics of judgment and treasure in *Pearl*. The use of jewels to denote appraisable treasure—both material wealth and, by spiritual metaphor, heaven's bounty—aligns the Middle English poem with the legend's core philosophy. Illustrated Apocalypses made in late medieval England, already well recognized as inspiring the *Pearl*-poet, very often also depicted scenes of the saint working miracles of gem and more. Keen-sighted and generously humane, the Divine Apostle knew how to assess every substance and detect every virtue. He avidly sought to deposit souls where proper valuation would set them: in heaven's treasury. Gifted with blessed insight, John displayed an uncanny aptitude for attributing right worth to all of Creation, from the natural to the sublime, from pebbles to eternal souls. The portrait given to Saint John the Evangelist in his *vita* implicitly casts him as Divine Jeweler and as master-explicator of the pearl of great price. Knowing this rich hagiographical tradition, the *Pearl*-poet draws upon it to invoke the apostle as the sanctified model for the Jeweler-turned-visionary who narrates *Pearl*.

Conclusions

My conclusions here add to the consensus view of the *Pearl*-poet as a clerk or chaplain for aristocratic patrons. He hones a high poetic style in the vernacular in order to instill a biblical lesson. The parable of the pearl of great price inspires the poem's main conceit—the lost pearl—and informs how a narrator stricken by loss comes eventually to exchange worldly values for spiritual ones, that is, how he transcends an attachment to material things and learns to strive for his treasure in heaven. In exploiting all the poetic possibilities of this homiletic theme, the author certainly recognized the parable's prominent status in Saint John hagiography. Consequently, the apostle is brilliantly planted in *Pearl* not just as the Divine who beheld the Apocalypse, but also as the keen-eyed Evangelist who actively preached about true valuation, being himself the supreme appraiser of the virtues set by God in all matter. The narrator is made a Dreamer because he, like the Evangelist, will ultimately have a vision of the New Jerusalem, made expressible only by recourse to the saint's sublime words. And just as importantly, the narrator is made a Jeweler because he, like the Evangelist, knows all about gems and can judge earthly worth. In both arenas of the saint's expertise, the narrator in his frail humanity projects a shadow likeness of the holy apostle.

The poet's method for drawing the analogies is essentially diptych, with the Dreamer/Jeweler's incomprehension made evident in the poem's first half, to be superseded by the growing power of his vision (tutored by John's insights) in the second half. At the central turning-point, a wordplay on Godes *ryche*—kingdom and treasure—marks how the Dreamer/Jeweler's evaluative sensibilities inch forward from a sense-based surface materialism to a transformative sense of spiritual wonderment. While the Dreamer/Jeweler is *not* Saint John, he has by the end of the poem imbibed the saint's guiding spirit, now feeling himself to be Christ's *frende* and wanting to pay the Prince, that is, yield his pearl rather than grieve and complain. He becomes like the comprehending merchant-jeweler of the parable, or like the many confused followers of John's teaching in the legend, of whom only Edward the Confessor understood the core message immediately and instinctively. The Divine Apostle's Christian lesson on appreciating earthly wealth mainly as a means for charity, and on valuing one's soul as heavenly treasure, rests at the heart of a poem that, like the rich Apocalypses of the period, projects a luxurious aesthetic surface designed to please aristocratic sensibilities.

Lydgate's Jailbird

Corey Sparks
Indiana University

A cage went in search of a bird.

Robert Hass[1]

God loved the birds and invented trees. Man loved the birds and invented cages.

Jacques Deval[2]

IN JOHN LYDGATE'S FIFTEENTH-CENTURY BEAST FABLE, "The Churl and the Bird," a captive songbird laments her confinement, a hindrance to her will that destroys poetic joys. Arguing for her freedom, she complains to her churl(ish) captor that:

> Song & prisoun haue noon accordaunce,
> Trowistow I wole syngen in prisoun?
> Song procedith of ioie & plesaunce,
> And prisoun causith deth & destruccioun;
> Ryngyng of ffeteris makith no mery soun;
> Or how shold he be glad or iocounde,
> Ageyn his wil that lith in cheynes bounde?[3]

For their crucial comments and support, I thank Patricia Clare Ingham, Karma Lochrie, and Shannon Gayk as well as the Indiana University Early English Literature and Culture Forum. Thanks also to Sarah Stanbury and Anthony Bale for their encouragement at, respectively, the beginning and conclusion of this project. Finally, I would like to thank the two anonymous readers for *SAC* for helpful suggestions.

[1] Robert Hass, "September Notebooks: Stories," *Poetry* (February 2010), available at http://www.poetryfoundation.org/poetrymagazine/poem/238586 (accessed January 21, 2013).

[2] Jacques Deval, *Afin de vivre bel et bien* (Paris: A. Michel, 1970), 27.

[3] John Lydgate, "The Churl and the Bird," lines 99–105, in *The Minor Poems of John Lydgate*, ed. Henry Noble MacCracken, EETS 192, Vol. 2, *Secular Poems* (London: Oxford University Press, 1934), 464–85. Subsequent quotations from the poem will be cited in-text. The relative lack of critical attention to the poem from modern scholars does not reflect the contemporary popularity of Lydgate's poem. The poem exists in several manuscripts that date across the fifteenth and sixteenth centuries, and was printed six times, suggesting both immediate and relatively sustained popularity.

Studies in the Age of Chaucer 36 (2014):77–101

Having been caged by a gardening churl, who imagines refreshing music at his beck and call, the confined songbird clearly opposes imprisonment to poetic production. She argues that song can only be produced under conditions of joy and pleasure, and that prison affords no such condition. Instead, captivity constrains the otherwise happy—because naturally free—will. According to the newly minted jailbird's very logical account, a constrained will cannot produce pleasing song. If one's happiness, which is located in the pleasures of exercising one's will, is taken away, then one cannot produce "mery soun," anything pleasing to oneself or anyone else.

The songbird's willful protest against her captivity succinctly captures Lydgate's interest in how the space of the medieval prison raises questions about the unsettled (and thus unsettling) boundaries between discipline and desire, between what one may be forced to do and what one wants to do. In this essay I thus seek to deepen our understanding of the spatial imaginaries implicated in medieval prisons, explicating one late medieval poet's imagining of what a prison is and does. While engaged with a single poem, my larger argument points toward broader issues related to literary history as well as the history of prisons. Attending to Lydgate's careful thinking about the will in this poem suggests how the history of the prison and literary history are interconnected beyond literary works specifically known to have been written in prison. Literary works that take up questions about the will's capacious motivations and concomitant need for discipline speak directly to the evolving functions and contested meanings of late medieval imprisonment and captivity. Finally, because Lydgate's poem uses the birdcage as a figure for the medieval prison, this essay engages recent thinking in animal studies about the ways medieval animal figuration can give us something more than mere anthropocentrism. Lydgate, the peripatetic poet-monk of Bury St. Edmunds, a monastery closely associated with the Lancastrian dynasty, hardly pretends that "The Churl and the Bird" provides an autobiographical accounting of confinement, but he nevertheless gives us a compelling co-construction of the nature of imprisonment and poetic making in the later Middle Ages.[4]

[4]For recent work on late medieval prison literature, see Julia Boffey, "Chaucerian Prisoners: The Context of the *Kingis Quair*," in *Chaucer and Fifteenth Century Poetry*, ed. Boffey and Janet Cowen (London: King's College London, Centre for Late Antique and Medieval Studies, 1991), 84–102; Robert Epstein, "Prisoners of Reflection: The Fifteenth-Century Poetry of Exile and Imprisonment," *Exemplaria* 15, no. 1 (2003): 159–98; A. C. Spearing, "Prison, Writing, Absence: Representing the Subject in the

As my opening passage shows, Lydgate's jailbird articulates a logic of the cage in which confinement is easily imagined as posing a problem for the will of the captive. From simple stocks to elaborately sealed rooms, technologies of confinement restrict the will because they restrain the captive body. I understand the will as residing at the borders of the body: the ability to desire something and enact it in the world. Defining the will in this way stresses its status in the Middle Ages as a faculty of self that is both internal, pertaining to psychological dimensions, and external, pertaining to issues of agency. Moreover, this definition highlights the position of the will in medieval and contemporary debates about the extent to which people have the capacity to act and how they may be held responsible for their own actions. Spaces of confinement are a problem for those confined precisely because they *take away* the ability to exercise the will for one's own purposes. Careful to keep the confined body in view, historians of the medieval prison often retain an opposition between confinement and exercise of the will. Discussing imprisonment, Edward M. Peters argues, "Imprisonment of any sort and for whatever purpose is in essence the public imposition of involuntary physical confinement . . . [including] physical punishments that restrict the individual's freedom of movement."[5] No matter the form of physical restraint, agrees Jean Dunbabin, the point of captivity was that "Prisoners could not again enjoy their natural freedom of movement until they had satisfied the demands laid upon them [by their captors]."[6] The body's movement is notably labeled a "freedom" by Peters and deemed "natural" by Dunbabin. An apparently naturally occurring freedom of movement acts as the access point to the will; a lack of the capacity to move the body becomes a lack of the will's capacity. Furthermore, a prisoner himself cannot be satisfied, cannot fulfill his own desire; on Dunbabin's account, only captors and jailers can be "satisfied." Such attention to captors' possibilities for satisfaction suggests the degree to which confinement has historically been understood from the perspective of the captor, defining the work that confinement

English Poems of Charles d'Orléans," *MLQ* 53, no. 1 (1992): 83–99; and Joanna Summers, *Late-Medieval Prison Writing and the Politics of Autobiography* (Oxford: Oxford University Press, 2004).

[5] Edward M. Peters, "Prison before the Prison: The Ancient and Medieval Worlds," in *The Oxford History of the Prison: The Practice of Punishment in Western Society* (Oxford: Oxford University Press, 1995), 3–43 (3).

[6] Jean Dunbabin, *Captivity and Imprisonment in Medieval Europe, 1000–1300* (New York: Palgrave Macmillan, 2002), 1.

does in terms of the purposes, and thus the wills, of those who confine; the captor acts while the captive is acted upon.

Fierce debates over the will and the nature of agency erupted during the period of High Scholasticism and the rise of "voluntarist" philosophies in the late thirteenth and early fourteenth centuries. Voluntarism, often privileging the necessary freedom of the will, stands in contrast with the more "intellectualist" philosophy held by Thomas Aquinas.[7] John Duns Scotus, an insular Scholastic philosopher who spent time at both Oxford and Paris, questioned whether an individual can be held ethically responsible for his actions if the faculty in charge of pursuing and enacting one's desires—the will—is not free in its desiring and acting. Though Scotus is somewhat unique among voluntarist philosophers in arguing for a contextually determined, "rational" will, voluntarist accounts of the will tend to be aligned with discourses of freedom and choice.[8]

In a sort of limit case of the will's freedom both to desire and to act, Scotus argued that one's will was "naturally inclined" to love God (as

[7] Thomistic intellectualism and voluntarist accounts such as John Duns Scotus's assume a fundamental relation between intellect and will, but they disagree on the extent to which faculty drives action in the world. Other notable Scholastics connected to voluntarism, several of whom were insular like Scotus, include William de la Mare (d. 1285), Peter John Olivi (d. 1298), Henry of Ghent (d. 1293), and William of Ockham (d. 1347). It must also be pointed out that Scholasticism took pains to distinguish accounts of the human will and accounts of the divine will, and my summary here, as well as the focus of this essay, pertains to the human will. For cogent accounts of voluntarism, especially in relation to ethics, see Allan B. Wolter's introductory material in *Duns Scotus on the Will and Morality*, trans. Wolter (Washington, D.C.: Catholic University of America Press, 1986); Bonnie Kent, *Virtues of the Will: The Transformation of Ethics in the Late Thirteenth Century* (Washington, D.C.: Catholic University of America Press, 1995); and *The Cambridge History of Medieval Philosophy*, ed. Robert Pasnau, 2 vols. (Cambridge: Cambridge University Press, 2010), especially sections V and VI: "Will and Desire," and "Ethics," respectively.

[8] The divisions between intellectualist and voluntarist positions can easily be overstated, especially in accounts of voluntarist philosophy that understand Scotus as arguing for an irrational, anti-intellectual will. This overstatement of the will's freedom is the accusation regularly leveled at Thomas Williams's work on Scotus. For Williams's position see his series of articles from the late 1990s that culminates in "The Libertarian Foundations of Scotus' Moral Philosophy," *The Thomist* 62 (1998): 193–215. For criticism of Williams's position, see Mary Beth Ingham, "Letting Scotus Speak for Himself," *Medieval Philosophy and Theology* 10 (2001): 173–216. Ingham and Williams's debate has continued. I join Scholastic considerations of the will to confinement in this essay not to take a particular side in the philosophical debate; rather, I do so to show the activeness of such questions about the nature of the will in the fourteenth and fifteenth centuries.

opposed to supernaturally prompted through divine grace). It is inclined to do so both selflessly for God's attributes and more self-centeredly for the advantages such love brings.[9] Such a natural inclination, understood to be one aspect of a "dual-natured" will, would entail a preexisting directionality to the will. Given orthodox stances about divine creative power, such an inclination would itself be divinely created making one's human will ultimately subject to the will of God. Scotus was nevertheless concerned to preserve the will's free capacity both to choose God and to act ethically in the world; he would go on to argue, therefore, that even God could not violate free will.[10] For Scotus, then, the will cannot ever be "forced to will." Consequently, this fundamental freedom of the will suggests a potentially nuanced engagement with the confinements and coercions one would face in prison. Indeed, Scotus takes pains to deal with the complications imprisonment brings, arguing "no human act, properly speaking, can be coerced" even as a person's choices may be constrained by fear of "worse evils . . . such as death, imprisonment or captivity, serious mutilation, and the like."[11] The concerns about freedom and confinement that motivate such philosophical considerations of the will's capacities and boundaries are precisely what undergird late medieval literary accounts of the prison, of which Lydgate's poem is a captivating example. I suggest that the rise and persistence of voluntarism marks a historically situated investment in questions about the will, freedom, and confinement that are also at stake in Lydgate's beast fable about a jailbird's protestations, as well as more broadly in the literature of the fourteenth and fifteenth centuries.

"Jailbird" isn't a medieval coinage, but it should have been. The caged bird appears in myriad medieval Continental and insular texts and images across highly varied contexts and genres: the many texts

[9] My labels "selflessly" and "self-centeredly" suggest positive and negative connotations. However, I mean them more neutrally as they gloss Scotus's engagement with Anselm of Canterbury's concepts of *affectio iustitiae* (affection for justice) and *affectio commodi* (affection for the advantageous), which are themselves morally neutral concepts regarding the directions the will may take either in regard to self or God.

[10] One of the most forceful articulations of this stance from Scotus uses imprisonment-laden language; it goes thus: "sed voluntatem violentari includit contradictionem; igitur Deus non potest volitum a voluntate mea impedire" (But [to say] the will may be violated encloses a contradiction; therefore, God is not able to hinder the willing of my will). *Johannis Duns Scoti doctoris subtilis, ordinis minorum opera omnia*, Vol. 13, ed. Luke Wadding (Paris: Apud Ludovicum Vives, 1893), *Ord.*, II, dist. 37, q. 2.

[11] *Duns Scotus on the Will and Morality*, *Ord.*, IV, dist. 29, 151–52.

engaging Boethian imagery such as the *Roman de la rose* and Chaucer's *Manciple's Tale*;[12] a brief but crucial appearance in *The Seven Sages of Rome*; as well as marginal images found in various bestiaries and fifteenth-century books of hours.[13] The term, however, is attested to only beginning in the seventeenth century, seeming especially popular through the eighteenth century. In most of its appearances "jailbird" or "gaolbird" is associated with recidivism, long-term imprisonment, and reproach for criminal character. The post-medieval term thus signifies a "habitual criminality."[14] Across the seventeenth and eighteenth centuries, "jailbird" appears in places as diverse as Barten Holyday's *Juvenal's Saturday*; Daniel Defoe's *The True-Born Englishman: A Satyr*; a preface to the works of Milton; and newspapers such as the *General Evening Post*, the *London Evening Post*, and the *Public Advertiser*.

In one of "jailbird' "s more gruesome appearances, the *Argus* from November 20, 1798 relates the story of the bishop of Verdun, Guillaume de Harancourt. The story of that fifteenth-century bishop's fate at the hands of Louis XI opens with an adaptation of an Ovidian quote

[12] Boethius's image of the caged bird longing to be free from her cage appears in *The Consolation of Philosophy* at Book III, metrum 2; the imagery at least partly motivates Lydgate's poem. The Boethian image as it appeared in the *Roman de la rose* became a common site for visual depiction; a beautiful illustration of "a bird in a cage plots freedom" exists in the *Roman de la rose* manuscript, Oxford, Bodleian Library, MS Douce 332, fol. 131v. The image shows a caged bird longingly looking on several birds sitting together in trees nearby.

[13] For further studies of the ubiquity of bird imagery in the Middle Ages, see William Bundson Yapp, *Birds in Medieval Manuscripts* (London: Schocken Books, 1982); Wendy Pfeffer, *The Change of Philomel: The Nightingale in Medieval Literature* (New York: Peter Lang, 1985); W. B. Clark and M. T. McMunn, *Beasts and Birds of the Middle Ages: The Bestiary and Its Legacy* (Philadelphia: University of Pennsylvania Press, 1989); W. A. Davenport, "Bird Poems from *Parliament of Fowls* to *Philip Sparrow*," in Boffey and Cowen, *Chaucer and Fifteenth Century Poetry*, 66–83. French bestiaries from the later Middle Ages regularly have images of caged birds, especially blackbirds; see *Bestiaire d'amours* (Paris, Bibliothèque nationale de France [BNF], Fr. 1951, fol. 9), or *Bestiaire d'amours* (BNF, Fr. 12469, fol. 7), both from the thirteenth to fourteenth centuries, or the slightly later *Bestiaire d'amours* (BNF, Fr. 1444, fol. 259v), from the second half of the fourteenth century. For books of hours see, for instance, those owned by Catherine of Cleves (New York, Pierpont Morgan Library, M.917, fol. 247 [c. 1440]), available at http://www.themorgan.org/collections/works/cleves/manuscript.asp. Also see the Hours of Marguerite d'Orléans (BNF, Latin 1156 B, fol. 15), available at visualiseur.bnf.fr/ConsulterElementNum?O=IFN-7911707&E=JPEG&Deb=1&Fin=1&Param=C (accessed June 6, 2014).

[14] *OED*, s.v. *jail-bird* | *gaol-bird*, n., available at http://www.oed.com/view/Entry/100653. Moreover, the word "jail," or "gaol," while coming to refer to a space of imprisonment during the Middle Ages, originally referred to a birdcage; *OED*, s.v. *jail* | *gaol*, n., http://www.oed.com/view/Entry/100650.

about deserved fates—"[N]ec lex e[s]t justior ulla, Quam necis artifices arte perire sua."[15] The *Argus*'s parable-like tale about jailbirds and their cages continues thus, in its entirety:

> So it fared with PERILLUS, who, by the command of a TYRANT, in this respect—JUST made the first horrid experiment of his BRAZEN BULL; and so it fared with WILLIAM HARANCOURT, Bishop of VERDUN, the inventor of Iron Cages. The prelate paid dearly for his cruel ingenuity; for he was CAGED for fourteen years a miserable JAIL-BIRD in the Castle of Angers.[16]

The passage quickly does two things. It succinctly links a fifteenth-century French historical event with a classical tale.[17] The tale, from Ovid's *Ars amatoria*, relates the fate of Perillus, a Sicilian sculptor and inventor. Combining those talents, he constructed a hollow bronze bull in which prisoners of the tyrant Phalaris would be placed along with water. A fire would be lit beneath the bull, boiling the prisoners alive. Vents through the bull's nose and mouth would transform the boiling

[15] "Nor is there any law more just than that the artificers of death perish by their own art." The line appears in the story of Perillus and Phalaris in Ovid's *Ars amatoria*, I.647–58. Ovid returns to the story multiple times in his corpus: *Tristia*, 3.11.39–52, 5.1.51–54; *Epistulae ex Ponto*, 2.9.43–44, 3.6.41–42; and *Ibis*, 435–38.

[16] "Iron Cages," *Argus* 211 (November 20, 1789), available at *17th–18th Century Burney Collection Newspapers* (accessed April 5, 2012).

[17] Harancourt was accused of plotting against Louis XI during the tumult of French succession politics at the close of the fifteenth century. Along with Count Jean Balue, Harancourt was imprisoned for siding with and aiding Louis's cousin Charles the Bold, a charge for which he would spend (depending on the account) the next fourteen years caged. The story of Harancourt and his iron cage, like Ovid's famous tale, was a long-lasting and popular set piece. The bishop and his cage even earn an appearance in Victor Hugo's *The Hunchback of Notre Dame*. A longer account of iron cages appears a century later in the US. In 1889, the *New York Times* printed a condemnation of iron cages that relates Harancourt's fate in a bit more detail. Simply titled "The Iron Cage," the piece was written by someone claiming to have had "an eight month's taste of this kind of captivity," and it claims that Harancourt was put into the very first cage that he had constructed. "The Iron Cage," *New York Times*, September 15, 1889: 12. In a fascinating coincidence whereby song and prison are juxtaposed in the space of the page, the *Times* story about Harancourt's iron cage appears immediately after one about vocal training. Harancourt and his iron cage similarly provided an evocative example for nineteenth-century French historiography and publication of state archives. For instance, in *La Bastille: Histoire et description de bâtiments* (Paris: Imprimerie nationale, 1893), 106–14, Fernand Bournon connects Harancourt's caging with Louis XI's moves to consolidate and centralize royal power, especially in the king's development of the Bastille as a state prison (in contrast to the *Argus*'s placement of Harancourt at the Château d'Angers). A contemporary review of Bournon's text that spends some time discussing Harancourt soon appeared across the Channel: Rowland Edmund Prothero, *The Quarterly Review*, 186, no. 372 (1897): 357–93.

person's screams into bovine groans: the grisly, inhumane torture's product being a "reduction" of human powers of communication to incoherent animal noise.[18] The *Argus* then uses this link between late medieval event and horrific classical tale to evoke (rather than explicate) the nature of criminality within a vision of fated justice, an evocation captivated by bodily destruction even as it ostensibly critiques the willful invention of cruel implements of punishment and captivity.

"Habitual criminality" in the *Argus* anecdote is less about multiple acts accumulating into an individual's character since the anecdote relates nothing of repeated acts. Instead, it constructs criminality as fated. Perillus's single act of cruel invention seals his fate in the Ovidian story, and Harancourt is similarly destined to be a "miserable Jail-Bird" by inventing iron cages. In Harancourt's case, the passive construction "was CAGED" effaces any outside agent doing the caging, keeping the brief narrative's focus solely on the bishop's destiny. If "habitual" hints at some internal compulsion, the link of cage and jailbird in the *Argus* piece instead reorients caging as being externally enforced. The repeated "so it fared" moreover marks the ends of Perillus and Harancourt not merely as particularly deserved but as destined from the outset. In spectacularly succinct and circular reasoning, the *Argus* presents the jailbird as inescapably caged: a cage is where a jailbird goes, and caging confirms the jailed individual's identity as always already having been a "Jail-Bird." Instead of the cage searching out the bird, as Robert Hass says in the first of this essay's epigrams, the eighteenth-century jailbird inexorably searches out its cage.

The *Argus*'s post-medieval association between imprisonment and the production of criminal identity is familiar. It is the established account of penal development given by Michel Foucault in *Discipline and Punish*.[19] Key to Foucault's archeology of modern penal practice is his assertion that the prison produces criminals. For Foucault, hidden but thoroughgoing surveillance founds a system of discipline and correction worked out on guilty bodies and meant to render them docile subjects of state power. This essay suggests, though, that before modern penal praxis could be debated, legislated, and administered in the ways Foucault insightfully discusses, the premodern prison had to be imagined as

[18] On the language-destroying nature of torture, see Elaine Scarry, *The Body in Pain: The Making and Unmaking of the World* (Oxford: Oxford University Press, 1985).

[19] Michel Foucault, *Discipline and Punish: The Birth of the Prison*, trans. Alan Sheridan, 2nd ed. (New York: Vintage, 1995).

a space capable of producing effects on particular sorts of selves who could act and be acted upon in understandable and accountable ways. The medieval assemblage of confinement and the will at work with Lydgate's jailbird contributed to this broader production of subjects. Medieval historians of the prison have critiqued Foucault's work for essentially relegating the modern prison's predecessors, in the words of Guy Geltner, to "a hazy prehistory."[20] Modern penal theory and practice could paradoxically connect procedures and practices of punishment with those of correction, for instance, only because medieval spaces of confinement were themselves imagined, through poetic figures like the birdcage, to be tightly linked to issues of desire, agency, and the will. Lydgate's jailbird speaks to a late medieval working-through of how the prison collocates disciplinary coercion with self-discipline. The prison seen through the bars of the medieval birdcage is where the will's nature and correct ordering are compellingly at stake.

The nexus of bird, cage, and prison in Lydgate's "The Churl and the Bird," while similar in some respects to the *Argus* tale's investment in the birdcage's spatial and subjective exemplarity, provides different resonances for that space of confinement. For Lydgate, the cage raises questions about the nature of the will, but the caged bird's willfulness is soundly outside the realm of criminality fated for spectacular, cruel punishment. Lydgate gives us verbal jousting and poetic repartee instead of inchoate, tortured groans. The churl threatens to eat the bird when she refuses to sing, focusing his now punitive attentions on the bird's bodiliness,

> Or to the kechen I shal thi body bryng,
> Pulle thi ffetherys that be so brihte and cleere,
> And aftir roste, or bake to my dyneer
> (145–47)

The threat links the bird's caged body to the churl's agency and desire: "*I* shal . . . bryng" and "*my* dyneer." It is the churl who can enact his will on the body of the bird. The threat nevertheless falters in the face of the clever bird's rejoinders. The bird's answer inverts the will–body

[20] Guy Geltner, *The Medieval Prison: A Social History* (Princeton: Princeton University Press, 2008), 10. For similar critiques, see Dunbabin, *Captivity and Imprisonment*, esp. 157; and Trevor Dean, *Crime in Medieval Europe* (New York: Longman, 2001), esp. 118–221.

link used by the churl, underplaying the body while foregrounding the bird's own ability to enact her birdish will. She says, "Thou shalt of me haue a ful small repast" (152), suggesting punitive attention to her diminutive body will bring little satisfaction. She then gives a promise of reward for release, putting emphasis on her ability to provide more compelling compensation: "I shal the yeve a notable gret gwerdoun / Thre grete wysdames" (158–59). With this promise of reward, the songbird is not giving herself over to the churl's coercions. Rather, she subtly points out that she may be caged, but it is the churl who is lacking. The churl seeks the satisfactions of beautiful birdsong and, furthermore, thinks he may coerce it from the bird, but she reroutes her captor's threats through her own will—"thou wilt werkyn bi my counsail" (153). The quarrel between captor and captive suggests Lydgate is after a kind of Scotistic test case for the will: the ways caging provokes and engages the will instead of wiping it out. Instead of destroying body and emptying will in a display of spectacular human cruelty, Lydgate's birdcage is a space in which the will is at work.

Birds have long been associated with freedom, natural beauty, and the making of poetry.[21] In this essay, I would like to draw a bead on such associations, especially as they locate what Marianne DeKoven sees as a crucial space for animal studies' still-developing work on premodern animal figuration. "Analyzing the uses of animal representation," DeKoven argues, "can clarify modes of human subjugation that ideology might otherwise obscure."[22] Sarah Stanbury similarly argues for the productivity of turning to animal figures for thinking about human issues:

[21] The persistence and prominence of such associations are superbly reflected in the fact that US poet laureate Billy Collins recently edited an anthology of bird-centric poems: *Bright Wings: An Illustrated Anthology of Poems about Birds* (New York: Columbia University Press, 2009).

[22] Marianne DeKoven, "Why Animals Now?," *PMLA* 124, no. 2 (2009): 361–69 (363). The "now" of DeKoven's title suggests the newness of literary criticism's engagement with animal studies, a newness that perhaps too easily occludes the vibrant, varied, and long-standing discussions among medievalists about animals. See the recent colloquium on "Animalia," *SAC* 34 (2012): 309–58; Susan Crane, *Animal Encounters: Contacts and Concepts in Medieval Britain* (Philadelphia: University of Pennsylvania Press, 2012); *Rethinking Chaucerian Beasts*, ed. Carolynn Van Dyke (New York: Palgrave Macmillan, 2012); Karl Steel, *How to Make a Human: Animals and Violence in the Middle Ages* (Columbus: Ohio State University Press, 2011); the "Animal Turn" special issue of *postmedieval: A Journal of Medieval Cultural Studies* 2, no. 1 (2011); David Salter, *Holy and Noble Beasts: Encounters with Animals in Medieval Literature* (Cambridge: D. S. Brewer, 2001); Joyce E. Salisbury, *The Beast Within: Animals in the Middle Ages* (New York: Routledge, 1994); Beryl Rowland, *Blind Beasts: Chaucer's Animal World* (Kent, Ohio: Kent State University Press, 1971).

"Learning to read not just animal metaphor but *through* animal metaphor is thus poised, in the new animal turn, to rewrite the history of the human subject as constituted by a system of imagined affiliations with non-human life, and to rewrite as well a history of animal/human relations."[23] In its estranging otherness, the non-human animal and its figurations pinpoint social, subjective, or representational dynamics we might otherwise take for granted. Medievalists' recent work in animal studies demonstrates that attention to animal figuration need not uncritically reify anthropocentrism. For example, Susan Crane, in attending to the multifaceted encounters between cat and scholar or horse and knight, plumbs the crucial role animal figuration plays in "creaturely relations." The medieval animal–human relationship for Crane is fundamentally tied—though not reducible—"to the relationship of text and living practice."[24]

By juxtaposing songbird and prison, Lydgate rattles the bars of "the empire of the sign," wherein "animals [habitually] refer to values, norms, and morals."[25] The poem is explicitly moralistic, and yet it puts intense pressure on imagining both human and non-human animal agency. In Rosi Braidotti's terms, the animal acts "as a body that can *do* a great deal, as a field of forces, a quantity of speed and intensity, and a cluster of *capabilities*."[26] The medieval jailbird's figuration becomes a site for reconsidering the non-human animal as a body that does things, that by its nature can do things either analogous to humans (like sing) or impossible for them (like fly).

Although this essay tells a story about a human institution, it can only be told by considering birdish willfulness. The link of prison and willful songbird in "The Churl and the Bird" is not an anthropomorphic reduction of the human to the animal; rather, Lydgate imagines the late medieval prison through the caged songbird in order not only to get at thorny questions about the nature of the human will but also to question the seeming naturalness of the category of human creative agency. The modern prison seems normal, its existence unremarkable even if particular policies and penal practices are regular fodder for debate.

[23] Sarah Stanbury, "Posthumanist Theory and the Premodern Animal Sign," *postmedieval: A Journal of Medieval Cultural Studies* 2, no. 1 (2011): 101–14 (103). Emphasis added.

[24] Crane, *Animal Encounters*, 3.

[25] Rosi Braidotti, "Animals, Anomalies, and Inorganic Others," *PMLA* 124, no. 2 (2009): 526–32 (528).

[26] Ibid. Emphasis added.

Prison has seemed normal for a long time though its forms in the later Middle Ages were in flux.[27] What makes the modern prison seem normal, though, is an assemblage of associations, practices, and spaces that has a long history, a history reaching back into the Middle Ages. Furthermore, *analyzing* the prison now has an established place in scholarship and public discourse. The analysis of this space, especially as a marker of power relations and subjection, has thus also become normal. The history of the prison, we think, has been told. I'd like to suggest that it has not, and that, furthermore, the place to start in really telling it is a poem about a bird that does not want to be caged.

Scholars have noted a particular human and avian contiguity emphasizing the beauty and communicative power of birdish vocalizations. Susan Crane, for instance, focuses on the "preoccupations" medieval romance has with animal "contiguities . . . beyond mere physicality," namely the proximities of birdsong and human speech.[28] Even more importantly, I would add, in extension of Crane's thinking about animal desire in *The Squire's Tale*, such contiguities are constituted by the imbrications of free, beautiful birdly "kynde" within human accountings of pains and desires. In other words, while birdishness is imagined to be marked by freedom and beauty, especially in terms of birdsong and flight, birds' nature is often poetically figured in conjunction with the pains and pleasures of desire.[29]

The proximities of birdsong and human speech were discussed beyond poetry as well, especially in terms of attempts to differentiate the roles of reason and natural inclination in the production of pleasing sound. The later Middle Ages provide "the first unequivocal written

[27] Regarding modern distinctions among custodial, punitive, and coercive imprisonment, Ralph Pugh mentions in passing that "the three types tend to merge and in the middle ages [*sic*] were never clearly kept apart," in *Imprisonment in Medieval England* (Cambridge: Cambridge University Press, 1968), 1 n. 4; on the problems of applying modern taxonomies of imprisonment on the Middle Ages, see also Richard W. Ireland, "Theory and Practice within the Medieval English Prison," *The American Journal of Legal History* 31, no. 1 (1987): 56–67. Pugh's desultory comment often serves as an opening argumentative gambit for medievalists; for example, see Ireland, "Theory and Practice," 56; Dunbabin, *Captivity and Imprisonment*, 8; and Geltner, *The Medieval Prison*, 9.

[28] Susan Crane, "For the Birds," *SAC* 31 (2009): 23–41 (25–26).

[29] For a brief example, think of the status of the nightingale in Marie de France's *Laüstic*. The bird's song initially both marks and covers for illicit love between two neighbors. Then, the bird's body emblematizes the jealous husband's violent assertion of his own position. Last, once the murdered bird's body has been ensconced in a gold, bejeweled coffer, it becomes—like the lay itself—a beautiful artifact, a venerated and not-unproblematic relic of a now-passed tryst.

traces of birdsong being drawn into the sonic frame of reference of human musical practice," notes Elizabeth Eva Leach.[30] Although there are numerous and significant medieval poetic and philosophical considerations of human music in connection to birdsong, Leach argues, medieval music theory ultimately denied birdsong the status of music since birds lacked the powers of reason required to produce "music" as such. Medieval "singers [might] voice the songs of birds," but such sonic reproduction did not allow birds the status of reasoned music makers.[31] Birdish melodic production was instead understood, by Augustine for a prime example, to emerge from natural inclination. The collocation of bird and cage to which this essay attends rubs up against the divisions among abstract rationalism, embodiment, and natural inclination espoused by certain medieval musical ideologies; such ideologies "sought to contain the visceral force of music . . . while relying upon the sonority of the very flesh [they] explicitly denigrated."[32] Conversely, Lydgate's poem presents musical or poetic production as highly embodied, an animal embodiment inextricable from the activity of the will.

The evocative efficacy of birdsong, animal behaviorists have come to find, is not merely a literary trope but a natural phenomenon. That efficacy is, moreover, precisely located within the operations of birdish forms of desire. Recent work by animal behaviorist Meredith West demonstrates the power birdsong has to communicate, especially in terms of teaching information to newer generations.[33] West, along with others

[30] Elizabeth Eva Leach, *Sung Birds: Music, Nature, and Poetry in the Later Middle Ages* (Ithaca, N.Y.: Cornell University Press, 2007), 3.

[31] Ibid., 7.

[32] Bruce Holsinger, *Music, Body, and Desire in Medieval Culture: Hildegard of Bingen to Chaucer* (Stanford: Stanford University Press, 2001), 9.

[33] Such bird behavior in the wild is veritably impossible to document or recreate accurately. West describes attempts to refashion the birdcage in the crucial conjunction of space, natural environments, and balancing human and animal needs: "Our aim at the Animal Behavior Farm [is] to create circumstances allowing us to see animals at their best—to create contexts as conducive as possible to revealing hidden or non obvious capacities. To achieve this goal, we leave the typical laboratory cage behind and fashion semi-naturalistic environments, environments balancing our need to see an animal with the animal's need for space and security. Such settings reveal behaviors hard to see in the wild." "Animal Behavior Farm," available at http://www.indiana.edu/~aviary/ (accessed June 20, 2013). For behavioral scientists like West, the carefully constructed birdcage becomes a space necessary for the work of identifying and analyzing birdish desire. The cage used by the Animal Behavior Farm differs from that imagined in "The Churl and the Bird" in both construction and purpose. Nevertheless, I think we might usefully see the difference as one in degree rather than kind. (I would not want to push any connection too far, though, and there is not space in this essay to consider more fully the implications of the point.) The jailbird's gilded cage is an obvi-

like Todd M. Freeberg, has demonstrated that cowbirds learn and prefer "local" courtship songs that are passed down at least two generations by both males and females.[34] Given such findings, it is not an anthropomorphic step too far to argue that cowbirds' communicative powers are driven by the spatial and generational vagaries of desire.

In "The Churl and the Bird," however, the caged songbird *refuses* to sing, willfully demanding of her captor: "Trowistow I wole syngen in prisoun?" A space of constraint and coercion, prison is no place for song. The songbird strenuously opposes captivity to a sort of natural and unproblematic freedom. She lays it out clearly for her captor, reiterating that, "To syng in prisoun thou shalt me neuer constreyn" (135). Instead, she will only sing, "Tyl I have fredam in woodis vp and doun, / To flee at large" (136–37). Flight is freedom, and the natural habitat for that freedom of movement and song is the woods. While arguing for her release, Lydgate's songbird expounds the ways being caged goes against her nature, a nature specifically located outside the bounds of human artifaction:

> To be shet vp & pynned undir drede
> Nothyng accordith vn-to my nature;
> Thouh I were fed with mylk & wastelbred,
> And swete cruddis brouht to my pasture,
> Yit hadde I leuer do my besy cure
> Erly on morwe to shrape[n] in the vale.
> (120–25)

The captured songbird clearly desires her freedom over even potentially mitigating cultural products. Here, those products are delicious, cultured foods: "mylk," "wastelbred," and even "swete cruddis." These foods are not mere sustenance; they are gourmet dishes reserved for the upper classes. Wastelbread, for instance, was a cake made from the most finely ground flour, and being the most expensive bread, it was usually reserved for the upper classes; sweetened curds, along with sweetened

ously inappropriate habitat meant to render the songbird available to the churl's desire for song. It is, though, a carefully crafted space, and one meant to elicit the bird's "natural" inclination to song.

[34] See Andrew P. King, Meredith J. West, and David J. White, "Female Cowbird Song Perception: Evidence for Plasticity of Preference," *Ethology* 109 (2003): 865–77; also Todd M. Freeberg, "The Cultural Transmission of Courtship Patterns in Cowbirds, *Molothrus ater*," *Animal Behaviour* 56 (1998): 1063–73.

milk, were thought to be a soothing end-of-meal treat, something that aided digestion. The songbird understandably rejects the promise of cultured, expensive food because such dishes are obviously inappropriate fodder for her. Moreover, she rejects her caging even if her cage were a beautiful artifact, gold-forged and jewel-studded: "my cage forged were of gold, / And the pynaclis of berel & cristall" (92–93). The bird cleverly reinforces her nature's opposition to caging in the closing description of the landscape, which emphasizes light and openness in the use of "morwe" and "vale." She thus understands her desire for freedom not only as a momentary fancy, but as bound up with her very existence—an existence meant for the natural world, not the world of human culture, no matter how beautiful or tantalizing that world may seem from her human captor's perspective.

The depth and range of the bird's articulation of her desire for freedom are focused in her use of "leuer" as a term connected to issues of the will. "Leuer" could have a range of meanings: from "preference" or "I would rather"; to "desire," "dear," or "glad"; and even "beloved" in its associations with "leof." Given that she bookends "leuer" with a statement about "my nature" and the description of the natural world, the bird presents her desire as being less about a superficially willful preference and more a deep-seated inclination. Indeed, her argument here reiterates the passage with which I opened where she explicitly uses the word "wil," linking it to gladness and opposing it to lying in chains.

So powerful is the association between the birdcage and getting free that an obscure prison space in Oxfordshire called the "Bird Cage" only appears in the historical record when prisoners escape from it. In the small town of Thame was an inn called the Bird Cage, which was used regularly as a prison by the bishop of Lincoln.[35] The space was used as a prison for at least 200 years, and between the thirteenth and fifteenth centuries several escapes and a prison break were recorded: "In 1247 two cases of escape and flight to Tetsworth and Thame churches were reported. In 1268 a band of armed men broke open the prison and released a man. The prison is last recorded in 1453 when John Benett, bailiff of the liberty, let a man escape who had fled to Thame from Southwark."[36] Mary Lobel's account of the various escapes and prison

[35] Pugh, *Imprisonment in Medieval England*, 359.

[36] Mary Lobel, ed., "Thame Hundred," in *A History of the County of Oxford*, Vol. 7, *Dorchester and Thame Hundreds* (1962): 113–16, available at *British History Online*, http://www.british-history.ac.uk/report.aspx?compid=63772 (accessed January 24, 2012). That the bishop should hold a prison in the town would not be surprising, especially

breaks from the Bird Cage fascinatingly reinscribes the very language of the birdcage and birds. Prisoners do not just escape from the Bird Cage, they take flight. Lobel's language of "escape and flight" picks up on the use of "fugit" in the rolls of the justices-itinerant to describe the thirteenth-century escapees' movement from this "prisona de tame," which is also labeled "hospitatis."[37] Moreover, men don't just take flight from the Bird Cage, they fly *to* it. The man whom the bailiff John Benett released in 1453, notes Lobel, "had fled to Thame."[38] Seeking to escape Southwark, the unnamed man flees to Thame, where he must subsequently be released.

The mere presence of this space surprises, both for having existed under such a label and for having been completely ignored since Pugh's and Lobel's brief mentions in the 1960s. Indeed, Lobel remarks that the still-extant space is "among the oldest buildings" and "is one of the best preserved and most interesting" in the area.[39] The lack of attention to the Bird Cage Inn and consequent failure to consider such a space in connection with the highly visible and persistent presence of caged birds in late medieval representations of captivity suggest a lacuna in prison history as well as a suggestive route of examination for animal studies. Thinking through animal figuration—here the caged bird—productively calls attention to the complex imaginative, subjective, and literary resonances specific places of confinement could have in the later Middle Ages. This evocatively named Oxfordshire space provides material verification of the imagined linking of confinement with birdcages. Moreover, the space's presence within the historiographical record is evocatively constituted by escapes. If there is any animal figure that gives us the exact opposite of confinement, that signifies unfettered freedom, that figures Scotus's fundamentally uncoercible will, it is the bird. A bird's ability to fly, its ability to move through space in ways that we cannot, looks like a freedom about which we humans can only fantasize.

given that bishops of Lincoln regularly stayed in Thame (Lobel, *A History*, Vol. 7, 160–78).

[37] The relevant thirteenth-century records are London, The National Archives, *JUST* 1/700 and 1/703. More work remains to be done studying the language used in recording these small-scale spaces of confinement. Special thanks to Kerilyn Harkaway-Krieger, Cynthia Rogers, and Erin Sweany for help with paleography and translation.

[38] Etymologically, "to fly" and "to flee" are not related. However, the various forms are often confused. They were confused even in the Old English forms, suggesting that while the two verbs are not technically related, they have been and continue to be imagined as bound to each other; *OED*, s.v. *flee*, v., http://www.oed.com/view/Entry/71387.

[39] "Thame: Topography, Manors and Estates," in Lobel, *A History*, Vol. 7, 160–78.

If the jailbird so badly wants out of the cage, this prompts the question: Whence and whither does she want to fly? In "The Churl and the Bird," the caged songbird argues that she wants to get back to doing her "besy cure," in the "vale" in the "Erly morwe." Her introduction earlier in the poem paints an ostensibly bucolic setting in which she is free to sing. Perched in a laurel tree, the songbird is divinely beautiful with "sonnyssh fetheris brihter than gold" (59); she sings "toward evyn & in the daw[e]nyng" (62) and her birdsong "makith heuy hertis liht" (60). In this beautiful setting the bird regularly, naturally in harmony with the progression of the cosmos, produces pleasing songs. The songs have positive effects, working a musical magic of relief on hearers.

These easing songs, this beautiful setting, however, are immediately complicated as Lydgate aligns them with pain and compulsion. First, the songs come from the bird's pains: "She did hir peyn most amorously to syng" (63). I take this line to be saying more than "she sang beautifully about her pain." That is, the pain is not only a past pain which constitutes the current content of the bird's song. Rather, the singing itself is painful. She "takes pains" to sing beautifully. The bird's naturally occurring, beautiful, transportive songs both come from a place of pain and reproduce pain in their very making. This production of birdsong is "musical sonority as a practice of the flesh,"[40] painful as it is beautiful. For another poetic example of an embodied relationship between birdsong and pain, we might think here of the falcon in Chaucer's *Squire's Tale*. Chaucer's falcon movingly sings of the painful vicissitudes of being the unwilling recipient of a lover's cruel treatment, famously lamenting men's desire for "newfangleness." As she sings, the falcon "with hir beek hirselven so she prighte" so that she runs red with blood.[41] Her mid-song breast-tearing somatizes her anger not just over having been abandoned but at having given over her will to another—"that my wyl was his willes instrument; / This is to seyn, my wyl obeyed his wyl."[42]

Lydgate understands his bird's painful singing to be similarly wrapped up in constraints on the will. Instead of being driven by treach-

[40] Holsinger, *Music, Body, and Desire*, 2.

[41] *CT*, V.417, in *The Riverside Chaucer*, gen. ed. Larry D. Benson, 3rd ed. (Boston: Houghton Mifflin, 1987). Patricia Clare Ingham argues for the ways Chaucer's lamenting falcon figures the captivating and fraught connections among desire, romance, and medieval discussions of newness; see "Little Nothings: The Squire's Tale and the Ambition of Gadgets," *SAC* 31 (2009): 53–80.

[42] *CT*, V.568–69.

erous love, the bird in "The Churl and the Bird" sings according to the "natural" diurnal cycle of song: "Esperus afforcid hir corage" (64). Because she is "afforcid" to sing, the bird cannot do otherwise. The dawn is no mere prompt to poetize; she has no other choice but to sing every morning and evening. She is forced to sing because of an internal compulsion inherent to her very nature. The bird cannot help herself but sing, producing beautiful songs about her pain.

This internal compulsion is thus productive even as it operates as a constraint—the other meaning of "afforcid." If the bird is forced to sing, if nature *by nature* compels the will, then the production of pleasing song does not come from an exercise of a will that is somehow absolutely free of any constraint; rather, it emerges out of a will constrained (or confined) by compulsion. The songbird's seeming ensnarement in this natural space, a space shot through with compulsion, recalls "jailbird"'s associations with habitual imprisonment; while not physically trapped, the songbird seems unable to stop returning. This contrasts the bird's argument elsewhere that song depends on the exercise of an unconstrained will. Outside the cage the songbird is subject to wild oscillations between internal compulsion and the external imposition of repetition. She is compelled to produce beautiful song out in the natural world outside the cage twice a day; that compulsion to repeat which produces beautiful song cannot seemingly escape the pains of which the bird sings.

"Peyn," with its attendant complications of will and compulsion, reappears toward the poem's conclusion. After successfully arguing her release, the bird chastises the churl, first for foolishly letting her go and then for lamenting the loss of what was never really his in the first place. She chides,

> For who takith sorwe for losse in that degre,
> Rekne first his losse, & aftir rekne his peyne,
> Off oo sorwe, he makith sorwis tweyne.
> (215–17)

Here pain is something "reckoned"—something accounted for, that one can give an account of. Loss, pain, and sorrow are separated, each accountable in some way—able to be "counted" and also "doubled." But the increasing of any one of them depends on *giving an account*; that is, what doubles one's "sorwe" moves between the internal exercise of remembering and the external willing (and perhaps willful) constructing of a narrative of one's pain. Suggesting the compulsively crowed bon mot "Kepe wel thy tonge" of Chaucer's Manciple, the songbird implies a (non-therapeutic) injunction not to speak of it—to keep pain unreckoned, unaccounted for. To tell a story about one's pain, to reveal one's inner secrets, is to threaten, contra the Manciple, not externally imposed punishment but an unwilled internal (re)production of pain.

On this account of the production and reproduction of pain, we nevertheless also seem to find that one can choose one's response to loss. To reckon one's loss is to exercise the will. When one "takith sorwe" one takes up one's own sorrow, an act of the will. Moreover, it is seemingly a choice one doesn't have to make. The true marker of a free will, according to Scotus, is that it could have chosen otherwise.[43] If, as the songbird argues, one "takith" one's sorrows, there's the implied option that one doesn't have to take up sorrow. The songbird thus seems to claim that feeling pain is contingent on a choice to feel that pain, and if it is a matter of choice, then it is a matter of will and of self-discipline. The bird's lesson to the churl, then, contradicts the image of painful compulsion we found imagined in her natural habitat.

Another valence of compulsion appears in the bird's lesson-giving to the churl, wherein taking pleasure in the freedom to sing becomes hard to distinguish from painful compulsion. The bird first promises to sing the churl a great reward using language of volition: "Yiff thou wilt on-to my rede assent . . . I shal the yeve a notable gret gwerdoun . . . take heed what I do profre" (155, 158, 160). The caged bird sets the conditions in if/then terms that bind both churl and her in a promise. In this iteration, then, the bird declares her free choice to provide the churl with song, to reproduce for the churl the thing for which the bird was initially caged—if only the churl first release her. The promise functions as a site of compulsion wherein the bird's freedom from the cage nevertheless ties her to required performance. It seems the bird ultimately feels no obligation to fulfill these terms—she spends twenty-one lines contemplating the foolishness of hanging around and perhaps getting caught again. All the same, she makes good on her promise. This moment of articulation of willing choice to sing, however, discomfitingly parallels the scene of compulsive diurnal singing in the forest.

[43] Scotus discusses the will's potential to will opposites at length, for instance, in *Questions on the Metaphysics*, IX, q. 15.

Now free and having delivered her three lessons, she seems unable to quit the churl, "houyng above his hede" (224) and taunting him. Compulsion here seems much less connected to the pains of the forest; the now-free jailbird relishes the chance to lord it over the churl, calling out to him "O dulle cherl!" (299). Yet even after declaring "I am now free, to syngen & to flie" (271), the bird "gan ageyn retoorne" (297–98), the "ageyn" here recalling the painful compulsion "to syng ageyn" in the forest.

The jailbird declines to identify with the alignment of song and pain, however. Not only do prison and song "haue noon accordaunce," she avers, "Ryngyng of ffeteris makith no mery soun" (99, 103). Instead of a space in which one's pains may be reckoned through song, the bird argues that its cage functions as a space purely of punishment and discipline. The cage thus becomes the space in which oscillations between the externalities and internalities of compulsion are carefully delimited. That is, the figure of the medieval jailbird here marks the boundaries between what externally compels you and that which is internally compulsive. Even as the songbird is supposedly naturally "free," as the poem positions freedom in the natural world rather than the confining human world, and as that natural world is the space for the production of moving beauty, Lydgate invests the natural world with compulsion and pain. The figure of the caged bird ostensibly *clarifies* the difference between what someone else makes you do and what you yourself cannot help doing. Thus, strangely enough, it is confinement that elucidates while natural freedom is the site of problematic messiness. The jailbird's abnegation seeks to cordon off the cage's external imposition of discipline from the potential hazards of self-discipline. The external pains of the cage seem all too similar to the internal(ized) pains of her song. She does not want the caging to be internal. Keeping things external is much safer. Conversely, the picture we get of what happens to her outside the cage—the compulsive singing of beautiful, moving, painful songs—is, I have argued, a picture of the very blurred boundaries between outside and inside, between choice and compulsion.

Attending to the figure of the caged bird in "The Churl and the Bird" provides a compelling view onto Lydgate's thinking about and working through a profound philosophical and poetic question: what might it mean to understand poetic making as a form of agency that navigates the constraining compulsions seemingly inherent to one's "nature"? The question speaks to a history of the prison inextricable from literary production, inextricable from the exercise of creative agency caught in constraining circumstances. Given the numerous examples of late medieval prison writing and the ubiquity of the prison as a poetic image, Lydgate's question locates for us a core literary concern for writers in England in the later Middle Ages, writers who were often associated with or apprehensive about troubled royal courts, concerned about England's fraught international relations, and anxious to establish English as a literary language. One of the ways the prison has been understood to work is as a space for the production of poetry and authorial identity. Robert Epstein, discussing English prisoners James I of Scotland and Charles d'Orléans, says, "Exile and imprisonment . . . are, after all, particularly powerful images in the modern imagination, becoming in our own time figures for the condition of humanity in general and the poet in particular."[44] Joanna Summers argues that the variety of late medieval texts linking imprisonment and writing do so in the service of constructing, narrating, and presenting a textual self in order to persuade a prospective audience. An author's attempts to, as Summers puts it, "'market' his character and write himself out of confinement and subjection and into favor" certainly suggest the operations of desire and, like Lydgate's songbird, an agency invested in highly contingent poetic production.[45]

In that it understands the prison in conjunction with the production of poetry, the question also speaks to Lydgate's critical reception. Lydgate has been in so many ways a poet metaphorically confined. As a figure of literary history, he remains fascinatingly marked by discourses of confinement and compulsion, even by the current criticism that looks more favorably on him and his work. Maura Nolan calls Lydgate's poetry "narrower and more limited than Chaucer's," even as she argues that Lydgate's mummings and disguisings constitute an act of will, participating in "a turn away from a Chaucerian vision."[46] Making the case for bringing Lydgate "out of the shadow of Chaucer," Larry Scanlon and James Simpson argue, "to deny Lydgate all treatment as a major author, no matter how provisional, would ultimately mean reinforcing the trap

[44] Epstein, "Prisoners of Reflection," 161.

[45] Summers, *Late-Medieval Prison Writing*, 23.

[46] Maura Nolan, *John Lydgate and the Making of Public Culture* (Cambridge: Cambridge University Press, 2005), 5.

in which we currently find him."[47] Lydgate cannot seem to win for losing. In his brief consideration of the "The Churl and the Bird," Derek Pearsall calls the poem a "delight,"[48] suggesting that the work partakes in a kind of beauty. He immediately goes on to characterize that beauty, however, as not being Lydgate's own. Instead, the poem's modicum of beauty comes from Chaucer's influence as well as the nature of the poem's source. Lydgate cannot sing beautifully, but he cannot help but try: "like . . . a man compelled to stammer but with nothing to say."[49]

When declaring John Lydgate "perfectly representative of the Middle Ages," Pearsall fascinatingly associates the poet with birds. He argues that the Lancastrian poet-monk's work is like early scientific examinations of bird flight. He says:

> To understand in precise detail the mechanics of a bird's flight, biologists used film slowed down to record, frame by frame, the exact process at each stage. Lydgate provides us with something like the same sort of opportunity to understand the precise configurations and convolutions of a type of mind and of an intellectual and artistic tradition.[50]

In this unexpected and fantastically birdish analogy, Lydgate gives us the frame-by-frame of flight—a mechanical precision that is artistic but not beautiful. Caught in the frame and carefully gridded, like the motion studies to which Pearsall alludes, Lydgate the poet-monk is decidedly not taken to flights of fancy.[51] For the captivating beauty of bird-flight, to see a freer kind of poetry, poetry that moves and moves us, we must instead turn to Chaucer. We have here the Lydgate commonplace: a dull but learned poetics of the frozen frame that marks the

[47] Larry Scanlon and James Simpson, "Introduction," in *John Lydgate: Poetry, Culture, and Lancastrian England*, ed. Scanlon and Simpson (Notre Dame: University of Notre Dame Press, 2006), 1–11 (6). For two other recent reconsiderations of Lydgate's place in literary history, see Robert Meyer-Lee, *Poets and Power from Chaucer to Wyatt* (Cambridge: Cambridge University Press, 2007); and Mary C. Flannery, *John Lydgate and the Poetics of Fame* (Cambridge: D. S. Brewer, 2012).

[48] Derek Pearsall, *John Lydgate* (Charlottesville: University of Virginia Press, 1970), 199.

[49] Ibid., 214.

[50] Ibid., 14.

[51] Eadweard Muybridge's late nineteenth-century studies of locomotion are probably the most famous example of the process Pearsall describes here. Muybridge published voluminous photographic studies on the locomotion of both humans and non-human animals, paying special attention to horses and birds as well as humans.

confining and dulling analysis of something beautiful, inspiring, and free.

The compulsions that Lydgate plumbs in the "The Churl and the Bird" are thus easily seen as reinscribed within critics' accounts of Lydgate's position in literary history. Lydgate is effectively doubly confined: haunted by the external pressures of the Lancastrian regime and by possible routes of poetic production in relation to that regime, he is nevertheless compelled to produce poetry. And what beauty that poetry achieves is not because of anything he himself does, and in fact happens accidentally. Thus, like his songbird in its natural habit, Lydgate cannot help himself; compelled to poetize, he stacks line upon line, point upon point, moral upon moral. Instead, I argue that rather than reading Lydgate in this poem as uncritically cluttered and encyclopedically stammering, we should take his poem's account of compulsion seriously, locating as it does compulsion within a space cross-cut by natural inclination and literary creation, interiority and exteriority, freedom and confinement. But we can only read Lydgate in this way—we can only readjust our sense of literary history—if we read Lydgate through this willful jailbird.

The songbird's refusal to sing appears within a carefully crafted argument and ultimately efficacious escape. She gets free while mocking and educating the churl, teaching him three lessons about self-discipline and correctly ordering one's will: don't give immediate credence to new stories; don't sorrow over lost things; and, most provocatively for this essay's concerns, don't desire the impossible (197–217). The songbird, who previously complained about prison as externally imposed, schools the churl on how to regulate one's desire. That the bird ultimately wins her freedom has been read as political commentary, an understandable move given Lydgate's relation to and careful navigation of half a century of Lancastrian court politics. Helen Barr argues that the poem is largely one of social quietism or conservatism, as seen in an implied anti-peasant strain to the songbird's arguments.[52] The clever and learned bird reclaims her own "natural" position and puts the churl in his ignorant, rustic place. On this account, the songbird's ability to argue rings around the churl and ultimately win her freedom gives us the reassertion of a naturalized political order. Such an account understands the poem's

[52] Helen Barr, *Socioliterary Practice in Late Medieval England* (Oxford: Oxford University Press, 2001), 190.

figurations anthropocentrically; the caged songbird stands in for and comments on human politics. Honing in on the figure of the caged bird in Lydgate's poem suggests a healthy skepticism is needed in approaching any claims that position the poem as holding up a seemingly unproblematic "natural" order. As I've argued, we need to attend to the ways the poem renders the natural world as shot through with pain and compulsion, even as that world is presented as the site of natural inclinations and supposedly free exercise of the will that contrasts with the confinements of the gilded cage.

The account of poetic making in the poem, although focused on questions of human artifaction and agency, is nevertheless routed through a very specific animal figure that raises serious questions about what exactly it might mean to do something according to one's nature. Singing is what a bird does, whether it seems to want to or not, so what would it take for that bird to abstain? Lydgate's use of the figure of the caged bird suggests the ways in which poetic making is always already some sort of involuntary willfulness: a course of action taken in the face of opposition from others and one's own self that nevertheless cannot escape the constraints of one's condition, one's personal and literary history, one's bodily experience. Voluntary actions—the things that seemingly mark one as "one" because one is capable of even "own-ing" an action—escape or betray one's own control.

Complicating Duns Scotus's assertion of the will's fundamental uncoercibility, Lydgate implies, then, that it is precisely in a space of coercion that the will works. Though his jailbird argues that that "Song & prisoun haue noon accordaunce," Lydgate shows confinement to be complexly productive. Following Lydgate's lead, we might usefully reconsider the entanglement of confining space, faculties of self, and poetic production across myriad fourteenth- and fifteenth-century texts. The prison's coercions when put in dialogue with the compulsions foundational to one's nature thus seem to open a space for "more inventive and complex expression."[53] The bird's refusal to sing, "Trowistow I wole syngen in prisoun?," poetically uttered from the space of her gilded cage, rubs up against the compulsions that are part of the nature to which she wishes to return, with which she vehemently identifies. We might understand the jailbird saying, "I would rather be subject to the compulsions that mark me as me—even if such compulsions sit at the

[53] Epstein, "Prisoners of Reflection," 162.

event horizon of the spiraling rigors of self-discipline. I would rather be subject to *that* than be subject to another's will in this cage." "The Churl and the Bird" is Lydgate's rumination on the poetic and philosophical implications of taking up such a stance of willful refusal in the face of confinement. That rumination perturbs the clear distinctions in Jacques Deval's statement that heads this essay—"God loved the birds and invented trees. Man loved the birds and invented cages." Deval succinctly differentiates wood from cage in God and humanity's divergent creative energies toward birds. In "The Churl and the Bird" both woods and cage have at stake the making of poetry as an act of the will in the face of constraint. Lydgate's jailbird's willful stance of refusal imagines the medieval prison as a space in which the will crucially matters, and not, contra received accounts of the medieval prison, because bodily constraint can so easily be equated with coercive evacuation of the will.

Dictators of Venus: Clerical Love Letters and Female Subjection in *Troilus and Criseyde* and the *Rota Veneris*

Jonathan M. Newman
Bishop's University

Introduction: Pandarus and the Pragmatics of Love

THE CONSCIOUS ATTENTION TO the rhetoric of seduction in *Troilus and Criseyde* puts it in a tradition of erotodidactic literature going back at least as far as Ovid's amatory poetry.[1] Medieval texts such as the *Facetus*, Andreas Capellanus's *De amore*, and parts of the *Roman de la rose* teach an Ovidian rhetoric of seduction described as *praeludia* to physical acts of love.[2] *Troilus and Criseyde* can itself be described as an *ars amandi*, and was treated as such well into the sixteenth century.[3] Unlike its predecessors, *Troilus and Criseyde* sets this erotodidactic tradition in a more serious fictional world by personifying that tradition in the voluble Pan-

I would like to thank the Social Sciences and Humanities Research Council of Canada and the Leslie Center for the Humanities at Dartmouth College for their support of the research that went into making this article. I would also like to thank Monika Otter, Peter Travis, Michelle Warren, Eyvind Rondquist, Al Shoaf, and Magda Hayton who read drafts at various stages and offered helpful suggestions.

[1] Written in Rome around 2 CE, the *Ars amatoria* is a playful handbook of seduction written in elegiac couplets. Learned, complex, and sophisticated, it offers its reader a cynical and pragmatic take on the conduct of love affairs among urban Roman men and women in the Augustan age.

[2] Andreas Capellanus, *De amore* (*On Love*, ed. and trans. P. G. Walsh [London: Duckworth, 1982]), 1.5.543. All citations and translations of *De amore* (unless otherwise noted) are from Walsh's edition, hereafter abbreviated to *DA*, and cited by book, section, and paragraph number.

[3] Martin Camargo, *The Middle English Verse Love Epistle* (Tübingen: Max Niemeyer Verlag, 1991), 85. See also Seth Lerer, who views its reception as an art of love in concert with its reception as a conduct and strategy guide for courtiers, in *Courtly Letters in the Age of Henry VIII: Literary Culture and the Arts of Deceit* (Cambridge: Cambridge University Press, 1997).

Studies in the Age of Chaucer 36 (2014):103–138

darus against the backdrop of the Trojan War. As the point of entry for Ovidian erotics into the narrative, Pandarus operates "in a naturalistic world where speech is action," fashioning the love-discourse between Troilus and Criseyde.[4] He takes Troilus's desire and Criseyde's resistance and gives them an Ovidian script.[5] The script also gives Pandarus the part of "go-between" played in the style of the Ovidian *praeceptor amoris*, a role that medieval clerics reformulated in terms of a third role, the master of rhetoric.[6]

Throughout the central and later Middle Ages, a master of rhetoric was a master of letter-writing. Letters are central to *Troilus and Criseyde* as they were to the literary, political, and cultural activity of the later Middle Ages.[7] Pandarus exercises coercive power through his three congruent roles: Ovidian seduction-teacher; comic go-between; and *dictator*, the professional letter-writer and master of the *ars dictaminis*.[8]

[4] Charles Muscatine, *Chaucer and the French Tradition: A Study in Style and Meaning* (Berkeley: University of California Press, 1965), 145; John Fyler argues the obverse—that Pandarus's mediation between language and reality would dissolve the real world into the artifice of poetry. John M. Fyler, "The Fabrications of Pandarus," *MLQ* 41, no. 2 (1980): 115–30.

[5] Michael A. Calabrese, *Chaucer's Ovidian Arts of Love* (Gainesville: University Press of Florida, 1994), 33–80. For a more recent study on Ovid and Pandarus, see Colin Fewer, "The Second Nature: *Habitus* as Ideology in the *Ars amatoria* and *Troilus and Criseyde*," *Exemplaria* 20, no. 3 (2008): 314–39.

[6] "Ego sum praeceptor amoris." *Ars amatoria*, 1.17; citations and translations of *Ars amatoria* (hereafter abbreviated *Ars*) are from *Ovid: The Art of Love and Other Poems*, ed. G. P. Goold, trans. J. H. Mozley, 2nd ed. (Cambridge, Mass.: Harvard University Press, 1929). To Gretchen Mieszkowski, Pandarus is already a composite of two traditions of go-betweens, those who inhabit "idealized stories concerning emotions and loving relations," and those who inhabit "stories of love and conquest . . . about sex." *Medieval Go-Betweens and Chaucer's Pandarus* (New York: Palgrave Macmillan, 2006), 135. On Andreas as a cleric and rhetorician see Albrecht Classen, "Epistemology at the Courts: The Discussion of Love by Andreas Capellanus and Juan Ruiz," *NM* 103, no. 3 (2002): 341–62; Peter Dronke, "Andreas Capellanus," *Journal of Medieval Latin* 4 (1994): 51–63; and Don A. Monson, "Andreas Capellanus and Reception Theory: The Third Dialogue," *M&H* 31 (2005): 1–13. On the figuration of Ovid's *praeceptor* in *Roman de la rose*, see Peter Allen, *The Art of Love: Amatory Fiction from Ovid to the "Romance of the Rose"* (Philadelphia: University of Pennsylvania Press, 1992), 80–109.

[7] Studies connecting letter-writing in *Troilus and Criseyde* to formal epistolary practice in the Middle Ages have been few but valuable: John McKinnell, "Letters as a Type of the Formal Level in *Troilus and Criseyde*," in *Essays on Troilus and Criseyde*, ed. Mary Salu (Cambridge: D. S. Brewer, 1979), 73–89; Martin Camargo, "Where's the Brief?: The *ars dictaminis* and Reading/Writing between the Lines," *Disputatio: An International Transdisciplinary Journal of the Late Middle Ages* 1 (1996): 1–17, and Camargo more extensively in *The Middle English Verse Love Epistle*; Lerer, *Courtly Letters in the Age of Henry VIII*.

[8] Kathleen A. Bishop discusses the background of the go-between role in Latin comedy in "The Influence of Plautus and Elegiac Comedy on Chaucer's Fabliaux," *ChauR*

Martin Camargo describes the extensive mediation performed by the scribe in the process of both composing and receiving letters:

> Since the style and structure of medieval letters were highly conventional, a large part of their composition was . . . typically entrusted to a trained professional, who might but need not also serve as scribe. The "author" would first summarize what the letter should say; then the secretary or notary would reshape this oral précis so that the desired message was arranged in the standard sequence of clearly articulated parts . . . a similar process occurred when the letter reached its destination. The private reading of a written text was not the normal mode of reception for medieval letters. More typically, the letter would have been read in public, by the bearer if he were literate, or by some other mediator. And in many cases the bearer was expected to elaborate on the letter's contents, to respond to questions about them, or to supplement them with confidential information delivered (orally) in private.[9]

Pandarus performs all of these mediating tasks as he generates and shapes communication between Troilus and Criseyde.[10] As scribe and *dictator*, Pandarus uses his learned formulas to provide form, content, and motive to their letters. The roles played by Troilus and Criseyde are intersected by two authoritative clerical discourses: the art of love and the art of letter-writing.

These two protocols are also combined in the *De amore* of Andreas Capellanus (c. 1190), perhaps the most famous instance of medieval erotodidacticism. Andreas anticipates Pandarus in combining the Ovidian love tutor with the medieval social role of the clerical courtier. *De amore*'s scholastic prose is quite different from the urbane elegiacs of the *Ars amatoria*. Ovid's use of the term *praeceptor* smacks of ironic self-aggrandizement, but Andreas plays his pedagogical role straight, declaring honesty of character (*morum probitate*) and eloquence central to winning love—two attributes, of course, that fall squarely within clerical domains of expertise.[11] The *De amore* also reflects clerical expertise in the

35, no. 3 (2001): 294–317. On the *dictator* as a stable social and professional role in the Middle Ages, see Ronald Witt, "Medieval 'ars dictaminis' and the Beginnings of Humanism: A New Construction of the Problem," *RenQ* 35, no. 1 (1982): 1–35.

[9] Camargo, "Where's the Brief?," 4.

[10] "It is Pandarus who advises Troilus to write Criseyde a letter, and Pandarus's elaborate directions regarding its contents suggest that he is dictating its words to Troilus rather than vice versa"; ibid., 12.

[11] For detailed comparison of the two texts, see Chapter 2 of Allen, *The Art of Love*, 59–78; John Scattergood, "The Unequal Scales of Love: Love and Social Class in Andreas Capellanus's *De amore* and Some Later Texts," in *Writings on Love in the Later Middle Ages*, ed. Helen Cooney (New York: Palgrave Macmillan, 2006), 63–79 (65).

ars dictaminis: its "didactic preface [is] modeled after a letter to a student," and the individual speeches in its specimen dialogues are constructed in the dictaminal order.[12] Its model dialogues are grouped by social class in a way that reflects the organization of *artes dictandi*.[13] It features two fully elaborated letters in the dictaminal style.[14] The marks of the *ars dictaminis* on *De amore* are unsurprising; both issue from the great increase in education, textual production, and bureaucratic complexity in full swing at the turn of the thirteenth century. The *ars dictaminis* touched on all these developments; by playing the Ovidian *praeceptor amoris*, Andreas got the chance to demonstrate his facility with *dictamen* and other clerical discourses such as disputation.

The Ovid of the *Ars* and the *Remedia amoris* was thus reimagined by medieval clerics as one of them. Andreas's adaptation of the *Ars*'s cynical attitude to the intellectual methods and textual procedures of his own day contributes to the medieval conception of Ovid as the clerk of Venus; Pandarus belongs to this tradition.[15] An emblematic if lesser-

[12]Monson, "Andreas Capellanus and Reception Theory," 4; Classen, "Epistemology at the Courts," 359; Antonio Cortijo-Ocaña, "Introducción," in *Boncompagno: "El tratado del amor carnal"; o, "Rueda de Venus." Motivos literarios en la tradición sentimental y celestinesca (ss. XIII–XV)*, ed. with Spanish translation Cortijo-Ocaña (Pamplona: Ediciones de Universidad de Navarra, 2002), 24.

[13]Treatises on *ars dictaminis* talked so extensively about the alignment of social and linguistic order that Giles Constable describes them as constituting a first-order descriptive sociology in "The Structure of Medieval Society according to the *Dictatores* of the Twelfth Century," in *Law, Church, and Society: Essays in Honor of Stephan Kuttner*, ed. Kenneth Pennington and Robert Somerville (Philadelphia: University of Pennsylvania Press, 1977), 253–67.

[14]In a metafictional moment, the *homo nobilior* and *mulier nobilis* first appeal to the authority of Andreas the chaplain, and then refer their disputation to the judgment of the countess of Champagne (*DA*, 1.6.389–94). Their letter and the countess's response meet all the formal requirements of the dictaminal letter, and also show the dramatic potential of letters in comparison to the abstract pseudo-philosophical dialogues of *DA*, 1.6.

[15]Ovid's own poetry is steeped in the learning of his day, making this appropriation more possible. Alessandro Schiesaro, "Ovid and the Professional Discourses of Scholarship, Religion, and Rhetoric," in *The Cambridge Companion to Ovid*, ed. Philip R. Hardie (Cambridge: Cambridge University Press, 2002), 62–78. Based on a passage in *Troilus and Criseyde* in which Criseyde rails against those who view jealousy as the essence of love (*TC*, III.1023–29), Dronke suggests that Chaucer read Capellanus: "The perverse thesis—jealousy is love—is unusual enough in this categorical form for me to think that Chaucer had Andreas in mind; and Criseyde (or Chaucer through her) sees straight to the dishonest, equivocal, even ugly quality that lurks within Andreas's view"; "Andreas Capellanus," 62. At the very least, Pandarus, who is attempting to deploy this view of jealousy as love in the course of Criseyde's seduction, is Chaucer's characterization of a cynical tradition of clerical love-discourse that includes *De amore*. All Chaucerian references are to *The Riverside Chaucer*, gen. ed. Larry Benson, 3rd ed. (Boston: Houghton Mifflin, 1987).

known specimen of this tradition of clerical erotodidacticism is the *Tractatus amoris carnalis Rota Veneris nuncupatus* (or *Rota Veneris*) written by the thirteenth-century Tuscan rhetoric master Boncompagno da Signa.[16] This text is ostensibly an instruction manual for writers of love letters, and its combination of erotodidactic literature with the textual protocols of clerical work culture provides an unexplored perspective on the moral dimensions of love narrative in *Troilus and Criseyde*. It specifically sheds light on how Criseyde is constructed as the love-object and hidden subject of the erotodidactic tradition.

Epistolary Erotodidacticism and the *Rota Veneris* of Boncompagno da Signa

Boncompagno da Signa's *Rota Veneris* presents itself to the reader as a letter-writing handbook, offering precepts and models, but unlike other *artes dictandi*, treats love letters exclusively.[17] These letters form narrative sequences, so the *Rota*'s *dictator* is also a narrator who resembles Pandarus (and the narrator of *Troilus and Criseyde*) in several ways this essay will explore. The love affairs composed by Boncompagno escape His control and generate consequences that Ovidian erotics cannot anticipate. The *Rota Veneris* and *Troilus and Criseyde* both prompt their readers to meditate on the capacity of the love letter to generate voices—textual subjects—that overpower the controlling desire of the *dictator* or *praeceptor*. Both Boncompagno and Pandarus implicate Chaucer's narrator in a tradition of writing about love that represents women as objectives. Reading these texts together suggests an authorial ambivalence—Chaucer simultaneously rejects and adopts the role of Ovidian cleric—that complicates too pat an understanding of *Troilus and Criseyde* as illustrating, through Troilus's double sorrow, a double flight from

[16] Based on *De amore*'s stylistic features, internal references, textual history, and references to it in other texts, Dronke argues that "Andreas the chaplain" is a literary persona, the court of Marie de Champagne is a fictional setting, and the actual context of production and reception was among arts students at Paris in the 1230s. If this is true, that would mean that *De amore* was written after the *Rota Veneris* of Boncompagno da Signa. Dronke, "Andreas Capellanus," 56.

[17] Camargo offers the following distinctions in terminology when discussing the field of the medieval *ars dictaminis*: *dictamen* refers to prose composition; *ars dictaminis* is the discipline that cultivates the study of prose composition; *ars dictandi* is a specific work treating the *ars dictaminis*; a *dictator* is a teacher of the *ars dictaminis*, a clerical functionary in charge of composing letters, or both. Martin Camargo, *Ars dictaminis, ars dictandi* (Turnhout: Brepols, 1991), 17–19.

earthly to heavenly love, from the narrow perspective of Ovid to the wider perspective of Boethius.[18]

A brief look at Boncompagno's career will give a more precise idea of what I mean by "clerical." He was born in 1170 in the village of Signa outside Florence; was educated in grammar, rhetoric, and law at Florence and then Bologna; and joined the faculty at Bologna around 1190 as its first doctor of the *ars dictaminis*.[19] Bologna had long been a center for the study of *dictamen*; at least ten *artes dictandi* came out of Bologna in the first half of the twelfth century.[20] After the 1150s, the *ars dictaminis* came to France, Germany, and England, and "the literary classicism of late twelfth-century France left its marks in the elaborate style of French letters and dictaminal practice."[21] In Bologna, however, it remained "a practical art, 'the business program in the medieval university,'" flourishing alongside the notarial arts.[22] Boncompagno and other Italian *dictatores* did not enter religious orders; to speak of his discourse and training as "clerical" is to indicate the word's technical rather than religious aspect.[23] Technical prowess elevated Boncompagno to prominence in Bologna. He claims he was popular with students, but not so much with colleagues, who falsely accused him of fraud (out of envy, naturally) in order to drive him from Bologna at the height of his career.[24] After a

[18] See Calabrese, *Chaucer's Ovidian Arts of Love*, 71–80.

[19] Josef Purkart, "Boncompagno of Signa and the Rhetoric of Love," in *Medieval Eloquence: Studies in the Theory and Practice of Medieval Rhetoric*, ed. James Murphy (Berkeley: University of California Press, 1978), 320.

[20] Robert L. Benson, "Protohumanism and Narrative Technique in Early Thirteenth-Century Italian 'Ars dictaminis,'" in *Boccaccio: Secoli di vita. Atti del Congresso Internazionale Boccaccio 1975, Università di California, Los Angeles, 17–19 ottobre 1975*, ed. Marga Cottino-Jones and Edward F. Tuttle (Ravenna: Longo, 1977), 32.

[21] Ibid.

[22] Ibid. The cited text is Louis J. Paetow, *The Arts Course at Medieval Universities, with Special Reference to Grammar and Rhetoric* (Urbana-Champaign: University Press of Illinois, 1910), 67. In a similar vein, Witt remarks that "the close alliance between rhetoric and the notarial art brought into being the *dictator*, who either taught the technique of writing prose or, himself the product of such a discipline, had a career as a chancery official where he utilized those skills"; "Medieval 'ars dictaminis,'" 25.

[23] On *clericus* as denoting a professional competence rather than a pastoral role, see M. T. Clanchy, *From Memory to Written Record: England 1066–1307* (London: Edward Arnold, 1979), 179. The *dictator* of medieval Italy was often a civic functionary presiding over the production and disposition of documents whose elaborate formal requirements necessitated a class of experts. Witt, "Medieval 'ars dictaminis,'" 4–6. Legal deeds, for example, were technically letters, and shared certain compulsory features with letters expressing diplomatic overtures, anathema, affection, requests for money, spiritual counsel, or intellectual exchange; Giles Constable, *Letters and Letter-Collections* (Turnhout: Brepols, 1976), 20–25; 31–38.

[24] Josef Purkart, "Introduction," in Boncompagno da Signa, *Rota Veneris: A Facsimile Reproduction of the Strassburg Incunabulum*, trans. Purkart (Delmar, N.Y.: Scholars' Facsimiles and Reprints, 1975), 14.

period (1204–15) serving at the court of Wolfger of Erla, patriarch of Aquileia, Boncompagno returned to Bologna where he long remained.[25] He later applied to work in the papal curia, but was rejected and died alone and poor in a Florentine hospital in 1240 at the age of seventy.[26]

Boncompagno was a preeminent master of the *ars dictaminis* at a time when the practice and teaching of that art were undergoing a "rapid and massive change," a "proto-humanistic" moment that combined renewed interest in rhetoric for its own sake, an active civic culture, and a self-regarding community of scholars competing for prestige and lucrative posts.[27] Rather than a flash of accidental precocity anticipating actual (as opposed to "proto-") humanism, the rhetorical culture of Boncompagno's Tuscany consolidated the preceding century's achievements in producing, organizing, and interpreting texts, and also transformed these achievements into the basis of a competitive culture of performance. Men trained at elite institutions in Paris, Orléans, and Bologna identified with a burgeoning transnational work culture, confident in and proud of their professional expertise.[28] Boncompagno earned celebrity among such men by the virtuosity of his fifteen works, including *artes dictandi*, Ciceronian meditations on friendship and old age, and a history of the siege of Ancona in 1172.[29] His most popular work, the *Rhetorica antiqua sive Boncompagnus*, survives in eighteen known manuscripts, followed by the *Rota Veneris*, which survives in eight manuscripts and an incunabulum printed in Strasburg around 1473.[30]

The *Rota Veneris*, an amatory adaptation of the dictaminal treatise, is a learned *jeu d'esprit* produced for and by this clerical work culture, and demonstrates that culture's fascination with its own intellectual meth-

[25] Wolfger "was not only known as a generous supporter, host, and patron of *ioculatores*, *histriones*, *mimi*, and *cantores*, but also held a most important office as emissary and negotiator used by the Empire and Papacy." He is also a documented patron and benefactor of Walther von der Vogelweide; ibid., 26.

[26] Purkart, "Boncompagno of Signa and the Rhetoric of Love," 320. Perhaps his professional troubles had to do with his personality—the Franciscan chronicler Salimbene described him as a *ioculator* and as the greatest trickster of the Florentines; Salimbene de Adam, *Cronica*, ed. Oswald Holder-Egger, MGH SS 32 (Hanover: Hahn, 1913), 77: "more Florentinorum trufator maximus." Cited in Purkart, "Introduction," 28.

[27] Benson, "Protohumanism," 35.

[28] See John D. Cotts, *The Clerical Dilemma: Peter of Blois and Literate Culture in the Twelfth Century* (Washington, D.C.: Catholic University of America Press, 2009), esp. 4–12.

[29] Purkart, "Introduction," 12–13.

[30] This incunabulum is available in facsimile with English translation by Josef Purkart. See note 24.

ods. At a little over 5,000 words, it is relatively short. Its incunabular printing takes up eighteen pages and some manuscript versions fill only three folios.[31] Though brief, it is dense and intricate, at once *ars amandi*, *ars dictandi*, and dream-vision. It begins with the narrator wandering in a *locus amoenus*; Venus appears (whom the narrator first mistakes for a virgin!) to ask him why he has not written a book of "salutaciones et delectabilia dictamina . . . que viderentur ad usum amancium pertinere" ("salutations and delightful prose . . . which might seem to pertain to the use of lovers").[32] Boncompagno assents, providing advice for writing love letters with examples linked in several narrative sequences. Near the end, Venus returns to bless his efforts and commend them to all women; he in turn briefly holds forth on the gestural vocabulary of lovers and concludes with a disclaimer: the Fathers of the Church taught the faithful to read the Canticle for the edification of the spirit rather than the lasciviousness of the flesh (*RV*, 16.7).[33]

After Venus's initial appearance, Boncompagno describes salutations and exordia suitable to achieve *captatio benevolentiae* in love letters.[34] The *ars dictaminis* was preoccupied with this goal; the precise arrangement of formulaic salutations by rank of sender and recipient in *artes dictandi* was designed to achieve this.[35] Boncompagno, on the other hand, writes, "Ceterum si vellem secundum uniuscumque vitam et conditionem genera ponere narrationum, primo deficeret tempus quam sermo" (*RV*, 3.1)

[31] Cortijo-Ocaña, "Introducción," 62–65.

[32] Boncompagno da Signa, *Rota Veneris*, 1.1. Citations of the Latin text of the *Rota Veneris* (hereafter abbreviated *RV* and cited parenthetically) are by section and page number according to the edition in *El tratado del amor carnal*, ed. Cortijo-Ocaña. The MGH edition by Friedrich Baethgen is available online at *Medieval Diplomatic and the 'ars dictandi,'* ed. Stephen M. Wight, available at http://scrineum.unipv.it/wight/index.htm (accessed July 30, 2014). English translations, unless otherwise noted, are from Josef Purkart's 1975 translation (see note 24).

[33] Purkart, "Boncompagno of Signa and the Rhetoric of Love," 320. The brevity of this animadversion suggests a subtle mockery of such self-exculpating clauses as those found in *De amore*. As Alfred Karnein states, the *Rota Veneris*, like *De amore*, may have its origins in a serious clerical struggle against courtly and chivalric ideas about women and erotic love, but it does not follow that these texts endorse rigoristic views of sexuality; "Andreas, Boncompagno, und andere," in *Mittelalterbilder aus neuer Perspektive: Diskussionsanstösse in der Dichtung und Strategien des Erzählens. Kolloquium Würzburg, 1984*, ed. Rudolf Behrens and Ernstpeter Ruhe (Munich: W. Fink, 1985), 31–42. John P. Hermann discusses the apposition of Boncompagno's treatment of gestures to the ambivalent significations of the lovers' gesture in *Troilus and Criseyde*; "Gesture and Seduction in *Troilus and Criseyde*," *SAC*, 7 (1985): 107–35.

[34] I call the narrator Boncompagno; he is addressed by Venus as a writer of rhetorical handbooks, and names himself author at the work's conclusion (*RV*, 16.7).

[35] Camargo, *Ars dictaminis, Ars dictandi*, 22.

("If I wished to enumerate the varieties of content in accordance with each and everyone's life and condition, time would run out before I would run out of words"). He instead organizes models according to two temporalities, *ante* and *post factum*, before and after seduction (*RV*, 3.3). The section on letters written *ante factum* begins with a comprehensive list of appropriate metaphors for compliments (*RV*, 4). These are put to use in the first series, narrating a love affair that culminates in a lady's inviting her lover to meet secretly in a walled garden through the maneuvering of a go-between (*RV*, 7.3). This narrative combines elements of elegiac comedy, romance, and fabliau.[36] Its rich imagery and elaborate codes belong to romance, but an Ovidian (and comic) naturalism undercuts the lovers' sublime words, as does the dictator's wry commentary: "Consueverunt autem amantes ad maiorem delectationem dicere se vidisse per somnium quod fecerunt" (*RV*, 7.4) ("Lovers, moreover, have, to their greatest delight, been wont to say that they have witnessed in a dream what they have done").[37] In their *post factum* exchange of letters, playfully exultant in tone, the man writes that he had a dream about entering the lady's chamber; she invites him to visit again so she can help him to interpret it (*RV*, 7.5, 7.6). This playful conclusion gives way to a series of contingent possibilities—distance, parental prohibition, relegation to a convent, etc.—that frustrate and defy lovers (*RV*, 8.1–14.2). This arc of contingencies descends through various catastrophes to bottom out with satiric portraits of grotesque lovers (*RV*, 14.2).[38]

In the next section, I will examine those elements of clerical Ovidianism found in the *Rota* that also inform Chaucer's portrayal of Pandarus. Both refract the Ovidian rhetoric of seduction through dictaminal practice, and thus make that practice an instrument for female subjection, and make its intellectual techniques continuous with violence. The *Rota* and *Troilus* share these features with other medieval erotodidactic

[36] Cortijo-Ocaña, "Introducción," 15–24.

[37] *RV*, 7.4. In *De amore*, the women are often the stewards of Ovid's naturalistic frankness. In one *demande d'amour* (1.6.538) a man is asked whether he would prefer a woman's lower or upper half if he had to choose. He high-mindedly claims he would take the upper part, for it is a woman's discourse that elevates a man. The woman tells him he is a mistaken fool; no man would take any interest in a woman's upper half if not for the lower.

[38] These fall under two chapter headings: "Suasio pro muliere propter abundanciam diviciarum" and "Dissuasio contra virum propter senectutem." The prose under these headings integrates traditional satirical topoi with rhetorical school exercises; on the lineage of these portraits, see Cortijo-Ocaña, "Introducción," 26–27.

texts—Marilynn Desmond has argued that eroticized violence is an elementary part of Ovidian erotics—but the two have in common a trait they uniquely share, a narrative chaos generated by the ontology of the letter as a material form, and by resistance to the clerical *dictator*'s control that the material form gives to female voices and women's self-narration.[39]

Clerical Work Culture, Masculine Performance, and Female Subjection

Boncompagno enmeshes erotic discourse with the intellectual procedures of his professional life. He explains that the occupations of lovers—except knights, who are permitted the love of women—should be concealed in love letters because it would seem *ineptum* if the dignity of any cleric or the office of any merchant should be revealed by a woman.[40] A term of art like *ineptum* serves as both stylistic and social judgment; if the sender is revealed, his social identity is spoiled. Metonymically, the letter is described as spoiled—"epistola deluderetur."[41] This entails the equally regrettable outcome that his efforts at seduction go to waste. Boncompagno's solution is not chastity, but that the cleric or civic official conduct love affairs in secret and communicate with lovers by code:

> Nec etiam ipsi debent, cum scribunt mulieribus alicuius lascivie causa, suas dignitates vel officia nominare, quia male cum antecedenti concordaret illatum et sic per consequens epistola deluderetur. Clerici autem, qui frequenter super nature incudem feriunt cum malleo repercussorio nec valent motus renum de facili refrenare, ponant in salutacionibus aliqua *occulta signa*, que *propria nomina sibi sub ymagine* representent.
>
> (*RV*, 2.3; emphasis added)

[39] Marilynn Desmond, *Ovid's Art and the Wife of Bath: The Ethics of Erotic Violence* (Ithaca, N.Y.: Cornell University Press, 2006), esp. chapters 2 and 3.

[40] "Sed videtur michi, quod omnia officia preter miliciam sunt in salutacionibus tacenda, quia hoc ineptum videretur, si alicuius clerici dignitas vel negociatoris officium a muliere aliqua diceretur" (*RV*, 2.3). (But it seems to me that all official designations—except that of knight—ought to be omitted from the salutation, because it would seem inappropriate were the dignified rank of some cleric or the official business of the suitor to be mentioned by some woman.) The translation here is altered from Purkart's.

[41] Ami warns of this outcome if the lover's desire should be disclosed to Malebouche. Guillaume de Lorris, Jean de Meun, and Armand Strubel, *Le roman de la rose* (Paris: Librairie générale française, 1992), 7277ff.

[Nor, indeed, ought they, in writing to women for some lascivious reason, make mention of their dignified ranks or official duties, for this sort of thing would ill agree with what has preceded, and thus, consequently, the letter would be spoiled. The clerics, however, who repeatedly pound upon the anvil of nature with a rebounding hammer and cannot easily curb the movements of their loins, should put other, hidden signs in their salutations to represent, in symbols, their real names.]

The replacement of names and titles by secret codes recalls the *senhal* of Occitan love lyric, but here, in a secretarial rather than courtly world, the motive for secrecy is to protect the man's reputation. This motive is more cynical than protecting the lady's honor, and suggests that political ambitions and seductive play occupy the same sphere of experience. Secrecy in love letters, moreover, benefits from the advanced intellectual techniques of manipulating and deciphering "occulta signa" and "propria nomina . . . sub ymagine." These terms put the erudite language of allegoresis to the practical service of concealing an illicit love affair. Conversely, secret love affairs offer clerics an occasion to perform their expertise. From the integumentary reading practices of advanced arts masters to the strategic privacy of diplomats and merchants, the cleric finds in the game of seduction a low-stakes arena for the demonstration of his professional skills.[42] Furthermore, by omitting the titles and marks of status that emphasize hierarchy in the *ars dictaminis* and inscribe it into the dictaminal letter, the writer of love letters signals that this is a specialized form of discourse with its own hierarchy, one that makes the *dictator*, as *praeceptor*, master rather than servant. The art of love is a literary game, to be sure, but not one walled off in a garden of poetic fantasy; it belongs to clerical work culture as a game of textual self-performance whose players can demonstrate their prowess to peers and colleagues, those who can appreciate clever manipulations of shared formulae. This game contributed in many ways to the institutional self-regard and social identity of clerical administrators, a group of men often eccentric both to lay courts and Church institutions.

[42] Andreas Capellanus plays on the verbal relation between *secreta* and *secretarius*: "Similiter si visitationis inter se amantes utantur epistolis, propriorum nominum etiam scriptione abstineant . . . sed et mutuas sibi invicem missas epistolas proprio non debent insignire sigillo, nisi forte habuerint *secreta* sigilla quae nulli nisi sibi sint *secretarius* manifesta (*DA*, 2.7.21; emphasis added). ("Likewise if lovers keep in touch by letter, they should refrain from writing their own names . . . nor should they stamp letters sent to each other with their own seals, unless they have secret ones known to none except themselves and their confidants.")

Boncompagno's treatment of the art of love combines the specialized language of literature with the working language of his dictaminal profession. Analytical philosophers distinguish between *object language*, which refers to the extralinguistic world, and *metalanguage*, which refers to linguistic codes themselves. John Lucy distinguishes a third category, *metacommunicative* discourse, that takes relationships between people as its object.[43] The *ars dictaminis* is a metacommunicative discourse, treating language as the embodiment of relationships between people. It thus lends itself to the verbal game of love that is one of the enduring medieval legacies of Ovid's amatory poetry. Boncompagno goes beyond the mixing of language and human relationships to conflate lovers' desirous language with their desiring and desired bodies. His performance does not so much tease out the implicit carnality of clerical discourse as it assimilates acts of love to dictaminal textuality. Boncompagno brags to his reader what they can achieve with his instruction: "Inprimis namque taliter potest amator *exordiri*, *narrare* atque *petere* illam quam desiderat habere" (*RV*, 3.3; emphasis added) (And so from the outset, the lover in this way can *undertake*, *narrate/describe*, and *pursue* her whom he desires to have).[44] *Exordiri*, *narrare*, and *petere* are the names of the three parts of a letter's body turned into verbs, and therefore characterized as actions rather than things.[45] These actions do not take as their object the body of a text but the body of the woman, "illam quam desiderat habere." Seduction is an act of composition demanding the mediating skills of the *dictator*. The technical metalanguage of the *dictator* is transformed into an erotic object language, the professional competence of the cleric into the erotic competence of the lover. In reference to the letters of Abelard and Héloïse, Desmond argues that "the prescriptive tradition of the *ars dictaminis* provided a rhetorical script for the power relations of amatory discourse."[46] Similarly, the compositional control of the *dictator* becomes sexual dominance in the

[43] Gregory Bateson, "A Theory of Play and Fantasy," in *Steps to an Ecology of Mind* (San Francisco: Chandler, 1972), 178. Cited in John Lucy, "Reflexive Language and the Human Disciplines," in *Reflexive Language: Reported Speech and Metapragmatics*, ed. Lucy (Cambridge: Cambridge University Press, 1993), 15.

[44] My own translation.

[45] The *Oxford Latin Dictionary* offers meanings for *petere* that range across domains of law, courtship, and conquest: beg, beseech, request; strive for, seek; fall upon, attack; demand, exact, require, sue.

[46] Desmond, *Ovid's Art and the Wife of Bath*, 62.

ars amandi, but this power is limited if not illusory, for the rhetorical view of love in the *Rota Veneris* and in *Troilus and Criseyde* is contradicted by a narrative view of love. Narrative comprehends, as rhetoric cannot, the chaotic chain of contingencies that love generates.

This narrative chaos is an inevitable result of Boncompagno's combination of *ars amandi* with *ars dictandi*, and it anticipates the complexities generated by Chaucer's combined treatment of these two authoritative discourses in *Troilus and Criseyde*. As didactic genres, the *ars dictandi* and *ars amandi* both offer examples to imitate—in the one, specimen letters, and in the other, illustrative dialogues. Both are narrative fragments that invite extension and completion by the reader, and both in concert shaped the medieval conception of love letters. Though often criticized by modern critics as formulaic and utilitarian, the *ars dictaminis* had a literary potential that was cultivated by medieval practitioners. In the Orléans school of the twelfth century, model letters took on a fictional, sometimes fantastical character.[47] Boncompagno criticizes the Orléans school at times, but was the first Italian *dictator* "to construct more elaborate fictions in the letters" and make them a "display of literary virtuosity."[48] This virtuosity was elaborated in the creation of "epistolary sequences, ranging in length from two letters to seven or eight."[49] There are classical antecedents to the epistolary sequence as narrative genre, most famously Ovid's *Heroides*, already imitated by Baudri of Bourgueil and Abelard and Héloïse. Robert Benson nevertheless claims for Boncompagno a distinct place as "the inventor of the epistolary novella as a genre within the literary tradition of the Latin West, and . . . its first fully successful practitioner."[50] The *Rota* is a conspicuous example of this success. Its epistolary sequences provide a narrative frame for rhetorical exempla that in turn dramatize the narratives; the overall effect is a lightness and charm that, like Ovid's poetry, does not compensate for but results from its didactic flavor.

[47] These probably derived from the *suasoriae* and *controversiae* of rhetoric schools, exercises in composing fictitious speeches on mythological and historical themes. On these, see James J. Murphy, *Rhetoric in the Middle Ages: A History of Rhetorical Theory from Saint Augustine to the Renaissance* (Berkeley: University of California Press, 1974), 38–40. Cortijo-Ocaña suggests that these exercises inform the dialogism of both Latin and vernacular medieval literature from the eleventh century onward; "Introducción," 12.

[48] Benson, "Protohumanism," 35–36.

[49] Ibid., 41.

[50] Ibid.

Boncompagno begins his didactic program by demonstrating complimentary metaphors in a florid love letter.[51] The list of compliments in the first letter's exordium may seem excessive, but in more utilitarian *artes dictandi*, such lists function as template menus, offering options for the user to select. But this list also comes at the beginning of a narrative sequence, which makes the list's exhaustiveness feel excessive, one of several didactic elements that disrupts the capacity of readers to be absorbed into the fiction. Even more disruptive is the *dictator*'s own self-interruption to discuss the appropriate variations when writing to virgins, married women, nuns, widows, peasants, etc. (*RV*, 2.3). Despite these interruptions and changes of direction, the narrative advances, for each letter is itself a narrative event, a material token of linked bodily acts of composition, transmission, and reception.

A letter of response makes the narrative less fragmentary and more involving. The next letter features the desired woman's response; she tells him to go away and stop bothering her:

In epistole tue serie fatigasti pro nichilo, credens per quedam adulatoria verba et pulchritudinis mee commendacionem benivolenciam captare. Sed nichil est quod credis et semina mandas arene.

(*RV*, 5.2)

[In your series of letters you have worn yourself for nothing, believing you could capture my goodwill through some flattering words and complimenting my beauty. But what you believe is to no end, and you commit your seeds to sand.][52]

Her rejection is unsurprising. The entire erotodidactic tradition is predicated on the notion that men pursue and women resist.[53] Seduction is

[51] "Manus longe, digiti exiles, nodi coequales et ungule sicut cristallum resplendentes totius stature augmentabant decorem. Verum quia primo deficeret commendator quam pulcritudinis immensitas, stilum verto ad sapientie vestre magnitudinem" (*RV*, 4). ("Your long hands, your slender fingers, your well-shaped knuckles, and your nails, resplendent as crystal, enhanced the seemliness of your whole figure. But in truth, since he who praises is more likely to be lacking than is the immensity of beauty he is praising, I shall turn my pen towards the magnitude of your wisdom.")

[52] The translation is my own. The woman's rejoinder that he is wasting his effort echoes a constant refrain of the female interlocutors in *De amore* as well.

[53] For a discussion of this resistance in Roman erotic elegy, see Susannah Giulia Brower, "Gender, Power, and Persona in the Poetry of Baudri of Bourgueil," Ph.D. diss. (University of Toronto, 2011), 32–34, available at https://tspace.library.utoronto.ca/bitstream/1807/31697/1/Brower_Susannah_G_201111_PhD_thesis.pdf (accessed May 13, 2014).

pursuit and evasion, conquest and resistance, and these ruling metaphors cast the lover in traditionally masculine roles like soldier or hunter.[54] In the *Rota*'s first narrative sequence, the man's success is inevitable because it is an axiom of erotodidactic writing that a woman's refusal is a dissembling ploy in a game. Boncompagno says as much:

Preterea sciendum est quod unaqueque mulier, cuiuscumque sit ordinis vel condicionis, negat inprimis quod facere peroptat. Unde si aliquo modo mittenti rescribere velit, intelligas ipsam concedere velle, licet hoc neget verbis.

(*RV*, 5.1)

[Furthermore, it should be known that any woman whatsoever, of whatever station or condition she may be, refuses at first what she actually wishes to do. Hence, if she is willing to write back to the sender in any way at all, you should understand that she herself is willing to yield, although she denies it with her words.]

The *dictator* assures his reader that the very fact that she responds (even if with mockery) means that she has ratified the process of her own seduction: "Hac siquidem epistola perpendere poterit amans, quo suum procul dubio desiderium adimplebit" (*RV*, 5.3) ("From this type of letter, the lover will be able to discern that his desire shall doubtless be fulfilled"). As the lover responds with increasingly elaborate rhetoric, she rejects him with increasing vehemence. She declares herself stunned by his insolence but finally relents and arranges a rendezvous, demonstrating that the force of her engagement, be it positive or negative, discloses the truth of her reciprocated desire. This idea is at least as old as the *Ars amatoria*, in which Ovid declares that if a woman even so much as reads a love letter, she confirms her reciprocal desire:

Legerit, et nolit rescribere? Cogere noli:
  Tu modo blanditias fac legat usque tuas.
Quae voluit legisse, volet rescribere lectis:
  Per numeros venient ista gradusque suos.
Forsitan et primo veniet tibi littera tristis,
  Quaeque roget, ne se sollicitare velis.

[54] *Ars*, 1.38, 1.45; *DA*, Praef.2, 1.6.312. Desmond discusses the performative masculinity of these roles in terms of imperial and colonial politics. See *Ovid's Art and the Wife of Bath*, 37.

Quod rogat illa, timet; quod non rogat, optat, ut instes;
Insequere, et voti postmodo compos eris.
(*Ars*, 1.479–86)

[Suppose she has read, but will not write back: compel her not; only see that she is ever reading your flatteries. She who has consented to read will consent to answer what she has read; that will come by its own stages and degrees. Perhaps even an angry letter will first come to you, asking you to be pleased not to vex her. What she asks, she fears; what she does not ask, she desires—that you will continue; press on, then, and soon you will have gained your wish.]

The same idea can be found in another medieval erotodidactic text, the *Facetus*, an anonymous poem that is part *ars amandi* and part conduct manual. This work's narrator assures the reader that any lady's rejection is temporary and insincere.[55]

In romance and lyric, this faux-resistance is idealized as *daunger*, an attitude or pose central to the "olde daunce" of love and courtship, but in the twenty-first century we view this idea—that no means yes—as the logic of rape. The *Ars amatoria* affirms this judgment with an extended digression describing the rape of the Sabine women as paradigmatic of courtship (1.101–34).[56] Elsewhere in the same work, Ovid directly justifies physical coercion on the premise that women enjoy it: "Vim licet appelles: grata est vis ista puellis: / Quod iuvat, in vitae saepe dedisse volunt" (1.673) ("You may use force; women like you to use it; they often wish to give unwillingly what they like to give"). Clearly, the *praeceptor amoris* is the lover's friend, not the lady's; his claims about feminine psychology support his friend's sexual conquest. As author, he can demonstrate by narrative exemplum that his view of women's sexual desire is accurate, that his techniques are effective, that in fact, no means yes. The woman represented in the *Facetus* yields with pleasure to the lover's persistence. The lover persists not in the hope that she will change her mind, but in the assumption that she already wants him but must make him prove his desire.

Forsitan illa sagax sic verba superba loquetur,
Ut quod mente cupit per sua verba tegat:

[55] "The *Facetus*; or, The Art of Courtly Living," ed. and trans. Alison Elliot Goddard, *Allegorica* 2 (1977): 27–57, lines 183–84.

[56] "[T]he rape of the Sabines programmatically points to the violence of the *ars* professed by the *praeceptor*." Desmond, *Ovid's Art and the Wife of Bath*, 51.

"Stulta petis, juvenis, frustra laudas mea membra;
  Si sum pulcra satis, cur tibi cura fuit?
Vade, recede cito, ganeam me forte putasti,
  Et nunquam facias tu michi verba magis."
Tunc dicat juvenis: "Cur me, dulcissima rerum,
  Morte perire facis? Hoc tibi crimen erit.
Munera magna peto, tamen hec sunt digna favore;
  Si me forsan amas, nil tibi quippe nocet."
Inquiet illa quidem: "Fateor non horreo quemquam
  Teque libenter amo, nil michi plura petas."[57]

[Perhaps the clever girl may respond with a haughty speech to conceal her heart's desire with her words: "Young man, you're seeking something silly. In vain you praise my figure; perhaps I am passing fair—what concern is that of yours? Go away, go quickly—perhaps you think me a strumpet—and never speak to me again!"

Then let the youth reply, "Why, sweetest creature, do you condemn me to death? This crime will be yours. I am seeking a great reward, but nevertheless these things are worthy of favor. If you should chance to love me, no harm would come of it."

Then she will answer him, "I admit that I do not fear anyone, and I willingly love you; now seek nothing more!"]

Once again, the lover's verbal persistence is continuous with the use of physical force to overcome her resistance, force that the narrator thoroughly eroticizes.[58] The author of the *Facetus*, like Ovid, presumes to speak the woman's mind. In the fictional world of erotodidactic texts, women's roles are pre-scripted; the writing of their responses, moreover, is an erotic act in itself.

Female subjection undergirds the masculine performance of rhetorical prowess to which Ovidian erotics gives occasion. The eroticism of Ovid is already suffused in the professional techniques of law and rhetoric: "disce bonas artes" (*Ars*, 1.459), the *praeceptor* teaches, because they are

[57] *Facetus*, lines 243–54.

[58] "Sic postquam ludens fuerit calefactus uterque, / Vestibus ejectis, crura levare decet. / Vim faciat juvenis, quamvis nimis illa repugnet, / Nam si desistat, mente puella dolet" (ibid., lines 293–96). ("After play such as this both will be warm with passion; having thrown off their clothes, he then should lift her legs. Let the youth employ force although she strenuously resists, for if he should stop, the girl would grieve.")

as useful for wooing a woman as they are for defending a client.[59] Ovid's rhetoricized eros means that the literate cleric's professional competence makes him also a master of love. Ovid cultivates a tongue-in-cheek magisterial pose throughout the *Ars amatoria*; declaring himself the "praeceptor amoris" (1.17) or tutor of love at the beginning, he ends the first and second books of *Ars amatoria* with the tag "NASO MAGISTER ERAT" (2.744, 3.812). *De amore* and the *Facetus* contain even more schoolroom discourse, and that other famous Ovidian *praeceptor*, Ami in the *Roman de la rose*, twice refers to his seduction lore as his "arz et science."[60] Clerical erotodidacticism transforms love into a sphere in which intellectual methods and values, especially textual ones, are paramount; clerical identity is masculinized, and masculinity is clericalized. As Ovid writes, "dabit eloquio victa puella manus" (*Ars*, 1.462)—to eloquence the vanquished girl will give her hand. What these erotodidactic texts elide is the subjectivity and autonomous desire of women. The circumscribed world of their amatory fictions does not require it; in this world, the woman's role is simply to reward the eloquent and persistent lover.

This subject (and subjected) position for women is presupposed by generic constraints, yet Ovid himself, with his characteristic "tension and uncertainties," points in the *Ars* to the inaccessibility and uncontrollability of women's desire in real life.[61] In its treatment of love letters, the *Ars* refers to the myth of Cydippe: "Littera Cydippeu pomo perlata fefellit, / Insciaque est verbis capta puella suis" (1.457–58) ("A letter carried in an apple betrayed Cydippe, and the maid was deceived unawares by her own words"). Acontius writes the words "I swear by the sanctuary of Diana to marry Acontius" on an apple thrown before Cydippe's feet. She picks up the apple, reads it aloud, is overheard, and bound thus to her accidental oath, her utterance no less binding for all its lack of intentionality. This figures how erotodidactic literature writes

[59] Desmond argues that the *praeceptor* teaches violence as an erotic skill parallel with and analogous to rhetoric; I suggest that erotodidactic writing depends not just on analogy but on continuity between violence and rhetoric, persuasion and threat. *Ovid's Art and the Wife of Bath*, 46.

[60] *Roman de la rose*, lines 8285, 9651.

[61] The *De amore* diverges from this pattern, because the woman's role in that text is to maintain the social order, including class distinctions, which will trump eloquence and virtue alike. See Toril Moi, "Desire in Language: Andreas Capellanus and the Controversy of Courtly Love," in *"What Is a Woman?" and Other Essays* (Oxford: Oxford University Press, 1999), 408, 411–12.

women. It gives them the words to act as accomplice to their own seduction, and even physical resistance is assimilated to the script. By contrast, Cydippe's lament in the *Heroides* articulates the inner life and self-directed desire of a woman who resists being a love-object.[62] Criseyde also manifests this inner life, as we shall see, precisely in her resistance to being scripted as a love-object by an exchange of letters dictated by Pandarus, the self-styled *praeceptor amoris*.

The opening epistolary sequence of the *Rota Veneris* discloses in a small way the inner life of its represented woman; when the woman describes her correspondent as "credens per quedam adulatoria verba et pulchritudinis mee commendacionem *benivolenciam captare*" (5.2; emphasis added), she reveals her awareness of the part she is given as object and target of rhetorical art. With the phrase "benevolenciam captare," she appropriates the discourse of the *dictator*. She is on to her lover's game, aware of its techniques, and can even play too, quoting Ovid herself: "you cast your seed in the sand."[63] Being a player rather than just an objective in this game undercuts her subjection to some extent, even if the rules put her at a disadvantage, even if her sarcasm is ultimately nothing more than the resistance that makes the game worthwhile for the men to whom it belongs.

To represent a woman's voice, even in dramatizing the process of her seduction, is to generate the possibility of her resisting or reshaping her assigned role, a possibility underscored by the echoes of the *Heroides* in erotodidactic writing beginning with Ovid's own. If coerced to accept this role or overpowered by literal force, she at least voices her knowledge that the process sweeping her along cares about neither her experiences nor hopes. This woman's voice has a bodily presence, a materiality that can resist the *praeceptor*'s fantasies and disrupt his script. As Boncompagno's model letters respond to one another, the epistolary dialogue in the *Rota Veneris* gropes toward being a narrative. However much the *dictator* treats each letter as a diaphanous specimen, a disposable possibility in a forking trail of outcomes, the presence of voices in the durative matter of physical letters urges readers to link letters as chains of events.

[62] The letters of Acontius and Cydippe are the subject of *Heroides*, 20 and 21. Interestingly, Cydippe's lament closes the *Heroides*, a palinode, perhaps, to the amatory phase of Ovid's poetic career.

[63] "[Q]uid harenae semina mandas?"; *Heroides*, 5.115. Ovid, *Heroides and Amores*, ed. and trans. Grant Showerman (Cambridge, Mass.: Harvard University Press, 1963).

These resistant voices are a surplus effect of magisterial performance; the rhetorician's success is precisely the source of his failure, the loss of control that undermines erotodidactic love as a rule-bound imaginary game. Boncompagno's virtuoso epistolary variations in the *Rota Veneris* generate this narrative excess; at a certain point, it becomes absurd to claim that his narrative sequences can be taken as generic models for letter-writers. One letter is from a woman asking her husband to come back from his travels because their family is out of money and their daughters might have to prostitute themselves (14.2).[64] Another is from a nun who has been forced by her father to take the veil and longs for her lover to come climb her convent walls and rescue her (11.3). Each letter is not a formula to adapt, but a petitioning voice evoking a fictional world. The maker of formularies provides a blank as a first person subject—it should belong to the formulary's user, as it clings to the author who is its origin.[65] And yet, even as a textual effect, this voice takes on its own life as a resistant subject, not fully available to author or user, to *praeceptor* or pupil.

Textual Subjects, Presence Effects, and Narrative Contingencies

To write a letter, even a model letter, is to textualize a subject position. To say or write "I" is an act of deixis with a *presence* effect, an assertion of existence and presence before an addressee. "I" is a mark produced as an indexical sign of bodily and social presence. Hans Ulrich Gumbrecht describes the Middle Ages as a period in which an aesthetics of *presence* predominates over an aesthetics of *meaning*.[66] The former prioritizes the "materiality" or "mediatic modality . . . of each object of aesthetic experience" over the hermeneutic, "metaphysical" dimension of the "meaning-component"; in medieval culture, Gumbrecht argues, the material medium has more aesthetic effect, more heft, than the immate-

[64] This passage is in the Cortijo-Ocaña but not the Baethgen edition.

[65] According to Carolyn Dinshaw, Chaucer associates reading with masculine control of the feminine; *Chaucer's Sexual Poetics* (Madison: University of Wisconsin Press, 1989), esp. 28–64. On the tensions of authorial attachment to the generic voice of the formulary, see Ethan Knapp, *The Bureaucratic Muse: Thomas Hoccleve and the Literature of Late Medieval England* (University Park: Pennsylvania State University Press, 2001), 32–36.

[66] Hans Ulrich Gumbrecht, *Production of Presence: What Meaning Cannot Convey* (Stanford: Stanford University Press, 2004), 31ff.

rial idea it represents.[67] The dominant self-reference in "presence culture" is not the mind but the body.[68] Since letters were understood in the Middle Ages as a proxy for the body, they invoke presence. This is suggested by the quantitative expressions of passion that surround letters in the Middle Ages; in a presence culture, claims Gumbrecht, feeling or affect can be meaningfully intensified through quantitative expression.[69] We see this enumeration in *Il filostrato* and in *Troilus and Criseyde* itself; when Troilus kisses the letter he has written to Criseyde, "a thousand tymes er he lette, / he kiste tho the lettre that he shette" (*TC*, II.1089–90)—it is already an emblem of the body into whose presence it will come.[70] The letter is a proxy for *his* body, which makes it a proxy for *her* body; its contiguity between both their bodies across time is metonymical for their eventual physical union.

Letters reproduce presence because they result from absence and distance. The expression of anguish in love letters and lyrics often touts distance as its cause, as in troubadour lyrics of *amor de lonh*.[71] In the Middle Ages, epistolary correspondence was described as *sermo absentium*, a deficient proxy for face-to-face interaction imposed by the regrettable necessity of distance.[72] Yet the absence that prompts letters generates their presence effect, their durative and sensible materiality necessary for unaltered transmission.[73] The letter becomes a proxy for the writer's body, particularly in the case of love letters, and the medium of parchment—animal skin scraped smooth—must certainly have contributed

[67] Gumbrecht is careful to hedge this categorical statement by pointing out that meaning and presence cultures always exist in tension with each other: "I assume that there are always specific distributions between the meaning-component and the presence-component—which depend on the materiality (i.e. on the mediatic modality) of each object of aesthetic experience." Ibid., 108.

[68] Ibid., 78–79.

[69] "The concept of intensification [as in the Eucharist] makes us understand that it is not unusual, for presence cultures, to quantify what would not be available for quantification in a meaning culture: presence cultures do quantify feelings, for example, or the impression of closeness and absence, or the degrees of approval and resistance." Ibid., 85–86.

[70] *Il filostrato*, II.107, in Geoffrey Chaucer and Giovanni Boccaccio, *"Troilus and Criseyde," with Facing-Page "Il filostrato,"* ed. Stephen A. Barney (New York: W. W. Norton, 2006).

[71] See also *DA*, 2.7.14.

[72] Constable, *Letters and Letter-Collections*, 13–14.

[73] Constable examines some medieval remarks on the untrustworthiness of oral messengers and the preferability of letters (even over speech) in "Medieval Letters and the Letter Collection of Peter the Venerable," in *The Letters of Peter the Venerable*, Vol. 2, ed. Giles Constable (Cambridge, Mass.: Harvard University Press, 1967), 1–45.

to that sense, as would the wax tablet scratched by the lover's body. This sensual mediation contributes to the intimacy of reading and writing letters. For this reason, Pandarus's offer to sew up Criseyde's first letter to Troilus causes a shock of violation that resembles his remaining in the young lovers' bed-chamber when they consummate their desire. The capacity of the letter to simulate bodily presence was acknowledged in *artes dictandi*; Guido Faba (possibly a student of Boncompagno) writes in the *Summa dictaminis* that the letter "absentes quantumcumque remotos inducit tamquam simul essent presentia corporali" ("unites those absent, no matter how distant from each other, as if they were bodily present together").[74]

The bodily presence reproduced by the letter is one dimension of its presence effect; the other is its deictic invocation of the first- and second-person pronouns, *I* and *you*. The first-person pronoun links the letter's physical form with a speaking subject as the source of the utterance—even, perhaps especially, in writing.[75] This contiguity of a letter with the living voice it reproduced was central to the letter's documentary authority in the Middle Ages.[76] The *salutatio* names the sender and recipient and defines the relationship between them; like the wax seal, it bears the imprint of the author's social and bodily presence, which a presence culture conflates.[77] Boncompagno's first example of a salutation activates both dimensions of the letter's presence effect, materiality and deixis: "Gloriosissime ac preciosissime domine G.—, amice dulcissime, I.— salutem et id ineffabile gaudium mentis, quod aliqua voce vel actu exprimi numquam potest" (*RV*, 2.2) ("To the most glorious and precious mistress G.—, sweetest darling, I.— sends that ineffable joy of the mind which cannot be expressed by any word or deed, voice or gesture"). This model salutation demonstrates how letters not only

[74] Martin Camargo, "Where's the Brief?," 2, 15. Camargo cites and translates Guido Faba from "Guidonis Fabe *Summa dictaminis*," ed. Augusto Guadenzi, in *Il propugnatore* n.s. 3 (1890), Part 1, 287–388, Part 2, 345–93 (1.296–97). Gumbrecht asserts that "the meaning-dimension will always be dominant when we are reading a text—but literary texts have ways of also bringing the presence-dimension of the typography, of the rhythm of language, and even the smell of paper into play." *Production of Presence*, 108.

[75] Derrida meditates on the capacity of writing relative to speech for manifesting the presence and desire of subjects, in *Of Grammatology*, trans. Gayatri Chakravorty Spivak (Baltimore: Johns Hopkins University Press, 1997), esp. 152–54. I thank Peter Travis for bringing this to my attention.

[76] The documentary authority attached to the deictic "I" is still a part of wills and affadavits: "I, ——— , being of sound mind and body . . . ."

[77] The physical imprint is literalized in *TC* when Troilus mixes his tears into the wax (II.1086–88).

replace but surpass bodily expressions of love like voice and gesture. The letter is constantly available to the reader's touch, manipulation, kisses, and rereading. The initial that stands for a name recalls the dictaminal frame; as in a formulary, the "I" and "you" of the document are theoretically available for appropriation by anyone, but the erotic physicality of the love letter resists this appropriation in the *Rota Veneris* as it does in *Troilus and Criseyde*.

The subject positions of the model letters in *Rota Veneris* are presented by Boncompagno as ciphers, filled by the masterful presence of the mediating *dictator* and the desiring will of the manual's user. The deictic naming of "I" and "you," however, creates a sense of presence and positionality that frustrates this will. The shifting formulaic adaptability of "I" and "you" is frustrated by the letter's deictic presence effect, its capacity to "presentify" eroticized bodies, and the narrative contingencies afflicting those bodies. Blank subject positions become resistant subjects as the letters embodying them join as narrative. Initials ("domina G.—") in *Rota Veneris* become not blanks to be filled in, but codes, *occulta signa*, concealing and protecting the *haeccitas*, the unique "thisness" of the entities they summon.[78] In the middle section of the *Rota*'s model letters (11–15), as love is frustrated by various circumstances, epistolary subjects take on an elaborate specificity that defies the pretext that these are generic models for the reader's use. The sequence draws in the reader whom it then confronts with jarring developments—sequences of alternatives, forking pathways of love-narrative introduced by the connective "pone quod" (grant that), a phrase that continuously reasserts the *dictator*'s and the reader's presence: "Grant that she has married another and does not wish to sport further with him" (8.1), or "grant that she should become pregnant before that man marries her" (9.1).

Near the beginning of the *Rota*, Boncompagno writes that "distinguenda sunt amandi tempora et amancium genera" (3.1) ("distinctions must be made among situations for loving and kinds of lovers"). The letters, as formulae, are organized not only according to social roles (in

[78] J. Allan Mitchell discusses the connection between medieval literature and the medieval idea of *haeccitas* (as found especially in Duns Scotus and interpreted by Heidegger) in *Ethics and Eventfulness in Middle English Literature* (New York: Palgrave Macmillan, 2009), esp. 24–26. The unrepeatability of this *haeccitas* resembles the "ephemerality" of presence, which, according to Gumbrecht (also reading Heidegger), describes the self-concealing or "withdrawing" of presence at the moment of self-disclosure. *Production of Presence*, 78.

the typical dictaminal fashion) but according to *tempora amandi*, times or occasions in the course of love.[79] Colin Fewer has recently described the Ovidian view of love as belonging to a world-order of "radical contingency" where *casus* (chance) rules rather than Virgilian *fata*.[80] Along similar lines, Cortijo-Ocaña describes how Boncompagno insists on the necessity of love, which, as in stoic doctrine, moderates and unites the warring elements of the world; Boncompagno thus calls the work *Rota Veneris*: "Rota Veneris volui nominari, quia cuiuscumque, tamquam in rota orbiculariter volvuntur et pertimescunt omni tempore plurimum, quoniam perfectus amore continuum parit assidue timorem" (1) ("[I] wished to call [it] the Wheel of Venus, for people of whatever kind are bound together by love as if on a wheel, are turned in a circle, fearing the worst at all times, since perfect love always engenders perpetual fear"). Love, like fortune, confronts human desire and moral action with something like pure contingency. As J. Allen Mitchell puts it, "love is ever emergent and under construction, demanding future decisions all the time."[81] To link *tempora amandi* as a succession of situations and decisions is to sew situations together as narrative events; this is precisely what happens when individual letters are linked in a sequence of mutual response.

The *praeceptor amoris* would attempt to impose order on the radical contingency of love by making it an art, for "arte regendus amor" (*Ars*, 1.4) ("love should be ruled by art"). Colin Fewer speaks of Ovidian seduction as a matter of habituation, of bringing the love-object to heel by degrees.[82] Yet habit requires an expectation that situations repeat themselves; to isolate *tempora amandi* from each other is to make them abstracted situations like the hypothetical social contexts of the *ars dictaminis* (e.g., instructions for a priest writing a bishop with a request). The epistolary frame of the *Rota Veneris* links such situations together in causal succession; situations become events, eruptions of unrepeatable novelty that resist categorical abstraction. Events clump together as narrative despite the controlling efforts of the *dictator* to separate them. The reader is prompted to look for and impose connections between letters,

[79] In this respect, the *Rota Veneris* differs considerably from *De amore*'s illustrative dialogues.

[80] Fewer, "The Second Nature," 322.

[81] Mitchell, *Ethics and Eventfulness*, 56.

[82] Fewer, "The Second Nature," 322; compare to Ovid's description of the effects of love letters: "Per numeros venient ista gradusque suos" (*Ars*, 1.482) ("[Her consent] will come by its own stages and degrees").

even across separate sequences. Virgins therefore become married women, adulteresses, abandoned wives, widows, or nuns, in narrative arcs that linger and dissipate in a chaos of alternating voices; from this chaos emerge desiring and forlorn voices expressing the contingency and eventfulness of love, "a generous sign discharging ecstatic energy."[83] Love is experienced through narrative, not rhetoric. But Boncompagno stops short of following his narratives to any lasting or definite culmination—at every point where they threaten to overwhelm the dictaminal frame, he interrupts them, alters the situation, and a new story soon gets under way. Chaucer, to the contrary, introduces his *dictator*, Pandarus, into the flow of events, and makes him witness the consequences of his rhetoric.

The Ovidian Cleric and Female Subjection in *Troilus and Criseyde*

Like the *Rota Veneris*, *Troilus and Criseyde* is informed by traditions of love narrative, amatory didacticism, and formal letter-writing; Pandarus is another Ovidian *praeceptor amoris* refracted through the clerical social role.[84] Like the narrator of the *Rota Veneris*, he is master of the practical rhetoric of letter-writing and acts as letter-writing secretary and messenger to the lovers.[85] Like Boncompagno, Chaucer encountered erotodidactic literature mediated through a clerical textuality imbued by the discourse of schools and notaries. Pandarus is the condensation of this textual discourse, the *Rota*'s *dictator* made flesh, and his frantic activity prompting and shuttling the letters forms the center of Book II's narra-

[83] Mitchell, *Ethics and Eventfulness*, 4; this is in fact Mitchell's description of fortune, but it applies equally to love, which was associated with Fortune in the Middle Ages, as demonstrated in Howard Rollin Patch, *The Goddess Fortuna in Mediaeval Literature* (1927; repr. New York: Octagon Books, 1967), 95–97.

[84] McKinnell, "Letters as a Type of the Formal Level." R. A. Shoaf notes the resemblance of Pandarus to the "dictaminist," as the combination of poet, rhetorician, and lawyer, in *Dante, Chaucer, and the Currency of the Word: Money, Images, and Reference in Late Medieval Poetry* (Norman: Pilgrim Books, 1983), 116.

[85] This is a role Chaucer himself may have played or at least witnessed closely. "He must have received a thorough training" in the *ars dictaminis* to be a diplomat and civil servant, even if, as John McKinnell claims, it was "usual in England to obtain such training rather from Italian collections of specimen letters than from the *artes dictandi* themselves"; "Letters as a Type of the Formal Level", 79 n. 15. On dictaminal treatises in fourteenth-century England and their influence on the fully reported letters of Troilus and Criseyde, see Norman Davis, "The *Litera Troili* and English Letters," *RES* 16, no. 63 (1965): 233–44.

tive action.[86] He speeds the words that speed the lovers; his actions are words and those words become the actions of Troilus and Criseyde. Pandarus is the magisterial voice of the *dictator* incarnated on the same level of representational reality as the lovers, and therefore he is himself mediated by Chaucer's narrator.[87] Chaucer's narrator refers to himself as the servant of the servants of the God of Love (I.15)—a profanation of a specifically epistolary formulation of papal authority that links clerical rank and letter-writing with erotodidacticism.

Love letters are crucial to plot development and characterization in *Troilus and Criseyde*. The love affair begins in Book II, in which Pandarus solicits letters, delivers them, hovers as they are read, and tries to direct their interpretation. First he advises Troilus to assume a style that is natural and spontaneous rather than learned and ornate:

> Towchyng thi lettre, thou art wys ynough.
> I woot thow nyl it dygneliche endite,
> As make it with thise argumentes tough;
> Ne scryvenyssh or craftyly thow it write[.]
> (II.1023–26)

This letter-writing advice echoes the *Ars amatoria*:

> Sed lateant vires, nec sis in fronte disertus;
> Effugiant voces verba molesta tuae.
> Quis, nisi mentis inops, tenerae declamat amicae?
> Saepe valens odii littera causa fuit.
> (1.463–66)

[But hide your powers, nor put on a learned brow; let your pleading avoid troublesome words. Who, save an idiot, would declaim to a tender sweetheart? Often has a letter been a potent cause of hate.]

For Pandarus, as for Ovid's *praeceptor*, love is a game of acquisition, not an ennobling sentiment, so all manners of deception are fair game.[88]

[86] This activity, and its differences from that of Boccaccio's Pandaro, are described succinctly in Camargo, *The Middle English Verse Love Epistle*, 54.

[87] I suggest that the clownishness of the leaping and japing Pandarus, well described by Charles Muscatine, is mimetic adaptation—an *embodiment*—of the rhetorical excess of the clerical writer of the High Middle Ages. Charles Muscatine, *Chaucer and the French Tradition: A Study in Style and Meaning* (Berkeley: University of California Press, 1965), 140–42.

[88] On the pervasive deception of the fictional world described in Ovid's *Ars amatoria*, see Allen, *The Art of Love*, 18, 26–28, 34.

The illusory artlessness and self-concealing labor that the *praeceptor* recommends to the letter-writer he also recommends to a woman arranging her hair (*Ars*, 3.133–48). Nevertheless, Troilus's letter is such a conventional and overwrought affair that, unlike in the *Filostrato*, the narrator of *Troilus and Criseyde* abridges the letter's content through indirect discourse:

> First he gan hire his righte lady calle,
> His hertes lif, his lust, his sorwes leche,
> His blisse, and *ek thise other termes alle*
> *That in swich cas thise loveres alle seche*;
> And in ful wise, as in his speche,
> He gan hym recomaunde unto hire grace;
> To tell al how, it axeth muchel space.
> (II.1065–71; emphasis added)

Troilus assumes the subject position of *Rota Veneris*'s generic lover. The narrator paraphrases Troilus's first letter with the editorial summary "That in swich cas thise loveres alle seche." If he says things all lovers say, this is still a situation and not yet an event. Following Pandarus's directions, Troilus imbues the seal of the letter with his own bodily fluids, making it an index of his body as well as a symbol of his social identity:

> and with his salte teris gan he bathe
> The ruby in his signet, and it sette
> Upon the wex deliverliche and rathe.
> (II.1086–88)

But Troilus goes further, kissing this extension of his own body a thousand times, since this incarnation of his desire will be brought into the presence of his lady. As Camargo points out, the "letter becomes a surrogate Troilus, physically present to beg his lady's mercy."[89] The letter-writer, however, manifests not only his own presence in the letter, but that of the recipient, for whom the letter thus becomes a surrogate to him.

> Therwith a thousand tymes er he lette
> He kiste tho the lettre that he shette,

[89] Camargo, *The Middle English Verse Love Epistle*, 56.

> And seyde, "Lettre a blisful destine
> The shapyn is: my lady shal the see!"
> (II.1089–92)

As in the *Rota Veneris*, there is a suggestion of self-gratification about male textuality as it is depicted here; in fact, Troilus is adoringly kissing his own words, an act that, as we shall see, mirrors the onanism of the Ovidian cleric.[90]

Troilus's letter mediates between lover and desired lady precisely as a body; so does the body of the man who carries that letter, Pandarus. Embodying the clerical *dictator* and *praeceptor amoris* as a fictional persona, Pandarus manifests the ridiculous elements of that figure, the "supersubtle trickster and grimacing 'roynish clown'" (as Dronke describes Andreas Capellanus).[91] He also embodies the role's domineering, patriarchal elements, which derive from the *praeceptor* persona and are given culturally authoritative form by association with the stable institutional discourses of clerical work. This is made disturbingly plain when Pandarus and his niece are making small talk in the garden; he suddenly plucks out Troilus's letter, and, like a living paratext providing an *accessus* to Troilus's intentions, asks her to read it and write back at once—otherwise, "pleynly for to seyne, / He may not longe liven for his peyne" (II.1126–27). What follows next recalls the erotodidactic tradition's premise about seduction—that any response whatsoever to a lover's plea is a signal of consent. Just as the recipient of the letter in the *Rota* is fully aware of the conventions her lover is using to "obtain her goodwill," Criseyde's reaction to Pandarus likewise suggests her full awareness of the part required of her. She is not pleased:

> Ful dredfully tho gan she stonde stille,
> And took it nought, but al hir humble chere
> Gan for to chaunge, and seyde, "*Scrit ne bille*,
> For love of god, that toucheth swich matere,
> Ne bring me noon; and also, uncle dere,

[90] Shoaf sees this verbal self-gratification as not exclusive to clerical masculinity: "Every man loves his own 'engyn' and the 'fantasie' [III.274–75] it affords him. He need not literally indulge 'solitary sex,' to have always to hand this potential escape from separateness." R. A. Shoaf, "'The Monstruosity in Love': Sexual Division in Chaucer and Shakespeare," in *Men and Masculinities in Chaucer's "Troilus and Criseyde,"* ed. Tison Pugh and Marcia Smith Marzec (Cambridge: D. S. Brewer, 2008), 183–94 (191).

[91] Dronke, "Andreas Capellanus," 62–63.

> To myn estat have more reward, I preye,
> Than to his lust; what sholde I more seye?"
> (II.1128–34; emphasis added)

For her, this is not a game but an event that threatens to sweep her in its path without regard for her desires. Her "humble chere," a word combining affect and expression, begins to change under the weight of dread, a word of great affective force.[92] Her reaction, the physical shock described in II.1128–29, bears witness to the potent corporeal presence of the letter. The physical presence of her lover's desire in her hand transforms the *praeceptor*'s abstract situation into an event. The *ars dictandi* and *ars amandi* both have the capacity to constrain roles within their self-contained fictional worlds, but the delivery of the letter transforms that constraining authority into coercive force. Criseyde begins to "chaunge" not from Pandarus's patter but from the physical presence of the letter and the presence effect of the lover's body it evokes.[93]

Criseyde's response, "Scrit ne bille," makes plain her awareness of the coercive nature of this petition and the predetermined position it assigns her: a "bille" is a formal document, a plea, charge, petition, receipt, or contract.[94] The term discloses the dominating power of a lover's petition as codified by the clerical *praeceptor*. The love letter solicited and delivered by Pandarus echoes the erotodidactic texts produced by the apparatus of clerical power for the amusement of clerics.[95] Saying "Scrit ne bille," Criseyde expresses her hope that if she can keep herself out of the textual role dictated to her, if she can refuse the letter, she can maintain her autonomy and security, her "estat." This suggests a provisional limit to the constraining power of discourses—we can sometimes refuse the roles offered us if we see them for what they are. But Pandarus will not have that; he demonstrates that the controlling potential of discourse is

[92]The contrast with Boccaccio's depiction of the same scene is marked: "Stette Criseida temorosamente / sanza pigliarle; un poco il mansueto / viso cambiò" (*Il filostrato*, 2.110, in Giovanni Boccaccio, *Tutte le opere*, gen. ed. Vittore Branca [Milan: Mondadori, 1964]); where Boccaccio minimizes the affect ("un poco"), Chaucer heightens ("*Ful* dreadfully . . . *al* hir humble chere"; *TC*, 1128–30, emphasis added).

[93]Troilus has a very different reaction to the bodily presence of the letter—arousal (*TC*, II.1331–37). See Lerer, *Courtly Letters in the Age of Henry VIII*, 9.

[94]*MED*, s.v. *bille*, available at http://quod.lib.umich.edu/m/med/ (accessed June 7, 2012).

[95]We see a similar dynamic at work in the dialogues of *De amore* when a higher-ranked man is addressing a lower-ranked woman (1.6.166). See Moi, "Desire in Language," 407.

actuated by violence.[96] The fact that the letter is proxy for the lover's body gives an added charge to Pandarus's grabbing Criseyde and thrusting the letter down the front of her garment:[97]

> "But for al that that ever I may deserve,
> Refuse it nought," quod he, and *hente hir faste*,
> And in hir bosom the lettre doun he thraste[.]
> (II.1149–55; emphasis added)

Pandarus then secures the efficacy of this violation of Criseyde's self by daring her to reach into her gown and cast it away where people might see (II.1178). In *De amore*, secrecy is a way to secure a private domain for ladies to engage with lovers on equal or superior terms, protected from the violation of exposure.[98] Here, secrecy is instead enlisted by Criseyde's uncle as a technique to coerce her precisely through the fear of such a violation. Jill Mann points out how Troilus's mildness is achieved "by transferring the coercive elements in the wooing to Pandarus, who manipulates, coaxes, threatens, and deceives with unflagging energy."[99] Physical coercion, rather than a last resort when the rhetoric of seduction fails, is in fact the culmination of that rhetoric. Criseyde, like Cydippe, is compelled to read, and by reading is drawn, like it or not, into a "paynted proces" (II.425) that will yield defeat and dishonor all around.[100]

Criseyde's reaction to the letter itself reflects an effort to remain withdrawn; it is to Troilus's *epistolary style* rather than his message that she responds in order to keep the affair in the realm of textuality (II.1177–79).[101] But Pandarus has arranged for "a carefully controlled dose of

[96] Gumbrecht talks about power being a potential in discourse, whereas violence is "the actualization of power, that is, power as performance or as event." *Production of Presence*, 114.

[97] "Even without bearing in mind the letter's function as stand-in for Troilus, one recognizes in this scene a surrogate rape." Camargo, *The Middle English Verse Love Epistle*, 57.

[98] See *DA*, 2.7.18.

[99] Jill Mann, *Feminizing Chaucer* (Cambridge: D. S. Brewer, 2002), 83.

[100] Shoaf discusses the word *proces* as touching on the double aspect of Pandarus as mediator—both artist (painter or poet) and functionary (notary or lawyer). *Dante, Chaucer, and the Currency of the Word*, 116.

[101] We might understand Criseyde's retreat into textuality as a way to appropriate control for herself of the meaning of the process; as Gumbrecht puts it, "there is no emergence of meaning . . . that does not alleviate the weight of presence." *Production of Presence*, 90.

Troilus's physical presence" to ride past her window, drawing her out of the safety of pure textuality and compelling her to write him back.[102] Her letter roundly rejects his advances, announcing that she will love him only as a sister (II.1221–25). Her rejection may be "candour itself" but this is finally irrelevant.[103] When Pandarus returns her letter to Troilus, he glosses it as a "charm" for healing his sickness, and so makes it conform, regardless of her message, to the familiar script of seduction (II.1313–16). Criseyde's conscription is inevitable. The Ovidian notion that a woman's resistance to seduction is but "sweet, reluctant, amorous delay" (in Milton's phrase) informs Pandarus's coercive power.[104] Her role is prescribed by clerical discourses of which Pandarus is master.[105]

Troilus reads her letter over and over again, and, finally, takes the advice proposed by Ovid and elaborated by Boncompagno da Signa; he recognizes that any response from Criseyde, even a seeming refusal, equals her consent to his desire.

> But finaly, he took al for the beste
> That she hym wroot, for somewhat he byheld
> On which hym thoghte he myghte his herte reste,
> Al covered she the wordes under sheld.
> (II.1324–27)

This recalls the elaborate paraphrases for "no means yes" found in the erotodidactic tradition. Furthermore, Troilus's understanding of her very straightforward message as "wordes under sheld" recalls the allegoresis of secrecy, the *occulta signa* prescribed by the *Rota Veneris* (2.3). By imposing an allegorical meaning on her words, Troilus rewrites her intention and purpose. We see fulfilled the promise of the *Rota*'s dictator that his methods will teach the lover to *exordiri*, *narrare*, and *petere* the woman he desires—to compose her as a text. It is customary to distinguish Pandarus's "Ovidian pragmatism" from Troilus's "courtly idealism," but Troilus is tainted by the mediation he consents to use to serve his desire, as is further suggested by Pandarus's remaining in the room when Troilus and Criseyde have sex.[106] According to Carolyn Dinshaw,

[102] Camargo, *The Middle English Verse Love Epistle*, 55.

[103] McKinnell, "Letters as a Type of the Formal Level," 82.

[104] *Paradise Lost*, IV.311.

[105] Camargo likewise sees parallels with both *Ars amatoria* and Boncompagno's *Rota Veneris*; *The Middle English Verse Love Epistle*, 64.

[106] "[I]t should hardly surprise us that Troilus becomes an exact copy of his friend Pandarus"; Shoaf, "The Monstruosity in Love," 192.

"the narrator, Pandarus, and Troilus are all characterized as readers of feminine texts."[107] I suggest that they are writers too, seeking to make the woman into a text, to rewrite her own self-composition according to a familiar erotodidactic template.[108]

Conclusion: Chaucer as *Praeceptor amoris*

The consequences of Pandarus's game outlive its successful prosecution. To view seduction as a literary game of make-believe, an arena for rhetorical performance, is a kind of moral evasion in which *Troilus and Criseyde* implicates not only Pandarus and Troilus, but the narrator and even Chaucer himself. Calabrese argues in a Robertsonian vein that Chaucer's portrayal of Pandarus reveals the limitations of viewing erotic love as a game; these limitations are thrown into relief by the epic backdrop of doomed Troy and the transcendent realizations of a dying Troilus. This may be so, but I suggest that Pandarus's moral failures show how even earthbound love has its ethical demands.[109] The *Rota Veneris* is the virtuoso performance of a master rhetorician, directed not only toward inducing a listener to believe a certain thing, but also toward showing off, reveling in its own competence. This mode of rhetoric is not intended to be (despite Ovid's and Pandarus's advice) inconspicuous; verbal bravura is as much the intended outcome as persuasion. Boncompagno's performance weaves together multiple kinds of communicative competence: worldly experience in seduction, clerical expertise, and literary cultivation. This combination results in a masculine self-performance that is competitive and self-assertive. At the same time, in its excess, and in the incongruities among the different types of expertise on display, it is a clownish performance. James J. Murphy attaches to Boncompagno da Signa the epithet of "dictaminal buffoon" (if to defend him from it); perhaps he is reading Boncompagno backwards through Pandarus.[110] The Italian *dictator*'s persona is certainly a prototype of Chaucer's Pandarus, another self-performing clerical mediator obsessed with love and full of pedantic ostentation.

To the various psychosexual motives suggested to explain Pandarus's

[107] Dinshaw, *Chaucer's Sexual Poetics*, 29.

[108] "Her love does not arise ex nihilo but seems to entail subjection to a dominant discourse of late medieval culture." Mitchell, *Ethics and Eventfulness*, 42.

[109] Calabrese, *Chaucer's Ovidian Arts of Love*, 42–50.

[110] Murphy, *Rhetoric in the Middle Ages*, 362.

vicarious participation in his friend's seduction of his niece, let me add one more: he is fundamentally onanistic, but as a pornographer rather than a mere voyeur.[111] The story of seduction that begins in Book II and culminates in Book III, his *proces*, is the expression of his expertise, and he takes his pleasure in seeing his *proces* work, in the act of mediation itself, in the eros of writing. The carnal materiality of letters issues in the carnal love of Troilus and Criseyde. But the story does not end when the *proces* does; the material contingency of life invades the pleasure-garden of erotodidactic love, even as it does in the *Rota Veneris*, and Pandarus, like Boncompagno, can no longer control the story. If performance is understood only as the assumption of responsibility for communicative competence, Pandarus is a successful performer, but Chaucer, a consummate performer himself, suggests that a competence not responsible to its effects is morally inadequate.

Pandarus rejects this moral demand. As in the *Rota Veneris*, the narrative pressure of the letters and the mimetic depth of their represented subjects disrupt the generic formulas of dictaminal and erotodidactic treatises; consequently, as in the *Rota*, external contingencies (the fortunes of war, the machinations of Calkas and Diomede) disrupt the simple love plot. Unlike Boncompagno, however, Pandarus cannot wipe the slate clean and start a new story; he is not in charge of the fictional world in which he lives. In Mitchell's words, "fidelity to the event . . . remains always limited and compromised by generic understanding."[112] Pandarus is more beholden to his generic understanding than to the people overtaken by events. Loyal finally to the male desire on which his erotodidactic discourse depends, he would regard the resistant female subject as an aberration to be annihilated. He says to Troilus:

[111] See Sarah Stanbury, "The Voyeur and the Private Life in *Troilus and Criseyde*," *SAC* 13 (1991): 141–58; A. C. Spearing, *The Medieval Poet as Voyeur: Looking and Listening in Medieval Love-Narratives* (Cambridge: Cambridge University Press, 1993), 120–40. Shoaf points out the sexually self-gratifying character of Pandarus's ability as a fantasist in "The Monstruosity in Love," 191.

[112] Mitchell, *Ethics and Eventfulness*, 22; I am using performance here in the sense used by the linguistic anthropologists Richard Bauman and Charles Briggs as described by John Lucy: "performance . . . is a reflexive mode of communication which consists of the assumption of responsibility for displaying communicative competence, that is, for speaking well in socially appropriate ways. Recognition that one is assuming responsibility in this way is keyed or indicated by a confluence of signals in the verbal forms themselves rather than by the presence of a simple diagnostic mark." Lucy, "Reflexive Language and the Human Disciplines," 21, describing Richard Bauman and Charles Briggs, "Poetics and Performance as Critical Perspectives on Language and Social Life," *Annual Review of Anthropology* 19 (1990): 59–88.

> "If I dide aught that myghte liken the,
> It is me lief; and of this tresoun now,
> God woot that it a sorwe is unto me!
> And dredeles, for hertes ese of yow,
> Right fayn I wolde amende it, wiste I how.
> And fro this world, almyghty God I preye
> Delivere hire soon! I kan namore seye."
> (V.1737–43)

Pandarus's clerical mastery of the conventional discourses of love does not give him the knowledge to control events as they progress. Criseyde cannot be dictated, so he wills her destruction, and beyond this, he can say no more. In marked contrast to his previously bumptious and noisy performance, the narrator—for it is no longer Pandarus's narrative—leaves him for good, still and silent at last.

The discourse of Pandarus, like that of *Rota*'s dictator, is an art of seduction overwhelmed by the narratives its precepts generate. Pandarus, however, is only one learned mediator at work in *Troilus and Criseyde*. Another is the narrator, and the final one is Chaucer, who in relating the process of seduction, undertakes an ethical reevaluation of the literary role of the mediating cleric, the man whose mastery of textual, literary, and social discourse makes him likewise the master of love and seduction. If, as Lee Patterson wrote, the tales of Melibee and Thopas represent Chaucer's attempt to slough off two superannuated authorial roles, we might see Pandarus as another such role.[113] Once an innovative and culturally transformative figure, the learned *ioculator* and clerical *praeceptor amoris* is now domesticated and constricting, an inadequate cliché of literary authority.

Though he was a governmental administrator under Richard II, Chaucer does not identify his extraliterary role as clerk in the manner of his contemporaries Gower and Hoccleve, referring to himself by that term in only the highly artificial context of his invocation to Venus ("Whos clerc I am") in the proem to Book III of *Troilus and Criseyde*.[114] By calling himself a clerk of Venus, however, he does identify himself with Ovid,

[113]Lee Patterson, "'What Man Artow?': Authorial Self-Definition in *The Tale of Sir Thopas* and *The Tale of Melibee*," *SAC* 11 (1989): 117–75.

[114]This is a central topic of Andrew James Johnston, *Clerkes and Courtiers: Chaucer, Later Middle English Literature and the State Formation Process* (Heidelberg: Universitätsverlag C. Winter, 2001).

who is called "Venus own clerke" in *The House of Fame* (1487). While rejecting the role of the clerical-courtier as a dictaminal buffoon might have served the social jockeying of a shopkeeper's grandson at court, Chaucer the storyteller also had a compelling reason to reject it—fidelity to the *haeccitas*, the specificity and unrepeatability of the textual persons his narrative summoned, and out of honor for their material resistance. The fiction of the *Rota Veneris* is governed by the conceit that it is an instruction manual, and this fiction underlies Pandarus's self-delusion, revealed when set in the larger frame of *Troilus and Criseyde*. The final sidelining of Pandarus is not just a matter of *caritas* triumphing over *cupiditas*, Boethius over Ovid; it manifests Chaucer's changing moral and aesthetic conception of the role of a writer as a mediator.

As for letters, Chaucer gives the last one to Criseyde, writing Troilus from the Greek camp:

> Yet preye ich yow, on yvel ye ne take
> That it is short which that I to yow write;
> I dar nat, ther I am, wel lettres make,
> Ne nevere yet ne koude I wel indite.
> Ek gret effect men write in place lite;
> Th'entente is al, nat the lettres space.
> And fareth now wel. God have yow in his grace!
> La Vostre C.
> (V.1625–31)

Her letter ends with a letter that rejects the capability of letters to communicate. The signature initial belongs once more to her, aligns once more the indexical mark of the body with the symbol of her inviolable inner self. This, her "entente," is an uninterpretable mystery to Troilus, because he has run out of scripts to conform the letter to his desires:

> This Troilus this lettre thoughte al straunge
> Whan he it saugh, and sorwfullich he sighte;
> Hym thoughte it like a kalendes of chaunge.
> (V.1632–34)

This "chaunge" was set in motion when Pandarus urged on Criseyde the first letter, when all her "humble chere / Gan for to chaunge" (II.1130), but Criseyde no longer belongs to Pandarus's composition.

She concludes the poem's final letter with the letter C, recalling the formulaic blanks of the *Rota*'s model salutations: shall we supply Criseyde? Chaunge? Chaucer? The letter is another cipher, an *occulta signa*, unmediatable, concealing an "entente" that was never expressed because it was never asked for—not by Pandarus, not by Troilus. And not by Chaucer either, though he diffidently acknowledges this oversight, claiming that his sources do not tell him Criseyde's thoughts (III.575). In truth, Chaucer, like Boncompagno and Pandarus, is as constrained by the Ovidian script as his characters. The love story depends on the narrator's playing Pandarus, on Chaucer's acting as mediating *dictator*; he can displace the role onto Pandarus and then, for its moral error, sideline and silence his proxy author-in-the-text. But he cannot fully absolve himself from Pandarus. In the *Ars amatoria*, "the masculinities elicited in heterosexual performance are mocked for their excess" by Ovid's narrator, just as Pandaric masculinity is mocked in *Troilus and Criseyde* by the narrator.[115] But even if the *praeceptor*'s erotic writing of female subjection is bracketed by irony—by Ovid, Boncompagno, and Chaucer alike—all three authors indulge themselves no less in its pleasure.

[115] Desmond, *Ovid's Art and the Wife of Bath*, 44.

The Legend of Thebes and Literary Patricide in Chaucer, Boccaccio, and Statius

Leah Schwebel
Texas State University

CHAUCER'S REFUSAL TO NAME Boccaccio in *The Knight's Tale* and elsewhere in his poetry has often been interpreted as a strategic attempt to lend his writings more substantial authority.[1] As a recent author writing in a vernacular language, Boccaccio's name lacks the solemnity of a "Lollius," a "Corynne," or even an anonymous "old book." Critics have generally agreed, therefore, that Chaucer invents these sources for the same reason that medieval historiographers such as John of Salisbury or Guido delle Colonne feigned reliance on ancient *auctores* while camouflaging signs of recent invention: to bolster the authenticity and credibility of his works.[2] I want to propose in this essay

My sincere thanks to Fiona Somerset, David Coley, and David Benson, all of whom repeatedly read and commented on earlier versions of this paper. I am also grateful to *SAC*'s two anonymous readers, whose suggestions on my argument were both thorough and engaged.

[1] See especially Robert Edwards, *Chaucer and Boccaccio: Antiquity and Modernity* (Houndmills: Palgrave, 2002), 17; Donald R. Howard, *Chaucer: His Life, His Works, His World* (New York: Fawcett Columbine, 1987), 189–91; and C. David Benson, "The 'Knight's Tale' as History," *Chaucer Review* 3 (1968): 107–23. William E. Coleman, "The Knight's Tale," in *Sources and Analogues of the Canterbury Tales*, ed. Robert M. Correale and Mary Hamel, 2 vols. (Cambridge: D. S. Brewer, 2002), 2:87–247 (109) speculates that perhaps Chaucer's copy of the *Teseida* lacked Boccaccio's name. Critics have similarly attributed Chaucer's erasure of Boccaccio in *Troilus and Criseyde* to Boccaccio's insufficient authority. See especially George Kittredge, "Chaucer's Lollius," *Harvard Studies in Classical Philology* 28 (1917): 47–133 (49); Alastair Minnis, *Chaucer and Pagan Antiquity* (Cambridge: D. S. Brewer, 1982), 24–25; David Wallace, *Chaucer and the Early Writings of Boccaccio* (Cambridge: Cambridge University Press, 1985), esp. 152.

[2] To provide a few examples of this practice: John of Salisbury conjures up a pseudo-classical and fictional source-text, Plutarch's *Institutes of Trajan*, in the *Polycraticus* (V.2). Benoît de Sainte-Maure (although not a historiographer in the strictest sense of the word) minimizes his role in the creation of the *Roman de Troie* by presenting himself as a translator of ancient sources—in this case Dares's *De excidio Troiae historia* and Dictys's *Ephemeris belli Troiani*—despite his handsome elaboration of both texts (*Résumé du poème*). Guido delle Colonne relies almost singularly on the *Roman de Troie* for the *Historia destructionis Troiae*, yet he makes no mention of Benoit's text, purporting instead to

Studies in the Age of Chaucer 36 (2014):139–168

that Chaucer's erasure of Boccaccio has a separate origin and purpose. I suggest that Chaucer learns his aesthetic of erasure from Boccaccio, who playfully conceals his debt to Statius in the *Teseida* under the premise of translating an anonymous old book, vowing—with no small irony—that "no Latin author has told his story before."[3] As for why Boccaccio and Chaucer erase their sources, they do so in order to participate in a tradition of authorial usurpation practiced by the Latin epicists, to develop an epic genealogy for their poems. Unlike the medieval historiographers, then, who minimize signs of poetic license, Boccaccio and Chaucer call attention to authorial erasure as a literary trope, situating their vernacular poems in a classical tradition while suggesting their preeminence as modern poets writing in a new, literary language.

But when Boccaccio and Chaucer erase their sources, whom do they expect to notice? Questions of Chaucer's anticipated and actual reception have often framed the way we have discussed his engagement with his sources. Paul Strohm in particular reminds us to consider in any discussion of Chaucer's reception the poet's "consciousness both of an immediate audience . . . and an audience of posterity."[4] It is this second audience for whom I think Chaucer conceals his source. To clarify, I do not imagine that either Boccaccio or Chaucer expected all of his patrons and readers to pick up on the implications of this erasure. Rather, these poets—indeed, all poets—compose with their literary descendants in mind, the writers who will follow them and will invoke these same genealogical strategies to warrant their places in an ongoing literary tradition.[5] And if there is something patricidal about this behavior, there is also something suicidal about it, since Chaucer writes not only to efface

translate Dares and Dictys directly (*Prologus*). Geoffrey of Monmouth credits his information to the discovery of an invented *liber vetustissimus* (*Historia regum Britanniae*, I.1).

[3] "Una istoria antica . . . che latino autor non par ne dica." The Italian text is taken from *Tutte le opere di Giovanni Boccaccio*, gen. ed. Vittore Branca, 10 vols. (Milan: Mondadori, 1964), 2:254 (I.2); further quotations of the *Teseida* are from this edition. All English translations will be taken from Bernadette Marie McCoy, *The Book of Theseus: Teseida delle nozze d'Emilia* (New York: Medieval Text Association, 1974).

[4] Paul Strohm, "Chaucer's Audience(s): Fictional, Implied, Intended, Actual," *Chaucer Review* 18 (1983): 137–45 (138).

[5] To adopt Walter Ong's famous phrase, the poet "fictionalizes" an audience receptive to his rhetorical strategies (*Interfaces of the Word: Studies in the Evolution of Consciousness and Culture* [Ithaca, N.Y.: Cornell University Press, 1977], esp. 53–81). Or, in the words of Gian Biagio Conte, *The Rhetoric of Imitation: Genre and Poetic Memory in Virgil and Other Latin Poets*, ed. Charles Segal (Ithaca, N.Y.: Cornell University Press, 1986), 10, the poet "presupposes" and "establishes the competence of [his] Model Reader."

Boccaccio but also to be effaced by a worthy successor, an ambition we will see gratified by Lydgate. It is from this Oedipal series of erasures and un-erasures, of literary patricides and poetic resurrections, that poets understand their authorial legacies emerging. What this means for our present study is that Chaucer, and Boccaccio before him, would seem to conceive of literary lineage in both a retrospective and prospective sense. In mimicking Boccaccio's intertextual poetics, in other words, Chaucer not only binds his work to a previous literary tradition, but also takes steps to ensure his own perpetuity.

That we can trace a pattern of authorial obfuscation from Antiquity to the Middle Ages, or from Virgil to Lydgate, as I will do here, speaks to the efficacy of this device. In resituating Chaucer's famous occlusion of Boccaccio within a genealogy of erasure, I aim to add a new understanding of Chaucer's presentation of himself in relation to a literary tradition that includes not only his ancestors—contemporary and ancient—but, equally important, descendants, in a way that other poets may have appreciated even if we have missed it.

The Humility Topos and the "Little Book" Motif

I will begin with Boccaccio's envoy to the *Filocolo* (1339). In this final farewell to his poem, Boccaccio refers to Statius in a way that suggests his sincere reverence for the earlier poet, a display of modesty that becomes increasingly mediated as we peel back the layers of allusion to discover its literary precedents. Boccaccio cautions his "piccolo libretto" not to aspire to match Virgil in verse, Lucan and Statius in poems of war, Ovid in works of love, or Dante in vernacular poetry. The role of his little book, Boccaccio suggests, is to follow behind these authors as a "minor servant":

> Ché, con ciò sia cosa che tu da umile giovane sii creato, il cercare gli alti luoghi ti si disdice: e però agli eccellenti ingegni e alle robuste menti lascia i gran versi di Virgilio. . . . E quelli del valoroso Lucano, ne' quali le fiere arme di Marte si cantano, lasciali agli armigeri cavalieri insieme con quelli del tolosano Stazio. E chi con molta efficacia ama, il sermontino Ovidio seguiti. . . . Né ti sia cura di volere essere dove i misurati versi del fiorentino Dante si cantino, il quale tu sì come piccolo servidore molto dei reverente seguire.

[For since you were created by a humble youth, it is not for you to seek out higher places. So leave the great verse of Virgil to the excellent wits and vigorous minds. . . . And those verses of mighty Lucan, in which the fierce arms of Mars are sung, leave them to martial knights, along with those of Statius from Toulouse. And whoever loved with great purpose, let him follow Ovid of Sulmona. . . . And do not be concerned to aspire to be where the measured verses of the Florentine Dante are sung, whom you ought to follow very reverently as a minor servant.][6]

While this passage points toward Boccaccio's diverse literary influences, ranging from Ovid to Dante, it especially evokes the epilogue of the *Thebaid*, in which Statius asks his epic to trudge behind the *Aeneid* at a reverential distance: "vive, precor; nec tu divinam *Aeneida* tempta, / sed longe sequere et vestigia semper adora" ("Live, I pray, and essay not the divine *Aeneid*, but ever follow her footsteps from afar in adoration").[7] In a witty nod to his textual archetype, Boccaccio even cedes Statius a place among his own *bella scola*. Since Statius betrays no outward interest in outpacing Virgil, and nor does Boccaccio divulge a corresponding rivalry with Statius, Boccaccio would seem to place himself in a tradition of poets paying homage to their literary models. Nevertheless, both Statius's and Boccaccio's declarations of meekness are at odds with their overall presentation of themselves as poets of equal or superior rank in relation to their predecessors.

In the process of denying any rivalry between his own and Virgil's work, Statius recycles the language Virgil gives to Aeneas as he relates the loss of his wife Creusa: "et longe servet vestigia coniunx" ("and let my wife follow our steps afar").[8] Statius's echo of the *Aeneid* at the precise moment he announces its sovereignty over his poem complicates just such a gesture of humility. Rather than acknowledge his textual borrowing, Statius silently absorbs the language of the *Aeneid* into the fabric of his work, insinuating a desire to match Virgil, maybe even to

[6] The Italian text of the *Filocolo* is taken from Boccaccio, *Tutte le opere*, 1:674 (V.97). The English translation is by Donald Cheney, *Il filocolo* (New York: Garland Library of Medieval Literature, 1985), 470.

[7] Statius, *Thebaid*, XII.816–17, in *Statius*, ed. and trans. D. R. Shackleton Bailey, 3 vols. (Cambridge, Mass.: Harvard University Press, 2003), 3:308–9. The Latin texts of Statius's *Thebaid* and *Silvae*, as well as the English translations, are taken from this edition.

[8] The Latin text of the *Aeneid*, as well as the translation, is taken from *Virgil: In Two Volumes*, trans. H. Rushton Fairclough (Cambridge, Mass.: Harvard University Press, 1960), 1:342–43 (II.711). According to Michael Putnam, this passage indicates the "'inferiority' topos of poets' pronouncing their inability to compete with Virgil as Paragon" (Jan M. Ziolkowski and Michael C. J. Putnam, eds., *The Virgilian Tradition* [New Haven: Yale University Press, 2008], 59).

move beyond him as an archetype in verse.[9] Equally notable are the words that follow: Statius observes that fame is transient, passing from one poet to the next, and he consoles his *Thebaid* that "tibi si quis adhuc praetendit nubila livor, / occidet, et meriti post me referentur honores" ("if any envy still spreads clouds before you, it shall perish, and after me you shall be paid the honours you deserve").[10] Statius imagines that time will grant him due honor and fame, even if, at present, he must pay lip-service to the *Aeneid*, an admission that undermines his previous claim of Virgil's preeminence.[11] In the glare of this proviso, the grandeur of the *Aeneid* appears to stem from the temporary favor of the masses, and not from its intrinsic worth.

In a more explicit challenge to Virgil's poetic authority, Statius concludes an ode from the *Silvae* by claiming that his *Thebaid*

Multa cruciata lima
temptat audaci fide Mantuanae
gaudia famae.

[Tortured by much filing, essays with daring string the joys of Mantuan fame.][12]

Here Statius discharges his epic from the "etiquette of deference" to the *Aeneid* that we saw at play in the earlier work.[13] Instead, he twists his

[9] For a reading of Statius's use of allusion in the *Thebaid* to subvert the *Aeneid*, see Randall T. Ganiban's study, *Statius and Virgil: The "Thebaid" and the Reinterpretation of the "Aeneid"* (Cambridge: Cambridge University Press, 2007). See also Karla F. L. Pollman, "Statius' *Thebaid* and the Legacy of Vergil's *Aeneid*," *Mnemosyne* 54 (2001): 10–24.

[10] *Thebaid*, 3:308–9 (XII.818–19).

[11] See Robert Edwards, "Medieval Literary Careers: The Theban Track," in *European Literary Careers: The Author from Antiquity to the Renaissance*, ed. Patrick Cheney and Frederick A. de Armas (Toronto: University of Toronto Press, 2002), 108, who writes of this passage that Statius eschews open rivalry to "[wager] on time as the medium of both fame and vindication. He denies outright envy only to introduce poetic competition; and in the image of his poem's reverently trailing behind the *Aeneid* ('longe sequere'), we glimpse the revisionary poet stalking his source, marking its steps, and measuring the distances still unfulfilled between them."

[12] *Silvae*, 1:290–91 (IV.7.25–28). Virgil was born near Mantua; "the joys of Mantuan fame" is the *Aeneid*.

[13] Steven Hinds, *Allusion and Intertext: Dynamics of Appropriation in Roman Poetry* (Cambridge: Cambridge University Press, 1998), 93. See also Kathleen Coleman's edition of *Silvae*, IV. In her commentary on the phrase "audaci fide" (IV.7.27), Coleman notes that whereas in the epilogue of the *Thebaid* Statius was "displaying conventional modesty in presenting his new work before the public, here the circumstances are different" and he can take "legitimate pride in its success" (*Statius: Silvae IV* [Oxford: Clarendon Press, 1988], 204).

words from the *Thebaid* ("nec tu divinam *Aeneida tempta*") to imply a new relationship between himself and Virgil in which both poets stand on equal footing: "*temptat* audaci fide Mantuanae / gaudia famae"—attempt Virgilian fame. A second ode addressed to his father reflects a similar ambition. Statius writes, "non posthabuisset Homero, / tenderet aeterno <et> Pietas aequare Maroni" ("Piety mayhap would have accounted (me) not inferior to mighty-mouthed Homer and striven to match (me) with immortal Maro").[14] Tempering his pride in his poetry with a father's expected indulgence of his son, Statius places himself on a par with the poetic exemplars of western civilization. It would seem that his earlier prostration before Virgil was at least partly ceremonial, since in these odes Statius vies for equivalence.

Like Statius's initial deference to Virgil, Boccaccio's words of praise for Statius in the *Filocolo* corrode under scrutiny. After concealing his extensive debt to Statius under the cover of translating an "istoria antica," in the envoy to the *Teseida* (1339–41), Boccaccio declares himself first to sing in the Italian vernacular "the toils endured for Mars":

> Poi che le Muse nude cominciaro
> nel cospetto degli uomini ad andare,
> già fur di quelli i quai l'esercitaro
> con bello stilo in onesto parlare,
> e altri in amoroso l'operaro;
> ma tu, o libro, primo a lor cantare
> di Marte fai gli affanni sostenuti,
> nel volgar lazio più mai non veduti.

[Since the Muses began to walk unclothed before men's eyes, there have been those who employed them, with graceful style in virtuous discourse, while others used them for the language of love. But you, my book, are the first to bid them sing in the vernacular of Latium what has never been seen thus before: the toils endured for Mars.][15]

As early as the Renaissance, readers recognized that Boccaccio's assertion of primacy responds to Dante's call for an Italian poet of arms in *De vulgari eloquentia*. Listing the three subjects worthy of poetic treatment as love, virtue, and arms, Dante notes that while Cino da Pistoia

[14] *Silvae*, 1:350–51 (V.3.62–63).
[15] *Teseida*, 661 (XII.84); trans. McCoy, 329.

has written on love, and himself on virtue, "arma vero nullum latium adhuc invenio poetasse" ("I find no Italian up to now who has any poetry on deeds of arms").[16] Boccaccio steps forward to fill this vacancy in the *Teseida*, transposing his vision of a vernacular trinity onto the topography of literary giants to whom he paid homage in the *Filocolo*. Where Virgil, Statius, Lucan, and Ovid once reigned, now stand Dante, Boccaccio, and Cino, with Boccaccio claiming the title of martial poet for himself. But in making this move, Boccaccio departs from the trinity of poets suggested in *De vulgari eloquentia*, occluding the names of Dante and Cino in his work and acknowledging only his own vernacular poetic achievement. Thus presenting the *Teseida* as first in its class among an anonymous majority, Boccaccio privileges his accomplishment over even that of his Italian peers.

Yet Boccaccio does not dispense with his humble façade from the *Filocolo* entirely in the *Teseida*. As before, he instructs his poem to "pay homage, as to an elder, to each one who has preceded you, as you will give cause for those who come after you to do"—advice that reprises his command to the *Filocolo* to "follow reverently" behind his models. However, in this advice lurks the hint of a retraction. Not only do his predecessors remain unnamed here, but, as with Statius's insistence in the *Thebaid* that time will grant him due fame, Boccaccio also insinuates that he will eventually rise to a position of prominence. His language is that of generational progression: by treating other books as elders, he will set an example for those who follow, and younger poets will at a later point keep pace behind *him*. Like Statius before him, Boccaccio identifies a pattern of allusive usurpation, and he develops Statius's move to overtake Virgil in the *Thebaid* by expunging Statius from his succession of literary models in his own *Teseida*. Literary fame, Boccaccio implies, is at least partially a textual construction, achieved through the open imitation and appropriation of past literary models, and crystalized by later poets' participation in similar patterns of homage and ascendancy. Boccaccio cements Statius's position within an authorial lineage and articulates his own future in that same lineage with a single poetic gesture.

[16]The Latin text of *De vulgari eloquentia* is taken from Italo Borzi's *Dante: Tutte le opere*, 2nd ed. (Rome: Newton, 2010), 1017–70 (1045 [II.2]). The English translation is by Marianne Shapiro, *De vulgari eloquentia: Dante's Book of Exile* (Lincoln: University of Nebraska Press, 1990), 72.

"I will be the first to Sing (what has been Sung before)": Revolutions of Primacy in Antique Poetry

By claiming to be "the first to sing of arms in the vernacular" Boccaccio recycles another refrain associated with *translatio studii*, in which poets announce their primacy as translators of Greek culture and then crown themselves with the laurel. In *Georgics*, III, for example, Virgil declares himself first to bring the poetic muses from Greece to Italy:

> Primus ego in patrium mecum, modo vita supersit,
> Aonio rediens deducam vertice Musas;
> primus Idumaeas referam tibi, Mantua, palmas.

[I first, if life but remain, will return to my country, bringing the Muses with me in triumph from the Aonian peak. First I will bring back to you, Mantua, the palms of Idumaea.][17]

Paradoxically, Virgil's claim of "firstness" recapitulates Ennius's earlier declaration that it was *he* who first brought the Greek Muses to Italy, as Lucretius reports to us in *De rerum natura*:

> Ennius ut noster cecinit, qui primus amoeno
> detulit ex Helicone perenni fronde coronam
> per gentis Italas hominum quae clara clueret.
>
> [As our loved Ennius sang, who first brought down
> from lovely Helicon garlands ever green
> to grow in fame wherever Italians live.][18]

Later in the poem, Lucretius echoes this refrain—only this time with regard to his *own* primacy ("et hanc primus cum primis ipse repertus / nunc ego sum in patrias qui possim vertere voces" ["I've been found the first of all, / able to tell them in our native tongue"]).[19] Indeed, Horace

[17] The Latin text of the *Georgics*, as well as the translation, is taken from *Virgil: In Two Volumes*, 1:176–77 (III.10–12).

[18] Titus Lucretius Carus, *De rerum natura libri sex*, ed. Cyril Bailey (Oxford: Clarendon Press, 1950), 1 (I.117–19). The translation is by Frank O. Copley, *The Nature of Things* (New York: Norton, 1977), 3. For an excellent reading of these lines, see Hinds, *Allusion and Intertext*, 52–55.

[19] *De rerum natura*, 11 (V.336–37); trans. Copley, 120.

claims for himself the same achievement in *Odes*, III.30.10–16; he insists that he was first to bring Greek song to Italy ("princeps Aeolium carmen ad Italos"), and demands to be crowned with the laurel.[20]

Each poet's declaration of primacy relies on, yet undermines, its earlier models. As Steven Hinds says of the *Georgics*, while on the one hand "Virgil's claim to be first is 'authorized' by its association with Ennius' claim," on the other hand "the Ennian precedent can be argued precisely to disqualify the Virgilian claim," since only one poet can truly be first.[21] Virgil's recycling of Ennius's words thus binds his work to a literary tradition at the same time as it calls attention to his own imposture, for if we admit the allusion then we concede the lie. While seemingly self-abnegating, this paradox tells us something about how Hellenizing revolutions operate in Roman poetry; as Hinds explains, "they operate through a revision of previous Hellenizing revolutions, a revision which can be simultaneously an appropriation and a denial."[22] Through the percussive repetition of a literary trope, in other words, a poet can at once invoke and subvert the authority of his models.

Boccaccio glances back at the literary pantheon he established in the *Filocolo* only to disable it in the *Teseida*. His poetic enterprise now paramount, he portrays himself as the sole representative of martial song. The exemplary authors of the *Filocolo*—so imposing in the former poem—here remain unnamed. At the completion of his literary odyssey Boccaccio reaches out to claim his prize. Guided by the light of the starry bear, he awaits the garlands of the laurel:

[20] *The Odes of Horace*, ed. and trans. David Perry (New York: Farrar, Straus, and Giroux, 1997), 254. Horace makes a similar claim to primacy in his *Epistles* (I.19.23). See also Propertius, *Elegies*, III.1. For a modern analogue, we can turn to Milton's invocation in Book I of *Paradise Lost*. Milton claims that his song will pursue "things unattempted yet in Prose or Rhime" (I.13–16), a literal translation of Ludovico Ariosto's promise in *Orlando furioso*, "Cosa non detta mai in prosa nè in rima" (I.2). Moreover, Ariosto himself is alluding to Matteo Maria Boiardo's *Orlando innamorato*, in which the narrator declares at the conclusion of Book II that his reader will hear things never before recounted in verse or prose (XXX.1). For a discussion of the textual history of this line, see especially Daniel Shore, "Things Unattempted . . . Yet Once More," *Milton Quarterly* 43 (2009): 195–200. Many thanks to William Robins for bringing this example to my attention.

[21] Hinds, *Allusion and Intertext*, 54. On the motif of "firstness" in Roman poetry see also Tony Woodman, "*EXEGI MONVMENTVM*: Horace, *Odes* 3.30," in *Why Horace?: A Collection of Interpretations*, ed. William Scovil Anderson (Wauconda: Bolchazy-Carducci Publishers, 1999), 205–22, esp. 11–12.

[22] Hinds, *Allusion and Intertext*, 55.

Però che i porti disiati
in sì lungo peleggio già tegnamo,
da varii venti in essi trasportati,
le vaghe nostre vele qui caliamo,
e le ghirlande e i don meritati,
con l'ancore fermati, qui spettiamo,
lodando l'Orsa che con la sua luce
qui n'ha condotti, a noi essendo duce.

[Since we have now reached the harbors for which we yearned on such a long voyage while we were borne there by varying winds, we now furl our wandering sails, and with anchors set fast, we await the garlands and the merited rewards, praising that starry Bear that has been our leader, guiding us by its light.][23]

With nothing to pay homage to but the laurel crown, and no one at this point to keep pace behind but the North Star, Boccaccio, the sole identifiable figure among a sea of forgotten sages, claims more for his poem than Statius dared apportion to his *Thebaid.* Whereas Statius couched an argument for equivalence in the verses of his *Silvae*, Boccaccio claims for his *Teseida* poetic dominion.

A Tradition of *Fingendo* and the *Genealogia deorum gentilium*

Hidden beneath a seemingly benign statement of subservience or a declaration of firstness lies a rhetoric of allusive usurpation that allows Boccaccio to latch onto a prior literary tradition while declaring its members antiquated. Boccaccio thus suggests his movement beyond a Statian model by mirroring—and developing on—Statius's earlier treatment of Virgil, praising Statius in one poem only to erase him conspicuously from a second, and following an anonymous "istoria antica" instead of naming his source. In the glosses to the *Teseida*, Boccaccio flags his concealment of Statius in a new way: he takes credit as the author not only for his own material but also for material deriving from the *Thebaid.* In the gloss to Book I.14, for example, Boccaccio claims that his explanation of the shield of Tydeus, which he describes in Book I as pinned to a tree in a forest outside Thebes, is his poetic invention, despite its origins in *Thebaid*, II.704–26. Boccaccio explains in the gloss that the

[23] *Teseida*, 662 (XII.86); trans. McCoy, 329.

author of the *Teseida* "vuole . . . mostrare, *poeticamente fingendo*, qual fosse la cagione che movesse Teseo contra le donne amazone a fare guerra" ("wants . . . to show by a poetic fiction the provocation that moved Theseus to make war against the Amazon women").[24] The provocation, Boccaccio clarifies, is Tydeus's victory over fifty of Eteocles' men, the knowledge of which inspires Theseus to besiege Scythia. On the one hand, by suggesting that the event that sets the cogs of the siege of Thebes in motion likewise spurs the Amazonomachy, Boccaccio anchors his *Teseida* to the *Thebaid* by way of teleological necessity. Yet, on the other hand, by describing this event as his own poetic fiction—"poeticamente fingendo"—Boccaccio severs this passage from the moorings of its Statian source.[25] *Fingendo* in this context implies not only authorial agency but also innovation, both of which are antithetical to the historiographer's cause.[26] We could not ask for a clearer indication that the "istoria antica" is not merely an authenticating device than Boccaccio's emphasis on his *fictio* in the glosses.

Boccaccio's celebration of his "poeticamente fingendo" anticipates his later work, the encyclopedic *Genealogia deorum gentilium*, in which he defends poetry before the *vulgus ineptum* and imperious censors alike.[27]

[24] *Teseida*, 258 (I.14, gloss); trans. McCoy, 48.

[25] In the *Thebaid*, it is Athena, not Mars, to whom Tydeus dedicates the spoils of his conquest (II.704–6), and Tydeus fastens his victims' armor, not his own shield, to the tree (II.710–12). These changes would seem minor; however, because Boccaccio does not acknowledge the *Thebaid*, they take on the aspect of an alternative account, and one that stands in contrast to the original and even discredits it. It is also worth noting that the Statian passage makes a direct comparison between Athena and Mars—with Mars held as the inferior god (II.715–25). By substituting Athena for Mars, aligning himself with Tydeus, meanwhile reversing the priorities of the Statian scene, Boccaccio inscribes his own superior power as the patron poet of arms. The shield that Tydeus consecrates to Mars—a symbol of victory in the *Teseida*—here signifies Boccaccio's erasure of Statius, with the *istoria antica* taking Statius's place as the authority on Thebes.

[26] *Fingendo* derives from the Latin verb *fingere*, which means "form out of original matter, create," "compose (poems and other literary works)," and "invent." But it could also mean "make up, feign" and "produce insincerity." P. W. Glare, ed., *Oxford Latin Dictionary* (Oxford: Oxford University Press, 1996), 702–3 (s.v. *fingere*, senses 2; 6[a and b]; 9[a and b]; and 10[b]).

[27] Boccaccio lists these as his opponents in the opening of Chapter 2: "Concurrent, ut fit, ad spectaculum novi operis non solum vulgus ineptum, sed et eruditi convenient homines. . . . Sunt hi, ut reliquum sinamus vulgus, homines quidam insani, quibus tanta loquacitas est et detestabilis arrogantia, ut adversus omnia quorumcunque probatissimorum hominum presumant clamoribus ferre sententiam" (Around my book, as usual at the sight of a new work, will gather a crowd of the incompetent. The learned will also attend. . . . There are, among others in this crowd, certain madmen so garrulous and detestably arrogant that they presume to shout abroad their condemnation of everything that even the best man can do). Boccaccio, *Genealogie deorum gentilium*, XIV.2.1, 2.2, in *Tutte le opere*, Vol. 7/8, 1360, 1362. All Latin citations are taken from Boccaccio,

First vindicating poetry against claims that it is unprofitable, insignificant, and immoral, Boccaccio suggests that innovation is the very foundation of his craft. He grants that poets invent stories; however, he qualifies this in that they invent stories in the service of a greater truth. We must therefore look beyond the superficial fiction to see the deeper, more profound, truth within.[28] First of all, Boccaccio establishes the "honorable origins" of poetry: " 'Fabula' igitur . . . a 'for, faris' honestam sumit originem, et ab ea 'confabulacio,' que nil aliud quam 'collucutio' sonat" ("the word *fabula* has an honorable origin in the verb *for*, *faris*, hence 'conversation' [*confabulatio*], which means only 'talking together' [*collocutio*]").[29] Boccaccio then offers an example from the Gospel of Luke, in which two disciples spoke together, and Christ himself came to walk with them. Boccaccio concludes that if it is a sin to compose stories (*fabulari*), then it is a sin to converse (*confabulari*), which, he adds, only the biggest fool would admit.[30] Boccaccio then makes a particular case for the value of epic poetry. Of the four kinds of *fabula*, he explains, there is one that

> Hystorie quam fabule similis est. Hac aliter et aliter usi poete celebres sunt. . . . Et hec si de facto non fuerint, cum communia sint esse potuere vel possent.
>
> [Is more like history than fiction, and famous poets have employed it in a variety of ways. . . . If the events they describe have not actually taken place, yet since they are common, they could have occurred, or might at some time.][31]

Naming Homer and Virgil as among the "famous poets" who have employed this style of historical writing, and adding Christ himself to the list ("my opponents need not be so squeamish—Christ, who is God, used this sort of fiction again and again in his parables!"),[32] Boccaccio

---

Tutte le opere, Vol. 7/8. The English translation is taken from *Boccaccio on Poetry*, trans. Charles G. Osgood (Princeton: Princeton University Press, 1930), 17–18; all further translations are from this edition. We do not have an exact date for Boccaccio's completion of this work. See Jon Solomon's new edition (in the I Tatti Renaissance series), *Genealogy of the Pagan Gods* (Cambridge, Mass.: Harvard University Press, 2011), 1:viii–ix for the *Genealogia*'s history.

[28] Petrarch justifies poetry in similar terms in *Familiares*, X.4. I am extremely grateful to Michael Papio for his help and suggestions on this section.

[29] *Genealogie deorum gentilium*, 1412 (XIV.9.3); trans. Osgood, 47.

[30] *Genealogie deorum gentilium*, 1412 (XIV.9.4); trans. Osgood, 47.

[31] *Genealogie deorum gentilium*, 1414 (XIV.9.7); trans. Osgood, 48–49.

[32] The editor notes that the phrase ("Nec fastidiant obiectores . . . usus est") follows in the margins of cod. Plut. LII 9 (an autograph manuscript), but is suppressed in the *Vulgata*; *Genealogie deorum gentilium*, 1707 n. 99. Osgood includes these words in the body of the text of his translation, 49.

advocates convincingly for poetry that takes on the guise of historical reality. On a grander scale, he makes an argument for *fingendo* as the common element connecting poets in a glorious and transcendent display of "confabulation."

To this end, Boccaccio's marriage of the two terms *poetes* and *fingere* to describe his reference to the shield of Tydeus is a happy one, since his *fingendo* positions him in a tradition of illustrious poets. In fact, shortly after confessing his own recourse to poetic pretending in the glosses to the *Teseida*, Boccaccio reiterates the term "poeticamente fingendo" to describe the fiction of the ancients. The phrase recurs in his annotation on the temple of Mars, which, Boccaccio explains, is housed in the frigid mountains of Thrace to accommodate the god's hot temperament. Boccaccio derives this description from *Thebaid*, VII.34–42, where, on Jupiter's orders, Mercury makes an unpleasant journey to the seat of this frozen shrine. But Boccaccio does not credit his material to Statius. Instead, he ascribes it to the fiction of the ancients:

> Scrivono fingendo i poeti che la casa di Marte, dio delle battaglie, sia in Trazia, a piè de' monti Rifei. Alla quale fizione volere intendere . . . che l'ira e il furore s'accende più fieramente e più di leggiere negli uomini ne' quali è molto sangue, che in quegli ne' quali n'è poco.
>
> [Poets feign that the house of Mars, god of battles, is in Thrace, at the foot of the Ripheus mountains. This fiction is to be understood to mean that . . . wrath and fury are more violently and more easily enkindled in men in whom there is much blood than in those in whom there is little].[33]

Boccaccio's qualification of this account as *fictio*—and his allegorical/humoral interpretation of the location of the house of Mars in Thrace—heightens our awareness that, at least in the *Teseida*, poetic authorities are not invoked only to lend a degree of authenticity. Instead, Boccaccio appeals to *i poeti* to call attention to their, and his own, *fingendo*.[34] What is more, Boccaccio's recycled use of the term *poeticamente fingendo*, earlier used to highlight his own art and subsequently adapted to describe the *fingendo i poeti*, positions him in a line-up of ancient poets as a fellow

[33] *Teseida*, 259 (I.15, gloss); trans. McCoy, 49.

[34] Cf. Barbara Nolan, *Chaucer and the Tradition of the "Roman Antique"* (Cambridge: Cambridge University Press, 1992), 165, who claims that Boccaccio aligns himself here with his classical forebears, and with the French authors of the *romans antiques*, so as to cloak himself in the "authority of the philosophers educated in the liberal arts."

author, versed in the art of *inventio*. Boccaccio's *fingendo* is justifiable vis-à-vis a poetic standard of "confabulation"—his predecessors made up stories in the service of their poetry, and so, too, shall he. And in this circumstance, where his "poeticamente fingendo" is used, as with the "istoria antica," to showcase his concealment of the *Thebaid*, implicit in Boccaccio's definition of poetry is the practice of not only *inventio* but also, in some cases, *deletio*.

Lest we fail to notice the many signs of the *Thebaid*'s erasure, Boccaccio dedicates a final tribute to his silenced source. In an addendum to the poem, Boccaccio labels his verses the "Teseida di nozze d'Emilia," *Theseid* of the Nuptials of Emilia, a Latinate title deliberately reminiscent of the *Thebaid*, and the closest Boccaccio comes to naming his epic model in the whole work. Announcing that his *Theseid* will bring him "in ogni etate fama immensa" ("vast fame in every age"),[35] Boccaccio recalls Statius's final farewell to his epic at the same time as he disqualifies it: "iam . . . praesens tibi Fama benignum / stravit iter coepitque novam monstrare futuris" ("Already . . . Fame has strewn a kindly path before you and begun to show the new arrival to posterity").[36] Like claims of primacy, declarations of literary immortality have a definite expiration date—they wither at the behest of a usurping heir. Accordingly, Boccaccio's pronouncement of his *Theseid*'s everlasting fame not only evokes the silenced *Thebaid*, in which Statius predicts his eternal glory, but also influences how we interpret Chaucer's subsequent elision of Boccaccio, which, as I will demonstrate, is meant to revisit Boccaccio's earlier erasure of Statius. In his challenge to his predecessor, Boccaccio perpetuates a tradition of authorial expurgation, and thus sets in motion the course of his own literary exile. Moreover, in extending this maneuver by concealing Boccaccio's influence under the pretense of translating "olde stories" (the English equivalent of Boccaccio's "istoria antica"), Chaucer corroborates Boccaccio's place in this tradition, and so offers himself as Boccaccio's ideal reader.[37]

The Silenced Author of Chaucer's *Knight's Tale*

In his encounter with the *Teseida*, Chaucer witnesses Boccaccio erase Statius under the premise of translating a fabricated ancient book.

[35] *Teseida*, 664 (*Riposta delle Muse*); trans. McCoy, 331.

[36] *Thebaid*, 3:306–7 (XII.812–13).

[37] Geoffrey Chaucer, *The Riverside Chaucer*, gen. ed. Larry D. Benson, 3rd ed. (Boston: Houghton Mifflin, 1987), I.859; Chaucer also claims to rely on "olde bookes," or

Unlike other writers whom Chaucer may have observed doing something similar, however, Boccaccio introduces his *istoria antica* at the precise moment in which acknowledging Statius as his principal source would be entirely apt, even desirable: his account of the siege of Thebes and its aftermath, for which he draws on the *Thebaid* so extensively, and with such frequency, that we cannot ignore its influence.[38] Instead of capitalizing on the *Thebaid*'s very real authoritative clout, however, Boccaccio implies the *un*-reliability of Statius's epic by treating it as other writers treat their more dubious material: he buries it beneath the assertion that he is translating an anonymous, ancient source. Chaucer, I argue, mimics and develops this trope of erasure. There is a distinct progression from Statius, who presents Virgil as his superior in the *Thebaid* yet implies his own equivalence in the *Silvae*; to Boccaccio, who names Statius as the exemplary poet of arms in the *Filocolo* only to omit all mention of him in the *Teseida*; to Chaucer, who sustains his erasure of Boccaccio throughout his poems, despite relying on him repeatedly as his principal source.

Yet Chaucer would appear unsatisfied with simply perpetuating a device found in the works of his predecessors. He thus reveals a further interest in recovering Boccaccio's silenced source from the *Teseida* by celebrating Statius as the predominant authority on Thebes. While not exclusive to *The Knight's Tale*, this maneuver is most prominent in this poem, in which Chaucer indicates the imposing influence of the *Thebaid* from the outset.[39] Nearly all of the authoritative manuscripts include a passage from *Thebaid*, XII as a motto or gloss to the first segment:

"bookes olde," three times in *The Knight's Tale*, at I.1198, 1463, and 2294. All quotations from Chaucer's works will be from this edition and cited in the text.

[38] On the relationship between the *Teseida* and the *Thebaid* see especially David Anderson, *Before the Knight's Tale: Imitation of Classical Epic in Boccaccio's "Teseida"* (Philadelphia: University of Pennsylvania Press, 1988), 38–191.

[39] To provide a few examples, in *The House of Fame* Chaucer records Statius as the sole author holding up the "fame of Thebes" (1460–62). In the *Anelida and Arcite*, a shorter work beginning as a translation of the *Teseida*, Chaucer corrects Boccaccio's earlier suggestion that "no Latin author" had told his story before by claiming to translate an "olde storie, in Latyn which I finde" (10). Chaucer then names "Stace," as well as "Corynne," as one of the two *auctores* whom he will follow (21), suggesting, as Barbara Nolan points out, that Chaucer recognized Boccaccio's debt to Statius in the *Teseida* and attempted a "similar exercise in creative imitation" (*Chaucer and the Tradition of the "Roman Antique,"* 247). Chaucer names "Stace" as one of the poetic models of whom he will "kis the steppes" in the epilogue to the *Troilus*, a passage modeled on the envoy to the *Filocolo*. In recuperating Statius to this assembly of literary exemplars, Chaucer expunges Boccaccio from his own line-up of authors. His adulation of Statius thus involves—even hinges on—the implicit suppression of his Boccaccian source.

Iamque domos patrias, Scithice post aspera gentis
Prelia, laurigero [subeuntem Thesea curru
laetifici plausus missusque ad sidera vulgi
clamor et emeritis hilaris tuba nuntiat armis.]

[And now Theseus drawing near his native land in laurelled car after fierce Battling with the Scithian folk (is heralded by applause and the trump of warfare ended)].[40]

With this reference to the *Thebaid*, Chaucer signals his deviation from Boccaccio, whose poem, though saturated with allusions to the epic, at no point includes a direct citation of the Latin text. Nor is the passage itself insignificant; these lines mark the introduction in the *Thebaid* of Theseus, a figure who remains peripheral to the main action of the epic even as he plays a necessary role in its conclusion. As Chaucer himself will do, Statius all but forgoes mention of Theseus's whereabouts prior to his battle with Creon, referring to the Amazonomachy only in passing in his description of the hero's triumphal return home.[41] Boccaccio, on the other hand, devotes the first two books of the *Teseida* to Theseus's attack on Scythia, his marriage to Hippolyta, and finally his assault on King Creon. This passage thus contains the seed from which Boccaccio develops the opening of his poem. In beginning with these lines, Chaucer reveals to us the process of Boccaccio's poetic invention, evoking both the original context of Theseus's journey to Thebes and Boccaccio's amplification of this storyline. Perhaps in the spirit of restoration, Chaucer folds the excess material back into its Statian proportion, a mere footnote to a chapter on Theban history.[42] Choosing Theseus's return home for his starting-point, Chaucer relegates the Amazonomachy to

[40] Chaucer takes this citation from *Thebaid*, XII.519–22. The Latin passage is also included in the *Anelida and Arcite*, between lines 21 and 22.

[41] Anderson, *Before the Knight's Tale*, 201, argues that Chaucer's alterations to the *Teseida* "generally reflect a concern with preserving and accentuating the *Thebaid*-like structure and themes of Boccaccio's narrative." With regard to Chaucer's use of *abbreviatio*, Anderson notes that Chaucer "shortens [the *Teseida*] in ways that maintain, or even increase, the underlying patterns from the *Thebaid*" (202).

[42] Cf. Stephen H. Rigby, *Wisdom and Chivalry: Chaucer's "Knight's Tale" and Medieval Political Theory* (Leiden: Brill, 2009), 135, who sees Chaucer's editorial adjustment as a way of ennobling Duke Theseus's achievement: "in massively compressing his source, Chaucer does not have to confront the problems involved in having the chivalrous Theseus overcome a kingdom of women, something which might be considered . . . an achievement of 'litel worschepe.' "

the margins of his poem. He then declares the battle (and, obliquely, the first two books of the *Teseida*) extraneous.

If Chaucer follows Statius in beginning his story after the conquest of the Amazons, then he is unique in showcasing this material before he discards it. Opening with the invocation of fictional, ancient source-texts—"whilom, as olde stories tellen us" (I.859)—he launches into an account of the duke's Scythian interlude, describing

> The grete bataille for the nones
> Bitwixen Atthenes and Amazones;
> And how asseged was Ypolita,
> The faire, hardy queene of Scithia;
> And of the feste that was at hir weddynge;
> And of the tempest at hir hoom-comynge.
> (I.879–84)

The sum of this story, the Knight implies, is of little consequence. He casually dismisses this prefatory material as "to long to heere" (I.875; an amusing assessment, considering that the final detail of this summary, the "tempest at hir hoom-comynge," is Chaucer's own invention) before elaborating on the things he would have said, were it not for the time constraints of his journey. "I *wolde* have toold yow fully . . . How wonnen was the regne of Femenye," he insists for a second time (I.876–77; emphasis added). Yet although the Knight flouts the structural integrity of the *Teseida* by omitting the poem's beginning, he hardly gives the rejected portion a quiet burial. Rather, in first presenting and then retracting his offer to speak of the siege against the Amazons, Chaucer calls attention to the restructuring of his source, rendering the very things he deems unnecessary conspicuous by their absence.[43]

Having opened his story with a passage from the *Thebaid* and then justified his truncation of the *Teseida* based on the shortness of time, in the second part of *The Knight's Tale* Chaucer takes his erasure of Boccac-

[43] For Chaucer's aesthetic of omission in *The Knight's Tale*, see Mark Sherman, "The Politics of Discourse in Chaucer's *Knight's Tale*," *Exemplaria* 6 (1994): 87–114. Sherman explains that *The Knight's Tale* "must be read . . . with an eye for what is *not* articulated and is in fact blatantly suppressed." By cataloguing the things he *will not* tell us, moreover, the Knight "heighten[s] the reader's awareness of excluded narratives to such a degree that the unsaid exerts greater narrative force than the said, that the utterance stands in the shadow of what it obfuscates" (91, 94).

cio to a whole new level. He names "Stace of Thebes and these bookes olde" as his source for a scene deriving from the *Teseida*, in which Emilia/Emelye goes to the Temple of Diana to pray:

> Smokynge the temple, ful of clothes faire,
> This Emelye, with herte debonaire,
> Hir body wessh with water of a welle.
> But hou she dide hir ryte I dar nat telle,
> But it be any thing in general;
> And yet it were a game to heeren al.
> To hym that meneth wel it were no charge;
> But it is good a man been at his large.
> Hir brighte heer was kembd, untressed al;
> A coroune of a grene ook cerial
> Upon hir heed was set ful fair and meete.
> Two fyres on the auter gan she beete,
> And dide hir thynges, as men may biholde
> *In Stace of Thebes and thise bookes olde.*
> (I.2281–94; emphasis added)

Chaucer follows the *Teseida* rather closely here, embellishing his source only in the Knight's hesitancy to provide the specifics of Emelye's ritual, and in his attribution of the episode to "Stace."[44] Still, Chaucer's reference to Statius is not the outright falsification that it would seem. Boccaccio himself derives the details of Emilia's ritual from a corresponding scene in the *Thebaid*, in which the prophet Tiresias performs a series of rites in a forest sacred to Diana with the hope of ascertaining the outcome of the war (*Thebaid*, IV.416–73).[45] When his initial efforts at necromancy fail, Tiresias warns Apollo that he is not above invoking darker forces:

> Ne tenues annos nubemque hanc frontis opacae
> spernite, ne, moneo: et nobis saevire facultas.

[44] *Teseida*, 478 (VII.72–74). In the original Italian, in addition to perfuming the temple, crowning her hair with cereal oak, and lighting two pyres, Emilia sacrifices turtle doves and lambs, draining the blood from their bodies and tossing the entrails and viscera of the dead animals into the fire. Her proceedings closely echo the process of Tiresias's sacrifice in the *Thebaid*. Chaucer removes these more gruesome details from her rites.

[45] For a concise description of some of the parallels between these two episodes, see Anderson, *Before the Knight's Tale*, 80.

scimus enim [et] quidquid dici noscique timetis
et turbare Hecaten (ni te, Thymbraee, vererer)
et triplicis mundi summum, quem scire nefastum.
illum—sed taceo: prohibet tranquilla senectus.

[Do not, I warn you, do not contemn my thinning years and the cloud upon my darkened brow. I too have means to be cruel. For I know whatever you fear spoken or known. I can harry Hecate, did I not respect you, Lord of Thymbra, him too, highest of the triple world, whom to know is blasphemy. Him—but I hold my peace: tranquil eld forbids.][46]

At this point, Manto interrupts her father, as the earth opens to reveal a scene from the underworld. Among these phantoms are mythical figures in varying states of horror and despair: Semele holding her womb; Agave in a state of Bacchic frenzy, chasing her son Pentheus; Actaeon, horns protruding from his brow, fighting off the hounds that still tear at his limbs; and Niobe, madly tallying the bodies of her dead children. Finally, the old Theban King Laius arrives, with a neck wound marking the patricide of Odysseus, to prophesize that Thebes alone will survive this bloody war. These visions, each more frightening than the last, set the tone for the final books of the *Thebaid*, in which the siege grinds toward its inevitable, tragic conclusion. As the model for Emilia's ritual in the *Teseida*, however, the episode is strikingly inappropriate.

Clearly a transgressive figure, Tiresias is a curious prototype for Emilia. Still, Boccaccio transfigures this scene of horror and necromancy into one of piety and devotion; if Tiresias is arrogant and impetuous, then Boccaccio's Emilia sacrifices "più divotamente" (most devoutly) of all three who sacrifice to the gods.[47] Pious and reverent, she displays not only respect for Diana but also an acceptance of her fate, asking the goddess,

Se' fati pur m'hanno riservata
a giunonica legge sottostare,
tu mi dei certo aver per iscusata,
né dei però li miei prieghi schifare.

[If the Fates have decreed that I be subjected to the law of Juno, you must certainly forgive me for it. Do not reject my prayers on that account.][48]

[46] *Thebaid*, 2:544–45 (IV.512–17).
[47] *Teseida*, 477 (VII.70); trans. McCoy, 180.
[48] *Teseida*, 481 (VII.83); trans. McCoy, 182.

Even as Boccaccio opts to tell a less sinister tale, however, Emilia's rites retain the prior whiff of necromancy. In addition, by modeling her devotion on a necromantic ritual, Boccaccio makes himself complicit in Tiresias's original trespass, conveying by proxy what is wrong to know. In his commentary on the *Thebaid* (of which we know Boccaccio possessed a copy), Lactantius Placidus notes numerous allusions in this passage to scenes of necromancy from Virgil's *Aeneid*, Ovid's *Metamorphoses*, Lucan's *Pharsalia*, and Seneca's *Oedipus*. This foundation of references makes it all the more difficult for Boccaccio to insist on Emilia's piety, since her ritual follows a long line of occult behavior. As though in response to this tradition, the Knight pares down the episode to a minimum, tepidly insisting that "how [Emelye] dide hir ryte *I dar nat telle*," although it is no doubt a "game to heeren al".[49] It is as if he wishes to distance his tale from its transgressive origins as much as possible. Perhaps as a point of compromise, the Knight directs us to "Stace of Thebes and thise bookes olde" for the specifics of how Emelye "dide hir thynges." And while we will not discover the niceties of Emelye's ritual in the *Thebaid*, we do find its root, and, accordingly, the identity of Boccaccio's "old book," in Tiresias's original trespass.

Naming the ultimate source of his source but not his immediate author, Chaucer participates in a kind of genealogical leapfrog, further associating Statius with the phrase under which Boccaccio concealed him in the *Teseida*, "thise bookes olde." This mention of Statius demonstrates the extent to which Chaucer has enhanced a trope of erasure learned from his predecessors. In reviving Boccaccio's silenced author in the figure of "Stace," Chaucer renders this device more conspicuous, more metapoetic, than it appeared in previous forms, so as to show clearly the tradition of occlusion whence he came. Still, I suspect that Chaucer discovered the idea of crediting a Boccaccian passage to "Stace" in *Teseida*, VI, in which Boccaccio likewise passes over his immediate source in favor of naming an earlier model. This maneuver is relatively muted in the *Teseida*. Boccaccio describes the arrival of noblemen to the tournament in which Palamon and Arcite will fight, and among these men is "Idas the Pisan." As Boccaccio explains in the glosses, the character of Idas is based on Virgil's description of Camilla (*Aeneid*, VII.803–11): "della leggereza che qui pone l'autore che avea questo Ida, scrive

[49] Coleman, "The Knight's Tale," 2:93, claims that by citing Statius, "the remote source for the passage," Chaucer is "making the point that Statius is available in two forms in the *Knight's Tale*: directly and at second-hand via the *Teseida*."

Virgilio di Camilla, e quindi fu tolto ciò che qui se ne scrive" ("of the swiftness that the author here ascribes to Idas, Virgil writes of Camilla, and what is written here is taken from him").[50] As it so happens, this reference to Virgil is the only explicit mention of an ancient poet in the entire *Teseida*: a suggestive detail, because the figure of Idas the Pisan is original to Statius, not Virgil.[51] Recently crowned with an Olympic wreath, Idas is a fearsome competitor in the games of *Thebaid*, VI.550–645, triumphing over Parthenopaeus in the first footrace. Boccaccio clearly invokes this figure, dwelling on Idas's recent triumph in the Olympic games, and describing his exploits in the race (*Teseida*, VI.52–53). Yet no scholar has thought to look beyond Camilla for a textual model, because Boccaccio names Virgil as his source (although Piero Boitani notes that Boccaccio's citation of Virgil here is "curious" for the very reason that he "never acknowledges his much more substantial debt to Statius").[52] In naming Virgil, however, Boccaccio brings to the surface of his poem a Virgilian prototype that remains unacknowledged by his author. Not only does Statius's Idas possess qualities reminiscent of Virgil's Camilla—Idas, for example, runs as fast as a speeding arrow (*Thebaid*, VI.596–97), and Camilla can outrun the wind (*Aeneid*, VII.806–7)—but the games of *Thebaid*, VI are themselves modeled on Virgil's description of the athletic tournament in *Aeneid*, V, as Lactantius Placidus informs us.[53] Given how closely these authors were reading

[50] *Teseida*, 436 (VI.53, gloss); trans. McCoy, 163. Coleman, "The Knight's Tale," 2:113, suggests that Chaucer's version of the *Teseida* may have lacked Boccaccio's original commentary. However, his suggestion is primarily based on negative evidence—what Chaucer would have "responded to in some way" if he had found it in his manuscript. Coleman ultimately suggests that the "most prudent conclusion regarding the question of Boccaccio's glosses is that the case is not proved" (2:113–14).

[51] While the name of Idas is common in epic poetry, the figure of Idas the *Pisan*, an Olympian who competes in a footrace, is particular to the *Thebaid*. See Johannes Jacobus Smolenaars's commentary on *Thebaid*, VII (Leiden: Brill, 1994), 266, which lists these examples of other figures with this name: *Iliad*, IX.558; *Aeneid*, IX.575 (Trojan); X.351 (Thracian); *Metamorphoses*, V.90; *Fasti*, V.701 (Argonaut).

[52] Piero Boitani, *Chaucer and Boccaccio* (Oxford: Society for the Study of Mediaeval Languages and Literature, 1977), 27. Anderson, *Before the Knight's Tale*, 115–16, mentions Statius's Idas in his discussion of Boccaccio's games, yet he claims that Boccaccio translates only Virgil here.

[53] "PRIMVS SVDOR EQVIS: Vergilius <Aen. V 66>: 'prima citae classis ponam certamina Teucris.' " R. D. Sweeney, ed., *Lactantius Placidus in Statii Thebaida commentum: Anonymi in Statii Achilleida commentum. Fulgentii ut fingitur Plancidas super Thebaiden commentariolum*, Vol. 1 (Stuttgart and Leipzig: B. G. Teubner, 1997), 406 (VI.296). For Boccaccio's use of Lactantius, and the existence of a copy of the *Thebaid* containing Lactantius's commentary in Boccaccio's possession, see Anderson, *Before the Knight's Tale*, 4, 38 n. 1.

each other, it is likely that Boccaccio was aware of Statius's debt to the *Aeneid*, and that he names Virgil as his source so as playfully to allude to this debt. Chaucer appears to have recognized this maneuver and amplified it in his own poem. If Boccaccio discreetly credits Virgil for a figure taken from the *Thebaid* in the glosses to his poem, then Chaucer closely translates a passage from the *Teseida* before misattributing it twice; first, to Boccaccio's occluded author, "Stace," and second to the proxy Boccaccio had invented to perform this occlusion, "thise bookes olde."

The consideration and humor Chaucer puts into concealing his source suggests that he anticipated an audience who would recognize the intricacies of his intertextual poetics. I imagine it was Chaucer's anticipation of just such an audience that led him to connect his erasure of Boccaccio in *The Knight's Tale* with his similar occlusion of Boccaccio in other works, most explicitly in the *Troilus*. For example, Chaucer gives the exiled Arcite of *The Knight's Tale* the alias of "Philostrate," Chaucer's silenced Boccaccian source for the *Troilus*, instead of the name assigned to him in the *Teseida*, "Penteo" (IV.3).[54] Perhaps it is no accident, then, that (Ph/)Filostrato(e)/Arcite is quite literally "buried" by the end of the work, with Mars, Boccaccio's patron god of the *Teseida*, enlisted to guide his soul home (I.2815), and a "coroune of laurer grene" placed on his brow (I.2875). This final detail—the laureation of Philostrate—may even be Chaucer's way of paying homage to his occluded author without explicitly naming him. In the epilogue to the *Troilus*, moreover, Chaucer repurposes the envoy from the *Filocolo* to praise the very author whom Boccaccio erased in the *Teseida*. Chaucer directs his "litel bok" to kiss the steps of Virgil, Ovid, Homer, Lucan, and Statius (V.1786–92), unceremoniously ousting Boccaccio from his own line-up of authors to make room for the exiled "Stace," meanwhile usurping Boccaccio's post as the "sixth of six" poets.[55]

But it is not Boccaccio's role as "poet of arms" that Chaucer covets; in fact, Chaucer makes explicit elsewhere in the *Troilus* that he would prefer *not* to sing of war.[56] Instead, it is Boccaccio's status as an interme-

[54] There is some debate on the chronology of *The Knight's Tale* and the *Troilus*. Yet, the fact that the two poems share many lines speaks to the proximity, perhaps even overlap, of their composition. See Vincent DiMarco, "Explanatory Notes for the *Knight's Tale*," in *The Riverside Chaucer*, 826.

[55] See David Wallace, *Chaucer and the Early Writings of Boccaccio* (Woodbridge: D. S. Brewer, 1985), 50–53, for a discussion of poets naming themselves sixth of six authors.

[56]
And if I hadde ytaken for to write
The armes of this ilke worthi man,

diary poet—the vernacular arbiter in a line-up of ancients—that Chaucer seeks to assume, and in doing so establish his place in an epic tradition. Note that Chaucer removes not only Boccaccio but also Dante from his line-up of literary models, severing Boccaccio's connection to the classical *auctores*. This second elision makes room for a new vernacular poetics. Again in the *Troilus*, Chaucer stresses the very *Englishness* of his poem:

> And for ther is so gret diversite
> In Englissh and in writyng of oure tonge,
> So prey I God that non myswrite the,
> Ne the mysmetre for defaute of tonge;
> And red wherso thow be, or elles songe,
> That thow be understonde, God I biseche!
> (V.1793–98)

In a business where being *myswriten* is an occupational hazard, Chaucer no doubt intends his appeal for comprehension to be taken quite literally, but his plea for his book to be "understonde," "wherso thow be [read], or elles songe," also announces "oure tongue" as a literary language—a language that is accessible and coherent to all.[57] Chaucer then directs the *Troilus* for correction to his *English* counterparts, "moral Gower" and "philosophical Strode," casting aside the Latin poets and their "corsed olde rites" (V.1856, 1857, 1849). In a poem where the principal source receives no mention, the importance of this dedication cannot be overemphasized. Naming himself poet of love (V.1769), Strode poet of philosophy, and Gower author of moral works, Chaucer rewrites Dante's list of worthwhile literary subjects as love, philosophy, and virtue, removing not only Boccaccio but also the entire category of martial poetry from this list. The effect of this dedication, of course, is to establish an English equivalent of the Florentine *tre corone*.

Anchoring his *Troilus* in a classical past yet ultimately suggesting the primacy of a new vernacular literature, Chaucer performs a maneuver

---

> Than wolde ich of his batailles endite;
> But for that I to writen first bigan
> Of his love, I have seyd as I kan—
> (V.1765–69)

[57] Although we can only speculate on Chaucer's knowledge of *De vulgari eloquentia*, his plea for the *Troilus* to be understood echoes Dante's insistence on the superiority of Italian based on its universal capacity to be understood (*De vulgari eloquentia*, I.1).

similar to Boccaccio in his Theban poem. After elevating a standard of ancient literary models in the *Filocolo*, Boccaccio suggests a corresponding, even predominant, Italian literary tradition in the *Teseida*, evoking the memory of his ancient models *in absentia*. In the epilogue to the *Troilus*, Chaucer, in turn, develops an intricate web of allusions to his Italian forebears, Dante and Boccaccio, incorporating references to the *Commedia*, the *Filocolo*, the *Filostrato*, and the *Teseida* in a span of less than 100 lines. Far from acknowledging his literary debts here, however, Chaucer removes the names of Dante and Boccaccio from his list of authorial influences. He presents his poem as a distinctly English work following in the footsteps of the classical *auctores*, "Virgile, Ovide, Omer, Lucan, and Stace," whom he names only to condemn for their "corsed olde rites." Finally, Chaucer looks forward to an English posterity, inviting his friends, patrons, and readers to receive—and in Gower and Strode's case, correct—his work. Chaucer parades his literary models before us, but in a way that requires our attention to the prevalence of his poetry in relation to previous writings.

Go, Little Quire

I will conclude this study with Lydgate, but before doing so I will invoke an example of authorial occlusion from the writings of Chaucer's near contemporary, Petrarch. This example, concerning Petrarch's famous silence toward Dante in his writings, and Virgil's earlier silence toward Homer, suggests the existence of a pattern of authorial concealment outside a series of interconnected works on Thebes, and corroborates what I imagine to be poets' motivation behind perpetuating this trope: to position themselves within a genealogy of erasure, and, in the process, to locate their works within an illustrious tradition of great writings.

In *Familiares*, XXI.15 (1359), Petrarch responds to Boccaccio's suggestion that perhaps his frequent recommendation of Dante rankled with the older poet by denying jealousy of any man, including Virgil and Homer, but especially not Dante, who writes for the "ydiotas in tabernis et in foro."[58] In the course of this letter, Petrarch gestures at Dante multiple times, yet he never once names him. This is typical

[58] Francesco Petrarca, *Le familiari*, ed. Vittorio Rossi and Umberto Bosco, 4 vols. (Florence: G. C. Sansoni, 1933–42), 4:94–100 (XXI.15). Further quotations are from this edition.

behavior for Petrarch, who, despite engaging with Dante consistently in his poetry, avoids mentioning him throughout.[59] As Giuseppe Mazzotta notes, were it not for his reticence to name Dante, there would be nothing in this letter that would lead us to doubt Petrarch's sincerity.[60] One year following this exchange, however, Petrarch makes abundantly clear that his silence toward Dante is not accidental—to the contrary, it bespeaks his profound understanding of authorial erasure as a literary device.

In a separate letter addressed to the deceased Homer, *Familiares*, XXIV.12 (1360), Petrarch defends Virgil for neglecting to mention the Greek bard anywhere in his writings, drawing us "irresistibly . . . to the implied homology" between these two instances of authorial erasure.[61] Petrarch concedes that Virgil's behavior does, on the surface, appear extraordinary. Lucan, Flaccus, Ovid, Juvenal, and Statius all acknowledge their debt to Homer, while Virgil, overladen by the weight of Homer's spoils, does not.[62] Nor is Virgil consistent in his ingratitude; indeed, he courteously mentions other poets, including his contemporaries, Varus and Gallus, which, Petrarch claims, Virgil never would have done if he were possessed by jealousy. Still, Petrarch cautions Homer not to draw the obvious conclusion—that is, that Virgil's refusal to name him was a deliberate attempt to undermine his poetic authority. What happens next is rather remarkable: Petrarch offers Homer a clearly fallacious explanation for Virgil's silence, deflecting, rather than engaging in, a legitimate conversation on authorial borrowing and

[59] Petrarch names Dante only twice in all his poetry, and both times in conjunction with other vernacular love poets writing for the vulgar masses. On these instances, see especially Kevin Brownlee, "Power Plays: Petrarch's Genealogical Strategies," *JMEMSt* 35 (2005): 467–88.

[60] Giuseppe Mazzotta, "Petrarch's Dialogue with Dante," in *Petrarch and Dante: Anti-Dantism, Metaphysics, Tradition*, ed. Zygmunt G. Barański and Theodore J. Cachey, Jr. (Notre Dame: University of Notre Dame Press, 2009), 181.

[61] Ibid. This letter was to an unknown correspondent, in response to a letter written in Homer's name; yet Petrarch addresses the recipient as Homer throughout. Aldo Bernardo explains that Petrarch shared his letters, and especially those addressed to the ancients, with his literary friends. We know, for example, that Boccaccio was allowed to copy certain letters from *Familiares*, XXIV, Petrarch's series of letters to the ancient poets. See Aldo Bernardo, "Introduction," in Francesco Petrarch, *Rerum familiarium libri: I–VIII* (Albany: State University of New York Press, 1975), xxiii.

[62] Petrarch, *Le familiari*, 4:258 (XXIV.12). The translation of this letter is taken from *Francesco Petrarca: Letters on Familiar Matters. Rerum familiarium libri XVII–XXIV*, trans. Aldo Bernardo (Baltimore: Johns Hopkins University Press, 1985), 342–50 (45); further translations are taken from this edition. (Although Homer is named in the *Juvenalia*, these poems are thought to be apocryphal, and not by Virgil at all.)

occlusion. Petrarch claims that Virgil was reserving for Homer a place of honor in his poetry, but unfortunately died before he could grant him this tribute:

Posuisset, michi crede . . . nisi mors impia vetuisset. Licet autem alios ubi occurrit atque ubi commodum fuit annotasset, tibi uni, cui multo amplius debebat, non fortuitum sed certum certoque consilio destinatum reservabat locum. Et quem reris, nisi eminentiorem cuntis atque conspectiorem? Finem ergo preclarissimi operis expectabat, ibi te suum ducem tuumque nomen altisonis versibus laturus ad sidera.

[He would have done so, believe me . . . were it not that death interfered. Though he mentions others where it is opportune and convenient, for you alone, to whom he was much more indebted, he was reserving a special place selected after careful consideration. And what was this, do you suppose, if not the most prominent and distinguished place of all? He thus was waiting for the end of his outstanding work, where he intended to exalt your name to the heavens as his guide in sonorous verses.][63]

To substantiate his claim, Petrarch points to the *Thebaid* as an example. As Virgil took Homer as his model, so too was he chosen by Statius as a model for the *Thebaid*, and yet Statius did not acknowledge Virgil until the very end of his work: "nec tamen ingenue ducem suum nisi in fine poetici itineris recognovit" ("yet he did not openly acknowledge him as his guide except at the end of his poetic journey"). Of course, Statius's mention of Virgil at the end of his epic belies a complicated program of erasure of his own, as we have seen, and Petrarch acknowledges this in his phrasing: "illic tamen bona fide totum grati animi debitum benemerite persolvit Eneydi" ("it was [only] at the close that he openly and in good faith paid the full debt of his grateful mind to the *Aeneid*").[64] Rather than support his case in defense of Virgil, then, in petitioning the *Thebaid* Petrarch aggravates any cause for Homer's resentment. He implies that Virgil's silence was not only deliberate, but it was also recognized and perpetuated by a successor.

Petrarch uses his letter to Homer to establish a clear precedent for his reticence to name Dante, and so to align himself with a classical

[63] *Le familiari*, 4:259 (XXIV.12); trans. Bernardo, 346.
[64] *Le familiari*, 4:259 (XXIV.12); trans. Bernardo, 346.

tradition of occlusion. He implies a correlation between himself and Virgil, and between Dante and Homer, all the while playing up the unique implications of his own situation: as Petrarch is still among the living, his silence toward Dante cannot be explained—however ironically—by an early death.[65] This is not to suggest that Petrarch's distaste for Dante's poetics was disingenuous, or that he lacked an "all too real desire to . . . eclipse [Dante] and cancel his presence," but rather that he relied on an existing trope of erasure to act on these propensities.[66] In other words, Petrarch solicits our attention to a notable example of erasure from a classical past to corroborate his own silence. In doing so, he affiliates himself with his literary predecessors, meanwhile suggesting that his erasure of Dante is intentional.

I have included this example from the *Familiares* because it points to the existence of a trope of erasure beyond the specific strand that I have followed in this study. Moreover, it suggests that poets rely on one another not only for their material but also for their very method of authorial engagement. As Petrarch conjures up an example of literary occlusion from Antiquity to gloss his silence toward Dante, so Chaucer deposes Boccaccio using Boccaccio's own poetics of intertextuality, expanding on a trope of erasure adapted from his predecessors to render this excision complete and multifaceted.

Turning at last to the fifteenth century, we see that Chaucer's greatest reader, John Lydgate, frequently employs a strategy of erasure in his engagement with Chaucer. We need look no further than the *Siege of Thebes*, Lydgate's added Canterbury tale, for an example of this. Writing his poem as a preface to *The Knight's Tale*, Lydgate restores to the *Siege* the material contained in the first two books of the *Teseida*, which Chaucer had dismissed as "to long to heere." At the point when Lydgate's narrative would intersect with the Knight's, moreover, he indulges in a little *praeteritio* of his own, summarizing the parts of the story he would have told if they did not fall beyond the scope of his narrative. Instead,

[65] Nor is Dante the only poet whom Petrarch erases. Andrew Laird, "Re-inventing Virgil's Wheel," in *Classical Literary Careers and Their Reception*, ed. Philip Hardie and Helen Moore (Cambridge: Cambridge University Press, 2010), 150, points us toward Petrarch's "strategic occlusion" of Virgil, his "clear model" for the *Africa*. Wherever in the *Africa* "one might expect references to the story of the *Aeneid* to prompt an overt or positive acknowledgement of its poet," he notes, "that expectation is confounded" (147).

[66] Mazzotta, "Petrarch's Dialogue with Dante," 181–82.

Lydgate directs us to his "mayster Chaucer," and to the beginning of the "Knyghtys Tale," for these details.[67]

But this reference constitutes the sole mention of Chaucer in the entire *Siege of Thebes*. Although Lydgate alludes implicitly to Chaucer as the "floure of poetes thorghout al Breteyne" in line 40 of the preface, he does not actually *name* Chaucer until the very end of the poem. This omission, which prompted A. C. Spearing to suggest that the "implicit claim of the *Siege* is that in it Lydgate *becomes* the father whose place he usurps," recapitulates Statius's deferred acknowledgment of Virgil to the epilogue of the *Thebaid*.[68] Moreover, it is made all the more striking by Lydgate's frequent references to Boccaccio throughout his poem. Each time invoked as a source or authority, "Bochas" is named no fewer than seven times in the *Siege*, a gesture that calls attention to Lydgate's sustained silence toward Chaucer, and echoes Chaucer's previous treatment of Boccaccio and Statius.[69]

Lydgate experiments with a strategy of elision elsewhere, naming Chaucer among a succession of illustrious poets in the *Fall of Princes* only to erase him from a similar catalogue in the *Life of Saint Alban and Saint Amphibal*. In the first case, openly alluding to the epilogue of the *Troilus* and its literary antecedents, Lydgate identifies Chaucer as the most excellent of his literary predecessors:

> I nevir was acqueynted with Virgyle,
> Nor with the sugryd dytees of Omer
> Nor Dares Frygius with his goldene style,
> Nor with Ovyde, in poetrye moost entieer,
> Nor with sovereyn balladys of Chauceer
> Which among alle that euere wer rad or songe,
> Excellyd al othir in our Englysh tounge.[70]

[67] *John Lydgate: The Siege of Thebes*, ed. Robert R. Edwards (Rochester: TEAMS, 2001), lines 4501, 4524. James Simpson, "'Dysemol daies and fatal houres': Lydgate's *Destruction of Thebes* and Chaucer's *Knight's Tale*," in *The Long Fifteenth Century: Essays for Douglas Gray*," ed. Helen Cooper and Sally Mapstone (Oxford: Clarendon Press, 1997), 15–33 (29), notes that this maneuver forces us to reinterpret *The Knight's Tale* through the lens of the *Siege*, reinserting Chaucer's text into an "unequivocally historical, political narrative; it equally places the most severe constraints on whatever glimpses of prudential wisdom the *Knight's Tale* might have seemed to offer."

[68] A. C. Spearing, "Renaissance Chaucer and Father Chaucer," *English* 34 (1985): 1–38 (26).

[69] These instances are as follows: lines 199, 213, 1541, 3171, 3201, 3510, 3541.

[70] John Lydgate, *The Fall of Princes*, ed. Henry Bergen, 4 vols., EETS e.s. 121–24 (London: Oxford University Press, 1924–27), IX.3401–7.

Although Lydgate would seem to exempt himself from this pantheon of great authors by denying any affiliation with its members ("I nevir was acqueyted with . . ."), in "endorsing Chaucer's claim as the first 'poet' of stature to 'kiss' Parnassan steps," Lydgate "firmly enters his own 'poetrye' into this extraordinary company" with what Christopher Cannon aptly describes as only "ostensible modesty."[71] But Lydgate takes this strategy of self-authorization one step further in the *Life of Saint Alban and Saint Amphibal*. Here, he recapitulates a similar succession of authors from the *Fall of Princes*, claiming that he lacks the poetic skills of Lucan, Virgil, Homer, Cicero, and Petrarch, only this time he *omits* Chaucer from the list. The implication is that now it is Lydgate who is sixth of these six great authors, and who excels "al othir in our Englysh tounge":

> I nat acqueyntid with Musis of Maro,
> Nor with metris of Lucan nor Virgile,
> Nor sugrid ditees of Tullius Chithero,
> Nor of Omerus to folwe the fressh stile,
> Crokid to clymb over so hih a stile,
> Or for to folwe the Steppis Aureat
> Off ffranceis Petrak, the poete laureat.[72]

Lydgate's omission of Chaucer from his succession of literary models whose steps he will follow is accentuated in the following line, with a reference to Chaucer's poem, *The House of Fame* ("The golden trumpet of the hous of ffame, / . . . / Hath blowe ful fer the knyhtly mannys name").[73] Presented without mention of its author, this reference may show Lydgate cheekily complying with the narrator of *The House of Fame*'s request to remain anonymous after witnessing Lady Fame's arbitrary dispensation of either glory or slander to her petitioners. When questioned, Chaucer refuses to identify himself so that "no wight have my name in honde" (1877). (Although, since earlier in the same poem Chaucer names himself [729], we may take this demonstration of humility lightly.)

Nor is this the first time that Lydgate excises Chaucer from a cata-

[71] Christopher Cannon, *The Making of Chaucer's English: A Study of Words* (Cambridge: Cambridge University Press, 1998), 185.

[72] John Lydgate, *The Life of Saint Alban and Saint Amphibal*, ed. J. E. Van der Westhuizen (Leiden, Brill: 1978), 8–14.

[73] Ibid., 15–17.

logue of his authorial models. In the *Mumming for the Mercers of London*, Lydgate names a succession of six poets: Cicero, Macrobius, Virgil, Ovid, Petrarch, and Boccaccio (29–33). Lydgate's lineage includes Boccaccio, but it leaps gracefully over Chaucer, an omission that has been read by Maura Nolan as Lydgate's attempt to suggest his unmediated relation to a European poetic tradition.[74] But perhaps, in light of Chaucer's naming of Statius but not Boccaccio, and Boccaccio's naming of Virgil but not Statius, more central to Lydgate's purpose than the tradition Nolan has identified is one of authorial erasure. This may not accord with our perception of Lydgate as a poet plagued by anxiety, more likely to follow Chaucer slavishly than to exploit his poetics, but it would suggest that Lydgate deeply understood the implications of Chaucer's refusal to name Boccaccio, and that he perpetuated a trope of concealment in this and other works so as to affiliate his poems with those of his predecessors. Indeed, this perspective dovetails with the increasing scholarly impulse to see Lydgate as a canny, even playful, interlocutor of his English and Italian sources.[75] At the very least, the repeated acts of erasure committed by (and performed upon) Statius, Boccaccio, Chaucer, and Lydgate—acts, we might say, of deliberate literary patricide—remind us that authorial occlusion need not signify a poet's concern over his source's inadequacy, but rather can be used to indicate the active tradition whence he came, and which will continue long after him. Indeed, while Oedipus may now give his name to a psychological complex, we would do well to remember that he existed first as a character in an "olde storye" about Thebes.

[74] Maura Nolan, *John Lydgate and the Making of Public Culture* (Cambridge: Cambridge University Press, 2005), 103.

[75] See, for example, Robert Meyer-Lee, *Poets and Power from Chaucer to Wyatt* (Cambridge: Cambridge University Press, 2007); Jennifer Summit, *Memory's Library* (Chicago: University of Chicago Press, 2008); and Mary C. Flannery, *John Lydgate and the Poetics of Fame* (Cambridge: D. S. Brewer, 2012).

Practices of Satisfaction and *Piers Plowman*'s Dynamic Middle

Ryan McDermott
University of Pittsburgh

IAN MCEWAN'S NOVEL *Atonement* seems to end with the scene of its invention, the moment its fictional author, Briony Tallis, begins to write the book we have just read. She writes in order to exonerate her sister's lover, the man she has fatefully and wrongly accused of rape, before his conviction in the court of law can irreversibly ruin his life: "She knew what was required of her. Not simply a letter, but a new draft, an atonement, and she was ready to begin."[1] It turns out that the story we have read was meant to set the legal record straight and restore justice. However, the book does not end there. It begins again on a new leaf, where Briony confesses, now in the first person, that the people she injured had died long before they could enjoy the relatively happy reunion narrated in the previous thirty pages. Briony has been revising her story, her confession, for fifty-nine years, always too late. Her decision to write a happy ending came late in life and seemed to her the only way to satisfy the "love of order" that inspired her to write as a girl and that "shaped the principles of justice."[2] "As long as there is a single copy," Briony writes near the real end of the book, "a solitary transcript of my final draft, then my spontaneous, fortuitous sister and her medical prince survive to love."[3] Briony has to settle for giving literary immortality to those she has wronged because literature by her definition cannot atone. "There is no one, no entity or higher form that [the novelist] can appeal to, or be reconciled with, or that can forgive her."[4]

Atonement's ending registers Briony's grief not only for unreconciled

[1] Ian McEwan, *Atonement* (New York: Doubleday, 2001), 330.
[2] Ibid., 7.
[3] Ibid., 371.
[4] Ibid.

Studies in the Age of Chaucer 36 (2014):169–207

sin, but also for the loss of a cosmos in which a sinner can make satisfaction even if the injured party cannot forgive. Even as Briony recognizes the medieval distinction between satisfaction directed to God and legal satisfaction, or restitution, directed to an offended party, her quandary is particularly modern. She stands near the extreme end of a history of satisfaction: after Gratian and Peter Lombard had formalized it as one of the three parts of penance;[5] after Thomas Cranmer's prayer book had obviated human practices of penance on account of Christ's "full, perfect, and sufficient sacrifyce, oblacion, and satysfaccyon;"[6] after the Roman Catholic Church introduced the confessional box, signaling "the decay of the idea that sin was a social matter;"[7] after both sacred and secular "institutionalizations of charity" evacuated of their efficacy the practices and languages of satisfaction;[8] and after the modern subject tamed truth so that it could no longer transfigure the self or give subjectivity.[9] If Martin Luther disrupted medieval complacency about the sufficiency of sacramental satisfaction, Briony Tallis is desperately certain that nothing can ever satisfy.

It is tempting to read Briony as a figure for modern failures of acknowledgment, recognition, and communal reconciliation, alienated by at least one epoch from the medieval school of forgiveness, the peni-

[5] See Joseph Goering, "The Scholastic Turn (1100–1500): Penitential Theology and Law in the Schools," in *A New History of Penance*, ed. Abigail Firey (Boston: Brill, 2008), 219–37.

[6] Church of England, *The Boke of the Common Praier and Administratio{n} of the Sacramentes and Other Rytes and Ceremonies of the Churche, after the Vse of the Churche of Englande* (Worcester: John Oswen, 1549), fol. 161r; available at *Early English Books Online*, eebo.chadwyck.com/home (accessed May 5, 2013).

[7] John Bossy, "Practices of Satisfaction, 1215–1700," in *Retribution, Repentance, and Reconciliation: Papers Read at the 2002 Summer and 2003 Winter Meeting of the Ecclesiastical History Society*, ed. Kate Cooper and Jeremy Gregory (Woodbridge: Boydell Press, 2004), 106–18 (111). See also John Bossy, "The Social History of Confession in the Age of the Reformation," *Transactions of the Royal Historical Society* 5, no. 25 (1975): 21–38 (29–33).

[8] Ivan Illich, *The Rivers North of the Future: The Last Testament of Ivan Illich*, ed. David Cayley (Toronto: House of Anansi Press, 2005), 175–200. Illich's arguments are best appreciated in the haunting recordings of the radio series, *The Corruption of Christianity: Ivan Illich on Gospel, Church and Society*, produced by Cayley for *Ideas* (Toronto: Canadian Broadcasting Corporation, 2000).

[9] "If we define spirituality as being the form of practices which postulate that, such as he is, the subject is not capable of the truth, but that, such as it is, the truth can transfigure and save the subject, then we can say that the modern age of the relations between the subject and truth begin when it is postulated that, such as he is, the subject is capable of truth, but that, such as it is, the truth cannot save the subject." Michel Foucault, *The Hermeneutics of the Subject*, ed. and trans. Frederic Gros (New York: Palgrave Macmillan, 2005), 19.

tential system in which the living and the dead practiced the social grammar of reconciliation.[10] Briony rightly grieves. Too late, Briony! Too late for a tribunal, too late for a confessional, too late for God. "Is't not too late?," asked a sixteenth-century Lutheran doctor, hoping it might not be. "Too late," said the Evil Angel. "Never too late," said the Good Angel, "if Faustus will repent."[11] Briony might not have a good angel to turn to, but Marlowe's post-penitential drama reveals how her despair presumes a certain periodization of history and structure of time. "Behold, now is the acceptable time," Paul wrote, "now is the day of salvation," but Briony's window of opportunity for effective satisfaction has passed, and she lives and writes after the "now," after religion.[12] Briony subscribes, then, to a subtraction story of secularization, according to which modernity is what remains after religion has dwindled away.[13] To be modern means to come after religion and its trappings, to live—if now is the day of salvation—after the now. It is always too late, even if she wants to repent.

But this essay seeks to postpone and assay the consequences of such a foreclosure by allowing several medieval, early modern, and contemporary voices to speak about satisfaction alongside one another and challenge each other. This method of speculative, transhistorical conflict is designed not so much to narrate a shift in religious forms as to cast a series of flash-bursts from a variety of angles that reveal by a manifold of shadow and contrast the contours of belief about and practices of

[10] See Sarah Beckwith, *Shakespeare and the Grammar of Forgiveness* (Ithaca, N.Y.: Cornell University Press, 2011), 20–33.

[11] Christopher Marlowe, *The Tragedy of Doctor Faustus, B-Text*, in *Doctor Faustus and Other Plays: A Text*, ed. David Bevington and Eric Rasmussen (Oxford: Oxford University Press, 2008), 2.3.75–78.

[12] 2 Corinthians 6:2. All English biblical quotations are cited from the Challoner revision of the Douay-Rheims, and Latin from the Stuttgart Vulgate; both are available in parallel online at www.latinvulgate.com (accessed 24 February 2014).

[13] On subtraction narratives, see Charles Taylor, *A Secular Age* (Cambridge, Mass.: Belknap Press, 2007), 569–79. I find Taylor's critique of subtraction narratives compelling. However, from the perspective of medieval religious history, Taylor tends toward the opposite error, imaginatively adding to the Middle Ages a surplus of faith sufficiently robust to sustain all of modernity's subtractions and still persist. While not reductively Weberian, Taylor's account also avoids the reason for continuity most religions themselves give: that God continues to exist and work in the lives of humans and their institutions. This exaggeration occurs mostly in Chapter 1, "The Bulwarks of Belief." For more cautious accounts of medieval faith and practice, see 90–95. For an alternative account of medieval belief, explicitly contrasted to Taylor's, see Steven Justice, "Did the Middle Ages Believe in Their Miracles?," *Representations* 103 (2008): 1–29.

satisfaction. These new vantages grant, in turn, a new perspective on *Piers Plowman* as a key text in the history of satisfaction and as a poem structurally as well as authorially invested in writing for the sake of satisfactory participation in salvation history.

My larger argument about the history of satisfaction in late medieval and early Reformation literary culture centers on a major point of disagreement among *Piers Plowman*'s readers across the centuries, namely, how to understand the work as a whole in light of the apparent failures that dominate its ending. Like Briony's story and the larger story of satisfaction's demise, *Piers Plowman* suggests glum conclusions. The poem ends in disaster with the total corruption of the Church and the undoing of the penitential self as the pitiful Contrition abandons his own allegorical essence and "clene forȝete to crye and to wepe."[14] No wonder some of the poem's best readers have identified failure as its chief engine of invention and closure.[15] Yet I argue in this essay that Langland designs the poem to reframe failure within a history of salvation in which Christians can participate sacramentally to redeem failure, especially by penitential satisfaction.[16] Satisfaction, then, not failure itself, motivates the poem's inventive impulse. Langland conceives of sacramental and literary satisfaction not as the termination of a discrete penitential sequence (contrition, confession, satisfaction), but as an ongoing, open-ended habit of beginning again and making good ends.

[14] William Langland, *Piers Plowman*, C XXII.369. Unless otherwise noted, I quote from *Piers Plowman: The C Version*, ed. George Russell and George Kane (London: Athlone Press, 1997); *Piers Plowman: The B Version*, ed. George Kane and E. Talbot Donaldson (London: Athlone Press, 1988); and *Piers Plowman: The A Version*, ed. George Kane (London: Athlone Press, 1960). I have also consulted *Piers Plowman: A Parallel-Text Edition of the A, B, C and Z Versions*, ed. A. V. C. Schmidt, 2 vols. (Kalamazoo: Medieval Institute Publications, 2011).

[15] See especially Anne Middleton, "Narration and the Invention of Experience: Episodic Form in *Piers Plowman*," in *The Wisdom of Poetry: Essays in Honor of Morton Bloomfield*, ed. Larry D. Benson and Siegfried Wenzel (Kalamazoo: Medieval Institute Publications, 1982), 91–122; D. Vance Smith, *The Book of the Incipit: Beginnings in the Fourteenth Century* (Minneapolis: University of Minnesota Press, 2001), 82–86; D. Vance Smith, "Negative Langland," *YLS* 23 (2009): 33–59; and Nicolette Zeeman, *"Piers Plowman" and the Medieval Discourse of Desire* (New York: Cambridge University Press, 2006).

[16] For a reading of the ending as dominated by the pattern of failure, rebuke, and loss, see Zeeman, *"Piers Plowman" and the Medieval Discourse of Desire*, 263–83: "For a brief phase, the poem's protagonists are all 'patient' enough to allow the redemption to happen. It is doubly notable, therefore, that a narrative of failure reappears again at the end of the poem. . . . Once more Piers is gone. Once more Conscience departs. Such narratives of denial and loss have shaped the poem since its inception, and it is no surprise that one more such narrative brings the poem to its famously gaping close" (283). Zeeman's book ends here.

In support of these claims, I interpret both formal and historical evidence, and demonstrate how the two kinds of evidence mutually support each other.[17] Formally, *Piers Plowman* employs chiastic structures to resist purely linear reading and to reinscribe patterns of failure into larger histories of redemption. I will identify chiastic structures at work locally in alliterative patterning and more broadly in the plot of the poem, especially the visionary and liturgical climax where the dreamer Will witnesses and participates in the signal events of salvation history: Christ's Passion, descent to hell, Resurrection, Ascension, and Pentecost. Historically, *Piers Plowman* develops a currently underappreciated, capacious understanding of penitential satisfaction. Drawing on late medieval penitential liturgy and literature and on the work of historians of penance, I retrieve an understanding of satisfaction according to which writing a poem such as *Piers Plowman* can constitute a work of mercy and therefore count as sacramental satisfaction. These two kinds of evidence are linked by *Piers Plowman*'s unique announcement of its writtenness in the midst of its most significant chiastic structure. When the dreamer Will announces that he woke up and wrote what he had dreamed, he does so in the context of penitential participation in the history of salvation through liturgy. Will's dream of that history merges with the real-time Holy Week liturgies. If Will and William Langland are writing as an act of penitential satisfaction, then they occupy what may seem like a strange place in the medieval economy of salvation, both outside the clerically controlled sacrament of penance, yet also seeking that sacrament's benefits. The central part of this essay, then, seeks to make that place seem less strange and to articulate how Langland's questionable vernacular making both stands outside clerical sacramental authority and stakes a claim to being legitimate *lele labour* as a penitential practice.

If we can understand Langland's writing as satisfactory, we can better

[17] While I am adducing two kinds of evidence for this argument—formal and theological-historical—a third type of evidence could further support the argument for the importance of Langland's writing from the middle, namely, evidence of *Piers Plowman*'s order of composition and revision, though I do not have the space to develop the relationship here. For an argument from the evidence of revision that Langland's making is essentially penitential, see Alan Fletcher, "The Essential (Ephemeral) William Langland: Textual Revision as Ethical Process in *Piers Plowman*," *YLS* 15 (2001): 61–84. My analysis here suggests that Fletcher should shift his focus from contrition to satisfaction. I discuss the potential for corroboration with Lawrence Warner's hypotheses about *The Lost History of Piers Plowman* in note 103 below.

appreciate the failures and successes of penance in the late Middle Ages, and better recognize practices of satisfaction across the Reformation that narratives of decline and loss tend to overlook.[18] *Piers Plowman*'s eschatological vision of hope and satisfaction beyond personal and institutional religious failure challenges Briony's self-binding temporality, her *post*-apocalyptic sense of belatedness that rebukes hope and occludes present help. The poem also challenges Faustian histories of the Reformation and modernity—not necessarily those that register loss and shed a contrite tear, but those that less than halfway through the play say, "*Consummatum est*" (2.1.74) and so see devils holding down repentant hands and cannot see the angels there all along.

The history of modernity within which we necessarily practice criticism and historiography is not yet finished and likely holds many surprises. We do not know its end, and therefore we do not know how "late" we really are. If the age of reform had its unintended consequences, as Brad Gregory has argued, it also had its unrealized intentions and multiple futures—futures that may not yet even have arrived.[19] This essay is designed to recognize some of those futures by studying practices of satisfaction not only over a long duration of literary and religious texts, but in the manifold permutations, returns, and possibilities inscribed in the texts themselves and in the futures they collaborate in inventing. The next section looks closely at two forms of permutation and return in *Piers Plowman*, a text that resists simple linear reading toward an ending and instead invites readers to layer their inter-

[18] I include some of the most influential of these narratives in notes 7, 8, and 9. For a similar approach to continuity and change, see Katherine C. Little, "Transforming Work: Protestantism and the *Piers Plowman* Tradition," *JMEMSt* 40, no. 3 (2010): 497–526, which explores continuities and transformations of labor and works across the Reformation.

[19] Brad S. Gregory, *The Unintended Reformation: How a Religious Revolution Secularized Society* (Cambridge, Mass.: Belknap Press, 2012). This admirably ambitious work tells multiple overlapping, and at times conflicting, stories about the origins of modernity, marshaling an impressive array of primary and secondary texts to do so. Taken as a whole, the book wields nuanced explanatory power. Yet its powerful method prevents it from treating its primary texts as more than markers of historical developments. The book must perforce move on with its arguments; it cannot linger with a text, respond to its recursive invitations, or tease out its multiple possible futures in disparate communities of interpretation. This book, which illuminates the sources and contours of modern pluralism, cannot itself give a good account of the plural possibilities of its primary texts. (I am grateful for a conversation with Will Revere in which he articulated this perspective.) *Piers Plowman* stands at the center of this essay because it is a text that invites its readers to return, revise, and layer their responses, as its reception history bears out.

actions with it, repeatedly returning to certain structural "middles" that produce the meaning of the poem more than its actual ending.

Chiasmus and *Piers Plowman*'s Dynamic Middle

For all the attention that has fruitfully been lavished on the forms and energies of beginning and ending in *Piers Plowman*, it is a surprisingly centripetal poem. To be sure, the center does not hold. But the poem begins again so many times because it is constantly trying to return to a center of gravity. That center is the Incarnation of Christ, as Cristina Maria Cervone has argued in her study of "Incarnational poetics" in Middle English poetry. "In making the hypostatic union so central to the work that form does, an Incarnational poetic encourages a process of thought that comes back again to that good and fundamental beginning. In all of these poems, . . . the Incarnation is the pivot point around which thought and form coalesce."[20] In *Piers Plowman*, the Incarnation comprises a narrative structure of exit and return, of the Son's descent from the Father into human flesh and ultimately the region of the dead, and of his ascent by way of the Resurrection to the right hand of the Father in heaven. That narrative structure provides a template for humanity, which fell from grace in Adam and Eve, suffered death, but through Christ can rise again and ascend not only into heaven but even into union with the triune God. As the patristic dictum puts it, "God became man that man might become God."[21] That famous saying absorbs the symmetry of the narrative structure of the Incarnation into its syntactic structure, producing the poetic figure of chiasmus. This section of the essay explores how William Langland employed metrical, syntactic, and narrative chiasmus to give *Piers Plowman* an incarnational form that directs readers' attention repeatedly back to the middle, the place of salvific exchange between God and humanity.

Modern literary scholars have been cautious about chiasmus on historical and methodological grounds. Historically, there has been little evidence of conscious chiastic patterning by literary writers, though new

[20] Cristina Maria Cervone, *Poetics of the Incarnation: Middle English Writing and the Leap of Love* (Philadelphia: University of Pennsylvania Press, 2013), 208.

[21] Cf. Athanasius, *De incarnatione Dei Verbum*, 54.3; in *Select Writings and Letters of Athanasius, Bishop of Alexandria*, ed. Archibald Robertson (Grand Rapids, Mich.: Eerdmans, 1953); available at Christian Classics Ethereal Library, http://www.ccel.org/ccel/schaff/npnf204.vii.ii.liv.html (accessed February 18, 2014).

research in the past fifteen years has begun to change that.[22] Methodologically, the fear is that once you start looking for chiasmus, you see it everywhere. I use the term advisedly, with due historical caution. I employ the term chiasmus to name an array of parallel and concentric reversals or reciprocity, from syntactical arrangements grouped in medieval rhetorical manuals under the figure *commutatio* to larger structural patterns that reflect the semantic symmetry David Howlett has noted as one mark of "biblical style" in early medieval writings such as Saint Patrick's *Confessio*.[23] Langland's chiastic effects depend on a complex interplay of line-level chiasmus, larger structural chiasmus, and conceptual or narrative chiasmus as found in the basic Christian plot of Creation, Fall, Incarnation, redemption.

Medieval poetics and rhetoric hardly register the term chiasmus (it became popular only with Renaissance rhetoric).[24] More common are the figures *isocolon*, *antimetabole*, *commutatio*, and *annominatio*. In the widely cited definition of the *Rhetorica ad Herennium*, *commutatio* "occurs when two discrepant thoughts are so expressed by transposition that the latter follows from the former although contradictory to it."[25] In this strict sense, *commutatio* must occur at the sentence or line level, where two opposing ideas are expressed using the same root word or words. But such a line can still express larger chiastic structures, even plot structures, as in "that was tynt thorw tre, tre shal hit wynne" (C XX.143). In this line, the plot of salvation history and its central events of winning and losing revolve around a tree—or two trees: the Tree of Life in the Garden of Eden and the tree of the cross on Golgotha. I therefore speak of chiasmus as an umbrella term to describe the wide

[22] On chiastic structure in medieval meditative theology and poetry, see Robert McMahon, *Understanding the Medieval Meditative Ascent: Augustine, Anselm, Boethius, and Dante* (Washington, D.C.: Catholic University of America Press, 2006), 36–42. For a study of chiasmus based on late medieval and early modern mnemonic culture, see William E. Engel, *Chiastic Designs in English Literature from Sidney to Shakespeare* (Burlington: Ashgate, 2009).

[23] See *Liber epistolarum Sancti Patricii episcopi: The Book of Letters of St. Patrick the Bishop*, ed. D. R. Howlett (Dublin: Four Courts Press, 1994); and D. R. Howlett, *British Books in Biblical Style* (Dublin: Four Courts Press, 1997).

[24] Medieval awareness of the Greek *chiasmos* comes across primarily in the figure of *isocolon*. See Heinrich Lausberg, *Handbook of Literary Rhetoric: A Foundation for Literary Study*, ed. David E. Orton and R. Dean Anderson (Leiden: Brill, 1998), 322.

[25] *Rhetorica ad Herennium*, 4.28.39; "Commutatio est cum duae sententiae inter se discrepantes ex transiectione ita efferuntur ut a priore posterior contraria priori proficiscatur." In *Ad C. Herennium: De ratione dicendi (Rhetorica ad Herennium)*, trans. Harry Caplan (Cambridge, Mass.: Harvard University Press, 1964), 324.

array of symmetrical, reciprocal, or concentric parallelisms and antitheses that Langland deploys not only in his rhetoric, but also in his disposition of salvation history and the events that constitute the plot of *Piers Plowman*, in his marking of topographical ascents and descents, and in the various metrical balancing tactics he enlists to create a range of effects with his alliterative lines.[26] While one can appreciate the methodological objection that once we start looking for chiasmus, we find it everywhere, it is significant that in the case of *Piers Plowman*, we do not find chiasmus everywhere. We find it in strategic places, in the middles to which Langland wants us to return in our meditative reading habits, and especially in the middle on which this part of the essay focuses, a middle between two episodes dominated by the figure of Christ's cross.

Chiasmus has long been associated with the cross. The term derives from the Greek letter χ (*chi*) because chiasmus involves a crossing of elements in a symmetrical array. The crossing may be expressed *abba* or in diagram form (Figure 1). Early Christians associated the letter *chi* with Christ; the *Chi Rho* Christogram, derived from the first two letters of the Greek *Christos*, predated the cross as the central Christian symbol. New Testament scholars have found chiasmus to be an essential rhetorical structure of the Gospels, especially John.[27] *The Dream of the Rood* anchors structural chiasmus with single-verse chiasmus, such as "Rod wæs ic aræred. Ahof ic ricne cyning" (As a cross was I raised up | lifted

Fig. 1

[26] For an even more capacious understanding of chiasmus, anchored in pre-Socratic thought and formal logic, see Patrick Lee Miller, *Becoming God: Pure Reason in Early Greek Philosophy* (New York: Continuum, 2011), 1–42.

[27] See John Breck, *The Shape of Biblical Language: Chiasmus in the Scriptures and Beyond* (Crestwood: St. Vladimir's Seminary Press, 1994).

I the mighty king).[28] Beyond the line level, cruciform symmetries structure many Middle English meditative lyrics such as "The Four Leaves of the Truelove," which conveys a cross-patterned homily on the saving love embodied in the flower truelove and Christ's form "spred on a Crosse," or Thomas of Hales's "Love Rune" with its cryptic inscription of the sign of the cross at the precise numerical center of the hermetic *roune*.[29] In *Piers Plowman*, deep within the Incarnation's narrative chiasmus, Mercy sets the dream's larger structure on a pivot around the cross in a line-level chiasmus: "And that was tynt thorw tre, tre shal hit wynne" (C XX.143). At the end of the same passus Will exhorts his wife and daughter to participate in an Easter Sunday liturgy that involves creeping to the cross and kissing it. The next passus begins with a dream of Christ, dressed in Piers's armor, bearing a cross. It is to these particular crosses and this chiastic crossing that Langland draws our recursive, meditative attention. These crosses are particularly poignant because they frame the first explicit announcement of the poem's writtenness, which allows us to understand how the work of writing relates to the cross by means of penitential liturgy.

In order to appreciate how and why Langland creates intense chiastic effects in this part of the poem, we first need to step back and consider what is going on in the larger plot of Will's dreams. The pivotal first line of C XXI is also the first line of the *Vita de Dobest*, the final movement of the poem as rubricated in most B and C manuscripts. The line is situated between two passus comprising vivid dreams of biblical-liturgical action. They begin with Will alienated from community, going along "ylike a lorel al my lyf tyme" (C XX.3), and they end with the Church, the king, and the commons alienated from each other. The plot of the two passus progresses from spiritual dryness and disorder to intense

[28] *The Dream of the Rood*, ed. Michael Swanton (Manchester: University of Manchester Press, 1970), line 44. "This line . . . divides the active Christ from the passive one and the passive cross from its active role. It also bisects the four portions of the narrative so that they form a chiasmus, the central juxtaposed scenes depicting the dual acts of Christ ascending the cross and of the cross raising Christ and being pierced by the nails, the framing scenes being on the one side the enemies raising the cross and on the other side the friends taking down Christ and burying the three crosses." Carol Braun Pasternack, "Stylistic Disjunctions in *The Dream of the Rood*," *Anglo-Saxon England* 13 (1984): 167–86 (178).

[29] "The Four Leaves of the Truelove," in *Moral Love Songs and Laments*, ed. Susanna Greer Fein (Kalamazoo: Medieval Institute Publications, 1998), line 199. Fein argues that Hales's line 100—"Est and west, north and suth!"—"may be meant to invoke the sign of the Cross and thereby sanctify the rune. . . . If this interpretation is correct, the line is integral to the cryptic, runic nature of the poem" (41 n. 100).

liturgical and visionary participation in the events of Holy Week and Pentecost, and back again to spiritual dissolution.[30] More immediately, Will wakes and writes between two liturgies involving the cross. At the end of Passus XX, six lines earlier, Will urges his wife and daughter to "arise and go . . . crepe to þe croes on knees and kusse hit for a iewel" (C XX.470–71). Then at the beginning of Passus XXI, seven lines later, Will falls asleep in the middle of mass and dreams "That Peres þe plouhman was peynted al blody / And cam in with a cros before þe comune peple" (C XXI.6–7). It is fitting and significant that this chiastic structure—with writing in the middle framed on either side by liturgical devotion—should depend on the cross and, as we shall see, on Langland's distinctive theology of the cross. The next section of this essay develops an understanding of how Langland's use of chiasmus in the alliterative line performs theological argument about Christ's Passion and frames the signal moment when Will wakes and writes. The following section takes up the question of what it means, given this framing, to wake up and write.

Alliterative Chiasmus and Langland's Theology of the Cross

The standard alliterative long-line is notably unbalanced. Like *Piers Plowman* itself, the end of an alliterative line swerves away from the prior pattern of stress: *aa*|*ax*. But Langland was able to enlist the alliterative line to produce a wide variety of effects, including balance and symmetry, as Macklin Smith has demonstrated in his studies of Langland's "balancing tactics."[31] These tactics include line-level alliterative meter as well as chiastic "frames" established by interlinear alliteration. Smith demonstrates that alliterative stress can perform the function that polyptoton—deploying a word or form of the word twice to different

[30] The significance of this liturgical, penitential, and Eucharistic setting for the poem's central problems cannot be overstated. For an appreciation of how penance and Eucharist finally and fittingly support each other here, see David Aers, *Sanctifying Signs: Making Christian Tradition in Late Medieval England* (Notre Dame: University of Notre Dame Press, 2004), 29–51.

[31] Some of these tactics are discussed in Macklin Smith, "Langland's Alliterative Line(s)," *YLS* 23 (2009): 163–216 (190–93). I rely also on Smith's unpublished working papers and personal correspondence, including "Chiastic Form in *Piers Plowman*," Forty-Fourth Annual International Congress on Medieval Studies (Kalamazoo, May 9, 2009); and "Balancing Tactics in *Piers Plowman*," Fifth International *Piers Plowman* Conference (Oxford, April 16, 2011).

effects[32]—performs in standard *commutatio*. Instead of repeating the same words in reverse order to express opposed thoughts, those thoughts can be opposed or apposed by different, yet alliterating, words. This is precisely what occurs at C XXI.14.

Here Conscience tells Will that his vision of Piers "peynted al blody" and bearing a cross at mass "Is Crist with his croes, conquerour of Cristene" (C XXI.14). This "enriched" line, with its *aa|aa* alliterative patterning, is the closest Langland usually comes to alliterative chiasmus, but it nevertheless capitalizes on the full potential for symmetry that the four-beat line bears.[33] The chiastic alliterative structure can invite speculation about conceptual chiasmus: in what ways might the inner and outer full staves, when paired, produce effects of symmetry, balance, antithesis, or parallelism? A. V. C. Schmidt notes the line's "heavily emphatic enriched fourth lift growing, as it were, out of the root *Crist* planted as the (anticipated) first *k* lift."[34] Taking the "commutative property" of this alliterative *commutatio* even further, "Crist" and "Cristene" can be interchangeable in the economy of salvation as a consequence of the identity that obtains between the inner alliterating terms, "croes" and "conquerour." Christ is the conqueror and belongs to all Christians ("conquerour *of* Cristene"), and by commutation these properties apply also to the cross: it is a conqueror, it belongs to all Christians, and they conquer under its sign. Because the cross is the conqueror, Christ and Christians are *at one*; through the atonement humanity completes the second half of the great Patristic chiasmus, "God became man that man might become God."[35] Through the crossing of Christ's Passion, humanity crosses back to its original *telos* of participation in the divine life.

The line's chiastic argument does not just recapitulate, however neatly and heuristically, Chalcedonian Christology.[36] Rather, it chiasti-

[32] See Lausberg, *Handbook of Literary Rhetoric*, 288–92.

[33] I use A. V. C. Schmidt's terminology, which indicates that the line alliterates as usual on the first three lifts and then enriches or "fills" the final lift of the *b*-verse with another alliterating syllable. See A. V. C. Schmidt, *The Clerkly Maker: Langland's Poetic Art* (Cambridge: D. S. Brewer, 1987), 32. There are only ten *ab|ba* lines in *Piers Plowman* B, but three of them do not map on to the stress pattern. See Tomonori Matsushita, ed., *A Glossarial Concordance to William Langland's "The Vision of Piers Plowman," The B-Text*, 3 vols. (Tokyo: Yushodo Press, 1998–2000), 3:700.

[34] Schmidt, *Clerkly Maker*, 47.

[35] Athanasius, *De incarnatione*, 54.3.

[36] The Council of Chalcedon's (451 CE) articulation of the hypostatic union depended on the notion of *communicatio idiomatum*, the exchange of attributes between Christ's divine and human natures, expressed in Leo the Great's influential *Tome* (449 CE): "Thus

cally substantiates the claims in the previous passus that the cross completes the incarnation. C amplifies the argument of B that "God . . . Bicam man of a mayde . . . to se þe sorwe of deying" (B XVIII.213) with the even bolder claim that God's knowledge was incomplete without experiencing human death and suffering:

> Ne hadde God ysoffred of som oþer then hymsulue,
> He hadde nat wist witterly where deth were sour or swete.
> (C XX.217–18)

The omniscient God could not have proper knowledge of death without becoming a human. The line's chiastic structure absorbs and focuses reverberations from these bold soteriological overtures elsewhere in the poem, illustrating Smith's argument that

> the occasional crisscross patterns in *Piers Plowman* communicate *extra*, higher meanings at play in—or over—the course of this complex, recursive, experiential, messy, and pervasively imbalanced poem. . . . Langland . . . seems to have theorized his frames and symmetries, using them to suggest Providential forms and even . . . to describe God's essence and agency. In other words, Langland also theorizes chiasmus, translating it, as it were, from rhetoric into theology, via poetics.[37]

This particular line in fact transposes the thematic chiasmus of salvation history into an alliteratively chiastic line, thus translating theology into poetics. The soteriological commutation of "Crist" and "Cristene" across the middle terms of "cross" and "conquerour" contributes to the larger centripetal force of the Holy Week liturgy as it bears out the chiastic structure of Incarnation and redemption centered around the

in the whole and perfect nature of true man was true God born, complete in what was His own, complete in what was ours. And by 'ours' we mean what the Creator formed in us from the beginning and what He undertook to repair." "Letter 28," trans. Charles Lett Feltoe, in *Leo the Great, Gregory the Great*, ed. Philip Schaff and Henry Wace, Nicene and Post-Nicene Fathers, Second Series 12 (Buffalo: Christian Literature Publishing, 1895); available online, rev. and ed. Kevin Knight, at http://www.newadvent.org (accessed June 10, 2011). Langland elaborates the anthropological consequences of the hypostatic union in terms of consanguinity. As Christ says during the Harrowing of Hell, "Ac to be merciable to man thenne my kynde hit asketh / For we beth brethrene of bloed" (C XX.417–18). This is significant in Will's dream because Christ bearing the cross not only wears Piers's armor, but is "al blody," with the blood covering and presumably making indistinguishable what is Christ and what is Piers.

[37] Smith, "Chiastic Form," 1–2.

triumphant defeat of the Crucifixion and descent into hell. Such a grand defeat can result in triumph only thanks to the hinge-like properties of the Incarnation, which can be expressed poetically in a line of chiastic alliteration. The normative alliterative line is unbalanced (*aa|ax*), just as defeat does not normally balance itself out with victory. Yet for those rare defeats that result in victory there are rare balanced and chiastic alliterative lines. This one functions as a hinge mechanism for the poem's entire plot, opening onto the victory of the cross and transferring the benefits of that victory to those in need of salvation.

On the other side of the chiastic fold between passus XX and XXI, another alliteratively balanced line binds repentant sinner to saving God across their asymmetrical relationship. As we have seen, upon waking from his dream of the Harrowing of Hell, Will exhorts his wife and daughter, Kitte and Calote,

> Arise and go reuerense godes resureccion
> And crepe to þe croes on knees and kusse hit for a iewel.
> (C XX.470–71)

The first line of Will's exhortation could hardly be more imbalanced thematically. The *a*-verse's imperatives put Kitte and Calote in a passive, penitential position even as the *b*-verse comprises God's greatest action. Yet chiastic, contrapuntal alliteration yokes the two halves together, facilitating commerce between penitent sinners and glorified God.[38] Three full staves alliterating on {r} are counterpointed with a secondary alliteration on {g} in the *a*-verse and a corresponding, stressed {g}-syllable in the *b*-verse position normally reserved for the key-stave: "A**r***ise* and **g**o **r***eu*erense | **g***od*es resu**r***ec*cion" (*a{b}a|ba*).[39] The following line amplifies this exhortation, identifying the object of reverence as the cross, which stands in for "godes resureccion," thus converting the instrument of death into the sign of life.

Langland's contemporaries might have appreciated a similar transla-

[38] Schmidt, *Clerkly Maker*, 62–67.

[39] This is a rare line indeed, one that the standard typology would not admit if scanned *aa|xa*. ("The minimum requirement of metricality is that two full staves must appear in the *a*-verse and the first stave in the *b*-verse must be full." Hoyt N. Duggan, "Notes toward a Theory of Langland's Meter," *YLS* 1 {1987}: 41–70 {43}.) Nor does "godes" here submit to the distinction between full, mute, and blank staves. It cannot be full since it does not alliterate on the primary {r} sound. It cannot be mute since it has stress. And it cannot be blank since it *does* alliterate on the secondary {g} sound.

tion in the liturgical chronology, for although the ceremony of creeping to the cross was occasionally observed on Easter morning, it was much more commonly associated with Good Friday. Whichever practice was familiar to Langland's readers, the Easter morning veneration of the cross renders the instrument of defeat the sign of victory, not only by carrying it across the cosmic reversal of the Harrowing of Hell on Holy Saturday, but also by making the cross available to penitents for participation. For the victory of the cross can only be complete when sinners repent, take up their crosses, and follow Christ—when their rising and going alliterates in counterpoint, as it were, with God's own Resurrection. In this sense, the line's highly anomalous absence of a key-stave invites alliterative participation. God ("godes") occupies the key position, alliterating only with the secondary, unstressed, human-oriented "go" of the *a*-verse. Whereas the key-stave normally "unlocks" the primary alliterative pattern of the *a*-verse, here what it reveals about the *a*-verse is the urgency of human agency, the tropological imperative that makes every "go" in the Gospels faintly echo with Jesus' exhortation, ". . . and do thou in like manner" ("vade et tu fac similiter," Lk 10:37). To "go" in this line is to alliterate with "godes," and so to participate in "godes resureccion."

The two chiastic, crucicentric lines just analyzed frame with a rough symmetry the clearest signal in all of *Piers Plowman* that Will and William Langland are self-consciously making a public literary artifact. At the middle of this crucicentric middle, at the middle of the chiastic fold between passus XX and XXI, between cross and cross, Will says, "Thus y wakede and wrot what y hadde ydremed" (C XXI.1). In this line, writing—"wrot"—is situated directly between waking and dreaming; it is in fact the numerical center of the line's nine words. Will enjoys one of his precarious, always interstitial waking moments eight lines after waking and just four before falling asleep again. This middling site of writing becomes, in turn, a frame in its own right, reappearing in similar form at the end of the passus to bracket the poem's climactic vision of the Resurrection's communal consequences.

Critics have gravitated to this juncture between C XX and XXI (B XVIII and XIX) as a site of heightened interpretive vision even as the poem proceeds to its irresolute ending. Morton W. Bloomfield writes, "In a profound sense, the powerful scene of the Harrowing of Hell is the true end of the poem, of the quest for Christian perfection which this poem exemplifies."[40] But the poem does not end with B XVIII/C XX in any of the extant manuscripts. If the quest for Christian perfection from the ethical-soteriological crises of the "fair feld ful of folk" (C Prol.19) culminates in B XVIII/C XX, then the final two passus mirror that development in reverse, declining from the perfect unity of Pentecost to the ruin of Holy Church. This plot of Fall-to-redemption, redemption-to-Fall bears a broadly chiastic pattern. Thus Anne Middleton notes "the latent similarities, a pattern of cyclical return, of theme and form that joins the beginning to the end of the poem, markedly enhancing a broad chiastic symmetry between the two opening visions and the two post-Resurrection visions that conclude both long forms of the poem."[41] Middleton recognizes that something happens around the beginning and ending of *Piers Plowman* that keeps the beginning and ending from fully determining the work's *ratio*. Beginning and ending do not map on to the work's first and final causes, and they can give a misleading sense of the formal and efficient causes. I have focused on the literary form of chiasmus as a formal cause that refuses the determinations of beginning or ending. The centripetal force of chiasmus invites a new critical perspective on *Piers Plowman*, one that reads middles as at least equally productive of its *sentence* as its beginnings and ends. If Bloomfield and Kathryn Kerby-Fulton's early work read Langland through his endings, and Middleton and D. Vance Smith read him through his beginnings, then I am arguing for a reinvigorated focus on the middle.[42]

My argument about the chiastic middle where Will wakes and writes hovers around the end of *Piers Plowman*. But other structural and thematic middles earlier in the poem—from its numerical mid-point to Will's middle age to the theological middle of the Incarnation—have prepared for this late, crucicentric middle. This late middle is particu-

[40] Morton W. Bloomfield, *"Piers Plowman" as a Fourteenth-Century Apocalypse* (New Brunswick: Rutgers University Press, 1961), 125.

[41] Anne Middleton, "Acts of Vagrancy: The C Version 'Autobiography' and the Statute of 1388," in *Written Work: Langland, Labor, and Authorship*, ed. Steven Justice and Kathryn Kerby-Fulton (Philadelphia: University of Pennsylvania Press, 1997), 208–317 (269).

[42] Bloomfield, *"Piers Plowman" as a Fourteenth-Century Apocalypse*; Kathryn Kerby-Fulton, *Reformist Apocalypticism and "Piers Plowman"* (New York: Cambridge University Press, 1990); Middleton, "Narration and the Invention of Experience"; Smith, *The Book of the Incipit*. Middleton also reads from the end in "Making a Good End: John But as a Reader of *Piers Plowman*," in *Medieval English Studies Presented to George Kane*, ed. Edward Donald Kennedy et al. (Wolfeboro: D. S. Brewer, 1988), 243–63.

larly significant because it dilates the most prevalent middle in the poem, the Incarnation, and makes it available to literary and sacramental participation. Will wakes and writes between two penitential liturgies—one in waking life, one in a dream—that involve the Incarnation and the cross. Because Will and his wife and daughter are here able to participate in the drama of the Incarnation, this chiastic middle consummates the dozen or so visionary, metaphoric, and figural accounts of the Incarnation earlier in the poem.[43] I call this middle "dynamic" because it is not anchored to a point in the sequence of reading or of composition. Rather, this incarnational and crucicentric middle bears a centripetal force that draws the poem's acts of invention and the readers' acts of interpretation back to it. And because this middle becomes a middle by virtue of readers' recursions to it in their own lives of sacramental participation in crucicentric satisfaction, it dynamically moves outside the text.

This crucicentric middle stands out for its framing of the poem's writtenness, and its connection of writing to penitential liturgy and therefore to satisfaction. Because this middle comes near the end, it concerns *novissimis*, the poem's internal eschatology, its hope for an ending, and its anagogical *ratio* of invention, according to which, as the Latin term suggests, last things entail new things, new hopes. By chiastic patterning, Langland draws the focus due a poem's ending away from the actual ending, reorienting it to a site at the middle of the ending where Will participates intensely in the salvific work of doing well. Writing in the middle is important for Langland because it becomes the chief activity by which Will does well. The writer and the readers might do well beyond the poem in countless ways, but writing is the most appropriate form of labor by which to model doing well in a literary work. Making *Piers Plowman* performs the work of penance that Langland goes out of his way to articulate in some detail. Langland renders Will's writing as one kind of satisfaction, the literary way to fulfill the "silent middle term" of Truth's laconic pardon, the assurance that mercy abounds for sinners who repent.[44] So it becomes especially urgent to understand what it means, in Langland's literary milieu and in the context of the poem thus far, to say, "I waked and wrot."

[43] On some of these figural and metaphoric middles, see Cervone, *Poetics of the Incarnation*, Chapter 5: "'He is in the mydde point': Poetic Deep Structure and the Frameworks of Incarnational Poetics," 159–208.

[44] Traugott Lawler, "The Pardon Formula in *Piers Plowman*: Its Ubiquity, Its Binary Shape, Its Silent Middle Term," *YLS* 14 (2000): 117–52.

What Does It Mean to Say, "I woke up and wrote"?

Up to the point of Will's announcement that he woke up and wrote, Will has been identified as someone who writes only three times in the A- and B-texts combined, and not at all in C. The A-text represents Will as a copyist in the service of merchants.[45] When Imaginatif accuses Will in B of meddling with making "bokes" to "telle men what dowel is, dobet and dobest boþe," Will does not deny the charge (B XII.16–22b). Later in B, Will worries that priests "wol be wrooþ for I write þus" (B XV.489). On the whole, as Wendy Scase has observed, "there is only sporadic internal conceptualization of the poem as a written text."[46]

The waking and writing scenes that bookend B XIX/C XXI therefore stand out for their literary self-consciousness, and so they participate in a rich, late medieval tradition of waking and writing in dream-visions. Like the dreamer in Chaucer's *Book of the Duchess*, Will hears bells in his dream that wake him up to a scene of composition:

> Ryght thus me mette, as I yow telle,
> That in the castell ther was a belle,
> As hyt hadde smyten houres twelve.
> Therwyth I awook myselve
> And fond me lyinge in my bed;
> And the book that I hadde red,
> . . .
> I fond hyt in myn hond ful even.
> Thoghte I, "Thys ys so queynt a sweven
> That I wol, be processe of tyme,
> Fonde to put this sweven in ryme
> As I kan best, and that anoon."
> This was my sweven; now hit ys doon.[47]

Chaucer's dreamer describes his waking, his reflections on his dream, and his resolution to write it down in rhyme. The last line of the poem

[45] "Þanne were marchauntis merye; many wepe for ioye, / And yaf wille for his writyng wollene cloþis; / For he copiede þus here clause þei couden hym gret mede" (A VIII.42–44).

[46] Wendy Scase, "Writing and the Plowman: Langland and Literacy," *YLS* 9 (1995): 121–31 (127).

[47] Geoffrey Chaucer, *The Book of the Duchess*, in *The Riverside Chaucer*, gen ed. Larry D. Benson, 3rd ed. (Boston: Houghton Mifflin, 1987), 1321–34.

indicates that what we have just read constitutes the work the dreamer set himself to do when he awoke from his dream.

As in many medieval dream-visions, Chaucer and Langland both "focused attention on a human experience clearly linked to literary process, and the reader of a dream vision was prepared for a poem that, examining the dream experience, might also examine its own status as poetry."[48] Like Chaucer, Langland indicates the two waking moments on either end of B XIX/C XX as prompts to writing. But Langland's scenes of waking composition differ from Chaucer's and those of most other medieval dream-visions in that they do not neatly conclude the poem. Will's writing functions as more than a frame that links dreaming to literary process. Writing here constitutes part of the plot, part of Will's spiritual and ethical itinerary.

Langland's momentary etiology of the poem's invention also pointedly avoids the didactic rhetoric of some prophetic dream-visions in which dreamers are called to make known certain teachings and judgments to the powers that be.[49] In *Mum and the Sothsegger*, the bee-keeper evinces none of Imaginatif's caution about making when he exhorts the dreamer,

> Loke thou write wisely my wordes echone;
> Hit wol be exemple to sum men seuene yere here-after.
> . . .
> And make vp thy matiere, thou mays do no better.
> Hit may amende many men of theire misdeedes.
> Sith thou felys the fressh lete no feynt herte
> Abate thy blessid bisynes of they boke-making[.][50]

The bee-keeper places the vision in the tradition of political counsel books, the various "mirrors of princes" that convey wisdom to the powerful so that they may "amende . . . theire misdeedes," solving the problem of disordered action by supplying right knowledge. The bee-keeper

[48] Steven F. Kruger, *Dreaming in the Middle Ages* (New York: Cambridge University Press, 1992), 135.

[49] On prophetic and apocalyptic visionary vocations and their significance in *Piers Plowman*, see Richard Kenneth Emmerson, "The Prophetic, the Apocalyptic, and the Study of Medieval Literature," in *Poetic Prophecy in Western Literature*, ed. Jan Wojcik and Raymond-Jean Frontain (Cranbury: Associated University Presses, 1984), 40–54.

[50] *Mum and the Sothsegger*, in *The "Piers Plowman" Tradition: A Critical Edition of "Pierce the Ploughman's Crede," "Richard the Redeless," "Mum and the Sothsegger" and "The Crowned King,"* ed. Helen Barr (London: J. M. Dent, 1993), 1268–69, 1278–81.

betrays a naïvely Platonist anthropology, according to which agents must only know the good in order to do it, while the work as a whole expresses a satirist's cynicism about the likely impact his truth-telling will have on society. The dreamer awakes confident that his visions were

> nedeful and notable for this newe world,
> and eeke plaisant to my pay for thay putten me reste
> Of my long labour and loitryng aboute.
> (1295–97)

But instead of writing down his dream, the narrator proceeds to unpack "a bagge" of "poyse," "Of vice and of vertue fulle to the margyn" (1343, 1344, 1346), and these fragments of satire and moral allegories ramble on for 400 inconclusive lines. Since he never directly links his dream to the invention of the foregoing lines, they merge into the ragtag collection of "poyse." As A. C. Spearing puts it, "ultimately the dream has been used as an excuse for the collapse of literary form into a mere catalogue."[51] Unlike B XIX/C XXI of *Piers Plowman*, *Mum and the Sothsegger* fails to incorporate the invention of the poetry and the act of writing into a plot of ethical and spiritual development. This may be why "boke-making" remains for the bee-keeper an unambiguous good: writing never promises to take on the responsibility of sacramental penance.

Guillaume de Deguileville's *Pèlerinage de la vie humaine* comes closer to the liturgical context of waking and writing in B XIX/C XXI. As at the end of B XVIII/C XX, liturgical bells also wake de Deguileville's dreamer, inspiring him to write down his dream:

> Algates up I ros me and to Matines I wente, but so tormented and weery I was þat I mihte nothing doo þere. My herte I hadde so fichched to þat I hadde met þat me thouhte, and yit do, þat swich is þe pilgrimage of dedliche man in þis cuntre, and þat he is ofte in swich periles—and þerfore I haue sett it in writinge in þe wise þat I mette it.[52]

[51] A. C. Spearing, *Medieval Dream-Poetry* (Cambridge: Cambridge University Press, 1976), 166.

[52] Guillaume de Deguileville, *The Pilgrimage of the Lyfe of the Manhode*, ed. Avril Henry, 2 vols. (New York: Oxford University Press, 1985), 1:174. On Langland's awareness of and indebtedness to de Deguileville, specifically in the waking moments, see Stephen A. Barney, *The Penn Commentary on "Piers Plowman,"* Vol. 5, *C Passūs 20–22; B Passūs 18–20* (Philadelphia: University of Pennsylvania Press, 2006), 104–5; and J. A. Burrow, *Langland's Fictions* (Oxford: Clarendon Press, 1983), 113–18.

Like Will at the start of B XIX/C XXI, when he wakes up, the dreamer of the *Pèlerinage* promptly goes to church, however reluctantly, and has trouble concentrating on the prayers because the dream has wearied him and still demands his affective attention. He had so affixed his heart to what he had dreamed that he perceived its profound affinity to waking life: "me thouhte . . . þat swich is þe pilgrimage of dedliche man in þis cuntre." To "sett" the dream "in writinge" cements the connection between dream life and waking life and renders the dream available to others' participation.

Will's writing also opens his dream to others' participation, but in a mode more closely united to penitential liturgy in the intricate Holy Week and post-Resurrection plotting of passus B XVIII–XIX/C XX–XXI. As Míċeál Vaughan and Raymond St.-Jacques have established, the intricate plot of passus B XVIII–XIX/C XX–XXI follows the Holy Week liturgies by quoting from and alluding to them.[53] The Holy Week and Pentecost liturgies set the itinerary for Will's progress through the scenes of redemption history, with Conscience as his guide. Along the way, Will participates in these quasi-historical events by making liturgical acts of devotion, such as kneeling at the coming of the Holy Spirit. When, upon waking from his dream of the Four Daughters of God, Will sends his wife and daughter to "go reuerense godes resureccion / And crepe to þe croes on knees and kusse hit for a iewel" (C XX.470–71), he is inviting them to participate in the drama of redemption he has just witnessed in his dream. They are to participate liturgically by creeping to the cross and kissing it, a practice so integrated into penitential culture that it was treated simultaneously as an expression of contrition and work of satisfaction in the thirteenth-century Constitution of Giles of Bridport, bishop of Salisbury and codifier of the Sarum Use: "Let no one presume on Easter Day to approach the Body of Christ unless he has first confessed and adored the cross."[54] The liturgical con-

[53] Míċeál F. Vaughan, "The Liturgical Perspectives of *Piers Plowman* B, XVI–XIX," *Studies in Medieval and Renaissance History* 3 (1980): 87–155; Raymond St.-Jacques, "Conscience's Final Pilgrimage in *Piers Plowman* and the Cyclical Structure of the Liturgy," *Revue de l'Université d'Ottawa* 40, no. 2 (1970): 210–23; and Raymond St.-Jacques, "Langland's Bells of the Resurrection and the Easter Liturgy," *ESC* 3, no. 2 (1977): 129–35.

[54] Henry John Feasey, *Ancient English Holy Week Ceremonial* (London: Thomas Baker, 1897), 120; available at *Internet Archive*, archive.org/details/ancientenglishho00feas (accessed May 25, 2011). Here adoration of the cross is the fitting expression of contrition and satisfaction, the other parts of penance in addition to confession.

text of this waking interlude draws all prior and subsequent episodes into its orbit—just as the Triduum encompasses and reframes the entire Christian liturgical year. Whatever comes beyond this point will necessarily have to refer back to the centrality of the cross and the penitential participation by which the cross effects salvation. By signaling the writtenness of the poem at this theologically pivotal moment of the work, Langland unites his work of making to a penitential practice of satisfaction. Will's writing in the waking state corresponds to the textually encoded liturgical actions of kneeling and creeping to the cross. Langland connects this marker of invention, of written labor, to the penitential liturgy of devotion to the cross and to the sacrament of the Eucharist by placing the first explicit acknowledgment of the poem's writtenness in the chiastic fold between two liturgies.

Sacramental Penance and Literary Satisfaction

Having situated the writing of *Piers Plowman* within theologically significant chiastic patterning that unites the work of writing the poem to the work of penitential liturgy, I now turn to the evidence from historical theology concerning practices of satisfaction. Langland invests so much in these formal dynamic middles perhaps because he is chiefly concerned with the lives of the spiritual middle class, the *mediocriter boni* who have not given themselves over to evil, nor reached the state of perfection, but who must repent and rely on God's mercy if they are to make it to heaven.[55] Truth's pardon, the poem's most succinct soteriological statement, assigns those who do good to heaven and those who do evil to hell, leaving the vast middle category of sinners who repent for further explication.[56] This middle category is vast indeed, for the Christian life, even the life of a saint, requires continuous conversion. It is always lived in and from the middle, *in via*.[57] Traugott Lawler has

[55] See Giles Constable, *Three Studies in Medieval and Religious Social Thought: The Interpretation of Mary and Martha, the Ideal of the Imitation of Christ, the Orders of Society* (New York: Cambridge University Press, 1995), 342–60.

[56] The pardon Truth gives to Piers comprises two lines of Latin from the Athanasian Creed: "Et qui bona egerunt ibunt in vitam eternam; / Qui vero mala in ignem eternum" (C IX.286a–b). A priest looking on glosses the Latin: "do wel and haue wel, and god shal haue thy soule / And do yuele and haue euele and hope thow non oþere / Bote he þat euele lyueth euele shal ende" (C IX.290–92).

[57] As Alan Fletcher has argued, drawing on evidence of Langland's practice of revision from version to version, "if the *conversio morum* and its socially desirable by-products were to be sustained, contrition must ever be renewed. It was not a once-off event. And such ongoing contrition is necessarily a project that only a fluidly adaptive text is likely to succeed in enabling: a continuing *conversio morum* requires a coextensive *conversio textus*;

demonstrated how Langland articulates this middle option throughout the poem, especially in revisions from the B- to the C-text.[58] Peace and Mercy carry the day in their debate with Truth and Righteousness (B XVIII/C XX) precisely because Christ's mercy extends to sinners who repent, and extends to them for the sake of their salvation. Lawler summarizes the soteriology thus: "if to do penance is to do well, and to do well is to enter eternal life, then those who sin but do penance will enter eternal life."[59]

Langland identifies the public penitential work of *Piers Plowman* by drawing on the pastoral theology of satisfaction in all its diversity. Penitential practices and theology figure prominently in *Piers Plowman*. Patience explicitly rehearses the conventional penitential theology:

> *Cordis contricio* cometh of sorwe of herte
> And *oris confessio* cometh of knowlechyng and shrifte of mouthe
> And *operis satisfaccio* for soules paieth and alle synnes quyteth.
> (C XVI.29–31)

Satisfaction remains largely undefined in *Piers Plowman*, and its conventional tripartite analysis as prayer, fasting, and almsgiving does not readily correspond to the work many readers understand the poem to be doing. Scholars have given much more attention to confession because this part of the sacrament clearly corresponds to the poem's narrative of failure.[60] But three themes from the pastoral literature on

---

it demands an ongoing, restless adaptation, a re-making by and in the agents of its manufacture. Writing, and the unending business, until death, of repenting and doing well in the real world, may for Langland have been reciprocal activities, and this reciprocity, I would suggest, yields another way of accounting for why he was drawn repeatedly back to his poem. His repeated acts of 'making' may in themselves have embodied a moral venture as much as they indulged some guiltily self-absorbed pleasure in the writing of poetry." Fletcher, "The Essential (Ephemeral) William Langland," 67–68.

[58] Lawler, "The Pardon Formula in *Piers Plowman*," 128–31. Lawler adduces evidence from emphatic C-text revisions, such as this amplification of Repentance's prayer on behalf of the repentant *commune*:

> [W]hat tyme we synnefole men wolden be sory
> For dedes that we han don ylle dampned sholde we ben neuere
> Yf we knowlechede and cryde Crist þerfore mercy:
> *Quandocumque ingemuerit peccator omnes iniquitates eius non recordabor amplius.*
> (C VII.145–47a)

[59] Lawler, "The Pardon Formula in *Piers Plowman*," 140.

[60] Of the three parts of penance, confession has received the most attention in studies of *Piers Plowman*. Its first lines signal that the work involves confession. The narrating "I" reflects back on another time from a particular moral vantage, one from which the "werkes" of his past seem "vnholy" (C Prol.3). The Londe of Longynge episodes, espe-

satisfaction complicate and enrich an understanding of satisfaction as prayer, fasting, and almsgiving, and illuminate how Langland understands satisfaction.

First, one aspect or "part" of satisfaction is contrition for and recollection of past sins *in prayer*, apart from and subsequent to auricular confession to a priest. As the Good Samaritan tells Will, "sorwe of herte is satisfaccion for suche þat may nat paye" (C XIX.604). The fourteenth-century preaching manual *Fasciculus morum* suggests the narrative quality of prayerful satisfaction:

> Therefore, the words of the Psalm apply well to these and others who thus grieve for their sins: "I will recount to you all my years," and so forth; add: the years I have spent in vain endeavors, for which I have held the eternal years in my mind which I have lost with their glory, and therefore I have kept them firmly in my contrite mind.[61]

This kind of contrite recollection *as satisfaction* could describe much of what readers of *Piers Plowman* have typically and problematically treated as confession. To understand *Piers Plowman*'s narratives of failure as confession is problematic because auricular confession must be made to a priest, and so any analysis of *Piers Plowman* in terms of confession has had to use an analogy to confession, rather than the sacrament itself. If we understand the narratives of failure as satisfaction, we can see how Will within the poem and William Langland as author could both be performing the work of satisfaction by recounting "the years I have spent in vain endeavors."

---

cially, can be read as the extended confession of error. Vaughan argues that *Piers Plowman* "is one man's confession of mouth, his contrite narration of his past life of sleeping, of misunderstanding, ignorance, and sin, from which he finally 'gan awake.'" Míċeál F. Vaughan, "'Til I gan awake': The Conversion of Dreamer into Narrator in *Piers Plowman* B," *YLS* 5 (1991): 175–92 (191). See also Vaughan, "Liturgical Perspectives," 87–101. John Bowers doubts whether Will has the requisite contrition to make a good confession, arguing that his sleepiness in the early passus represents a slothful disposition that resists contrition; John Bowers, *The Crisis of Will in "Piers Plowman"* (Washington, D.C.: The Catholic University of America Press, 1986), 61–77. Katherine C. Little leaves the poem's penitential work to one side to focus on its critical function, arguing that "Langland's portrait of confession [in B V] underlines the magnitude of the task of reform as well as 'some misgivings' about it." Katherine C. Little, *Confession and Resistance: Defining the Self in Late Medieval England* (Notre Dame: University of Notre Dame Press, 2006), 27. For a consideration of the poem's lived theology of penance ordered toward reconciliation, see Rachael Deagman, "The Formation of Forgiveness in *Piers Plowman*," *JMEMSt* 40, no. 2 (2010): 273–97.

[61] *Fasciculus morum: A Fourteenth-Century Preacher's Handbook*, ed. and trans. Siegfried Wenzel (University Park: Pennsylvania State University Press, 1989), 525.

Second, by the fourteenth century the category of "almsgiving" had greatly expanded to include all the corporal and spiritual works of mercy, with the latter including "to teach the uneducated, give counsel to people who are in doubt, console the sorrowing, correct the sinner, forgive those who offend, support those who are burdened, and pray for all."[62] The meaning of "alms" is similarly dilated in *Piers Plowman*, where the *lorelles* who do not want to help Piers plow his half-acre pray that his grain will multiply, in exchange for his "Almesse þat ȝe ȝeuen vs here" (C VIII.133). The material alms Piers might give the *lorelles* are later transfigured into the fruits of his scriptural plowing as the seeds of virtues that he plants grow into good deeds (C XXI.258–75). Likewise, *Fasciculus morum* turns the parable of the sower and the seed to consider satisfaction by almsgiving: "Next you must . . . put on it some soil that is rich and fertile, called *marl* in English, which is true and just penance for this and that sin. And then let us sow the seed of good works."[63] Alms, dilated to include all the spiritual and corporal works of mercy, resist the privatization of satisfaction. Satisfaction by alms is oriented toward the person or community offended, making it a public action rather than a private transaction of the kind satirized throughout *Piers Plowman*, the "pryue payement" that Friar Flatterer accepts from Contrition at the low point of the final passus (C XXII.364). Furthermore, the works of mercy prominently include edification, counsel, and fraternal correction. *Piers Plowman* is full of such works of mercy and therefore the writing of the poem constitutes the work of "alms" as penitential satisfaction.

Third, *Piers Plowman* holds a mechanistic understanding of penance up to critique, promoting instead what I call open-ended satisfaction. Priests from at least the thirteenth century frequently imposed, in addition to a specific penance, this general penance as part of the absolution: "May whatever good you do and suffering you endure be for the remission of your sins."[64] Thomas Aquinas praised this penance for its psycho-

[62] Ibid., 529.

[63] Ibid., 549.

[64] This is the rubric as it was eventually formalized after Trent in the penitential rite of Paul V: "Passio Domini nostri Iesu Christi, merita beatae Mariae Virginis, & omnium Sanctorum, & quicquid boni feceris & mali sustinueris sint tibi in remissionem peccatorum, augmentum gratiae, & praemium vitae eternae." *Rituale romanum Pauli Quinti* (Rome, 1636), 48–49; available at Google Books, http://books.google.co.uk/ (accessed October 4, 2014). The exact wording varies in pre-Tridentine sources. Relevant to England is this rubric for absolution in the Sarum Pontifical: "Passio Jesu Christi, merita beatae Mariae, et omnium sanctorum, et totius ecclesiae catholicae, quicquid etiam boni

spiritual sensitivity, noting that the debt of sin is often so great that a fittingly heavy penance would extinguish the small flame of contrition. Better, he thought, "that the priest should tell the penitent how great a penance ought to be imposed on him for his sins; and let him impose on him nevertheless something that the penitent could tolerably bear." Then if the penitent does more good beyond the penance, those works will avail for the remission of sins because the priest has endowed them with the expiatory power of the keys.[65] By 1614 this general penance was enshrined in the mandatory Roman penitential rite, but it was in widespread use in the late Middle Ages.[66] This meant that when wisely

---

feceris et mali sustinueris pro dilectione Dei et proximi, cedant tibi in remissionem istorum et aliorum peccatorum tuorum, in augmentum gratiae, et praemium vitae aeternae." *Monumenta ritualia ecclesiae Anglicanae; or, Occasional Offices of the Church of England According to the Ancient Use of Salisbury*, Vol. I, ed. William Maskell (London: W. Pickering, 1846), 228.

[65] Thomas Aquinas, *Quaestiones de quodlibet*, quodlibet III q. 13 art. 1; available at http://www.corpusthomisticum.org/q03.html (accessed January 15, 2011). This quodlibetal question, composed during Thomas's second regency in Paris, 1268–72, is the earliest record of the rubric I have found, besides the Sarum Use (see previous note). Thomas suggests that the rubric is already in widespread use: "These things which he does beyond the expressed command more greatly receive the power of the expiation of present sins from that general imposition that the priest says: *May whatever good you do be for the remission of your sins*. So it is praiseworthy that many priests became accustomed to saying this—although they do not have the greater power to grant remedy against future sin; and insofar as such satisfaction is sacramental in this case, it expiates [already] committed sins by the power of the [office of the] keys" ("et haec quae praeter iniunctionem expressam facit, accipiunt maiorem vim expiationis culpae praeteritae ex illa generali iniunctione qua sacerdos dicit: *quidquid boni feceris, sit tibi in remissionem peccatorum*. Unde laudabiliter consuevit hoc a multis sacerdotibus dici, licet non habeant maiorem vim ad praebendum remedium contra culpam futuram; et quantum ad hoc talis satisfactio est sacramentalis, in quantum virtute clavium est culpae commissae expiativa").

[66] The rubric seems to have become more closely united with routine absolution and more widely used over the course of the fourteenth and early fifteenth centuries. The Sarum Pontifical, which likely has its roots in the early thirteenth century, gives this rubric in the context of the reconciliation of excommunicates (see note 64 above). In *Pupilla oculi* (1385), an influential manual for priests, John of Burgh, chancellor of the University of Cambridge, assumes that the rubric is being used regularly for the penance of lay communicants. He remarks that "after the imposition of the specific penance, priests are accustomed to say, 'May whatever good you do be for the remission of your sins,'—and this practice is extremely praiseworthy" ("Solent namque sacerdotes post iniunctam penitentiam specialem sic dicere, Quicquid boni feceris sit tibi in remissionem peccatorum et valde laudabiliter"). John of Burgh, *Pupilla oculi* (Strasburg: Schott, Knobloch, and Götz, 1516), xl; available at Bayerische Staatsbibliothek, gateway-bayern.de/VD16+J+374 (accessed June 13, 2013). The Middle English verse adaptation of *Pupilla oculi*, John Mirk's *Instructions for Parish Priests* (c. 1400), includes the rubric in Latin as an intrinsic part of the absolution, with no comment on its laudability. See John Mirk, *Instructions for Parish Priests*, ed. Gillis Kristensson (Lund: Gleerup, 1974), 162–63. To situate the mainstream adoption of this rubric in the broader historical development of penance, see Henry Ansgar Kelly, "Penitential Theology and Law

applied, the three parts of penance did not constitute a closed sequence with a discrete beginning and end, confined to the parish church during obligatory annual shrift in Holy Week, but permeated all of life, since every good work and every suffering could avail for the remission of sins.

Piers Plowman is not the only fourteenth-century example of writing as an alms-deed, a spiritual work of mercy in an open-ended, lifelong practice of satisfaction. According to Richard Rolle's *Form of Living*, alms-deeds involve "nat only to gyf pouer men met or drynke, bot for to . . . enfourme ham how þay shal do þat ben in poynt to perisshe."[67] *Piers Plowman* is if nothing else an effort to "enforme" those who will some day face death "how þay shal do" by making of the phrase a question and enacting the search for its answer in the quest for Dowel, Dobet, and Dobest. Rolle's penitent can "enfourme ham how þay shal do" by "clennesse . . . in hert, in mouth, and in werke," three spheres of the spiritual life that continuously interact in "honest occupacioun and profitable," and in "litelle . . . speche." The economy of speech Rolle envisions cannot be achieved until "þi hert be stablet in þe loue of Ihesu, so þat þe þynke þat þou lokest euer on hym [Christ], wheþer þou spek or noȝt." This means that the task Holy Church enjoins on Will—"Lere hit thus lewed men . . . : / Than treuthe and trewe loue is no tresor bettre" (C I.135)—might constitute a work of satisfaction, an "almes dede" of "clennes of mouth," but not without great travail and habituation: "Bot such a grace may þou noght haue in þe first day, bot with longe trauaille and gret bisinesse to loue, and with custume."[68] To do well in such work will require lifelong practice.

While Rolle's immediate audience was the anchoress Margaret Kyrkeby, his conception of *clene speche* as a lifelong work of satisfaction extends to the project Nicholas Watson finds him sharing with Dante: "to engage in complex processes of reinterpretation of their lives and writings in order to present them as patterned in meaningful ways . . . creating retrospective patterns where none were before."[69] As Watson notes, the evangelistic goals of such a project require author and literary

at the Turn of the Fifteenth Century," in *A New History of Penance*, ed. Abigail Firey (Leiden: Brill, 2008), 239–98.

[67] Richard Rolle, *The Form of Living*, in *Richard Rolle: Prose and Verse*, ed. S. J. Ogilvie-Thomson, EETS o.s. 293 (Oxford: Oxford University Press, 1988), 13.

[68] Ibid.

[69] Nicholas Watson, *Richard Rolle and the Invention of Authority* (New York: Cambridge University Press, 1991), 267.

persona to overlap, connecting the subjectivities and work of invention inside the poem to the work of an author outside the poem, thus rendering the fictive material real and publicly available for use and participation. Middleton has also recognized that "the visionary duration of Will's life, the making of the poem that records it, and a life of penitential self-knowledge through confession are . . . rendered synonymous."[70] This obliquely autobiographical connection causes the internal, fictional work of the poem—Will's quest—and, eventually, his writing, to participate in the external work of its invention, composition, and disposition: William Langland's work of satisfaction, understood as a lifelong project to "kenne it aboute" (C I.88) "how þai sall do"—in Rolle's terms—by "clennes of mouth."[71] Rolle's and Langland's shared sense of the lifelong, open-ended nature of satisfaction anticipates the expansion of the absolution rubric in Mirk's *Instructions to Parish Priests* (c. 1400) to emphasize just this aspect of satisfaction. Mirk integrates the "whatever good you do" rubric with the traditional absolution and makes explicit what was only implied in earlier versions of the rubric: "may all the good deeds which you have done *and will do up to the end of your life* be for the remission of these and all your other sins."[72] Langland approaches the relationship between penance and Dowel, Dobet, and Dobest from this open-ended perspective on penance, this sense of satisfaction as ongoing and potentially imbuing all of life.[73] The poetry's representational mode absorbs the form of the sacrament. The writing of the poetry can then become a means of enacting the sacrament of penance, of doing well for the remission of sins.

Making Satisfaction across the Reformation

If we wanted an image of a pivotal juncture between Langland's practice of making satisfaction, Conscience's tears in the final passus "for the

[70] Anne Middleton, "William Langland's 'Kynde Name': Authorial Signature and Social Identity in Late Fourteenth-Century England," in *Literary Practice and Social Change in Britain, 1380–1530*, ed. Lee Patterson (Berkeley: University of California Press, 1990), 15–82 (60).

[71] Rolle, *The Form of Living*, 13.

[72] Mirk, *Instructions for Parish Priests*, 163 (my italics). The full rubric after the traditional absolution reads, "Ista humilitas et passio domini nostri ihesu christi / et merita sancte matris ecclesiae, et omnes indulgencie / tibi concesse, et omnia bona que fecisti et facies vsque / in finem vite tue, sint tibi in remissionem istorum et / omnium aliorum peccatorum tuorum. Amen" (162–63).

[73] Larry Scanlon has recognized this dynamic in the B V pageant of the Seven Deadly Sins, where the penitential "discourse this piece of poetry draws on offers no moment where semiosis stops. Langland's personifications of penitential discourse are drawn into

failure . . . of the penitential system,"[74] and Briony Tallis's authorial despair over the impossibility of atonement, we might turn to Sir Thomas Wyatt's *A Paraphrase of the Penitential Psalms*, written likely in the wake of a revision of penitential theology by the 1536 *Articles about Religion* (commonly known as the Ten Articles). In passages of connecting commentary, as well as in the Psalm paraphrases themselves, Wyatt dwells on the incommensurable difference between God and man, and the impossibility of satisfying the infinite debt not only of David's grave sins, but of any sin whatsoever.

> But when he weigh'th the fault and recompense,
> He damn'th his deed and findeth plain
> Atween them two [David and God] no whit equivalence
> Whereby he takes all outward deed in vain
> To bear the name of rightful penitence,
> Which is alone the heart returned again
> And sore contrite that doth his fault bemoan,
> And outward deed the sign of fruit alone.[75]

---

an endless signifying loop by the requirement of doctrines no less than by their poetic complexity." Larry Scanlon, "Personification and Penance," *YLS* 21 (2007): 1–29 (29).

[74] Nicholas Watson, "*Piers Plowman*, Pastoral Theology, and Spiritual Perfectionism: Hawkyn's Cloak and Patience's Pater Noster," *YLS* 21 (2007), 83–118 (116). Watson labels this interpretation of Conscience's cries as "Lutheran" or more generally "post-Reformation," and after interrogating the post-Lateran IV "pastoral project" and its failures, he concludes that "even in crisis, Langland's commitment to the universalism of the pastoral project remains unshaken." As evidence, he turns to the chiastic passages that have occupied much of this essay: "the sacrament of the Eucharist survive[s] untouched, given renewed emphasis by Will's reintegration with the church through the Mass in passūs 18–19, as he experiences the life and death of Christ and lives the same events liturgically in his waking life (especially B.18.427–33, 19.1–4)" (117). According to my reading here, *Piers Plowman* embraces and transcends penitential "failure," absorbing it in the ongoing life of sanctification and satisfaction, not only for individuals, but for the corporate Church as well—a topic for another essay. Langland's understanding of open-ended satisfaction, as I have developed it here, resists Watson's understanding of the meaning of pastoral and institutional failure in *Piers Plowman*. The poem is not just a critique of a failed project, nor a desperate act of hope predicated on an overrealized eschatology (ibid., 96). Rather, it contributes to the pastoral project and articulates an eschatological horizon in which the failures of the institutional Church must constantly be repaired and atoned for in a penitential quest for union with the crucified Lord. The pastoral project is not a progressive nor an apocalyptic project, and therefore need not be abandoned when it does not succeed in effecting or witnessing an "imminent transformation of the world" (ibid.). To apply a phrase of Protestant coinage to Langland, *Ecclesia semper reformanda est* (the Church must always be reformed).

[75] Sir Thomas Wyatt, *A Paraphrase of the Penitential Psalms*, in *The Complete Poems*, ed. R. A. Rebholz (Harmondsworth: Penguin, 1978), 648–55.

Wyatt's suspicion of the "outward deed" echoes the 1536 *Articles*' emphasis that works cannot of themselves merit anything: "not as though our contrition, or faith, or any works proceeding thereof, can worthily merit or deserve to attain the said justification."[76]

Reading both of these texts from the perspective of later developments in radical Puritan thought, James Simpson notes that for Wyatt's David, "nothing but grace, or God's unprovoked, unmerited gift, defines the relation between sinner and God. . . . Grace, in this account, renders the virtuous accretions of the individual life entirely redundant, or at best a 'sacrifice.' "[77] To be sure, certain strains of English theology would develop in this direction, and Thomas Cranmer's Forty-Two Articles of 1552 would exclude penance from the sacraments, grouping it among those practices "grown partly of the corrupt following of the Apostles," leaving only the "dominical" sacraments of baptism and Eucharist.[78] Yet the 1536 *Articles* include penance in the triad of sacraments "instituted of Christ in the New Testament as a thing so necessary to man's salvation, that no man which after his Baptism is fallen again, and hath committed deadly sin, can, without the same, be saved, or attain everlasting life."[79] While the Ten Articles consider that the sinner "hath no works or merits of his own, which he may worthily lay before God, as sufficient satisfaction for his sins,"[80] they emphatically endorse practices of satisfaction that might as well find their place in a medieval Catholic penitential manual:

> all men truly penitent, contrite, and confessed, must needs also bring forth the fruits of penance, that is to say, prayer, fasting, almsdeeds, and must make restitution or satisfaction in will and deed to their neighbour, . . . and also must do all other good works of mercy and charity, . . . or else they shall never be saved.[81]

[76] *Articles about Religion, Set Out by the Convocation, and Published by the King's Authority*, in *Formularies of Faith Put Forth by Authority during the Reign of Henry VIII*, ed. Charles Lloyd (Oxford: Oxford University Press, 1856), 12; available at Google Books, http://books.google.co.uk/ (accessed February 14, 2012).

[77] James Simpson, *The Oxford English Literary History*, Vol. 2, *1350–1547: Reform and Cultural Revolution* (Oxford: Oxford University Press, 2004), 324.

[78] Gerald Lewis Bray, *Documents of the English Reformation 1526–1701* (Cambridge: James Clarke, 2004), 299.

[79] *Articles about Religion*, 8.

[80] Ibid., 9.

[81] Ibid., 10–11.

In the political welter of subsequent decades, the Ten Articles' palpable tension between the real social consequences of sin, the gratuitousness of salvation, and penitential cooperation with grace in works of satisfaction would appear to have been no more than "a careful, if finally incoherent, compromise between radical and conservative views."[82]

But Langland's practices of satisfaction—performed as contrite, questing, and edifying works of mercy—suggest another view on Wyatt's penitential poetic, a view from which the Ten Articles appear surprisingly coherent. Langland's careful development of the relationship between doing well, poetic making, and sacramental satisfaction finds an echo in Wyatt's penitential poetics. For David's contrite heart does more than just feel contrition; it "doth his fault bemoan" (654), not only in acknowledgment of wrongdoing, but in recognition and announcement of God's mercy, to "lere[n] hit thus lewed men," in Holy Church's terms (C I.135): "Sinners I shall into thy ways address, / They shall return to thee and thy grace sue" (486–87). Wyatt's David echoes the penitential manuals' understanding of edification as a work of mercy because medieval penitential theology was itself derived in part from the penitential Psalms—a salutary reminder that reformist preference for scripture often did not effect a rupture with tradition, which was also based on scripture. While Wyatt interjects his own concern about outward show—"But thou delights in no such gloze / Of outward deed as men dream and devise" (498–99)—he also uses the Psalm that would become the Book of Common Prayer's morning canticle to work out how deeds, and especially his own public, poetic practice of satisfaction, can constitute authentic "sacrifice." The key is God's grace cooperating within him to generate deeds that God can accept outwardly:

> Thou must, O Lord, my lips first unloose,
> . . .
> Make Zion, Lord, according to thy will,
> Inward Zion, the Zion of the ghost.
> Of heart's Jerusalem strength the wall still.
> Then shalt thou take for good these outward deeds
> As sacrifice thy pleasure to fulfil.
> Of thee alone thus all our good proceeds.
> (494, 503–8)

[82] Simpson, *Reform and Cultural Revolution*, 324.

Wyatt takes such pains to parse outward show and inward true contrition because he keenly perceives the danger of what Sarah Beckwith has called "the mind's retreat from the face" in early modern England—the widening gap between personal belief and collective uniformity, between private dissent and public allegiance, between authentic religion and perfunctory rites, between the invisible and the visible Church.[83] For Wyatt's David, sin is the name for this retreat, and insofar as it is a retreat from the face of God, the remedy for sin is to be healed and strengthened from inside out—not just inside.[84] Sin has not lost its public dimension, nor has reconciliation.[85]

The radical Protestant Robert Crowley, who edited, glossed, and printed three editions of *Piers Plowman* B in 1550, seems to have concurred.[86] To be sure, he identifies Lady Mede's ability to finagle cheap grace as "the fruites of Popish penaunce," and he labels as "the olde satisfacion" Lechour's preposterous rehab plan to "drynke but wiþ þe duck" for seven years of Saturdays.[87] But despite Crowley's periodization, he aligns the Protestant present with Langland's deeply conventional critique of penitential abuses, revealing a fundamental continuity between the two authors' reforming impulses. And at what is perhaps *Piers Plowman*'s most "Catholic" moment, when Christ entrusts the office of the keys to a very Petrine Piers (B XIX.182–90), Crowley's only gloss actually intensifies the penitential logic of *redde quod debes*, by

[83] Beckwith, *Shakespeare and the Grammar of Forgiveness*, 20–33.

[84] On the same issue of inner and outward actions, Erasmus believed, according to Jennifer Herdt, that "To imitate exemplary virtues—the charity of Christ and the saints—is not to do something merely 'external'; to honor and admire exemplary virtue without imitating it is." Jennifer Herdt, *Putting on Virtue: The Legacy of the Splendid Vices* (Chicago: University of Chicago Press, 2008), 109. Where Wyatt could differ—and where Herdt locates a fatal development in early modern ethical theory—is on the capacity of outward deeds to effect inward change. For Erasmus, "what is 'exterior,' what appears, can shape what is 'interior,' the character of our hearts" (109).

[85] As Simpson remarks, in David's efforts to reconcile himself with God we can also perceive Wyatt's suit to regain Henry VIII's favor. While the analogy renders "the relationship between [temporal] lord and servant . . . massively disproportionate," it also presents Wyatt's work of poetry as secular satisfaction for his political offenses. Simpson, *Reform and Cultural Revolution*, 327.

[86] See R. Carter Hailey, "'Geuyng light to the Reader': Robert Crowley's Editions of *Piers Plowman* (1550)," *PBSA* 94 (2001): 483–502; Sarah A. Kelen, *Langland's Early Modern Identities* (New York: Palgrave Macmillan, 2007), 26–36; Little, "Transforming Work," 508–13.

[87] Robert Crowley, *The Vision of Pierce Plowman, nowe the seconde tyme imprinted by Roberte Crowlye . . . Whereunto are added certaine notes and cotations in the mergyne, geuyng light to the Reader* (London: Robert Crowley, 1550) (*STC* 19907a), fols. 12v, 21v; *Early English Books Online*, eebo.chadwyck.com/home (accessed February 15, 2012).

which "hath Pierce power . . . / To bynde and unbinde, both here and els where / And assoylen menne of all synnes" (fol. 106v). In the margin adjacent to this controversial Catholic claim, Crowley notes, "Pierces pardon is, pai that thou oweste."[88] While the gloss could seem subtly to redirect the passage toward purely juridical restitution, Crowley elsewhere chimes in with Patience's commentary on David's penitential Psalm 32 to affirm that "Satisfaction kylleth sinne" (fol. 73r; B XIV.95–96).[89] Crowley's sideline cheer for satisfaction might bespeak uneasiness about the efficacy of auricular confession, but it resonates not at all with the interiorization and privatization of sin and forgiveness that Langland and Crowley both see as threats to authentic Christian living.

That the discourses of sacramental and literary satisfaction were alive and well in the early Reformation should not surprise. As historian Thomas N. Tentler has remarked,

> The polemics of the Reformation and confessional age were bitter and prolonged precisely because the opposing parties agreed on fundamentals: that there must be ecclesiastical rites of expulsion and reconciliation, dogmatic theological formulas and causal explanations of the justification of sinners, a comprehensible psychological description of the experience of that forgiveness, and belief in the eternal consequences of the success or failure to "achieve" that forgiveness.[90]

Martin Luther may have been driven to desperation by the impossibility of ever fully atoning for his sins, but once he rediscovered grace through faith, lifelong repentance turned from bane to boon, the very way of the cross, as the opening salvo of the Ninety-Five Theses attests:

> 1. Our Lord and Master Jesus Christ, when He said *Poenitentiam agite*, desired that the whole life of the faithful be penance.

[88] Larry Scanlon cogently surmises that "Crowley tolerates the ecclesiological claims because . . . Langland is poetically extending Catholic authority and not simply affirming it, and because as the passus continues he will use this poetic extension to demonstrate that virtuous social action is an imperative of individual conscience." Larry Scanlon, "Langland, Apocalypse, and the Early Modern Editor," in *Reading the Medieval in Early Modern England*, ed. Gordon McMullan and David Matthews (New York: Cambridge University Press, 2007), 51–73 (69).

[89] "And satisfaction seketh oute the rote, and both sleeth and voydeth / And as it never had ben, to nought bringeth dedly syn" (fol. 73r).

[90] Thomas N. Tentler, "Postscript," in *Penitence in the Age of Reformations*, ed. Katharine Jackson Lualdi and Anne T. Thayer (Burlington: Ashgate, 2000), 240–59.

2. This saying cannot be understood concerning sacramental penance, i.e., confession and satisfaction, which is administered by the priests.

3. Yet he means not only interior [penitence]; indeed, interior [penitence] is nothing, unless one outwardly performs manifold mortifications of the flesh.[91]

Langland's understanding of open-ended satisfaction, as I have developed it here, would make a very intriguing gloss on Luther's second thesis. One scandal of Truth's pardon—"Dowel and have well and God shal have thy soul"—is that it seems to elide the penitential system, as does Luther's second thesis. But the dynamic middle of *Piers Plowman*, saturated with both sacramental penance and the grace of faith, absorbs the penance administered by priests into a much larger picture, the "whole life of the faithful" living the *evangelium crucis*, Luther's mark of the authentic Christian life.

Nor did only the Lutherans exhibit affinities with Catholic penitential practices. Later English Reformed writers stressed lifelong sanctification as participation in the life and death of Christ. Granting that hardline Calvinist election soteriology could seem to obviate a Christian's growth in holiness, pastoral practice in many branches of the Reformation cultivated a lively and robust sense of how the good a Christian might do, or the suffering she might endure, could avail for saving participation in Christ.[92] As Deborah Shuger argues, many Tudor Protestants believed that "the road to heaven is paved with good works."[93] Where Catholic

[91] "1. Dominus et magister noster Iesus Christus dicendo 'Penitentiam agite &c.' omnem vitam fidelium penitentiam esse voluit. 2. Quod verbum de penitentia sacramentali (id est confessionis et satisfactionis, que sacerdotum ministerio celebratur) non potest intelligi. 3. Non tamen solam intendit interiorem, immo interior nulla est, nisi foris operetur varias carnis mortificationes." Martin Luther, "Disputatio pro declaratione virtutis indulgentiarum" (1517); available at Project Wittenberg, http://www.projectwittenberg.org (accessed October 4, 2014).

[92] Peter Lake characterizes the "ordo paenitendi" of the moderate Puritan Abdiel Ashton as an open-ended experience by which "God always employed the faults of his children to their ultimate spiritual advantage, since each lapse provided the occasion for a fresh turning to God through a recapitulation of the processes of repentance. . . . Not only was Christ responsible, through his sacrifice on the cross, for our freedom from the imputation of sin, he was also the moving force in our gradual liberation from our own sins, in the process of sanctification." Lake, *Moderate Puritans and the Elizabethan Church* (New York: Cambridge University Press, 1982), 164–65.

[93] Deborah Shuger, "The Reformation of Penance," *HLQ* 71, no. 4 (2008): 557–71 (561). Shuger likens Edmund Spenser's penitential theology to Langland's, noting how Una entrusts the Redcross Knight "to the care of Mercy, who guides him to a 'holy hospital' where 'seven beadmen that had vowed all / Their life to service of high heaven's

and Protestant could most readily disagree was on the possibility of condign merit—whether good works performed by grace could avail for a soul's salvation—and on the necessity of the priestly office.[94] But all believed on the basis of biblical evidence that good works and sufferings would receive at least rewards in heaven (e.g., Lk 6:23, 35).

By arguing that we should recognize continuities in the practice of efficacious satisfaction as open-ended growth in holiness characterized by works of mercy, literary or otherwise, I do not mean to occlude the many convolutions of penitential practice and theology wrought by the cultural revolutions of the late medieval and early modern periods.[95] But if we are to understand penance as a sacrament, then we cannot reduce its history to the mere sum of variable practices and discourses. One brief example from recent history suggests how we might consider a changing phenomenon such as satisfaction to exceed social and intellectual history's range of vision.

The *Joint Declaration on the Doctrine of Justification* (1999) was the fruit of ecumenical dialogue between the Roman Catholic Church and the main historical branches of the Reformation that has been taking place seriously since at least the 1960s. In it, Lutherans and Catholics "confess together" that even after Baptism:

> the justified must all through life constantly look to God's unconditional justifying grace . . . and are not exempt from a lifelong struggle against the contradiction to God within the selfish desires of the old Adam (cf. Gal 5:16; Rom 7:7–10). The justified also must ask God daily for forgiveness as in the Lord's Prayer (Mt 6:12; 1 Jn 1:9), are ever again called to conversion and penance, and are ever again granted forgiveness. . . . We confess together that good works—a Christian life lived in faith, hope and love—follow justification and

King' instruct the knight in the seven works of mercy, so that 'Mercy in the end his righteous soul might save.' Here, as in Langland, this saving mercy is at one and the same time the righteous soul's own mercifulness and the mercy of God extended to the merciful; the syntax insists upon the interlacings of human and divine initiative" (561).

[94] For a good example of this argument, see Thomas More, *The Confutation of Tyndale's Answer*, in *The Complete Works of St. Thomas More*, ed. Louis Martz et al., 15 vols. (New Haven: Yale University Press, 1963–97), 8.1:90–91.

[95] For an appreciation of these changes that emphasizes rupture, see Thomas N. Tentler, *Sin and Confession on the Eve of the Reformation* (Princeton: Princeton University Press, 1977), 345–70.

are its fruits. When the justified live in Christ and act in the grace they receive, they bring forth, in biblical terms, good fruit.[96]

Absent from this formulation is agreement on the function of the office of the keys, and the *Declaration* avoids explicit discussion of the distinction between temporal and eternal *poena* and *culpa*.[97] But it recognizes as common to both traditions a fundamental sense of penance as an ongoing, open-ended practice of good works as a way of participating more fully in Christ. The framers of the *Joint Declaration* refuse to paper over the Reformation-era disagreements; the mutual "condemnations are still valid today and thus have a church-dividing effect."[98] But neither side thought it too late to move toward reconciliation. Nor are the *Declaration*'s "binding decisions" the end, for the Church is still *in via*, "on the way to overcoming the division . . . toward that visible unity which is Christ's will."[99] The *Declaration* was subsequently ratified by the World Methodist Federation and has been widely acknowledged as valid by Anglicans.[100]

The principle of continuity on which these bodies based their agreement was not so much a convergence of social practices or hindsight equivocation of intellectual discourses. Rather, they understood themselves to be enhancing the incomplete "visible unity" of the universal Church, which receives its coherence only from the future, from the

[96] Lutheran World Federation and the Catholic Church, *Joint Declaration on the Doctrine of Justification*, 4.44, 47, http://www.vatican.va/roman_curia/pontifical_councils/chrstuni/documents/rc_pc_chrstuni_doc_31101999_cath-luth-joint-declaration_en.html (accessed February 2, 2012).

[97] For a modern Lutheran's very "Catholic" view of the office of the keys in early Lutheranism, see David Yeago, "The Office of the Keys: On the Disappearance of Discipline in Protestant Modernity," in *Marks of the Body of Christ*, ed. Robert W. Jenson and Karl E. Braaten (Grand Rapids: William B. Eerdmans, 1999), 95–122.

[98] Lutheran World Federation and the Catholic Church, *Joint Declaration*, Preamble.1.

[99] Ibid., Preamble.4, 5.44. The decisions shed significant "new light":

> the doctrinal condemnations of the 16th century, in so far as they relate to the doctrine of justification, appear in a new light: The teaching of the Lutheran churches presented in this Declaration does not fall under the condemnations from the Council of Trent. The condemnations in the Lutheran Confessions do not apply to the teaching of the Roman Catholic Church presented in this Declaration. (5.41)

[100] On Anglican agreement, see R. William Franklin, "A Model for a New Joint Declaration: An Episcopalian Reaction to the *Joint Declaration on Justification*," in *Justification and the Future of the Ecumenical Movement*, ed. William G. Rusch (Collegeville: Liturgical Press, 2003), 35–46 (37–38).

promised end of Christ's high-priestly prayer "ut sint unum" (Jn 17:11)—that all may be one. For the two churches, the phenomenon of sacramental penance appears fully only when seen in eschatological perspective. The two churches can recognize satisfaction and its attendant works and mortifications as an essential part of the Christian life because they are revealed in Christ, whom both churches hold to be continuously present in his extended body, the Church universal—though not with the fullness that will be manifest in the Kingdom of Heaven. As Paul writes, Christians are "always bearing about in our body the mortification of Jesus, that the life also of Jesus may be made manifest in our bodies" (2 Cor 4:10). So it is finally the Pauline logic of the always-present but not-yet-fulfilled body of Christ, rather than historical agreements, that underwrites the *Joint Declaration*'s agreement about lifelong, open-ended satisfaction as growing participation in the life of Christ.

This example suggests that inquiry into religious continuity across Renaissance and Reformation should not function primarily on a logic of conservation versus loss, though it certainly involves those dynamics. Rather, on either side of the Reformation, God and the human, united in Christ, are the dual principles of continuity. A history that does not enter sympathetically into this self-understanding is capable of measuring greater or lesser degrees of change in social practices and intellectual discourses, but not of seeing continuity in the way the communities it studies see it.

To read *Piers Plowman* from its dynamic, crucicentric middle, where loss and gain hang in the balance, refreshes the temporality of penance so that even in its dismal final passus it is not too late to cry after grace, for the crucicentric middle ensures that even failure can be turned to satisfaction. Piers may end up a "presence-become-absence" by the end of the poem, but that ending is not the poem's "conclusion."[101] Conscience's quest might seem endless, doomed to failure because he seeks to endow the very religious orders that brought ruin to the penitential system and the pastoral project commenced in 1215.[102] But as Con-

[101] David Aers, "Langland on the Church and the End of the Cardinal Virtues," *JMEMSt* 42, no. 1 (2012), 59–81 (73). For a close reading of the final passus's penitential crisis that concurs with Aers and lends detail to my argument here, see Deagman, "The Formation of Forgiveness," 90–94.

[102] Aers, "Langland on the Church," provides the most comprehensive account of the final passus's institutional and sacramental failures, and the various ecclesial options.

science sets off on his new search for Piers, crying after Grace, he and his readers know much more than they did back in the fair field full of folk. They know where to look. In his new quest, Conscience knows to seek again the dynamic middle where the search for Dowel, Dobet, and Dobest prompts continual repentance and renewal in the sacraments and fosters growth in holiness, and where Piers's life of *lele labour* merges with Christ's life lived unto death for humanity.[103]

How else could the poem end, when the principle of continuity that will leap across the Reformation intact, the only available goal for Conscience to seek after at the end of *Piers Plowman*, is a Pauline figure of the Church as the suffering body of Christ, both conquered and conqueror in the doubled illumination of eschatological hope?

> . . . Peres þe plouhman was peynted al blody
> And cam in with a cros before þe comune peple
> And riht lyke in alle lymes to oure lord iesu.
> . . .
> Quod Conciense and knelede tho, "this aren Peres Armes,
> His colours and his cote armure; ac he þat cometh so blody
> Is Crist with his croes, conquerour of Cristene."
> (C XXI.6–8, 12–14)

Piers or Christ?, Will asks. The answer is both, in chiastic relation to each other. At the beginning of Will's dream, Piers looks "riht lyke" the Lord Jesus in his physical appearance, "in alle lymes," while in Conscience's response, Christ looks like Piers in the visible marks of identity, his arms, and insignia. Here the chiastic relation formally enacts the

[103] These poetic and theological considerations stand to gain intriguing support from Lawrence Warner's proposal that the B-text as we know it acquired its final two passus from the C-text. Warner gives us a scenario in which Langland sits for some years on the satisfactory, heavenly conclusion of B XVIII, and then adds a new ending that includes both the clearest realization of ecclesial unity in this world in the Pentecost scene of C XXI *and* the crisis of dissolution in C XXII. This new ending resituates the previous ending as an intermediate phenomenon. The addition of the final two passus then would render the old conclusion as the middle term, the balancing point for the chiastic structure I have been exploring here. In other words, by reinventing *Piers Plowman*'s ending, Langland would simultaneously introduce open-ended irresolution *and* embed the anagogical climax of the work *in the middle*. And if he was indeed undertaking such ambitious additions and revisions, then it is highly significant that instead of unraveling the conclusion of B XVIII, Langland left the reconciliation of the Four Daughters of God and his Easter morning waking intact. See Lawrence Warner, *The Lost History of "Piers Plowman": The Earliest Transmission of Langland's Work* (Philadelphia: University of Pennsylvania Press, 2011).

commercium divinum of the hypostatic union by which God and humanity enter into the eternal mutuality reflected in the patristic dictum, "God became man that man might become God." The dictum finds an image in Piers, but becoming happens in the search, in the crying after grace, in the open-ended work of satisfaction. *Piers Plowman* ends with an open-ended quest and a cry:

> "By Crist!" quod Consience tho, "y wol bicome a pilgrim
> And wenden as wyde as þe world rennet
> To seke Peres the Plouhman . . ."
> And sethe he gradde [cried, prayed] after grace tyl y gan awake.
> (C XXII.380–82, 86)

Conscience's cry and prayer echo across epochs, down to Marlowe's Faustus and even to McEwan's Briony: it is still not too late; now is the acceptable time. Langland's open-ended, recursive practice of satisfaction speaks to at least part of Briony's grief, witnessing that writing can participate in atonement. Perhaps, if atonement requires a God in which to participate, and that God does not exist, then Briony is still right that her writing cannot atone. But then it is not a matter of being too late. Periodization will not put to rest the question of faith.

Dismal Science: Chaucer and Gower on Alchemy and Economy

Robert Epstein
Fairfield University

ALCHEMY HOLDS A FASCINATION for modern times, as the forerunner of chemistry and perhaps the precursor of modern science, as a lore of the occult, or as a model for alternative spiritual or psychological systems.[1] But alchemy is most often invoked as a metaphor, usually in one of two ways. It can stand for a mysterious and magical process, or it can serve as an emblem of deliberately deceptive hokum. In particular, it functions as a metaphor for the perpetually abstruse processes of the commercial economy. For Marx, alchemy is the master trope for the inexorable power of capitalism to convert all things into commodities: "Not even are the bones of saints, and still less are more delicate res sacrosanctae, extra commercium hominum able to withstand this alchemy."[2] On the other hand, George Soros, one of the most successful

[1] The literature on the history of alchemy and its relation to the rise of science is voluminous; some notable contributions include: Frances A. Yates, *Giordano Bruno and the Hermetic Tradition* (Chicago: University of Chicago Press, 1964); Robert P. Multhauf, *The Origins of Chemistry* (London: Oldbourne, 1966); Allen G. Debus, *The Chemical Philosophy: Paracelsian Science and Medicine in the Sixteenth and Seventeenth Centuries* (New York: Science History Publications, 1977); Betty Jo Teeter Dobbs, *The Janus Face of Genius: The Role of Alchemy in Newton's Thought* (Cambridge: Cambridge University Press, 1991); William R. Newman and Lawrence M. Principe, *Alchemy Tried in the Fire: Starkey, Boyle, and the Fate of Helmontian Chymistry* (Chicago: University of Chicago Press, 2002). On the current standing of alchemy in the history of science, see two recent assessments: Lawrence M. Principe, "Alchemy Restored," *Isis* 102 (2011): 305–12; William R. Newman, "What Have We Learned from the Recent Historiography of Alchemy?," *Isis* 102 (2011): 313–21. Principe and Newman critique the ahistorical nature of much nineteenth- and twentieth-century occult and mystical reception of alchemy in "Some Problems with the Historiography of Alchemy," in *Secrets of Nature: Astrology and Alchemy in Early Modern Europe*, ed. Newman and Anthony Grafton (Cambridge, Mass.: MIT Press, 2001), 385–431.

[2] Karl Marx, *Capital: A Critical Analysis of Capitalist Production*, trans. Samuel Moore and Edward Aveling (Moscow: Progress Publishers, 1965), 1:132. Marx also uses alchemy as a metaphor for the fraud underlying capitalist accumulation; he says of a colonial governor in India, "His favorites received contracts under conditions whereby they, cleverer than the alchemists, made gold out of nothing" (704). On alchemical language and thought in Marx, see Karen Pinkus, *Alchemical Mercury: A Theory of Ambiv-*

Studies in the Age of Chaucer 36 (2014):209–248

private financiers in history, entitled his first book *The Alchemy of Finance*.[3] And the recent book by the economics columnist Neil Irwin about the central bankers who used every legal and fiduciary means at their disposal to address the global financial crisis of 2008 is called *The Alchemists*.[4] Then there are the comments of Larry Summers, economic adviser to President Obama, on Mitt Romney's budget plan during the 2012 United States presidential election: "This is alchemy . . . Lead cannot be turned into gold. Two plus two cannot equal five . . . And 20 percent across-the-board tax cuts cannot be squared with balanced budgets without raising middle-class taxes or eviscerating government."[5] Alchemy is that which is obscure in its operation, but somehow works; it is also that which seems to work, but does not.

In the late Middle Ages, alchemy's social position was shifting and uncertain. It had an ancient lineage and an extensive written tradition, but it was never incorporated into the standard curricula of schools or universities; it was variously condemned and endorsed by scholarly authorities; its practitioners were notorious in popular imagination for delusion and chicanery, but they could also be patronized by courts and princes.[6] Alchemy and alchemists appear only occasionally in medieval literature, but the art figures at significant points in the two great tale collections of fourteenth-century England.[7] John Gower praises it in the fourth book of *Confessio Amantis*. Chaucer, after a number of pejorative

alence (Stanford: Stanford University Press, 2010), particularly Chapter 6, "Reading *Capital I* Alchemically," 141–57.

[3] George Soros, *The Alchemy of Finance: Reading the Mind of the Market* (New York: John Wiley and Sons, 1994). Soros does not use the metaphor of alchemy casually, and he does not employ it as a shorthand for occult wisdom. Rather, he sees alchemy as analogous to market analysis in that it is practical without being scientific or even entirely rational: "Scientific theories are judged by the facts; financial decisions are judged by the distorted views of the participants. Instead of scientific method, financial markets embody the method of alchemy" (304).

[4] Neil Irwin, *The Alchemists: Three Central Bankers and a World on Fire* (New York: Penguin, 2013).

[5] Bonnie Kavoussi, "Larry Summers: Mitt Romney's Budget Plan is 'Alchemy,'" *The Huffington Post*, October 23, 2012, available at http://www.huffingtonpost.com/2012/10/23/larry-summers-mitt-romney_n_2005026.html (accessed June 30, 2014).

[6] See Will H. L. Ogrinc, "Western Society and Alchemy from 1200 to 1500," *Journal of Medieval History* 6 (1980): 103–32; William R. Newman and Anthony Grafton, "Introduction: The Problematic Status of Astrology and Alchemy in Premodern Europe," in *Secrets of Nature*, 1–38.

[7] Of course, alchemy has its own literature, including alchemical poetry. See the two-part article by Didier Kahn, "Alchemical Poetry in Medieval and Early Modern Europe," Part 1, "Preliminary Survey," *Ambix* 57 (2010): 249–74, and Part 2, "Synthesis," *Ambix* 58 (2011): 62–77.

asides, abruptly and belatedly introduces alchemy into the *Canterbury Tales* and then debunks it at considerable length in *The Canon's Yeoman's Prologue and Tale*.

Critics attempting to explain such literary uses of alchemy have frequently and rightly taken it as metaphorical for economic operation. But the medieval authors understood neither alchemy nor economics in the same manner that later writers would. Like moderns, Gower and Chaucer saw in alchemy analogies to the commercial economy. But unlike most modern thinkers, Gower and Chaucer interpreted alchemy as an inverted analogy, seeing its processes as opposite to the workings of economic forces. The poets' very different depictions of alchemy and alchemists therefore reveal the profound contrasts in their views of money and economy.

Gower: "The science of himself is trewe"

Two thirds of the way through Book IV of *Confessio Amantis*, Genius chooses to counterbalance his indictment of Sloth with some praise of its opposite, industriousness. What follows is a catalogue of various fields of liberal arts, natural philosophy, and technology—from poetry, music, painting, and sculpture, to fishing, metallurgy, textiles, augury, and cuisine. For each of these Gower identifies, though sometimes rather idiosyncratically and obscurely, the legendary or mythical founder of the discipline. But at one point, Gower expounds, at much greater length, on:

thilke experience,
Which cleped is alconomie
Wherof the selver multeplie
Thei made and ek the gold also.
(IV.2458–61)[8]

"Alconomie," according to Gower, posits seven material elements, each associated with a planet. These elements exist in a continuum, running from gold at one extreme to silver at the other:

[8] All quotations of *Confessio Amantis* are taken from the edition of Russell A. Peck, vols. 1–3 (Kalamazoo: Medieval Institute Publications, 2000–2004).

For as the philosphre tolde
Of gold and selver, thei ben holde
Tuo principal extremites
To whiche alle othre be degres
Of the metalls ben acordant.
(IV.2487–91)

There are, Gower says, three "philosophers' stones." The first two are the *lapis vegetabilis*, which has the power "to kepe and to preserve / The bodi fro siknesses alle / Til deth of kinde upon him falle" (IV.2538–40), and the *lapis animalis*, which is able to heighten and maintain the five senses, "wherof a man mai hiere and se / And smelle and taste in his degré, / And for to fiele" (IV.2545–47).[9] It is the third stone, the mineral stone, that has the power to refine any metal, removing any impurities (IV.2555–56).[10] Since gold and silver are the purest extremes in the continuum of metals,

This mineral, so as I finde,
Transformeth al the ferste kynde
And makth hem able to conceive
Thurgh his vertu, and to receive
Bothe in substance and in figure
Of gold and selver the nature.
(IV.2559–64)

This increase of gold, Gower acknowledges, is the ultimate goal of alchemy and alchemists: "For to the rede and to the whyte"—standard alchemical figures for gold and silver—"This ston hath pouer to profite. / It makth multiplicacioun / Of gold" (IV.2571, 2573–74).

Gower, like many medieval writers, credits Hermes Trismegistus with the founding of alchemy. He also cites Geber, Ortolan, Morien, and Avicenna as authorities on the craft. Gower's own sources seem to have included Vincent of Beauvais, Arnaldus of Villanova, Roger Bacon,

[9] On Gower's alchemical philosophy, see George Fox, *The Mediaeval Sciences in the Works of John Gower* (1931; repr. New York: Haskell House, 1966), 114–35.

[10] Gower seems to equate the "mineral stone" and the "elixir"; in other sources, the elixir is a substance made from the philosophers' stone and used for transmutation. The three distinct stones seem to be unique to Gower; they may derive from his misinterpretation of passages in other sources describing categories of materials used to create the philosophers' stone. See ibid., 127–28.

the *Libellus de alchimia* ascribed to Albertus Magnus, and other widely circulated texts.[11] His descriptions of alchemy, therefore, could be called, as they often have been, conventional—but for the fact that there were competing conventions.

Gower was approaching alchemy at an unstable period in its history. The craft was introduced to Europe via Arabic texts in the twelfth century and would flourish in the early modern period, but in the thirteenth century alchemy had become a point of intellectual controversy.[12] Thirteenth-century authorities, notably Albertus Magnus, wrote generally favorably of alchemy, and Roger Bacon defended it vigorously. But other Scholastics, including Giles of Rome, expressed reservations about the value of its supposed productions, and a Latin translation of an Arabic anti-alchemical text was widely received as the work of Albert.[13] After convening a debate on the issue, Pope John XXII condemned the practices of alchemists in a decretal in 1317, declaring, "Poor themselves, the alchemists promise riches which are not forthcoming; wise also in their own conceit, they fall into the ditch which they themselves have digged."[14] In the fifteenth century several European countries would ban the practice of alchemical transmutation; Henry IV of England passed such a decree in 1404.[15]

Poets of the thirteenth and fourteenth centuries varied in their representations of alchemy. Jean de Meun, in his discussion of the powers of Art and Nature, says that Art "may learn enough alchemy to be able to colour every metal, but she would kill herself before she could transmute the species, unless she first reduced them to their elemental matter; if

[11] See ibid., and Peck's note to *Confessio Amantis*, IV.2468–78.

[12] See Lawrence M. Principe, *The Secrets of Alchemy* (Chicago: University of Chicago Press, 2013), 51–82. See also Ogrinc, "Western Society and Alchemy," 104–7; Multhauf, *Origins of Chemistry*, 143–200; Debus, *Chemical Philosophy*, 11–14.

[13] See William R. Newman, *Promethean Ambitions: Alchemy and the Quest to Perfect Nature* (Chicago: University of Chicago Press, 2004), 43–54. See also Principe, *Secrets of Alchemy*, 58–62.

[14] Quoted in Edgar H. Duncan, "The Literature of Alchemy and Chaucer's Canon's Yeoman's Tale: Framework, Theme, and Characters," *Speculum* 43 (1968): 633–56 (636). See also Principe, *Secrets of Alchemy*, 61; J. R. Partington, "Albertus Magnus on Alchemy," *Ambix* 1 (1937): 3–20. The Latin text of the decretal is printed in *Sources and Analogues of Chaucer's "Canterbury Tales,"* ed. W. F. Bryan and Germaine Dempster (1941; repr. New York: Humanities Press, 1958), 691–92.

[15] Principe, *Secrets of Alchemy*, 62. Petitioners were occasionally granted license to practice alchemy; the ban was ultimately lifted in 1689. See Duncan, "Literature of Alchemy," 634; D. Geoghagen, "A License of Henry VI to Practise Alchemy," *Ambix* 6 (1957): 10–17.

she worked all her life she would never catch up with Nature." But he then adds, "It is worthy of note, nevertheless, that alchemy is true art, and that anyone who worked at it seriously would discover great marvels."[16] Petrarch, in *Remedies for Prosperity*, addresses alchemy in a dialogue of Hope and Reason:

> HOPE: I hope for good results with alchemy.
> REASON: It is surprising that you hope for something which never happened to you or anyone else. All reports that it happened to some are fabricated by people who have found it expedient to believe so . . .
> HOPE: The alchemist promises me great things.
> REASON: Tell him to perform for himself what he promises to others, and to cure his own poverty first. Alchemists are an indigent lot who admit that they are paupers but wish to enrich others as though the poverty of others were more troublesome to them than their own. Wretched themselves, they protest impudently that they take pity on others and promise great things, sometimes even to people they do not know at all. O what rotten promises, what stupid credulity![17]

In Gower's England, Langland apparently harbors the popular suspicion that alchemy is a form of dark magic. In the *Piers Plowman* A-text, Dame Study warns Will against three sciences that are mere "fybicches" (tricks) that she invented solely to mislead human minds:

> Yut are thre fybicches of forels of manye mannys wittes,
> Of experimens of alkonomye, of Albertes makyng,
> Nigramauncie and permancie, the pouke to reyse;
> Yif thou thinke Dowel, del therwith nevere.
> Al these sciences, sikerly, I myself founded—
> Founded hem formest folk to deseyven.[18]

[16] *The Romance of the Rose*, trans. and ed. Frances Horgan (Oxford: Oxford University Press, 1994), 248–49. On Jean de Meun's treatment of alchemy, see Newman, *Promethean Ambitions*, 77–82.

[17] Conrad H. Rawski, *Petrarch's Remedies for Fortune Fair and Foul: A Modern English Translation of "De remediis utriusque Fortune," with a Commentary*, Vol. 1 (Bloomington: Indiana University Press, 1991), 299–300.

[18] William Langland, *Piers Plowman: The A Version*, ed. Míceál F. Vaughan (Baltimore: Johns Hopkins University Press, 2011), XI.161–66. A slightly different version

Gower, therefore, has no single, conventional path when approaching alchemy. He chooses to praise it at length. He does ultimately declare that the contemporary practice is unwise and that those who pursue alchemy are unlikely to be able to duplicate the successes of the ancient practitioners, making it essentially a lost art:

Bot now it staunt al otherwise;
Thei speken faste of thilke ston,
Bot hou to make it, nou wot non
After the sothe experience.
And natheles get diligence
Thei setten upon thilke dede,
And spille more than thei spede;
For allewey thei finde a lette,
Which bringeth in poverte and dette
To hem that riche were afore.
The lost is had, the lucre is lore,
To gete a pound thei spenden fyve;
I not hou such a craft schal thryve
In the manere as it is used:
It were betre be refused
Than for to worchen upon weene
In thing which stant noght as thei weene.
(IV.2580–96)

Yet Gower is acknowledging that alchemy is at heart a "sothe experience"—empirical fact—and he is at pains to insist that alchemical theory and its lore are natural, authoritative, and genuine:

For thei be whom this art was founde
To every point a certain bounde
Ordeignen, that a man mai finde
This craft is wroght be weie of kinde,
So that ther is no fallas inne.
(IV.2505–9)

What makes this curious is that Gower uncharacteristically ignores the moral questions that haunted alchemy in the late Middle Ages. Con-

appears in B X.212–21; see *Piers Plowman: The B Version*, ed. George Kane and E. Talbot Donaldson (Berkeley: University of California Press, 1988).

temporary authorities did not merely question whether some practicing alchemists were charlatans or fools. They also expressed reservations about what alchemy actually achieved when it was successful, and the moral and social ramifications of the art.

The concern of intellectual critics in Gower's time was not so much that alchemists were unable to perform the functions they claimed, but that alchemy, if efficacious, might be false and misleading. As William Newman has explained, the debate hinged on a perceived conflict between Art and Nature—the question of whether any product of human artifice could equal, or even improve, received creation, a question ultimately of profound importance to humanistic thought and to conceptions of science and technology.[19] A point of debate among Scholastics like Albert Magnus and Giles of Rome was whether the precious metals produced by alchemists were *true* gold and silver or synthetic and therefore artificial gold and silver, differing in some fundamental (though perhaps imperceptible) way from the real metals.[20] As Aquinas comments:

> Gold and silver are costly not only on account of the usefulness of the vessels and other like things made from them, but also on account of the excellence and purity of their substance. Hence if the gold or silver produced by alchemists has not the true specific nature of gold and silver, the sale thereof is fraudulent and unjust, especially as real gold and silver can produce certain results by their natural action, which the counterfeit gold and silver of alchemists cannot produce . . . If however real gold were to be produced by alchemy, it would not be unlawful to sell it for the genuine article, for nothing prevents art from employing certain natural causes for the production of natural and true effects, as Augustine says . . . of things produced by the art of the demons.[21]

In either case, critics saw economic implications in the validity of the precious metals that secured the value of currency. If alchemical gold were false, it could force true gold out of the marketplace, destabilizing the value of currency; if alchemists were to produce true gold in significant quantities, it could potentially devalue currency by deflating the

[19] See Newman, "Alchemy and the Art–Nature Debate," in *Promethean Ambitions*, 34–114.

[20] Ibid., 51–54.

[21] Saint Thomas Aquinas, *Summa theologica: Translated by Fathers of the English Dominican Province* (New York: Benziger Brothers, 1947–48), 4701.

value of gold.[22] Alchemists, therefore, could be seen as a kind of counterfeiters. In his decretal, Pope John XXII declares that "though there is no such thing in nature, they pretend to make genuine gold and silver by a sophistic transmutation; to such an extent does their damned and damnable temerity go that they stamp upon the base metal the characters of public money for believing eyes."[23]

It is for these reasons that Dante confines alchemists in one of the deepest portions of hell, the tenth and final *bolgia* of the eighth circle, "where the ministress of the High Lord, infallible Justice, punishes the falsifiers" (XXIX.55–57).[24] Here, where the air is poisoned with contagion and there are "spirits languishing in divers heaps" (XXIX.66), Dante encounters two souls. The first says that he was executed by Albero of Siena for falsely claiming that he could teach him to fly, adding, "But, for the alchemy I practiced in the world, Minos, to whom it is not allowed to err, condemned me to this last pouch of the ten" (XXIX.118–20). The second points even more explicitly to the deceitful art of alchemy: "I am the shade of Capocchio, who falsified the metals by alchemy; and you must recall, if I rightly eye you, how good an ape of nature I was" (XXIX.136–39).

Note that Dante is not condemning alchemists for falsely claiming to be able to transmute metals. Rather, Dante's alchemists are languishing at the bottom of the eighth circle because the precious metals that they transform other metals into are not the true gold and silver that they seem to be, and this makes them a species of falsifiers or counterfeiters.

And yet Gower, normally as concerned as Dante with adjudging and critiquing the moral status of individuals and classes, has only praise for alchemy's inventors and original practitioners. Gower emphasizes the truth and indeed the virtue of the craft:

> Bot noght forthi, who that it knewe,
> The science of himself is trewe
> Upon the forme as it was founded,
> Wherof the names yit ben grounded

[22] See Principe, *Secrets of Alchemy*, 59–60. See also Newman, *Promethean Ambitions*, 131.

[23] Duncan, "Literature of Alchemy," 637. See also Principe, *Secrets of Alchemy*, 61.

[24] Dante Alighieri, *The Divine Comedy: Inferno*, trans. Charles S. Singleton (Princeton: Princeton University Press, 1970). It is worth noting that Dante and Virgil left the usurers sitting on burning sands back in the seventh circle, with sinners against nature—plenty deep, but not nearly so deep as falsifiers like the alchemists.

Of hem that ferste it founden oute;
And thus the fame goth aboute
To suche as soghten besinesse
Of vertu and of worthinesse.
(IV.2597–604)

It is perhaps not so surprising that in a section devoted to disciplines of science and learning Gower chooses the side of human artifice in a debate between Art and Nature. But what makes his defense of the empirical and moral validity of alchemy particularly puzzling is its position within the *Confessio*. This section, late in Book IV, comes just before the mammoth Book V, and its extended critique not just of the sin of avarice but specifically of commerce and money.

Gower's economic critique derives ultimately from Aristotle's *Politics*. In the *Nicomachean Ethics*, Aristotle studies the power of money to create equivalencies. It facilitates the exchange of goods, even goods of widely disparate natures and values. It also provides a way of finding equivalent values of abstract concepts, such as labor and time. "It measures all things," he says.[25] It is obvious, Aristotle insists, that exchange took place before there was money. Money simply facilitates exchange: "Money, then, acting as a measure, makes goods commensurate and equates them."[26]

In the *Politics*, on the other hand, Aristotle makes a distinction between the art of getting wealth and "household management" (literally, *economics*).[27] Barter, the kind of exchange that he says in the *Ethics* has always existed, entails the exchange of "the necessities of life and nothing more." But, he goes on, "When the use of coin had once been discovered, out of the barter of necessary articles arose the other art of wealth-getting, namely, retail trade."[28] So, there is the good and appropriate getting of wealth, the acquisition of the commodities needed for the proper maintenance of the household; and there is the art of accu-

[25] *An Introduction to Aristotle*, ed. Richard McKeon (New York: Modern Library, 1947), 409.

[26] Ibid., 410.

[27] A particularly valuable review of Aristotelian economic thought and its medieval reception is provided by Lianna Farber in *An Anatomy of Trade in Medieval Writing: Value, Consent, and Community* (Ithaca, N.Y.: Cornell University Press, 2006); see especially 12–37.

[28] *Introduction to Aristotle*, 568.

mulating wealth through money and trade. This other art of wealth-getting is unnecessary and undesirable. It is, Aristotle says, "unnatural," here in the sense of being against the natural order. It is not a "natural part of the management of the household."[29] Money is an instrument for the measure of value; it has no value in and of itself because it has no use except as a method of measure. Money is therefore not useful as a commodity, so there is no natural benefit to its accumulation. And as it lends itself to pure accumulation, the search for monetary profit knows no natural limits: there is no point at which one could be said to have enough. In fact, it is simply "a mode by which men gain from one another," and it is therefore a mode of exploitation culminating in usury.[30] And all of this is true not generally of gold or wealth or property but specifically of coined money:

> Originating in the use of coin, the art of getting wealth is generally thought to be concerned with it and to be the art which produces riches and wealth; having to consider how they may be accumulated. Indeed, riches is assumed by many to be only a quantity of coin, because the arts of getting wealth and retail trade are concerned with coin. Others maintain that coined money is a mere sham, a thing not natural, but conventional only, because, if the users substitute another commodity for it, it is worthless, and because it is not useful as means to any of the necessities of life, and, indeed, he who is rich in coin may often be in want of necessary food. But how can that be wealth of which a man may have a great abundance and yet perish with hunger, like Midas in the fable, whose insatiable prayer turned everything that was set before him into gold? Hence men seek after a better notion of riches and of the art of getting wealth than the mere acquisition of coin, and they are right.[31]

These two Aristotelian positions are not necessarily irreconcilable.[32] But in the Middle Ages these passages inspired dual traditions of interpretation. Scholastic philosophers provided commentary on *Ethics*, V, and as Joel Kaye has shown, this text served as a springboard for some very sophisticated economic analysis by some fourteenth-century schol-

[29] Ibid., 570.
[30] Ibid., 571.
[31] Ibid., 568–69.
[32] An extensive argument for the unity and coherence of the passages in *Politics* and *Ethics* is provided by Scott Meikle, *Aristotle's Economic Thought* (Oxford: Clarendon Press, 1995).

ars.[33] But the *Politics* held greater sway over moral philosophy and canon law.[34]

But the canonists and other moral theologians of the late Middle Ages seem to have been inclined to seek accommodation with the burgeoning money economy, by emphasizing those portions of Aristotle that were most amenable to it, and where necessary by revising Aristotle's positions. Lester K. Little, in a well-known study, explains the high medieval innovation of religious poverty in the context of the money economy that emerged in twelfth- and thirteenth-century Europe.[35] Little demonstrates that the ideal of religious poverty was inspired by, predicated on, and informed by the logic of the commercial economy. Furthermore, Little shows that the scholastic philosophers, so many of whom were in the fraternal orders, were predisposed, because of their urban and commercial origins, to see commercial exchange as logical and natural. These fraternal thinkers, therefore, were at the forefront of the effort throughout the later Middle Ages to accommodate money and profit to Christian ethics.[36]

Aquinas, in addressing the question of fraud in the *Summa theologica*, restates Aristotle's distinction from the *Politics* between money as mea-

[33] Joel Kaye, *Economy and Nature in the Fourteenth Century: Money, Market Exchange, and the Emergence of Scientific Thought* (Cambridge: Cambridge University Press, 1998).

[34] Ibid., 53.

[35] Lester K. Little, *Religious Poverty and the Profit Economy in Medieval Europe* (Ithaca, N.Y.: Cornell University Press, 1978).

[36] Jacques Le Goff provides a counter-argument to Little and others in *Your Money or Your Life: Economy and Religion in the Middle Ages*, trans. Patricia Ranum (New York: Zone Books, 1988). In "trying to show that an ideological obstacle can fetter or delay the development of a new economic system" (69), Le Goff maintains that Scholastic thinkers, inheritors of ancient Hebraic and Patristic suspicions of wealth and profit, consistently resisted commerce and the fiduciary innovations of the money economy, and thereby inhibited the rise of capitalism. However, in a subsequent book, *Money and the Middle Ages: An Essay in Historical Anthropology*, trans. Jean Birrell (Cambridge: Polity Press, 2012), Le Goff, while expanding on this topic, also concedes that "the pursuit and the use of money by individuals and by states was gradually justified and legitimized by the institution that inspired and governed them, the Church, despite the conditions it attached to this justification" (2). See also Martha C. Howell, *Commerce before Capitalism in Europe, 1300–1600* (Cambridge: Cambridge University Press, 2010). The most comprehensive analysis of Scholastic economic thought has been provided in a series of works by Odd Langholm: see *Wealth and Money in the Aristotelian Tradition: A Study in Scholastic Economic Sources* (Bergen: Universitetsforlaget, 1983); *Economics in the Medieval Schools: Wealth, Exchange, Value, Money and Usury according to the Paris Theological Tradition, 1200–1350* (Leiden: Brill, 1992); "The Medieval Schoolmen (1200–1400)," in *Ancient and Medieval Economic Ideas and Concepts of Social Justice*, ed. S. Todd Lowry and Barry Gordon (Leiden: Brill, 1998). See also John T. Noonan, Jr., *The Scholastic Analysis of Usury* (Cambridge, Mass.: Harvard University Press, 1957).

sure, which is necessary and useful, and money as ends, an object of accumulation, which is useless and dishonorable. But then Aquinas provides an additional stipulation:

> Profit which is the purpose of trade, while it does not in itself involve something honorable or necessary, also does not of its own nature imply something vicious or contrary to virtue. Nothing prevents profit from being directed to a necessary or even honorable goal, so that trade is thereby made licit. For example someone may seek to secure a moderate profit through trade to maintain his household or to support the poor or he may also engage in trade for the public welfare to provide his country with the necessities of life and seek profit not as his goal but as a recompense for his labor.[37]

What had begun in Aristotle as a principle of the unfairness of inequitable exchange has become in Aquinas a justification of the profit of the merchant.

This is an example of what R. Howard Bloch has termed "the scholasticism of exchange":

> The rise of scholasticism as an integral part of the urban revival of the High Middle Ages was even accompanied by what might be called a "scholasticism of exchange." Canonists and theologians struggled, against a long anticommercial tradition, to make the kinds of distinctions and connections by which profit could be justified and by which even fraud might be exculpated.[38]

From a starting-point where money and profit were considered wrong, there was an effort to make finer and finer moral distinctions, each of which made the general practice of commerce incrementally more natural and licit. At first, the seller's profit was *prima facie* evidence of the inequality of the transaction; soon enough, an exchange was unjust only if the seller intended fraud.[39]

Lianna Farber has recently made the case that fourteenth-century writers, both within the schools and in vernacular literature, were approaching a consensus on the legitimacy of trade and commercial

[37] *St. Thomas Aquinas on Politics and Ethics*, ed. and trans. Paul E. Sigmund (New York: W. W. Norton, 1988), 73–74.

[38] R. Howard Bloch, *Etymologies and Genealogies: A Literary Anthropology of the French Middle Ages* (Chicago: University of Chicago Press, 1983), 170.

[39] See also Kaye, *Economy and Nature*, 82–83, on the move in the thirteenth century toward adjudging usury solely on the basis of intention.

economy, based on common notions of value, community, and consent.[40] One can see such a perspective informing Gower's earlier poetry. Both *Mirour de l'omme* and *Vox clamantis* contain, in their depictions of the third estate, extensive anti-commercial satires. In both works, the corruption of merchants is embodied in allegorical figures. But in both cases the figure represents not money or profit (or Mede) but rather fraud—*Triche* in the *Mirour*, *Fraus* in the *Vox*.[41] Nothing in these poems questions the legitimacy of commerce per se. The introduction of *Triche* is prefaced by an assertion that merchants are not only necessary but divinely ordained:

Si une terre avoir porroit
Tous biens ensemble, lors serroit
Trop orguillouse, et pour cela
Dieus establist, et au bon droit,
Qe l'une terre en son endroit
Del autry bien busoignera:
Sur quoy marchant dieus ordina,
Qui ce q'en l'une ne serra
En l'autre terre querre doit;
Pour ce qui bien se gardera,
Et loyalment marchendera,
De dieu et homme il est benoit.
(25189–200)[42]

If one country had all goods together, then it would be too proud. And therefore God established, quite rightly, that any one country would properly have need of others. Thereupon God ordained merchants, who would go seek in another country whatever any one country did not have. Therefore, he who conducts himself well and trades honestly is blessed by God and man.[43]

[40] Farber, *Anatomy of Trade*, 1–8 and passim.

[41] See Roger A. Ladd, "The *Mirour de l'omme* and Gower's London Merchants," in *Antimercantilism in Late Medieval English Literature* (New York: Palgrave Macmillan, 2010), 49–75. See also Craig E. Bertolet, "Fraud, Division, and Lies: John Gower and London," in *On John Gower: Essays at the Millennium*, ed. R. F. Yeager (Kalamazoo: Medieval Institute Publications, 2007), 43–70.

[42] *The Complete Works of John Gower: The French Works*, ed. G. C. Macaulay (Oxford: Clarendon Press, 1899).

[43] *Mirour de l'omme (the Mirror of Mankind), by John Gower*, trans. William Burton Wilson, ed. Nancy Wilson Van Baak (East Lansing, Mich.: Colleagues, 1992).

Chaucer's Parson, in his discussion of Avarice, expresses almost exactly the same sentiment:

> Of thilke bodily marchandise that is leveful and honest is this: that, there as God hath ordeyned that a regne or a contree is suffisaunt to hymself, thanne is it honest and leveful that of habundaunce of this contree, that men helpe another contree that is more nedy./ And therfore ther moote been marchantz to bryngen fro that o contree to that oother hire marchandises./ That oother marchandise, that men haunten with fraude and trecherie and deceite, with lesynges and false othes, is cursed and dampnable. (X.777–79)[44]

In *Confessio Amantis*, however, Gower is staking out positions closer to those of Aristotle in the *Politics*, and more conservative even than those of Aquinas. Book V of the *Confessio* begins by depicting a world fallen from an edenic state. It has fallen, though, not from innocence into corruption through sin, but from commonality into private property through money:

> Ferst whan the hyhe God began
> This world, and that the kinde of man
> Was falle into no gret encress,
> For worldes good tho was no press,
> Bot al was set to the comune,
> Thei spieken thanne of no fortune
> Or for to lese or for to winne,
> Til Avarice broghte it inne;
> And that was whan the world was woxe
> Of man, of hors, of shep, of oxe,
> And that men knewen the moneie.
> (V.1–11)

The introduction of money, according to Gower, led people to stop seeing material as commonly owned and intended for the common good, and instead to see it as a commodity destined for private property. Money does this, Gower says, by making hoarding both possible and appealing. In the *Confessio*, Gower does not seem to see money as functioning to facilitate exchange. On the contrary, he sees it as separating

[44] Quotations of the *Canterbury Tales* are taken from *The Riverside Chaucer*, gen. ed. Larry D. Benson, 3rd ed. (Boston: Houghton Mifflin, 1987). On this passage, see Ladd, *Antimercantilism*, 78.

wealth from usable material in a way that inhibits the useful exchange of goods. What it promotes is the accumulation of wealth in and for itself. This leads to greed and to division—to the construction of battlements to protect hoarded wealth and to war to gain more. But as it does not correspond to use, the wealth of money brings no profit even to those who accumulate it. Gower says of the avaricious man:

So is he povere, and everemore
Him lacketh that he hath ynowh:
An oxe draweth in the plowh,
Of that himself hath no profit;
A schep riht in the same plit
His wolle berth, bot on a day
Another takth the flees away
Thus hath he that he noght ne hath,
For he therof his part ne tath.
(V.40–48)

Since he can neither spend his wealth nor, ultimately, preserve it, the avaricious man profits from commerce no more than the ox profits from the plow. Speaking of plows and plenitude, contrast this passage from Chaucer's *Shipman's Tale*:

But o thyng is, ye knowe it wel ynogh
Of chapmen, that hir moneie is hir plogh.
We may creaunce whil we have a name,
But goldlees for to be, it is no game.
(VII.287–90)

In the Chaucerian image, money is the plow, the harvest is credit, and the merchant is the plowman. (This is the merchant of Saint-Denis speaking, so it may not represent an unmediated Chaucerian perspective.) In the Gowerian image, the harvest is profit—but the merchant is the ox. Chaucer, clearly, has a sense of productive capital. Gower's view is more broadly philosophical, but his claim that the man can no more profit from an abundance of wealth than an ox can profit from the plow or the sheep from its wool derives from Aristotelian views of the accumulation of money as unnatural since it does not necessarily correspond to any practical use. Scholastic writers also emphasized the infertility of money, its inability to produce fruitful profit, and where they acknowledged that money was quite remarkable in its ability to reproduce itself, they characterized this as an unnatural fecundity.[45]

Hewing to Aristotle's anti-pecuniary critique from the *Politics*, the first tale Gower tells in Book V is that of Midas. His source is Ovid's *Metamorphoses*, Book XI, but Gower glosses the tale almost precisely as Aristotle does:

And thus, thogh that he multeplie
His gold, withoute tresorie
He is, for man is noght amended
With gold bot if it be despended
To mannes us.
(V.133–37)

Particularly notable here is Gower's use of the phrase "multeplie / His gold." The meaning here is that the increase of money is vain and fruitless unless the money is converted to useful ends. And yet Gower had used the same terms in Book IV to praise alchemists:

And also with gret diligence
Thei founden thilke experience,
Which cleped is alconomie,
Wherof the selver multeplie
Thei made and ek the gold also.
(IV.2457–61)

But the purpose in Book V is to negate the value of such multiplication; the function of money is to separate wealth from use, so there is no true gain in the accumulation of gold.[46] Gower brings the point home most

[45] See Kaye, *Economy and Nature*, 53, on the Aristotelian characterization of money as infertile; see also Bloch, *Etymologies*, 173, and Le Goff, *Your Money*, 29, on the Scholastic amplification of the principle.

[46] "Multiplication" is a technical term of alchemy, referring to the process, distinct from transmutation, by which a substance is applied to a precious metal to increase the amount of the metal. See Principe, *Secrets of Alchemy*, 131; Duncan, "Literature of Alchemy," 634–35. But Gower's use of the word "multiplie" in both alchemical and economic contexts reveals the imagined link between money and alchemy as modes for the increase of wealth. Chaucer, somewhat more self-consciously, uses the word "multiplicacioun" in both senses, and critics have recognized that Gower in the *Confessio* is exploiting the same ambiguity. See *The General Prologue to "The Canterbury Tales" and The Canon's Yeoman's Prologue and Tale*, ed. A. V. C. Schmidt (New York: Holmes and Meier, 1976), 154.

vividly through the tale of Midas, the climax coming when his golden touch prevents him from eating, leading him to the brink of starvation.

Equally striking in Book V is Gower's repetition and amplification of Aristotle's claims from the *Politics* that greed and inequality, and in fact all strife, derive from the invention of money, and specifically from the minting of coinage:

> For this a man mai finde write,
> Tofor the time, er gold was smite
> In coign, that men the florin knewe,
> Ther was welnyh no man untrewe.
> (V.333–36)[47]

Coinage here is not the *sign* of avarice, but the actual cause of it. The problem is money itself: the intentional, artificial abstraction of wealth.

And yet, in the Book IV catalogue of founders of sciences, Genius credits Saturn with introducing—in addition to agriculture—coinage, and therefore commerce:

> Of chapmanhode he fond the weie,
> And ek to coigne the moneie
> Of sondri metall, as it is,
> He was the ferste man of this.
> (IV.2447–50)

This observation leads Genius to comment on metallurgy, and then directly to his account of alchemy. So, why are money, coinage, gold, and wealth assessed so differently in the context of alchemy than they are in the economic context of Book V?

We would be justified in judging these as philosophical inconsistencies in the sprawling poem; they would not be the only ones. We could also see Gower's position in Book V as essentially nostalgic. But it is a radical nostalgia, and its complaint against coin may actually be more historically situated than its original in Aristotle's *Politics*.

When Gower refers to a past "Tofor the time, er gold was smite / In Coign, that men the florin knewe" (V.334–35), is he referring to a

[47] John Peter links Gower's "nostalgic" tone in this passage to other complaints against money in the *Ubi sunt* tradition, including Bernard's *De contemptu mundi*; *Complaint and Satire in Early English Literature* (Oxford: Clarendon Press, 1956), 70.

legendary era of misty antiquity? Given that this passage follows the tale of Midas, we might be inclined to think so. As it happens, the Greeks did tell legends of the inventor of minting; he was Gyges, the sixth-century ruler of Lydia, who is described by Herodotus and whom some modern historians still credit as the first king to coin money.[48] The legends of Gyges, however, are not about minting, but rather about a ring that granted invisibility, and Gower does not tell his tale. Instead, he may have had a more precise and recent era in mind. For Gower, the time "before gold was smitten into coin, and men knew the florin" would be the time before the middle of the preceding century.

The word "florin" could be used generically by medieval writers to mean coins or money. But there is a reason that the florin became synonymous with minted money; it is not just any coin. Minted in Florence first in 1252 and for three centuries thereafter, it was the first widely circulated gold coin minted since Carolingian times. It quickly became the most popular coin in the medieval world, and was the standard unit of currency in western Europe through the early Renaissance. The minting of gold coins like the florin (along with the Genoese genovino and the Venetian ducat), made possible by an influx of gold from new mines in Hungary, greatly facilitated large-scale international transactions.[49] The increasing circulation of money, through trade as well as war and taxation (overseen by new state bureaucracies), laid the groundwork for what some have called the commercial revolution of the long thirteenth century.[50] Gower roots his critique of avarice in a complaint against coinage because he is indicting the money economy. From this perspective, Gower is justified in seeing the minting of gold into coins as the source of the social disruption he most bemoans. He most consistently satirizes divisiveness, and nothing is more divisive than the supplanting of the common profit that existed before money by the individual profit motive of the money economy. This is embodied by Dame Avarice's courtier Covoitise, who:

> takth non other hiede,
> Bot that he mai pourchace and gete.

[48] See David Graeber, *Toward an Anthropological Theory of Value: The False Coin of Our Own Dreams* (New York: Palgrave, 2001), 101–2; Marc Shell, "The Ring of Gyges," in *The Economy of Literature* (Baltimore: Johns Hopkins University Press, 1978), 11–62.

[49] See Peter Spufford, *Money and Its Use in Medieval Europe* (Cambridge: Cambridge University Press, 1988).

[50] See Le Goff, *Money and the Middle Ages*, 33–60.

His conscience hath al forgete,
And not what thing it mai amonte
That he schal afterward acompte.
(V.2010–14)

In fact, for Gower "the time, er gold was smite / In Coign" was more recent than the early thirteenth century. Gold coins were minted for the first time in England in 1344. The first issue was an imitation of the florin and was sometimes called an English florin, but it was a failed specie and was quickly recalled.[51] It was replaced by the "noble," which was a tremendous success, becoming one of the most popular coins in Europe and the mainstay of English currency until the time of the Tudors.[52] The image on the obverse of the noble, virtually unaltered for more than a century, depicted the king enthroned on a ship. This was taken to commemorate Edward III's naval victory at Sluys, and more generally as figuring the confluence of imperial military ambitions, monarchical authority, and national economic expansion through overseas trade—all of which were in fact abetted by the issuance of this coinage.[53] Explaining the proliferation of the noble, Peter Spufford observes, "In the 1350s and 1360s they were struck in enormous numbers as the ransoms and other profits of a successful war were remitted back to England in gold, along with the continuous proceeds of the sale of English wool."[54] As Donald Baker notes, the ship design on the noble "was also probably intended to inspire the merchant navy in the wool trade with Flanders."[55] The overall nationalistic effect can be seen in a passage from the early fifteenth-century *Libelle of Englyshe Policye*:

For foure things our noble sheweth to mee—
King, ship, and swerd and power of the sea.
—But King Edward made a siege royall

[51] Donald C. Baker, "Gold Coins in Mediaeval English Literature," *Speculum* 36 (1961): 282–87 (83).

[52] Spufford, *Money and Its Use*, 282 and 379–80; Baker, "Gold Coins," 284.

[53] Baker, "Gold Coins," 284. The motto on the noble read "IHC AUTEM TRANSIENS PER MEDIUM ILLORUM IBAT" ("He [Jesus Christ], however, passed through the middle of them"). This has been taken to refer to the victory at Sluys, but Shell (*Economy of Literature*, 70–71) argues that it also alludes to the Ring of Gyges and its ability to grant invisibility, and that the motto links Edward III to Gyges as a minter of coins.

[54] Spufford, *Money and Its Use*, 282. See also Le Goff, *Money and the Middle Ages*, 87.

[55] Baker, "Gold Coins," 284.

And wann the town and in special
The sea was kept, and thereof he was lord,
Thus made he nobles coined of record.[56]

Russell Peck has claimed that "Gower formulated his ideas of good and bad kingship during the reign of Edward III."[57] Gower, Peck argues, was contemptuous of Edward for what he saw as the king's weakness and moral lassitude, and also for his war policies. In *Confessio*, Book V, the "division" caused by coin is seen equally in individual pursuit of profit and in war. Before gold coinage,

Tho was ther nouther schield ne spere
Ne dedly wepne for to bere;
Tho was the toun withoute wal,
Which nou is closed overal;
Tho was ther no brocage in londe,
Which nou takth every cause on honde.
So mai men knowe, hou the florin
Was moder ferst of malengin
And bringere inne of alle werre.
(V.337–45)

Of course, the social changes brought by the money economy were very real and profound. In particular, the rise of wage labor, with the formation of a class of wage laborers in the towns and the expectation of cash payment for agricultural labor, altered social relations in ways that Gower and his contemporaries were acutely aware of. There was also more immediate instability caused by the fluctuations in cash values; the fourteenth century has been seen as a period of monetary crisis.[58] According to the historian Mavis Mate, "The introduction of a gold coinage had just as much impact on the English economy as the outbreak of the Black Death."[59]

[56] Quoted in ibid., 285. On the economic nationalism of this poem, see John Scattergood, "*The Libelle of Englyshe Polycye*: The Nation and Its Place," in *Nation, Court and Culture: New Essays on Fifteenth-Century English Poetry*, ed. Helen Cooney (Dublin: Four Courts Press, 2001), 28–49; Ladd, *Antimercantilism*, 112–19.

[57] Russell A. Peck, "The Politics and Psychology of Governance in Gower: Ideas of Kingship and Real Kings," in *A Companion to Gower*, ed. Siân Echard (Cambridge: D. S. Brewer, 2004), 215–38 (224).

[58] See Le Goff, *Money and the Middle Ages*, 82–93.

[59] Mavis Mate, "The Role of Gold Coinage in the English Economy, 1338–1400," *The Numismatic Chronicle* 18 (1978): 126–41 (126).

But Gower would never have seen the problems wrought by gold currency or even the disruptions of the money economy as purely economic issues. The *Confessio* consistently depicts the ethical inextricably bound up with the political, and the governance of the individual mirroring the governance of the state. James Simpson has argued that "the whole poem outside Book VII is a discussion of ethics and economics, a discussion which leads inevitably to the explicit political discourse of Book VII."[60] The economics that Simpson refers to, Gower's "iconomique," means, as it does in Aristotle, the governance of the household, but in Gower it is, like the self, a microcosm of society. "The *Confessio amantis* as a whole," Simpson says, "reveals that there is no escape from politics."[61] It is entirely consistent, therefore, that in decrying the power of commerce to divide the social fabric and to undermine the common profit, Gower would focus on the minting of gold coins, which in his time was sanctioned by the king as both the symbol and the instrument of state power wedded to mercantile ambition. Gower's perspective is fundamentally nostalgic, but he is nonetheless farsighted enough to see how much power would soon be invested in the centralized state through capitalism, and how difficult it would become to maintain the cherished ideal of kingly moral leadership when royal interests were married to the expansion of the national commercial economy.

This would explain why Gower criticizes money and coinage in Book V of the *Confessio* while praising alchemy and its quest for wealth in precious metals in Book IV. While anti-alchemical treatises accused the alchemists of artificially generating imitation gold, and therefore counterfeiting wealth, the alchemists themselves and their supporters insisted that they were augmenting the true content of metals through entirely natural processes. Gower therefore emphasizes that alchemy works in accordance with "kinde"—nature:

> This craft is wroght be weie of kinde,
> So that ther is no fallas inne.
> (IV.2508–9)

[60] James Simpson, *Sciences and the Self in Medieval Poetry: Alan of Lille's "Anticlaudianus" and John Gower's "Confessio Amantis"* (Cambridge: Cambridge University Press, 1995), 220. See also Russell A. Peck, *Kingship and Common Profit in Gower's "Confessio amantis"* (Carbondale and Edwardsville: Southern Illinois University Press, 1978), 99–123.

[61] Simpson, *Sciences and the Self*, 264.

These olde Philosophres wyse
Be weie of kinde in sondri wise
Thre stones maden thurgh clergie.
(IV.2531–33)

Ther is algate founde a wyte,
So that thei folwe noght the lyne
Of the parfite medicine,
Which grounded is upon nature.
(IV.2622–25)

For Gower, as for Scholastic defenders of alchemy such as Albertus Magnus,[62] alchemy is not supernatural, nor is it "artificial," in the sense of invented. It is empirical; Gower refers from the start to the "experience / Which cleped is alconomie" (IV.2458–59). And as Gower repeatedly states, all of the metals exist on a continuum, with silver and gold at the two extremes. So the alchemical process is not one of "transmutation," but rather of multiplication: "It makth multiplicacioun / Of gold" (IV.2573–74). Alchemy seeks to "multiply" the gold or silver in a substance by bringing out its essential nature. Alchemists perfect the substance, by leading it to the ideal it naturally longs for. "For thei tuo"—that is, gold and silver—"ben th'extremetes, / To whiche after the propretes / Hath every metal his desir / With help and confort of the fyr" (IV.2565, 2567–70). Alchemy does not make something out of nothing, and it does not change one substance into another. It increases what is essentially already there.

Gower begins Book V of the *Confessio* with the words "Obstat auaricia nature legibus" (Avarice obstructs the laws of nature). He endorses alchemy before he excoriates money because alchemy stands in contrast to mercantilism as a myth of natural wealth. Alchemy in Book IV is everything that money in Book V is not: ordered, organic, bounded by natural extremes, rational, obedient to consistent laws, commensurable, and equitable. One of the qualities of money that most disturbed ancient and medieval thinkers was that, through exchange and interest, it seemed to be able to multiply itself, and therefore to create wealth *ex nihilo*, without labor or material.[63] But in Gower's understanding, the

[62] See Newman, *Promethean Ambitions*, 45–48.
[63] See Le Goff, *Your Money or Your Life*, 29–30.

alchemist's labor leads the material, through "the comfort of the fire," to the ideal form it most desires.

Some of the greatest minds of the thirteenth and fourteenth centuries worried that alchemy, by increasing the amount of (natural or synthetic) gold and silver, could destabilize the money economy. Gower seems to have harbored greater concerns about the destabilizing effects of the money economy itself. Alchemy for Gower was a myth of profit without money or exchange, of value that is absolute rather than relative, of wealth that is organic, natural, universal, elemental, and inalienable from the innate value of material. Alchemy allowed him, as it must have allowed many of his contemporaries, to entertain a vision of labor, wealth, and profit while maintaining his belief in a moral social system rooted in ancient concepts of justice and fair exchange. The elixir, Gower says, can refine every metal, "And pureth hem be such a weie / That al the vice goth aweie" (IV.2555–56).

But, it is also lost. The science itself is true, but we cannot recover it to the modern world, which, even by Gower's time, was thoroughly monetized.

Chaucer: "That slidynge science"

"But al be that he was a philosophre," Chaucer says of the Clerk in *The General Prologue*, "Yet hadde he but litel gold in cofre" (I.297–98). The joke reveals that Chaucer associates practical philosophy with alchemy, and alchemists with dishonest wealth. This offhand remark at the beginning of the *Canterbury Tales*, though, hardly prepares the reader for the extensive attack on alchemy that arises abruptly near the end.

There is much that is anomalous about *The Canon's Yeoman's Prologue and Tale*.[64] There is, first, the sudden intrusion into the Canterbury pilgrimage of an additional wayfarer, as the burned and bedraggled Yeoman and his heavily sweating Canon come galloping up to join the fellowship as they are passing Boughton-under-Blee. The Yeoman, identifying himself to the curious Host, begins subtly to reveal the Canon as an alchemist, and the Canon flees in consternation, leaving the Yeoman to expound at much greater length. The anomalousness continues with what the Ellesmere confusingly labels parts 1 and 2 of *The Canon's Yeo-*

[64] See Judith Scherer Herz, "*The Canon's Yeoman's Prologue* and *Tale*," *MP* 58 (1961): 231–37.

man's Tale—really a confessional Prologue and related Tale, in the manner of the Wife of Bath and the Pardoner.[65] In Part 1, the Yeoman bitterly recalls the time, effort, and money he has lost in the workshop of his alchemical Canon, and indicts the hopelessly complicated obfuscations of alchemical theory. In Part 2, the Tale, he tells of an alchemical canon—a different one, he insists, and a pure charlatan—who cons a London priest.[66] The Yeoman's choler is unusual as well. Chaucer's portraits of scoundrels are typically in the first person, or at least from the scoundrels' own perspectives rather than those of their victims, and often colored with a not entirely feigned admiration for their ingenuity; in general, he just gives them enough rope to hang themselves.

As the pilgrims wonder what is so urgent in the pair's sudden appearance, readers have wondered what is so important in alchemy as a theme to merit its unusual and abrupt introduction so late in the Canterbury frame scheme, as well as the Yeoman's vehement denunciations. There has been no sufficient explanation for why Chaucer goes out of his way to excoriate alchemy. His stance has sometimes been labeled conventional, but as Gower's treatment of the topic reveals there were actually competing conventions.[67]

[65] See Joseph E. Grennen, "Saint Cecilia's 'Chemical Wedding': The Unity of the *Canterbury Tales*, Fragment VIII," *JEGP* 65 (1966): 466–81.

[66] The London setting, too, is an anomaly. Other than the abortive *Cook's Tale*, the Canon's Yeoman's is the only tale Chaucer sets in the city itself, a point explored by David Wallace in "Chaucer and the Absent City," in *Chaucer's England: Literature in Historical Context*, ed. Barbara Hanawalt (Minneapolis: University of Minnesota Press, 1992), 59–90 (esp. 81–83).

[67] Ogrinc, "Western Society and Alchemy" (106) notes that the thirteenth-century tale collection attributed to "Il Novellino" includes a story of a man swindled by an alchemist. There are several recensions of this collection, however, and the dating of specific novellas within it is problematical; the alchemical story could date from as late as the sixteenth century. On the traditional perception of alchemists as frauds, see also Tara Nummedal, "On the Utility of Alchemical Fraud," in *Chymists and Chymistry: Studies in the History of Alchemy and Early Modern Chemistry*, ed. Lawrence M. Principe (Sagamore Beach, Mass.: Science History Publications, 2007), 173–80. Stanton J. Linden remarks that "enough has been written to redirect attention, once and for all, from conjecture about Chaucer's possible victimization at the hands of a real alchemist to explain the sudden appearance of a Yeoman and his Canon in the company of those with whom they alone did not set out from Southwark" (*Darke Hierogliphicks: Alchemy in English Literature from Chaucer to the Restoration* [Lexington: University of Kentucky Press, 1996], 42). That conjecture dates at least to the eighteenth century (see Linden, *Darke Hierogliphicks*, 305 n. 24) and was elaborated, naturally, by John M. Manly in *Some New Light on Chaucer* (New York: Holt, 1926), 246–47. An even older tradition, from the fifteenth century, holds that Chaucer's detailed knowledge of alchemical lore reveals him as an adept and practitioner of the craft. See Robert M. Schuler, "The Renaissance Chaucer as Alchemist," *Viator* 15 (1984): 305–33; Edgar H. Duncan, "The Literature of Alchemy and Chaucer's Canon's Yeoman's Tale: Framework, Theme, and

Perhaps because of this, and perhaps also because the Yeoman's critique of alchemy is in parts nearly as recondite as its object, *The Canon's Yeoman's Tale* has been less studied than many of the *Canterbury Tales*. In recent years, though, interest has increased in the Canon's Yeoman's sequence, and much of the analysis has been acute. Three analyses in particular share both this critical standard of excellence and also a fruitful focus on science, technology, and economics as the text's most significant themes.

Britton Harwood offers a Marxist reading of *The Canon's Yeoman's Tale* as a "mystification of work," an example of Chaucer's refusal to dramatize "productive capital"—payment for labor to make a product that is not owned by the laborer but is sold by the investor for profit.[68] For Harwood, the Yeoman is "the only wage laborer anywhere in Chaucer—the only laborer hired to make a commodity," and alchemy mimics industrial labor only to obscure it with magic and exoticism.[69] Lee Patterson also sees the Yeoman as exploited labor, "a personal servant, perhaps even an apprentice."[70] Expanding on Harwood's analysis, Patterson claims that alchemy in the Tale offers the promise not only of wealth but of a theoretical and empirical advancement in the human condition, that is, of technology, and when it proves false the Yeoman is disabused but maintains this technological view of human practice as well as a technologized sense of himself as a modern individual, making him the ideal subject to embrace modernity and capitalism. And Peggy Knapp links Chaucer's text to Ben Jonson's *The Alchemist*, for their emphasis on work and their use of alchemy to satirize nascent capitalism.[71] Like Harwood and Patterson, Knapp sees the Yeoman as a laborer in the Canon's tech-

---

Characters," *Speculum* 43 (1968): 633–56 (particularly 656); Gareth W. Dunleavy, "The Chaucer Ascription in Trinity College, Dublin MS D.2.8," *Ambix* 13 (1965): 2–21; Anke Timmermann, "New Perspectives on 'The Chaucer Ascription in Trinity College, Dublin MS D.2.8,'" *Ambix* 53 (2006): 161–65. Despite caveats like Linden's, this view continues to attract adherents; see Jonathan Hughes, *The Rise of Alchemy in Fourteenth-Century England* (London: Continuum, 2012), 75–76. Others, such as Principe, make the more reasonable claim that "Chaucer does not . . . conclude that transmutational alchemy is false; rather, it is a privileged kind of knowledge with which only a select few should dare to meddle" (*Secrets of Alchemy*, 182), but I think that much more accurately describes Gower's positions than Chaucer's.

[68] Britton J. Harwood, "Chaucer and the Silence of History: Situating the Canon's Yeoman's Tale," *PMLA* 102 (1987): 338–50 (342).

[69] Ibid., 343.

[70] Lee Patterson, "Perpetual Motion: Alchemy and the Technology of the Self," *SAC* 15 (1993): 25–57 (30).

[71] Peggy Knapp, "The Work of Alchemy," *JMEMSt* 30 (2000): 575–99.

nological industry, but in the Yeoman's rebellion against his lord she also sees the Marxian potential for the demystification of the workings of the capitalist process and the self-actualization and liberation of the worker. Knapp concludes that "modernity inhabits this tale."[72]

All of these approaches share a very fruitful emphasis on science, technology, and economics in the Canon's Yeoman sequence. But they also share a progressive view of economics, a Marxian view of labor and capital, and a view of alchemy as a metaphor for both capitalism and for industrial technology, all of which may not be entirely appropriate to this text, and may in fact obscure Chaucer's own particular fourteenth-century understanding of science, technology, and economics.

It is necessary, first, to reconsider the reading of the Yeoman as industrial wage laborer. The critical tradition of taking the Yeoman to be the Canon's paid employee or indentured apprentice seems to derive primarily from the meaning in other contexts of the word "yeoman."[73] Everything in the Yeoman's own description of the alchemical workshop suggests a collective enterprise:

I wol speke of oure werk.
Whan we been there as we shul exercise
Oure elvysshe craft, we semen wonder wise,
Oure termes been so clergial and so queynte.
. . .
Oure orpyment and sublymed mercurie,
Oure grounden litarge eek on the porfurie,
Of ech of thise of ounces a certeyn—
Noght helpeth us; our labour is in veyn.
Ne eek oure spirites ascencioun,
Ne oure materes that lyen al fix adoun,
Mowe in oure werkyng no thyng us availle,
For lost is al oure labour and travaille;
And al the cost, a twenty devel waye,
Is lost also, which we upon it laye.
(VIII.749–52, 774–83)

The Yeoman's language suggests, most conspicuously in his pervasive use of the first-person plural, that he is not merely a servant but a partner in the endeavors of the Canon's workshop. In fact, while he com-

[72] Ibid., 584.
[73] See Patterson, "Perpetual Motion," 30.

plains of the time and pains and injuries of his labor, he quite explicitly figures himself as a capital investor in the alchemical enterprise. After yet another kiln explosion ruins another attempt to realize the Canon's theories, the Yeoman imagines one of his anonymous partners asserting,

> Us moste putte oure good in aventure.
> A marchant, pardee, may nat ay endure,
> Trusteth me wel, in his prosperitee.
> Somtyme his good is drowned in the see,
> And somtyme comth it sauf unto the londe.
> (VIII.946–50)

The Yeoman and his collaborators do not *think* they are wage laborers or servants.

Is this just the false consciousness of an essentially proletarian worker? There is a greater problem with thinking of the Yeoman as the alienated laborer of industrial capitalism. Even if the Canon were paying the Yeoman for his services, it would not really be appropriate to characterize alchemy as "productive capital" in as much as, from Chaucer's perspective—and this is the core of the Yeoman's entire discourse—alchemy does not and cannot produce anything.[74] Lawrence Principe, reacting to a modern tradition that has often taken alchemy as essentially a set of philosophical or theoretical tropes, emphasizes that in its historical contexts alchemy was "a *productive* enterprise. Producing new materials and transforming or improving common ones forms a central theme within alchemical tradition."[75] For historians of science, this is key, as the empirical practices of alchemy can be shown to lay the groundwork for much later science, particularly in chemistry. But for understanding Chaucer, it is more important to recognize that his Canon's Yeoman does not believe alchemy capable of anything but wasting one's time, labor, and money. The Yeoman's primary complaint is not of being exploited by the Canon but of being deceived by alchemy.[76]

[74] What this might indicate is that *not even* the Canon's Yeoman is a wage laborer, and that productive capital is even more thoroughly erased from the *Canterbury Tales* than Harwood claims. If so, this would point toward some of the facts of economic life in a market society that Chaucer was not conscious of and that mark his work with their absence. But if we want to know what Chaucer *did* think about alchemy and economics, productive capital and wage labor are not the keys.

[75] Principe, *Secrets of Alchemy*, 208 (emphasis Principe's). See also Newman and Principe, *Alchemy Tried in the Fire*, 38–44.

[76] See Richard Firth Green, "Changing Chaucer," *SAC* 25 (2002): 27–52.

Patterson acknowledges that "the discourse of alchemy raises the problem of the verbal representation of truth with a special intensity and sophistication."[77] But he and other critics, including Knapp, see alchemy as fostering a technologized mentality that laid the groundwork for modernization. In this, they are again following historians of science, notably Principe and Newman, who advance an "empiricist" understanding of alchemy. No one denies that the pursuit of the "multiplying" of metals was vain or that many alchemists were crackpots or charlatans, but the empiricist view holds that alchemy, often in defiance of a more hidebound hierarchy that privileged only textual authority, nonetheless combined theory and practice in a novel way that anticipated modern science. Newman claims that "the alchemists of the Middle Ages developed a clearly articulated philosophy of technology, in which human art is raised to a level of appreciation difficult to find in other writings until the Renaissance."[78] Principe also argues for the integral role of alchemy in the development of technological and scientific modes of thought, and he places the arrival of alchemical lore in western Europe within the context of the "Renaissance of the Twelfth Century." But Principe acknowledges that alchemy was only one of many fields of technical learning that became available or more widely accessible to western Europeans at the same time: "Muslim scholars had made their own considerable advances, providing Europeans with a wealth of additional knowledge and ideas in astronomy, medicine, mathematics, physics, mechanics, botany, engineering, and fields completely new to Europe—such as *al-kimiya'*. In the twelfth century, Europe not only accepted these ideas but hungered for them."[79] A case can be made that the experimental protocols and empirical processes of alchemy made special contributions to the birth of scientific thought.[80] But the question is why we should consider the discipline important to Chaucer's

[77] Patterson, "Perpetual Motion," 39.

[78] William Newman, "Technology and the Alchemical Debate in the Late Middle Ages," *Isis* 80 (1989): 423–45 (433). See Patterson, "Perpetual Motion," 51.

[79] Principe, "Secrets of Alchemy," 52. See also Edward Grant, *The Foundations of Modern Science in the Middle Ages: Their Religious, Institutional, and Intellectual Contexts* (Cambridge: Cambridge University Press, 1996), particularly 168–206; Marie-Thérèse d'Alverny, "Translations and Translators," in *Renaissance and Renewal in the Twelfth Century*, ed. Robert L. Benson and Giles Constable, with Carol D. Lanham (Cambridge, Mass.: Harvard University Press, 1982), 421–62 (esp. 439–57).

[80] One of the strongest arguments for this view is made by William R. Newman in *Atoms and Alchemy: Chymistry and the Experimental Origins of the Scientific Revolution* (Chicago: University of Chicago Press, 2006).

intellectual development when he is so overtly hostile to it. There is, I think, another technology that better fits the bill, one that Chaucer demonstrates a keen interest in throughout the *Canterbury Tales*, that functions efficaciously in everyday practice, and that was inspired by and also inspired complex theoretical and analytical thought, often in a context that associates it with proto-scientific views of nature and with analytical measurement of natural phenomena. That technology is money.

The case for money as a technology has been made by Joel Kaye. Kaye specifically refers to "the technological form of money in exchange." In this form, Kaye maintains, money amounts to "an extendable, divisible, graded, and numbered continuum used as a common measuring scale, capable of expressing constantly shifting and diverse values in common numerical terms, and thus facilitating relation between seemingly incommensurable goods and services in exchange."[81] In this technological form, Kaye is able to locate in money the rationalist and scientific impetus that Newman and the literary critics who follow him find in alchemy.

Kaye's project is to construct a social context for a remarkable branch of thought in the first half of the fourteenth century. During this period, a group of scholars known later as the "Oxford Calculators" as well as some of their contemporaries at the University of Paris engaged in a range of studies of measurement and quantification of a wide variety of social and natural phenomena. The impetus for this "measuring mania," Kaye maintains, was money. Although as university scholars they were presumably removed from the world of the marketplace, these thinkers could not help, if only because of the exigencies of university administration, being immersed in the thoroughly monetized society of the thirteenth and fourteenth centuries.

Scholars were already engaged in debates on Aristotelian theories of money, business, and ethics, as well as problems of measurement of a physical universe they conceived as existing along series of continua not divisible into discrete units. Their practical experience with money in the commercial economy exposed them to a system that made equivalencies among widely disparate objects and ideas—commodities and products; time and effort; labor and expertise; scarcity and demand. Through this, Kaye argues, scholars came to see money in its technological form:

[81] Kaye, *Economy and Nature*, 171. See also Multhauf, *Origins of Chemistry*, 151–52.

> When people of the fourteenth century looked at coined money in their hand, they saw a round, discrete object—in rough geometrical terms, a point. However, as writers on money from Aristotle through the scholastic theorists to the twentieth century have realized, money in fact functions as a *line*, a connecting *medium* (to use the word attached to it by Aristotle and the scholastics), a measuring scale composed of a divisible and expandable *continuum* of value.

Through the use of money, therefore, and the observation of its quotidian operation, people had access to a technical system that could be used to impose rational order on complex natural processes and social interactions, even those that might otherwise seem immeasurable in their vastness, unruliness, or fluidity.

Philosophers in Oxford and Paris produced treatises of considerable subtlety and complexity, which they then shared and debated. Such economics inspired these scholars to analyze a range of phenomena and systems in the social and natural worlds, applying from economics methods of measurement with abstract but discrete units. "Every 'quality' capable of increase or decrease, whether physical or mental, came to be visualized as a divisible, continuous magnitude in the process of expansion or contraction," Kaye explains. "In Oxford and Paris, elaborate logical and mathematical languages were devised to describe and conceptually measure quantified qualities now conceived as divisible continua."[82] This application of analytical measurement to the natural world, Kaye concludes, laid the foundation for the scientific advances of subsequent centuries.

Chaucer, of course, was no "Oxford Calculator." He did not attend university; he was a layman and a secular poet; he wrote in the second half of the fourteenth century. But he was immersed in the world of money and commerce throughout his life, very often in the kind of administrative position that Kaye sees as key to the perspectives of fourteenth-century Scholastics. (He would therefore have dealt daily with what Kaye calls "the technological form of money in administration": "a continuous numbered scale superimposed by the administrator on a given problem in measurement and gradation, to the end of finding ranges of equalization and points of proportional division.")[83] Much of Chaucer's poetry—notably in *The Shipman's Tale*—reveals an interest in the workings of money and commerce, and of remarkably sophisticated

[82] Ibid., 166–67.
[83] Ibid., 174–75.

forms of monetary valuation and exchange—what modern economists call "financial instruments." Also, throughout his career—from the complicated disquisitions on acoustics in *The House of Fame* to the technological instruction of the *Treatise on the Astrolabe*—he demonstrated an interest in science and the measurement of natural phenomena. And we can see the confluence of these two interests in, among other places, *The Summoner's Tale*, where the friar's pursuit of a reasonably divisible sum of money is converted through the "unexpected gift" into an obscene and seemingly absurd challenge of dividing into equal quantities an apparently intangible substance: "To parte that wol nat departed be / To every man yliche" (III.2214–15).[84]

What I am proposing, then, is that Chaucer had considerable experience with the "technological form of money," that he was interested enough in it to represent its operations complexly and in detail in much of his work, and that he on some level also comprehended it as an application of a theoretical system that we might (though he did not) call economics.[85] Furthermore, his understanding of the social technology of money abetted his comprehension of the phenomenological systems of the natural world, such that he saw that natural processes could be perceived as measurable, predictable, and rational, and that this amounted to an incipiently scientific worldview.

If so, then Chaucer would not need alchemy to gain a technological or scientific perspective. On the contrary, in comparison to more practical technologies, alchemy would appear to him to be misleading and insufficient. And on the evidence of the Canon's Yeoman's sequence, it did.

The Yeoman complains first and foremost of the frustration inherent to the practice of alchemy.[86] Faced with failure after failure in their

[84] See Robert Epstein, "Sacred Commerce: Chaucer, Friars, and the Spirit of Money," in *Sacred and Profane in Chaucer and Late Medieval Literature*, ed. Robert Epstein and William Robins (Toronto: University of Toronto Press, 2010), 129–45.

[85] Naturally, Chaucer also had experience with the physical form of money, that is, with coin, and he could characterize it in a tone that recalls Gower. For instance, when the Pardoner's three "riotours" seek Death under an oak, they find "floryns fyne of gold ycoyned rounde" (VI.770). Not all of Chaucer's references to coinage are so pejorative; the Miller says of Alisoun, "Ful brighter was the shynyng of her hewe / Than in the Tour the noble yforged newe" (I.3255–56). See Baker, "Gold Coins," 282, 286. Notably, when the canon in the *Canon's Yeoman's Tale* persuades the priest to hazard his gold in the prospect of multiplying it in the canon's laboratory, the priest fetches his store of English gold coins: "This preest the somme of fourty pound anon / Of nobles fette" (VIII.1364–65).

[86] On Chaucer's treatment of alchemy, see John Reidy's explanatory notes to *The Canon's Yeoman's Prologue and Tale* in *The Riverside Chaucer*, 946–51. See also Edgar H. Duncan, "The Yeoman's Canon's 'Silver Citrinacioun,'" *MP* 37 (1940): 241–62, as well as Duncan, "Literature of Alchemy."

efforts to produce the desired metallurgical effects, the Yeoman and his partners find themselves in the impossible position of trying to reproduce erroneous results, and ever hopeful, they are rewarded only with lost materials and oven explosions, and wasted time and effort, and expense. If we were to seek a modern analogue to alchemy as conceived by the Canon's Yeoman, it would be neither commercial manufacturing, as Harwood suggests, nor chemical engineering, as Patterson and Newman imply. It would instead be cold fusion—a seemingly scientific process that leads its hopeful adherents down a rabbit hole of impossible duplication.

But the Yeoman also stresses that alchemy is as flawed in theory as it is in practice. Alchemical doctrine seems at first convincingly concrete, with a vast lexicon of materials and methods, and a philosophy, rejecting magical thinking, that places it firmly in the realm of natural process and invariable universal laws. But the deeper it is pursued, the more it deliquesces into evasiveness and obscurantism, the alchemist's notorious "secree" and "privetee." The "cursed craft" (VIII.830) is simply impervious to direct investigation, as the Yeoman illustrates with an anecdote of a disciple of Plato,

> That on a tyme seyde his maister to,
> As his book Senior bere witnesse,
> And this was his demande in soothfastnesse:
> "Telle me the name of the privee stoon."
> And Plato answerde unto hym anoon,
> "Take the stoon that Titanos men name."
> "Which is that?" quod he. "Magnasia is the same,"
> Seyde Plato. "Ye, sire, and is it thus?
> This is *ignotum per ignocius*.
> What is Magnasia, good sire, I yow preye?"
> "It is a water that is maad, I seye,
> Of elementes foure," quod Plato.
> "Telle me the roote, good sire," quod he tho,
> "Of that water, if it be youre wil."
> "Nay, nay," quod Plato, "certein, that I nyl."
> (VIII.1449–63)[87]

[87] On Chaucer's invention of this anecdote, see Reidy, explanatory notes to *CYPT*, 951; and Julius Ruska, "Chaucer und das Buch Senior," *Anglia* 61 (1937): 136–37. The book Chaucer refers to is a Latin translation of a tenth-century Arabic work by Muhammad ibn Umail, *Epistle of the Sun to the Crescent Moon*. Reidy, citing an unpublished paper by Edgar H. Duncan, explains that Chaucer's understanding of the title of the work as *Senior* and the author as Plato derives apparently from the annotations in a fourteenth-

Ultimately, the Yeoman concludes, alchemical theory can offer nothing more than *ignotum per ignocius*, a logical fallacy of explaining the unknown with more unknowns—deception by infinite regress.

Thus the Canon's Yeoman's "Plato" explains to his skeptical disciple why he cannot reveal to him the ultimate source of the "privee stoon":

> "The philosophres sworn were everychoon
> That they sholden discovere it unto noon,
> Ne in no book it write in no manere.
> For unto Christ it is so lief and deere
> That he wol nat that it discovered bee,
> But where it liketh to his deitee
> Men for t'enspire, and eek for to deffende
> Whom that hym liketh; lo this is the ende."
> (VII.1464–71)

Chaucer is apparently untroubled by the anachronism of Plato claiming that alchemy is "unto Christ . . . so lief and deere." This is an exemplary anecdote in the Canon's Yeoman's critique, meant to illustrate the ways in which alchemists sophistically lead their acolytes on while always refusing to ground their claims in observable fact. The claim that God loves the secret too much to allow it to be discovered, except when it mysteriously and unpredictably "liketh to his deitee" to reveal it in order to provide inspiration, is merely "Plato"'s last rhetorical gambit, after which he tries to cut off further questions: "lo, this is the ende."

Oddly, "Plato"'s assertion that "unto Christ it is so lief and deere" has frequently been taken as Chaucer's own avowal of the ultimate holiness and authenticity of alchemy. But the Canon's Yeoman's own conclusion makes it clear that he finds alchemy insupportable:

> Thanne conclude I thus, sith that the God of hevene
> Ne wil nat that the philosophres nevene
> How that a man shal come unto this stoon,
> I rede, as for the beste, lete it goon.
> For whoso maketh God his adversarie,
> As for to werken any thyng in contrarie

century English manuscript. But Chaucer seems very deliberately to have fashioned a few sentences of Latin alchemical lore into his exemplum of an alchemical Plato and his deployment of *ignotum per ignocius*. The relevant passages from Chaucer's Latin source-text are published in Bryan and Dempster, *Sources and Analogues*, 697–98.

Of his wil, certes, never shal he thryve,
Thogh that he multiplie terme of his lyve.
And there a poynt, for ended is my tale.
God sende every trewe man boote of his bale!
(VII.1472–81)

This bears some resemblance to Gower's assertion that modern men should not seek after the secrets of alchemy, but it is fundamentally different. Gower's claim is that alchemy is an authentic, empirical discipline, asserting that "The science of himself is trewe" (IV.2598) and that "ther is no fallas inne" (IV.2509). In Gower's telling, alchemy was discovered and perfected by the ancients, but it is now entirely a lost art. But Chaucer (through a wholly unauthorized alteration of sources) depicts Plato, among the most authoritative of *ancient* philosophers, as unable and unwilling to ground the claims of alchemy in empirical observation. The Canon's Yeoman's conclusion, that God does not wish philosophers to identify the process of coming to the stone, is his way of saying that this supposedly secret knowledge simply is not accessible to man through the systematic observation of natural processes. He who seeks the secrets of alchemy, he says, "maketh God his adversarie"—not, primarily, in the sense that this occultism is cursed, but rather in that God has not allowed its supposed truths to be accessible through the application of reason to the created world—which is to say, it is not scientific.

Alchemy is, in the Yeoman's term, "That slidynge science" (VIII.732), that slippery science, that maintains the appearance of rationality and holds out the promise of practicality but cannot deliver. Chaucer comes to alchemy with a notion of what science should be, derived from other sources—including, I am suggesting, the operation of money in a market economy. It entails regular measurement of results along consistent continua, observable phenomena, and logically accessible rules that can explain and predict results. Historians may well demonstrate that medieval alchemy manifested all of these qualities, but Chaucer seems not to have seen it so. And alchemy therefore looks to him like a pseudo-science.

And yet, in this context, I think the economic elements of alchemy are even more central to the significance of *The Canon's Yeoman's Tale*. In fact, the most important part of the Tale is one that is seldom noted even by those who have shown an interest in this understudied text. It is not the ostensible "actual work" of the alchemical workshop—the priest and the canon laboring to manipulate metals in the flames—but rather the lure that the canon uses to take in the priest in the first place.

The canon, of course, is playing a con. At the core of every con is not the betrayal of the mark's confidence but rather the rapport that the conman constructs in order to obtain that confidence. The concept is best described by another arch-conman of fiction, the veteran grifter Mike, played by Joe Mantegna, in David Mamet's film *House of Games*: "The basic idea is this: it's called a '*confidence*' game. Why? Because you give me your confidence? No. Because I give you *mine*."[88] At the conclusion of his Tale, Chaucer says as much of his crooked canon: "Thus maketh he his introduccioun, / To brynge folk to hir destruccioun" (VIII.1386–87).

Therefore, in what is by far the cleverest part of *The Canon's Yeoman's Tale*, the canon goes about gaining the priest's trust by first approaching him to ask for a loan. Chaucer tells us precisely one thing about this priest of London who is the canon's target:

> In Londoun was a preest, an annueleer,
> That therinne dwelled hadde many a yeer,
> Which was so plesaunt and so servysable
> Unto the wyf, where as he was at table,
> That she wolde suffre hym no thyng for to paye
> For bord ne clothyng, wente he never so gaye,
> And spendynge silver hadde he right ynow.
> (VIII.1012–18)

The most obvious point here is that the priest has enough cash on hand to make him a worthwhile mark for a conman. But the passage also reveals that the priest has the kind of mentality to make him a likely mark. The priest's landlady finds him "so plesaunt and so servysable" that she suspends his contractual obligation to pay for his board. The priest responds not by recognizing any obligation to return the landlady's generosity, but by blithely embracing the windfall as a personal profit. What this tells us is that the priest is accustomed to benefiting

[88] David Mamet, *House of Games: The Complete Screenplay* (New York: Grove Press, 1985), 34. This initial part of the standard con is called the "rope" by the early twentieth-century American conmen in David Maurer's classic sociological study, *The Big Con: The Story of the Confidence Man* (1940; repr. New York: Anchor Books, 1999).

materially from a suspension of the usual economic rules. The canon must see this as well, and recognizes in him the quintessential quality of a mark: a sense of entitlement.

The canon's "introduccioun" to the priest could hardly be more simple. He asks the priest to lend him a mark, and promises to pay it back in three days. The priest agrees, and three days later, the canon pays him back the mark. The priest is tremendously impressed by this. It shows him that the canon "so trewe is of condicioun / That in no wise breke wole his day; / To swich a man I kan never seye nay" (VIII.1039–41). "What!" replies the canon,

sholde I be untrewe?
Nay, that were thyng yfallen al of newe.
Trouthe is a thyng that I wol evere kepe
. . .
God thanke I, and in good tyme be it sayd,
That ther was nevere man yet yvele apayd
For gold ne silver that he to me lente,
Ne nevere falshede in myn herte I mente.
. . .
Syn ye so goodlich han been unto me,
And kithed to me so greet gentillesse,
Somwhat to quyte with youre kyndenesse.
(VIII.1042–44, 1048–51, 1053–55)

The canon offers to reveal to the priest the "pryvetee" of his "philosophie." Later, the canon will "allow" the priest to perform alchemical maneuvers with his own hands "in tokenyng I thee love" (VIII.1153).

The tricks that the canon performs in the rest of the Tale, the trade secrets of alchemy that the Yeoman is betraying, turn out not to be particularly impressive in their sophistication or ingenuity. The canon employs no dazzling mental one-upmanship, but rather ready-made props, like a hollowed-out ember in which silver filings are hidden, and sleight-of-hand, and sometimes simply the crudest form of misdirection; the canon merely gets the priest to look away, and substitutes a silver ingot for a copper ingot. Anyone but a willing gull would see through these tricks easily; they work only because the priest's confidence has already been established.

For the Yeoman, the moral is clear: "Ful sooth it is that swich profred servyse / Stynketh" (VIII.1066–67). Unrequested favors stink. It is the motto of all conmen; Mamet's Mike puts it only slightly differently: "Don't trust nobody."[89] The London priest's particular folly is to think that because the canon repays his debt on time and without having to be hounded, it indicates that the loan established a personal relationship beyond the economic transaction. After a simple monetary exchange—the priest lends the canon one mark; the canon pays it back—the canon gets the priest to slide into the romantic language of honor, fealty, and obligation: "trouthe"; "bileve"; "gentillesse"; "kyndenesse"; "love tokenyng."[90] The confidence in this confidence game is based on the priest's assumption that the usual rules of economic relationships do not apply to him and the canon, but that he can get rich quick anyway. Before he is a fool for false science, he is first a fool for false economics.

This nexus of alchemy, economy, and greed is central to the Yeoman's own moralization of his Tale:

> Considereth, sires, how that, in ech estaat,
> Bitwixe men and gold ther is debaat
> So ferforth that unnethes is ther noon.
> This multiplying blent so many oon
> That in good feith I trowe that it bee
> The cause grettest of swich scarsetee.
> Philosophres speken so mystily
> In this craft that men kan nat come therby,
> For any wit that men han nowe-a-dayes.
> . . .
> A man may lightly lerne, if he have aught,
> To multiplie, and brynge his good to naught!
> (VIII.1388–96, 1400–1401)

[89] Mamet, *House of Games*, 37.

[90] Although the canon is, in terms of his plan, earning what we term the priest's "confidence," to the priest's understanding the canon is establishing his "credit"—a word that was coming to connote both moral character and commercial reliability. Martha C. Howell remarks that "in this culture personal honor, what was coming to be called a man's 'credit,' was not only the mark of social legitimacy but also the essential guarantor of market integrity" (*Commerce before Capitalism*, 151). The canon's romance language, though dramatically ironic as well as jarring to the modern reader, arises organically from the fiduciary context that the canon has created for the priest. As Howell notes, "A man of credit had become a man of honor" (29). See also Craig Muldrew, *The Economy of Obligation: The Culture of Credit and Social Relations in Early Modern England* (New York: St. Martin's Press, 1998).

As in Gower, the word "multiplying" signals the convergence of alchemical and economic discourses.[91] In all estates, Chaucer says, "Bitwixe men and gold ther is debaat," due, obviously, to man's irrational but inevitable greed. So "blent" and deluded, they misunderstand natural processes (as through alchemy) and social processes (like the economic forces of the marketplace). Thus a desire for "multiplying" is paradoxically the cause of "scarsetee." As Kaye's model suggests, an analytical and practical understanding of the economic world could lead Chaucer to an understanding of the laws and principles governing the natural world. Alchemy, in contrast, is false economics that leads to false chemistry. For Chaucer, alchemy is where pseudo-science meets pseudo-social-science.

What alchemy is *not*, for Chaucer, is a metaphor for capitalism. It is, to a large extent, its opposite. The forces of a collective market in which each agent pursues individual self-interest—that is, economics—are, if properly observed, rational, explicable, and open to analysis. Alchemy, with its chicanery, self-delusion, and magical thinking, is not.

This is not to say, though, that Chaucer possesses a classical understanding of economics. Classical economists, and to an even greater extent neo-classical economists, see the market as universal, transhistorical, and inevitable—in other words, as natural. But a technological conception of money should lead one to see market economics as an *artificial* phenomenon—not false, but not natural. It is man-made. Aristotle says as much in the *Ethics*, where he concedes that money is not natural, but he emphasizes that it is artificial in the sense not that it is a violation of nature but that it is a man-made convention, which, like other inventions, can be used for the good. The name "money" (*nomisma*), he notes, derives from *nomos*, "law," "because it exists not by nature but by law, and it is in our power to change it."[92] In *The Canon's Yeoman's Tale*, market transactions and monetized relationships are not the only possible kinds of human interactions. One can, like the canon, assume that "profred servyce stynketh," and treat others instrumentally in interactions designed for personal profit. Or one can behave like the priest's landlady, who, out of a sense of personal connection, gives the priest his board and ignores his contractual obligation to repay her. Her actions

[91] See *The General Prologue*, ed. Schmidt, 162; *The Works of Geoffrey Chaucer*, ed. W. W. Skeat (Oxford: Clarendon, 1900), V.420. Duncan, "Literature of Alchemy," sees the term "multiplicacioun" as key to the Tale's meaning.

[92] *Introduction to Aristotle*, 409.

are based not on personal profit, but on the social value of granting exemptions, thereby affirming and extending relationships that are independent of competition and calculation of a market transaction. She treats her interaction with the priest essentially as a gift relationship. The folly of the priest is to think that he can individually profit from the money economy while naïvely maintaining associations and values from earlier and different systems—like the gift values of his landlady, or the faux-courtly devotion of the canon. Chaucer could learn from the functioning of market economics to apprehend rational and measurable patterns in the natural world. But I also think that he understood that economics describes human behaviors in one particular context, the market and the money economy, a context that was in his time relatively new. It was new enough for Chaucer to know that there are other value systems besides the market, and other choices for rational agents besides individual, competitive self-interest. But society and the self must therefore not be *naturally* defined by money or market competition. So, while Chaucer's economic imagination is not that of Marx, it is also not that of Adam Smith, and even less that of Friedrich Hayek.

Just as important, Chaucer's economics are not Gower's. Alchemy is, for both Chaucer and Gower, an essential trope for understanding economics. But whereas Gower idealizes alchemy as a vision of natural increase and pure wealth that is the opposite of the monetized economy, Chaucer reviles alchemy as the obscurantist antithesis of both scientific technology and economics, which are logical systems that, while artificial, can only be understood rationally and empirically.

When Scribes Won't Write: Gaps in Middle English Books

Daniel Wakelin
University of Oxford

"Ther lakketh no thyng to thyne <gap> eyen"

GEOFFREY SPIRLENG, who copied the *Canterbury Tales* with his son in Norfolk in the 1470s, had a special concern with finishing. As he completed his copy, he wrote an elaborate colophon in a decorative handwriting modeled on textura, with a prayer ending "amen" and a proud description of himself and his son. Sadly he had stopped too soon. Because of problems in his exemplars, he had duplicated two tales and omitted two entirely. He noticed this omission and so crossed out his colophon with a note explaining that "the book of Cant*er*bury is nat yet ended," and added the missing tales after.[1] The wording is telling. A scribe should not stop when the text "is nat yet ended"; a scribe should copy all of the text and only stop when it does. That makes it odd, then, that Spirleng does sometimes stop writing not at the end, nor even at the joins between Chaucer's tales which gave many scribes pause, but in the middle of the text. He stops writing in the middle of lines before carrying on, leaving a gap or blank space: "Ther lakketh no thyng to thyne <gap> eyen," he writes, for instance. The missing word is "outter." He leaves a gap like this thirty-six times for passages shorter than

[1] Glasgow, University Library, MS Hunter 197 (U.1.1) (hereafter Gl), fols. 102v, 115v. Richard Beadle, "Geoffrey Spirleng (c. 1426–c. 1494): A Scribe of the *Canterbury Tales* in His Time," in *Of the Making of Books: Medieval Manuscripts, Their Scribes and Readers; Essays Presented to M. B. Parkes*, ed. P. R. Robinson and Rivkah Zim (Aldershot: Scolar Press, 1997), 116–46, describes Spirleng's work in detail, with further comment in Daniel Wakelin, *Scribal Correction and Literary Craft: English Manuscripts 1375–1510* (Cambridge: Cambridge University Press, 2014), 46, 49, 61–62, 109, 230–31. For very helpful feedback, I would like to thank the anonymous readers for *SAC* and those present at a MEMORI seminar in Cardiff in January 2013 where I first discussed this topic.

Studies in the Age of Chaucer 36 (2014):249–278

a line. Four other times he leaves a gap for a whole line.[2] Spirleng is not alone among the copyists of English in leaving these little gaps of a line or less; lots do it. These are not, on inspection, erasures of words; the words were simply not written in the first place. What is going on when scribes won't write?

There are (as emerges below) two main causes for these gaps. The first sort of gap occurs when a scribe thinks that there is text missing from his exemplar and so leaves a space in order to slot in what's missing later. As it happens, one of Spirleng's exemplars survives, so we can see that there was one occasion when he left a whole line blank where his exemplar had skipped a line; he worked out that something was lost and so in his copy left room to supply it.[3] There is a dislike of incompleteness here like that which made him retrieve two omitted tales after he had finished. The second sort of gap, though, occurs when a scribe does find the text in his exemplar but does not believe it is right or that he has read it rightly and so leaves a gap to solve the puzzle later. For instance, in nineteen other gaps for which Spirleng's exemplar survives, the exemplar does have the word required but Spirleng leaves space for it. This second sort of gap is the main focus of this article. For leaving a gap deliberately seems odd, given his concern for completeness elsewhere. What were he and other scribes thinking when they refused to write the words they saw in their exemplars?

Given the effort needed to let the pen jump forward, not writing thus looks like a conscious choice. As such, the gaps raise a larger question about how far scribes exercised agency in their work, and about the forms that agency might take in concentration, attention, precision, improvisation, intellection, invention. Did scribes think as they put pen to paper and, if so, what did they think about, how did they think? Matthew Fisher stresses that "writing is always intended. Whether that writing is composition or copying, medieval manuscripts did not come

[2] Citing Gl, fol. 59r (*CT*, VIII.498). All line references to *CT* refer to *The Riverside Chaucer*, gen. ed. Larry D. Benson, 3rd ed. (Boston, Mass.: Houghton Mifflin, 1987). Some gaps were filled by an eighteenth-century antiquary.

[3] Gl, fol. 106v (*CT*, IV.89), following Cambridge University Library (hereafter CUL), MS Mm.II.5, fol. 146v. Gl, fols. 75v (VII.3312), 78v (VII.184), and 85r (VI.1408) also leaves three gaps for a missing line, in a part of the manuscript for which the exemplar does not survive, and where no extant manuscript lacks these lines, according to *The Text of the Canterbury Tales, Studied on the Basis of All Known Manuscripts*, ed. John M. Manly, Edith Rickert, Mabel Dean, Helen McIntosh, and Margaret Josephine Rickert, 8 vols. (Chicago: University of Chicago Press, 1940) (hereafter M–R), in their collations for B.1374, B.4502, and F.1408.

into being by accident."[4] Yet the intention in copying can be invisible, especially when scribes do copy what is in front of them, in what Fisher calls "replicative" copying or Richard Beadle calls "*verbatim* copying."[5] Such copying entails following the exemplar from the beginning through to the end, in every word; it involves reproducing other people's words and not one's own; so the evidence for what the copyist thinks is sparse and implicit. In the smooth surface of the accurate text, it is only wrinkles that reveal the scribe's presence—moments where he adds paratexts, such as annotations or new titles, or where he disrupts the text by revision, when he pursues what has been called "professional" or "active reading."[6] At these points where scribes change what they copy, we can see them thinking. Among the points that reveal the scribes deliberating over their work are those where they refuse to write, leaving a blank space. The gaps offer a fleeting glimpse of the effort and intelligence behind the seemingly automatic process of copying smoothly from beginning to end. As often in paleography it is these interruptions of the scribes' normal procedure that can tell us how that normality was maintained. As Ralph Hanna puts it, the scribe's "customary modes of procedure" become "second nature" to us too, so we need to be "arhythmically disconcerted": "it is the disruptions to expected rhythms that may introduce the researcher to particularly interesting topics."[7] The explanation for such disorder might turn out to be simple and everyday; but even everyday events can reveal the unarticulated assumptions and experiences of people in the past.

Such close reading of scribal activity, to evaluate scribal thinking,

[4] Matthew Fisher, *Scribal Authorship and the Writing of History in Medieval England* (Columbus: Ohio State University Press, 2012), 13, and similarly 15.

[5] Fisher, *Scribal Authorship*, 37–38; Richard Beadle, "Some Measures of Scribal Accuracy in Late Medieval English Manuscripts," in *Probable Truth: Editing Texts from Medieval Britain*, ed. Vincent Gillespie and Anne Hudson (Turnhout: Brepols, 2013), 223–39 (238). Daniel Wakelin, in "Writing the Words," in *The Production of Books in England 1350–1500*, ed. Alexandra Gillespie and Wakelin (Cambridge: Cambridge University Press, 2011), 34–58 (50–55), and in *Scribal Correction*, 45–53, also argues that such *verbatim* replication is common. All commentators distinguish this *verbatim* reproduction of substantives from the much rarer practice of *literatim* copying, which reproduces the exemplar letter by letter in every detail of spelling.

[6] For these models, see Kathryn Kerby-Fulton, Maidie Hilmo, and Linda Olson, *Opening up Middle English Manuscripts: Literary and Visual Approaches* (Ithaca, N.Y.: Cornell University Press, 2012), 207–44; and B. A. Windeatt, "The Scribes as Chaucer's Early Critics," *SAC* 1 (1979): 119–41 (122).

[7] Ralph Hanna, *Introducing Medieval English Book History* (Liverpool: Liverpool University Press, 2013), 60–61.

offers a useful supplement to our knowledge of the external conditions of scribes' work: who they were, where they worked, where they developed their orthography. Recent research has been answering those crucial biographical questions with increasing precision.[8] Alongside those enquiries about the context of writing, we might in addition interpret and evaluate the internal dimensions of scribes' activity. We could ask about such practical matters as how fast they wrote; how much they wrote in one stint; how accurate they were; how they emended errors; how they chose a script. We could also ask what they *thought* they were doing, why they did things, and what it felt like to do them.

In this particular case, while leaving a gap seems a failure of thought—not solving a puzzle, not understanding something—instead it suggests carefulness in copying. That might be counterintuitive: such gaps might seem to the editor inept disruptions of textual transmission or to the critic of variance delightful signs of scribal freedom from the tyranny of replication. It has been suggested that the gaps in one manuscript are signs of the scribe's "active revision" and his "freedom to intervene in the creation of the text."[9] But conversely (this article will suggest) the intention in not writing is *not* to disrupt the text nor to rewrite it but to preserve it better without rewriting. That's because the scribes imagine the text as something that exists outside the material realities of the exemplars they copy and their ability and work as copyists. While we in our research often focus on the material text—on the necessary mediation of the text by the book—in the white space of the gap the scribes imagine something like an immaterial text, as though seeking to transcend the imperfections of book production. As such, they also suggest a concern with preserving the text with as little variation, caused by the exemplar or by the copyist, as possible. These inaccuracies suggest a commitment to accurate copying, and an interest in the text as it might exist in a version other than that witnessed in the material forms the scribe possessed.

[8]Preeminently for the fifteenth century by Linne R. Mooney and Estelle Stubbs, *Scribes and the City: London Guildhall Clerks and the Dissemination of Middle English Literature, 1375–1425* (York: York Medieval Press, 2013); and by the website they have created with Simon Horobin, *Late Medieval English Scribes*, available at http://www.medievalscribes.com, ISBN 978-0-955-78766-9 (accessed June 13, 2014).

[9]Patricia R. Bart, "Intellect, Influence and Evidence: The Elusive Allure of the Ht Scribe," in *Yee? Baw for Bokes: Essays on Medieval Manuscripts and Poetics in Honor of Hoyt N. Duggan*, ed. Michael A. Calabrese and Stephen H. A. Shepherd (Los Angeles: Marymount Institute Press, 2013), 219–43 (233, 235).

In the fourteenth and fifteenth centuries and in the vernacular, with a seeming lack of rules or orderly systems for textual dissemination, such an interest in the non-varying text is not to be taken for granted. One thing we know about scribes of English at this period is that they change things; the texts of English works tend to vary from one manuscript to the next, in small details and large points of content. Most studies of scribal practice have focused on their variation, which has long been the subject of editorial untangling and more recently been subjected to interpretative analysis.[10] The most powerful accounts of scribal practice stress that it was one of "essential variance": the text in the hands of scribes was "manipulated, always open and as good as unfinished."[11] Indeed, it has been well observed that we now rather "take for granted the *mouvance* of medieval literary culture and the variance of medieval textual culture."[12] It is true that many scribes at many times either did not mind varying or even liked to vary what they copied. This is the crucial context within which we must consider the procedure of leaving gaps—and against which, in the end, the motive for leaving gaps seems striking. But an interpretation of the gaps can at least challenge our assumption or orthodoxy that scribes varied all the time and willingly; the gaps suggest that they also—not *instead* or *only*, just *also*—sometimes intended not to vary.

Introducing Gaps

That claim cannot, of course, be made for the intentions of all scribes across the centuries. First, the focus here is solely on the copying of English literary and learned works—poetry, history, religion, science—from the late fourteenth to the early sixteenth centuries. More practical or documentary genres might differ, the copying of Latin and French might differ, and earlier processes of copying might do so too. Even within this narrow set of manuscripts, the small phenomena of gaps

[10] Derek Pearsall, "Variants vs. Variance," in *Probable Truth: Editing Texts from Medieval Britain*, ed. Vincent Gillespie and Anne Hudson (Turnhout: Brepols, 2013), 197–205 (197–201), summarizes this scholarly tradition.

[11] Bernard Cerquiglini, *In Praise of the Variant: A Critical History of Philology*, trans. Betsy Wing (Baltimore: Johns Hopkins University Press, 1999), 21, 33–34; Bernard Cerquiglini, *Éloge de la variante: Histoire critique de la philologie* (Paris: Seuils, 1989), 42.

[12] Siân Echard and Stephen Partridge, "Introduction: Varieties of Editing; History, Theory, and Technology," in *The Book Unbound: Editing and Reading Medieval Manuscripts and Texts*, ed. Echard and Partridge (Toronto: University of Toronto Press, 2004), xi–xxi (xii).

cannot by themselves satisfactorily explain which scribes sought to prevent variance and which did not; a full study of their copying and exemplars would be needed for that. Indeed, it is important to note that the decision to introduce gaps is not taken often: the phenomenon, though fascinating, is not common. Yet the aim here is not to compile a comprehensive history of scribes' gaps, or of other aspects of their practice, but to interpret such gaps as do occur for what they suggest about their behaviour and intentions.

It is informative, though, to get some impression of how common these gaps are, through a rough survey. As a fair sample of Middle English books, I began by studying all the fifty-two once separate Middle English manuscript books in the Huntington Library. Studying one library's holdings in full gives an impression of the frequency of a phenomenon without starting by selecting juicy oddities.[13] Of the fifty-two manuscripts in the Huntington Library, only four contained spaces left for a whole line or more. The four were all Chaucer's or Chaucerian rhyming verse.[14] Rhyme is important for revealing where a line or more has gone astray; and perhaps the ambitions of post-Chaucerian poems won them this sort of careful attention. Then as well as these larger gaps, twelve of the fifty-two books had smaller gaps for just a word or few. Most scribes leave only one or two such gaps; and even the scribes who leave the most among the Huntington Library's books only leave half a dozen or so. This phenomenon is not, then, common in any one book nor across this whole collection. Yet it is not limited to only one kind of book: in the Huntington Library alone, these little gaps occur in two copies of the prose *Brut*, an herbal, a treatise on urine, two books

[13] Wakelin, *Scribal Correction*, 11–15, discusses the advantages and disadvantages of such a survey.

[14] San Marino, Henry E. Huntington Library (hereafter HEHL), MS Ellesmere 26.A.13, fol. 28v (Thomas Hoccleve, *The Regiment of Princes* [hereafter *Regiment*], 603–9; all subsequent line references are to the edition by Charles R. Blyth [Kalamazoo: Medieval Institute Publications, 1999]); MS HM 114 (as noted in note 33 below); MS HM 140, fol. 39r (John Lydgate, *Saint Albon and Saint Amphibalus*, ed. George F. Reinecke [New York: Garland, 1985]), III.752; MS HM 268, fol. 96v (John Lydgate, *The Fall of Princes* [hereafter *Fall*], IV.2483–85; all subesequent line references are to the edition by Henry Bergen, 4 vols., EETS e.s. 121–24 [London: Oxford University Press, 1924–27]), fols. 128v (VI.1320), 144v (VII.561). Six of the fifty-two once separate books are now bound into pairs, making forty-nine shelfmarks in total; the distinction largely follows the catalogue by C. W. Dutschke, *Guide to Medieval and Renaissance Manuscripts in the Huntington Library*, 2 vols. (San Marino: Huntington Library, 1989), available at http://sunsite.berkeley.edu/hehweb/toc.html.

of religious prose.[15] In verse they occur in a mystery cycle, *The Siege of Jerusalem*, verse homilies, the famous so-called Ellesmere Chaucer, and one book containing both Chaucer's *Troilus and Criseyde* and Langland's *Piers Plowman*.[16] They range from the grim to the glorious in genre of text and quality of manuscript production.

We might also wonder about the frequency of these gaps in a less random sample of books of intrinsic interest. Happily, one group of editors of Chaucer's *Canterbury Tales* has given some measure—not an accurate one but a first impression—of the frequency of gaps in their textual apparatus. John M. Manly and Edith Rickert's collations of manuscripts in volumes 5 to 8 of *The Text of the Canterbury Tales* often record where the scribes leave a "space," as they call it. They record "space" 156 times. A glance at many manuscripts reveals that Manly and Rickert do not have a full record of gaps in manuscripts of the *Tales*; gaps are easy to miss and the collation by Manly and Rickert was not designed to record them especially.[17] In particular, Manly and Rickert often miss gaps that fall at the end of lines of verse, which they simply list as a word being omitted ("om.") without signaling that space is left

[15] HEHL, MS HM 58, fols. 14r (*Agnus castus*, 175.18), 14v (*Agnus castus*, 176.3), and later filled in a paler ink on fols. 10v (*Agnus castus*, 171.28: "yeolo") and 14r (*Agnus castus*, 175.14: "wort"); MS HM 136, fols. 5v (*Brut*, 11.27), 15v (*Brut*, 37.12), 30r (*Brut*, 72.11), 156r–v (*Brut*, 391.14); MS HM 127, fol. 46v (Rolle, *Form of Living*, 666); MS HM 149, fol. 95v (Love, *Mirror of the Blessed Life*, 198.14); MS HM 505, fol. 72r, later filled (Daniel, *The Dome of Urynes*: "moyst"); MS HM 39872, fol. 9v (Jacques le Grand, *Le livre des bonnes meurs*, I.iii). Debatable are gaps on HM 113, fol. 1v (*Brut*, 5.5, 5.6, and 5.8): two gaps are for proper nouns ("troy," "eneas," and "greek") and the gaps only occur on the first page, so they may be part of an abandoned plan to write these words in rubric.

[16] HEHL, MS HM 1, fols. 67v (*Towneley Plays*, 20.77), 81v (later filled; *Towneley Plays*, 22.345–46); MS HM 128, fol. 206v (later filled; *Siege of Jerusalem*, 173–76); MS HM 129, fols. 7v (later filled; *Northern Homily Cycle*: "oure way"), 26v (later filled; *Northern Homily Cycle*: "esk"); MS Ellesmere 26.C.9, all later filled by different hands, on fols. 37r (*CT*, I.3461: "Thomas"), 74v (III.1116: "gentil man"), 143r (VI.951: "fond"), 188r (VIII.220: "of lilie"). Jordi Sánchez-Martí, "Pynkhurst's 'Necglygence and Rape' Reassessed," *ES* 92 (2011): 360–74 (367–68), spots the second of these four filled gaps in the Ellesmere Chaucer; his suggestion that it is the work of the scribe of *Sir Gawain and the Green Knight* in London, British Library (hereafter BL), MS Cotton Nero A.x is unconvincing. Gaps in the related Hengwrt Chaucer, all later filled, are listed by A. I. Doyle and M. B. Parkes, "Palaeographical Introduction," in *The Canterbury Tales: A Facsimile and Transcription of the Hengwrt Manuscript with Variants from the Ellesmere Manuscript*, ed. Paul G. Ruggiers (Norman: University of Oklahoma Press, 1979), xix–xlix (xlvi). See also HEHL, HM 114, in note 33 below.

[17] A. S. G. Edwards, "Manly–Rickert and the Failure of Method," *Studies in the Age of Chaucer* 32 (2010): 337–44 (342), notes problems in the accuracy and inclusiveness of M–R's corpus of variants.

for it. At least fourteen more such gaps at the ends of lines could be added to their tally.[18] Nonetheless, Manly and Rickert's collations are a useful gauge, according to the methods of one group of scholars, of the frequency of gaps, or "space"; the proportions of the different sorts of gap; and the places where they occur. The gaps fall into the two main sorts (indicated above): those where the exemplar was almost certainly lacking, and those where the exemplar might have been lacking or where it might have had the word but the scribe nonetheless chose not to write. Of the gaps Manly and Rickert record, fifty-nine are whole lines of verse left blank; also, two manuscripts share a gap in *The Tale of Melibee* as long as a line of prose, and five share a gap of a whole stanza in *The Monk's Tale*.[19] That suggests a possible proportion of about two-fifths (65 of 156, or 42 percent) emerging where scribes spotted large passages missing from the exemplar. The remainder, just over half, are gaps of one word or just a few, shorter than a line. Either they could be prompted by smaller omissions in the exemplar or they could be prompted by the second cause for gaps: by some reluctance to copy through incomprehension or doubt. Given the possibility of either cause for even these small gaps, it might be only a minority of gaps that reflect a decision to leave something out when it had been present in the exemplar. And in proportion to the length of the *Canterbury Tales* and the numerousness of the manuscripts, gaps where scribes decided not to copy are not common. But that does not make them uninteresting; indeed, it might make them more curious. Regardless of its frequency relative to other things, this phenomenon is intriguing in itself and for what it reveals about the normal scribal practices it disrupts.

[18] E.g., they occur three times in Holkham Hall, MS 667, fols. 53r (*CT*, III.520), 54r (III.704), 68r (IV.1686, not even "om."); and eleven times in Oxford, Bodleian Library (hereafter BodL), MS Arch. Selden B.14 (hereafter Se), fols. 9r (I.359), 50r (I.3316, not even "om.," and I.3336), 109v (III.1937, III.1938, III.1941), 135r (V.232), 200r (VII.2345/B.3535), 248r (VI.890), 259r (VI.1387), 259v (VI.1437). This is not only a problem of Manly and Rickert's terminology. At the end of lines of verse, it is possible that the scribe did not deliberately leave a gap but simply skipped a word unwittingly; however, while the turn at the line-end from one line to the next might interrupt his flow, it might also demand his attention. Also, the rhyme seems often to have acted as a check on the scribes' accuracy in other respects (as Wakelin, *Scribal Correction*, 194, 229–30, 253–55, 267, 273, argues), for instance by revealing where something is missing, which makes it less likely that scribes would omit rhymes unwittingly. M–R also miss gaps in other positions: e.g. CUL, MS Gg.IV.27, fol. 375r (also foliated "353") for *CT*, VIII.158, left at the end of the stanza after VIII.161, which M–R describe (their G.158) simply as "Out," or missing.

[19] M–R's B.2967 in sigla Hg, Ht (*CT*, VII.1777) and B.3197–3204 in Cp, Hg, MC, and Sl^2 (VII.2007–14).

Anyway, while gaps are not present in a majority of books in English from this period, they are not limited in their occurrence to just a few quirky books or to one circumscribed milieu or genre. It is difficult to link the tendency to leave gaps with any one group of scribes. There are some likenesses among a few of the people who leave gaps (described below). For instance, Richard Osbarn was one of the London-based bureaucrats of the early fifteenth century who propagated copies of Ricardian verse; Geoffrey Spirleng was also a bureaucrat by training; yet that is not a tight comparison: Spirleng copied his Chaucer half a century later and in Norfolk, within very different networks. And the other gaps in the Huntington Library's manuscripts occur in diverse kinds of works, from medical texts copied roughly, perhaps for the scribe's own use, to luxurious manuscripts of Lydgate's verse illuminated for a wealthy purchaser. Even the various copies of the *Canterbury Tales* vary in quality of production and in script, from hurried anglicana and poor parchment to calligraphic bastard secretary and elegant decorations. So it is unwise to homogenize the external contexts of such men's work; instead, the gaps tell us something about the internal dynamics of copying that many scribes shared.

Other Kinds of Omission and Repair

It is also important to distinguish these two sorts of gaps—for text which the exemplar lacked or for text which the scribe could not copy—from similar-looking but different phenomena. As well as leaving gaps on the page, scribes sometimes left out passages of the text, without any space for it, when they chose to excerpt, abridge, or abandon works. This excision of text is a different phenomenon from the insertion of blank space. Sometimes scribes omit passages for brevity or to suit new purposes. For instance, one copyist of Ezechiel and the Minor Prophets in the Early Version of the Wycliffite Bible excerpts and abridges them and marks the places where he skips sections by trailing off with "*et* c*etera*."[20] There are also instances of what looks like the hostile repudiation of the text. One scribe of a chronicle stops when he reaches the politically sensitive recent decades of the fifteenth century and notes "I dar write no Forther."[21] A scribe of the *Canterbury Tales* stops copying

[20] Manchester, John Rylands Library (hereafter JRL), MS Eng. 89 passim, e.g., fol. 2v, col. 1, lines 10 and 14.

[21] Champaign-Urbana, University of Illinois, MS 82, fol. 218v.

The Squire's Tale after a few lines because he, or perhaps his patron, judges it absurd: "Ista fabula est valde absurda in terminis et ideo ad presens pretermittatur nec vlterius de ea p*ro*cedat*ur*" (This tale is very absurd at the end and so for now let it be laid aside and not continued further).[22] Some people, then, did stop writing in acts of willful variance.

Yet usually when scribes abridge or truncate texts, they conceal it; they neither comment nor leave a blank space. Such interruptions and abandonments, then, differ from the leaving of visible gaps. If the cause for the omission were censorship or bowdlerization, a gap or comment showing that something had been cut would draw unwanted, teasing attention to it.[23] If the abbreviation were designed to save materials, leaving a blank space would defeat that purpose, as there would now be paper or parchment wasted.[24] And if the goal of omission were to compose a new, shorter work, then a blank space could distract readers and invite invidious comparisons with the longer text that was the source. Abridgments, then, are often invisible, and thus differ in appearance from the decisions of scribes to leave gaps.

Indeed, gaps might suggest that the text were unfinished, and there is evidence that scribes and readers did not like the impression that they had incomplete or interrupted texts. When scribes of English comment explicitly on their text—that is, when they make a meta-discursive comment about it, rather than copying or changing it, which is merely an implicit comment—the most common thing they say, with dismay, is that something is lacking. They frequently note that something *caret* or *deficit* or, in English, *lacketh*, *faileth*, or *wanteth*.[25] Just occasionally they say a little more: for instance, in a colophon that is often quoted, another scribe of the prose *Brut* chronicle worries that his copy has stopped too soon: "Here is no more . . . and þat is because we wanted

[22] Paris, Bibliothèque nationale de France, MS fonds anglais 39, fol. 57r (*CT*, VI.28). See similarly fol. 73v, cutting short *The Monk's Tale* (VII.2022).

[23] George Kane's introduction to William Langland, *Piers Plowman: The A Version; Will's Visions of Piers Plowman and Do-Well*, ed. George Kane, rev. ed. (1960; repr. London: Athlone, 1988), 137–38, articulates the general tendency.

[24] When the purpose of abridgment was to save time, too, then leaving space might defeat the purpose: it might require ever so slightly more pause for thought and mental effort than just continuing to write adjacent.

[25] E.g., among a few MSS of *The Canterbury Tales*, CUL, MS Dd.IV.24, fol. 204r (*CT*, VIII.711); BL, MS Harley 1758, fols. 167v thrice (VII.800, VII.814, VII.824), 168r (VII.888); BL, MS Harley 7335, fol. 99r (VIII.553); BL, MS Royal 18.C.ii, fol. 107v (III.188–94); BL, MS Sloane 1686, fols. 104v (II.1055), 196r (V.880); Philadelphia, Rosenbach Museum and Library, MS 1084/1, fol. 7v (*Gamelyn*, 281–83). On this phenomenon, see Wakelin, *Scribal Correction*, 258–61.

þe trewe copy þer of."[26] Similar are some comments beside incomplete tales in a few copies of the *Canterbury Tales*. While one scribe cut short *The Squire's Tale* (as noted above), another wrote nervously by the interrupted fiction "Squyers tale for Chawser made no more."[27] That is, he stresses that this is Chaucer's incompletion, and not his own.

Moreover, as is well known, scribes often tried to rectify omissions. They incorporated spurious bits into the *Canterbury Tales*, whether recognizing and seeking to conceal incompleteness or thinking they had found a more complete copy.[28] Similarly, people conflated the versions of Langland's *Piers Plowman* in order not to leave anything out.[29] On a local level, when they found single lines missing they were not averse to devising a new line to remedy the omission. For instance, one scribe of the *Canterbury Tales* leaves a gap for a missing line, but then later in a different ink adds into the space something spurious:

> The Iuge onswerd of this in his absence
> ⌐This to graunt were grete offence¬

Such additions, if measured against what modern editors think is authorial, are wrong; but they are not wildly wrong. This scribe rightly spots that he needs a rhyme and his guess of what the line will say is good: here the judge refuses to judge until the accused is brought forward.[30] Although there is a spurious invention here, the impetus seems to be to

[26] BL, MS Egerton 650, fol. 111r, discussed by Kathleen L. Scott, "Limning and Book-Producing Terms and Signs *in situ* in Late-Medieval English Manuscripts: A First Listing," in *New Science out of Old Books: Studies in Manuscripts and Early Printed Books in Honour of A. I. Doyle*, ed. Richard Beadle and A. J. Piper (Aldershot: Scolar Press, 1995), 142–88 (147–48).

[27] Princeton University Library (hereafter PUL), MS 100, fol. 60v. And on *The Cook's Tale*, see Aberystwyth, National Library of Wales, MS Peniarth 392, fol. 57v; and BL, MS Harley 7333, fol. 60r.

[28] Described by Stephen Partridge, "Minding the Gaps: Interpreting the Manuscript Evidence of the *Cook's Tale* and the *Squire's Tale*," in *The English Medieval Book: Studies in Memory of Jeremy Griffiths*, ed. A. S. G. Edwards, Vincent Gillespie, and Ralph Hanna (London: British Library, 2000), 51–85; and Simon Horobin, "Compiling the *Canterbury Tales* in Fifteenth-Century Manuscripts," *ChauR* 47 (2013): 372–89 (384, 389).

[29] Among many accounts, see Ralph Hanna III, *Pursuing History: Middle English Manuscripts and Their Texts* (Stanford: Stanford University Press, 1996), 204–13; John M. Bowers, "Two Professional Readers of Chaucer and Langland: Scribe D and the HM 114 Scribe," *SAC* 26 (2004): 113–46 (140); Lawrence Warner, *The Lost History of "Piers Plowman": The Earliest Transmission of Langland's Work* (Philadelphia: University of Pennsylvania Press, 2011), xv, 15, 20.

[30] BL, MS Add. 25718, fol. 50v (*CT*, VI.171–72). *The Riverside Chaucer* has this as "The juge answerde, 'Of this, in his absence / I may nat yeve diffynytyf sentence.'"

avoid the appearance—perhaps the patron's accusation—that they have not written the whole text.

Elsewhere, then, sometimes scribes rewrite the text deliberately, by omitting passages with no space or intent to reinstate them; at other times they conceal omissions deliberately, by supplying spurious text, or protest about them nervously. Given this dislike of incompleteness, and the willingness to remark upon gaps or to invent something to fill them, the decision to create or preserve gaps in one's copy seems more puzzling.

Two Types of Gap: Missing Text or Mystifying Text?

It is possible to imagine (as was noted) two broad motives for doing so. The first sort of gap left for whole lines or more is simpler to explain than the second. Like the notes that something *deficit*, gaps are usually left for whole lines because the scribe of an exemplar had omitted something and a copyist spotted that and left room to restore it. For such a long gap, spotting an omission seems the likelier cause; it would be unlucky for a scribe not to understand his exemplar for as long a stretch as this. The problem with the exemplars emerges, for instance, in the manuscripts of John Hardyng's verse chronicle, where such gaps often recur from copy to copy, as A. S. G. Edwards has noted. Scribes recognize the shortfall and invent lines to patch it up or (as considered here) leave a gap.[31] Sometimes the scribes of surviving copies spot omissions for themselves; sometimes they follow exemplars in which somebody had already realized and marked it in another way, for instance by writing *caret*. For example, in the so-called Devonshire Chaucer the scribe leaves a line blank where his exemplar merely signaled the jump in the text with little crosses in boxes in the margin.[32] But whoever first spots the lacuna, how do they do so? Because these long gaps tend to occur for a line or more of verse, as in the books of the Huntington Library (noted above), it seems to be the rhyme-scheme or stanzaic pattern of verse that reveals the jump in the text. Tellingly, people often leave these gaps for whole lines too late, only at the end of a couplet or stanza:

[31] A. S. G. Edwards, "The Manuscripts and Texts of the Second Version of John Hardyng's *Chronicle*," in *England in the Fifteenth Century: Proceedings of the 1986 Harlaxton Symposium*, ed. Daniel Williams (Woodbridge: Boydell, 1987), 75–84 (79–82).

[32] Tokyo, Takamiya Collection, MS 24, fol. 125v (*CT*, IV.2020); BL, MS Egerton 2726, fol. 133v. For another gap, see Tokyo, Takamiya Collection, MS 24, fol. 58v (II.328–29).

they do so at this point, because it is only when a couplet or stanza ends that one can see whether it has its full complement of rhymes, and so of lines. It is the incompleteness of the rhyme-scheme that reveals that the exemplar is lacking.

Some corroboration that lines were missing in an exemplar comes from the work of a scribe who copied the same work twice: Richard Osbarn, a scribe of the Guildhall, part of the bureaucracy of the City of London, who copied literary manuscripts on the side, as a mixture of freelance extra earning and fanatical hobby. Among other things, he wrote all of one copy of Chaucer's *Troilus and Criseyde* and contributed to a second, collaborative copy. In his single-handed copy, he did not leave a gap the first four times a line was missing but he did for the later five times.[33] When he copied part of the poem in the other, collaborative copy, he again left gaps for the later omissions but also for some of the earlier ones now, and he marked one of the earlier ones with the note *caret*.[34] The fact that many of the lines are missing in both copies suggests that they were missing in some exemplar he had to hand; it also looks as though the omissions were not always marked in his exemplar, for with two of them he notices and leaves a gap or *caret* in one copy and not another. That suggests that he spotted the problem and introduced the gaps for himself, rather than just blithely reproducing gaps he found in an exemplar, at least in the earlier omissions. Moreover, the fact that this was a problem with an exemplar and not with the scribe's comprehension is suggested by the fact that some of these gaps later got filled. In his solo copy, Osbarn filled all the five gaps for whole lines and also added in the margins the four lines for which he had not left gaps. In his collaborative copy, another scribe—scribe C of that copy, who seemingly checked the others' work—filled some of Osbarn's gaps with the missing lines.[35] It looks as though Osbarn and

[33] HEHL, MS HM 114, not leaving a gap on fols. 209v (*TC*, II.26: nearly identical), 212v (II.250: totally different from the modern editor's text), 216v (II.509), or 217r (II.537), but leaving one on fols. 225r (II.1083), 239v (III.292), 255v (III.1375), 274v (IV.790), and 310r (V.1377). All are identical to the modern edited text, except where marked. There are also smaller gaps left and later filled on fols. 210r (II.55, II.64—on which see note 49 below), 258v (III.1574), and 265r (III.169), and further gaps in this MS's copy of Langland's *Piers Plowman*, discussed by Bart, "Intellect," 235.

[34] BL, MS Harley 3943, fols. 20r (II.250: gap left; scribe C fills), 23v (II.509: missing and marked *caret*), 31v (II.1083: gap left; scribe C fills), 45v (III.292: gap left; scribe C fills).

[35] See notes 33 and 34.

his colleague checked another source in order to do so,[36] so there might seem little more to say: the problem lay with the exemplars. But it is worth noting that the solution lay not only with finding better exemplars but with the scribes' intelligence as well. Osbarn had to realize that gaps would be useful when he found a fuller text, and sometimes he did not work it out. Similarly, two passages with missing lines, for which Osbarn had left gaps in his solo copy, in the collaborative copy were written by a different scribe who left no such gaps. So it was not automatic but effortful to do this; not all scribes were equally intelligent, nor was any scribe consistently intelligent. Even leaving gaps for something missing, which might seem more passive than deliberate, required agency.

The practice of leaving gaps for whole lines is, though, consistent in cause. For smaller gaps of a word or few, no general pattern is found, whether in the content—not regularly the verse line—or in the thinking process—from the verse-form—that prompts the scribe to leave room. When the gap extends only to one or a few words, it was likely left for one of three reasons. Some of these shorter gaps occurred where the exemplar was missing something. Others occurred where the exemplar had the text, but in some mangled form, and the person copying it refused to reproduce the nonsense. Finally, other gaps occurred when the scribe who devised the gap might have had an exemplar that made perfect sense but about which he was himself uncomprehending. Given this variety of causes, to explain these short gaps as a group we need to generalize at a level that is riskily aloof from the *text* but that does bring us close to the *scribes* and what they think and do. Though the three reasons for small gaps—omission in the exemplar, muddle in the exemplar, uncertainty on the part of the copyist—are different, and one of them to the scribes' discredit, overall these small gaps suggest, as do the longer ones, the scribes' intelligent interest in accurate copying.

First, some small gaps might occur where the scribe spots little lacunae in the text he inherits. This seems the case, for instance, in a copy of the anonymous poem *The Court of Sapience*, from the later fifteenth century. The handwriting is modeled on bastard anglicana of a calligraphic quality, although with **g** from secretary script. The quality sug-

[36] And in fact Osbarn's solo copy has been heavily corrected by checking an exemplar from a different strand in the textual tradition: Ralph Hanna III, "The Scribe of Huntington HM 114," *SB* 42 (1989): 120–33; Mooney and Stubbs, *Scribes and the City*, 30–37.

gests that the scribe wrote for a living, as does the fine quality of some of the other books he made.[37] In his copy of *The Court of Sapience*, he leaves nine gaps for just a word or two, some of them likely where something was lost from his exemplar. Notably in the line "What nedeth drinke w[-]{h}ere thirst hath no <gap>," he leaves a gap for the word "powere," which should come at the end of the line, and he writes "d" in the margin.[38] The letter "d" might stand for the Latin *deficit*, which is commonly written (as noted) where text is lost. A few scribes and users evidently felt familiar enough with *deficit* to abbreviate it to "def" or "de" with a superscript "t"; one scribe wrote "+d" and "defect*us*" either side of the same line, which suggests that "d" did often note that something *deficit* or *is missing*.[39] So the scribe might here leave a gap because he spots that "powere" is lacking from his exemplar. He might have recognized that "were" two lines earlier needed a rhyme, or the syntax might have told him that the determiner ("no") lacks its following noun, as do the article "the" and the preposition "for," each followed by gaps elsewhere in this copy.[40] Or the syntax and sense might together reveal an incomplete doublet or list, as where the scribe leaves a gap for the word "reygne" after "vniu*er*se" and "Cite," in a description of "thre" places, which suggests that another spatial dimension is needed ("in vniu*er*se | Cite *and* <gap> thise be the thre diu*er*se"). Interestingly, although grammar can suggest that something is missing, it cannot suggest what, especially when these gaps occur in doublets or lists. In such synonymy or hyponymy, the rhetorical effect comes from

[37] New York, Columbia University Library, MS Plimpton 256 (hereafter Pl), with the scribe's oeuvre identified by Carol Meale, "Patrons, Buyers and Owners: Book Production and Social Status," in *Book Production and Publishing in Britain 1375–1475*, ed. J. J. Griffiths and Derek Pearsall (Cambridge: Cambridge University Press, 1989), 201–38 (212, 230–31 n. 64), and Kathleen L. Scott, *Later Gothic Manuscripts* (London: Harvey Miller, 996), II.331–32 (no. 124). There is some variation in the handwriting, notably in the use of **g** in BodL, MS Fairfax 4, another of his MSS.

[38] Pl, fol. 6v; *The Court of Sapience*, ed. E. Ruth Harvey (Toronto: University of Toronto Press, 1984), line 374. The letter **h** in "w[-]{h}ere" is written over erasure, as my diacritics show.

[39] Respectively BL, MS Harley 7335, fol. 90r (*CT*, at a jump between III.2294 and VIII.1); BL, MS Harley 1758, fols. 167v (*CT*, VII.814), 168r (VII.888); PUL, MS Taylor 2, fol. 25v/a34 (*Fall*, I.4024, which lacks the negative particle *not*); HEHL, MS HM 115, fol. 26r.

[40] Pl, fol. 22r (*Court*, 1431, 1452). Likewise, in BL, MS Harley 326, fol. 83r, this scribe leaves a gap where syntax suggests something is missing; in fact *The Three Kings' Sons*, ed. Frederick J. Furnivall, EETS e.s. 67 (London: Kegan Paul, Trench, Trübner, 1895), 136, line 8, prints this passage without any corresponding gap, but adds an editorial comma betraying that the syntax is awkward.

the piling up of words in copiousness and not from any particular choice of word, so it is difficult to guess which words would fill out the trope. For instance, it is tricky to guess which animal will be listed in the gap here, because the surrounding lines list fauna as diverse as:

> The broke the pantere *and* the dromedare
> The ase the camell and the full of sight
> The boore the swyne the <gap> *and* the hare
> The fox tigir of moost spedy myght [41]

In such a menagerie how would the scribe of *The Court of Sapience* guess that he needed a "whesel"? So he leaves a gap.

Yet the inventive vocabulary in synonymy or in tropes such as similes might not only impede the scribe from guessing when a word was missing; it might also worry him even if the word were present. After all, this scribe is not entirely alert to things missing: he is not sharp-eyed enough, ironically, to see the missing lynx in the line before the weasel ("the lynx ful of syght," the line should say). So he might not be noting omissions but might instead be baffled by things that are present but that he cannot read. He might refuse to write "whesel" even if it is in the exemplar, if the letters are formed so that they are visually illegible; or the spelling might be garbled so that it cannot be parsed; or the word might be legible and correct but the copyist be unable to decode it either visually or intellectually, say, if he does not know the word or think it is legitimate in this context. You might not expect a "whesel" among these other beasts or might not recognize its spelling. The word *weasel* seldom began with <wh> in fifteenth-century English, as it does in the other manuscript of this poem used by the editor.[42] The names of animals sometimes baffle scribes: for example, scribes of Lydgate's *The Fall of Princes* leave gaps for a "cowe," where it is the animal painted on the hull of a ship, and for "a stynkyng hound," to which a villain is compared; neither animal seems the only or the obvious choice at these points, and whatever is or is not in the exemplar the scribes refuse to guess.[43] In *The Court of Sapience*, we might suspect that this scribe was

[41] Pl, fol. 22r (*Court*, 1450–53).

[42] According to the forms listed in *OED*, *weasel*, *n.*, and illustrated in *MED*, *wesel(e* (n.).

[43] Respectively BL, MS Add. 21410, fol. 134r (*Fall*, VII.1087); JRL, MS Eng. 2, fol. 9v (*Fall*, I.1704, later supplied in different ink).

baffled, because several of the gaps are for Latinate or francophone words that might be unfamiliar: "enourne," "venym," "zemeth," "raveyn," and maybe "reygne," as well as the archaic "whatkyns."[44] It may seem unlikely that some of these words would give a fifteenth-century person pause for concern, but in the other copies of this poem other scribes gloss two of these words: "reygne" as "*scilicet* gou*er*ner" (namely *governor*) and "quatkyn" as "what qualis" (in both English and Latin). Maybe these words were confusing, then, to the scribe who left the gaps; or maybe an exemplar had interlinear glosses that confused him as to which word was right.[45] The scribe's incomprehension emerges in the gap for "enourne," where the poet says he "can not please paynt <gap> ne endite."[46] Here nothing in syntax or sense would reveal that anything is missing, for the "ne" (meaning *nor*) already links three things in *synonymia*. Rather, whoever first left the gap was probably able to see something in his exemplar, even if garbled or damaged, that he did not understand, for he left room for it. The poet says that he "can not please paynt <gap> ne endite," and his rhetorical gesture of humility is made real by the scribe who refuses to "enourne" or embellish by guessing words he does not know.[47] As George Kane remarked, scribes were sometimes "reluctant to copy faithfully, letter by letter, something that they could not understand": but as well as causing them to vary what they wrote, that reluctance might also have caused them not to write at all.[48]

What prompted this uncertainty seems to be (looking more widely)

[44] Pl, respectively fols. 2r (*Court*, 68), 16r (1043), 16v (1083), 21v (1403), and maybe 2v (98) and 28v (1854). Though French in etymology, "powere" (fol. 6v, 374) is less likely to be misunderstood than missing from the exemplar, as "d" attests (as discussed above). Also this scribe writes "powere" and "power" without trouble in BL, MS Cotton Vespasian B.ix, fol. 41r, line 16, and fol. 75v, line 32; *The Book of the Foundation of St. Bartholomew's Church in London*, ed. Sir Norman Moore, EETS o.s. 163 (London: Oxford University Press, 1923), e.g., 1, line 13, and 60, line 21.

[45] BL, MS Harley 2251, fol. 287v (*Court*, 98: modern pencil foliation); Cambridge, Trinity College, MS R.3.21, fols. 51r (98 again), 79v (1854). There are other glosses on BL, MS Harley 2251, fol. 287v and throughout Cambridge, Trinity College, MS R.3.21, on fols. 51r, 68v, 75v, 77v, 79r–v, and 80v, but no more on words omitted from Pl. BL, MS Harley 2251, and a different part of Cambridge, Trinity College, MS R.3.21, are by the so-called Hammond scribe, on whom see an entry in Mooney, Stubbs, and Horobin, *Late Medieval English Scribes*, and note 71 below.

[46] Pl, fol. 2r (*Court*, 68). Without "enourne" the line is not decasyllabic, but the syllable-count varies throughout the MS, so meter is unlikely to be the prompt for a gap here.

[47] Pl, fol. 2r (*Court*, 68).

[48] Kane, in Langland, *Piers Plowman: The A Version*, 132.

very diverse, and every single gap can reveal particular words that tested scribes, say, for their orthography, archaism, neologism, or stylistic decorum. Nonetheless a few patterns emerge from these particulars. Among them, a sizeable minority of gaps is left for foreign-derived words, like "enourne," and especially for outright foreign names of people or places. For instance, as well-informed a scribe as Richard Osbarn twice left a gap for the name of Procne, once working it out and filling it later ("proygne"), once having the gap filled by a colleague with a commonplace word ("Songe").[49] A scribe of Lydgate's *The Fall of Princes* leaves gaps for four classical figures.[50] Most strikingly, in one well-decorated copy of the *Canterbury Tales*, the scribe left thirty-one gaps, of which seventeen were for classical and foreign people and places such as "Alocen and Vitulon," "Thelophus," "Pirrus," and five times "Odenake."[51] This is not a blanket ignorance of foreign names: the same scribe does in adjacent passages copy the names of Aristotle, Achilles, and more.[52] This is important because it suggests that the proper nouns were not left blank simply in order to highlight them by writing them in red ink or a display script later, as one would suspect if all the names were blank.[53] Instead, there is some distinction: the scribe recognizes the more famous classical and foreign figures, such as Aristotle, but not the obscure ones, such as Alhazen and Witulo, the Arabic and Polish scientists. It is as though the scribe were not sure whether the exemplar had got these exotic words right and so would not copy them. Chaucer hints at their outlandishness by saying that some of these names are ones that "knowen thei / that han here bookes herde," but the scribe has evidently

[49] HEHL, MS HM 114, fol. 210r (*TC*, II.64), filled by Osbarn in a different ink; BL, MS Harley 3943, fol. 17r, filled by scribe C of that MS wrongly.

[50] JRL, MS Eng. 2, fols. 3v (*Fall*, I.538), 9v (I.1636), 19v (I.3615), 66r (III.1230), discussed by Wakelin, "Writing the Words," 56.

[51] Se, fols. 135r (*CT*, V.232, V.238), 145r (II.288), 199r–v (VII.2272, VII.2291, VII.2295, VII.2318, VII.2327). See also fol. 171r (VII.964, "Sophie"), 200r (VII.2345, "Thymalao"), 244v (VII.603, "Stilboun"; VII.604, "Corynthe"), 248r (VI.889, "Avycen"), 258v (V.1379, "Mecene"), 259r (V.1387, "Aristoclides"; V.1411, "Gawle"), 259v (V.1437, "Nicerates wyf").

[52] Se, fol. 135r (*CT*, V.233, V.239).

[53] Contrast HEHL, MS HM 39872, fols. 14v (*Livre des bonnes meurs*, I.iv), 40v (I.xv), 85v (IV.v), 90v (IV.vii), 96r (IV.x), 97v (IV.xi), 122r (V.ix), where the scribe consistently leaves a gap after a Latinate word and begins each gap with ".i.," the usual abbreviation for *id est* (that is); these look like gaps for glosses in a different ink or script. This MS also has a gap for the missing or misunderstood word *teipsum* in a Latin quotation of *nosce teipsum* (fol. 9v, I.iii: "the seid vois seid Notis <gap> ¶ That is as much to sey . as know thou thi self"), as listed in note 15 above.

not heard.[54] It should be stressed: these foreign proper nouns lie behind only a small proportion of the gaps left in Chaucer's verse.[55] But they do form a distinct group, distinguished by their unfamiliarity, and they suggest most clearly that the scribes' uncertainty may lie behind various other sorts of gap.

The gaps, then, are comparable with the scribes' well-known habit of replacing rarer vocabulary with plainer by unconscious substitution.[56] The gaps could suggest the limits of the scribe's imagination or his vocabulary, as he is unable to recognize and guess a word. Yet these gaps also suggest, more positively, that scribes refuse to do a job poorly—to reproduce what they do not comprehend or what look like other people's errors; to guess and intrude their own words—and so they write nothing. The white space of not writing is not intended as willful variance of an extreme sort; it is intended as non-intervention, not stupid but thoughtful.

Signs of Thinking

That thought-process is sometimes visible. While the exemplar seldom survives to show what made scribes leave gaps—something missing or something mystifying—a few copies themselves show traces of the decision-making. One of the gaps in the copy of the *Canterbury Tales* with the foreign names left blank tells us about the thinking of the scribe.[57] When he omitted the name of the philosopher Avicenna (Chaucer's "Avycen"), another foreign proper noun, he did not omit it entirely; he included the initial letter "a" at the start of the space.[58] That single "a" suggests that he saw something in his exemplar—perhaps the name wrongly subdivided as though an imaginary common noun with an indefinite article ("a vycen"), perhaps just the name Avicenna, which he did not know, or in a cryptic spelling. There are other instances in copies of the *Canterbury Tales* in which scribes leave gaps after beginning

[54] Se, fol. 135r (*CT*, V.235).

[55] M–R's collations record nineteen gaps for foreign names, among their 156 in total, at their B.57, B.288, B.305, D.737, E.48, F.238, F.1379, F.1411, C.603, C.604, C.889, B.2157, B.3310 twice, B.3426, B.3481, B.3485, B.357, B.3517. Apart from their E.48 in Holkham Hall, MS 667, fol. 58r (*CT*, IV.48, "Poo" for the River Po), these gaps all occur in Gl or Se (their sigla too).

[56] Windeatt, "Scribes," 125–29.

[57] That could be the scribe of the surviving copy or the scribe of an exemplar whose gap he reproduces perfectly.

[58] Se, fol. 248r (*CT*, VI.889).

to write a few letters. Manly and Rickert's collation counts eleven overall. The practice of Geoffrey Spirleng shows that such abandoned copying could occur where the words were present in the exemplar: he writes simply "s" and leaves a gap where his exemplar has the full word "spell," meaning *speak*.[59] One scribe is especially prone to this practice and leaves six of these gaps after starting and abandoning certain words.[60] At these points he is not responding to something absent from his exemplar but is vexed by something present in it. An early scribe of the *Tales*, who signs his name as "Wytton," makes clear what is going on, even when the word is not obviously unfamiliar, as the name Avicenna is. He writes "Shu," for instance, before a gap where modern editors require the world "Soul" (meaning *solitary*):

> But eu*ere* lyue as a wydewe / in clothes blake
> Shu <gap> as the Turtyl / that lost hath hire make

What makes sense of his muddle is comparing the variants found in other manuscripts: numerous surviving copies have the word *should* here, even though it makes no grammatical sense.[61] So it is likely that this scribe had an exemplar with that error, and that his false start with "Shu" and perplexed abandonment of it for a gap are explicable; his alertness to the error is commendable, and his decision not to write is a sign of care and judgment. While it may seem that not writing reflects nugatory and almost non-existent effort, these false starts make visible the fact that often the scribe was trying to decipher his exemplar in difficult circumstances.

The process of reading and thinking about the exemplar is evident too when a very few scribes leave little prompts alongside their gaps.

[59] Gl, fol. 18v (*CT*, I.3480), following CUL, MS Mm.II.5, fol. 38r. See also BodL, MS Laud. misc. 600, fol. 126v (II.57, which M–R, as their B.57, record as simply a space without letters); Oxford, Corpus Christi College, MS 198, fol. 245v (VII.2661/B.3851); Oxford, Trinity College, MS 49, fol. 26v (*CT*, I.1922); and those in notes 60–61 below. M–R seem to suggest that gaps follow incomplete words in CUL, MS Gg.IV.27, at VII.1280 (M–R's B.2470), and BL, MS Royal 1.D.xv, fol. 99r (V.221), but I could not see gaps there.

[60] Holkham Hall, MS 667, fols. 17r (I.3896), 77v (III.1943), 58v (IV.120), 68r (IV.1686), 71r (IV.2104), 29v (IX.40).

[61] CUL, MS Dd.IV.24, fol. 115v (IV.2080), with a cross in the margin. M–R's collation records other MSS' variants at this line (their E.2080). Orietta Da Rold, "The Significance of Scribal Corrections in Cambridge, University Library MS Dd.4.24 of Chaucer's *Canterbury Tales*," *ChauR* 41 (2007): 393–438, analyses this scribe's work in detail.

Twice where Geoffrey Spirleng leaves gaps, he adds the correct word in the margin anyway ("mannysh'; "marche" for the name *Mardocheus*).[62] Likewise, in another copy of the *Canterbury Tales*, a Flemish saying is quoted: "But soth pley is <gap> pley as þe fle*m*myng saith." A gap was left for "quad" and the word "quade" was first written in the margin. That was done by somebody with spindly handwriting and a different form of letter **a** who seems to have been collaborating with the scribe, for he wrote many marginal corrections and cues for rubrication.[63] It would be understandable if the scribes could make out the letters of *Mardocheus* and *quad* but did not recognize them as legitimate English words. These phenomena—the attempted copying of just a few letters and marginal prompts for later writing—are even rarer than the phenomenon of leaving gaps. But such oddities throw light on normal practice; they show what is suppressed in the usually empty space of the gap. They show that gaps need not reflect a real inability to decode the graphic marks in the exemplar; they reflect caution about one's own abilities to interpret those marks.

They also suggest that scribes are wary of their exemplars. They do not trust the manuscripts that are the actual record of the text, and wonder whether there might be a better text that exists not in their hands but somewhere else, perhaps in another manuscript, but also in their own mind as an aspiration. The scribes are interested in that immaterial and absent text. Indeed, their dispreference for the material book is evident in their willingness to leave a blank space, even though such interruptions suggest that they had not completed their work and mar often quite luxurious pages. At these fleeting moments, the scribes seem more interested in the text as an idea than the book as a commodity or visual artifact.

Filling the Gaps

That is, of course, a paraphrase of what the scribes were doing in terms they are unlikely to have used. That paraphrase also, in its speculation

[62] Gl, fol. 36r (*CT*, II.782), fol. 40v (IV.1373): both words are present in the proper place in the exemplar, CUL, MS Mm.II.5, fols. 86v, 101r.

[63] BodL, MS Hatton donat. 1, fol. 64r (*CT*, I.4357). The gap was filled later but remains visible because it was longer than the inserted word, and because the filling "quad" has one-compartment **a** from secretary instead of two-compartment **a** from anglicana, as used by the scribe. The collaborator's marginal corrections are on fols. 6v (I.504), 8r (I.687), 27r (I.2326); interlineations on fols. 42r (I.3604), 64v (I.4393); and cues for rubrics on fols. 64r and 65v, not all of them filled in.

about attitudes to the text, overlooks the practicalities of making books. These prompts served some practical purpose: they would help somebody to complete the copying later; they suggest that gaps were left with the expectation of filling them in the future. That expectation is evident in another set of prompts that are less voluble but clearly designed to be useful for future stages of work. In the copy of the *Canterbury Tales* with many gaps for foreign names, there is a small cross in the margin next to six of the gaps. It is not possible to be sure that such skimpy marks were made by the scribe, but he does make crosses elsewhere and the ink looks identical in colour now (though that could be the effect of drying over time). Tellingly, these crosses by gaps occur only where the gap falls at the end of the line of verse. In verse, which ends with a ragged right-hand margin, gaps in this position might not be as clearly visible as they would be mid-line. So, while not all the gaps that need a cross get one, the crosses only occur in this copy where they're needed.[64] Whoever writes these prompts is thinking logically about which gaps will be tricky to spot for filling later. That is, the effort of not writing at first might well reflect the expectation of more writing later.

That was a fair hope for a scribe given that book production regularly involved more than one stage of work.[65] Scribes or their colleagues often went through their copies adding corrections, red ink, or illustrations in later stages of work, and they or their colleagues often wrote prompts in the margins to guide themselves or others in making these corrections and decorations. They would also leave blank spaces for inserting these rubrics, initials, or keywords in other inks and for illustrations.[66] Gaps for words to be added in rubric, in particular, can look a lot like the gaps for text that the scribe thought was missing or misunderstood.

[64] Se, fols. 50r (*CT*, I.3316, I.3336), 200r (VII.2345), 248r (VI.890), 259r (V.1387, V.1411). Where there is no cross by a gap at a line-ending, either the gaps come in quick succession (Se, fol. 109v: III.1937, III.1938, III.1941) or the incomplete line is very short (fols. 9r, I.359; 259v, V.1437), so that the disruption is visible.

[65] Aliza Cohen-Mushlin, "A School for Scribes," in *Teaching Writing, Learning to Write: Proceedings of the XVIth Colloquium of the Comité Internationale de Paléographie Latine*, ed. P. R. Robinson (London: King's College Centre for Late Antique and Medieval Studies, 2010), 61–87, summarizes ways in which people training junior scribes gave them half-completed leaves or initials to fill in.

[66] As described by, e.g., Phillipa Hardman, "Reading the Spaces: Pictorial Intentions in the Thornton MSS, Lincoln Cathedral MS 91, and BL MS Add. 31042," *Medium Aevum* 63 (1994): 250–74 (esp. 251–52, 258).

Many of the manuscripts of English works with gaps also have rubrication and illumination that were likely completed later; in such cases, envisaging completion of the text, as well, later would be sensible.[67] How that might work emerges in another book by the scribe of *The Court of Sapience* (discussed above), a copy of Roger of Waltham's *Compendium morale*: in this he left twenty-one gaps; but somebody began correcting the text and wrote prompts for filling these gaps, as for other corrections, in the margins. The scribe then inserted the correct text into the longest gap, in ink visibly different in colour.[68] As it happens, he overlooked other prompts for corrections and so left those gaps unfilled; and all the correction petered out in the fifth quire.[69] But leaving gaps could lead to the writing of prompts and the filling of gaps, in turn: gaps, then, expressed a plausible aspiration to perfect the book in stages.

The gaps were sometimes filled well. After skillful filling, it is not always easy to tell whether there was once a gap beforehand, and this probably means that gaps have been identified less frequently than they occurred. But happily for us, such invisible mending is difficult to do: sometimes the gap was wrongly sized or the filling was in a different ink or handwriting. For instance, the early scribe of the *Canterbury Tales*, "Wytton" (mentioned above), left a gap for a line missing from his exemplar of *The Summoner's Tale*; he did then work out what that line should be and wrote it in the gap at a later stage: "Who eu*er*e herde / of swich a thyng or now." The former gap is visible because the added line is in ink that is noticeably darker, and because the space left for it was too cramped, so that the added letters overlap the descenders of the letters on the line above. Just as leaving a gap reflects the thinking-process of a scribe, the filling of that gap attests to further development in his or others' thinking. For instance, "Wytton" evidently found an exemplar that could supply his line from *The Summoner's Tale*, but also then better understood where to put it: he realized that he had left the gap too late, in the second rather than the first half of a couplet; so he added the line anyway in the gap, as needs must, but reordered the two

[67] E.g., BodL, MS Hatton donat. 1, in note 63 above.

[68] BodL, MS Fairfax 4, fol. 17v.

[69] BodL, MS Fairfax 4, fols. 18v, 32r. The corrective prompts also peter out after fol. 37v, late in the fifth quire, so the later gaps have none: they are on fols. 38r, 60v (twice), 61r, 61v, 74r, 81r, 96r, 138v, 139r, 145v, 150r, 157r, 166r (three times), 172r, 177r.

lines with the construe-marks *a* and *b* in the margin, revealing his growing comprehension of what had gone wrong and how to fix it.[70]

Things did not always go so smoothly. First, access to the same exemplar to decode it later or to another exemplar to find missing text was not common enough, and many gaps went unfilled. Then sometimes the scribe filled his gap—perhaps wary of incompleteness—and got it completely wrong. For instance, the so-called Hammond scribe made two copies of John Lydgate's poem *The Horse, the Goose, and the Sheep*: in one copy he duplicated a line in error and erased it, leaving a gap; in another he left a gap in that place without any correction. It is unclear whether he caused the omission in the first copy by repeating a line, and then used his faulty copy as the exemplar for another, or whether he inherited the omission in both his copies from a third manuscript. What is clear is that he never later had access to a better exemplar to recover what should go in this gap. He did write something in one of the gaps, at a late enough stage to use ink mixed to a different hue; but he filled it with something unique, and so probably invented:

> ¶ High and lowe . were made of oo nature
> Of erth we cam to erth we shal ageyne
> ⌐Of kynges and princes . take we no cure¬
> With theyr victories and tryumphes in certayne[71]

Although he seems to have had access to multiple exemplars of some other works, he seems not to have had any further exemplar or access to the original exemplar of *The Horse, the Goose, and the Sheep*, and so was limited in his capability to rectify as big an omission as a whole line.[72] The invented line is not silly; it fits the syntax, sense, and rhyme.[73] But

[70] CUL, MS Dd.IV.24, fol. 91v (*CT*, III.2229), discussed by Da Rold, "Significance," 407, who notes (430) another gap filled further down the page (*CT*, III.2254). The line that this MS lacked was lacking in many MSS of the *a* branch of the textual tradition.

[71] BL, MS Add. 34360, fol. 36v, skipping John Lydgate, *Minor Poems*, ed. Henry Noble MacCracken, 2 vols., EETS o.s. 107, 192 (London: Oxford University Press, 1911–34), II.565 (no. 23, line 638); compare his error in BL, MS Harley 2251, fols. 286v–287r. Linne R. Mooney, "A New Manuscript by the Hammond Scribe Discovered by Jeremy Griffiths," in Griffiths, Gillespie, and Hanna, *The English Medieval Book: Studies in Memory of Jeremy Griffiths*, 113–23, lists his known MSS.

[72] Eleanor Prescott Hammond, "A Scribe of Chaucer," *MP* 27 (1929): 26–33 (29), traces his access to more than one exemplar of the *Canterbury Tales*.

[73] Because this scribe's two MSS both have the variant "nature" in the rhyming line, instead of "mateer" preferred by the editor (Lydgate, *Minor Poems*, II.565, no. 23, line 638), the spurious line rhymes with the invented "cure" better than the editor's preferred one would have. That could perhaps have prompted the gap and replacement.

without another, fuller exemplar, even a well-informed scribe such as this one cannot fill the gap accurately.

As well as being filled by the scribes themselves, it is far commoner for gaps to be filled by readers or users of the books.[74] Yet these people did not usually have access to the exemplar from which the books were copied, nor to any other copy, so they were even worse at filling gaps with the usual text. Sometimes they did well: in another copy of the *Canterbury Tales*, a line for which the scribe left a gap, somebody else then supplied, and that person worked out how to reorder the lines as required with construe-marks *a* and *b* (above), just as the scribe "Wytton" did.[75] But usually when a gap was filled by somebody other than the scribe it went awry. For example, in the manuscript of the *Canterbury Tales* with frequent gaps for foreign names, the scribe left five gaps in *The Monk's Tale* for the name of Odenake—that is, Odenatus, the husband of Zenobia, whose story Chaucer obtains from Boccaccio's *De mulieribus claris*. Then a person with handwriting of the very late fifteenth or early sixteenth century filled these gaps with the banal words *prince* and *noble*. He did not intervene without thinking, for he knew how to fit his additions to the grammar: in one line "To <gap> a prince of that contre" he added "a nobill" in the gap and so had to cross out the second indefinite article "a," which was no longer grammatical: "To ⌐a nobill¬ ~~a~~ prince of that contre." His motive for deleting that "a" is intriguing. Did he think that "a" was one of the stray, incomplete attempts at copying that accompany some other gaps, such as this scribe's "a" before a gap for *Avicenna* (discussed above)? Did he think that this "a" indicated that a common noun with the indefinite article "a" was needed here, such as he supplied ("⌐a nobill¬ ~~a~~ prince"; *a noble prince*)? Or did this "a" make him realize that he was adding something that did not really fit? As the passage went on he stopped filling the last two gaps for "Odenake": did he see that this was not going to work?[76] It is impossible to say exactly what he was thinking, but it is evident that, while he lacked knowledge, he was not without thoughtfulness.

When the gaps left are longer, the fillings can be even more inaccu-

[74] Of course, the difference of their handwriting and ink might make the filling of gaps by other people more visible.

[75] Lincoln Cathedral Library, MS 110, fol. 101r (*CT*, III.757). See also fol. 103v (III.932) and smaller corrections on fol. 101r (III.759). Horobin, "Compiling," 384–85, notes attempts to fill in missing parts of the frame-narrative in this MS.

[76] Se, fol. 199v (*CT*, VII.2272). He also fills VII.2291 and VII.2295 (fol. 199r) but not VII.2318 or VII.2327 (fol. 119v).

rate. Even when the scribe was well connected it could go wrong, as it does, for instance, in two fillings of gaps by Thomas Hoccleve in one of the copies of the *Canterbury Tales* by Adam Pinkhurst—men whom one might expect to know better.[77] Likewise, in a copy of the *Canterbury Tales* with twenty-two gaps, three were filled by somebody else with errors of placement or content. The scribe left a gap for a line missing from a stanza in *The Man of Law's Tale* and the later user's addition is revealing: the scribe left the gap too late, but the user blithely filled the gap in its wrong position, whereas the scribe "Wytton" knew how to reorder his lines *a* and *b* to incorporate things later. Also, whereas "Wytton" found the established text somewhere, this anonymous reader had to invent something, and yet something much less inventive than the poet's own line. Editors think that Chaucer's line was starkly allegorical in describing the heroine's kindness ("Humblesse hath slayn in hire al tyrannye"), but the added line is flatly literal ("And all so deboner a mongys all company").[78] This person makes another addition that is even blander: it fills a gap left for Chaucer's line "Love wol nat been constreyned by maistrye," one of his big principles, with the following:

> That frendes eu*er*yth other muste obeye
> If they woll longe holden companye
> ⌐This ys trew that I yow sertefy¬
> Whenne maystry comth the god of loue anone
> Beteth his winges and farewell he ys gone[79]

Many copies omit the line, so the scribe's gap is forgivable. But the reader's invented replacement is of a lambent dullness that is unforgivable. It is also tempting to suggest that it even unconsciously hints at its own fakery with its assertions of verity: "This ys trew that I yow

[77] E.g., National Library of Wales, MS Peniarth 392 (the Hengwrt Chaucer), fols. 138v, 150r, as printed by Mooney and Stubbs, *Scribes and the City*, 126. A third filling of a gap, on fol. 83v, which Mooney and Stubbs foliate as fol. 88v, is not spurious (contrary to Doyle and Parkes, "Palaeographical Introduction," xlvi).

[78] Holkham Hall, MS 667, fol. 43r (*CT*, II.165). (I consulted this MS from a facsimile stored in the British Library.) This person imitates the scribe's handwriting, but unconvincingly, with more broken strokes and a loopless **d**, which might suggest a date later in the fifteenth century or greater care in forming graphs, perhaps trying too hard.

[79] Holkham Hall, MS 667, fol. 32r (*CT*, V.764). M–R report that five other MSS and Caxton's first edition omit this line (their F.764), so this scribe's gap is explicable. Also on fol. 40r (V.339) he fills a gap where a king should return to his "revel" with a reference to him returning to his "horse."

sertefy." When spurious lines are supplied, they are normally of a telltale blandness like this, with phatic phrases and recapitulations—language used just to fill space. They replace the required proper nouns with common nouns, complex grammatical apposition with a single noun-phrase, going on a "revel" with getting on a "horse," bold humility with everyday politeness, maxims on love with flat asseverations. There's a telling example when a reader fills a gap in a copy of Lydgate's *The Fall of Princes* where Phaedra accuses Hippolytus of rape:

> she hath accused yonge Ipolitus
> . . . With full bolde chere *and* a plein visage
> Hou he purposed <gap> ⌐in plaine language¬
> Only be force here beaute to oppresse.

The gap was left for the words "in his furious rage," but the later reader expected Hippolytus to speak "in plaine language."[80] That blandness or bluntness suggests that this guesswork is not creative ambition but is an attempt to complete the text as fully as possible in the most likely, which is to say the most commonplace, way. Just as the scribes pause before exotic words, wary of the limits of their imagination decoding them, similarly when users fill those gaps they keep their imaginations in check.

The Value of Nothing

Of course, scribes too can achieve this banalization, when they drift in copying into autopilot and write something simpler than the poet's own words; textual criticism has long recognized that.[81] Nor need anybody have worried about it. As the mistaken filling of gaps reminds us, this was a culture that did allow scribes and readers to vary the texts they encountered. Variance was, it should be recalled, an acceptable and common part of manuscript textuality. Indeed, when the scribes left gaps for things, they created more variance of the most dramatic sort—they did not transmit some words at all—and they made room for others to vary things further by inventing replacements. The fact that the

[80] BL, MS Add. 21410, fol. 4r (*Fall*, I.2833). Of course, for anybody who knows the myth, this could be ingenious: Phaedra's accusation is false and Hippolytus is more likely to use "plaine language" than "rage."

[81] Kane describes this in Langland, *Piers Plowman: The A Version*, 132–34.

gaps were filled, and the fact that the scribes left those gaps to be filled, might suggest a sanguine openness to—literally, an open space for—intervention. If a later stage of book production never occurred as was hoped, with the tidy consultation of authoritative exemplars, then it might be better for one of the book's users to intrude something than to have nothing. A filled gap seems preferable to a gap: the rhyme is preserved, always; something sensible is said, if boring; there is less visual distraction on the page from white space among the words.

But that makes it all the more curious that, when first writing, in these few moments the scribes restrain themselves from replacing, inventing, intervening. Why would they not do so? Whatever the chaotic outcome, the intention (I suggest) was to prevent or even to put right variance. When scribes saw words in their exemplars but did not copy them, they seem to have worried that they would mangle them, or that they were already mangled, and so to have refused to write them until they could be sure that they would get them right. The gap reveals that scribes could be aware of the risk of omitting, simplifying, and misrepresenting the poet's words. Though scribes were free to rewrite or emend, they could restrain themselves from doing so. That suggests that scribes did not universally welcome scribal interventions, or else they could have supplied omissions or interpreted obscurities with their own invention. They did not.

Nor did they often return to fill their gaps. That being the case, one might wonder whether they were that bothered with completing the text. We might compare the spaces left unfilled for initials and illustrations: of them, Phillipa Hardman has asked audaciously "whether there ever was a real intention to provide rubricated initials in these spaces, or whether the purpose of a large initial . . . could not just as effectively be served by an unfilled space: whether . . . the pre-rubrication stage of production came to be seen as an acceptable convention in itself."[82] Does this imaginative insight throw light by analogy on the purpose of gaps left for text? Rather than failing to find any better exemplar or expertise with which to solve their textual puzzle, the scribes might not have cared to solve it. The gap alone is an implicit comment that they recognized and strove to solve the puzzle, and restrained themselves from fraudulent solutions, and that might be enough to soothe the scribe's conscience or satisfy his patron. That might explain why the

[82] Hardman, "Reading the Spaces," 258.

gaps were left even in books of expensive quality: rather than being shoddy workmanship in outcome, they would make visible the careful workmanship as a process behind that outcome. This would be the "workmanship of risk" described by the craftsman David Pye, in which the flaws in handcrafted objects have their own aesthetic interest, for their contrast with the smoother workmanship reveals the processes behind, and formal ingredients within, the artwork.[83] Or if that seems too aestheticist or anachronistic, might there be a religious significance? This was a culture that believed that all human effort was flawed until it was completed by grace; so there might be satisfaction in not copying the perfect text but humbly aspiring to perfection yet falling from it.

To sketch the aesthetic or religious attitudes behind gaps would require a much wider inquiry than this. But for now it might be possible to infer the attitudes to textuality that underpin them. The gaps suggest an interest not in the text as the copy in hand but in the text as an intellectual structure. This need not be an *ideal* text, for the resulting manifestation is holey, incomplete; but it is an ideational text, an idea in the mind. The gaps allow the reader to imagine how it would rhyme, what it would say, how complete it would be. The gaps might thereby better evoke the text as an idea—invisible, intangible, non-existent—than the copying does as an achieved object. This is an airy suggestion but it might explain the self-restraint of not guessing or inventing something to fill the gap: a reverence for the text as something that survives somehow outside the mangled material instantiations one has of it.

If there is such reverence when scribes won't write, then might a similar reverence underpin the rest of their copying which proceeds more smoothly? Despite our focus on variance, invariant reproduction is far more predominant in the proportion of words scribes copied.[84] It is, though, difficult in the humanities to describe sameness. Might the gaps allow us not to take those accurate copies for granted? Leaving gaps suggests the attention and concentration and intelligence that are going on when the scribe is at work, even if he is merely reproducing. The scribe must be awake enough to notice when not to write. Might

[83] David Pye, *The Nature and Art of Workmanship*, with an introduction by John Kelsey (1968; repr. London: Herber Press, 1995), 34–35, 63. David Ganz, "Risk and Fluidity in Script: An Insular Instance," in Robinson, *Teaching Writing, Learning to Write*, 17–23 (18), applies Pye's work to paleography.

[84] As Kane concedes in Langland, *Piers Plowman: The A Version*, 126, and as observed in note 5 above.

we, alongside our praise of variance, praise this copying? The gaps are usually only a latent possibility; usually there are none present and all goes well. But even the possibility of gaps suggests the tension behind the seemingly seamless process of accurate copying. The scribes' agency is present in copying smoothly others' words, in continuous expression, but is only visible when they interrupt that copying. Despite the variance widespread in English manuscripts of the late fourteenth and fifteenth centuries, those scribes sometimes strove not to rewrite, if they could help it, by leaving a gap. Whereof they could not write, thereof they chose to be silent.

REVIEWS

ARTHUR BAHR. *Fragments and Assemblages: Forming Compilations of Medieval London*. Chicago: University of Chicago Press, 2013. Pp. x, 285. $45.00 cloth.

The book consists of an introduction followed by four chapters that discuss: manuscripts produced by (or "supervised by") a fourteenth-century Londoner, Andrew Horn; the Auchinleck MS; Chaucer's *Canterbury Tales*; and the Trentham MS of Gower. These seem reasonably well researched, although research is not really the goal here; rather, each defined corpus (a group of manuscripts, a single manuscript, a literary text) is subjected to a critical reading—what I suppose could be styled the codicological version of the very New Critical readings of a distant and undefined scholarly past from which Bahr struggles at several points to distinguish himself. What links these four disparate subjects is stated in the keywords of the title: "Fragments," "Assemblages," "Compilations," "London."

I will state from the outset that I am very skeptical of this kind of study and the assumptions that underlie it, whether the subject is manuscript collections (I claim no particular expertise here) or those compilations of printed books known as "tract volumes," or *Sammelbände*, with which I am more familiar. Bahr's interest and the intellectual task from which he claims to derive "delight" (256–57) lie in the readings themselves, and the value of the book depends on them; I am more interested in the method and assumptions (admittedly a secondary concern for Bahr), and that is what I will focus on here.

The reasons texts were put together in single manuscripts or bound volumes of printed books vary. These reasons are sometimes irrecoverable (why anyone did anything in history is rarely clear), and when they are recoverable, they are often not always that interesting or illuminating. One way to approach this problem is simply to look at other compilations: when you survey a number of them (whether manuscripts or printed *Sammelbände*) you can begin to see distinctions and differences; you can see (or imagine) types of composite volumes, perhaps a scale on which these might form a continuum. Volume X is intentional, Volume Y, by contrast, accidental. Volume Z is authorial. Another one is scribal.

Thus Bahr's apparent method—to bring various types of compilations together—has potential. You might be able to say something about the nature of one compilation by contrasting it with another. What Bahr does here is different: each of his four different compilations is given what appears to be an independent close reading. The relations are not really dealt with, even when they are obvious (Chaucer/Gower), nor when they are apparently remote (how is Horn's corpus of manuscripts in any way comparable to the *Canterbury Tales* as represented in modern editions?).

The following theses and assumptions are stated repeatedly in the introduction: "This book . . . contends that we can productively bring comparable interpretive strategies to bear on the formal characteristics of both physical manuscripts and literary works" (1) (i.e., manuscript compilations are "texts"); "I define *compilation*, not as an objective quality . . . but rather as a mode of perceiving such forms so as to disclose an interpretably meaningful arrangement" (3) (i.e., historical objects are critical objects); "a compilation relies on the perspective of its readers" (11). (I believe this is also the implication of the syntax of the subtitle, where a close reading reveals that the implied agent of "forming" is the modern scholar.) Onto these main assumptions is grafted what I'll call a thematic assertion: all these compilations have to do in some way with civic matters, whether the city of London, or the royal succession. "They are thus four compilations from medieval London, that, when assembled and apprehended together, become a compilation of medieval London" (4). This is not much of a thesis—it is rather a recent popular topic (David Wallace's *Chaucerian Polity* [Stanford: Stanford University Press, 1999]; Ralph Hanna's *London Literature, 1300–1380* [Cambridge: Cambridge University Press, 2005]). And to assert that the *Canterbury Tales* is about the city of London in some way, as is Horn's *custumal*, or as is any other of the millions of literary works written in London, is not to say very much.

Other themes and ancillary theses are suggested: Fragment I of the *Canterbury Tales* introduces a "Low Countries" motif that leads to a second thread in the work, linking *The Pardoner's Tale*, *The Squire's Tale*, *Sir Thopas*, and *The Cook's Tale*. This sounds productive, but becomes silly once we hear it named: "Franco-Flemish-tinged Knight–Squire compilational thread" (184) (which sounds, I believe, like a Gilbert and Sullivan patter song), or the variant "Cook-inflected Knight–Squire thread" (192). The London *puy* is somehow reminiscent of the Arras *puy* of the thirteenth century (32, 88), and this in turn justifies or echoes that Franco-Flemish aspect of the *Canterbury Tales*. Bahr's introduction has some extensive and enthusiastic references to Walter Benjamin's *Arcades Project*. Benjamin then appears, completely out of the blue, in every subsequent chapter—every chapter, that is, except the last, which was written first. This type of name-dropping association illuminates neither the medieval subject at hand nor the Frankfurt critics who had no interest in these subjects. The same could be said of many of the cited authorities here. Obviously, the subject matter here is in part legitimized by Hanna's *London Literature*, which discusses Horn, the Auchinleck MS and Chaucer within the context of the "city." To continue Hanna's project (or critique it) seems to me to be a worthwhile endeavor; yet, there is no sustained critique or even discussion of it here. Does Bahr agree with Hanna? Disagree? Is his method the same? Different? Was Hanna right or wrong to select his subjects as he did? Readers are left to determine that on their own.

Bahr is at several points concerned with distancing himself from anything that smacks of New Criticism, however that might be defined (e.g., 217). But few New Critics wrote in accordance with their caricatures by "post" New Critics. Most of them did exactly what Bahr does—seek for subtle meanings, structures, and themes in a given text (however that "text" is defined) with eclectic references to historical context whenever they might help. Bahr's casual associations of the terms "literary," "aesthetic," "close reading"; his explicit denial that he is engaged in "codicological New Criticism" (217); and his dismissive rejection of Mary A. and Richard H. Rouse's *Authentic Witnesses* (which Bahr rightly or wrongly thinks could be cited against his approach [103])—none of this is clearly enough presented to critique in any serious way. Surely an author might "care about how a manuscript appeared." But that does not in and of itself constitute literariness: it might be an economic consideration, an aesthetic one, or a psychological one. I don't see that such an imagined concern necessarily implies a thematic relation of the texts involved. By the same token, a writer could produce a vast tissue of allusions, parodies, and self-reflections, with little concern for the physical appearance of the final product (most of us have likely produced these ourselves).

Furthermore, what Bahr means by "codicological" matters is not as clear as it might be. Most readers will assume that he is giving close readings of a literary text (or texts) in light of its codicological form as materially embodied in a manuscript. But I'm not sure what this material object turns out to be. All citations in this book are to printed editions, even nineteenth-century ones, or, in the case of the Auchinleck MS, the facsimile. The codicological evidence, thus, has been thoroughly textualized (in the sense that it has been made reproducible) before becoming a subject of discussion.

Finally, I am most unsettled by what may be a stylistic matter, but what I believe masks the most important assumption here—the frequent claims that these medieval compilations, texts, or manuscripts, agented or not, are perfect expressions of our own interests and sensibilities. Bahr's compilations repeatedly "invite" us to do, well, precisely what we as professional critics like to do. Each is a "potential source of aesthetic resonance and an invitation to literary analysis" (11). They suggest things, problematicize them, "defer . . . the prospect of closure" (106), "[encourage] more creative forms of interpretation" (60). They exhibit "strongly textual self-representation," (159); they are "shifting and allusive," and "receptive to the kinds of close readings that have generally been reserved for texts, self-consciously literary or otherwise" (155). They are "invitations to compilational constructions" (155), "physical incitements to rereading" (115). They show "precise and subtle concatenations of theme and image," "teasingly encouraging [their] audience to engage in precisely such interpretation of the text itself" (135); are "invitations to think of . . . texts in terms of and against one another" (105). It is as if all these entities have lain dormant for over 600 years waiting for their ideal readers who just happen to be professional academics working on their résumés today. In short, and resoundingly: the compilation "begs to be analyzed . . .we have obliged" (105).

I reiterate: this review is directed only at the method, not at the four individual close readings, which seem perfectly professional and competent. But to me, this book thus turns out to be (reversing Bahr's own phrase on page 255) less than the sum of its parts. The otherwise competent readings are seriously undermined when put together like this, where the weakness of any overriding thesis and the shallowness of the method and assumptions are most exposed. So what if Benjamin's *Arcades Project* is like three of the four choices? So what if works written in London allude to London? How can we attribute intent and selection to a compilation such as Horn's corpus when we do not have a clear idea of what he selected from? What do these manuscripts look and smell like? How long do libraries allow you to examine them? Who/

what is/are the *Canterbury Tales*? How can the apparently displaced and conspiratorial agency in all these works have been missed until today? It will likely sound more condescending than I mean it to be to state that I am in some sympathy with the professional requirements placed on younger scholars. I could write a "compilation," "assemblage," "set of fragments"—all these now fashionable things—with no overriding thesis whatsoever; after brow-beating enough presses, I might get someone to give in. I don't believe history is all that coherent, and I am luckily, through no particular virtues of my own, in a position to express that belief formally. Junior scholars do not have that luxury and are far more constrained by the monograph genre, which increasingly is the only form recognized by dull-headed administrators and their well-meaning minions on tenure and promotion committees. An overriding thesis or *grand récit* will almost inevitably imply an overriding logic or coherence in the history that is its subject. The banality of that required thesis and associated assumptions then gets in the way, as it surely does here, of what are otherwise perceptive, intelligent, and well-considered observations on particular literary subjects and texts.

JOSEPH A. DANE
University of Southern California

ROBERT BARTLETT. *Why Can the Dead Do Such Great Things? Saints and Worshippers from the Martyrs to the Reformation*. Princeton: Princeton University Press, 2013. Pp. xviii, 637. $39.95.

Robert Bartlett's compendious account of saint worship from the martyrs to the Reformation explores the connection between the spread of western Christianity and the phenomenal development of a huge pantheon of Christian saints. Saints were a ubiquitous presence in medieval life, celebrated at shrines and churches; in processions and festivals; and in an "opulent visual culture" (490) that included wall and panel paintings, statues, stained-glass windows, vestments, reliquaries, textiles, and—for the well-to-do—illuminations. There was a steady growth of literary narratives devoted to the lives of saints as well, from third-century accounts of Roman persecutions; to martyrologies, Miracle Books, and sermons in both Latin and European vernaculars from the third through the fifteenth centuries; to the long-lived *Legenda aurea*, first compiled in the 1260s and replicated often thereafter in both manuscript and print editions. Indeed, Bartlett makes a persuasive case that the size and duration of the cult of the saints helped instigate a common Christian culture in Europe.

At the outset, Bartlett claims that "of all religions, Christianity is the one most concerned with dead bodies" (1). Unlike the antecedent gods of paganism, he argues, Christian saints were mortal and subject to bodily vicissitudes, including death. The challenge of Christian holiness was to detoxify mortality by repudiating bodily pleasure, thereby denying the body's material dominance over the spirit. Accordingly, the lives of the saints inverted ordinary social values by hypostasizing virginity over marriage; by promoting "radical asceticism" (634); and by offering a torturous, bloody template for martyrdom. Pagans (and later Reformers) were repelled by what they saw in saints' stories as an obsession with the mechanics of pain and with the unsavory afterlife of the body. Bartlett acknowledges this morbidity but seeks to situate it more broadly within what he calls the "breathtaking physicality" (250) of early Christian belief.

Certainly, as its critics charged, the cult of the saints seemed to revel in bodily mutilations and punishments. The litany of horrors associated with virgin martyrs is a case in point:

> Juliana is stretched on a wheel until her bones break and the marrow comes out, then plunged into hot lead. Margaret is strung up and beaten, first with rods and then with instruments with iron teeth, until her bones are laid bare. Later she is burned with flaming torches, "as far as her inmost parts" . . . Euphemia is placed on a fiery wheel, hung by the hair, crushed between stones, thrown to the beasts. Cecilia is placed in boiling water. (536)

Medieval Christians viewed such ready submission to unthinkable pain (common to male as well as to female martyrs) as well beyond ordinary human capabilities—as, for that matter, was a life of sexual denial and penitential practices. In their unsullied purity and resolute fearlessness, martyrs were emphatically larger than life.

At the same time, however, as Bartlett points out, martyrs and other saints were woven into the fabric of everyday life as friends and as intercessors with Christ. In these avatars, saints were accessible, their bodies humanized through the detailing of familiar body experiences—Saint

Catherine of Siena agreeing "to wash her face more often and fix her hair" (522) in deference to the wishes of a reproachful sister; the Forty Martyrs of Sabaste, stranded on a frozen lake, hugging their naked bodies against the cold and gazing longingly at a distant fire. Such attention to mundane concerns did not, however, diminish the superhuman status of the saints or soften the contours of their violent martyrdoms. On the contrary, as Bartlett seeks to demonstrate, the macabre, the mundane, and the resplendent were all aspects of a single—and singular—physicality.

The splendid juxtaposition of the macabre and the resplendent is readily apparent in the medieval showcasing of body relics. As Bartlett explains it, body relics were produced by cutting away "detachable and movable body parts" (102), including blood, and by salvaging objects that had been in contact with the saint's corpse, such as pieces of clothing and splinters from deathbeds. However repellent (and unavoidable) the sight and smell of an ordinary corpse might have been to medieval Christians, the detritus of saints' bodies was imaginatively transmuted and revered. Thus, remnants of bone and blood, supposedly invested with supernatural power to cure the sick and to exorcize demons, were often housed in splendid reliquaries, some containing whole arms or heads, others in the shape of tombs—"gruesomeness enshrined in gold" as Bartlett aptly puts it. Exhibited triumphantly in saints' day processions, reliquaries in effect transported the corpse to the center of celebratory ritual.

A similar dynamic governed popular worship at tomb-shrines—commonly erected over the crypts of saints. On one hand, "crowds came from far and wide" (261), a desperate procession of the blind, deaf, paralyzed, and diseased to plead with the saints for miraculous interventions. But the shrine itself, notwithstanding its function as a tomb, was "a numinous and extraordinary site" (253), decorated with rich fabrics and precious jewels, lighted with a profusion of candles, and strewn with fragrant herbs. In contrast to the file of suffering petitioners, shrines were cynosures, emanating "a glittering glory that shone out into a world unaccustomed to such brilliance" (276), much like the radiance of reliquaries transfiguring the body parts within.

Perhaps the most compelling instance of the medieval glorification of the macabre was located in the mass, where the reenactment of Christ's Crucifixion culminated in the Eucharistic feast, that is, the consumption by the faithful of Christ's transubstantiated body and blood. As Bartlett points out, the Eucharist came to dominate Christian devotion after the institution of the feast of Corpus Christi in 1264, which brought in its wake a new Christocentric imagery of bleeding hosts and bloody sacrifice—motifs absorbed, in turn, by the cult of the saints. When considered from this perspective, the spectacular violence of the later saints' lives was a mode of acknowledging the agony at the heart of the mass and the sanctity of sacrifice in Christian belief. Thus it follows, Bartlett claims, that critics, early and late, of medieval devotional excesses fail to comprehend the faithful's wholehearted embrace of Christianity's "breathtaking physicality." Indeed, this principle is the crux of Bartlett's argument, that is, that the cult of the saints—a "vast and swelling tidal wave of devotion" (162) that "suffused the imagination of worshippers" (637)—bore witness to the honesty and amplitude of medieval belief.

The only criticism that I would make of Bartlett's study is that his theoretical perspectives are frequently occluded by the wealth of descriptive detail. For example, I would have found it helpful if Bartlett had amplified the summarizing commentaries at the end of each topical section, and integrated these more fully into his concluding "Reflections." But this is a minor caveat. As both reference work (there is an impressive listing of primary and secondary sources) and critical commentary, Bartlett's study ranks as a magisterial response to the provocative query of his title.

SUSAN ZIMMERMAN
Professor Emerita, Queens College, CUNY

E. JANE BURNS and PEGGY MCCRACKEN, eds. *From Beasts to Souls: Gender and Embodiment in Medieval Europe*. South Bend, Ind.: University of Notre Dame Press, 2013. Pp. 280. $38.00 paper.

This collection is groundbreaking, not least for its intellectual generosity: in asking what happens to gender in narratives that challenge the boundaries of the human, essays in this volume connect the driving questions of posthumanism to feminist, queer, and postcolonial methodologies. In so doing, this anthology denudes posthumanism of some of its claims to novelty and singularity: investigating the limits of *the human* becomes less abstract and grandiose when these authors—from

French, history, English, German, and women's studies—pursue the myriad ways in which cross-species, shape-shifting, and in/organic bodies prompt us to think more precisely about gender's connection to embodiment. This is the best kind of achievement for a critical anthology: across eight chapters considering bodies as diverse as desirous stones, winged penises, and nursing animals, *From Beasts to Souls* offers a welcome answer to all those conference panels that for the past decade have been asking "w(h)ither feminism, queer theory, or postcolonialism?" By tracking the specificities of gender in bodies that confound any categorical articulation of the human, articles in this essay collection establish posthumanism as a theoretical methodology deeply indebted to the medieval past, and vitally important to the future of medieval studies.

Posthumanism's imbrication in medieval European sources is perhaps most evident in Chapter 1, "The Sex Life of Stone," by Jeffrey Jerome Cohen. Here Cohen investigates the motility and potential desire of stones to ask, "Could such a stone be gendered?" (17). In thinking about this question through the Pygmalion myth, medieval lapidaries, and *Mandeville's Travels*, Cohen builds a case for seeing stone as part of a "queer ecological materialism" (23), which grants stone agency and desire, powers that remain independent of human obsessions and manipulations. To establish this possibility, Cohen investigates those human fantasies of gender and sexuality that render stone inert, passive, a reflection of human fantasies of stability and permanence. The contrast between these views and those of medieval lapidaries, which invest stones with an active, elementary form of *vertu*, allows Cohen to connect Mandeville's discussion of diamonds to a vibrant, nonhuman world of desire, reproduction, and gender. And although Cohen does not fully acknowledge it (his essay is too focused on establishing the independence of lithic desire, in my view), the chapter is masterful at showing how misogyny and heteronormativity seek to shape bodies that cannot fully be known.

In Chapter 2, "Nursing Animals and Cross-Species Intimacy," Peggy McCracken considers the animality that mother's milk potentially confers in the Old French Crusade Cycle, the *Decameron*, *Hayy Ibn Yaqzan*, and a Krakow altarpiece entitled *The Punishment of Unfaithful Wives*. These diverse narratives share the belief that cross-species nursing should only be predicated by need. Because mother's milk is understood to pass on maternal virtues or faults, stories of nursing deer, or of women who suckle animals, must be overcome with a return to humanity. In *La naissance du Chevalier au cygne*, like the *Decameron* and *Hayy Ibn Yaqzan*, the animal intimacy of nursing must ultimately be abandoned. In the Krakow altarpiece, by contrast, the "unnatural" act of adultery is punished by forcing women to nurse puppies in public. Animal intimacy is a risk to humanity, but it also uncovers the misogynist assumption that women are more closely connected to animals. Through her deft readings, McCracken shows how women are distanced from humanity through the intimacies of maternity itself. While the stories are meant to provide limit cases, "These stories suggest a mixing—of person and animal, of the human and the bestial" that is persistently associated with women in the Middle Ages (43).

Chapter 3, "The Lady and the Dragon in Chrétien's *Chevalier au lion*," by Matilda Tomaryn Bruckner, pursues a more figural interspecies mingling. By exploring the tale's central image—"the fire-breathing dragon who holds a lion by its tail" (66), this essay considers the intermixture of animal and human, man and woman, Yvain and Laudine. As Bruckner observes, "Even as the romance accepts 'man' as the measure of the human, it problematizes that abstraction by exploring male and female differences lodged in their common human nature" (67). The lion and the dragon, and the struggle that links these figures in Yvain's adventure, suggest the ways that passions differently animate bodies across gender, species, and society. These beasts, like the humans they represent, are bound by "a mutual pact of aggression and nonaggression" that tames both "to form a *conjointure*, like the romance itself, of violence and love, animal and human" (83). In reading cross-species struggle and alliance as they animate the erotic coupling of *Yvain*, Bruckner affirms the relevance of animality to treatments of gender in key medieval texts.

Dyan Elliott, in Chapter 4, "Rubber Soul: Theology, Hagiography, and the Spirit World of the High Middle Ages," asks what happens to gender after the body dies. She treats a number of doctrinal accounts that insist upon the spirit's genderless state after death. As she notes, "the soul as a spiritual substance was necessarily sexless" (92). By contrast to writers whose antimaterialism enforced an antifeminist account of the separation of body and soul, Elliott looks to Beguine hagiography for "a permanent bridge between living and dead, confirming both the continuity of identity of the deceased and Christianity's commitment to the integral nature of a body and soul" (90). While the soul was still posited as immaterial, and therefore genderless, hagiography made the soul recognizable, and created "an irresistible continuity of identity that accommodated not just specific individuals but even their circle of friends" (112). The gendering of the soul resisted accounts that implicitly condemned women through an anticorporeal bias. But, it also meant that earthly hierarchies remained relevant in heaven, making merit a gendered ladder in the celestial realm, too. In moving beyond the human body, Elliott cannily demonstrates, one does not necessarily transcend gender's differential structures.

Chapter 5, "Kissing the Worm: Sex and Gender in the Afterlife and the Poetic Posthuman in the Late Middle English 'A Disputacion betwyx the Body and Wormes,'" by Elizabeth Robertson, is also interested in how gender encodes embodiment after death. Her focus is on material embodiment, however, and the poems that seek to negotiate the vexed partition of the soul and body in the Middle Ages. Though this genre has a lengthy history, Robertson devotes the bulk of her analysis to the fifteenth-century "Disputacion" because it differs from others: the soul is female in this debate poem, and gender difference becomes a means to communicate both the body's dissolution and the soul's surrender after death. In figuring the worms that penetrate the corpse as male, the poem sets up a homology that uses rape to represent the body's surrender to decay, as well as the soul's surrender to God. Though we are beyond the human once again in this chapter, Robertson insightfully demonstrates poetry's ability to link living and dead. Because all poetry is, in a sense, "corpse poetry," this chapter shows how truisms about gender difference might allow audiences to come to grips with the difficulties that attend death's destruction of the body's material substance.

In Chapter 6, "Hybridity, Ethics, and Gender in Two Old French Werewolf Tales," Noah Guynn examines *Bisclavret* and *Melion* for their use of hybrid, indeterminate bodies as these reflect upon the tales' misogyny and constructions of masculine sovereignty. Though other stories associate animality with bestial inhumanity, in these tales werewolves are noble, and it is the betraying women who are revealed to be less than human. In the familiar narrative of *Bisclavret*, moreover, Guynn uncovers "the consequences for a woman of being judged according to assumptions and appearances, of being perceived as a monster and then treated like one" (169). When the werewolf bites off her nose, this disfigurement is punishment for her lack of humanity, which, for a woman, is her lack of obeisance to her husband. *Melion* uses hybridity to link colonial subjects to the obeisance demanded of women: the Irish, conquered by the titular hero, are meant to show submission and are subjected to violence as a consequence. In both tales, though, the werewolves establish their humanity by displays of yielding that endear them to their respective sovereigns. As Guynn concludes, "the fact that [Melion's] doggish gestures of obedience lead to his reinstatement as Arthur's *privez* suggests that chivalry itself is a mode of domestication, that knights are made to submit to their lords in much the same way women are made to husbands or Irish barbarians to Norman reformers" (173). Here animality reinforces human structures of sovereignty.

The *Roman de Mélusine* is similarly invested in hybridity's ability to expand power, as E. Jane Burns demonstrates in Chapter 7, "A Snake-Tailed Woman: Hybridity and Dynasty in the *Roman de Mélusine*." In reading this tale against religious narratives that depict the serpent in the Garden of Eden as a female-faced hybrid, Burns contests the idea that cross-species creations are necessarily malevolent. Instead, her analysis shows the political advantages of feminine hybridity. Mélusine is depicted as courtly, able, and bounteous—she expands the Lusignan line and secures the territories they govern. Consequently, Burns suggests, this story provides "a tantalizing hybrid in which political boundaries are as expansive as the female body that here redefines them so productively" (211). This story challenges narratives that associate feminine hybridity with the "unnatural," or with the deceptive serpent who beguiles Eve. The fecundity of Mélusine's body, instead, shows us the ways that animal–human crossings expand political power, familial control, and courtly society. This chapter provides a fascinating counter to suggestions that the non/human is always monstrous, ever outside the norms that govern human society. In emphasizing the secular productivity of female hybridity, Burns demonstrates the heterogeneity of what does or should constitute "the human" in medieval discourse.

In Chapter 8, "Moving beyond Sexuality in Medieval Sexual Badges," Ann Marie Rasmussen defamiliarizes the human by examining representations of bodies that are reduced to a single, procreative part. Sexual badges, which frequently feature vulvas on stilts, or flying penises, refine how we might think of hybridity. Since many of these badges cross human, animal, and vegetal domains, they resist admixture. Instead, using Caroline Walker Bynum's notion of hybridity, Rasmussen emphasizes the ways in which these badges hold different elements in visible tension. When penises have limbs, or when vulvas grow on trees, they become "autonomous, though different, beings" (232). Some penis badges are ridden, cooked, or worn by female figures; these examples, Rasmussen argues, make women agents, and allow them to take up a form of "female masculinity when they are shown wearing crowns made up of penises or phalluses, the sign of masculinity" (233). Gender as a hybrid, one that makes the human seem strange unto itself, is signified across this genre of everyday ornamental art. By wearing the body in pieces, consumers of these artifacts show that gender can be reconfigured within different communities.

In their introduction, Burns and McCracken observe the stubborn persistence of binary gender: "To be sure, medieval literature offers many examples of gender mutability, but not usually within stories about shape-shifting protagonists or cross-species transformation" (4). What becomes evident through essays in the volume, however, is the flexibility that sustains gender's curious staying power. Scholars have sometimes wondered why gender has endured (if it is a social construction, one based on contingent individual performances that might be done as well as undone, then how does it continue to lodge itself within material structures?), but this collection helpfully foregrounds embodiment in ways that allow us to understand gender's vivacity and durability. Bodies may transform, disperse, or coalesce in productive, unsettling, or expansive ways. They might even upend or reinscribe what it means to be human. As authors in this collection show, and in thrilling, detailed fashion, getting past human embodiment might make us see gender anew, and might allow us to investigate how different bodies come to matter. Posthumanism has the potential to "[spur] us to move beyond the feminist challenge of thinking through the all-too-human body and to imagine bodies that include the animal, vegetal, and even inanimate aspects of embodiment . . ." (7). The capacious analysis of gender in *From Beasts to Souls* also has the potential to activate the insights of posthumanism in other contexts: through its wide-ranging readings of hybrid, monstrous, and in/organic bodies, this collection returns us to the ethical question of what makes different genders matter in various medieval contexts.

HOLLY A. CROCKER
University of South Carolina

CRISTINA MARIA CERVONE. *Poetics of the Incarnation: Middle English Writing and the Leap of Love*. Philadelphia: University of Pennsylvania Press, 2012. Pp. 312. $69.95 cloth.

Cristina Cervone's immensely learned and sensitively written book takes several well-known works of late medieval English literary theology—William Langland's *Piers Plowman*, Julian of Norwich's *Revelations of Divine Love*, and Walter Hilton's two-part *Scale of Perfection*—and puts them into a productive dialogue with several much less well-known works—the "Long Charter of Christ," the "Short Charter of Christ," and several anonymous lyric poems—in order to demonstrate persuasively that, for these late medieval literary compositions, poetic form does important theological work. Poetic form, as Cervone puts it, is not merely ornamental, but is indeed foundational to the doing of vernacular theology in the late English Middle Ages. Cervone taps into a wide range of sources—prose treatises; first-person prose narratives; and allegorical, narrative, and lyric poetry. The formal and generic variety of her examples and the diversity of the authors she considers add considerable weight to Cervone's claim that literary form was widely seen as a vital resource for theological speculation and instruction. As its title suggests, *Poetics of the Incarnation* manifests a broad sociocultural interest in showing the importance of poetic form to the late medieval vernacularization of Christian theology—particularly the theology of the Incarnation.

Incarnational theology, of course, brings with it certain core challenges: explaining how God becomes man requires explaining how spirit becomes flesh, how the eternal becomes temporal, how the abstract becomes concrete, and how being becomes action-in-the-world. These challenges, in Cervone's view, are precisely why poetic language is an optimal vehicle for doing theological work. Poetic language consists of textures—layered; sensory; and, most importantly, metaphorical. Because of its formal complexity, poetic language produces what Cervone terms, borrowing adroitly from cognitive science, "linguistic dilation." This is when "language gains enough agency to achieve near-personification" (85). Poetic form, for instance, enables a narrative to generate a secondary narrative within itself, a new concrete figuration underneath a larger and often more abstract idea. Poetic form can also enable multiple temporalities to coincide in a single narrative, so that the "then" of Christ's Incarnation is made palpably coterminous with the "now" of the moment of reading. Finally, poetic form enables a reader to access, at once, language's immediate, concrete, material signification and a deeper, subtler, more spiritual meaning. Poetic form, that is, is quite literally the stuff of Incarnational theology.

Rather than being organized with one major text in each chapter, Cervone's chapters cluster around particular thematics of Incarnational theology and how they play out in poetic form. This organization has the advantage of allowing us to see how a set of texts explore a single Incarnational dynamic, and what poetic forms seem most useful to a particular text. The first chapter analyzes how Hilton's *Scale of Perfection*, *Piers Plowman*, and Julian's *Revelations* all work through, in the vernacular, the problematics of signification that Augustine sets out in his treatment of "enigma" in the *De Trinitate*. Cervone shows that Hilton deliberately mimics Augustine's techniques for making "Jhesu" available to readers as the word of God; she shows that, for Langland, enigmatic language, embodiment, and cognition are all linked through deliberately figural language; and she demonstrates that Julian's substitution of a bodily/ghostly dialectic for the traditional literal/figurative one "allows for specially suitable alignment of the material with the immaterial" (40). For all of these authors, as Cervone sees it, the capacity of poetic language to mean more than one thing at the same time—its innate polysemy—affords it a particular purchase on their doing of vernacular Incarnational theology.

Before moving into her next chapter, Cervone delves into cognitive theory, to ground her explanations of how contemporary theory discusses poetic language's interaction with the mind. This cognitive theory pays dividends in the second chapter, in which Cervone shows how polysemy makes theological meaning in the "True-love" tradition (e.g.: "In a Valley of This Restless Mind," a poem from British Library, MS Harley 7322, "Flourdelys," *Piers Plowman*, Julian's *Revelations*, and the "Long Charter of Christ"). In all of these late Middle English works, polysemy enables an elision of the abstract and the concrete. That elision, in turn, helps the reader to make cognitive sense of the nearly incomprehensible truth of Christ's Incarnation. Cervone's third chapter turns to explore the metaphorics of deeds—conceived both as charters in particular and as acts in general—and how those metaphorics inform the literature of medieval English Incarnational theology. The charter metaphor, Cervone finds, "reinforces Christ's lordship, his aristocratic heritage, and his concomitant lordly responsibilities" (88); this dynamic of textually guaranteed nobility and generosity is particularly apparent in the "Charters of Christ." But Cervone also examines how Christ's deeds—his actions—are depicted in *Piers Plowman* through its participation in the "leap of love" tradition and in Julian's *Revelations* through repetitions of images of the Crucifixion. In all cases, what Christ *does* in the Incarnation is inseparable from who he *is*, showcasing how poetic language can be used by literary theologians to compress the distance between acting and being.

The fourth chapter examines how poetic form can also compress the distance between history and eternity. Examining Passus XVIII of *Piers Plowman*, and Julian of Norwich's master-and-servant parable, Cervone demonstrates that "temporal fluidity" for Langland and "timelessness and placelessness" for Julian are primary problematics in wrestling with Incarnational theology, and that both authors rely heavily on poetic form in order to do so. Cervone's final chapter leaves off from the dialectical studies of the previous three (abstraction/concreteness; being/acting; timelessness/time) in order to dig more deeply into three image systems mentioned only briefly earlier: Christ's body as language, as clothing, and as botanical growth. Focusing now on the Charters of Christ; select religious lyrics; Hilton's *Scale*; and, interestingly enough, medieval visual arts, Cervone explores how these three images are in fact master metaphors for the literature of the Incarnation.

Poetics of the Incarnation is a thought-provoking and persuasive account, as well as an elegant defense of the importance of formalism in the study of Incarnational theology. It is true that Cervone's formulations are often immensely complex—usually owing to the complexity of her ideas and the ambitious scope of her project—but that complexity seems strangely apt to a project that suggests that the kind of affective devotion to the Passion that has received a good deal of attention in scholarship is *not* the only means of vernacular theological work that was going on in late Middle English literature. Cervone reminds us that there was also a thriving brand of high-flown and intellectual vernacular theology, concerned less with making us feel the suffering of Christ in his final human hours, and more with making us understand the significance of his Incarnation in the first place.

In that insistence on the importance of Incarnational theology, I suspect the book will be important not only for literary scholars, but for scholars of the history of theology, much in the same way that Gail McMurray Gibson's *The Theater of Devotion: East Anglian Drama and Society in the Late Middle Ages* (Chicago: University of Chicago Press,

1989) has been. Moreover, Cervone's book will not simply appeal to scholars of the medieval world: because of her deep familiarity with and fluency in cognitive theories of how poetry works on the mind, coupled with her commitment to articulating those theories carefully and tracing them out in her discrete readings, I would think that her book will appeal to scholars of poetics from all historical disciplines.

ELEANOR JOHNSON
Columbia University

SUSAN CRANE. *Animal Encounters: Contacts and Concepts in Medieval Britain*. Philadelphia: University of Pennsylvania Press, 2013. Pp. viii, 271. $59.95.

Susan Crane has been at the forefront of developments in the field of medieval animal studies. At the New Chaucer Society's Congress in 2010 she organized a lively strand of sessions devoted to "Animal Discourses," select papers from which were collated into a symposium in *New Medieval Literatures* in 2011. In the same year, *postmedieval* dedicated a special issue to "The Animal Turn," to which Crane contributed an essay that now features, in revised form, in the book currently under review. The following year saw the publication of a virtual colloquium on "Animalia" within the pages of this journal, in which the author again participated. Crane's latest study, *Animal Encounters*, represents an exceptionally rich and insightful intervention in these ongoing debates, one that will be a point of reference for years to come.

Animal Encounters responds to a number of key concerns in critical animal studies. First, Crane hopes to rectify what she sees as a tendency to "forget" the animal in literary analysis, by striving, as she puts it in her opening paragraph, "to redirect attention from the animal trope's noisy human tenor back to its obscure furry vehicle" (1). Even a genre such as beast fable, which has generally been viewed as inhospitable to an animal-centered perspective, gets reconfigured in Crane's analysis as a space where animals matter. Additionally, Crane is motivated to reconsider human specificity in relation to (other) animals. What happens when traditional markers of human distinctiveness, such as language or reason, can be shown also to exist among nonhuman animals?

What are the implications, ethical or otherwise, of these encounters with animality beyond the confines of the human? Furthermore, Crane resists the notion of a univocal medieval "paradigm," or the idea that, between the earlier and later Middle Ages, there was a "paradigm shift" in attitudes to animals. Readers are invited instead to envisage a complex and contradictory terrain, crisscrossed by multiple sites of animal encounter—spaces in which animals never *simply* operate as figures.

This plurality derives not only from Crane's engagement with a multiplicity of genres, milieus, and timeframes, but also from her application of approaches developed outside literary studies. These include, as outlined in the introduction, "evolutionary biology, taxonomy, language acquisition, ethology, and environmental studies" (3). For instance, in the chapter on second-family bestiaries, information derived from scientific DNA analysis, evolutionary biologist Stephen Jay Gould's work on taxonomy, and Jorge Luis Borges's imaginary "Chinese" encyclopedia are cited in support of the view that the bestiary can be interpreted as an exercise in taxonomic thinking. Crane also conveys with admirable clarity possible resonances between medieval texts and modern critical theories, notably Jacques Derrida's influential critique of philosophy's dichotomy between human and animal. Each chapter incorporates sensitive analyses of visual material (mainly manuscript illuminations), which, like the texts that are the book's main focus, call into question the idea of a single human/animal "boundary" in medieval culture. Crane calls the materializations of animal presence she collates "fragments" (8), and concludes by describing the project as one of "recovering and reconsideration" (169); this is reflected in the book's eschewal of a central methodology in favor of a more eclectic range of approaches.

The opening chapter, which centers on Irish and Northumbrian hagiography, resists the assumption that saintly encounters with animals in these early medieval *vitae* are ultimately only human in significance. Animals have not simply been enlisted as participants in a "divine puppet show" (38), Crane submits. Rather, figures such as Saint Cuthbert are also envisaged coming into contact with animals whose species-specific behavior is enlisted as a site of wonder. Chapter 2, focusing on relations between humans and wolves, takes as its point of departure the contrast between the fable of "The Priest and the Wolf" by Marie de France, and a courtly lai, *Bisclavret*, possibly also authored by the same Marie, about a werewolf whose body shifts between human, lupine, and canine states. Although even the fable can be read against the grain, as expressing zones of proximity between humans and other animals, it is in the adventures of the lai's species-crossing protagonist, Bisclavret, that Crane discovers a clear correlation with Derrida's deconstruction of the human/animal boundary. Taxonomy is a central term in Chapter 3's exploration of the second-family bestiary, thoughtfully deployed as a means of getting beyond the dichotomy usually assumed to exist in these manuscripts, between religious and moral instruction on the one hand, and zoological knowledge or natural history on the other. Inspired by the Wallace Stevens poem "Thirteen Ways of Looking at a Blackbird," Crane explores the different meanings attributed by the bestiarist to the stag, convincingly demonstrating the genre's investment in modes of anthropomorphism that not only reinforce the "cut" between humans and other animals but also potentially revise or even reject it. The aspects of mentality and behavior often assumed to be uniquely human, these books imply, can sometimes also be detected across the classificatory divisions separating humans from other animals. Chapter 4, concentrating on late medieval hunting treatises, is a lightly revised version of an essay first published in 2008 that focuses on the ritual aspects of the hunt *à force*. Here, Crane aims to bring into focus the ideological function of this ritualized form, namely as a "space in which nobility mimes its own myth of itself" (107). Of special interest here is Crane's analysis of a miniature in a French manuscript of Gaston of Foix's *Livre de chasse* depicting huntsmen sniffing stag dung during a breakfast assembly in the forest. Imagery of this kind demonstrates the mastery of domestic and wild creatures to which noble huntsmen exclusively lay claim, but the emphasis on *informed* mastery also troubles the idea that hunting is simply an exercise in violent domination.

The final chapters return to issues raised in the opening ones concerning motifs of cross-species cohabitation. Now, though, the "relationships are ethically problematic, raising questions about compassion, fellowship, and responsibility" (120). The point of reference in these chapters is the genre of romance, as mediated in Chaucer's *Squire's Tale* and the *Romance of Sir Beves of Hamtoun*. Chapter 5, drawing on ideas presented in the author's Biennial Chaucer Lecture in 2006, puts Canacee's relationship with the falcon in *The Squire's Tale* under the spotlight, specifically insofar as it raises questions about hospitality and interspecies compassion. Chapter 6, presenting material first encountered in the aforementioned special issue of *postmedieval*, brings into focus the "complexly coordinated material relationship" (137) between knight and horse in chivalry. Especially illuminating here is Crane's observation that the embodied interaction between knight and horse, as exemplified by Bevis's relationship with his beloved mount Arondel, "carries the knight into a zone of consciousness and an ethical awareness that are not exclusively human" (167). Also perceptive is Crane's analysis of the "horsly" qualities, sexed status, and vivacity of *The Squire's Tale*'s steed of brass, which, she argues, captures something of the enlivened physicality of the chivalric horse. Such examples demonstrate how traces of the "living animal" can be found in unexpected places in medieval literature, even in contexts where the animal referent has seemingly been displaced by a machine-like analogue.

Animal Encounters blazes a trail for a new kind of literary analysis centered on animals, in which the "furry" vehicle of the animal trope becomes the star attraction rather than its human tenor. Anthropomorphism itself is shown, by Crane, to be more than simply a means of reinforcing animal difference: animal and human are revealed as unsettled, mutually defining categories. In closing, I would simply like to observe, in this connection, that the living beings most frequently disregarded in literary analysis are critters of the non-furry variety, animals such as insects and invertebrates. To date, these life forms have not inspired the same levels of critical reflection as Derrida's cat or Marie de France's werewolf, but if, as Crane suggests, there is no thinking that can entirely "forget" the living creature, then these animals, too, may be deserving of scholarly attention in the future.

ROBERT MILLS
University College London

CAROLYN DINSHAW. *How Soon Is Now? Medieval Texts, Amateur Readers, and the Queerness of Time*. Durham, N.C.: Duke University Press, 2012. Pp. 272. $84.95 cloth; $23.95 paper.

In the preface of *How Soon Is Now?*, a New York Medieval Festival attendee's awkward bathrobe costume catches Carolyn Dinshaw's eye. Dinshaw reads the bathrobe not as a goofy mistake but as a strangely touching "medievalist act" that shows the interweavings of past, present, and future in the bathrobe's accidental similarity to medieval designs (xii). A few pages later, Dinshaw interprets the 1984 song "How Soon Is Now?" by The Smiths as an investigation of the "temporal conundrum" of the fleeting present (2). With a start like this, readers can expect a book that artfully jumps the tracks of the usual monograph, and they are not disappointed.

How Soon Is Now? offers a provocative mix of analyses of medieval texts, examinations of their reception by amateur readers, theoretical investigations, autobiographical reflections, and calls for change in the academy. These elements are united by the central project of "claim[ing] the possibility of a fuller, denser, more crowded *now*" (4). On the one hand, the book identifies moments in medieval texts that depict the experience of living in a complex and multiple "now." On the other, the book examines the personal engagements of amateur medievalists who have found comfort or distress in medieval literature's odd temporalities. Dinshaw observes that both medieval texts and their later readers embrace "forms of desirous, embodied being . . . out of sync with the ordinarily linear measurements of everyday life" (4). Professional scholars, the book movingly asserts, have much to gain from affirming such queerly amateur experiences in their own work.

True to the book's open-ended spirit, Dinshaw shapes her chapters not as "definitive models" but as "provocations" (5). Following the preface's bathrobe anecdote, the introduction surveys theories of time's multiplicity, analyzing the difficult nature of the present in the titular Smiths song alongside Aristotle's *Physics* and Augustine's *Confessions*. Dinshaw also notes the book's debts to recent scholarship on temporality, queerness, and historicity. Dipesh Chakrabarty's work stands out as an especially notable influence in the introduction and in subsequent chapters. Playfully reminding readers of the forgotten importance of the amateur, the introduction also discusses the founding figure of contemporary Chaucer studies, Frederick James Furnivall. Furnivall, Dinshaw observes, was himself regarded with suspicion by established scholars, and his many editorial projects were motivated by a desire to reach an audience of passionate amateurs.

Chapter 1 develops Dinshaw's claim that medieval texts and their amateur readers can provide us with "a more capacious and positive sense" of the present (41). It dwells on "asynchrony stories," medieval narratives whose present is malleable or plural. In particular, Dinshaw examines a monk's slip into the future in the *Northern Homily Cycle*, the century-crossing Seven Sleepers of Ephesus from Caxton's version of the

Golden Legend, and the temporally adrift army of King Herla from Walter Map's *De nugis curialium*. The chapter's conclusion then points out a similar asynchrony in Henry Wadsworth Longfellow's adaptation of the story of the monk in his verse drama *The Golden Legend*, showing how "Longfellow enters into a temporally complex *now* through medieval poetry and prose" (68).

Time and politics cross paths in the second chapter, which dwells on the temporalities of empire and colony. Dinshaw tracks the role of time in *The Book of John Mandeville*, examining that text's discussions of the Fountain of Youth and of Eden as examples of "curiosity and longing to experience another kind of time" (76). The second part of the chapter considers adaptations of Mandeville by nineteenth-century British bureaucrat-amateurs who riffed on "Sir John" to consider their own "eastern" moments. Andrew Lang, for example, wrote a faux-Middle-English letter to John Mandeville, correcting Sir John's errors and informing him about the progress of the British Empire. In this "amateur medievalist" letter, Dinshaw sees Lang using the medieval past to express his own affective engagement with imperialism (95). M. R. James is also treated here. Dinshaw examines both James's creation of a parodic lost fragment of Mandeville and his famous ghost stories as examples of how "the colonial, the philological, and the amateur" connect with queer experiences of time (99). Dinshaw concludes this chapter by meditating on her own experience of postcolonial "not-quite-white queerness," exploring the links between contemporary medieval studies and colonial legacies (104). The autobiographical material, here and throughout, is especially powerful. It puts into practice the book's call for affective "amateur" engagement on the part of scholars and it reveals the rich interconnections of the personal and professional.

In the third chapter, Dinshaw turns to *The Book of Margery Kempe* to unravel its discussion of the present. Beginning with Margery's exclamation that the death of Christ "is as fresch to me as he had deyd this same day," Dinshaw argues that Margery's "multiple temporalities" can provide new "temporal avenues" for readers (106, 108). The rest of the chapter examines the experiences of two such readers caught up with Margery: Hope Emily Allen, the independent scholar and amateur who was Margery's first editor, and Dinshaw herself. Here, Dinshaw considers the different times experienced by amateurs. While professionals labor within measured deadlines, Dinshaw claims, expert but amateur scholars like Allen can luxuriate (or drown) in "multiplicity and open-endedness" (22).

The fourth and final chapter weaves together "asynchrony stories" that cross centuries. It starts with Dinshaw's encounter with a gravestone knocked out of place (and time) by a Catskill flood, then moves along briskly from Washington Irving's "Rip Van Winkle" to the medieval pursuits of Irving's persona Geoffrey Crayon, the narrator of Irving's *Sketch Book of Geoffrey Crayon, Gent*. Geoffrey Crayon's pilgrimage-like visit to the chambers where James I of Scotland was imprisoned then leads to an examination of Boethian time in James's *Kingis Quair*. The effect of this chapter is kaleidoscopic, demonstrating time's queerly circuitous ways of connecting texts and events. One last amateur appears in the book's epilogue, to match with the preface's "bathrobe guy." Dinshaw champions the invitation to "other ways of world making" exemplified by the character Thomas Colpeper, the embarrassingly (and adhesively) enthusiastic amateur historian of the 1944 Powell and Pressburger film *A Canterbury Tale* (170).

Allying itself with recent work on the ties between professional study and popular enthusiasm, Dinshaw's book encourages scholars to reaffirm the personal commitments often concealed beneath an expert persona. The insights of *How Soon Is Now?* could be expanded productively by comparing them to the Chaucer enthusiasts documented in Candace Barrington's *American Chaucers* (New York: Palgrave Macmillan, 2007). Dinshaw's amateurs align well with a figure such as Kathrine Gordon Sanger Brinley, who, as Barrington recounts (126–42), recited Chaucer to largely female audiences in the 1920s with the erudition of a scholar and the zeal (and medieval garb) of an amateur.

As several online discussions have already noted, Dinshaw's categories of amateur and professional blur when applied to some of the realities of our contemporary crisis of employment. Faculty at non-research institutions are only nominally rewarded for their publications, and so undertake their projects in the time of amateurs, while, for the precariat, the promise of the rationally rewarded time of a professional seems as distant as Mandeville's earthly paradise.[1] Such elaborations attest to the

[1] I owe my thoughts on this topic to these discussions: Karl Steel, "SMITHS NERD," *In the Middle*, March 29, 2013, http://www.inthemedievalmiddle.com/2013/03/smiths-nerd.html; and Rick Godden, "Nerds, Love, Amateurs: Reflections on *How Soon Is Now*," *Modern Medieval*, March 29, 2013, http://modernmedieval.blogspot.com/2013/03/nerds-love-amateurs-reflections-on-how.html.

power of the book's central idea. *How Soon Is Now?* provokes an important debate about how scholars might redefine the relationship of their work to the *love* that, as Dinshaw reminds us throughout the book, gives us the word "amateur."

How Soon Is Now? makes a valuable argument about the presence of asynchrony in medieval literature, and, more crucially, dares medievalists to examine the relationship between time, personal commitment, and the centuries-old texts that we teach. Fittingly, the book is lovingly capacious in its outreach to multiple audiences. Non-medievalists looking for work on temporality studies will find the book accessible because of its reader-friendly summaries and translations. Medievalists, on the other hand, will discover a revealing mirror of their own engagements. The book would be perfect to teach in an introductory graduate seminar since its combination of accessibility and provocation would inspire wide-ranging discussion about the future of the field. With its question-mark title and its as-yet unrealized dreams of a different kind of scholarly life, *How Soon Is Now?* issues a call. Readers may find themselves moved to affirm this call with some more lines from The Smiths about strange loves, queer interests, and the amateur pursuit of the past: *A dreaded sunny day, so let's go where we're happy and I meet you at the cemetry gates*.

BRANTLEY L. BRYANT
Sonoma State University

GEORGIANA DONAVIN. *Scribit Mater: Mary and the Language Arts in the Literature of Medieval England*. Washington, D.C.: The Catholic University of America Press, 2012. Pp. xii, 315. $69.95 cloth.

As Georgiana Donavin points out in her introduction to *Scribit Mater*, Marian studies have undergone some notable changes in the course of the past half-century, with many postmodern critics treating the emphasis on Mary's virginity as signal evidence of patriarchal misogyny, its determination to encourage women's passivity, and the repression of female sexuality. More recent scholarship has aimed to reconsider and to recuperate Mary's authority within the Christian tradition, and has relied on a wide range of medieval Marian literature. This scholarship has also revisited the entire ideal of virginity, which, it has argued, may in fact be seen as empowering. We all remember from *Hali Meiðhad* the vividly portrayed woes of marriage and the attendant advantages of virginity.

In the literature considered by Donavin, the sapient Virgin is shown not only to be free of the duress of the conventional married state, but also to be enthroned as the inspiration for the *trivium*: "a steeping in Marian language . . . resulted in representations of the Virgin as a purified grammarian, an accomplished rhetorician, an inspired muse, and a mentor for writers" (17).

Donavin's introduction is thorough in its presentation of the points that will be made in the course of her study's six chapters, which cover a wide range of medieval English literature, from "The English Lives of Mary" to "Margery Kempe and the Virgin Birth of her *Book*." At the introduction's close, Donavin explicitly challenges "the paradigm of Kristeva's abject mother," as she announces her own determination to counter the "scholarly denigration of medieval constructs of virginity." *Scribit Mater* "represents the Virgin as a powerful linguistic intermediary and occasionally as a force for a radical literature that realigns spiritual and social roles" (26). Indeed, Donavin's work proves to be an effective refutation to the commonly accepted stereotype of the submissive Mary.

Her goal is clarified by the first sentence of her first chapter: "[In the course of this book] I will show how throughout medieval English literature, the Virgin Mary is associated with academic and narrative arts of speech, . . . her superior knowledge and its impact on salvation history" (27). Specifically, the chapter is dedicated to a consideration of a variety of lives that focus on Mary and her "superior spiritual understanding" (74).

In the English lives considered by Donavin, the Virgin is anything but a passive vessel: she explains the Christian mysteries, and is the crucial "vehicle for Christ's coming to earth, . . . a teacher of providence's progress" (29, 30). Her virginity is an active source of strength. The chapter covers a broad chronological period, from the Anglo-Saxon *Advent Lyrics* to Lydgate's *Life of Our Lady*. While this might at first seem a rather wide net to cast, Donavin, to the contrary, convincingly establishes a pervasive tradition that "illustrate[s] the divergent audiences—ecclesiastical and lay, courtly and popular—that took Mary to be the mother of wisdom" (28–29).

Scribit Mater's next chapters deal with John of Garland and his pedagogical poetry: Walter of Wimborne, John of Howden, and Richard Rolle, and how they contributed to "northern medieval English traditions for a Marian meditative poetry" (115); and "Chaucer and the Dame School," in the "era when primary education took place under the Virgin Mary's wing" (163).

Donavin focuses on Garland's *Epithalamium Beate Virginis Marie* and *Parisiana poetria*, both of which reveal the Virgin to be instrumental in the teaching of the liberal arts, and of writing itself. "[His] Mary—his book, muse, and teacher—embodies both Wisdom and Word, attributes of Christ, as she bears the Christ child" (113). Garland, attributing his own rhetorical powers to the Virgin's inspiration, figures her "as a warrior for Christian virtues [whose] divine message . . . depends on conquering the vices"—"an icon of . . . learning and a Christian Lady Rhetorica" (115).

Walter and John—discussed in "The Musical Mother Tongue in Anglo-Latin Poetry for Meditation"—were thirteenth-century contemporaries, whose poetry abounds with Marian imagery. Both "meditate upon . . . the Mother so that her tongue might speak for all to the divine audience" (119). Placing emphasis on music and song, both write of Jesus' life from his mother's point of view.

Walter's *Ave Virgo Mater Christi* "explains that Mary herself is the language upon which his Franciscan devotional verse is built" (127). Within her womb, "Mary reenacted creation [and] became the best of moral rhetoricians" (131). John's Marian poetry is, as demonstrated by Donavin, more romantic than Walter's. His songs, as seen in the *Philomena*, "compare to the reflections of troubadours upon an exalted love" (142); his "Marian verses are more effusive [than Walter's], erupting in imagery" (143). He listens as she sings lullabies to her child: "Mary is the mother of lyric, of both music and words" (153).

This chapter concludes with a consideration of Rolle and his *Canticum amoris*. In contrast to Walter and John, Rolle "is the Virgin's enamored devotee . . . he desires total union with her" (157). Yet in all three poets we find "a formal presentation of compelling Marian epithets whose images unlock a lyrical language and a personal ritual for meditation" (159).

In Chapter 4, Donavin considers Chaucer's *An ABC*, *The Prioress's Tale*, and *The Second Nun's Tale* as representations of a continuum of Marian learning. While *An ABC* assumes "the Virgin Mary's presence at the beginning of language instruction" (182), *The Prioress's Tale* offers the opportunity for the uneducated "to learn a song of Marian praise." The spectrum culminates in *The Second Nun's Tale*, which—as Saint Cecilia converts so many, and so roundly defeats Almachius in their debate—aims to demonstrate "the intellectual power of female asceticism," as well as Cecilia's individual courage. Together these three Chaucerian works serve to present Mary as "an accomplished, heavenly school mistress . . . at the head of the language curriculum" (219).

Chapters 5 and 6 deal with Mary's voice in the Middle English lyrics; and with "Margery Kempe and the Virgin Birth of her *Book*." The lyrics, in a variety of dialects, celebrate the Virgin not as biblical student, but as an "icon of beautiful speech and song" (221). Frequently, Marian verses are presented as appropriate subjects for hymns and sermons. What is shared by these lyrics—which reveal Mary in a variety of settings linked to relevant liturgical feasts—is a "performative nature . . . oral repetition must have been common" (224). They reassert her "linguistic prowess in oral ways" (249).

Magnificent Margery comes last, her *Book* being "very much a maternal act" (251) that reflects her "determination to perpetuate a Marian model of lay piety" (253). Donavin's treatment of Margery and her "labowrs," as she "ascends spiritually in the ranks of the holy family and establishes her major role as handmaid to the handmaid" (263), is careful and caring. She clearly respects Margery and her visionary experiences. "In all, *The Book of Margery Kempe* is conceived through Kempe's *imitatio Mariae*, and as the Word of Christ, offers the fruit of the Virgin Birth" (286).

Scribit Mater is an impressive work. Donavin's thesis is repeatedly verified as she weaves through centuries and genres, dealing with an enormously complex body of literature. As she demonstrates, the Virgin is indeed central to "a variety of trends in pedagogical and popular culture . . . an icon of rhetorical excellence" (287). Donavin's scholarship, as it must be in such a project, is meticulous. Her writing is compelling and incisive, which is why I have included so many quotes: why try to paraphrase when the original is so good?

FRANCES BEER
York University, Toronto

MARY C. FLANNERY. *John Lydgate and the Poetics of Fame*. Cambridge: D. S. Brewer, 2012. Pp. 206. $90.00.

To explain when and why vernacular poets stepped out from the shadows of anonymity that had been their shelter during the earlier Middle Ages and began to claim for themselves a place in both contemporary public conscience and future literary posterity must be a major objective of late medieval literary history. In a pan-European context, Petrarch, the poet who, in Lydgate's words, "be writying . . . gat hymsilff a name / perpetuelli to been in remembraunce," looms particularly large. It is the contention of Mary C. Flannery's new book that, for English poetry, Lydgate is himself a pivotal figure.

Flannery's argument, in its essence, is that Lydgate was aware of and admired the laureate Petrarch's insistence on the fame due to poets. In the *Fall of Princes* particularly, Lydgate locates the power of poets in their ability not merely to report the fame of their subjects, but also to create it and to maintain it against the vicissitudes of fortune. These arguments are worked out in Chapters 4–6, which constitute the meat of her book. Through a series of sensitive close readings of the *Fall* and other texts from Lydgate's oeuvre, Flannery makes a convincing case that Lydgate is not "dull" (in the sense David Lawton has used the adjective), but instead "brimming with confidence and ambition."

Chapter 4, "The Poet's Verdict," examines Lydgate's quasi-judicial role in assessing fame in the *Fall of Princes*, focusing particularly on his account of Queen Brunhilde in Book IX. Here, Flannery contrasts Lydgate's confidence in the power of the poet to manipulate fame with Chaucer's deterministic submission to fortune. Chapter 5, "Promotion and Self-Promotion," places Lydgate's poetics of fame alongside the work of Italian writers like Dante, Petrarch, and Boccaccio and their classical forebears, before tracking laureate traces in Book IV of the *Fall*, the prologue to *The Troy Book*, and two of Lydgate's mummings. Chapter 6, "Lydgate's Fortune in the House of Fame," explores Lydgate's presentation of the encounter between Bochas and the goddess Fortune in Book VI of the *Fall*, to argue that, for Lydgate, unlike Chaucer, poets were capable of subduing the forces of chance. Indeed, the clarity with which the book, beginning with Chapter 1, "Chaucerian Fame," distinguishes Lydgate from Chaucer (for whose Clerk, remember, Petrarch was irrevocably "deed and nayled in his cheste") is one of the book's great strengths.

These parts of the book live up to its title and offer a sophisticated and thought-provoking account of Lydgate's self-positioning as a poet. More questionable is the relevance of the two other chapters. Chapter 2, "Fame and the Advisory Tradition," discusses the status of "fame" in mirror-for-princes texts like the *Secreta secretorum* and Hoccleve's *Regement of Princes*. Chapter 3, "Loose Tongues in Lydgatean England," provides an overview of the late medieval legislative framework for the prosecution of slander, and briefly discusses three of Lydgate's short poems on deviant speech. As the necessity of using quotation marks around "fame" hints, these chapters are not about fame in its present-day sense, but rather the Latin *fama*, with its wide range of meanings, from report to rumour to reputation to renown, good or bad. As it stands, the book is more accurately described by the title of the 2007 Cambridge Ph.D. thesis in which it originated, "Rumour and Renown: *Fama* in John Lydgate's *Fall of Princes* and Its Successors."

The origins of the book in a thesis on *fama* are latent even in the chapters that focus most directly on Lydgate's pursuit of literary fame. The following comments are not intended to impugn these chapters, but rather to outline two of the important, difficult, but unresolved aspects of poetic fame that they raise. One issue is that the semantic field of "fame or renown" is not mapped in its entirety. Flannery begins with a brief, helpful discussion of *fame*, yet Middle English writers used a number of other words for the same concept, including (taking *The Historical Thesaurus of English* as our starting-point): *hereword*, *lose* (< OF *los* < L *laudes*), *renown*, *name*, *renomee*, *enpress*, and *note*. Furthermore, as is evident from Flannery's discussion of the preface to Boccaccio's *De mulieribus claris*, where he states that he will use *claritas* to denote not only *virtus*, but also other kinds of popular fame, "fame" could be denoted in Latin by words other than *fama*. A full account of the late medieval vocabulary of fame across Latin, French, and English—not to mention Italian—is a major but necessary undertaking for a study of poetic renoun.

Another issue concerns the importance of Lydgate's poetics of fame to English literary history more generally. Flannery's conclusion, subtitled "Lydgatean Fame after the Fifteenth Century," reads the *Mirror for Magistrates* and several other early modern works indebted to Lydgate's *Fall of Princes* to argue that sixteenth-century *de casibus* texts repeatedly effaced their model's confidence that poets could shield their subjects' reputations against fortune. While these rewritings certainly problematize the very particular poetics of fame Flannery attributes to Lydgate, this argument raises the question of how Lydgate's self-presentation fits within the broader developments in poetic self-fashioning outlined at the beginning of this review.

Attractively produced and helpfully indexed, this is an important and interesting book that will provide thought-provoking reading for anyone interested in Lydgate and the literary cultures of the Middle Ages and Renaissance.

MARK FAULKNER
The University of Sheffield

MARY C. FLANNERY and KATIE L. WALTER, eds. *The Culture of Inquisition in Medieval England*. Cambridge: D. S. Brewer, 2013. Pp. viii, 194. $99.00.

This cogent, exciting collection of essays argues for the centrality of inquisition to England's cultural and literary imagination in the late Middle Ages. The editors claim that inquisition "has been the subject of historical rather than cultural investigation," and so they offer this collection, which persuasively and persistently shows inquisition to have been a creative activity for ecclesiastical authorities, jurists, and vernacular authors alike. In doing so, the collection argues both that inquisition dialogues often assumed a kind of "literary" quality and that vernacular literature often took inquisition as an imaginative opportunity to explore constructions of authority, interiority, and community.

Although the essays display a range of interpretive approaches and objects of analysis, two thematic threads emerge throughout. First, as the introduction makes clear, inquisition here functions broadly as a flexible discourse, rather than as a specific legal practice. Second and more specifically, inquisition is conceptually and procedurally affiliated with confession, insofar as it negotiates between a private self and a public persona. Thus the collection seeks to "recognize the potential of inquisition alongside confession to form a hermeneutics for medieval subjectivity and narrativity." Edwin Craun's essay, which reads *summae confessorum* alongside canon law, most clearly explores affinities between confession and inquisition, though all of the essays pursue the overlaps and frictions between the two to some degree.

The collection is organized chronologically, moving from the fourteenth century into the sixteenth. Its narrow temporal and geographical focus is both its strength and its limitation. Although inquisition was first codified as a legal process in the 1215 Fourth Lateran Council, most of these essays (with the notable exceptions of H. A. Kelly's and Ian Forrest's) gloss over the thirteenth century. Moreover, although many essays gesture to the specificity of England's use of inquisitional procedures compared to the way they were used on the Continent, none provides a sustained discussion of the particular ways English law absorbed and reframed inquisition. This focus permits the collection to be coherent overall, but it doesn't quite do justice to inquisition's long history, nor does it explain why England should be of special interest to scholars thinking about inquisition.

Nonetheless, the collection compellingly describes how inquisition worked and the ways it seeped into the late medieval consciousness in England. Indeed, H. A. Kelly's wide-ranging opening essay is essential reading for anyone thinking about medieval inquisition. In it, Kelly disabuses common, erroneous assumptions about the principles and processes of inquisition, including the all-too-easy conflation of inquisition and heresy inquisition, and he outlines the peculiarities of English inquisitional procedures. By establishing when and how inquisition became the primary form of prosecution in English ecclesiastical courts, Kelly provides a critical overview that supports the following essays' interpretive work. In the next essay, Craun likewise offers a broad view that marks conceptual distinctions between confessional systems, which sought to rehabilitate the sinner through private penance, and legal systems, which sought to establish legal and ethical norms by making private sins available for public admonishment. Craun surprisingly reveals that sacramental confession and juridical inquisition both operated according to charitable impulses, seeking to protect the innocent from sins/crimes and to persuade the offender to amend his or her life.

Subsequent essays offer arguments that are more historically or textually specific. Forrest and Diane Vincent both track the use of inquisition in the persecution of Lollardy. Forrest argues that the problem of heresy in late fourteenth- and fifteenth-century England revived English churchmen's interest in provincial canon law and resulted in a flurry of scribal and juridical productions. He rightly points out that the "energetic updating of old manuscript volumes containing provincial constitutions and the intensive production of new ones" has not been fully explored either in Lollard studies or in canon law scholarship; this is a rich field for further work.

Vincent shows that heresy inquisitions against Lollards offered Wycliffites an opportunity to assume authorial control over the inquisitional process. She looks particularly at Wycliffite use of public bills and broadsheets as a way to shape public opinion regarding inquisition itself, provocatively arguing that "the public imagination of the process was just as important as the public knowledge of the verdict." In addition, she shows that literary texts were as likely to participate in these debates as legal or bureaucratic ones; Vincent reads Capgrave's *Abbreuiacion of Cronicles* and Hoccleve's "To Sir John Oldcastle" to reveal the multiple sources and methods by which public opinion about the legality and fairness of inquisitional process was formed.

The next three essays concentrate on how inquisition emerged as a crucial discourse through which interiority and authority could be articulated. In "'Vttirli Onknowe'? Modes of Inquiry and the Dynamics of Interiority in Vernacular Literature," Mary C. Flannery and Katie L. Walter emphasize one of the collection's unifying claims: that inquisition, like confession, sought to root out the individual, private intentions of the sinner. They distinguish inquisition from confession through the role of community: whereas confession ideally maintains the privacy of the individual sinner, inquisition requires that sin become common knowledge. Inquisition's external focus puts pressure on sacramental confession, they argue, insofar as it reframes selfhood as a dialogic relationship between interior and exterior knowledge. Strikingly, for Flannery and Walter, this relationship is most profoundly explored in pastoral and literary texts like *Dives and Pauper* and Lydgate's *Fall of Princes*; in these texts, the differences between confession—a process devoted to the interior self—and inquisition—a process devoted to communal knowledge—suggestively blur.

Jenny Lee offers a different take on the distinction between confession and inquisition: "Broadly speaking," she writes, "whereas sacramental confession led to the effacement of sins, inquisitorial discourse led to the defacement of their subjections, their names, their bodies, their lives." Turning to Thomas Usk's *Appeal* and *Testament of Love*, Lee argues that Usk exploits the first-person voice of inquisitional form to represent the legal constraints upon the confessing subject (in the *Appeal*) and to take control of legal discourse and thus reclaim the public authority of the confessing subject (in the *Testament*). In the *Erle of Toulouse*, as James Wade shows, inquisition likewise negotiated private and public lives, particularly in terms of sexual practices and ethics.

The final two essays turn to the sixteenth century to examine how inquisition offered important vocabularies for constructing authorial personae in Protestant England. Genelle Gertz's essay examines heretics' abjurations to explore how they constructed an interior self in the service of legal and ecclesiastical institutions. In contrast, she argues, those abjurations written or revised by heretics themselves registered heretics' opposition to the proceedings and offered the opportunity to assert control over their public image. In "Imitating Inquisition: Dialectical Bias in Protestant Prison Writings," Ruth Ahnert emphasizes the self-consciously fictional quality of the writings produced by imprisoned heretics in the sixteenth century. Mapping the strategies deployed in prisoners' accounts of their trials, Ahnert shows that these documents vindicated the prisoners' theological and political positions under the guise of "fair reporting."

Emily Steiner's concluding response, which focuses on *The Legend of Good Women*, reminds us of the role of pleasure both in the power dynamics inherent in inquisition and in our own, occasionally self-interested, historiographies of medieval law. Indeed, the collection as a whole explores the sometimes surprising ways power and authority are navigated and transferred in inquisitional practices, and throughout it emphasizes that medieval inquisition itself was creative; dynamic; imaginative; and even, in some ways, pleasurable.

JAMIE TAYLOR
Bryn Mawr College

ALAN J. FLETCHER. *The Presence of Medieval English Literature: Studies at the Interface of History, Author, and Text in a Selection of Middle English Literary Landmarks*. Turnhout: Brepols, 2012. Pp. 302. €80.00.

This volume consists of six substantial essays bookended with an introduction and conclusion, which explain the overarching idea that is pursued within each: an exploration of "the presence of the text's original age within it in tandem with its presence to its age" (259). With the exception of the sixth essay, on Malory, all of these pieces have been published before, some relatively recently; in the preface Alan Fletcher states that all have been revised, updated, and rewritten for the present purpose, and collectively they reflect a career's worth of engagement with the subject in terms of both research and teaching. The texts discussed (*The Owl and the Nightingale*; *Sir Orfeo*; *Pearl*; *Piers Plowman*; the *Canterbury Tales*; Malory's *Morte Darthur*) earn their place in the book by dint of their present-day value in the canon of medieval English literature. As a criterion, this in itself reveals much about Fletcher's own sense of the canon and about the particular late twentieth-century environment in which he taught. Whilst *Sir Orfeo* remains a staple of introductory Middle English courses, and the canonical position of the *Canterbury Tales* is unassailable, fewer undergraduate courses now routinely include the more challenging *Pearl* and *Piers Plowman*, Malory's *Morte Darthur* is now more frequently encountered through extracts rather than in its entirety, and how many places now teach *The Owl and the Nightingale*? If the poles of the teaching canon are less firmly fixed than Fletcher's collection of essays suggests, and there is also little reference here to those newer staples of Middle English courses such as women's prose writing, there is, however, a great deal of sustained engagement in these pages with current research and with modern critical developments.

Those who do not know all of these texts will find Fletcher's discussions helpful in providing an overview in each case of the key points of intellectual inquiry that goes far beyond the usual parameters of the introductory survey; those whose acquaintance with the texts is deeper will find much to engage with in these essays. Thus, for example, his account of *The Owl and the Nightingale* reviews the evidence for the poem's date in support of a later dating to the 1270s, and explores the work's early readership (really just one identifiable reader) and the likelihood that its author may have been a Dominican. In the case of the better-known *Sir Orfeo*, Fletcher focuses on the troubling episode at the heart of the poem: the chamber of horrors peopled by the undead in the Fairy King's castle, and seeks to explain how medieval audiences might have made sense of this chaos. The poem itself offers no guidance in this regard, but Fletcher identifies three late medieval discourses that might have helped: Christianity (particularly Christian teaching on death), astrology (particularly the Ptolemaic theory of malign planetary influence), and notions of fairyland. He then offers a fourth possible discourse, that of performance, noting that harpers were the most socially well-positioned of the minstrel class in the reign of Edward I, and connects this to a discussion of the poem's origins, favouring either London or a center in touch with London culture.

A brief comment on the lack of agreement as to the origins of *Pearl* (provincial or metropolitan product?) is offered at the start of Fletcher's analysis of this landmark text, which he rightly describes as "complex beyond any one single category" (89). He fully endorses the view that the poem's author was some kind of cleric, and whilst acknowledging the various biographical contexts that have been put forward to reveal the identity of the Pearl-Maiden (the death of Anne of Bohemia; the enclosure of Isabella of Woodstock), he argues that the poem's resonances with the concept of the Holy Innocents would have been far more powerful to a contemporary audience. Much recent research has focused on the poem's liturgical echoes of the feast of the Holy Innocents, but here Fletcher puts forward evidence drawn from the preaching prepared for this day, specifically citing an early fourteenth-century sermon by Nicholas de Aquevilla; this is translated into English, with an edition of the Latin also offered in an appendix. In the fourth chapter, on *Piers Plowman*, Fletcher revisits the question of Langland's relation to preaching, beginning with Passus V and the sermon on contrition. Novice readers will find Fletcher's deft summary of the poem's complex transmission history very useful, whilst more experienced medievalists will enjoy the links that he draws between the poem's textual history and the ever-receding goal of a definitive critical edition. Fletcher also draws parallels between those "participatory" scribes who made revisions to the poem and the situation that obtains in the sermon tradition where a preacher may have returned again and again to his material, rearranging and reshaping it over time, resulting in a similarly convoluted textual history in which the search for authentic readings is doomed to be a vain one.

By far the longest chapter (almost seventy pages) is that devoted to Chaucer, covering some parts of the *Canterbury Tales* (treating especially the Pardoner, Friar, Summoner, Monk, and Parson), and also *An ABC* and the Prologue to *The Legend of Good Women*. Here Fletcher's topic is Chaucer's relation to contemporary religious radicalism, first exploring the principal ways that Chaucer responded to and enlisted the culture of heresy in his writings, pointing to notions of *errour* and "glose," and then speculating about Chaucer's personal investment in this culture.

This chapter was first published a decade ago in *SAC* (25 [2003]); it is here revised with one very significant addition: a new section, "Dr. Jekyll and Mr. Pynkhurst," inserted to respond to Linne Mooney's identification of Chaucer's scribe as Adam Pinkhurst, and to draw in Fletcher's own contention that another manuscript attributable to Pinkhurst may be Trinity College Dublin, MS 244: a volume of Lollard tracts. A final substantive chapter treats Malory's *Morte Darthur* and argues that this is a text preoccupied with authority. Fletcher explores this preoccupation in terms of tropes and formulas, paying particular attention to Malory's use of various tomb epitaphs.

Perhaps the most striking feature of this collection is its chronological range. Although the meatiest part of the volume is undoubtedly its analysis of the "big three" authors of late fourteenth-century England, Fletcher eschews the safer option of narrowly inhabiting the Ricardian period and is equally comfortable discussing texts from both the late thirteenth and the late fifteenth centuries. This generous chronological span ensures that all the major literary bases (debate, romance, dream-vision; Chaucerian and non-Chaucerian poetry; prose; secular and religious writing) find themselves covered in the collection. A strong linking thread is provided by Fletcher's natural application of his considerable knowledge of sermons and medieval preaching, and it is this above all that unifies these interpretations of the major extant vernacular literary texts from late medieval England.

MARGARET CONNOLLY
University of St. Andrews

FRANK GRADY and ANDREW GALLOWAY, eds. *Answerable Style: The Idea of the Literary in Medieval England*. Columbus: Ohio State University Press, 2013. Pp. vii + 341. $74.95 cloth, $14.95 CD.

This volume in honor of Anne Middleton collects essays on a variety of approaches to medieval literary style, with an emphasis on the works of Chaucer and Langland. Written in the spirit of the festschrift, a number of the essays critically engage with both Middleton's work and the practice of new formalism in medieval literary studies, offering a welcome contribution to the discipline. As the editors Frank Grady and Andrew

Galloway caution: medievalists began to turn their attention to the formal elements of style long before the movement of new formalism supposedly began. The volume nevertheless assembles a collection of essays with the goal of pursuing the literary as such.

The book is divided into two sections, with the first group of essays focusing on vernacular literary style as it employs and often departs from Latin literary style. The second half focuses more exclusively on English vernacular expressions of style. The volume has been published by Ohio State University Press as part of the series Interventions: New Studies in Medieval Culture, which includes theoretically inflected works on animal studies, gender, law, translation studies, and politics. The essays largely exercise, to borrow Levinson's phrase, a kind of activist formalism, carefully attuned to historical context but never dominated by it in the practice of literary analysis.

Rita Copeland's excellent discussion of the shift in the reception of Horace's *Ars poetica* from the Middle Ages to the early modern period inaugurates the collection. The *Ars poetica*, she argues, moved from the status of grammar school manual to universalizing classic of critical theory because of a shift in its use and therefore its perceived status. Once other style manuals, such as Geoffrey of Vinsauf's *Poetria nova*, became more frequently employed in the classroom, Horace's poem was dislodged from the practical and repetitive doldrums of schoolwork. For this reason, the *Ars poetica* could be "rediscovered" as a humanist classic in the sixteenth century since it was no longer connected to the lower status of grammar school composition manual. Copeland's essay, which builds on her earlier work on rhetoric and pedagogy, offers valuable insight into discussions of style by examining the reception of theories of style.

Ralph Hanna employs a similar methodology for thinking about genre in "*Speculum Vitae* and the Form of *Piers Plowman*" and also offers a compelling response to Nicholas Watson's influential theory of vernacular theology. While Watson had emphasized the growth of a culture of censorship at the hands of Archbishop Thomas Arundel after 1409 as the major factor in shaping English vernacular writings about theology, Hanna suggests that perhaps simply a change in tastes might be the factor that best explains why catechetical works such as the *Speculum vitae* fell out of favor with writers. These texts had exhausted the possibilities for writing about virtues and vices within the genre of catechetical writing and Hanna argues that writers like Langland sought new forms for thinking about practical or applied religious issues. Hanna's approach offers readers a theory that should spark further debate on the genres of religious writing that emerged in England in the later Middle Ages.

Katherine Zieman's essay, "Escaping the Whirling Wicker: Ricardian Poetics and Narrative Voice in *The Canterbury Tales*," in addition to advancing excellent analyses for those who work in the field, also gives an overview of scholarly debate on character and narrative voice in Chaucer that would be especially useful to graduate students. She responds to Middleton's idea of "public poetry" in Ricardian literature, focusing on the rhetorical strategies Chaucer employs to create an impression of a fully realized character. *The Man of Law's Tale* offers moments of narrative interruption that call attention to the narrator, and in doing so, create a sense of character. These moments of interruption, however, should also be examined as an effect that creates the impression of truth or authenticity. Direct address that interrupts the flow of narrative is one such strategy that can leave us with the impression of truth. Thinking about rhetorical effect can in turn allow for greater reflection on how an audience's sense of the intentions and desires of individual characters and narrators is formally achieved. Zieman unifies older forms of scholarship on subjectivity with the renewed interest in formalism in her engaging essay.

Steven Justice offers a similar approach to style and effect in "Chaucer's History-Effect." How does Chaucer create a sense of a Criseyde who seems "real" in the *Troilus*? He begins his essay with a joke from the *Troilus* that elicits laughter from Criseyde and Pandarus, but that is likely to cause confusion for readers. Justice argues that our isolation from the joke is in fact what gives Criseyde and Pandarus an air of "realness." An inside joke suggests a shared history, a sense of experience that lies outside the reader's own experience and even outside the world of the poem. The *Troilus*, as work that emphasizes the reader's far-reaching knowledge of the characters and their predicaments before the plot even begins to unfold, nevertheless offers "imprecisions that Chaucer cultivates," gaps in the reader's knowledge that together formally create a "subjectivity-effect." Such lacunae generate uncertainty about any given character's intentions, which in turn create a more fully "felt" character. These approaches to a character's individual history correspond to the way that the poem evokes the historical difference of ancient Troy. Like Zieman's, Justice's essay on the *Troilus* offers useful formalist approaches to the question of character and subjectivity that have been explored by Lee Patterson and others.

The space of this review unfortunately does not allow for a fair treatment of all of the essays in this strong volume. David Lawton in "Voice and Public Interiorities" calls for scholars to consider in greater formal and historical depth voice as a literary tool, offering an excellent close reading of *The Book of the Duchess* and its relationship to questions of voice and the figure of Orpheus. Lee Patterson reconsiders the definition of "tragedy" as it applies to the *Troilus* in "*Troilus and Criseyde*: Genre and Source." Andrew Galloway's unexpected reading of the Petrarchan and Chaucerian versions of *The Clerk's Tale* aims to connect Griselda's emotional self-mastery to a poetics of renunciation. Chaucer critiques the sadism of Petrarch's tale, Galloway argues, by offering a narrator who "seems to simmer with resistance" to the story he tells. Moreover, Chaucer's narrator reacts to the aesthetic excesses of the Petrarchan version, thus evincing a control of form in his own narrative that corresponds to Griselda's masterfully controlled presentation of self.

What does new formalism mean to medieval studies? Does it simply become a history of aesthetics? How can medievalists navigate the need for understanding the context of an often alien social or political environment without running into the biases that new historicism can produce? This volume invites debate on the role of the new formalist movement in medieval studies. The editors ultimately suggest that rather than marking a departure, the return to form builds on the work of a generation of scholars like Anne Middleton. As a celebration of form, the essays offer enriching readings that will be useful in scholarly debate and in the classroom. As an inquiry into literary style and genre, the essays advance discussions about the changes that literary expression underwent in late medieval England.

KATHLEEN SMITH
American Univeristy, Washington, D.C.

JONATHAN HSY. *Trading Tongues: Merchants, Multilingualism, and Medieval Literature*. Columbus: Ohio State University Press, 2013. Pp. xii, 237. $59.95.

This book makes a solid contribution to the increasingly crowded discussion of language contact and conflict in the later Middle Ages, and it shares with many recent works a particular focus on England. The terminology of such discussion—bilingualism, diglossia, multilingualism, code-switching, contact zone—has become familiar, and the accretion of books and essays on the subject has generated a more and more complex, sophisticated treatment of it. Jonathan Hsy's book does not match its most notable predecessors in range and amplitude: Ardis Butterfield's *The Familiar Enemy* (2009), and the French of England project, especially as it is embodied in the scholarly work of Jocelyn Wogan-Browne and the collection of essays she edited on *Language and Culture in Medieval Britain* (2009). But it does, in a series of concise and interesting chapters, fill in details in a usually convincing and often quite illuminating fashion.

The book's punning title, as Hsy says in his introduction, "illustrates how profoundly commerce in medieval contact zones, particularly in cities and coastal environments, shapes how language is used in literary texts." It also means to illustrate how medieval writers traded tongues "by moving across languages—and combining them—in the texts they created," including the languages of law and commerce, using "different languages to develop distinct expressive registers, to stylize certain types of speech, or to evoke a vivid sense of place" (5–6). As a preface to his consideration of major texts, Hsy discusses two short works in which macaronic verse captures the variegated multiplicity of London: *The Stores of the Cities* and *London Lickpenny*, which "associates different linguistic communities with particular urban spaces: Latinate and French-speaking legal professionals work in Westminster; Flemish vendors outside the gates of Westminster Hall negotiate two related Germanic vernaculars; and retailers in Chepe and bargemen in Billingsgate cry out in Middle English" (16). For this picture of a polyglot London, Hsy cites and echoes the work of Laura Wright on "medieval Thames vocabulary," and more generally that of Ardis Butterfield and Christopher Cannon. In his view, *London Lickpenny* anticipates Walter Benjamin's account of the modern city as a "theatre of new, unforeseen constellations," a space for linguistic and literary experiment (21–22).

The second chapter looks at Chaucer, overlapping—though only minimally—with Mary Catherine Davidson's recent book on *Medievalism, Multilingualism, and Chaucer* (2010). Hsy focuses on *The Shipman's Tale* and *The House of Fame*, unsurprising choices because of their shared concern with commerce and the city. This chapter takes a while to get going, and on the whole its readings seem less memorable than those in the rest of the book, perhaps because Chaucer fits Hsy's argument less well than, for example, Gower does. Hsy makes a suggestive comparison of the dreamer's Aldgate house, where the Eagle accuses him of too much study, "inhabiting a world of silence despite his apparently noisy urban surroundings," with the silent space inside Fame's discordant palace (30); and he also compares the merchant of Saint Denis in *The Shipman's Tale* to the dreamer of *The House of Fame*, like him a bookish, "solitary figure curiously isolated from the busy world that surrounds him" (52). This tale, more than *The House of Fame*, is certainly tailor-made for a discussion of mercantile language and exchange, though I'm not persuaded that the Shipman's undoubted familiarity with the patois of "sea-terms" explains Chaucer's assigning the tale to him.

The following chapter opens with a brief account of the anonymous lyric "Dum ludis floridus" in which "By traversing three languages, the Harley lyricist conveys a speaker who is fixed in his thoughts of love even as he is physically in motion. At the same time, the poet's frequent and abrupt code-switching dramatizes the distress and disorientation that the lover feels" (62). Hsy's focus then shifts to the story of Constance, "a seafaring female protagonist" (65), as it is told by Nicholas Trevet, Gower, and Chaucer: Constance, in this reading, is similarly fixed while perpetually on the move, and her "maner Latyn corrupt" is the lingua franca of merchants' speech. The chapter ends with Charles d'Orléans, an English poet while in England but one who left English—and his manuscript written in English—behind when he finally returned to France after his long exile.

The third chapter examines "Translingual Identities in John Gower and William Caxton," and is perhaps the best in the book, showing how each writer "invests a considerable amount of thought into how his own translingualism informs an ever-shifting literary persona" (92). Both, much more than Chaucer, are writers concerned with London; both are writers who "trade in tongues" by focusing on merchants, and in Caxton's case by being himself both author and printer (128). Chapter 4 discusses *The Book of Margery Kempe* as "an intricate work of travel writing," which "explores translingual and intercultural modes of perception and understanding" (132), including Margery's "seaborne prayers" (146). The texts examined in Chapter 5, "Merchant Compilations," include a farrago of prose and various verse forms, in Latin, French, and English, making these collections "not only multilingual but also multifunctional" (158). These compilations, by the draper Robert Fabyan, the grocer Richard Hill, and the mercer John Colyns, show the "wide-ranging interests" and "diverse linguistic capacities" of their authors (191), as mercantile producers with aesthetic as well as practical concerns.

The book's "Coda" returns to Charles d'Orléans, as he negotiates the divide in status between French and English to achieve, in Susan Crane's formulation, "an early, elite version of post-colonial hybridity" (quoted on 195). Hsy explicates the intriguing image on his book's cover, reprinted on 208, which is from British Library, MS Royal 16 F.II, a manuscript of Charles's French and English poetry. It shows Charles writing in captivity in the Tower of London, surrounded by the boat-filled Thames and the London cityscape, with Charles himself, a "poet in perpetual motion," represented three times: writing his text while seated at a long table; at a window of the Tower looking out; and standing outside, handing his text to a kneeling recipient. All of this "evinces the poet's parallel existence on solid ground and water; his capacity to think across terrestrial and fluid domains of linguistic difference" (207–9)—and the image serves as a fitting reprise of Hsy's argument.

JOHN M. FYLER
Tufts University

MICHELLE KARNES. *Imagination, Meditation and Cognition in the Middle Ages*. University of Chicago Press, 2011. Pp. 280. $50.00 cloth.

Michelle Karnes has written a thought-provoking argument for the elevation of the role of the imagination in our perception of late medieval contemplative and devotional thought. Specifically, she argues that a synthesis of elements of Scholastic and Augustinian psychology achieved by Bonaventure led to the promotion of the power of imagination from its lower role (as it is usually conceived) in the memory and projection of sense impressions into the cognitive faculty, so that it came to have a function in the higher cognition of those ideas that are eternally in the mind of God: that it is through the functioning of the power of imagination that we know the highest truths that the human mind is capable of knowing. This synthesis worked out in Bonaventuran psychology,

Karnes goes on to point out, characterizes Bonaventure's authentic works of devout, imaginative meditation, and further influences the circle of works attributed to him in the later Middle Ages, like the *Stimulus amoris* and the *Meditationes vitae Christi*. But it was dismissed by later medieval English writers like Walter Hilton (if it was indeed he who wrote the *Prickynge of Love*) and Nicholas Love, in whose vernacular versions of these pseudo-Bonaventuran works imagination was reduced once more to the lower rank that it had held in the monastic tradition as a helpful but problematically illusory aspect of sensuality.

Karnes's study is divided into six chapters: the first provides an overview of classical and early medieval thought on the imagination, beginning with Plato and the Neoplatonists; focusing on Aristotle; and continuing through the medieval Aristotelian/Scholastic tradition, including Avicenna, Averroes, and Aquinas. The second chapter treats first of Augustinian thought on imagination (particularly in *De Trinitate*) before proceeding to deal with Bonaventure's philosophical writings. The third shows how the Bonaventuran philosophical position on imagination expressed itself in the devotional writings that were assuredly written by him; the fourth follows this emanation of influence into the most prominent Latin devotional writing in the "Bonaventuran" tradition, the *Stimulus amoris* and the *Meditationes vitae Christi*, as well as Suso's *Horologium sapientiae* and Ludolph of Saxony's *Vita Christi*. The sixth chapter follows directly on from this, demonstrating what happened to the Bonaventuran strand of imaginative contemplation in the two prominent Middle English versions of the *Stimulus* and the *Meditationes*, the *Prickynge of Love* and Nicholas Love's *Mirror of the Blessed Life of Jesus Christ*. The fifth chapter interrupts the flow of this argument, in an excursus on "Imaginatif" in *Piers Plowman* that demonstrates the usefulness of this study to those other than specialists in contemplative and devotional literature.

The crux of Karnes's argument lies in her observation that Bonaventure synthesized the late medieval Aristotelian conceptualization of the operation of the agent intellect in illuminating the intelligible species abstracted from common sense perception as phantasmata by a higher-level form of imagination, with Augustine's trinitarian psychology, according to which reason illuminates the intelligible species that reside eternally in memory. For Augustine, as Karnes demonstrates with admirable lucidity, the soul is a created trinity made in the image and likeness of the uncreated Trinity: memory in the individual human soul is the image of the Father, in whom eternal truth resides; reason is the image of the Son, the Word in whom/which eternal truth expresses itself; and will is the image of the Holy Spirit, the love that flows from this truth to this truth. For Bonaventure, as Karnes argues, the Son, the Word of the Augustinian Trinity—through which we know the ideas ("verba" or "species") that reside properly in the Mind, the Father (to the limited extent that we do know them)—functions in the individual human soul in the same way as the Aristotelian/Scholastic agent intellect in illuminating the intelligible species. I am not certain that I am convinced by this, but I will admit that my undergraduate study of medieval philosophy in a Jesuit university nearly half a century ago may have left me with too much of a Thomistic bias to be truly receptive to Bonaventure. I am not certain, when Augustine uses the word "image" in *De Trinitate*—as he does frequently in saying, for example, that Christ, the Word, is the perfect image of the eternal Truth that resides unexpressed within the Father, or that the created trinity of powers in the soul is the image of the uncreated Trinity—that he has imagination in mind. To recognize that the human soul is the image of the Trinity is a cognitive recognition, but is it also an act of imagination? On the other hand, from the Scholastic/Aristotelian side, might the suggestion that Christ functions as the same agent intellect in all human beings simultaneously be inappropriately Averroistic?

Granted Karnes's thesis, however, her observations on the primary role of imagination in Bonaventuran mystical theology are spot-on, as is her demonstration of the degradation of imagination in the Middle English versions of the *Stimulus amoris* and the *Meditationes vitae Christi* to a lower-order mental power dealing with the objects of sense perception. As she points out, the *Mirror of the Blessed Life of Jesus Christ* and the *Prickynge of Love*, although they occasionally include educated clerical readers within their intended audience, aim themselves primarily at a lay and female audience conceived of as limited in their intellectual (if not necessarily spiritual) capabilities. I do not disagree with the trajectory that Karnes describes, and her discussion is refreshingly complex (in particular, I appreciate her emphasis on Steven Justice's observation that "the vernacular has in itself no fixed ideological function (212)");[2]

[2] See Steven Justice, "General Words: Response to Elizabeth Schirmer," in *Voices in Dialogue: Reading Women in the Middle Ages*, ed. Linda Olson and Kathryn Kerby-Fulton (Notre Dame: University of Notre Dame Press, 2005), 377–94 (389).

my only demur is that I am not sure that the mid-point of the curve is quite as high as she sees it, or the end-point quite so low.[3]

All told, this is an excellent, very well-informed and well-argued study, a must-read for anyone who would understand the psychological assumptions underlying late medieval devotional and contemplative literature in particular, but also any literature of the period that deals with the cross-fertilization of imagination and spirituality—which is to say, with virtually all of late medieval literature.

MICHAEL G. SARGENT
Queens College and the Graduate Center
of the City University of New York

ALEX MUELLER, *Translating Troy: Provincial Politics in Alliterative Romance*. Columbus: Ohio State University Press, 2013. Pp. xiii, 253. $69.95 cloth; $14.95 CD-ROM.

Alex Mueller's learned and meticulous study of the long shadow of Troy upon alliterative romance joins a recent surge of scholarship in the politics of alliterative romance and late medieval vernacular romance more generally. Informed by anti-imperialist critical theory from Walter Benjamin and Hannah Arendt to Giorgio Agamben and Benedict Anderson, Mueller proceeds, through a combination of careful source comparison, manuscript analysis, and close reading, to situate late medieval alliterative romances within a historiographical tradition bifurcated between, on the one hand, the fantasies of empire he associates with Geoffrey of Monmouth and, on the other, the more ambivalent and skeptical anti-imperialist historiography that he associates with Guido delle Colonne. Mueller's argument thus reads the opening gestures that many alliterative romances make toward Troy as a significant claim about their historiographical sympathies, which almost assumes the potency of a party affiliation. The linchpin of Mueller's argument is to classify alliterative romances according to how they adapt the Troy

[3] See Ian Johnson's perceptive delineation of Nicholas Love's use of Augustine's *De agone Christiano* in "What Nicholas Love Did in His *Proheme* with St. Augustine and Why," in *The Pseudo-Bonaventuran Lives of Christ: Exploring the Middle English Tradition*, ed. Johnson and Allan F. Westphall (Turnhout: Brepols, 2013), 375–91.

legend and what those adaptations suggest about their attitudes toward *translatio* and aristocratic imperial genealogy. His search for a Guidonian counter-voice is intended as a corrective to the undue scholarly dominance of Galfridian historiographies.

Mueller's organizing metaphor is corporeal: he notes that Guido and various alliterative romances commonly homologize fractured bodies with equally fractured imperial foundations in particularly moralistic ways. Thus, far from acceding to the allure of Troy as illustrious origin, Mueller's argument traces Trojan historiography as a kind of pathology. Guidonian Troy is a burnt and dismembered body whose disintegrations invade and infect subsequent historiographies. I loved this reading and found it the most powerful and convincing through-line of Mueller's study.

Mueller builds upon the work of Patricia Clare Ingham, Geraldine Heng, Randy Schiff, and Christine Chism, among others. His book is structured as five chapters, one setting up the historiographical frame of Guido vs. Geoffrey, and then four more, which treat significant alliterative romances: John Clerk's *Destruction of Troy*, *The Siege of Jerusalem*, the *Alliterative Morte Arthure*, and *Sir Gawain and the Green Knight*. The introduction argues that northern and provincial alliterative romances draw upon Guido delle Colonne's influential *Historia destructionis Troiae* to critique the southern Galfridian English literary and historiographical traditions that instrumentalize Trojan historiography in the service of imperialism. Mueller posits that alliterative romances highlight the moral atrocity of empire-building by pinioning imperialism's favorite instruments of self-validation: genealogy, war, violence, heraldry, and territory. Chapter 1, "Genealogy," posits Mueller's Guidonian intervention into Galfridian historiography as a skeptical counter-discourse of infective, rather than productive, genealogy. Chapter 2, "War: Reviving Troy," compares John Clerk's *Destruction of Troy* to Guido's *Historia destructionis Troiae*, and another Middle English analogue, Lydgate's *Troy Book*. From this source study, Mueller concludes that John Clerk, while faithfully translating Guido's Latin prose text, justifies his own historiographical use of vernacular poetry, insisting that "vernacular poetry can appropriately and accurately express Guido's 'eyewitness truth' about historical events" (61). Moreover, where Guido attributes Troy's fall to a combination of fate and human choice, Clerk, by contrast, underscores the human error and malice that doom Troy, making the *Destruction* "a raw expression of human freewill" (66). Mueller ends with a vivid reading of Hector's embalmed body as a misguided attempt to immortalize Troy's highest chivalric ideals, which instead results in their zombification. Hector's corpse is displayed over his own monument, looking as he did in life while simultaneously putrefying, blighting visitors to his tomb and readers of the passage alike. Thus, in Clerk's adaptation of Guido, Troy's glory is lost in translation but its misjudgments transfer all too readily.

Chapter 3, "Violence," discusses *The Siege of Jerusalem* as an exposé of Roman imperial atrocity. Mueller links the seemingly non-Trojan poem to Trojan historiography both through imperial genealogies of *translatio* that link Troy with Rome, and within particular manuscripts, such as Cambridge University Library, MS Mm.V.14, which contain both *The Siege* and Troy material. Christ and the Jews become types of Agamben's *homo sacer*, and the Romans become wielders of a biopolitics of "corporeal didacticism" (110). Their punishment of Jewish bodies homologizes their destruction of the Jewish city and nation, in an obliteration so immoderate and exploitative that it implicates the conquerors themselves. Mueller usefully synthesizes and builds upon a range of previous criticism on the poem, particularly Elisa Narin van Court's discussion of the poem as a document of Augustinian and anti-Galfridian historiography. The chapter ends with an original and powerful reading of the

> polluted rivers of the Xanthus of Troy, Tiber of Rome, and the canals of Jerusalem, choked with the stinking bodies of the fallen to infect the cities' inhabitants with pathological sovereignties: The contamination of imperial currents represents the course of the narrative in which dismembered bodies emerge in gruesome succession, confounding sovereign succession and dooming the birth of Christian imperialism to come. (122–23)

Chapter 4, "Heraldry," convincingly resituates the *Alliterative Morte Arthure* within Guidonian rather than Galfridian historiography, by tracing to Guido the heraldic sign of the dragon associated unusually in the *Morte* both with Arthur and with Lucius. Mueller reads the dragon as a sign of its bearer's commitment to total war, or "comprehensive corporeal annihilation" (139). As well as the dragon, Mueller explores the poem's "necrological heraldry" (237), heraldic signs that signal the death of the wearer rather than bespeaking his noble identity, which are themselves destroyed and replaced by desperately brutal attempts at resanctification. As a result, it becomes impossible to idealize any of the combatants' campaigns; both Britain and Rome become indistinguishably "glorious and cruel" (147). Chapter 5, "Territory," delivers a rather moralizing reading of *Sir Gawain and the Green Knight* as a critique of claims of Trojan descent by the Arthurian characters, who blithely forget inconvenient blunders with chilling ease, as shown by their easy adoption of the girdle at the poem's end. Arthur and Gawain are also condemned for their domination of borderlands and provinces, and they come to figure aristocratic greed and violence, as indicated by the surfeiting of feast and the violence of hunting within fitts 2 and 3. Mueller uses the Cheshire and Welsh historiographies of Ranulf Higden and Gerald of Wales to contextualize the *Gawain*-poet's "provincial distaste for imperial designs, Trojan heritage, and assertions of gentility" (205). Ultimately, "from the historiographical perspective of the Trojan borderland, Gawain's failure in his test of *trawþe* is yet another 'blunder' that England 'forgets' in its claims to imperial 'blysse'" (205).

Mueller concludes his study by resituating his alliterative romances with reference to two roughly contemporary texts: Trevisa's translation of Higden's *Polychronicon*, which accords more with Guidonian skeptical historiography, and Geoffrey Chaucer's *Troilus and Criseyde*, a text that forgoes military fervor but is nonetheless readily assimilated within imperialist agendas because it does not put up an "unsavory" (228) resistance. Here, Mueller pushes further to extract two essential "voices" from his foundational historiographical opposition: the clerical vs. the aristocratic. The clerical voice lends itself to skeptical historiography and takes an unpopular moral stand against the excesses of the aristocracy, while the aristocratic voices, even when they are indifferent to imperialist agendas as Chaucer seems to be, do not resist and therefore lend themselves to absorption.

Mueller's reframing of alliterative romance through the skeptical historiography of Troy is provocative, but I think it tactically oversimplifies the diversity both of medieval historiography and of alliterative romance. Augustine and Orosius make occasional appearances, and Ranulf Higden, Gerald of Wales, and John Trevisa get cameos, but where are the other powerful historiographies that alliterative romances mobilize: Bede and ecclesiastical history, as present in *Saint Erkenwald*; exemplary history, hagiography, and accounts of monastic foundation; other matters of Antiquity, such as Alexander and Charlemagne and the rest of the biblical, classical, and crusading Nine Worthies; Gildas and providential history; Old Testament history; the visionary journey through heaven, hell, purgatory, and apocalypse; and the comparative diachronies of universal history that developed beyond Orosius into their own medieval kaleidoscopes of mutually decentering dynastic claims? Why, among them all, does Troy deserve this kind of structural preeminence—is it the only historiographical strain so politicized in the fourteenth century? Is British imperialism so powerful a cultural force at this point? I would have loved more discussion of these questions.

Furthermore, *Translating Troy*'s polarizing "Geoffrey vs. Guido" historiographical frame must under-read Geoffrey of Monmouth to get its work done. By this time, Geoffrey must be used to being everyone's historiographical whipping boy, but I think Mueller's case for Guido's historiographical importance is actually weakened by situating Guido in opposition to Geoffrey: because both Geoffrey and, arguably, Guido become oversimplified through their polarization. To Mueller, Geoffrey is optimistic, wild, fantastic, prophetic, and consonant with imperialist and aristocratic supersessional genealogies, while Guido is skeptical, ambivalent, moralizing, antiprophetic, and consonant with clerical disdain for the glory of the world in whatever imperial guise it may take. Yet scholars from Lee Patterson to Patricia Clare Ingham to Valerie Flint have noted the parodic, recursive, attritional, and anti-imperialist narrative counter-drives within Geoffrey's text, which yield their own anti-imperial aftermaths in Welsh appropriations and apocalyptic (rather than imperialist) vaticinations. In other words, while I don't want to reclaim Geoffrey as a historiographical master narrator and I think Mueller's attention to Guido is a useful and original scholarly corrective, I don't think Guido alone is responsible for the dark view of imperial war in texts like the *Alliterative Morte Arthure*. Geoffrey is just as insistent about its destructive capacities: in the aftermaths of Belinus and Brennius; Maximianus, who depopulates the aristocracy of Britain; and Arthur himself, who leaves decline, cannibalism, and cultural death in his wake. While Mueller's intervention is welcome, deeply learned, and provocative, I found his readings of alliterative romance more programmatic than I liked. The splits in scholarly consensus over texts like *The Siege of Jerusalem*, *Sir Gawain*, and the *Alliterative Morte Arthure* respond, I think, to indeterminacies that animate the texts, with their admixtures of historiographical bliss *and* blunder, their obvious pleasure-taking in crafting stories of war, even when depicting empire's horrific costs.

For Mueller, using Guidonian Troy as a historiographic filter marks alliterative romance as politically and regionally oppositional, even unsavory. Alliterative romance becomes a doomed voice crying in the wilderness, against Anglo-Norman, southern, and Lancastrian literary empire-building. As a result, Mueller's argument ultimately reechoes in a more theorized and clerical key J. R. Hulbert's thesis linking alliterative romance with provincial resistance. Anyone interested in British national fantasy, ideologies of empire and their discontents, vernacular politics, and deeply learned, well-written historiographical argument should read this book and judge for him or herself.

CHRISTINE CHISM
UCLA

BARBARA NEWMAN. *Medieval Crossover: Reading the Secular against the Sacred*. Notre Dame: University of Notre Dame Press, 2013. Pp. 416. $42.00.

There has been a flurry of recent interest in the category of the "secular" as it pertains to medieval literature, partly in response to the grouping of work on vernacular religious texts under the aegis of a "Religious Turn" and partly in response to the thriving debate about the secular in the fields of anthropology, political theory, sociology, and philosophy. In this debate, the secular is frequently defined in spatial terms, as a coordinate of the "public sphere," for example, or the nation state, whereas for medieval Christians the secular was primarily a category of time. This alternative definition suggests one contribution that medieval studies can make to current theorizing about the secular, and it is one framework in which to understand perhaps the broadest contribution of Barbara Newman's *Medieval Crossover*. Drawing on her formidable command of medieval literary and religious cultures, Newman argues for a complementary relationship between the secular and sacred in a range of texts and genres, a "both/and" model of "double judgment" that depends on their simultaneous presence, and that is thus antithetical to the figurative spatiality of the secular in modern discourses, with their strong presumption that the secular and sacred map discrete zones.

Medieval Crossover, developed from Newman's 2011 Conway Lectures in Medieval Studies at Notre Dame, positions itself as a correction of both "Robertsonian" "exegetical" readings that overvalue the influence of Latinate theology on the meaning of vernacular texts, and more recent interpretations that attend only to "subversive" responses to dominant Christian paradigms. This may seem to overlook the wealth of scholarship that falls into neither camp, but Newman's approach nevertheless represents a methodological advance in the way it accords roughly equal status to the "sacred" and "secular," neither crediting the cultural primacy that some theology claimed for itself, nor reading religion as merely epiphenomenal to "secular" economic or political formations.

Newman outlines three key conceptual frameworks in the introductory first chapter. She first posits a hermeneutic of "both/and" that echoes medieval dialectic and derives its authority, above all, from the idea of *felix culpa*, in which sin is seen in terms of its redemptive complement. A form of the secular emerges from the "conjointure" of pagan and Christian: that is, as a "meeting place for two rival forms of the sacred." Newman elaborates this strikingly original claim through a reading of *Sir Gawain and the Green Knight*, in which the secular "meeting place" materializes as the Green Knight's barrow-chapel, where the green man of pagan lore meets the Christian knight. In the spirit of "both/and," I wonder how one might reconcile this reading with an alternative one that recognizes the Green Knight's "paganism" less as a rival form of the sacred than as a sort of negative impression of Christianity that preserves—and thus naturalizes—some of its core assumptions about the status and function of religion: e.g., that religion is a mechanism for cultivating or revealing a private identity, or that it comprises a set of rituals whose external form can be distinguished from their real force. Rather than a point of conjunction between two antithetical religions, that is, Gawain's confessional encounter with the Green Knight may be seen to conceptualize religion as a category in Christian terms.

Hybrid texts and genres—crossovers between erotic and religious lyric, for example, or romance and saints' lives—provide a third model of "both/and." Newman attends not only to shared formal and representational strategies (such as the oft-remarked similarity between the virgin martyr and the lady of romance), but also to the distinctive relationship between ethics and allegory often cultivated in such hybrid texts. Thus in the *Life of Pope Gregorius*, the saint—the product of incest who inadvertently marries his mother—is redeemed not only through confession and penance, but also through the allegorical significance assigned to his sin: the saint and his mother signify Christ married to the Church. A violation of Christian ethics is revealed nevertheless to point to Christian truth. Newman develops a very useful hermeneutic for understanding texts such as this. But, as this case study suggests, the "double coding" of ethical transgression as confirmation of the sacred may also be read as evidence of a much more closed system than the model of "both/and" proposes. On the other hand, a text like the *Life of Pope Gregorius* may be read as an exploration of the tensions that attend the improbable linking of ethics (practices in the *saeculum*) and the supraethical sacred in Christian thought. As several of her case studies show, medieval literature repeatedly probes the contradictions that arise from rooting ethical systems in a sacred that is defined as that which transcends social norms.

Chapter 2 explores Arthurian romances, focusing especially on Lancelot, as he appears in Chrétien's *Knight of the Cart*; two thirteenth-century Grail romances, *Perlesvaus* and the *Queste del Saint Graal*; and Malory's *Morte Darthur*. The secular is here identified with a mythic paganism that surfaces in elements of the plot—the cart, the sword bridge, the abduction of the queen, etc.—whose elusive significance makes possible both Christian allegorical readings and those that celebrate erotic love. In later Grail romances, this structure contracts from the level of tradition to the individual plot: rather than ancient pagan lore rewritten by the poet as a vehicle for Christian significance, secular commitments of characters within a romance are "rewritten" by a sacred counterpart, as when Guinevere's girding of Lancelot is "recuperated" by Galahad, girded by Perceval's sister. Malory institutes further changes, crafting the *Morte Darthur* as both a pagan myth of Arthur and a hagiography of a saintly Lancelot, in part by taking advantage of the slippery relation between treason and sainthood in the volatile climate of fifteenth-century England.

Chapter 3 offers a brilliant analysis of the relationship between Marguerite Porete's *Mirror of Simple Souls* and vernacular literary traditions in Picardy with which it shares a vocabulary of desire, renunciation, freedom, excess, and annihilation, including the lyric poetry of the *puy* of Valenciennes, beguine poetry, and regional recensions of the *Roman de la rose*. The beautifully textured close readings in this chapter, which trace Porete's influence on secular literary culture as well as her immersion in it, make a powerful case against the segregation of women's mystical literature from other forms of vernacular literary production. The chapter closes with an analysis of the *Mirror* as a reading of the

Roman de la rose, "in reverse, de-eroticized and told from the perspective of the Rose" (161), and a stunning argument that the theologians who drew up the charges in Porete's heresy trial confused her theology with Jean de Meun's "libertine view of Nature," which extricates sex from a Christian paradigm of sin.

Chapter 4 explores three very different texts under the label of *parodia sacra*, by which Newman refers to sacred tropes or narratives repurposed for "profane" ends: the *Lai d'Ignaure*, the *Passion of the Jews of Prague*, and the *Dispute between God and His Mother*, the last two of which are edited in appendices to the book. Parody is, as Newman remarks, a mode that destabilizes meaning in ways intended and unintended, and her readings in this chapter are the ones most likely to provoke further debate. In *Ignaure*, the many women who have taken Ignaure as a lover are fed his penis and heart by their vengeful husbands, a narrative that Newman reads as a satire on women's eucharistic devotion, another "ritual feast on the body of the Beloved" (178). The *Dispute between God and His Mother* pitches "the Christ of the poor" against a bourgeois Mary who rebukes her son for his poverty, as the poem validates and mocks her prudence and his "divine prodigality" in equal measure. An account of the massacre of Jews in Prague in 1389, the *Passion of the Jews of Prague*, attributed to one "John the Peasant," affiliates the Jews with Christ, even as it celebrates the horrific violence against them. Newman considers this work a parody of the Gospel, a reading that she supports by pointing out the *Passion*'s Gospel intertexts, which, she argues, create a "textual unconscious" at odds with the work's evident purpose. Newman proposes that some medieval Christian readers might have been capable of recognizing the terrible irony of this savage text. A full analysis of the work as Gospel parody would also need to explain how it functions to construct a categorical difference between Jesus and the Prague Jews that codes the violence against them as legitimate.

The last chapter reads René of Anjou's devotional *Mortification of Vain Pleasure* and his *Book of the Love-Smitten Heart* against one another. In each, a heart—extracted from the Soul in *Mortification* and from the Lover in the *Book of the Heart*—undergoes a quest that ends in solitary prayer. In the context of the secular love allegory, this ending would be a mark of failure. In the context of the devotional allegory, however, it marks the achievement of the ultimate goal: devout renunciation located in the private self. Newman suggests that this conclusion reflects the "democratization of piety," as vernacular religious texts made a rigorous devotional life accessible to an increasingly broad lay audience. The secular beloved, in contrast, remained potentially inaccessible: "the lady, unlike God, reserved the right to say 'no'" (253).

In the conclusion, Newman generously identifies her work as laying a path to be pursued by others. In addition to the method it outlines, *Medieval Crossover* provides the ground for exploring why so many medieval texts and genres—in serious and playful registers—construct an inextricable relationship between the secular and the sacred, even when they seem most antithetical to one another. Part of the answer may lie in the way that these texts, individually and collectively, work to identify religion as both normative and counter-normative: in many of the vernacular articulations of the *felix culpa* and other forms of paradox that Newman discusses, secular ethics are instantiated, maintained, and elaborated, even as the moral judgment they presume is reversed by the sacred, a category frequently defined in contradistinction to secular ethical and social protocols. This understanding of religion may be so familiar as to seem to inhere in the category itself, but cultural theorists working in a postcolonial framework—e.g., Talal Asad and others—have taught us to recognize that the particular conjunction of belief and practice on which it relies is historically and culturally specific. In presenting a range of texts characterized by "double coding" and "double judgment," *Medieval Crossover* puts us in a position to ask why medieval literature endeavored so often, and in such varied forms, to conceptualize religion as the point of intersection between the ethical and the supraethical—or, to put it somewhat differently, to ask why medieval literature defined itself, at least in part and frequently in practice, in terms of its capacity to produce elegant, irreverent, and enigmatic renderings of that intersection.

CATHERINE SANOK
University of Michigan (Ann Arbor)

JOHN SCATTERGOOD. *Occasions for Writing: Essays on Medieval and Renaissance Literature, Politics and Society*. Dublin: Four Courts Press, 2010. Pp. 272. €55.00.

John Scattergood has produced another collection largely consisting of previously published items. In their original venues, the essays on Chaucer, on Andreas Capellanus, and on Langland have already had considerable impact. The conventional response to such a volume should be disapproval of its redundancy, especially in an age of widespread electronic access. Yet this collection works as well as any carefully planned book. One reason is the consistency of Scattergood's approach, often moving from a well-trodden topic or question in literary history and then taking one surprising turn or unexpected illustration after another. Another reason for the justification of such a collection is Scattergood's pioneering contributions over the decades. Many of the current preoccupations of our field, such as the long fifteenth century, the relation of nationhood and language, the political import of certain minor genres or authors, the significance of subjects outside the law, and the importance of spatial location and temporality in literary discourse, were predicted by Scattergood. Despite his generous acknowledgment of scholars whose work came after his own, and although he would object to the claim, it might be said that Scattergood forged a new historicism *avant la lettre*.

The book is divided into two parts: "Movements," dealing with relatively long-term developments, and "Incidents," dealing with local events and texts. "Redeeming English: Language and National Identity in the Later Middle Ages" adds to the critique of the old standard model that lamented the obliteration of English after 1066. Scattergood argues for a resistant continued usage, resulting in a hybrid sense of national identity articulated by thirteenth- and early fourteenth-century English writers. He ends with the paradoxical attempts by the English to impose their language on Ireland in the fourteenth century. " 'The Unequal Scales of Love': Love and Social Class in Andreas Capellanus' *De amore* and Some Later Texts" describes the later English reception of Andreas, with its characteristic emphasis on social class, ending with the ironically reversed situation of a Paston marriage. "Writing the Clock: The Reconstruction of Time in the Late Middle Ages" points to the conflict of methods of timekeeping, such as sundials and clocks, as time is subject to commodification and rationalization; writers such as Chaucer and Dafydd ap Gwilym are cited as examples of the complex literary responses to the new technologies.

Part 2 contains essays on authors and texts from the fourteenth through the sixteenth centuries. Several of these chapters deal with works, such as *The Libelle of Englyshe Polycye* and Skelton's *Magnyfycence*, on which Scattergood has written definitive studies elsewhere. "London and Money: Chaucer's *Complaint to His Purse*" dates the poem to before 1400, when Chaucer retires to Westminster. Its tone can be explained by the expense and chaos, physical and moral, of London at the Lancastrian accession. Here, Scattergood argues against Andrew Fennel's engaging speculation that Chaucer wrote from Westminster where he was evading his creditors. Another chapter argues that Sir John Oldcastle is regarded as much as a class traitor as a heretic, which explains certain erasures and silences in the records of Lollard persecution. "On the Road: Langland and Some Medieval Outlaw Stories" collocates the two travelers and the Samaritan episodes in *Piers Plowman* with *The Geste of Robyn Hood* and *Eustache the Monk* to demonstrate the importance of the road as medium and liminal place, both necessary and dangerous, and experienced in multiple ways by medieval subjects. Outlaws stand in for new economic forces that do not respect traditional institutions. Other chapters cover figures as far apart as Piers of Bermingham and Thomas Wyatt, also outlaws of sorts. A compelling chapter on John Leland argues that Leland's *Itinerary*, ostensibly rescuing the manuscripts of the great monastic libraries after their dissolution, actually records the physical changes in the English landscape as it is subject to new forms of appropriation. Scattergood's sense of an emerging national identity, however elegiacally expressed, supplements Richard Helgerson's *Forms of Nationhood*, although I could not find any citation to that study. Elsewhere, Scattergood carefully rehearses arguments he is refuting or refining, often stating their theses more clearly than the authors themselves.

Four Courts Press, publisher of other collections by Scattergood, has produced a handsome book, marred only by low paper opacity. The volume is prefaced by a moving and technically impressive sonnet in memory of Derek Brewer. Like Brewer, John Scattergood's career has also been a long one: from his classic 1971 *Politics and Poetry in the Fifteenth Century*—a book that heavily influenced me in graduate school—to the alert and responsive essays, most from the twenty-first century, collected in the present volume.

JOHN M. GANIM
University of California, Riverside

MYRA SEAMAN, EILEEN JOY, and NICOLA MASCIANDARO, eds. *Dark Chaucer: An Assortment*. Brooklyn, N.Y.: Punctum Books, 2012. Pp. vii, 203. $15.00.

This book is experimental, staging different ways of responding to Chaucer. While some contributions are mini-versions of fairly traditional scholarly essays, others use rhyme, refrains, and word-association; weave together different stories; or juxtapose Chaucerian texts with modern pornography or with more canonical modern literature. Beginning with a "poetic preface" (by Gary J. Shipley) that describes each essay in a short, poetic paragraph, *Dark Chaucer* is an idiosyncratic series of meditations on moments or scenes in Chaucer that speak to the dark side of life. They are "essays" in the sense of essaying something, trying something out.

The assortment is connected by the theme of darkness. The book aims to move away from comic, playful aspects of Chaucer and from the idea of resolution in Chaucer's work, and instead focuses on "small black pearls" (Joy and Masciandaro), dark moments in Chaucer's writings. A theme that recurs over and over again is Chaucer's interest in the liminal space between life and death: reanimated corpses; bodies that won't die when they should; sleeping, dream-like, death-like states. Lisa Weston focuses on zombies and *The Prioress's Tale*; Masciandaro on Cecilia's three-day half-death in *The Second Nun's Tale*; Ruth Evans and Myra Seaman on *The Book of the Duchess* and its uncanny bodies. As one might expect in a book about dark Chaucer, gender is also a recurrent theme, as authors explore some of the most disturbing female figures, abused women subjected to violence such as Constance, Virginia, Cecilia, and Dorigen. Several essays circle around art and artifice. Elaine Treharne, for instance, writes about the focus on artifice in *The Physician's Tale*, connecting this to what she terms Chaucer's "hagioclasm," arguing that the tale challenges and breaks the genre of hagiography. Myra Seaman interestingly compares *The Book of the Duchess* to *Sir Orfeo*, analyzing how both texts interrogate the relationship between art and mortality.

The collection is dedicated to Lee Patterson, but the greatest influence on the essays as a whole is Aranye Fradenburg, whose work on psychoanalysis and sacrifice permeates many of the essays. Indeed, the fact that two such different critics both gravitate toward the darkness in Chaucer in various ways indicates the potential within this theme. Many of the essays are interested in psychoanalytical and specifically

Lacanian and post-Freudian approaches, but the theoretical scope is wide. One essay (by Thomas White) focuses on manuscript layout and reading practices; another on the reception of Chaucer by African-American poets at the turn of the twentieth century (Candace Barrington). Several essays engage with ecocriticism and animal theory, and some of the most memorable insights in the collection come from these perspectives: Travis Neel and Andrew Richmond discuss the crow as a crow, rather than as a figure for the court poet; Brantley Bryant discusses the destruction of the grove in *The Knight's Tale* and the horror of the light itself as an example of "dark counter-thinking" (27); J. Allan Mitchell sensitively explores the lithic imagery of *The Franklin's Tale*. Often-neglected texts are brought to the fore in this collection: Leigh Harrison's essay focuses on "The Former Age," and fabliaux are sidelined in favor of the much less discussed tales such as *The Second Nun's Tale*, *The Physician's Tale*, and *The Tale of Sir Thopas*.

The diversity of the essays makes the book an assortment in many ways. While some essays are imbued with scholarship, others analyze texts without showing knowledge of the critical field at all. Others do not aim to be critical essays in this sense, but instead explore themes in creative ways. Lisa Schamess's essay begins with an associative prologue inspired by Beckett; Hannah Priest takes us through different versions of the Constance story and of connected stories, focusing on the theme of retelling through cloth and tapestry, as woman and cloth are made blank over and over again. The refrain-based structure of the piece itself mirrors this theme of cycles and returns as it foregrounds questions about control, storytelling, and recurrence. Bryant's essay uses Saturn and Theseus's attitudes to life (in *The Knight's Tale*) as a lens on the current state of the academic profession and the value we place on a certain kind of sociability, exploring the experience of depression through the words of several anonymous academics who have suffered from mental ill health.

Some of these contributions, then, are not the kind of essays that one usually—or ever—reads in collections about Chaucer; they are very much written in the spirit of Punctum Books' mission statement (http://punctumbooks.com/about/): "neo-traditional and non-conventional scholarly work that productively twists and/or ignores academic norms." Punctum aims to be a refuge for "the imp-orphans of your thought and pen"—to encourage creative engagement with the humanities in the broadest sense.

In other ways too, *Dark Chaucer* is an unusual book. It was first imagined by the editors in April 2011 and it was published in 2012. It is currently available free online on the Punctum Books website. Most of us are used to working within a publishing system in which, sometimes, we wait many months for readers' reports, copy-edits, and proofs, and, once the process has finally worked its way through many years, our books are priced at a level that makes them unaffordable for almost anyone except libraries. Punctum offers a challenge to this standard publishing model, just as it also offers an alternative to the kind of work we might do with, for instance, Chaucer. That isn't to say that all publishing needs to go down this route. Most scholarly work needs time to bed down and to be worked through; many essays and books are not ready for publication so soon after their conception. And, at a time when many of us are thinking about open-access papers and journals, there is much to be said for books costing money.

Open access sounds like a bastion of intellectual freedom and knowledge-sharing, something that only an old-school elitist could possibly be against, but that is not necessarily the case. In the UK, the recent, government-supported Finch Report suggested moving the costs of publishing articles from publisher or consumer to published (i.e. author), with the implication that only those articles that a university department decides to fund will get published. This is a serious threat to academic freedom. It would work against the basic principle that work should be published based on merit, not based on where a researcher works or on the stage of his or her career. Issues about open access for edited collections or monographs have not yet been foregrounded, but these are issues with which we will all have to grapple. Of course, impoverished students and independent scholars should have access to knowledge through well-funded libraries and library subscriptions; our books should be cheaper, and the onus is on presses to find ways to do that. But, I don't want them all to be free. Books are the products of many kinds of labor, and we should value that.

This is not a critique of Punctum Books, an innovative, blue-skies concept that is enriching and diversifying the world of book production. Rather, what I want to emphasize is that open access is problematic as a more general aim. Punctum should make older publishers think about how they can work on getting books out faster and more affordably. But text-workers—editors, copy-editors, typesetters, peer-reviewers—are worthy of their hire, even if their labor is not as physically grueling as it was for Hoccleve or Usk. Making a book is still a collaborative process, and we need all of these different kinds of text-workers if we want to be able to read actual books. It would be nice if government funding or infinite philanthropy could make books available to all, free at the point of use, but since that isn't happening, I think readers and libraries—rather than authors or their patrons—should pay for the production of books. Open access is a crucial and complicated issue: we need to ensure fair access for the institutionally less privileged, as both readers *and* as authors, and we also need to support our colleagues in the publishing industry if we want the book as material object to continue to be part of our scholarly landscape.

MARION TURNER
Jesus College, Oxford

A. C. SPEARING, *Medieval Autographies: The "I" of the Text*. Notre Dame: University of Notre Dame Press, 2012. Pp. viii, 347. $32.00 paper.

In this book, A. C. Spearing revisits the central claims made in his *Textual Subjectivity: The Encoding of Subjectivity in Medieval Narratives and Lyrics* (Oxford: Oxford University Press, 2005). The guiding conviction there and in *Medieval Autographies* is that modern critics of Middle English literature misrepresent the works that they attempt to explicate when they apply the same set of interpretative categories to their texts as those that were developed for the analysis of nineteenth- and twentieth-century novels and poems. In particular, Spearing asserts, unlike the dramatic monologues of Kazuo Ishiguro and Robert Browning, the "I" of a Middle English poem "*may* refer to a fictional individual . . . whose consciousness the writing purports to represent" but "it does not necessarily do so" and "rarely does so in any clear-cut or systematic way" (13, emphasis in original). Closely bound up with this argument is a rejection of the assumption, which Spearing finds commonplace, that a medieval author's purpose "would be to produce a text coherent in perspective and ideology," and that "he or she could normally be expected to be perfectly in control of the text in fulfillment of this aim" (3). Although "discovering planned intricacies of structure provides an endless supply of material for books and articles" (120), the time has now come to reconsider the pleasure that is produced by the improvised and arbitrary aspects of late medieval literary creation.

In *Textual Subjectivities*, Spearing divided his attention between the familiar generic groupings of Middle English narrative and lyric poetry. *Medieval Autographies* argues for the previously unrecognized coherence of a body of writing encompassing "extended, non-lyrical, fictional writings in and of the first person" (1), which Spearing calls "autography." The texts in this category are related to and perhaps anticipatory of the modern autobiography, but they distinguish themselves from works in that genre because, in the case of medieval works, "[autography] is first-person writing in which there is no implied assertion that the first person either does or does not correspond to a real-life individual" (7). What is of interest here is not whether the events recounted in a particular work actually happened to their author, but rather the means by which autography evokes proximity and something that Spearing calls "experientiality," that is, "the literary illusion of experience separable from any individual experiencing consciousness" (20). In a move that will doubtless prompt further work on the interrelation of French and English literature in late medieval England, Spearing suggests that Chaucer and his followers elaborated this mode of writing under the influence of the Middle French *dit*.

In order to make the case for his new generic category, Spearing offers detailed analyses of a handful of Middle English texts, including *Wynnere and Wastoure* (Chapter 1), the Knight's and the Reeve's prologues and tales (Chapter 2), the *General Prologue* and *The Wife of Bath's Prologue* (Chapter 3), the Prologue to Hoccleve's *Regiment of Princes* (Chapter 5) as well as his *Series* (Chapter 6), and Bokenham's *Legendys of Hooly Wummen* (Chapter 7). As was the case in *Textual Subjectivity*, many of the opening arguments in *Medieval Autographies* are corrective. The recent critical histories of the Knight's and the Reeve's texts are reviewed with the intention of exemplifying the putative misreadings that can proceed from the assumption that Chaucer uses his pilgrims' stories to flesh out their characterizations. Spearing likewise cites, largely in order to dismiss, claims for the thematic unity both of Hoccleve's *Regiment* and of Bokenham's *Legendys*. In each case, this ground-clearing precedes a welcome reevaluation of the work of the authors addressed, not as life-writers or as exponents of a particular *idée fixe*, but rather as poets actively engaged in the exploration of their own craft. The book's fourth chapter plays a crucial role in explaining this turn. Here, Spearing argues that, despite the strictures of grammarians such as Geoffrey of Vinsauf, whose *Poetria nova* is so frequently cited by both modern scholars and medieval writers, the forms assumed by much Middle English literature owe a good deal more to improvisation and experimentation than to forward planning. This shift of perspective allows Spearing to re-present his star authors as inventive risk-takers; as masters in the art of "free composition" (49); and, moreover, as writers who expect their readers to enjoy the spectacle of their work-in-progress. In Chapter 6, for example, Spearing highlights Hoccleve's detailed description of the compilation of his *Series* in the *Dialogue* section of that work. Indeed, while many scholars will remain sensitive to Hoccleve's insistence on the co-identity of his narrator and his historical person, Spearing's account of this writer's self-conscious artistry may be one of the most valuable insights offered in *Medieval Autographies.*

Readers will judge for themselves the degree to which Spearing's engagement with his fellow medievalists is constructive. My own feeling is that a more sustained interaction with book historians and codicologists could have strengthened the case for autography. I am thinking here of recent work on fifteenth-century habits of compilation that discusses the willingness among late medieval readers to conceive of the person of the author as the originator of a work or body of works—a phenomenon not confined to France but present in England as well (see, for example, Alexandra Gillespie's *Print Culture and the Medieval Author: Chaucer, Lydgate, and Their Books, 1473–1557* [Oxford: Oxford University Press, 2006])—a burgeoning discussion that is only briefly acknowledged in *Medieval Autographies* (63). An assessment of the diverse single- and multi-author manuscripts and the early print books in which Spearing's writers' works traveled might have helped him sharpen his readers' focus on the often ambivalent relationship he posits between the "I" of a Middle English text and its historical referent. Finally, notwithstanding Spearing's clear distrust of critical orthodoxies, some readers may be struck by what often feels here like a return to the Chaucerianism of mid-twentieth-century scholarship. Spearing attributes much that he finds worthy of notice in Hoccleve and Bokenham to the earlier poet's influence. Some of the connections he makes are illuminating: the Prologue to the *Regiment of Princes* may perhaps owe something to Chaucer's *Pardoner's Prologue*, for example. Other links feel more strained. Must the "chief model" (240) for

Bokenham's depreciation of his poetic skill be *The Franklin's Prologue*, especially when Bokenham names Cicero and Claudian as his points of reference in the same lines that Spearing cites?

Medieval Autographies does an excellent job of highlighting both the fluidity of the Middle English poetic "I" and the inventiveness of some of its more familiar wielders; the chapter on Bokenham offers a useful introduction to that neglected writer's output. Whether or not "autography" sticks as the term used to describe the poems addressed in this study, Spearing's sensitive close readings will ensure the abiding interest of his book. Particularly memorable among the many glowing examples of this mode of criticism here is Spearing's extended rendition of *The Wife of Bath's Prologue* not as Alisoun's speech, as we might be used to hearing it, but as the poet's own *dit*-inspired textual performance "as an English pantomime dame . . . Chaucer in drag" (86–87). At the same time as he illustrates the fruitfulness of his approach to Chaucer, Spearing also reassures his reader that abandoning familiar narrator-based readings of the author's work need not take all the fun out of explication.

RORY G. CRITTEN
University of Fribourg, Switzerland

EMILY STEINER. *Reading "Piers Plowman."* Cambridge: Cambridge University Press, 2013. Pp. 273. $85.00 cloth; $27.99 paper; $22.00 e-book.

Reading "Piers Plowman" is a much needed and welcome tool for scholars who teach and write about Langland's knotty poem. The book offers a sustained, insightful critique of the text's major movements and themes; at the same time, it makes the broader argument that the poem desires to redeem not just individual Christian souls but the English language itself. This is the well-told story of "how an English poetics can perform the work of Latin rhetoric, and in the process, fashion a truly literary theological vernacular" (210).

An informative prologue sets the stage for the detailed readings that follow. It documents the poem's use of the alliterative long line, its multilingual *habitus*, and its transformation of the French tradition of dream-vision allegory. The poet domesticates his Continental inheritance, creating a "vision that is all-inclusive and therefore supremely ethical, committed to the salvation of everyone" (12). Langland's salvational ecumenicalism is, however, insistently English, given its spiritual and geographical affinities with southern England, especially London and its environs.

The chapters comprise a narratively linear set of expositions exploring the poem's central motifs. The opening passus establish a Boethian world, one in which, according to Steiner, a complex allegory elevates work-horse homiletic material into sophisticated philosophical commentary. Holy Church's sermon on moderation and excess exposes the mechanics of several relations simultaneously: the extent to which material and immaterial values shape one another, how the individual good participates in the sovereign good, how sexual desire and greed undermine conscience, and how politics and religion both operate "through networks of service and reward" (49). In the episode of Lady Meed, Langland demonstrates what political counsel and penitential poetry have in common: each offers a model of rulership based on the analogy between temporal and spiritual profit. Penitential poetry has the advantage, however, because it alone can reveal the inherent problem with a model of kingship that seeks to balance the aristocratic value of magnificence against the ethical imperative to limit reward.

If the poem's opening poses pointed questions about how an earthly governor can aspire to imitate (however imperfectly) spiritual lordship, the second *visio* "shifts from society to community, or from the structures to the ethics of association" (60). Piers, plowman and pilgrim, emerges to test the limits of these social ties. His daily work raises larger concerns about how personal actions contribute to the common profit: can true labor actually unite the three estates? How does private penance incorporate the medieval Christian into a larger spiritual public?

Social contracts are uneasily analogized with their spiritual counterparts, and Truth appears to grant absolution to the unruly community. The pardon is designed to remind "Piers and his fellows that every one of them is implicated by a contract drawn up between humanity and its God" (68). Yet the B-version-Piers rips this pardon in half—apparently dissatisfied by its simple assertion that the good go to heaven, while the bad do not—and the pilgrim continues his spiritual journey alone, following the path of his own allegorical education.

It is in these middle passus that the poet is able to examine in detail how "the cruxes of salvation theology" resemble "the social dynamics of teaching and learning" (98). The narrator's encounter with a variety of allegorical figures—including abstractions from faculty psychology (Reason, Imaginatif), just pagans (Trajan, Aristotle), the university (Dame Study, Wit), and the Church (Scripture, Theology)—demonstrates the dreamer's own shortcomings together with those of the rational intellect more generally. Knowledge, whether spiritual or earthly, does not by itself lead to salvation. The promise of an educable self can only be realized once it is put into practice out in the material world, where temporality—the unfolding of the providential plan—impinges on our aspirations to moral virtue—the progressive development of our ethical selves. The poet then draws a series of surprising analogies between humans and animals in order to argue for the virtue of patient poverty. These middle passus engage in a kind of dialectical encyclopedism that makes both the spiritual and literary stakes of Langland's vision clear: "For the poet, the difficult project of representing a virtuous practice is bound up in a poetics that compulsively pursues every form of life—animal or human, Christian or heathen, rich or poor, beggar or saint—as a potential moral exemplar" (143).

The poem's later passus portray a panorama of biblical history from the Garden of Eden through to Christ's birth, Crucifixion, and Resurrection—events narrated by a series of witnesses that include Piers himself, Abraham, Moses, the Good Samaritan, and the Four Daughters of God, among others. For Langland, rehearsing sacred history allows him the freedom to formulate a Trinitarian theology that speaks back to the poem's earlier concerns with associational ethics, a "theology that teaches people how to love God and neighbor by analyzing the relationships among the three divine Persons" (191). This biblical compendium also serves to redeem individual believers even as it legitimates the poet's own allegorical project: "Sacred narrative restores a fallen humanity through the life of Christ, but it also rehabilitates narrative more generally," since narrative, like mankind's own history, always suffers from "incompleteness" (180).

The poem is perhaps most in need of such redemption in its concluding passus, where its apocalyptic energies disrupt the generic dream-vision drive to closure, resulting in an abrupt and notoriously incomplete ending. In a dizzying series of waking and dreaming episodes, the dreamer's earlier persona—the learned itinerant—returns to write down his dream, to witness a bloody Piers as Jesus usher in the Church Militant, only to see it fall before the forces of Antichrist, a dissolution that necessitates yet another pilgrimage, one announced in the poem's closing lines. For Steiner, this ending allows Langland to confront "some of the problems inherent in authorial revision and in the institutionalization of irregular lives" (216). This is an ingenious way of trying to make sense of the poem's chaotic non-ending, and one that invites further elaboration.

In terms of its audience, the book can be used profitably by those with a long-standing knowledge of the poem as well as those encountering it for the first time. Proficient at defining terms and texts, it could supplement or even replace John Alford's *A Companion to Piers Plowman*, a stand-by regularly assigned by many of us who teach the poem. To either their relief or their consternation, readers looking for a discussion of the complex relations among the poem's many manuscript versions will not find it here. The decision to discuss the B-text is dispatched briefly with the claim that this version "is the most formally and intellectually experimental of the three main versions" (2). Beyond the contextual basics, the book contains substantive new insights for those who have read and taught the poem for years, particularly on the subject of Langland's relation to other fourteenth-century writers such as the *Cursor mundi* poet, Rolle, Mandeville, Trevisa, and Chaucer.

Within literary studies, *Reading Piers Plowman* demonstrates the continuing vitality of the *explication de texte* genre in a publishing world largely dominated by thematic monographs that tend to wander vagrant-like across centuries and over national borders, corralling disparate authors and their works along the way. The book also performs a more local service. If *Piers Plowman* scholarship can occasionally seem like a closed shop, with scholars of the poem speaking mainly to other scholars of the poem, Steiner's book opens up this conversation to a wider audience, one that can, with her help, see why the poem is "a show-stopping example of medieval visionary poetics" (13).

KELLIE ROBERTSON
University of Maryland, College Park

KATIE L. WALTER, ed. *Reading Skin in Medieval Literature and Culture*. New York: Palgrave Macmillan, 2013. Pp. xx, 225. £53.00.

One of the most vibrant trends in recent medieval and early modern studies is the focus on the cultural history of the senses. In the past ten years the number of works dedicated to the matter has skyrocketed, and the fascination with the senses—in particular with the so-called "lower senses" (smell, taste, and touch)—does not seem to be waning. Although framed from a historicist perspective, studies of the (lower) senses in the Middle Ages and early modern period are consistently characterized by being both interdisciplinary and transcultural. In this sense, *Reading Skin in Medieval Literature and Culture*, included in The New Middle Ages—the very prolific series published by Palgrave and directed by Bonnie Wheeler—constitutes a rich and very timely contribution to the topic.

Among the senses, the history of touch is without a doubt the one that twentieth-century scholarship has neglected the most. In the past ten years, this oversight has not only been noted, but also repaired to a great degree. Nevertheless, there are still vast expanses of unexplored territory waiting to be charted. As the organ of touch, skin is, indeed, one of these vital and undermined areas of inquiry. *Reading Skin in Medieval Literature and Culture* represents the most substantial attempt to undertake this issue in recent Anglo-American scholarship. Following the lead of *La pelle umana/The Human Skin* edited by Agostino Bagliani and published in the series Micrologus (no. 13 [2005]), but also influenced by more general recent works by the likes of Nina Jablonski and Steven Connor, Walter's edited volume gathers essays that deal with skin in medieval culture, juxtaposing disciplines such as medicine, natural philosophy, literature, cultural history, the history of the book, visual culture, and others.

The approach to skin as a primal metaphor for mediation runs through the volume and gives the collection a sense of conceptual harmony that testifies to the proficiency of its editor. Such conceptual harmony, however, should not be confused with homogeneity; the essays contained in this volume cover a wide thematic spectrum, since the authors' shared understanding of skin as a liminal space helps them read a variety of cultural phenomena from a very unique perspective. As Walter herself says in the introduction, *Reading Skin in Medieval Literature and Culture* attempts to "meditate on the significance of skin for expressing the human condition as well as attending to questions of the relation of the human to the other in its various guises: the divine, the cultural or racial other, the animal, the monstrous, the inanimate or dead" (3). Walter adds that one of the aims of the collection is to engage twentieth- and twenty-first-century cultural theories, such as those of

Michel Serres, Giorgio Agamben, Jean-Luc Nancy, and Roberto Esposito. This is perhaps the least interesting aspect of the project, and most of the essays that do try to establish a dialogue between medieval texts and contemporary theory fall short of justifying the interpretative advantages of doing so.

The first essay, Lara Farina's "Wondrous Skins and Tactile Affection: The Blemmye's Touch," constitutes the strongest contribution in the volume. Farina finds in the image of a Blemmye—a headless body whose face is on its torso—from a manuscript copy of *Wonders of the World*, an illustration of a uniquely medieval way of understanding the sense of touch, which derives from contemporary readings of Aristotle. According to Farina, the monstrosity of the Blemmye, "an imaginative representation of a body organized by the sense of touch," challenges ocular perception and forces the spectator to ponder human sensation as a tactile, rather than as an ocular, phenomenon. Among other things, Farina stresses the connections among reading and touching, skin and parchment. Susan Small's brilliant essay, "The Medieval Werewolf Model of Reading Skin," likewise engages the question of monstrosity and skin, this time from a linguistic perspective. Small argues that the werewolf is not a marvel, but rather a text to be read. The relation among skin, parchment, and reading in the Middle Ages is quite pervasive throughout the volume, but is explored most succesfully in Virginia Langum's essay, "Discerning Skin: Complexion, Surgery and Language in Medieval Confession." Langum explores medieval examples of a discipline that flourishes in the Early Modern period with the works of Michele Savonarola and Giambattista Della Porta, namely, clinical physiognomy. This discipline construed the body as a text that, if properly deciphered, reveals the mysteries of the soul in its relations both to the material world and to the divine. A close look at medical and confessional texts by Saint Augustine, Alain de Lille, John Metham, and others allows Langum to differentiate among three hermeneutic approaches to skin: material (the skin itself and its unique idiosyncrasies), metaphoric (the skin as borderland, as envelope, etc.), and metonymic ("the skin not only covers the soul, but reveals it"). Langum develops a rich analysis of this third—and most interesting—"metonymic" approach, not only by focusing on the rather unexplored territory of medieval physiognomy, but also by appealing to Paul Ricoeur's analysis of metonymy as contiguity.

This is perhaps the only example in *Reading Skin in Medieval Literature and Culture* of a successful engagement with contemporary theory. Langum borrows a concept and succeeds in showing that it not only sheds light on the issue at hand without engendering anachronistic dissonance, but also opens up new paths for understanding the complex relationship between science and religion in the Middle Ages. The collection also includes Robert Mills's "Havelok's Bare Life and the Significance of Skin" and Katie L. Walter's "The Form of the Formless: Medieval Taxonomies of Skin, Flesh, and the Human," two essays that tackle fascinating topics related to medieval conceptions of the body. The former essay discusses extreme physical punishment; the latter examines the connection between skin and conceptions of race. Mills and Walter engage theoretical notions by Didier Anzieu, Agamben, Nancy, and Esposito, *and* Maurice Merleau-Ponty, but do not manage to convince the reader of the advantages of such "conversations." As for the remaining essays, they include Elizabeth Robertson's "*Noli me tangere*: The Enigma of Touch in Middle English Religious Literature and Art for and about Women," Isabel Davis's "Cutaneous Time in the Late Medieval Literary Imagination," and Julie Orlemanski's "Desire and Defacement in *The Testament of Cresseid*." The book ends with Karl Steel's response to the collection, which emphasizes the importance and urgency of the topic. Steel is right, and it is precisely here, and not in the ad hoc invocations to contemporary theorists, that the relevance of this book for twenty-first-century readers lies. The history of the lower senses, in particular touch and its organ, the skin—the largest, most complex organ in the human body—becomes ever more relevant as debates around corporeality, sexuality, gender, and race intensify. *Reading Skin in Medieval Literature and Culture* continues a long neglected and crucial chapter of this history.

PABLO MAURETTE
University of Chicago

DAVID WATT, *The Making of Thomas Hoccleve's "Series."* Exeter: University of Exeter Press, 2013. $99.95.

Writing poetry about writing poetry is a temptation that few poets have resisted. Thomas Hoccleve is not among that select few. In the middle of the twentieth century, Robert Graves dismissed "what passes as English poetry" as "the product of either careerism, or keeping one's hand in: a choice between vulgarity and banality." David Watt's book, *The Making of Thomas Hoccleve's "Series,"* attempts to uncover where along that spectrum we can place Hoccleve's literary labor and its products as aesthetic and material propositions.

Watt takes as his primary subject the process, not the product, of Hoccleve's writing, and to that end interrogates its material remnants and the poetic fictions of its composition. Watt begins his book with a bold observation: "This is not the book I initially planned to write. The version of this book that I had in my head was never the version on the page in front of me" (1). Such a statement is honest, and draws attention to the chasms between intentionality and execution that are at the heart of all creative and critical endeavors. At the same time, Watt implies that the book escaped his control in some way. Though he thus sets up a parallel for his arguments about the complexities of Hoccleve's compositional difficulties, it is a disturbing beginning. His frank honesty about the potential failures of process suggest that the product, too, may be problematic. The book offers a sustained engagement with the entirety of Hoccleve's *Series*, and though many of its points are locally persuasive, it does not quite succeed in offering a critical framework that can make compelling sense of the gap between anticipation and execution it perceives in Hoccleve's poetry.

More successful is Watt's attempt to focus on both the ephemeralities and the materialities of the poetic process. As Watt argues in the book's introduction, "the *Series* offers a reflection *on*, not a reflection *of*, his [Hoccleve's] conception of book production" (4). To this end, Watt marshals paleographical evidence along with careful close readings of the entirety of Hoccleve's *Series*, a sequence of five distinct and interrelated Middle English poems, the best known of which are the first two, the "Complaint" and "Dialogue." "Learn to Die" has occasioned some more recent criticism, but the remaining two poems, "The Tale of Jereslaus's Wife" and "The Tale of Jonathas," have warranted little critical attention over many years. A book-length study of Hoccleve's *Series* is a welcome contribution to the field. Watt is to be commended for his sustained focus on Hoccleve's complexly allusive poetry, and his careful encounter with the manuscript instantiations of that verse.

The three autograph manuscripts of Hoccleve's poetry (or possibly four, as Linne Mooney has recently argued in these pages) have been disproportionately subject to the kind of paleographically and codicologically grounded literary criticism that Watt assays. The first chapter of *The Making* attempts to construct Hoccleve's likely audience "in and for the *Series*" through the lens of San Marino, Huntington Library, MS HM 111. Watt reads the claims of Hoccleve's narrator persona "Thomas" as reflecting and responding to the issues faced by Hoccleve and his poetry, and its reception by a coterie readership among the clerks of the Privy Seal. Watt argues Hoccleve's poems "are meant to circulate among those at work in the Privy Seal and elsewhere in Westminster Hall" (31). That "elsewhere" ultimately covers quite a bit of ground, deriving from Ethan Knapp's exposition of Hoccleve's bureaucratic vision and Emily Steiner's Langlandian documentary imagination, and stretching back to the coterie audiences of *Piers Plowman* described by Steven Justice and Kathryn Kerby-Fulton and others. Watt asserts an imagined audience ranging from the king, to the upper echelons of the nobility, to Hoccleve's fellow clerks. His depiction of a stratified and plural audience for the *Series*, its multiple valences carefully crafted by Hoccleve, is surely spot on, but not a particularly remarkable claim for poetry very near the center of the networks of late fourteenth- and fifteenth-century English poetry.

Chapter 2 turns to the copy of "Learn to Die" surviving in another holograph manuscript, Huntington Library, MS HM 744. The chapter argues for a reading audience intimately familiar with the physical processes of making books. That is, Watt sets out Hoccleve's poem, and the process of reading it, as analogous to medieval bookmaking: a series of decisions made, a series of crises and cruxes resolved. By treating bookmaking as having duration (acknowledging the important thinking on the matter by Daniel Wakelin), Watt positions the bookmaker as having responsibility for decisions in the "early" and "late" stages of manuscript production. These arguments rely upon a somewhat odd notion of booklet production, claiming "The structural coherence of the *Series* as a *story* depends on its readers' ability to imagine it being made by a narrator who uses booklet production to defer making decisions about its final form as long as possible" (66). Medieval writers don't write bound books. Textual and structural mobility are made possible at the level of the quire and the booklet, but can also be integral to the imagined design of a manuscript, or come about as an afterthought in the very last moments before quires are bound together, or, indeed, take place after binding through annotations indicating misplaced blocks of text. Final decisions about medieval books are always deferred, not by booklet-based composition but by the duration of the material processes of book writing and binding. In this chapter, Watt also discusses the oft-repeated assessment of the economic precariousness of vernacular bookmaking in the early fifteenth century. As against the ubiquitous business of making Latin prayerbooks, the creation of vernacular books may well have been less common, but given how often critics have trotted this idea out, it cannot have been all that radical or risky an undertaking.

The peculiar gaps and lapses of Hoccleve's writings occupy Chapter 3. Watt sees in another Hoccleve holograph, Durham University Library, MS Cosin.V.III.9, the conceptual frame that makes sense of the decision to cease translating "Learn to Die"—"The perils of excessive thought" (116) in the theologically complex age of Arundel and Chichele. Moving away from the paleographical criticism of the previous chapters to read instead the *Series* against a broad textual and historical backdrop, Watt traces a shift in Hoccleve's *Series*, from writing about writing books, to instead writing about *not* writing particular books. Watt suggests that "this choice therefore allows Hoccleve to foreground the kind of anxiety that might be generated by the translation of a theological text in the vernacular during the period" (129). The argument is not wholly convincing, and Watt acknowledges this by hazarding that "it is tempting to read this scene as parody . . . [or as] being critical of the popularity of these texts or of the narrator for being overcautious" (129).

There is another, rather less studied manuscript in Hoccleve's hand: the formulary now preserved in London, British Library, MS Additional 24062. To this can be added the other manuscripts and documents that Linne Mooney, Simon Horobin, and Estelle Stubbs have ascribed to Hoccleve's hand as part of the online *Late Medieval English Scribes* project, though Watt does not address these most recent identifications. In Chapter 4, he does an excellent job of bringing out the conceptual richness of a physical book that is both copy and exemplar, one designed and organized to be accessed as a model for its maker, and also for future generations of makers. Watt reads *The Series* as offering a moralizing model grounded in book culture, one that enables the construction of an ethical, scribally minded readership. The heterogeneity of both Hoccleve's formulary and the *Series* as a whole is central to Watt's vision for that lesson. Ultimately, Watt sees in Hoccleve's poetry a modest argument about the difficulties of personal spiritual reform in a theologically complicated moment. That reform is not encountered as a nested series of spiritual crises as in *Piers Plowman*, but through the lens of a day job reading and writing in the cogs of the bureaucratic, text-producing machine of early fifteenth-century London.

MATTHEW FISHER
University of California, Los Angeles

SUSAN YAGER and ELISE E. MORSE-GAGNÉ, eds. *Interpretation and Performance: Essays for Alan Gaylord*. Provo, Utah: The Chaucer Studio Press, 2013. Pp. xxxii, 214. $60.00 cloth.

Alan T. Gaylord, Professor Emeritus of Dartmouth College, is a Chaucerian who merits a festschrift. Susan Yager and Elise E. Morse-Gagné have succeeded in assembling a band of highly respected scholars to pay tribute to Gaylord's achievements in the fields of Chaucerian and Middle English studies: achievements most emphatically, though by no means exclusively, connected with the issue of performing Chaucer's texts. The facet of "performance" that one most readily associates with Alan T. Gaylord is the practice of reading Chaucer aloud. Indeed, Gaylord's Kalamazoo seminars on how to present Chaucerian verse to an audience and how this kind of presentation matters in terms of understanding and interpreting Chaucer's texts have entered the world of scholarly legend. It comes as no surprise, then, that the volume embraces a notion of "performance" that follows closely in the footsteps of the approach so successfully championed by Gaylord himself.

This lends a certain coherence to the collection, though some readers would have been grateful for a more analytical and theorized take on the issue of performance. After all, "performance" has long ceased to be a scholarly field solely concerned with the theatricality or the public delivery of texts. The concept of performance has spread considerably beyond those original confines, so that nowadays notions of "the performative" have invigorated medieval studies in topics ranging from manuscript study to liturgy, from court culture to the rhetorical and disputational practices embedded in medieval Latin school texts. In other words, it could have been interesting to meditate on how these proliferating notions of performance relate to the more traditional understandings of the concept, such as the "staging" or "reading aloud" of literary works.

Elise E. Morse-Gagné's introduction offers generous and intelligent praise of Alan T. Gaylord, elegantly fulfilling the particular demands of the festschrift genre. Ann Astell pays tribute to Gaylord's Robertsonian origins by exploring the relevance of the Gospels to *The Prioress's Tale*. One example is Matthew 21:15–16, which depicts Jewish leaders chiding the children of Jerusalem for celebrating Jesus' entry into the city; another is a parallel passage in Luke 19:40, in which Jesus counters Jewish criticism of the disciples with the words "If these were silent, the very stones would cry out." In a beautiful interpretation of a literally central moment in *Troilus and Criseyde*, Winthrop Wetherbee expands the notion of the performative to the textual as he demonstrates how Chaucer, drawing on Dante's *Paradiso*, succeeds in creating a moment of spiritualized love right before the climax of the consummation scene in Book III. Thomas Ohlgren evokes the image of a ghostly performance as he traces Robin Hood elements in a story from Thomas Walsingham's *Chronicon Angliae*, in which the bishop of Lincoln, Henry Burghersh, atones for past sins by appearing in the green garb of a forester in the dreams of his former men-at-arms. The deceased ecclesiastic demands that the ills he did to his tenants during his lifetime be redressed. In a rhetorical tour de force, Betsy Bowden shows excellent horse sense by helping clarify the equestrian recklessness that Arcite displays on his victory ride after winning his tournament in various versions of the story related in Chaucer's *Knight's Tale*. Howell Chickering's excellent contribution draws, among other things, on Elizabethan Chaucer criticism in order to examine the exact nature of Chaucer's so-called "riding rhyme," the highly flexible precursor of the more restricted iambic pentameter. Chickering persuasively argues that Chaucer employs his version of decasyllabic couplets in the service of a narrative style that is particularly attentive to specific speech rhythms; this style achieves, moreover, a singular form of transparency by deemphasizing rhyme. Susan Yager offers an interesting analysis of the Host's blunt rhymes and demonstrates how Harry Bailly is singled out through his idiosyncratic style of speech. Yager highlights the degree to which the Host shapes both the pilgrimage and the pilgrims and sees him as an intratextual stand-in for Chaucer, the poet. Fascinating as this take on Harry Bailly is, it is perhaps not sufficiently attentive to the Host's incomparable series of misinterpretations and to the way in which Harry Bailly tends to get things wrong whenever he comments on a tale. Paul R. Thomas's reading of *The Nun's Priest's Tale*'s prosody is sensitive to the stress patterns, and hence the meaning, that result from Chaucer's self-conscious juxtaposition of frequently monosyllabic English words of Germanic origin with polysyllabic words of Latinate origin. Maura Nolan's highly perceptive article, arguably one of the two most important in the volume, perfectly encapsulates both the strengths and the weaknesses of this book as a whole. Nolan analyzes Lydgate's handling of his characteristic broken-backed version of Chaucer's pentameter line. She shows how the fifteenth-century poet uses what many critics have considered his inability to reproduce the mellifluent lines of his revered master for the purposes of constructing the Host in the Prologue to the *Siege of Thebes* not as an individualized character—like the Pardoner, for instance—but rather as an abstract marker of literary discourse whose "aggressive half-lines [are] designed to emphasize his discursive power" (113). According to Nolan, Lydgate—who had a strong interest in forms of medieval drama such as mummings—tends to construct characters as actors on a stage, whose poetic lines draw attention to their very artificiality. This is a truly impressive reading of Lydgate's dialogic engagement with Chaucer's *Canterbury Tales*, but, at the same time, Nolan's analysis seems to cry out for closer examination—nay, more rigid theorizing—of the notion of the performative and the way it is employed. Does Nolan's line of argument imply that the dramatic is by definition less capable of representing the subjective? And is Chaucer's text somehow less "performative" than Lydgate's?

Alan Baragona, Lorraine K. Stock, and Peter Beidler all demonstrate how performance matters in teaching. Baragona provides an insightful discussion of Chaucer's final *-e* and embeds this within the larger issue of what kind of poetic line Chaucer actually wrote. Arguing that the first line of the *General Prologue* has four stresses rather than being merely a looser version of iambic pentameter, Baragona reminds us of the degree to which Chaucer's verse imitates the rhythms of speech. Lorraine K. Stock explores the usefulness of introducing role-play and material props into the classroom, while Peter Beidler's personal version of *prodesse et delectare* takes us through a number of his conference papers, which include, among other things, live sword fights and, for a paper on *The Miller's Tale*, a wooden model of the type of window through which Alisoun would have displayed her physical charms. Laura

Hodges' contribution to the book establishes interesting parallels between the incongruous fabrics Sir Thopas is dressed in and the sound patterns that develop in the descriptions of them. William A. Quinn's essay may well constitute the other of the two most intriguing articles for readers interested in performance theory. His interpretation of *The Squire's Tale* as a narrative event exploiting various forms of textual performativity is important not least because it provides the volume with an altogether more rounded notion of "performance." The collection closes with a witty, original, and philologically impressive continuation of *The Cook's Tale* by Brian S. Lee.

A special treat that comes with the book is the CD with readings of Chaucer by some of the contributors. Although the CD is not essential for understanding the individual authors' arguments—and in their contributions hardly any of the contributors refer directly to the readings on the CD—it does serve as an interesting and effective illustration of the problems inherent in reading aloud. All the readers do a magnificent job despite the considerable differences in their reading styles. Whereas Susan Yager chooses a pragmatic approach typical of most present-day American Chaucerians and is, therefore, not too concerned with some of the niceties of Middle English phonology—she renders the short /u/ in words like "us" and "but" as one would do in present-day English and offers a spelling pronunciation of the short /u/ as represented by the letter <o> in Middle English words like "som" or "compaignye"—Alan Baragona's careful delivery offers a philologically near-perfect rendition of the Middle English sounds. And, though this may be considered too subjective a comment, both Paul Thomas and Lorraine K. Stock have beautiful voices that instill the poet's text with a degree of resonance and elegance that reaches beyond the scholarly.

And what is true of these two scholars' voices can also be said of the collection as a whole. The book persuasively urges us to continue thinking of Chaucer Studies—and Middle English Studies in general—as fields in which the issue of performance will increasingly yield interesting rewards.

ANDREW JAMES JOHNSTON
Free University of Berlin

Books Received

Adams, Robert. *Langland and the Rokele Family: The Gentry Background to "Piers Plowman."* Portland, Ore.: Four Courts Press, 2013. Pp. 160. $50.00.

Ashton, Gail. *Brief Lives: Geoffrey Chaucer*. London: Hesperus Press, 2011. Pp. 112. £7.99; $12.95.

Atkin, Tamara. *The Drama of Reform: Theology and Theatricality, 1461–1553*. Turnhout: Brepols, 2013. Pp. x, 198. £59.50; $109.00.

Boulton, Maureen B. M., trans. *Piety and Persecution in the French Texts of England*. Tempe: Arizona Center for Medieval and Renaissance Studies, 2013. Pp. 228. $64.00.

Brown, Katherine A. *Boccaccio's Fabliaux: Medieval Short Stories and the Function of Reversal*. Gainesville: University Press of Florida, 2014. Pp. 240. $74.95.

Calabrese, Michael A., Stephen H. A. Shepherd, and Hoyt N. Duggan, eds. *Yee? Baw for Bokes: Essays on Medieval Manuscripts and Poetics in Honor of Hoyt N. Duggan*. Los Angeles: Marymount Institute Press, 2013. Pp. x, 296. $65.00.

Camargo, Martin. *Essays on Medieval Rhetoric*. Farnham: Ashgate, 2012. Pp. 336. £90.00; $170.00.

Carney, Clíodhna, and Frances McCormack, eds. *Chaucer's Poetry: Words, Authority, Ethics*. Portland, Ore.: Four Courts Press, 2013. Pp. 204. $74.50.

Coleman, Joyce, Mark Cruse, and Kathryn A. Smith, eds. *The Social Life of Illumination: Manuscripts, Images, and Communities in the Late Middle Ages*. Turnhout: Brepols, 2013. Pp. xxiv, 552. £133.79; $189.00.

Elliott, Elizabeth. *Remembering Boethius: Writing Aristocratic Identity in Late Medieval French and English Literatures*. Farnham: Ashgate, 2012. Pp. 190. £60.00; $109.95.

Forni, Kathleen. *Chaucer's Afterlife: Adaptations in Recent Popular Culture*. Jefferson, N.C. and London: McFarland, 2013. Pp. 176. $40.00.

Fresco, Karen L., and Charles D. Wright, eds. *Translating the Middle Ages*. Farnham: Ashgate, 2012. Pp. 248. £60.00; $104.95.

Ganim, John M., and Shayne Aaron Legassie. *Cosmopolitanism and the Middle Ages*. New York: Palgrave Macmillan, 2013. Pp. 256. $95.00.

Gillespie, Vincent, and Anne Hudson, eds. *Probable Truth: Editing Medieval Texts from Britain in the Twenty-First Century*. Turnhout: Brepols, 2013. Pp. 563. £118.09; $196.00.

Hawkes, David, and Richard G. Newhauser, eds. *The Book of Nature and Humanity in the Middle Ages and the Renaissance*. Turnhout: Brepols, 2013. Pp. 322. £68.43; $110.20.

Johnson, Eleanor. *Practicing Literary Theory in the Middle Ages: Ethics and the Mixed Form in Chaucer, Gower, Usk, and Hoccleve*. Chicago: University of Chicago Press, 2013. Pp. 264. $40.00.

Johnston, Andrew James, Margitta Rouse, and Philipp Hinz, eds. *The Medieval Motion Picture: The Politics of Adaptation*. New York: Palgrave Macmillan, 2014. Pp. 256. $95.00.

Kirkham, Victoria, Michael Sherberg, and Janet Levarie Smarr. *Boccaccio: A Critical Guide to the Complete Works*. Chicago: University of Chicago Press, 2013. Pp. 576. $50.00.

Lenz, Tanya S. *Dreams, Medicine, and Literary Practice: Exploring the Western Literary Tradition through Chaucer*. Turnhout: Brepols, 2014. Pp. 212. £59.50; $102.00.

Little, Katherine C. *Transforming Work: Early Modern Pastoral and Late Medieval Poetry*. Notre Dame: University of Notre Dame Press, 2013. Pp. 264. $38.00.

Mitchell, J. Allen. *Becoming Human: The Matter of the Medieval Child*. Minneapolis: University of Minnesota Press, 2014. Pp. 288. $25.00.

Morrison, Stephen. *A Late Fifteenth-Century Dominical Sermon Cycle*. Oxford: Early English Text Society, 2012. Pp. 650. £130.00; $135.00.

Murrin, Michael. *Trade and Romance*. Chicago: University of Chicago Press, 2014. Pp. 344. $45.00.

Pringle, Denys. *Pilgrimage to Jerusalem and the Holy Land, 1187–1291*. Farnham: Ashgate, 2012. Pp. 464. £75.00; $134.95.

Rice, Nicole R., ed. *Middle English Religious Writing in Practice*. Turnhout: Brepols, 2013. Pp. 290. £78.81; $88.24.

Riehle, Wolfgang. *The Secret Within: Hermits, Recluses, and Spiritual Outsiders in Medieval England*. Ithaca, N.Y.: Cornell University Press, 2014. Pp. 448. $35.00.

Scase, Wendy, ed. *The Making of the Vernon Manuscript: The Production and Contexts of Oxford, Bodleian Library, MS Eng. poet. a. 1*. Turnhout: Brepols, 2013. Pp. 331. £96.40; $160.00.

Somerset, Fiona. *Feeling like Saints: Lollard Writings after Wyclif*. Ithaca, N.Y.: Cornell University Press, 2014. Pp. 336. $65.00.

Taylor, Jamie K. *Fictions of Evidence: Witnessing, Literature, and Community in the Late Middle Ages*. Columbus: Ohio State University Press, 2013. Pp. 256. $59.95.

Turner, Marion, ed. *A Handbook of Middle English Studies*. Chichester: Wiley-Blackwell, 2013. Pp. 464. £98.50; $154.95.

An Annotated Chaucer Bibliography, 2012

Compiled and edited by Stephanie Amsel and Mark Allen

Regular contributors:

Mark Allen, *University of Texas at San Antonio*
Michelle Allen, *Grand Rapids Community College* (Michigan)
Stephanie Amsel, *Southern Methodist University* (Texas)
Brother Anthony (Sonjae An), *Sogang University* (South Korea)
Tim Arner, *Grinnell College* (Iowa)
Rebecca Beal, *University of Scranton* (Pennsylvania)
Debra Best, *California State University at Dominguez Hills*
Matthew Brumit, *Southern Methodist University* (Texas)
Margaret Connolly, *University of St. Andrews* (Scotland)
John M. Crafton, *West Georgia College*
Stefania D'Agata D'Ottavi, *Università per Stranieri di Siena* (Italy)
Amy Goodwin, *Randolph-Macon College* (Virginia)
Jon-Mark Grussenmeyer, *Rowan University* (New Jersey)
Ana Sáez Hidalgo, *Universidad de Valladolid* (Spain)
Andrew James Johnston, *Freie Universität Berlin* (Germany)
Wim Lindeboom, *Independent Scholar* (Netherlands)
Hillary K. Miller, *University of Alabama at Birmingham*
Warren S. Moore III, *Newberry College* (South Carolina)
Lazio Nagypal, *Independent Scholar* (Hungary)
Teresa P. Reed, *Jacksonville State University* (Alabama)
Martha Rust, *New York University*
Gregory M. Sadlek, *Cleveland State University* (Ohio)
David Sprunger, *Concordia College* (Minnesota)
Anne Thornton, *Abbot Public Library* (Marblehead, Massachusetts)
Winthrop Wetherbee, *Cornell University* (New York)
Elaine Whitaker, *Georgia College & State University*
Susan Yager, *Iowa State University*
Martine Yvernault, *Université de Limoges* (France)

Ad hoc contributions were made by Candace Barrington of Central Connecticut State University, New Britain, Conn., and Nicole D. Smith of the University of North Texas, Denton, Texas. The bibliographers acknowledge with gratitude assistance from librarians, especially Evelyn Day, Hollie Gardner, and Rebecca Graf at Southern Methodist University.

This bibliography continues the bibliographies published since 1975 in previous volumes of *Studies in the Age of Chaucer*. Bibliographic information up to 1975 can be found in Eleanor P. Hammond, *Chaucer: A Bibliographic Manual* (1908; reprint, New York: Peter Smith, 1933); D. D. Griffith, *Bibliography of Chaucer, 1908–1953* (Seattle: University of Washington Press, 1955); William R. Crawford, *Bibliography of Chaucer, 1954–63* (Seattle: University of Washington Press, 1967); and Lorrayne Y. Baird, *Bibliography of Chaucer, 1964–1973* (Boston, Mass.: G. K. Hall, 1977). See also Lorrayne Y. Baird-Lange and Hildegard Schnuttgen, *Bibliography of Chaucer, 1974–1985* (Hamden, Conn.: Shoe String Press, 1988); and Bege K. Bowers and Mark Allen, eds., *Annotated Chaucer Bibliography, 1986–1996* (Notre Dame, Ind.: University of Notre Dame Press, 2002).

Additions and corrections to this bibliography should be sent to Stephanie Amsel, Department of English, Southern Methodist University, 111 Clements Hall, P.O. Box 750435, Dallas, Texas 75275-0435. An electronic version of this bibliography (1975–2011) is available via The New Chaucer Society web page at http://artsci.wustl.edu/~chaucer/, or directly at http://uchaucer.utsa.edu. Authors are urged to send annotations for articles, reviews, and books that have been or might be overlooked to Stephanie Amsel, samsel@smu.edu.

Classifications

Abbreviations of Chaucer's Works

ABC	*An ABC*
Adam	*Adam Scriveyn*
Anel	*Anelida and Arcite*
Astr	*A Treatise on the Astrolabe*
Bal Compl	*A Balade of Complaint*
BD	*The Book of the Duchess*
Bo	*Boece*
Buk	*The Envoy to Bukton*
CkT, CkP	*The Cook's Tale, The Cook's Prologue*
ClT, ClP, Cl–MerL	*The Clerk's Tale, The Clerk's Prologue, Clerk–Merchant Link*
Compl d'Am	*Complaynt d'Amours*
CT	*The Canterbury Tales*
CYT, CYP	*The Canon's Yeoman's Tale, The Canon's Yeoman's Prologue*
Equat	*The Equatorie of the Planetis*
For	*Fortune*
Form Age	*The Former Age*
FranT, FranP	*The Franklin's Tale, The Franklin's Prologue*
FrT, FrP, Fr–SumL	*The Friar's Tale, The Friar's Prologue, Friar–Summoner Link*
Gent	*Gentilesse*
GP	*The General Prologue*
HF	*The House of Fame*
KnT, Kn–MilL	*The Knight's Tale, Knight–Miller Link*
Lady	*A Complaint to His Lady*
LGW, LGWP	*The Legend of Good Women, The Legend of Good Women Prologue*
ManT, ManP	*The Manciple's Tale, The Manciple's Prologue*
Mars	*The Complaint of Mars*
Mel, Mel–MkL	*The Tale of Melibee, Melibee–Monk Link*
MercB	*Merciles Beaute*
MerT, MerE–SqH	*The Merchant's Tale, Merchant Endlink–Squire Headlink*

MilT, MilP, Mil–RvL	*The Miller's Tale, The Miller's Prologue, Miller–Reeve Link*
MkT, MkP, Mk–NPL	*The Monk's Tale, The Monk's Prologue, Monk–Nun's Priest Link*
MLT, MLH, MLP, MLE	*The Man of Law's Tale, Man of Law Headlink, The Man of Law's Prologue, Man of Law Endlink*
NPT, NPP, NPE	*The Nun's Priest's Tale, The Nun's Priest's Prologue, Nun's Priest Endlink*
PardT, PardP	*The Pardoner's Tale, The Pardoner's Prologue*
ParsT, ParsP	*The Parson's Tale, The Parson's Prologue*
PF	*The Parliament of Fowls*
PhyT, Phy–PardL	*The Physician's Tale, Physician–Pardoner Link*
Pity	*The Complaint unto Pity*
Prov	*Proverbs*
PrT, PrP, Pr–ThL	*The Prioress's Tale, The Prioress's Prologue, Prioress–Thopas Link*
Purse	*The Complaint of Chaucer to His Purse*
Ret	*Chaucer's Retraction {Retractation}*
Rom	*The Romaunt of the Rose*
Ros	*To Rosemounde*
RvT, RvP, Rv–CkL	*The Reeve's Tale, The Reeve's Prologue, Reeve–Cook Link*
Scog	*The Envoy to Scogan*
ShT, Sh–PrL	*The Shipman's Tale, Shipman–Prioress Link*
SNT, SNP, SN–CYL	*The Second Nun's Tale, The Second Nun's Prologue, Second Nun–Canon's Yeoman Link*
SqT, SqH, Sq–FranL	*The Squire's Tale, Squire Headlink, Squire–Franklin Link*
Sted	*Lak of Stedfastnesse*
SumT, SumP	*The Summoner's Tale, The Summoner's Prologue*
TC	*Troilus and Criseyde*
Th, Th–MelL	*The Tale of Sir Thopas, Sir Thopas–Melibee Link*

Truth	*Truth*
Ven	*The Complaint of Venus*
WBT, WBP, WB–FrL	*The Wife of Bath's Tale, The Wife of Bath's Prologue, Wife of Bath–Friar Link*
Wom Nob	*Womanly Noblesse*
Wom Unc	*Against Women Unconstant*

Periodical Abbreviations

AdI	*Annali d'Italianistica*
Anglia	*Anglia: Zeitschrift für englische Philologie*
Anglistik	*Anglistik: Mitteilungen des Verbandes deutscher Anglisten*
AnLM	*Anuario de Letras Modernas*
ANQ	*ANQ: A Quarterly Journal of Short Articles, Notes, and Reviews*
Archiv	*Archiv für das Studium der neueren Sprachen und Literaturen*
Arthuriana	*Arthuriana*
Atlantis	*Atlantis: Revista de la Asociacion Española de Estudios Anglo-Norteamericanos*
AUMLA	*AUMLA: Journal of the Australasian Universities Language and Literature Association*
BAM	*Bulletin des Anglicistes Médiévistes*
BJRL	*Bulletin of the John Rylands University Library of Manchester*
C&L	*Christianity and Literature*
CarmP	*Carmina Philosophiae: Journal of the International Boethius Society*
CE	*College English*
ChauR	*Chaucer Review*
CL	*Comparative Literature* (Eugene, Ore.)
Clio	*CLIO: A Journal of Literature, History, and the Philosophy of History*
CLS	*Comparative Literature Studies*
CML	*Classical and Modern Literature: A Quarterly* (Columbia, Mo.)
CollL	*College Literature*
Comitatus	*Comitatus: A Journal of Medieval and Renaissance Studies*
CRCL	*Canadian Review of Comparative Literature/Revue canadienne de littérature comparée*

DAI	*Dissertation Abstracts International*
DR	*Dalhousie Review*
ÉA	*Études anglaises: Grand-Bretagne, États-Unis*
EHR	*English Historical Review*
EIC	*Essays in Criticism: A Quarterly Journal of Literary Criticism*
EJ	*English Journal*
ELH	*ELH: English Literary History*
ELN	*English Language Notes*
ELR	*English Literary Renaissance*
EMS	*English Manuscript Studies, 1100–1700*
EMSt	*Essays in Medieval Studies*
Encomia	*Encomia: Bibliographical Bulletin of the International Courtly Literature Society*
English	*English: The Journal of the English Association*
Envoi	*Envoi: A Review Journal of Medieval Literature*
ES	*English Studies*
ESC	*English Studies in Canada*
Exemplaria	*Exemplaria: A Journal of Theory in Medieval and Renaissance Studies*
Expl	*Explicator*
FCS	*Fifteenth-Century Studies*
Florilegium	*Florilegium: Carleton University Papers on Late Antiquity and the Middle Ages*
FMLS	*Forum for Modern Language Studies*
Genre	*Genre: Forms of Discourse and Culture*
H-Albion	*H-Albion: The H-Net Discussion Network for British and Irish History, H-Net Reviews in the Humanities and Social Sciences* http://www.h-net.org/reviews/home.php
HLQ	*Huntington Library Quarterly: Studies in English and American History and Literature* (San Marino, Calif.)
Hortulus	*Hortulus: The Online Graduate Journal of Medieval Studies* http://www.hortulus.net/
IJES	*International Journal of English Studies*
JAIS	*Journal of Anglo-Italian Studies*
JBSt	*Journal of British Studies*
JEBS	*Journal of the Early Book Society*

JEGP	*Journal of English and Germanic Philology*
JELL	*Journal of English Language and Literature* (Korea)
JEngL	*Journal of English Linguistics*
JGN	*John Gower Newsletter*
JHiP	*Journal of Historical Pragmatics*
JMEMSt	*Journal of Medieval and Early Modern Studies*
JML	*Journal of Modern Literature*
JNT	*Journal of Narrative Theory*
L&LC	*Literary and Linguistic Computing: Journal of the Association for Literary and Linguistic Computing*
L&P	*Literature and Psychology*
L&T	*Literature and Theology: An International Journal of Religion, Theory, and Culture*
Lang&Lit	*Language and Literature: Journal of the Poetics and Linguistics Association*
Lang&S	*Language and Style: An International Journal*
LATCH	*LATCH: A Journal for the Study of the Literary Artifact in Theory, Culture, or History*
LeedsSE	*Leeds Studies in English*
Library	*The Library: The Transactions of the Bibliographical Society*
LitComp	*Literature Compass* http://www.literaturecompass.com/
M&H	*Medievalia et Humanistica: Studies in Medieval and Renaissance Culture*
MA	*Le Moyen Age: Revue d'histoire et de philologie* (Brussels, Belgium)
MÆ	*Medium Ævum*
Manuscripta	*Manuscripta: A Journal for Manuscript Research*
Marginalia	*Marginalia: The Journal of the Medieval Reading Group at the University of Cambridge* http://www.marginalia.co.uk/journal/
Mediaevalia	*Mediaevalia: An Interdisciplinary Journal of Medieval Studies Worldwide*
MedievalF	*Medieval Forum* http://www.sfsu.edu/~medieval/index.html
MedPers	*Medieval Perspectives*
MES	*Medieval and Early Modern English Studies*
MFF	*Medieval Feminist Forum*

MichA	*Michigan Academician* (Ann Arbor, Mich.)
MLQ	*Modern Language Quarterly: A Journal of Literary History*
MLR	*The Modern Language Review*
MP	*Modern Philology: A Journal Devoted to Research in Medieval and Modern Literature*
N&Q	*Notes and Queries*
Neophil	*Neophilologus* (Dordrecht, Netherlands)
NLH	*New Literary History: A Journal of Theory and Interpretation*
NM	*Neuphilologische Mitteilungen: Bulletin of the Modern Language Society*
NML	*New Medieval Literatures*
NMS	*Nottingham Medieval Studies*
NOWELE	*NOWELE: North-Western European Language Evolution*
NYRB	*The New York Times Review of Books*
Parergon	*Parergon: Bulletin of the Australian and New Zealand Association for Medieval and Early Modern Studies*
PBA	*Proceedings of the British Academy*
PBSA	*Papers of the Bibliographical Society of America*
PLL	*Papers on Language and Literature: A Journal for Scholars and Critics of Language and Literature*
PMAM	*Publications of the Medieval Association of the Midwest*
PMLA	*Publications of the Modern Language Association of America*
PoeticaT	*Poetica: An International Journal of Linguistic Literary Studies*
PQ	*Philological Quarterly*
Quidditas	*Quidditas: Journal of the Rocky Mountain Medieval and Renaissance Association*
RCEI	*Revista Canaria de Estudios Ingleses*
RenQ	*Renaissance Quarterly*
RES	*Review of English Studies*
RMRev	*Reading Medieval Reviews* http://www.rdg.ac.uk/AcaDepts/ln/Medieval/rmr.htm
RMSt	*Reading Medieval Studies*
SAC	*Studies in the Age of Chaucer*
SAP	*Studia Anglica Posnaniensia: An International Review of English*

SAQ	*South Atlantic Quarterly*
SB	*Studies in Bibliography: Papers of the Bibliographical Society of the University of Virginia*
SCJ	*The Sixteenth-Century Journal: Journal of Early Modern Studies* (Kirksville, Mo.)
SEL	*SEL: Studies in English Literature, 1500–1900*
SELIM	*SELIM: Journal of the Spanish Society for Medieval English Language and Literature*
ShakS	*Shakespeare Studies*
SIcon	*Studies in Iconography*
SiM	*Studies in Medievalism*
SIMELL	*Studies in Medieval English Language and Literature*
SMART	*Studies in Medieval and Renaissance Teaching*
SN	*Studia neophilologica: A Journal of Germanic and Romance Languages and Literatures*
SoAR	*South Atlantic Review*
SP	*Studies in Philology*
Speculum	*Speculum: A Journal of Medieval Studies*
SSF	*Studies in Short Fiction*
SSt	*Spenser Studies: A Renaissance Poetry Annual*
TCBS	*Transactions of the Cambridge Bibliographical Society*
Text	*Text: Transactions of the Society for Textual Scholarship*
TLS	*Times Literary Supplement* (London, England)
TMR	*The Medieval Review* http://www.hti.umich.edu/t/tmr/
Tr&Lit	*Translation and Literature*
TSLL	*Texas Studies in Literature and Language*
UTQ	*University of Toronto Quarterly: A Canadian Journal of the Humanities*
Viator	*Viator: Medieval and Renaissance Studies*
WS	*Women's Studies: An Interdisciplinary Journal*
YES	*Yearbook of English Studies*
YLS	*The Yearbook of Langland Studies*
YWES	*Year's Work in English Studies*

Bibliographical Citations and Annotations

Bibliographies, Reports, and Reference

1. Allen, Mark, and Bege K. Bowers. "An Annotated Chaucer Bibliography, 2010." *SAC* 34 (2012): 467–544. Continuation of *SAC* annual annotated bibliography (since 1975); based on contributions from an international bibliographic team, independent research, and *MLA Bibliography* listings. 323 items, plus listing of reviews for 80 books. Includes an author index.

See also nos. 70, 91.

Recordings and Films

2. Clements, Pamela. "Neomedieval Trauma: The Cinematic Hyperreality of Geoffrey Chaucer's *The Canterbury Tales*." In Carol L. Robinson, Pamela Clements, and Richard Utz, eds. *Neomedievalism in the Media: Essays on Film, Television and Electronic Games* (*SAC* 36 [2014], no. 107), pp. 35–54. Essay on adaptations of *CT*, focusing on *A Canterbury Tale* (1944), Piero Pasolini's *I racconti di Canterbury* (1972), and *A Knight's Tale* (2001), which treat *CT* in a "neomedievalist fashion" and also provide "Chaucerian commentary" on the time periods of these films.

3. Greenlaw, Lavinia, trans. *Troilus and Criseyde*. BBC Classic Serial. [North Kingstown, R.I.]: AudioGO, 2010. Sound recording; e-file. 1 hour, 53 minutes. Item not accessed; reported by WorldCat, with link to a commercial description: "A BBC Radio 4 full-cast [unabridged modernization] of Chaucer's *Troilus and Criseyde* by poet and writer Lavinia Greenlaw . . . . The cast includes Tom Ferguson as Troilus, Maxine Peake as Criseyde and Malcolm Raeburn as Pandarus. Also starring Kathryn Hunt, Kevin Doyle, Terence Mann and Declan Wilson. Directed by Susan Roberts." BBC 4 website reports that the initial broadcast began on April 26, 2009.

4. Yardley, David. *New Carols and Songs for Chaucer's Pilgrims*. Talisman, 2012. CD. Amazon and MP3 download. 57 minutes. Thirteen new pieces of music written by David Yardley, set to medieval writings that reflect "all walks of medieval life."

Chaucer's Life

5. Alexander, Michael. *Geoffrey Chaucer*. London: Scala, 2012. 39 pp. A brief guide to Chaucer's life, times, and works, with illustrations.

6. Brown, Peter. *Geoffrey Chaucer*. Oxford: Oxford University Press, 2011. xv, 254 pp. Comprehensive look at Chaucer's life and analysis of how cultural, literary, and historical events affected Chaucer's poetry.

7. Hardyment, Christina. *Writing Britain: Wastelands to Wonderlands*. London: British Library, 2012. 192 pp. Documents the British Library's exhibition of the same name (May–September 2012). Examines how the British landscape shapes literary texts, and how British authors depict the wide range of landscapes in English literature. Briefly discusses Chaucer's life in London and describes how readers in London would have related to *CT*. Includes color reproductions of *CT* manuscripts.

8. Johnson, Boris. *Johnson's Life of London: The People who Made the City that Made the World*. New York: Riverhead, 2012. 320 pp. The mayor of London reviews the history of London from the Celts to the present, organizing each developmental period around an historical person. The chapter on the later Middle Ages features Chaucer's connection to London, including his dwelling in Aldgate and the likelihood that he witnessed the end of Wat Tyler's rebellion.

9. Matheson, Lister M., ed. *Icons of the Middle Ages: Rulers, Writers, Rebels, and Saints*. Santa Barbara, Calif.: Greenwood, 2012. 2 vols. xviii, 705 pp. Available as e-text. Surveys lives and careers of iconic medieval characters. Includes chapter on Chaucer by Louise M. Bishop, pp. 175–204.

10. Mattern, Joanne. *Geoffrey Chaucer: Medieval Writer*. Huntington Beach, Calif.: Teacher Created Materials, 2012. 32 pp. Illustrated biography of Chaucer written for elementary and middle-school children.

11. Osberg, Richard H. "False Memories: The Dream of Chaucer and Chaucer's Dream in the Medieval Revival." *SiM* 19 (2010): 204–26. Examines the role of two "false memories" of Chaucer's life in the formation of nineteenth-century attitudes toward the poet and his reputation. The spurious incidents—Chaucer's exile and imprisonment and his "retirement" to a park at Woodstock—were repeated in biographical accounts and other popular materials, helping to create the idea of a romanticized poet.

See also nos. 60–61, 94, 108, 207.

Facsimiles, Editions, and Translations

12. Allen, Mark, and John H. Fisher, eds., with the assistance of Joseph Trahern. *A Variorum Edition of the Works of Geoffrey Chaucer Volume II. The Canterbury Tales: The Wife of Bath's Prologue and Tale*, Parts 5a and 5b. Norman: University of Oklahoma Press, 2012. 2 vols. Part 5a, xxviii, 424 pp. Part 5b, xvi, 315 pp. Part 5a includes a new text and set of collations for *WBPT*, based on the Hengwrt MS, with variants from landmark manuscripts and scholarly editions; also includes a Critical Commentary (pp. 3–148) that surveys critical tradition topically, a Textual Commentary (pp. 148–250) that describes the witnesses and surveys cruces, a Bibliographical Index (for Parts 5a and 5b), and a General Index (for Part 5a only). Part 5b includes explanatory notes keyed to individual lines and a General Index (for Part 5b only). Commentaries and notes cover materials published before 1997.

13. Amsel, Stephanie A. "The Art of the Bridwell Library Kelmscott *Chaucer*." *William Morris Society in the United States Newsletter* (2012): 8–9. Describes Southern Methodist University Bridwell Library's 1896 William Morris paper copy of the Kelmscott *Chaucer*. Includes details about letters, manuscript notes, drafts of illustrations and borders by Edward Burne-Jones, photographs, and other items associated with the provenance. Of special interest is Morris's inscription to Burne-Jones.

14. Boenig, Robert, and Andrew Taylor, eds. *The Canterbury Tales*. 2nd ed. Peterborough, Ont.: Broadview Press, 2012. 510 pp. Illus. rev. ed. of *CT* based on Ellesmere MS. Includes glossary, timeline of Chaucer's life, and bibliographical references.

15. Dane, Joseph A. *Out of Sorts: On Typography and Print Culture*. Philadelphia: University of Pennsylvania Press, 2011. xii, 242 pp. Chapter 5, "Fists and Filiations in Early Chaucer Folios (1532–1602)," pp. 105–117, reprints *SAC* 23 (2001), no. 13.

16. Faulkner, Peter. "The Kelmscott *Chaucer* and the Golden Cockerel *Canterbury Tales*." *Journal of William Morris Studies* 19, no. 1 (2010): 66–80. Compares the aesthetic experiences of confronting two illustrated editions of Chaucer as reproduced in facsimile, arguing that the Eric Gill edition of *CT* provides greater pleasure to a modern user than does William Morris's *Chaucer*.

17. Ford, Mark, ed. *London: A History in Verse*. Cambridge, Mass.: Belknap Press, 2012. xxvii, 745 pp. Anthology of poetry of London that includes *GP* and *CkPT* in Middle English.

18. Hopper, Vincent F., and Andrew Galloway, trans. *Chaucer's Canterbury Tales: An Interlinear Translation*. 3rd ed. Great Neck, N.Y.: Barron's Educational Series: 2012. xviii, 590 pp. Updated third edition includes new introduction by Galloway and four additional narratives.

19. Kalter, Barrett. *Modern Antiques: The Material Past in England 1660–1780*. Lanham, Md.: Bucknell University Press, 2012. viii, 251 pp. Examines how the long eighteenth century reflected "the emergence of a modern historical consciousness." Chapter 2, "Chaucer Ancient and Modern: Standardization, Modernization, and the Eighteenth-Century Reception of *The Canterbury Tales*," pp. 69–108, focuses on how political, literary, and social factors affected the standardization and modernization of *CT* during the eighteenth century.

20. Kick, Russell. *The Graphic Canon: From the "Epic of Gilgamesh" to Shakespeare to "Dangerous Liaisons."* New York: Seven Stories Press, 2012. Vol. 1. 501 pp., illus. Includes graphic adaptations of great works of western literature. Contains brief introduction to *CT*, with example of Seymour Chwast's *WBPT*.

21. Lázaro Lafuente, Luis Alberto. "Retelling Medieval Stories for Children in Franco's Spain." In Luminiţa Frenţiu and Loredana Pungă, eds. *A Journey through Knowledge: Festschrift in Honour of Hortensia Pârlog* (Newcastle upon Tyne: Cambridge Scholars, 2012), pp. 120–29. Analysis of Chaucer's tales (and Arthurian stories) as retold for Spanish children during the Francoist period. Focuses on the first translation of Chaucer (and its subsequent editions) by Manuel Vallvé, who translated J. Kelman's 1914 *Stories from Chaucer Told to the Children*. Comments on *FranT*, *KnT*, *ClT*, and *MLT* as depictions of pious behavior, virtue, and submission of women.

22. Osborn, Marijane, trans. *Nine Medieval Romances of Magic: Re-Rhymed in Modern English*. Buffalo, N.Y.: Broadview Press, 2010. x, 251 pp. Modern verse translations of romances in their original verse forms, with individual introductions and notes, a general introduction, and a commentary on the value of modern verse translation. Includes *WBT* and *Th*, along with Gower's "Tale of Florent," *Thomas of Erceldoune*, *Sir Orfeo*, Thomas Chestre's *Sir Launfal*, *Emaré*, *Sir Gowther*, and *Floris and Blanchefleur*. Appendix A includes two later analogous narratives: the ending of *Sir Libeaus and the Lamia* and "Tam Lin."

23. Peterson, William S., and Sylvia Holton Peterson. *The Kelmscott Chaucer: A Census*. New Castle, Del.: Oak Knoll Press, 2011. 272 pp. Complete census of all known extant copies of the Kelmscott *Chaucer*.

Explores late nineteenth- and twentieth-century book history, and provides anecdotal and bibliographic details of the *Chaucer*.

24. Strojan, Marjan, trans. *Canterburyjske Povesti*. Ljubljana: Cankarjeva založba, 2012. 481 pp. Item not seen; listed in WorldCat as a Slovenian translation of *CT*, with notes and apparatus.

25. Taylor, Andrew. "Thomas Tyrwhitt (27 March 1730–15 August 1786)." In Fran De Bruyn, ed. *Eighteenth-Century British Literary Scholars and Criticism*. Dictionary of Literary Biography, no. 356 (Detroit, Mich.: Gale, 2010), pp. 334–47. Biography of Tyrwhitt, with emphasis on his scholarly accomplishments, especially his 1775 edition of *CT*.

26. Utz, Richard. "The Colony Writes Back: F. N. Robinson's *Complete Works of Geoffrey Chaucer* and the *Translatio* of Chaucer Studies to the United States." *SiM* 19 (2010): 160–203. Uses a postcolonial approach to examine the publication and reception of Robinson's first edition of Chaucer's works (1933) in its historical context, focusing particularly on the rise of scholarly productivity in the United States and attitudes toward England and Germany between World War I and World War II.

See also nos. 50, 64, 86, 90, 184.

Manuscripts and Textual Studies

27. Blake, Norman F. "The Production of the First Copies of the *Canterbury Tales*." In Antonio R. Celada, Daniel Pastor García, and Pedro Javier Pardo García, eds. *Actas del XXVII Congreso Internacional de AEDEAN = Proceedings of the 27th International AEDEAN Conference* (Salamanca: Universidad de Salamanca, 2004), n.p. CD-ROM. Proposes that Chaucer probably started with a provisional notion of the overall order of *CT*, which he experimented with, adjusted, and had not completely sorted out before he died. The scribes copied the text in stints as the best way to adapt Chaucer's progress in producing the poem, which may indicate a close working relationship between Chaucer and his scribes.

28. Edwards, A. S. G. "Sir James Ware, the Collecting of Middle English Manuscripts in Ireland in the Seventeenth Century, and Chaucer's *Canterbury Tales*." *ChauR* 46 (2011): 237–47. A case study of the difficulty of identifying particular manuscripts in inventories, wills, catalogues, book lists, etc., surveying the Middle English manuscripts once

owned by seventeenth-century collector Sir James Ware, focusing on the items that include works by Chaucer. Tentatively suggests identification, but emphasizes uncertainties.

29. Hilmo, Maidie. "Illuminating Chaucer's *Canterbury Tales*: Portraits of the Authors and Selected Pilgrim Authors." In Kathryn Kerby-Fulton, Maidie Hilmo, and Linda Olson, eds. *Opening up Middle English Manuscripts: Literary and Visual Approaches* (*SAC* 36 [2014], no. 33), pp. 245–89. Examines illustrations of *CT* in several manuscripts, including the Hengwrt; Ellesmere; Bodley 686; and Tokyo, MS Takamiya 24 (formerly Devonshire); and portraits of Chaucer, exploring how manuscript illustrations "serve to shape the text and its reception." Includes discussion of various illustrations of Chaucer's pilgrims.

30. Holsinger, Bruce. "Parchment Ethics: A Statement of More than Modest Concern." *NML* 12 (2010): 131–36. Reports the finds of "Dr. Lollius," who reputedly discovered, through DNA analysis of "covertly obtained slivers of parchment and vellum," that several extant Chaucer manuscripts are "human skin." The pseudo-report is offered to provoke contemplation of the slaughter of animals for the purpose of preserving human culture.

31. Iyeiri, Yoko. "Additional Eighteenth-Century Materials on Middle English in the Hunterian Collection of the Glasgow University Library." *N&Q* 257 (2012): 332–35. Adds, to the group of manuscripts identified by Carl Grindley in 1995 (one of which was a concordance to the works of Chaucer), two more written in the same hand: MSS 621 and 622. The former is on the grammar of *Robert of Gloucester*, the latter on that of John Wyclif.

32. Kerby-Fulton, Kathryn. "Major Middle English Poets and Manuscript Studies, 1300–1450." In Kerby-Fulton, Maidie Hilmo, and Linda Olson, eds. *Opening up Middle English Manuscripts: Literary and Visual Approaches* (*SAC* 36 [2014], no. 33), pp. 39–94. Section 5, "Some of the Earliest Attempts to Assemble the *Canterbury Tales*," analyzes structural and scribal differences in *CT* manuscripts.

33. Kerby-Fulton, Kathryn, Maidie Hilmo, and Linda Olson, eds. *Opening up Middle English Manuscripts: Literary and Visual Approaches*. Ithaca, N.Y.: Cornell University Press, 2012. xxxii, 392 pp., illus. Richly illustrated text highlights issues that affected literary production, and focuses on how illustrations and glosses expand understanding of medieval English book culture. Introduction discusses different strategies of scribes in two versions of *CkT*: in the Hengwrt, fol. 57v; and Oxford,

Corpus Christi College, MS 198, fol. 62. For three chapters that focus on illustrated Chaucerian works, see 29, 32, and 37.

34. Miller, T. S. "Chaucer Abroad, Chaucer at Home: MS Arch. Selden B. 24 as the 'Scottish Ellesmere.'" *ChauR* 47, no. 2 (2012): 25–47. Focuses on how Chaucer was perceived in Scotland in the fifteenth century, and how deliberate misattributions of Chaucer's writings created a "vehicle for *Scottish* culture, identity, and nationalism."

35. Mooney, Linne R., and Daniel W. Mosser. "Another Manuscript by the Scribe 'Cornhyll.'" *JEBS* 15 (2012): 277–87. The scribe of Harley 1758 copied Pierpont Morgan Library, MS M.875.

36. Murray, Kylie. "Passing the Book: The Scottish Shaping of Chaucer's Dream States in Bodleian Library, MS Arch. Selden B.24." In Mark P. Bruce and Katherine H. Terrell, eds. *The Anglo-Scottish Border and the Shaping of Identity, 1300–1600* (*SAC* 36 [2014], no. 83), pp. 121–39. Considers the Scottish reception of *TC* and *PF* by close study of the annotations in Bodleian Library, MS Arch. Selden B.24. Sketches a network of Scottish aristocratic readers of Chaucer's work and argues that political and ethical concerns were their main preoccupations.

37. Olson, Linda. "'Swete Cordyall' of 'Lytterature': Some Middle English Manuscripts from the Cloister." In Kathryn Kerby-Fulton, Maidie Hilmo, and Olson, eds. *Opening up Middle English Manuscripts: Literary and Visual Approaches* (*SAC* 36 [2014], no. 33), pp. 291–354. Discusses monastic libraries and scribal communities where texts could be "copied and translated without repercussions behind the monastic walls of England." Also reveals how demand for vernacular writing increased in female convents. Section 2, "Monastic Manuscripts of Chaucer: Literary Excellence under Religious Rule," links Chaucer's works, including *PF*, *Astr*, *Bo*, and *CT*, to Augustinian, Benedictine, and Carthusian monastery collections, and to "the nuns of Syon."

38. Rogos, Justyna. "Transcribing and Editing Graphetic Details in the Manuscripts of Chaucer's *Man of Law's Tale*." In Marcin Krygier and Liliana Sikorska, eds. *Þe Comoun Peplis Language* (*SAC* 36 [2014], no. 100), pp. 79–86. Questions the precision of transcribing manuscripts in electronic editing as undertaken for the *Canterbury Tales* Project and the Middle English Grammar Project. Uses examples from *MLT* to demonstrate that even graphetic transcription does not represent manuscript details precisely, especially in the cases of abbreviations and word-end flourishes.

39. Rust, Martha. "Love Stories on Paper in Middle English Verse

Love Epistles." *JEBS* 15 (2012): 101–51. *TC* indicates that love letters were written on paper in England as early as the 1380s. Uses *TC* to frame connection of paper with verse love epistles and their fictions.

See also nos. 41, 184, 188.

Sources, Analogues, and Literary Relations

40. Beard, Drew. "Strange Bedfellows: The Chaucerian Dream Vision and the Neoconservative *Nightmare*." *Irish Journal of Gothic and Horror Studies* 8 (2010): n.p. (electronic publication). Describes medieval dream-visions, characterizes Chaucer's examples as simultaneously concerned with destabilizing assumptions and containing dissent, and compares aspects of Chaucer's dream-visions with the "postmodern" horror-movie series, *A Nightmare on Elm Street*.

41. Cannon, Christopher. "Chaucer and the Auchinleck Manuscript Revisited." *ChauR* 46, nos. 1–2 (2011): 131–46. Reconsiders Laura Hibbard Loomis's method for gauging Chaucer's familiarity with the Auchinleck manuscript—a method based on collocations shared by Auchinleck and *Th*—arguing that the method does not prove his familiarity with Auchinleck, but does evince his knowledge of Oxford, Bodleian Library, MS Laud misc. 108, or something like it. Evidence from the records of the *MED* help to demonstrate the variety of Chaucer's poetic styles.

42. Grimes, Jodi. "Arboreal Politics in the *Knight's Tale*." *ChauR* 47, no. 1 (2012): 340–64. Examines the grove in *KnT* in the context of hunting and forest laws; reveals how Chaucer alters Boccaccio's *Teseida* to turn the grove first into a politicized space of human discord and then into a space of destruction, evoking warfare among men and against the natural world. By presenting the grove as Theseus's space, Chaucer advocates a "custodial view of power" that finds models in positive interactions with nature, even as he suggests that humans are incapable of lasting harmony.

43. O'Connell, Brendan. "The Poetics of Fraud: Jean de Meun, Dante, and Chaucer." In Gerald Morgan, ed. *Chaucer in Context: A Golden Age of English Poetry* (*SAC* 36 [2014], no. 104), pp. 261–78. Traces Chaucer's and Dante's different responses to poetic "representation and authority" to Jean de Meun's *Le roman de la rose*, examining the "poetics of fraud" in *PardT* and *HF*.

44. Reynolds, Matthew. *The Poetry of Translation: From Chaucer and Petrarch to Homer and Logue*. New York: Oxford University Press, 2011. x, 374 pp. Explores the complexity of using literary translations, discussing Chaucer in relation to Dante, Petrarch, and Dryden in Chapter 15.

45. Rigby, Stephen H. "Aristotle for Aristocrats and Poets: Giles of Rome's *De regimine principum* as Theodicy of Privilege." *ChauR* 47, no. 1 (2012): 259–313. Examines Giles of Rome's social theory and its vision of unity and hierarchy, as well as the degree to which it might have been influential in Chaucer's time, commenting on the Wife of Bath's discussion of *gentilesse*. Also refers to *LGW*; *HF*; *KnT*; and the Wife of Bath, the Parson, and the Clerk in *GP*.

See also nos. 54, 82, 96, 101, 115, 122–23, 133, 140, 144, 151–53, 155, 163, 170–71, 174, 181, 193, 195, 197–98, 205, 209, 212, 222, 224, 228–29.

Chaucer's Influence and Later Allusion

46. Abbate, Francesca. *Troy Unincorporated*. Chicago: University of Chicago Press, 2012. 76 pp. Poetic narrative based on characters and plot of *TC*, set in contemporary Troy, Wisconsin.

47. Abdou, Angie. *The Canterbury Trail*. [Victoria, B.C.]: Brindle and Glass, 2011. 277 pp. Fiction loosely based on framework of *CT*, with unlikely group of ski enthusiasts brought together during a pilgrimage through backcountry British Columbia.

48. Barrington, Candace. "Dark Whiteness: Benjamin Brawly and Chaucer." In Myra Seaman, Eileen A. Joy, and Nicola Masciandaro, eds. *Dark Chaucer: An Assortment* (*SAC* 36 [2014], no. 110), pp. 1–11. Studies the poem "Chaucer" by Benjamin Brawly, an early twentieth-century African-American poet.

49. Behrman, Mary. "The Waiting Game: Medieval Allusions and the Lethal Nature of Passivity in Ian McEwan's *Atonement*." *Studies in the Novel* 42 (2010): 453–70. Identifies and assesses allusions to medieval literature in Ian McEwan's novel *Atonement* (2001), particularly Chaucer's works (*TC* and *ClT*) and Arthurian literature.

50. Chi-Fang, Sophia Li. "Inheriting the Legacy: Dekker Reading Chaucer." *ES* 93 (2012): 14–42. Argues that playwright Thomas Dekker, influenced by John Stow, refashioned the Chaucer legacy in the theater.

51. Doherty, P. C. *The Midnight Man: The Physician's Tale of Mystery and Murder as He Goes on Pilgrimage from London to Canterbury.* Sutton: Crème de la Crime, 2012. 217 pp. Historical detective fiction set in the frame of *CT*, in which a doctor, modeled on Chaucer's Physician, tells a story to the rest of the pilgrims about sorcery, exorcism, and deaths involved with the mysterious figure of the Midnight Man.

52. Flannery, Mary C. *John Lydgate and the Poetics of Fame.* Woodbridge: Boydell and Brewer, 2012. xi, 208 pp. Looks at fame in medieval texts and argues that although Lydgate was Chaucer's fifteenth-century successor, he "diverges from Chaucer's treatment" of fame by "constructing a more confident model of authorship."

53. Higl, Andrew. *Playing the "Canterbury Tales": The Continuations and Additions.* Farnham: Ashgate, 2012. 208 pp. Considers the "post-Chaucer continuations and additions" to *CT*, particularly so-called "spurious" links between tales, *Siege of Thebes*, *Tale of Beryn*, *Canterbury Interlude*, *Ploughman's Tale*, *Plowman's Tale*, *Tale of Gamelyn*, and alternative endings to *CkT*. Considers the *Tales* as interactive, dynamic, polyvocal, game-like, and "ergodic," and argues that readers should appreciate the post-Chaucerian additions to *CT* as part of its reception history.

54. Hollifield, Scott Alan. "Shakespeare Adapting Chaucer: 'Myn auctour shal I folwen, if I konne.'" *DAI* A71.11 (2011): n.p. Argues that Shakespeare's adaptations relied not only on understanding and knowing Chaucerian texts, but on his "memory of Chaucer" and Chaucerian ideas and practices, particularly his mingling of "sources and authorities" in *TC*.

55. Johnson, Kij. "Story Kit." In Jonathan Strahan, ed. *Eclipse Four: New Science Fiction and Fantasy* (San Francisco: Night Shade Books, 2011), pp. 51–62. Experimental retelling of the story of Dido and Aeneas that opens with references to *HF* and *LGW*, among other works.

56. Kuczynski, Michael P. "Another Medieval Scientific Manuscript Owned and Annotated by James Cobbes." *N&Q* 257 (2012): 160–63. Cobbes's dense annotations of Nicholas of Lynn's *Kalendarium* in University of North Carolina, Chapel Hill, MS 522 may reflect this seventeenth-century book collector's familiarity with the British Library, MS Additional 23002 text of *Astr.*

57. Martin, Priscilla. "Jack and John: *The Plowman's Tale.*" In R. F. Yeager and Toshiyuki Takamiya, eds. *The Medieval Python: The Purposive and Provocative Work of Terry Jones* (*SAC* 36 [2014], no. 118), pp. 207–13. This is a short story, told from the first-person point of view of Chaucer's

Plowman, who describes his early life, his distaste for his brother the Parson, and their pilgrimage to Canterbury.

58. McLane, Maureen N. *My Poets*. New York: Farrar, Straus, and Giroux, 2012. iii, 273 pp. Combines memoir with literary criticism to explore the importance of poetry in the examined life. Begins with discussion of *TC* and Chaucer's use of *kankedort*.

59. Pugh, Tison, and Angela J. Weisl. *Medievalisms: Making the Past in the Present*. London: Routledge, 2012. ix, 176 pp. Analysis of the influence of medieval literature and culture on contemporary film, literature, and various academic disciplines. Includes discussion of Chaucer's *CT*, *KnT*, *PF*, and *TC*.

60. Schamess, Lisa. "L'O de V: A Palimpsest." In Myra Seaman, Eileen A. Joy, and Nicola Masciandaro, eds. *Dark Chaucer: An Assortment* (*SAC* 36 [2014], no. 110), pp. 125–37. Experimental juxtapositioning of Virginia's rape in *PhyT*, Chaucer's interaction with Cecily Chaumpaigne, and *The Story of O* (1954), presented as a text caught in the act of being edited, complete with palimpsests of strikeouts, text additions, and so forth.

61. Spearing, A. C. "Was Chaucer a Poet?" *PoeticaT* 73 (2010): 41–54. Despite Chaucer's characteristic humility about his poetry and the absence of any references to poetry in his *Life-Records*, critics are wrong to deemphasize the respect that subsequent writers accorded to his writing. Imitation of Chaucer's poetic techniques is evidence that Chaucer was a master poet.

62. Stavsky, Jonathan. "John Lydgate Reads *The Clerk's Tale*." *SAC* 34 (2012): 209–46. Provides an "anatomy of Lydgate's engagement with" *ClT*, documenting his "many Griseldas": muse, "haughty beloved," "antithesis of contemporary women," "exemplary spouse," woman who "falls short of being the Virgin Mary," "victim of misrepresentation," and model for Lydgate's "own conception of poetry."

63. Stock, Lorraine, and Betty J. Proctor. "The Wife of Bath as Inspiration for Defoe's *Moll Flanders*: A Case of Eighteenth-Century Medievalism." *MedPers* 25 (2010): 103–23. Demonstrates Daniel Defoe's familiarity with *CT*, and documents the fundamental influence of Chaucer's Wife of Bath on the form and content of *Moll Flanders*.

64. Von Nolcken, Christina. "'Penny Poet' Chaucer, or Chaucer and the 'Penny Dreadfuls.'" *ChauR* 47, no. 1 (2012): 107–33. Discusses William Thomas Stead's 1895 publication of Masterpiece Library's *CT*,

part of the "Penny Poets" series, and its effects on the circulation of Chaucer's works.

65. Westerson, Jeri. *Blood Lance.* New York: Minotaur, 2012. 322 pp. Murder mystery in which Chaucer aids medieval detective Crispin Guest to solve the murder of a man who apparently was seeking the Spear of Longinus.

66. ———. *Troubled Bones: A Crispin Guest Medieval Noir*. New York: Minotaur, 2011. 288 pp. Murder mystery in which medieval detective Crispin Guest aids Chaucer and the Canterbury pilgrims in seeking a murderer.

See also nos. 11, 44, 68, 94, 128, 137, 145, 194, 205.

Style and Versification

67. Camargo, Martin. "Chaucer and the Oxford Renaissance of Anglo-Latin Rhetoric." *SAC* 34 (2012): 173–207. Surveys rhetorical approaches to Chaucer and documents the "renaissance in rhetoric" in late fourteenth-century England by surveying manuscripts that contain rhetorical treatises. The impact of this renaissance is evident in Chaucer's poetry: while his early poetry was relatively unconcerned with rhetoric, it is clearly evident in *TC*; present in *NPT* and *SqT*; and underlying the characterizations of the Franklin, the Pardoner, and the Monk.

68. Goldstein, R. James. "A Distinction of Poetic Form: What Happened to Rhyme Royal in Scotland?" In Mark P. Bruce and Katherine H. Terrell, eds. *The Anglo-Scottish Border and the Shaping of Identity, 1300–1600* (*SAC* 36 [2014], no. 83), pp. 161–80. Employs both stylistic and codicological analysis to consider Chaucer's inheritance of the French rhyme royal stanza form and his use of it in *TC*. Demonstrates how rhyme royal flourished in Scotland, initially in *The Kingis Quair*, and later in the compositions of Robert Henryson.

69. Kiser, Lisa J. "The Animals that Therefore They Were: Some Chaucerian Animal/Human Relationships." *SAC* 34 (2012): 311–17. Explores human affiliations with the "non-power" of animals in four Chaucerian images: capons in *PardT*, mouse in *WBP* (in contrast with lioness), stags in *KnT*, and carrion in *ClT*. Contrasts these with the brass steed as an image of power in *SqT*.

See also nos. 41, 72–73, 75, 158, 161.

Language and Word Studies

70. Bergs, Alexander, and Laurel J. Brinton. *English Historical Linguistics: An International Handbook*. Berlin: De Gruyter Mouton, 2012. 2 vols. 1197 pp. Comprehensive interdisciplinary and theoretical study of the history of the English language. Chapter 36 discusses Chaucer's language.

71. Ciszek, Ewa. "Some Aspects of Word Formation in Henryson's *Fables*." In Marcin Krygier and Liliana Sikorska, eds. *Þe Comoun Peplis Language* (*SAC* 36 [2014], no. 100), pp. 37–42. Analyzes abstract noun formation (adding suffixes) in Robert Henryson's *Fables* and offers some brief comparisons with data from works by Chaucer.

72. Frye, Northrop, and Robert B. Denham. "Intoxicated with Words: The Colours of Rhetoric." *UTQ* 81 (2012): 95–110. Chaucer is aware of poetic or aureate diction but seldom uses it. He is "essentially a poet of *occupatio*." Language change rapidly made Chaucer's meter difficult to imitate, even for Lydgate. Like other writers, Chaucer introduces new Latinate vocabulary, especially in prose, even as he tries to write simply. This essay, edited from Frye's holograph, apparently notes toward a history of English literature, in the Victoria University Library, University of Toronto. Refers to *Astr* and *Bo*.

73. Leitch, Megan G. "Locating Authorial Ethics: The Idea of the *Male* or Book-Bag in the *Canterbury Tales* and Other Middle English Poems." *ChauR* 46, no. 4 (2012): 403–18. In the five instances in which *male*, meaning "bag or pouch" or "holder of writing," appears in *CT*, the word can also mean "man, male gender, or genitals," "stomach," and "wrongdoing." Through this wordplay, Chaucer reveals his anxieties about the type of author he might be, and about the relationships between authorship and sinfulness and spirituality.

74. Machan, Tim William. "Chaucer and the History of English." *SP* 87 (2012): 147–75. Critiques traditional treatment of Chaucer's English as the main antecedent of modern English and the assertion that it is representative. Chaucer's English is more conservative than that of many of his contemporaries and of general spoken discourse. Chaucer's use of the second-person plural pronoun, rife with social implications, indicates that the T–V distinction was no more than part of Chaucer's stylistic toolbox and not a marker of linguistic change. Some attention is given to *TC*.

75. Moore, Colette. *Quoting Speech in Early English*. New York: Cam-

bridge University Press, 2011. xiii, 216 pp. Study of speech representation in English texts from 1350 to 1600. See case study, 1.3.1 (p. 70), for analysis of evolving punctuation in *MerT*.

76. Pakkala-Weckström, Mari. "Chaucer." In Andreas H. Jucker and Irma Taavitsainen, eds. *Historical Pragmatics*. Handbooks of Pragmatics, no. 8 (New York: Walter de Gruyter, 2010), pp. 219–45. Defines pragmaphilology as a field of study, explains why Chaucer is an important focus for study in the field, surveys the pragmaphilological work that has been carried out concerning Chaucer, and makes suggestions for future directions. Much of the work that has been done relates to speech acts (especially insults, threats, and promises), forms of address, and pronouns.

77. Phillips, Susan E. "Chaucer's Language Lessons." *ChauR* 46, nos. 1–2 (2011): 39–59. Examines the varying degrees and uses of multilingualism among the Canterbury pilgrims and the characters in their tales, commenting on the facile "linguistic posing" of several speakers (Pardoner, Parson, Wife of Bath, Summoner and his characters) and exploring in depth the link between "mercantile pragmatism and foreign language use" in *MLT*.

78. Smallwood, T. M. "*For gode* in Chaucer and the *Gawain* Poet." *ChauR* 46, no. 4 (2012): 461–71. Argues that the phrase *for gode* in *MilT* (I.3526) is not, as is often assumed, a misspelling meaning "by God," but rather an intentional use of a phrase appearing in unsophisticated texts of the period. The phrase has similarly been misunderstood in *Sir Gawain*, lines 965 and 1822.

79. Smith, Jeremy J. "Chaucer's Use of the Demonstrative." *ES* 93 (2012): 593–603. Discusses Chaucer's use of *this* (e.g., "this carpenter," "this sely man," etc.). Replaces its usual explanation as a colloquialism with a discussion of the changing meaning of demonstrative *this/that* from Old English onward and applies this to several lines in *PardPT*.

80. Zholudeva, Liubov. "*Li livres de confort de Philosophie* by Jean de Meun and *Boece* by Geoffrey Chaucer: The Use of Prepositions (de/of, a/to) and the Problem of French Influence on Middle English." In J. Martin Arista et al., eds. *Convergent Approaches to Medieval English Language and Literature* (*SAC* 36 [2014], no. 81), pp. 159–75. Comparative analysis of *Li livres de confort* and *Bo*, and study of French linguistic influence on English, with special focus on prepositions. The comparison shows a prevailing tendency to reproduce the structures and usages of French, though only in a measured way: Chaucer also substituted French words

and structures with indigenous ones in an attempt to develop English as a literary language.

See also nos. 58, 100, 129, 138, 140, 156, 159, 169, 185, 187, 190, 196, 205, 210, 214, 217.

Background and General Criticism

81. Arista, J. Martin, et al., eds. *Convergent Approaches to Medieval English Language and Literature*. Newcastle upon Tyne: Cambridge Scholars, 2012. xiv, 356 pp. Collection of essays presented at the 22nd International Conference of the Spanish Society for Mediaeval English Language and Literature (SELIM), seeking new perspectives on medieval language study. For two essays pertaining to Chaucer, see nos. 80 and 198.

82. Besserman, Lawrence L. *Biblical Paradigms in Medieval English Literature*. New York: Routledge, 2012. xv, 219 pp. Examines literary paradigms found in works from Caedmon to Malory. Chapter 4 discusses biblical analogies and the "language of love" in *TC*.

83. Bruce, Mark P., and Katherine H. Terrell, eds. *The Anglo-Scottish Border and the Shaping of Identity, 1300–1600*. New York: Palgrave Macmillan, 2012. xii, 235 pp. Contains two articles related to Chaucer. See nos. 36 and 68.

84. Burrow, J. A. *English Poets in the Late Middle Ages: Chaucer, Langland and Others*. Variorum Collected Studies Series. Burlington, Vt.: Ashgate, 2012. 356 pp. Reprints twenty-two of Burrow's essays on fourteenth- and fifteenth-century poetry, including several on Chaucer. Individual essays retain their original pagination.

85. Clements, Pamela, and Carol L. Robinson. "Neomedievalism Unplugged." *SiM* 21 (2012): 191–205. Includes a brief discussion of ways in which authors have integrated medievalist material into curricula of their undergraduate Chaucer classes.

86. Cook, Megan. "How Francis Thynne Read His Chaucer." *JEBS* 15 (2012): 215–43. Son of Chaucer's editor and contemporary of Robert Cotton, Francis Thynne, read as an antiquarian, as evidenced by his objections to Speght's 1598 edition and comparison of his annotations of *Works* (1598) with the annotations of humanist Gabriel Harvey.

87. Cooley, Alice Jane. "Get a Room: Private Space and Private People in Old French and Middle English Love Stories." *DAI* A72.07

(2012): n.p. Considers *TC*, *MilT* and *MerT* as part of an examination of the role of secret intermediaries and seclusion in the apparatus of courtly love.

88. Donavin, Georgiana. *Scribit Mater: Mary and the Language Arts in the Literature of Medieval England*. Washington, D.C.: Catholic University of America Press, 2012. xiii, 315 pp. Investigates "constructions of Mary as Lady Rhetorica, *magistra* for language studies, muse for poetry, and exemplar of perfected speech in a fallen world." Chapter 4, "Chaucer and Dame School," considers how *ABC*, *PrT*, and *SNT* "depict a hierarchy of Marian studies and the Virgin's intervention at every level of language learning," from elementary learning in dame schools to advanced study in the trivium.

89. Donoghue, Daniel, Linda Georgianna, and James Simpson. "C. David Benson: Progress Report." *ChauR* 46, nos. 1–2 (2011): 10–19. Celebrates the character and career of C. David Benson, surveying his publications and professional activities.

90. Elliott, Ralph W. V., ed. L. K. Lloyd Jones. *Chaucer's Landscapes and Other Essays: A Selection of Essays, Speeches, and Reviews Written between 1951 and 2008, with a Memoir*. North Melbourne: Australian Scholarly Publishing, 2010. xii, 422 pp. Anthology of reprinted publications, addresses, and a memoir by R. W. V. Elliott, with topics including Chaucer, the *Gawain*-poet, runes, Thomas Hardy, and others. Two of the three pieces that pertain to Chaucer were published previously, and one is printed here for the first time: "Chaucer: The Canterbury Tales—Printed by William Caxton, 1477" (pp. 287–92), an address to the National Library of Australia in 2002, which describes *CT* and Caxton's decision to print it twice.

91. Fein, Susanna, and David Raybin. "Introduction [to a special double issue]." *ChauR* 46, nos. 1–2 (2011): 1–9. Introduces the essays in a double-issue of *ChauR* dedicated to C. David Benson; includes a black-and-white picture of Benson and a bibliography of his publications.

92. Flood, John. *Representations of Eve in Antiquity and the English Middle Ages*. New York: Routledge, 2010. 193 pp. Traces background of how Eve was understood by Christians in Antiquity and the Middle Ages in England. Explores portrayals of Eve by Augustine, Aquinas, Dante, and Chaucer, and other lesser-known authors. See Chapter 6, "Middle English Literature," for discussion of Chaucer's *CT*.

93. Gilbert, Gaelan. "Chaucerian Afterlives: Reception and Eschatol-

ogy." In Myra Seaman, Eileen A. Joy, and Nicola Masciandaro, eds. *Dark Chaucer: An Assortment* (*SAC* 36 [2014], no. 110), pp. 43–57. Claims that "Chaucer is eschatological" with a recurrent focus on "death, judgment, hell, and heaven," but that he also anticipates in *Ret* how readers might associate Chaucer the author with Chaucer's texts, thus encouraging "a dynamic of textual dispossession."

94. Gorbunov, A[ndreĭ] N[ikolaevich]. *Choser Srednevekovyĭ* [*Chaucer's Medieval*]. Moscow: Labyrinth, 2010. 333 pp. Critical discussion of Chaucer's life and each of his major works, containing a section concerned with the resonances of his poetry in later literature, including Russian literature. Considers social and religious conditions of Chaucer's age, his narrative point of view, and his realism.

95. Hume, Cathy. *Chaucer and the Cultures of Love and Marriage.* Rochester, N.Y.: Brewer, 2012. 244 pp. Reads *CT*, *TC*, and *LGW* in the context of late medieval courtesy books, advice literature, and epistolary collections. Considers public and private marital honor in the Paston letters and *FranT*, and wifely obedience in *ClT*, *Menagier de Paris*, and *Livre de la vertu du sacrement de mariage. ShT* illustrates the limits of women's economic power often suggested by the Paston, Stonor, and Plumpton correspondence, and *MerT* suggests the possibility of rebellion against advice literature. *MLT* goes beyond the conduct books to recommend female acceptance of marital unhappiness. *KnT* presents a pragmatic notion of marriage for the greater sociopolitical good. *TC*, *The Book of the Knight of the Tower*, and Christine de Pizan's *Livre des trois vertus* question courtly ideals, and *LGW* dramatizes its heroines' quasi-comic misapplications of advice literature.

96. Kamath, Stephanie A. Viereck Gibbs. *Authorship and First-Person Allegory in Late Medieval France and England.* Cambridge: Brewer, 2012. ix, 209 pp. Chapter 2 analyzes *CT* briefly, and connects Chaucer's allegorical tradition with Thomas Hoccleve, John Lydgate, and earlier pilgrimage allegories of Guillaume de Deguileville. Discussion of Chaucer's "mediation" of *Rom*.

97. Kelly, Henry Ansgar. "Wives and Their Property in Chaucer's London: Testimony of Hustings Wills." *Studies in Medieval and Renaissance History*, ser. 3, 8 (2011): 81–195. Surveys some 5,000 wills available at the Guildhall Court of Hustings, documenting that, even though the practice was formerly prohibited, property was regularly acquired by wives in late medieval London through the deaths of their husbands.

Such data are paralleled by literary evidence found in *WBP*, *MerT*, and *TC*.

98. Kemmler, Fritz, and Courtnay Konshuh, eds. *Medieval English: Literature and Language*. 4th ed. Tübingen: Gunter Narr, 2008. 394 pp. (5th ed., online resource, 2012). Surveys Old English and Middle English works to determine interconnectedness of the language and texts. Brief discussion of Chaucer's *GP*. Includes glossary and bibliography.

99. Krummel, Mariamne Ara. *Crafting Jewishness in Medieval England: Legally Absent, Virtually Present*. New York: Palgrave Macmillan, 2011. xviii, 243 pp. Provides postcolonial reading of history of Jewish communities and anti-Semitic discourses in medieval England. Chapter 5, "Text and Context: Tracing Chaucer's Moments of Jewishness," discusses Jews in *CT*, focusing on *Th*, and *PrT*.

100. Krygier, Marcin, and Liliana Sikorska, eds. *Þe Comoun Peplis Language*. Frankfurt am Main: Lang, 2010. 154 pp. Eleven essays on Old and Middle English language and literature. For two essays that pertain to Chaucer, see nos. 38 and 71.

101. Lewis, Robert E. "Report of the Chaucer Library Committee." *ChauR* 46, no. 4 (2012): 482–83. Owing to waning interest, the Chaucer Library, which had sought to present the works Chaucer knew, will cease, following the publication of Boccaccio's *Teseida*.

102. McTaggart, Anne. *Shame and Guilt in Chaucer*. New York: Palgrave Macmillan, 2012. 192 pp. *HF*, *TC*, and *CT* more commonly represent shame (an exterior phenomenon) than guilt (an interior one); in dialogue with late medieval penitential theology, they suggest the narrative invisibility of guilt. *HF* and *TC* tackle the plausibility, in pagan contexts, of shame without guilt. *KnT* and *PhyT* correlate communal representations of honor with the necessity of sacrifice to efface communal shame. *WBT*, *FranT*, and *Mel* posit shame's redemptive role in romance. *PardT* plays an embodied narrative shame against the narrative breakdown of guilt-representation in *ParsT*.

103. McTaggart, Anne H. "Shame and Guilt in Chaucer." *DAI* A70.12 (2010): n.p. In Chaucer's poetry, guilt is represented as an "ethical ideal," whereas shame is often "portrayed as the psychological reality" that disrupts attempts to "realize the ideal." Throughout his poetry, but especially in *CT*, Chaucer articulates "the public and private aspects of these emotions," and the "injustice of guiltless shame" is depicted

recurrently in female victims such as Dido, Criseyde, Virginia, and Dorigen.

104. Morgan, Gerald, ed. *Chaucer in Context: A Golden Age of English Poetry*. New York: Peter Lang, 2012. xi, 307 pp. Collection of essays addressing various Chaucerian topics, including "textual authority, poetic design, political affiliations and sympathies, and religious convictions." For essays on Chaucer see nos. 43, 117, 119, 123, 133, 183, 218.

105. Neel, Travis, and Andrew Richmond. "Black as the Crow." In Myra Seaman, Eileen A. Joy, and Nicola Masciandaro, eds. *Dark Chaucer: An Assortment* (*SAC* 36 [2014], no. 110), pp. 103–16. Reviews Chaucer's three uses of a crow (in *ManT*, *PF*, and as a "metaphor for the very blackness of blood" at the end of *KnT*) as a "marker for silence, sterility, and death."

106. Partridge, Stephen B., and Erik Kwakkel. *Author, Reader, Book: Medieval Authorship in Theory and Practice*. Toronto: University of Toronto Press, 2012. vi, 305 pp., illus. Collection of essays related to medieval concepts of authorship, focusing on a variety of vernaculars, languages, and literatures, and the "relationship of authorship to readership." For two essays dealing with Chaucer, see nos. 195 and 197.

107. Robinson, Carol L., and Pamela Clements, eds., with Preface by Richard Utz. *Neomedievalism in the Media: Essays on Film, Television, and Electronic Games*. Lewiston: Edwin Mellen Press, 2012. 424 pp. Series of essays by members of the Medieval Electronic Multimedia Organization (MEMO) related to differing interpretations of neomedievalism in various forms of media. For an essay related to Chaucer, see no. 2.

108. Sánchez-Martí, Jordi. "Patronazgo literario en la Inglaterra medieval (ss. VII–XIV): Una visión panorámica." *Cuadernos del CEMYR* 20 (2012): 93–102. Analysis of literary patronage from the Anglo-Saxon times until the end of the fourteenth century, when royal patronage was essential for authors like Chaucer.

109. Scott-Macnab, David. "The Animals of the Hunt and the Limits of Chaucer's Sympathies." *SAC* 34 (2012): 331–37. Tallies Chaucer's depictions of hunting in *BD*, *LGW*, and *FranT*, and argues that these show a "marked lack of sympathy for animals as quarries," in contrast with other works in Middle English.

110. Seaman, Myra, Eileen A. Joy, and Nicola Masciandaro, eds. *Dark Chaucer: An Assortment*. Brooklyn, N.Y.: Punctum Books, 2012. vii, 201 pp. Available as e-text. A collection of essays highlighting

"dark," unsettling, and culturally unsavory elements across the Chaucer canon. See nos. 48, 60, 93, 105, 131, 150–51, 169, 173, 180, 184, 191, 199, 202, 225, 228.

111. Shuffelton, George G. "Chaucerian Obscenity in the Court of Public Opinion." *ChauR* 47, no. 1 (2012): 1–24. Addresses how Chaucer's bawdiness is perceived in the United States. Includes issues of censorship related to *CT*, with focus on curricula changes over the past few decades.

112. Smith, Nicole D. *Sartorial Strategies: Outfitting Aristocrats and Fashioning Conduct in Late Medieval Literature*. Notre Dame: University of Notre Dame Press, 2012. xi, 281 pp. Studies clothing in imaginative literature, arguing that writers of romances redirect the negative depictions of the courtly body found in clerical chronicles and penitential writings into positive images that convey virtue. While religious and political documents decried the immorality inherent in sumptuous clothing and attempted to restrain the behavior of individuals wearing stylish garments, writers (including Marie de France, Heldris of Cornuälle, the *Gawain*-poet, and Chaucer) reimagine fashion-savvy aristocrats as models of morally sound behavior in a pedagogical program advanced not by preachers but by poets.

113. Spearing, A. C. *Medieval Autographies: The "I" of the Text*. Notre Dame: University of Notre Dame Press, 2012. viii, 347 pp. Suggests we cannot necessarily assume that, in medieval texts, every instance of an "I" must represent a fictionalized narrator who has a persona that can be analyzed and ultimately held responsible for various details of, or problems within, the text. Refers to Chaucer throughout, particularly in Chapter 3, "Chaucerian Prologues and the Wife of Bath."

114. Van Dyke, Carolynn, ed. *Rethinking Chaucerian Beasts*. The New Middle Ages. New York: Palgrave Macmillan, 2012. xiii, 286 pp. Sixteen essays by various authors examine animals in Chaucer, with an Introduction and Afterword that describe the grounds for challenging the "anthropocentric perspective" and align this challenge with feminism and the rejection of hierarchical classifications. The volume includes an index. For the individual essays, see nos. 120, 132, 139, 158, 165–66, 176, 187–88, 200–201, 209, 211–12, 226, 229.

115. Waugh, Robin. *The Genre of Medieval Patience Literature: Development, Duplication, and Gender*. The New Middle Ages. New York: Palgrave Macmillan, 2012. xvi, 230 pp. Details the patience genre in medieval literature. Chapter 5 focuses on Chaucer's female patience

figures, including Griselda in *ClT* and female characters in *LGW*, and compares how Christine de Pizan and Chaucer treat the patience literature genre differently in their works.

116. Wenzel, Siegfried. *Elucidations: Medieval Poetry and Its Religious Backgrounds*. Louvain: Peeters, 2010. xviii, 374 pp. Reprints twenty-seven essays by Wenzel and adds one previously unpublished lecture, "Moral Chaucer?" (pp. 189–204), which considers the "moral life" of Chaucer's characters, focusing on the "decision-making" by the two main characters in *TC*, and including reference to Dorigen in *FranT*. The volume includes a Foreword by Nigel Palmer and a comprehensive index.

117. Windeatt, Barry. "Plea and Petition in Chaucer." In Gerald Morgan, ed. *Chaucer in Context: A Golden Age of English Poetry* (*SAC* 36 [2014], no. 104), pp. 189–216. Argues that petition is an integral part of the "narrative process and imaginative texture of Chaucer's poems," and that it greatly affects poetic meaning. Discusses *Purse* and the F and G versions of *LGWP*, among other poems.

118. Yeager, R. F., and Toshiyuki Takamiya, eds. *The Medieval Python: The Purposive and Provocative Work of Terry Jones*. The New Middle Ages. New York: Palgrave Macmillan, 2012. x, 265 pp. Eighteen essays make up an "*Un*festschrift" that celebrates Terry Jones as a comedian, cinematographer, historian, and Chaucerian. For five contributions that pertain to Chaucer, see nos. 57, 124, 126, 129, 207.

See also nos. 58, 130.

The Canterbury Tales—General

119. Duggan, Anne J. "The Hooly Blisful Martir for to Seke." In Gerald Morgan, ed. *Chaucer in Context: A Golden Age of English Poetry* (*SAC* 36 [2014], no. 104), pp. 15–42. Discusses the shrines and holy places the pilgrims would have visited along their pilgrimage in *CT*.

120. Fradenburg, Aranye. "Among All Beasts: Affective Naturalism in Late Medieval England." In Carolynn Van Dyke, ed. *Rethinking Chaucerian Beasts* (*SAC* 36 [2014], no. 114), pp. 13–31. In some modern views, and in John of Trevisa's *On the Properties of Things*, animals have feelings and communicate. Similarly, *CT* and *PF* demonstrate "the value and pleasure of minds speaking to other minds," whether human or

avian. Late medieval interest in encyclopedic listings of things, including animals, may be a cultural result of the plague.

121. Hagger, Nicholas. *A New Philosophy of Literature: The Fundamental Theme and Unity of World Literature: The Vision of the Infinite and the Universalist Literary Tradition*. Winchester: O-Books, 2012. ix, 529 pp. Surveys metaphysical and secular Universalist traditions in world literatures. Chapter 3, "The Literature of the Middle Ages," includes a summary of *CT* and argues that it depicts a "metaphysical quest" with "metaphysical and secular aspects" of a fundamental Universalist theme.

122. Hanks, Tom. "'His studie was but litel on the Bible': Today's Student and the Bible in *The Canterbury Tales*." *MedPers* 25 (2010): 50–67. Tallies a number of "significant" allusions to the Vulgate Bible in *CT* and offers pedagogical advice on how to remedy the problem of modern students missing these allusions or misreading them.

123. Hughes, Gavin. "Fourteenth-Century Weaponry, Armour and Warfare in Chaucer and *Sir Gawain and the Green Knight*." In Gerald Morgan, ed. *Chaucer in Context: A Golden Age of English Poetry* (*SAC* 36 [2014], no. 104), pp. 83–108. Looks at *CT* and *Sir Gawain and the Green Knight* from a "military historical and archeological perspective." Focuses on the Knight in *GP* and *KnT*, and on warfare scenes in *Th* and *Sir Gawain*.

124. Pearsall, Derek. "Medieval Monks and Friars: Differing Literary Perceptions." In R. F. Yeager and Toshiyuki Takamiya, eds. *The Medieval Python: The Purposive and Provocative Work of Terry Jones* (*SAC* 36 [2014], no. 118), pp. 59–73. Describes various depictions of monks and friars in late medieval English vernacular literature, observing that, despite prevalent anti-fraternal satire, friars "retained considerable support" in this literature. Because they were cloistered, monks generally "receive less attention." Comments on Chaucer's Monk, Friar, and *ShT*, as well as other works of the English Middle Ages.

125. Pitcher, John A. *Chaucer's Feminine Subjects: Figures of Desire in "The Canterbury Tales."* The New Middle Ages. New York: Palgrave Macmillan, 2012. xiv, 200 pp. Analyzes how Chaucer's rhetorical constructions decenter self-disclosure and resist simplistic notions of gender in *WBPT*, *ClT*, *FranT*, and *PhyT*. Figurative or allusive speech cannot adequately represent subjectivity and desire. Chaucer's treatments of the feminine subject are not univocal; however, his tales can both reinforce and undermine cultural and gender norms.

126. Quinn, William A. "The 'Silly' Pacifism of Geoffrey Chaucer and Terry Jones." In R. F. Yeager and Toshiyuki Takamiya, eds. *The Medieval Python: The Purposive and Provocative Work of Terry Jones* (*SAC* 36 [2014], no. 118), pp. 167–79. Corroborates Terry Jones's view that Chaucer was a pacifist, and argues that Jones and Chaucer both use humor and indirection against war. Chaucer was very earnest in his critiques of war in *Mel* and *ParsT*, but less direct in *KnT* and his description of the Knight. Chaucer was downright funny in *Th*, although equally critical of battle.

127. Tracy, Larissa. *Torture and Brutality in Medieval Literature: Negotiations of National Identity*. Cambridge: Brewer, 2012. x, 326 pp. Chapter 5 focuses on comic uses of brutality in *CT*, particularly in *MilT* and *KnT*. Also addresses how Chaucer refers to torture in *MLT*, but rejects excessive brutality in *PrT*.

See also nos. 27, 29, 32–34, 47, 53, 57, 59, 64, 69, 73, 77, 95–96, 102–3, 178, 207.

CT—The General Prologue

128. Leff, Amanda M. "Lydgate Rewrites Chaucer: The *General Prologue* Revisited." *ChauR* 46, no. 4 (2012): 472–79. Examines how Lydgate's *Legend of Dan Joos* recasts the opening of *GP* into a representation of eternal redemption in praise of Mary in his own aureate style.

129. Wallace, David. "Chaucer, Langland, and the Hundred Years' War." In R. F. Yeager and Toshiyuki Takamiya, eds. *The Medieval Python: The Purposive and Provocative Work of Terry Jones* (*SAC* 36 [2014], no. 118), pp. 195–205. Comments on how the Hundred Years War "infiltrates" *CT* by way of "the first trio of portraits" and their depictions of late medieval warfare. Clarifies the meaning of *chyvachie* in the description of the Squire and dilates upon the significance of the English occupation of Calais, which shared a border with the places where the Squire fought.

See also nos. 17, 45, 98, 113, 209.

CT—The Knight and His Tale

130. Brewer, Derek. "A Note on *The World of Chaucer*." *PoeticaT* 73 (2010): 1–8. Brewer comments on his professional visits to Japan; on

similarities between Japanese and European medieval cultures; and on promises, honor, and irony in Chaucer's poetry, especially *KnT*.

131. Bryant, Brantley L., et al. "Saturn's Darkness." In Myra Seaman, Eileen A. Joy, and Nicola Masciandaro, eds. *Dark Chaucer: An Assortment* (*SAC* 36 [2014], no. 110), pp. 13–27. Explores the contrast between Theseus and Saturn in *KnT* as a metaphor for the lives of modern academic Chaucerians.

132. Gutmann, Sara. "Chaucer's Chicks: Feminism and Falconry in 'The Knight's Tale,' 'The Squire's Tale,' and *The Parliament of Fowls*." In Carolynn Van Dyke, ed. *Rethinking Chaucerian Beasts* (*SAC* 36 [2014], no. 114), pp. 69–83. Although some falconers were female, the activity of training (often female) falcons is highly gendered. The necessity for the falcon to be tamed is paralleled in the need for Emelye in *KnT* to submit to heterosexual marriage, and for Canacee in *SqT* to be "managed" by powerful males.

133. Morgan, Gerald. "Chaucer's *Knight's Tale*: The Book of the Duke." In Morgan, ed. *Chaucer in Context: A Golden Age of English Poetry* (*SAC* 36 [2014], no. 104), pp. 153–88. Examines the characterization of Theseus in *KnT*, comparing it with that of Boccaccio's Teseo and arguing that Chaucer depicts an ideal of moral worth, aristocratic justice, knightly virtue, and nobility of conquest.

134. Morris, Max, ed. *Classic Love Poems*. Chichester: Summersdale, 2010. 222 pp. Anthology of romantic lyrics and excerpts from English language poets, from Chaucer to Elizabeth Barrett Browning. Includes lines from *KnT* in Middle English.

135. Rack, Melissa J. "'I nam no divinistre': Heterodoxy and Disjunction in Chaucer's 'Knight's Tale.'" *MedPers* 25 (2010): 89–102. Argues that Chaucer does not resolve in *KnT* the disjunction between Aristotelian natural philosophy and Christian theology that is found in medieval university discourse; instead, he amplifies the tension to allow the "freeplay of interpretation." Focuses on Arcite's death and Theseus's final speech.

136. Salter, David. "'We stryve as dide the houndes for the boon': Animals and Chaucer's Romance Vision." *SAC* 34 (2012): 339–44. Explicates comparisons between lovers and animals in *KnT*, suggesting that Chaucer uses them to expose human folly.

137. Teramura, Misha. "The Anxiety of *Auctoritas*: Chaucer and *The Two Noble Kinsmen*." *Shakespeare Quarterly* 63, no. 4 (2012): 544–76. Analyzes John Fletcher's and William Shakespeare's collaboration on

The Two Noble Kinsmen, an interpretation of *KnT*, and offers how *The Two Noble Kinsmen* represents a "meditation . . . of the vernacular literary canon," as it allegorizes the treatment of *auctoritas* and Chaucer's influence.

138. Wadiak, Walter. "Chaucer's 'Knight's Tale' and the Politics of Distinction." *PQ* 89 (2010): 159–84. Explores Chaucer's "engagement with romance by looking at his treatment of adventure—both the word and the idea." In his romances, particularly in *KnT*, Chaucer rejects the "symbolic capital" of popular adventure in order to claim "literary prestige," part of his agenda of "self-laureation." Adventure in *Th* helps to clarify its lack in *KnT*, and Arcite's rejections of material goods mirrors Chaucer's rejection of symbolic capital.

139. Withers, Jeremy. "'A beest may al his lust fulfille': Naturalizing Chivalric Violence in Chaucer's 'Knight's Tale.'" In Carolynn Van Dyke, ed. *Rethinking Chaucerian Beasts* (*SAC* 36 [2014], no. 114), pp. 173–83. In *KnT*, warriors are compared to animals, a seemingly desirable condition that would allow warriors to "discharge at will their power and violence." However, several references to shackled, confined, or endangered animals create a contrast between warrior self-identification with animals and animals' subjugation in the realm of chivalric warfare.

See also nos. 21, 45, 59, 69, 95, 102, 105, 123, 126, 127, 151.

CT—The Miller and His Tale

140. Hardwick, Paul. "Talking Dirty: Vernacular Language and the Lower Body." In Hardwick, ed. *The Playful Middle Ages: Meanings of Play and Plays of Meaning. Essays in Memory of Elaine C. Block* (Turnhout: Brepols, 2010), pp. 81–91. Explores intersections of vernacularity and scatology in *MilT* and *Til Eulenspiegel*, commenting on how use of the *kultour* in *MilT* plays upon the Knight's earlier reference to a plough and undermines clerical discourse in which the plough is a "traditional analogue of the preacher's word."

141. Hühn, Peter. "Geoffrey Chaucer: *The Miller's Tale* (ca. 1390–1400)." In Hühn et al., eds. *Eventfulness in British Fiction* (New York: Walter de Gruyter, 2010), pp. 17–30. Examines the tripartite plot structure of *MilT* and its "two oppositional" contexts, i.e., the ethical demands of its religious allusions and the subversiveness of its fabliau

genre. The combination produces a "complex event structure full of suspense" and a sense of "poetic justice" guided by reason.

142. Smith, Peter J. *Between Two Stools: Scatology and Its Representations in English Literature, Chaucer to Swift*. Manchester: Manchester University Press, 2012. xii, 292 pp. In "Turning the Other Cheek: Scatology and Its Discontents in *The Miller's Tale* and *The Summoner's Tale*," pp. 12–59, Smith uses farting in *MilT* and *SumT* to explore Chaucer's complex and refined "scatological rhetoric," a trope that has been obscured by frequent bowdlerizing of these tales.

143. Stanbury, Sarah. "Derrida's Cat and Nicholas's Study." *NML* 12 (2010): 155–67. Considers the cat in *MilT* as a device of demarcation between the domesticity of John's house and the privacy of Nicholas's "elite" study, observing links between this use of an animal as a device and Derrida's contemplations on his cat. Also considers connections between Nicholas's study and that of Petrarch, who treasured his cat enough to mummify it. Includes 5 black-and-white figures.

See also nos. 78, 87, 127.

CT—The Reeve and His Tale

CT—The Cook and His Tale

144. Cartlidge, Neil. "Wayward Sons and Failing Fathers: Chaucer's Moralistic Paternalism—and a Possible Source for the 'Cook's Tale.'" *ChauR* 47, no. 2 (2012): 134–60. Suggests possible sources for Chaucer's ideas on parenthood that influenced *CkT*, including the "Wisdom commentary of Dominican friar, Robert Holcot." Also compares Holcot's views on parental responsibility in *PhyT*.

See also nos. 17, 33.

CT—The Man of Law and His Tale

145. Birns, Nicholas. "'To Aleppo gone': From the North Sea to Syria in Chaucer's *Man of Law's Tale* and Shakespeare's *Macbeth*." *Exemplaria* 24 (2012): 364–84. In *MLT*, Custance's first husband is the "Sowdan of Surrye," and in *Macbeth* the witches plot to scourge a shipmaster who is "to Aleppo gone." That both texts treat Syria and the

northern reaches of Great Britain as complementary zones, in space as well as time, permits a plausible linkage between *MLT* and *Macbeth*, and a common awareness of Islamic and Christian otherness.

146. Donoghue, Emma. *Inseparable: Desire between Women in Literature*. New York: Knopf, 2010. x, 271 pp., b&w illus. A topically arranged survey of female same-sex desire in western literature, with a brief discussion of *MLT* as "perhaps the earliest example in English" where "mutual passion between two women . . . moves the story along."

147. Johnston, Andrew James. "The Exigencies of 'Latyn corrupt': Linguistic Change and Historical Consciousness in Chaucer's *Man of Law's Tale*." In Claudia Lange, Beatrix Weber, and Göran Wolf, eds. *Communicative Spaces: Variation, Contact, and Change: Papers in Honour of Ursula Schaefer* (Frankfurt: Peter Lang, 2012), pp. 133–46. Interprets Custance's use of "Latyn corrupt" to the natives of Northumbria in terms of Isidore of Seville's discussion of linguistic history and suggests that *MLT* takes an acutely historicist view of the development of medieval Christianity, questioning Christianity's imperial Roman heritage, and privileging instead its vernacular and local traditions.

148. Lynch, Kathryn L. " 'Diversitee bitwene hir bothe lawes': Chaucer's Unlikely Alliance of a Lawyer and a Merchant." *ChauR* 46, nos. 1–2 (2011): 74–92. Considers how the "professional identity" of the teller informs concerns with justice in *MLT*. Engagement with mercantile law, common law, natural law, divine intervention, and the "limitations of human justice" pervade *MLPT* and indicate an uncertain sense of their relations and hierarchy.

149. McGregor, Francine. "Abstraction and Particularity in Chaucer's *Man of Law's Tale*." *ChauR* 46, nos. 1–2 (2011): 60–73. Assesses the relations between universality and particularity as epistemological modes in *MLT*, exploring allegory and individuality, realism and nominalism, and generalization and specification in the characterization of Custance and how she is perceived by the other characters. The Tale offers no "unified theory of perception," suggesting instead that perception is "layered."

150. Priest, Hannah. "Unravelling Constance." In Myra Seaman, Eileen A. Joy, and Nicola Masciandaro, eds. *Dark Chaucer: An Assortment* (*SAC* 36 [2014], no. 110), pp. 117–23. Meditates fictively on Custance and her loss of identity.

151. Steel, Karl. "Kill Me, Save Me, Let Me Go: Custance, Virginia, Emelye." In Myra Seaman, Eileen A. Joy, and Nicola Masciandaro, eds.

Dark Chaucer: An Assortment (*SAC* 36 [2014], no. 110), pp. 151–60. Explores Custance, Virginia, and Emelye as women who recognize they are characters in someone else's narratives. Also suggests that Chaucer was similarly constrained by his sources, leaving him too without freedom to be his own self.

See also nos. 21, 38, 77, 95, 127, 154.

CT—The Wife of Bath and Her Tale

152. Brady, Lindy. "Antifeminist Tradition in *Arthur and Gorlagon* and the Quest to Understand Women." *N&Q* 257 (2012): 163–66. *Arthur and Gorlagon* and *WBPT* share numerous misogynist topoi as well as the plot element of a mission to understand women. The Latin romance is thus "a more significant analogue for the combined *Prologue* and *Tale* . . . than has been recognized."

153. Davis, Isabel. "Calling: Langland, Gower, and Chaucer on Saint Paul." *SAC* 34 (2012): 53–97. Explores relations between concepts of selfhood and notions of spiritual and, especially, secular vocation in *WBT*, Langland's *Piers Plowman*, and Gower's *Vox clamantis*. The "wide scope" of late medieval applications of the Pauline notion of being "called" includes both the need for renewal and the "spiritual recoverability of the imperfect life." Assesses the Wife of Bath as a provisional "advocate of the messianic life" and comments on vocation or calling in *HF*.

154. Ladd, Roger A. "Selling Alys: Reading (with) the Wife of Bath." *SAC* 34 (2012): 141–71. Explores Chaucer's strategy of satire in *WBPT*, arguing that in its concern with interpretation and discursive insensibility it is fundamentally similar to the anti-mercantile satire of *MerT*, *ShT*, and *MLT*. Reads the Wife in "a London context," associating her with guild-class silkwomen, and hypothesizes Chaucer's series of revisions to the Wife of Bath materials (including the manuscript glosses), which reduces mercantile concerns to those of gender and marriage while maintaining effective satire of the merchant estate.

155. Mandel, Jerome. "Conflict Resolution in *The Wife of Bath's Tale* and in Gower's *Tale of Florent*." *ES revista de filología inglesa* 33, no. 1 (2012): 69–79. Compares the resolutions of conflict in *WBT* and Gower's *Tale of Florent* and explores their methods of characterization. While Chaucer depicts characters through dialogue, argument, debate, and

negotiation with other persons, Gower's characters resolve conflicts through internal reflection on principles and the sanctioned rule.

156. Rigg, A. G. "The Wife of Bath's 'Sweet Because.'" *N&Q* 257 (2012): 315–16. Two Anglo-Latin "celibacy poems" use *quoniam* to mean the same thing that it means in *WBP*, prompting the question, might a "joke have been circulating among thirteenth and fourteenth century clerics, that every *quare* has its *quoniam*?"

157. Swinford, Dean. "*The Wife of Bath's Tale* (Geoffrey Chaucer)." In Blake Hobby, ed. *The Trickster*. Bloom's Literary Themes (New York: Bloom's Literary Criticism, 2010), pp. 229–39. Explores how *WBT* "ironizes the quest motif at the heart" of the romance genre and assesses the extent to which the loathly lady, the knight, and the Wife of Bath may be considered to be tricksters.

158. Wang, Laura. "Reimagining Natural Order in 'The Wife of Bath's Prologue.'" In Carolynn Van Dyke, ed. *Rethinking Chaucerian Beasts* (*SAC* 36 [2014], no. 114), pp. 131–42. Classical and medieval antifeminist texts disparagingly compare women and animals. In *WBP*, Alisoun "redeploys animal similes" to claim the privileges of animal-like status because she is naturally crafty and sly, impatient, and cannot be held responsible. Alisoun also "animalizes" Jankyn by comparing him to a lion and sheep, "deflating notions of masculine supremacy" and celebrating humans' animal nature.

See also nos. 12, 20, 22, 45, 63, 69, 77, 97, 102, 113, 125.

CT—The Friar and His Tale

159. Raybin, David. "'Goddes Instrumentz': Devils and Free Will in the *Friar's* and *Summoner's Tales*." *ChauR* 46, nos. 1–2 (2011): 93–110. The language and imagery of demonic temptation versus human free will connect *FrT* and *SumT* and gain dimension by comparison with *ClT*. Thomas of *SumT* is called "demonyak," but his scatological riposte to the friar is justified anger.

See also nos. 124, 179.

CT—The Summoner and His Tale

160. Crane, Susan. "Cat, Capon, and Pig in *The Summoner's Tale*." *SAC* 34 (2012): 319–24. References to animals presented as "sentient

beings" in *SumT* convey the friar's "spiritual weakness," perhaps reflecting oral traditions of Franciscan ideals.

See also nos. 77, 142, 159, 179.

CT—The Clerk and His Tale

161. Behrman, Mary. "Biding Time: Knowledge and the Balance of Power in *The Clerk's Tale*." *MedPers* 25 (2010): 7–20. Argues that Chaucer (like Michel Foucault) understands power to be, at times, in the control of the "traditionally powerless" (e.g., servants and women), largely because they have subversive knowledge of their subjugators' private behavior. In *ClT*, for example, Griselda warns the tyrannical Walter that she will reveal his secrets to the Bolognese aristocracy and thereby compels her husband to treat her in a new way, even though much of the warning is couched in wordplay.

162. Fernández Rodríguez, Carmen María. "*The Canterbury Tales* in the Nineteenth Century: Maria Edgeworth's *The Modern Griselda*." In Elizabeth Woodward Smith, ed. *About Culture* (Santiago de Compostela: Universidade de Coruña, 2004), pp. 139–46. Describes Maria Edgeworth's view of the education of women through her adaptation of *ClT* in *The Modern Griselda* (1805), intended as a warning against sensibility and defense of rational women.

163. Green, Richard Firth. "Why Marquis Walter Treats His Wife So Badly." *ChauR* 47, no. 1 (2012): 48–62. Presents a version of the Griselda story from Thomas III, Marquis of Saluzzo (c. 1355–1416) in *Le chevalier errant*, and analyzes how fourteenth-century audiences would have reacted to Chaucer's version in *ClT*. Includes a translation of Thomas's version of Griselda's story.

See also nos. 21, 45, 49, 62, 69, 95, 115, 125, 159.

CT—The Merchant and His Tale

164. McDonie, R. Jacob. "'Ye get namoore of me': Narrative, Textual, and Linguistic Desires in Chaucer's *Merchant's Tale*." *Exemplaria* 24 (2012): 313–41. Argues that genre and the discourses of desire in *MerT* prove too strong for the narrator, who is constantly conflicted about his

presentation not only of linguistic and narrative desires but also of the psychoanalytic displacements of these desires.

See also nos. 75, 87, 95, 97, 154.

CT—The Squire and His Tale

165. Schotland, Sara Deutch. "Avian Hybridity in 'The Squire's Tale': Uses of Anthropomorphism." In Carolynn Van Dyke, ed. *Rethinking Chaucerian Beasts* (*SAC* 36 [2014], no. 114), pp. 115–30. In *SqT* Chaucer practices a form of anthropomorphism that acknowledges its representational limits. The relationship of Canacee and the falcon shows "a commonality among living creatures" and offers a model of female friendship. Canacee nurses the falcon and the falcon warns Canacee about "male betrayal," providing an example of "protective and reciprocal care."

166. Stock, Lorraine Kochanske. "Foiled by Fowl: The Squire's Peregrine Falcon and the Franklin's Dorigen." In Carolynn Van Dyke, ed. *Rethinking Chaucerian Beasts* (*SAC* 36 [2014], no. 114), pp. 85–100. Themes of *trouthe* and *gentillesse*, as well as the threat of suicide, in the *SqT* falcon episode (V.409–631) anticipate major themes of *FranT*. Because *SqT* is prior in the narrative sequence, the human language of *FranT* parodies avian language rather than vice versa. The falcon episode is a "foil" for Dorigen's complaint (V.1355–1456).

167. Williams, Tara. "Magic, Spectacle, and Morality in the Fourteenth Century." *NML*12 (2010): 179–208. Argues that a "relationship between magic, spectacle, and morality . . . preoccupies a number" of fourteenth-century Middle English texts, focusing on the magical objects in *SqT* and other instances of magic in *CT* to exemplify the variety and complexities of the relationship. Considers at length how Canacee's ring links magic to morality because it "facilitates true communication."

See also nos. 67, 69, 129, 132.

CT—The Franklin and His Tale

168. Kao, Wan-Chuan. "Conduct Shameful and Unshameful in 'The Franklin's Tale.'" *SAC* 34 (2012): 99–139. Interrogates post-

Enlightenment understandings of shame, and argues that in *FranT* shame negotiates continua rather than dichotomies (men/women, courtly love/marriage, and public/private). Read in light of conduct literature, Arveragus's claims and actions expose the "gender asymmetries in companionate marriage," while Dorigen's complaint, by mimicking devotional programs, defers shame and she acquires "a queer female masculinity." The Franklin is "an effective but feminized manager of shame," and the "affective labor of shame" in his Tale regulates "selves within the middling household."

169. Mitchell, J. Allan. "In the Event of the *Franklin's Tale*." In Myra Seaman, Eileen A. Joy, and Nicola Masciandaro, eds. *Dark Chaucer: An Assortment* (*SAC* 36 [2014], no. 110), pp. 91–102. Demonstrates how the resolution of *FranT* turns on so much semantic play with *fre* that the ending itself remains unresolved or *fre*.

170. Otis-Cour, Leah. "True Lover/False Lover, 'franquise dete': Dichotomies in the 'Franklin's Tale' and Their Analogue in Richard de Fournival's 'Consaus d'amours.'" *ChauR* 47, no. 2 (2012): 160–86. Offers Richard de Fournival's *Consaus d'amours*, a thirteenth-century French *art d'aimer* (art of love), as a possible source for *FranT*.

171. Parsons, Ben. "No Laughing Matter: Fraud, the Fabliau and Chaucer's *Franklin's Tale*." *Neophil* 96 (2012): 121–36. The already diffuse mixture of accepted sources for *FranT* is complemented here with an argument favoring a debt to French fabliaux.

See also nos. 21, 67, 95, 102–3, 109, 116, 125, 166, 179.

CT—The Physician and His Tale

172. Pigg, Daniel F. "Does the Punishment Fit the Crime?: Chaucer's *Physician's Tale* and the Worlds of Judgment." In Albrecht Classen and Connie Scarborough, eds. *Crime and Punishment in the Middle Ages and Early Modern Age* (Berlin: Walter de Gruyter, 2012), pp. 347–58. Argues that *PhyT* not only addresses changes in the medieval social power structure, but also serves as a "critique of masculine power" within the medieval European court system.

173. Treharne, Elaine. "The Physician's Tale as Hagioclasm." In Myra Seaman, Eileen A. Joy, and Nicola Masciandaro, eds. *Dark Chaucer: An Assortment* (*SAC* 36 [2014], no. 110), pp. 161–71. Reads *PhyT*

as a deliberate inversion of hagiography, seen particularly in its failure to end with any positive consequences of the martyrdom.

174. Yeager, R. F. "Gower and Chaucer on Pain and Suffering: Jepte's Daughter in the Bible, the 'Physician's Tale' and the *Confessio Amantis*." In Esther Cohen, Leona Toker, Manuela Consonni, and Otniel E. Dror, eds. *Knowledge and Pain* (New York: Rodopi, 2012), pp. 43–62. Unlike their biblical source, Chaucer's and Gower's allusions to Jephthah's daughter indicate concern with pain and emotional suffering. Also considers the illustration in Pierpont Morgan Library, MS M.126 that accompanies Gower's tale of Virginia in *Confessio Amantis*.

See also nos. 51, 60, 102–3, 125, 144, 151.

CT—The Pardoner and His Tale

175. Coleman, Joyce. "Philippa of Lancaster, Queen of Portugal—and Patron of the Gower Translations?" In María Bullón-Fernández, ed. *England and Iberia in the Middle Ages, 12th–15th Century: Cultural, Literary, and Political Exchanges* (New York: Palgrave Macmillan, 2007), pp. 135–65. Argues that Philippa of Lancaster, married to King João I of Portugal in 1387, sponsored the Portuguese and Castilian translations of Gower's *Confessio Amantis*, and may have been responsible for an analogue to *PardT* found in Hermegildo de Tancos's *Orto do esposo*.

176. Feinstein, Sandy, and Neal Woodman. "Shrews, Rats, and a Polecat in 'The Pardoner's Tale.'" In Carolynn Van Dyke, ed. *Rethinking Chaucerian Beasts* (*SAC* 36 [2014], no. 114), pp. 49–66. The Pardoner is compared to a hare, goat, and horse, but his Tale refers to smaller animals usually considered vermin. The three gluttonous rioters are appropriately called shrews, and the poison used to kill them is ostensibly bought for rats and a polecat. In the exemplum, however, animals are innocent and it is the rioters, and the Pardoner himself, who are "vermin."

177. Henson, Chelsea. "Hyperreal Blessings: Simulated Relics in *The Pardoner's Tale*." *Quidditas* 33 (2012): 59–78. Viewed in light of Jean Baudrillard's *Simulacra and Simulation*, the Pardoner's relics are simulacra, which allows Chaucer to question their "realness." The textuality of *PardT* (and *CT* as a whole) is to be read as a hyperreality.

178. Rabiee, Robert Yusef. "Rhetoric of Hypocrisy: The Pardoner's Reproduction in His Critics." *Comitatus* 43 (2012): 79–94. Posits the

centrality of the Pardoner (rather than the marginality assumed by many critics) to *CT*. The "confidence game" of his narration parallels Chaucer's own rhetorical approach and informs those of his critics. Chaucer illustrates the self-negating nature of such rhetoric; the institutions (ecclesiastical, literary, academic) that enable and helpfully obscure narrative hypocrisy will inevitably be destabilized by that narrative.

See also nos. 43, 67, 69, 77, 79, 102.

CT—The Shipman and His Tale

See nos. 95, 124, 154.

CT—The Prioress and Her Tale

179. Ruud, Jay. "Chaucer, the Prioress, and the Resurrection of the Body." *MedPers* 24 (2009): 59–70. Looking at *FrT*; *SumPT*; *PardT*; and, primarily, *PrT* (particularly its presentation of martyrdom, sainthood, and virginity), argues that "Chaucer's attitude toward the doctrine of the resurrection is . . . consistently conservative," for he thinks "material continuity [is necessary] to preserve personal identity." Suggests that Chaucer's attitude is more Augustinian than Thomistic, Aristotelian, or Dantean.

180. Weston, Lisa. "Suffer the Little Children; or, A Rumination on the Faith of Zombies." In Myra Seaman, Eileen A. Joy, and Nicola Masciandaro, eds. *Dark Chaucer: An Assortment* (*SAC* 36 [2014], no. 110), pp. 181–90. Imagines the singing clergeon of *PrT* as a sort of zombie whose zombie faith is echoed by the Prioress.

See also nos. 88, 99, 127.

CT—The Tale of Sir Thopas

181. Best, Debra. "Chaucer's Sir Olifaunt and the Knowledge of Humorous Romance Giants." *MedPers* 25 (2010): 21–30. Exemplifies the traditional humor that derives from exaggeration in depictions of giants in Middle English romance, and argues that, in *Th*, Chaucer goes "one step further" in making Olifaunt ridiculous, largely because this giant is seen from the perspective of Sir Thopas, himself ridiculous.

Points out that Sir Olifaunt "is the only three-headed giant in Middle English literature."

182. Jager, Katharine. "'Som deyntee thyng': Poetry and Possibility In Chaucer's *Tale of Sir Thopas*." *MedPers* 24 (2009): 33–45. Focusing on poetic form, seeks "to combine both literary aesthetics and late medieval history in a new formalist reading of *Th*," considering the poem's "aestheticized, satirical and popular poetics" and its larger historical and socioeconomic contexts.

183. Scott-Macnab, David. "Sir Thopas and His Lancegay." In Gerald Morgan, ed. *Chaucer in Context: A Golden Age of English Poetry* (*SAC* 36 [2014], no. 104), pp. 109–34. Discusses the significance of Sir Thopas's lancegay as a weapon of choice, and why Chaucer chose this weapon.

184. White, Thomas. "The Dark Is Light Enough: The Layout of the Tale of Sir Thopas." In Myra Seaman, Eileen A. Joy, and Nicola Masciandaro, eds. *Dark Chaucer: An Assortment* (*SAC* 36 [2014], no. 110), pp. 191–203. Suggests that the textual layout of *Th* is authorial in the Ellesmere, Hengwrt, Cambridge MS Gg.II.27, and Dd.IV.24 copies of *Th*. Because other manuscripts do not adhere to this layout, they exemplify how scribes interpret texts rather than transmit them faithfully. Includes a diplomatic edition of the layout of *Th* as found in Oxford, Christ Church, MS 152.

See also nos. 22, 41, 99, 123, 126, 138.

CT—The Tale of Melibee

185. Hill, Thomas D. "Chaucer's Parabolic Narrative: The Prologue to the *Tale of Melibee*, Lines 953–58." *ChauR* 47, no. 1 (2012): 365–70. The semantic range of *proverbs*, and Chaucer's emphasis on the word, indicates that *Mel* is a series of parables, or allegorical narratives.

See also nos. 102, 126.

CT—The Monk and His Tale

186. Binski, Paul. "The Painted Chamber of Westminster, the Fall of Tyrants and the English Literary Model of Governance." *Journal of the Warburg and Courtauld Institutes* 74 (2011): 121–54. Discusses biblical

kings represented in the *camera depicta* of the Westminster Chamber, also treated in several literary works on kingship, including *MkT* and a short passage in *ParsT*. The Chamber's murals proclaim the Plantagenet kings to be "ideal just warriors" and warn that immorality in a royal family "becomes a pathology of the state."

See also nos. 67, 124.

CT—The Nun's Priest and His Tale

187. Browne, Megan Palmer. "Chaucer's Chauntecleer and Animal Morality." In Carolynn Van Dyke, ed. *Rethinking Chaucerian Beasts* (*SAC* 36 [2014], no. 114), pp. 203–15. *NPT* demonstrates the danger of reading "for a single abstract moral" by means of its emphasis on Chauntecleer's humanlike qualities. Among his most human attributes are experiencing and expounding a dream. If *men* refers to both humans and chickens, the tale treats both Chauntecleer and the widow as leading good, virtuous lives; the poem's *moralite* calls readers to live an engaged but reflective life.

188. Freeman, Carol. "Feathering the Text." In Carolynn Van Dyke, ed. *Rethinking Chaucerian Beasts* (*SAC* 36 [2014], no. 114), pp. 33–47. Describes the specific appearance of vellum, the types of quills used in creating a medieval manuscript, and animal-inflicted damage to manuscripts by mice, bugs, etc. Intersperses discussion of *NPT* with regard to Chauntecleer's appearance and animals' desires for sex and for freedom.

189. Landy, Joshua. *How to Do Things with Fictions*. Oxford: Oxford University Press, 2012. 266 pp. Applies understanding of literary texts, including Chaucer's *CT*, to ideas of everyday life. Chapter 1, "Chaucer: Ambiguity and Ethics," addresses the benefits of using *NPT*, in particular, to teach ethics and issues of morality.

190. Rudd, Gillian. " 'rather be used / than be eaten'? Harry Bailly's Animals and *The Nun's Priest's Tale*." *SAC* 34 (2012): 325–30. Comments on Umberto Eco's, Jacques Derrida's, and Marianne Dekoven's contributions to animal studies, and assesses the Host's references to *jade* and *trede-fowl* in *NPP* and *NPE* as "prime examples" of the "human habit of appropriating the animal world." Also assesses the chase scene in *NPT*.

See also no. 67.

CT—The Second Nun and Her Tale

191. Masciandaro, Nicola. "Half Dead: Parsing Cecilia." In Myra Seaman, Eileen A. Joy, and Masciandaro, eds. *Dark Chaucer: An Assortment* (*SAC* 36 [2014], no. 110), pp. 71–90. Considers the anonymous executioner and the three strokes required to execute Cecilia in *SNT*.

192. Robertson, Elizabeth. "Apprehending the Divine and Choosing to Believe: Voluntarist Free Will in Chaucer's *Second Nun's Tale*." *ChauR* 46, nos. 1–2 (2011): 111–30. Argues that *SNT* "presents conversion as a choice stimulated by apprehension of the divine through the senses" and accomplished by a "radical act of the will, unmediated and immediate, if not inherently violent."

See also no. 88.

CT—The Canon's Yeoman and His Tale

CT—The Manciple and His Tale

193. Gorst, Emma. "Interspecies Mimicry: Birdsong in Chaucer's *Manciple's Tale* and *The Parlement of Fowles*." *NML* 12 (2010): 147–54. Considers the speaking birds in *ManT* and *PF* for the ways they suggest the "destabilization of human identity." Also considers the topic in the late fourteenth-century tale, *The Woman and the Three Parrots*.

194. Hodder, Karen. "Wordsworth and Chaucer's *Manciple's Tale*." In Karen Hodder and Brendan O'Connell, eds. *Transmission and Generation in Medieval and Renaissance Literature: Essays in Honour of John Scattergood* (Dublin: Four Courts Press, 2012), pp. 141–52. Discusses Wordsworth's modernization of *ManT*, which was commissioned for Thomas Powell's *The Poems of Geoffrey Chaucer Moderniz'd* (1841) but eventually suppressed by Wordsworth's wife.

195. Obermeier, Anita. "The Censorship Trope in Geoffrey Chaucer's *Manciple's Tale* as Ovidian Metaphor in a Gowerian and Ricardian Context." In Stephen B. Partridge and Erik Kwakkel, eds. *Author, Reader, Book: Medieval Authorship in Theory and Practice* (*SAC* 36 [2014], no. 106), pp. 80–105. Describes Gower's and Chaucer's "metaphorical and historical connections to Richard II," as reflected in *ManT*.

See also no. 105.

CT—The Parson and His Tale

196. Thomas, Arvind. "What's *Myrie* about the Prose of the *Parson's Tale*?" *ChauR* 46, no. 4 (2012): 419–38. Analyzes the Parson's use of *myrie* in *ParsP* in terms of the "internal generic matrix" constructed by the Parson in the *ParsT*. Focuses on Tzvetan Todorov's and Paul Strohm's writings on genre.

See also nos. 45, 57, 77, 102, 126, 186.

CT—Chaucer's Retraction

197. Partridge, Stephen B. "'The Makere of this Boke': Chaucer's *Retraction* and the Author as Scribe and Compiler." In Partridge and Erik Kwakkel, eds. *Author, Reader, Book: Medieval Authorship in Theory and Practice* (*SAC* 36 [2014], no. 106), pp. 106–53. Argues that *Ret* elevates Chaucer's status as author, and creates the "illusion of Chaucer's presence and agency" for the reader of *CT*. Connects Chaucer's use of *Ret* to French literary culture, which helped define Chaucer's own sense of authorship.

See also no. 93.

Anelida and Arcite

A Treatise on the Astrolabe

See nos. 56, 72.

Boece

198. Gutiérrez Arranz, José María. "From O qui perpetua to Allas! I wepynge: A Long Journey into Boethius's Intimations with Philosophy." In J. Martin Arista et al., eds. *Convergent Approaches to Medieval English Language and Literature* (*SAC* 36 [2014], no. 81), pp. 293–311. Following a discussion of classical and medieval translation, imitation,

commentary, and glossing, tabulates the sources of *Bo*—with newly proposed titles that fuse *interpretatio* and *exercitatio*.

See also nos. 72, 80.

The Book of the Duchess

199. Evans, Ruth. "A Dark Stain and a Non-Encounter." In Myra Seaman, Eileen A. Joy, and Nicola Masciandaro, eds. *Dark Chaucer: An Assortment* (*SAC* 36 [2014], no. 110), pp. 29–41. Concentrates on Ceyx and Alcyone's encounter in *BD* as a communication failure that aligns with a series of other failed attempts at communication throughout the poem.

200. Judkins, Ryan R. "Animal Agency, the Black Knight, and the Hart in *The Book of the Duchess*." In Carolynn Van Dyke, ed. *Rethinking Chaucerian Beasts* (*SAC* 36 [2014], no. 114), pp. 159–72. Although anthropocentric, *BD* emphasizes the similarity of animals and humans under the law of *kynde*. They share an "embodied state and an ethical system as a result of their shared creation." The hart, object of the hunt, parallels the Black Knight's heart, and Chaucer uses this parallel to counsel John of Gaunt to overcome his grief.

201. Roman, Christopher. "Contemplating Finitude: Animals in *The Book of the Duchess*." In Carolynn Van Dyke, ed. *Rethinking Chaucerian Beasts* (*SAC* 36 [2014], no. 114), pp. 143–55. Animals figure prominently in *BD* but are more than mere symbols. Seys's dead body is also an "unnatural animal." The birds, horse, whelp, and hart invite, but also resist, interpretation. The juxtaposition of death and animalistic vitality evokes grief, which itself is the simultaneous awareness of being present in life and of death. The animals in the poem help us to "think about finitude."

202. Seaman, Myra. "Disconsolate Art." In Seaman, Eileen A. Joy, and Nicola Masciandaro, eds. *Dark Chaucer: An Assortment* (*SAC* 36 [2014], no. 110), pp. 139–49. Rejects conventional readings of *BD* as a demonstration that art can transcend suffering; instead shows how *BD* "enacts . . . a disconsolate poetics, in which pain and suffering perdure."

203. Takada, Yasunari. "Chaucer's Allergy." *PoeticaT* 73 (2010): 55–65. Argues that Chaucer is "constitutionally sensitive" to intellectual realism, preferring sensory experientialism instead. In *BD*, as in *HF* and

PF, inconclusiveness and tentativeness defer rather than console and encourage a "broader mundane perspective" than is traditional in the dream-vision genre.

See also no. 109.

The Equatorie of the Planetis

The House of Fame

204. Blake, Nicola. "Narrative Play: Medieval Dream Narrators and Poetic Process." *DAI* A72.12 (2012): n.p. Examines *HF* and other medieval dream-visions from a stand-point of performance theory, while considering the role of the narrator/dreamer as perceiver and creator of meaning, with ramifications for how narrative may be viewed as process, rather than as product.

205. Hardie, Philip. *Rumour and Renown: Representations of "Fama" in Western Literature*. Cambridge: Cambridge University Press, 2012. vi, 686 pp. Explores the meaning of Middle English *fama*, derived from the Latin, in relation to the spoken word. Chapter 15, "Chaucer's *House of Fame* and Pope's *Temple of Fame*," analyzes relations between the spoken and written word in these poems, as well as other dichotomies within Chaucer's poems, including truth and rumor as Chaucer compares his dream of Dido and Aeneas with Virgil's version. Discusses how both Chaucer and Pope engage with the Latin and Greek traditions and examines Pope's homage to Chaucer, as well as his divergence from Chaucer's text.

206. Lewis, Jacob. "Tools for Tomorrow: The Utopian Function in Middle English Literature, 1350–1420." *DAI* A71.05 (2010): n.p. Argues that fourteenth-century English allegories and dream-visions "open up utopic spaces" and enable proposals for social change. Considers a variety of texts, including *HF*, which "discusses the potential inherent in both art and language to shape a better world in birth."

See also nos. 43, 45, 55, 102, 153, 203, 207, 221.

The Legend of Good Women

207. Bowers, John M. "The Naughty Bits: Dating Chaucer's *House of Fame* and *Legend of Good Women*." In R. F. Yeager and Toshiyuki

Takamiya, eds. *The Medieval Python: The Purposive and Provocative Work of Terry Jones* (*SAC* 36 [2014], no. 118), pp. 105–17. Dates *HF* in the mid-1380s, positioning it as a "transitional work" between *TC* and *CT* and a reflection of Chaucer's status at the time as a king's man. Argues that *LGW* was written concurrently with *CT*, with *LGWP*-F as early as 1392, and revised as *LGWP*-G after 1394. *LGW* is addressed to Richard II and his court, *CT* to "literary posterity."

208. Hernández Pérez, Beatriz. "Sharing Spaces: Female Hospitality in Chaucerian Literature." In Sonia Villegas and Beatriz Domínguez, eds. *Literature, Gender, Space* (Huelva: Universidad de Huelva, 2004), pp. 131–42. Assesses the hospitality of female characters in *LGW*, showing that the betrayal suffered by these women is the result not of their fickleness but of a failure of the courtly code.

See also nos. 45, 55, 95, 103, 109, 115, 117, 215, 221.

The Parliament of Fowls

209. Elmes, Melissa Ridley. "Species or Specious? Authorial Choices and *The Parliament of Fowls*." In Carolynn Van Dyke, ed. *Rethinking Chaucerian Beasts* (*SAC* 36 [2014], no. 114), pp. 233–47. Compares the birds of *PF* to birds in medieval scientific texts, in sources or analogues (especially Alan de Lille's *De planctu Naturae*), and in the observable environment. Chaucer fills *PF* with birds known in England, classifying them by diet but also by class. The birds represent diverse species native to England as well as the diversity of human society, anticipating the estates satire of *CT*.

210. Havely, Nick. "Nature's *Yerde* and Warde: Authority and Choice in Chaucer's *Parliament of Fowls*." In Seeta Chaganti, ed. *Medieval Poetics and Social Practice: Responding to the Work of Penn R. Szittya* (New York: Fordham University Press, 2012), pp. 109–23. Reads the relationship between the formel and Nature in *PF* in light of late medieval practices of wardship, informed by attention to *yerde* as an emblem of authority. Comments on the formel's decision not to marry and on parallels between the formel and Criseyde in Book II of *TC*.

211. Kordecki, Lesley. "Chaucer's Cuckoo and the Myth of Anthropomorphism." In Carolynn Van Dyke, ed. *Rethinking Chaucerian Beasts* (*SAC* 36 [2014], no. 114), pp. 249–60. Argues that the cuckoo–merlin dialogue in *PF* deconstructs the traditional human–animal binary by

presenting a "fleeting realization of anthropomorphism gone awry." The cuckoo's "brood parasitism . . . resolves itself into a mode of communal profit" and the poem becomes a "parody of overclassification."

212. Matlock, Wendy A. "Talking Animals, Debating Beasts." In Carolynn Van Dyke, ed. *Rethinking Chaucerian Beasts* (*SAC* 36 [2014], no. 114), pp. 217–31. Explores anthropomorphism and the "connaturality" of human and nonhuman animals in *PF* and Lydgate's *Debate of the Horse, Goose, and Sheep*, noting the comments of medieval and modern philosophers on the traditional animal–human binary. Lydgate's poem was as popular as Chaucer's in the Middle Ages, and it is more "radical" in its "sympathy for animal suffering."

See also nos. 36, 59, 105, 120, 132, 193, 203.

The Romaunt of the Rose

213. Hernández Pérez, María Beatriz. "La traducción como transición: La huella del *Roman de la rose* en la poesía chauceriana." In Dulce María González Doreste and María de Pilar Mendoza Ramos, eds. *Nouvelles de la rose: Actualité et perspectives du "Roman de la rose"* (La Laguna: Servicio de Publicaciones, 2011), pp. 455–78. Assesses *Rom* as a translation and also as a key moment in Chaucer's literary career that will make him the father of English poetry.

See also no. 96.

Troilus and Criseyde

214. Arner, Timothy D. "*For Goddes Love:* Rhetorical Expression in *Troilus and Criseyde*." *ChauR* 46, no. 4 (2012): 439–60. Focuses on how the idiomatic phrase "for goddes love" is used in *TC* as "an expression of power" and how the phrase "appeals to a divine system of mercy and justice" when used by Troilus, Criseyde, and Pandarus.

215. Beck, Christian Blevins. "Reading Emotional Bodies: Love and Gender in Late Medieval English Literature." *DAI* A71.11 (2011): n.p. Analyzes history of emotions, phenomenology, and gender theory, and specifically discusses "feminine embodiment and the bodily expressions of love" in *TC* and *LGW*.

216. Boboc, Andrew. "Criseyde's Descriptions and the Ethics of

Feminine Experience." *ChauR* 47, no. 1 (2012): 63–83. Suggests Chaucer's portrayal of Criseyde challenges the "traditional *descriptio* as a restrictive benchmark of feminine beauty." Describes Criseyde's transformations in *TC* as an "experiential journey through love and war."

217. Horner, Patrick J. "To 'speken in amphibologies': Reading *Troilus and Criseyde*, Book V, 763." *ChauR* 47, no. 1 (2012): 84–94. Analyzes Criseyde, arguing that Chaucer forces the reader's "active engagement" with the language in Criseyde's soliloquy, which reinforces the ambiguity of her character.

218. Jacobs, Nicolas. "Criseyde's Last Word." In Gerald Morgan, ed. *Chaucer in Context: A Golden Age of English Poetry* (*SAC* 36 [2014], no. 104), pp. 279–94. Discusses Criseyde's "slipperiness and unreliability" in *TC*, focusing on her last letter to Troilus, which is "Chaucer's own addition," as a way of understanding her character.

219. Johnston, Andrew James. "Geschlechter-Lektüren: Emotion und Intimität in Chaucers *Troilus and Criseyde*." In Ingrid Kasten, ed. *Machtvolle Gefühle* (New York: Walter de Gruyter, 2010), pp. 246–59. Assesses the "relationship between reading, space and emotions" in *TC*, focusing on the two scenes of book-reading in the poem. Criseyde's reading in the paved parlor links her with "hermeneutical openness," while Pandarus's feigned reading of an old romance in the bedroom reduces texts to "mere instruments." In German, with English summary.

220. Marelj, Jelena. "Philosophical 'Entente' of Particulars: Criseyde as Nominalist in Chaucer's 'Troilus and Criseyde.'" *ChauR* 47, no. 2 (2012): 206–21. Argues that Criseyde is a "willful agent," who reveals "nominalist intentions" and is guided by her own desires and "misdirected will" in her love of Troilus.

221. McTaggart, Anne. "Shamed Guiltless: Criseyde, Dido, and Chaucerian Ethics." *ChauR* 46, no. 4 (2012): 371–402. Examines shame as a force in identity construction and a constraint on female agency, focusing on Criseyde in *TC* and Dido in *HF*, and briefly mentioning *LGW*. As an historical force, shame also determines narrative possibilities in these poems.

222. Nuttall, Jenni. *"Troilus and Criseyde": A Reader's Guide*. Cambridge: Cambridge University Press, 2012. ix, 205 pp. Introduction to *TC* designed for students. Provides scene-by-scene themes, key topics, and commentary, with recurrent attention to Chaucer's debt to Boccaccio's *Il filostrato*.

223. Reiner, Emily. "The Ambiguous Greek in Old French and Middle English Literature." *DAI* A71.04 (2010): n.p. Investigates various characterizations of Greeks in Old French and Middle English, including that of Diomede in *TC*, a depiction "informed by classical ideas and Chaucer's depictions of Jews and Saracens in other works." Troilus, in contrast, is proto-Christian.

224. Sáez-Hidalgo, Ana. "Chaucer's Litel Tragedye in Its Theoretical and Literary Context." In Antonio R. Celada, Daniel Pastor García, and Pedro Javier Pardo García, eds. *Actas del XXVII Congreso Internacional de AEDEAN = Proceedings of the 27th International AEDEAN Conference* (Salamanca: Universidad de Salamanca, 2004), n.p. CD-ROM. Analyzes Chaucer's notion of tragedy in *TC* against the background of classical and medieval conceptualizations of the genre and Chaucer's own rewriting of sources.

225. Valasek, Bob. "The Light Has Lifted: Trickster Pandare." In Myra Seaman, Eileen A. Joy, and Nicola Masciandaro, eds. *Dark Chaucer: An Assortment* (*SAC* 36 [2014], no. 110), pp. 173–80. Suggests that readers most identify with Pandarus in *TC* because he embodies the type of the folkloric trickster.

226. Van Dyke, Carolynn. "That Which Chargeth Not to Say: Animal Imagery in *Troilus and Criseyde*." In Van Dyke, ed. *Rethinking Chaucerian Beasts* (*SAC* 36 [2014], no. 114), pp. 101–12. *TC* includes references to animals through frequent analogy and extended imagery, but these are often generically inappropriate. Dreams about animals are largely unexplored. Comparison of Troilus to the horse Bayard not only emphasizes the hero's animal nature but also raises the horse to the level of rational being, suggesting the commonality of beings on earth.

See also nos. 3, 36, 39, 46, 49, 54, 58–59, 67–68, 74, 82, 87, 95, 97, 102–3, 116, 210.

Lyrics and Short Poems

An ABC

See no. 88.

Adam Scriveyn

227. Edwards, A. S. G. "Chaucer and 'Adam Scriveyn.'" *MÆ* 80, no. 1 (2012): 135–38. Suggests that the diction of *Adam* indicates that it was not written by Chaucer.

The Complaint of Chaucer to His Purse

See no. 117.

Former Age

228. Harrison, Leigh. "Black Gold: The Former and Future Age." In Myra Seaman, Eileen A. Joy, and Nicola Masciandaro, eds. *Dark Chaucer: An Assortment* (*SAC* 36 [2014], no. 110), pp. 59–69. Argues that *Form Age* transcends its sources to offer "its own glimmer of hope" for new textual communities.

229. Steel, Karl. "A Fourteenth-Century Ecology: 'The Former Age' with Dindimus." In Carolynn Van Dyke, ed. *Rethinking Chaucerian Beasts* (*SAC* 36 [2014], no. 114), pp. 185–99. *Form Age* shares thematic elements with Alexander legends, including vegetarianism and prohibitions against agriculture. In these poems humans live as, and eat as, animals do, a contrast to the mastery described in Genesis. The life described in these poems, one of "moral sensitivity without limits," would be not utopian, but wretched.

Chaucerian Apocrypha

See no. 53.

Book Reviews

230. Ashton, Gail. *Brief Lives: Geoffrey Chaucer* (*SAC* 34 [2012], no. 9). Rev. A. S. G. Edwards, *TLS*, February 2, 2012, p. 27.

231. Bale, Anthony. *Feeling Persecuted: Christians, Jews and Images of Violence* (London: Reaktion Books, 2010). Rev. Martin B. Schichtman, *SAC* 34 (2012): 362–65.

232. Beidler, Peter G. *Chaucer's Canterbury Comedies: Origins and Orig-*

inality (*SAC* 35 [2013], no. 46). Rev. Roger A. Ladd, *SCJ* 43 (2012): 551–52.

233. Brown, Peter. *Geoffrey Chaucer* (*SAC* 36 [2014], no. 6). Rev. Alcuin Blamires, *SAC* 34 (2012): 368–71.

234. Butterfield, Ardis. *The Familiar Enemy: Chaucer, Language, and Nation in the Hundred Years War* (*SAC* 33 [2011], no. 51). Rev. Marilynn Desmond, *SP* 87 (2012): 190–91; Warren Ginsberg, *CL* 64 (2012): 330–34; Tim William Machan, *JEGP* 111 (2012): 130–32.

235. Cawsey, Kathy. *Twentieth-Century Chaucer Criticism: Reading Audiences* (*SAC* 35 [2013], no. 49). Rev. Carolyn P. Collette, *SAC* 34 (2012): 380–83; Dan Mills, *Comitatus* 43 (2012): 172–74.

236. Clarke, K. P. *Chaucer and Italian Textuality* (*SAC* 35 [2013], no. 14). Rev. A. S. G. Edwards, *TLS*, January 17, 2012, p. 27; Karla Taylor, *SAC* 34 (2012): 384–87.

237. Cooper, Lisa. *Artisans and Narrative Craft in Late Medieval England* (*SAC* 35 [2013], no. 53). Rev. Jonathan Hsy, *SAC* 34 (2012): 387–90.

238. Copeland, Rita, and Peter T. Struck, eds. *The Cambridge Companion to Allegory* (*SAC* 34 [2012], no. 52). Rev. Katherine Breen, *SAC* 34 (2012): 390–93; K. P. Clarke, *N&Q* 257 (2012): 112–13.

239. Crocker, Holly. *Chaucer's Vision of Manhood* (*SAC* 31 [2009], no. 95). Rev. Robert S. Sturges, *JBSt* 51 (2012): 183–85.

240. Dane, Joseph A. *Out of Sorts: On Typography and Print Culture* (*SAC* 36 [2014], no. 15). Rev. Natalie Aldred, *Library*, 7th series, 13, no. 1 (2012): 100–101.

241. Donavin, Georgiana. *Scribit Mater: Mary and the Language Arts in the Literature of Medieval England* (*SAC* 36 [2014], no. 88). Rev. Gillian Adler, *Comitatus* 43 (2012): 182–84.

242. Edmondson, George. *The Neighboring Text: Chaucer, Boccaccio, Henryson* (*SAC* 35 [2013], no. 29). Rev. Gillian Adler, *Comitatus* 43 (2012): 184–86; K. P. Clarke, *RES* 63 (2012): 146–47; Erin Felicia Labbie, *SP* 87 (2012): 1186–88; Sarah Stanbury, *SAC* 34 (2012): 401–4.

243. Epstein, Robert, and William Robins, eds. *Sacred and Profane in Chaucer and Late Medieval Literature: Essays in Honour of John V. Fleming* (*SAC* 34 [2012], no. 123). Rev. E. A. Jones, *SAC* 34 (2012): 404–6.

244. Fein, Susanna and David Raybin, eds. *Chaucer: Contemporary Approaches* (*SAC* 34 [2012], no. 125). Rev. Deanne Williams, *SP* 87 (2012): 1191–93; Leonard Koff, *JEGP* 111 (2012): 538–44.

245. Flood, John. *Representations of Eve in Antiquity and the English Middle Ages* (*SAC* 36 [2014], no. 92). Rev. Mihaela L. Florescu, *Comitatus* 43 (2012): 193–94.

246. Ford, Mark, ed. *London: A History in Verse* (*SAC* 36 [2014], no. 17). Rev. Nick Laird, *NYRB*, September 27, 2012, pp. 72–75.

247. Fumo, Jamie C. *The Legacy of Apollo: Antiquity, Authority, and Chaucerian Poetics* (*SAC* 34 [2012], no. 128). Rev. Theresa Tinkle, *SP* 87 (2012): 217–19; Winthrop Wetherbee, *SAC* 34 (2012): 406–9.

248. Gillespie, Alexandra, and Daniel Wakelin, eds. *The Production of Books in England 1350–1500* (*SAC* 35 [2013], no. 17). Rev. Susan Powell, *JEBS* 15 (2012): 364–67.

249. Gust, Geoffrey W. *Constructing Chaucer: Author and Autofiction in the Critical Tradition* (*SAC* 33 [2011], no. 73). Rev. John M. Ganim, *JEGP* 111 (2012): 134–36.

250. Hall, Alaric, Olga Timofeeva, Ágnes Kiricsi, and Bethany Fox, eds. *Interfaces between Language and Culture in Medieval England: A Festschrift for Matti Kilpiö* (*SAC* 34 [2012], no. 21). Rev. E. G. Stanley, *N&Q* 257 (2012): 584–88.

251. Hanning, Robert W. *Serious Play: Desire and Authority in the Poetry of Ovid, Chaucer, and Ariosto* (*SAC* 34 [2012], no. 129). Rev. Warren Ginsberg, *SP* 87 (2012): 227–29; Gregory Heyworth, *SAC* 34 (2012): 412–16.

252. Hume, Cathy. *Chaucer and the Cultures of Love and Marriage* (*SAC* 36 [2014], no. 95). Rev. Mary C. Flannery, *TLS*, December 14, 2014, p. 29.

253. Kolve, V. A. *Telling Images: Chaucer and the Imagery of Narrative II* (*SAC* 33 [2011], no. 142). Rev. Suzanne Conklin Akbari, *JBSt* 51 (2012): 195–97.

254. Krummel, Mariamne Ara. *Crafting Jewishness in Medieval England: Legally Absent, Virtually Present* (*SAC* 36 [2014], no. 99). Rev. Lawrence Besserman, *SAC* 34 (2012): 416–19.

255. Mattern, Joanne. *Geoffrey Chaucer: Medieval Writer* (*SAC* 36 [2014], no. 10). Rev. Shelle Rosenfield, *Booklist* 109, no. 3 (2012): 79–80.

256. Minnis, Alastair. *Fallible Authors: Chaucer's Pardoner and Wife of Bath* (*SAC* 32 [2010], no. 247). Rev. Larissa Tracy, *SCJ* 43 (2012): 918–19.

257. Moore, Colette. *Quoting Speech in Early English* (*SAC* 36 [2014], no. 75). Rev. Lucy Perry, *SAC* 34 (2012): 419–22.

258. Peterson, William S. *The Kelmscott Chaucer: A Census* (*SAC* 36 [2014], no. 23). Rev. Michael Ryan, *College and Research Libraries* 73, no. 1 (2012): 101–2.

259. Phillips, Helen, ed., *Chaucer and Religion* (*SAC* 35 [2013], no. 68). Rev. Marleen Cré, *RES* 63 (2012): 666–68; Denise Despres, *Religion and Literature* 43, no. 2 (2011): 183–85; William Robins, *JEGP* 111 (2012): 413–16; Claire M. Waters, *JEGP* 111 (2012): 416–18.

260. Reynolds, Matthew. *The Poetry of Translation: From Chaucer and Petrarch to Homer and Logue* (*SAC* 36 [2014], no. 44). Rev. David Hopkins, *N&Q* 257 (2011): 294–96.

261. Rigby, Stephen H. *Wisdom and Chivalry: Chaucer's "Knight's Tale" and Medieval Political Theory* (*SAC* 33 [2011], no. 114). Rev. Maik Goth, *M&H* 38 (2012): 155–57.

262. Rosenfeld, Jessica. *Ethics and Enjoyment in Late Medieval Poetry: Love after Aristotle* (*SAC* 35 [2013], no. 33). Rev. Sarah Kay, *SAC* 34 (2012): 429–31.

263. Rossiter, William. *Chaucer and Petrarch* (*SAC* 34 [2012], no. 54). Rev. Piero Boitani, *MLR* 107 (2012): 1224–26; William Robins, *JEGP* 111 (2012): 413–16.

264. Scattergood, John. *Occasions for Writing: Essays on Medieval and Renaissance Literature, Politics and Society* (*SAC* 33 [2011], no. 318). Rev. Alexandra Barratt, *JEBS* 15 (2012): 396–98.

265. Smyth, Karen Elaine. *Imaginings of Time in Lydgate and Hoccleve's Verse* (*SAC* 35 [2013], no. 70). Rev. Jenni Nuttall, *SAC* 34 (2012): 435–38.

266. Tinkle, Theresa. *Gender and Power in Medieval Exegesis* (*SAC* 34 [2012], no. 163). Rev. Jennifer L. Sisk, *SAC* 34 (2012): 438–41.

267. Travis, Peter W. *Disseminal Chaucer: Rereading the Nun's Priest's Tale* (*SAC* 34 [2012], no. 262). Rev. Elizabeth Scala, *JEGP* 111 (2012): 132–34.

268. Urban, Malte. *Fragments: Past and Present in Chaucer and Gower* (*SAC* 33 [2011], no. 30). Rev. R. F. Yeager, *JEGP* 111 (2012): 251–52.

269. Vaught, Jennifer C. *Rhetorics of Bodily Disease and Health in Medieval and Early Modern England* (*SAC* 34 [2012], no. 242). Rev. Dan Mills, *Comitatus* 43 (2012): 294–96.

270. Whalen, Brett Edward, ed. *Pilgrimage in the Middle Ages: A Reader* (*SAC* 35 [2013], no. 96). Rev. Thomas R. Schneider, *Comitatus* 43 (2012): 256–58.

271. Williams, David. *Language Redeemed: Chaucer's Mature Poetry*

(*SAC* 31 [2009], no. 144). Rev. Katherine Curran Sweeney, *Touchstone: A Journal of Mere Christianity* 25, no. 1 (2012): 51–53.

272. Williams, Tara. *Inventing Womanhood: Gender and Language in Later Middle English Writing* (*SAC* 35 [2013], no. 92). Rev. Claudia Yaghoobi, *Comitatus* 43 (2012): 298–300.

Author Index—Bibliography

Index

Page numbers of illustrations are indicated in the index by *italics*.